HEAL
97/98

Eighteenth Edition

Editor
Richard Yarian
Towson State University

Richard Yarian is a health educator with extensive training in the area of biomedical health. He received his B.A. in biology from Ball State University. Before leaving Ball State University, he also received both an M.A. and an Ed.S. in the area of health education. He continued his academic training at the University of Maryland where he received his Ph.D. in biomedical health. Following completion of his doctoral program, he became an assistant professor at the University of Maryland and taught courses in the areas of personal health, stress management, drug abuse, medical physiology, and cardiovascular disease.

A Library of Information from the Public Press
Dushkin/McGraw·Hill
Sluice Dock, Guilford, Connecticut 06437

Visit us on the Internet—http://www.dushkin.com

The Annual Editions Series

ANNUAL EDITIONS is a series of over 65 volumes designed to provide the reader with convenient, low-cost access to a wide range of current, carefully selected articles from some of the most important magazines, newspapers, and journals published today. ANNUAL EDITIONS are updated on an annual basis through a continuous monitoring of over 300 periodical sources. All ANNUAL EDITIONS have a number of features that are designed to make them particularly useful, including topic guides, annotated tables of contents, unit overviews, and indexes. For the teacher using ANNUAL EDITIONS in the classroom, an Instructor's Resource Guide with test questions is available for each volume.

VOLUMES AVAILABLE

- Abnormal Psychology
- Adolescent Psychology
- Africa
- Aging
- American Foreign Policy
- American Government
- American History, Pre-Civil War
- American History, Post-Civil War
- American Public Policy
- Anthropology
- Archaeology
- Biopsychology
- Business Ethics
- Child Growth and Development
- China
- Comparative Politics
- Computers in Education
- Computers in Society
- Criminal Justice
- Criminology
- Developing World
- Deviant Behavior
- Drugs, Society, and Behavior
- Dying, Death, and Bereavement
- Early Childhood Education
- Economics
- Educating Exceptional Children
- Education
- Educational Psychology
- Environment
- Geography
- Global Issues
- Health
- Human Development
- Human Resources
- Human Sexuality
- India and South Asia
- International Business
- Japan and the Pacific Rim
- Latin America
- Life Management
- Macroeconomics
- Management
- Marketing
- Marriage and Family
- Mass Media
- Microeconomics
- Middle East and the Islamic World
- Multicultural Education
- Nutrition
- Personal Growth and Behavior
- Physical Anthropology
- Psychology
- Public Administration
- Race and Ethnic Relations
- Russia, the Eurasian Republics, and Central/Eastern Europe
- Social Problems
- Social Psychology
- Sociology
- State and Local Government
- Urban Society
- Western Civilization, Pre-Reformation
- Western Civilization, Post-Reformation
- Western Europe
- World History, Pre-Modern
- World History, Modern
- World Politics

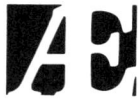

Cataloging in Publication Data
Main entry under title: Annual editions: Health. 1997/98.
    1. Hygiene—Periodicals. I. Yarian, Richard, comp. II. Title: Health.
ISBN 0-697-37281-2   613'.05   81-643582

© 1997 by Dushkin/McGraw-Hill, Guilford, CT 06437, A Division of The McGraw-Hill Companies.

Copyright law prohibits the reproduction, storage, or transmission in any form by any means of any portion of this publication without the express written permission of Dushkin/McGraw-Hill, and of the copyright holder (if different) of the part of the publication to be reproduced. The Guidelines for Classroom Copying endorsed by Congress explicitly state that unauthorized copying may not be used to create, to replace, or to substitute for anthologies, compilations, or collective works.

Annual Editions® is a Registered Trademark of Dushkin/McGraw-Hill,
A Division of The McGraw-Hill Companies.

Eighteenth Edition

Cover image © 1996 PhotoDisc, Inc.

Printed in the United States of America

Printed on Recycled Paper

Editors/Advisory Board

Members of the Advisory Board are instrumental in the final selection of articles for each edition of ANNUAL EDITIONS. Their review of articles for content, level, currentness, and appropriateness provides critical direction to the editor and staff. We think that you will find their careful consideration well reflected in this volume.

EDITOR

Richard Yarian
Towson State University

ADVISORY BOARD

Jerry L. Ainsworth
Southern Connecticut State University

Charles R. Baffi
Virginia Polytechnic Institute and State University

F. Stephen Bridges
University of West Florida

Susan W. Butterworth
University of Portland

Annette L. Caruso
Pennsylvania State University Ogontz Campus

Carlton M. Fancher
Central Michigan University

Anita Farel
University of North Carolina Chapel Hill

Kenneth R. Felker
Edinboro University

Nicholas K. Iammarino
Rice University

Allen Pat Kelley
Essex Community College

Judith McLaughlin
University of Georgia

M. Jane McMahon
Towson State University

Syble M. Oldaker
Clemson University

Judy Peel
University of North Carolina Wilmington

Glen J. Peterson
Lakewood Community College

Ruth P. Saunders
University of South Carolina

Richard G. Schlaadt
University of Oregon

Donna J. Schoenfeld
Rutgers University

Alex Waigandt
University of Missouri Columbia

Staff

Ian A. Nielsen, Publisher

EDITORIAL STAFF

Roberta Monaco, Developmental Editor
Addie Raucci, Administrative Editor
Cheryl Greenleaf, Permissions Editor
Deanna Herrschaft, Permissions Assistant
Diane Barker, Proofreader
Lisa Holmes-Doebrick, Program Coordinator
Joseph Offredi, Photo Coordinator

PRODUCTION STAFF

Brenda S. Filley, Production Manager
Charles Vitelli, Designer
Shawn Callahan, Graphics
Lara M. Johnson, Graphics
Laura Levine, Graphics
Mike Campbell, Graphics
Juliana Arbo, Typesetting Supervisor
Jane Jaegersen, Typesetter
Marie Lazauskas, Word Processor
Kathleen D'Amico, Word Processor
Larry Killian, Copier Coordinator

To the Reader

In publishing ANNUAL EDITIONS we recognize the enormous role played by the magazines, newspapers, and journals of the *public press* in providing current, first-rate educational information in a broad spectrum of interest areas. Many of these articles are appropriate for students, researchers, and professionals seeking accurate, current material to help bridge the gap between principles and theories and the real world. These articles, however, become more useful for study when those of lasting value are carefully *collected, organized, indexed,* and *reproduced* in a *low-cost format,* which provides easy and permanent access when the material is needed. That is the role played by ANNUAL EDITIONS. Under the direction of each volume's *academic editor,* who is an expert in the subject area, and with the guidance of an *Advisory Board,* each year we seek to provide in each ANNUAL EDITION a current, well-balanced, carefully selected collection of the best of the public press for your study and enjoyment. We think that you will find this volume useful, and we hope that you will take a moment to let us know what you think.

America is in the midst of a revolution that is changing the way millions of people view their health. Traditionally, most people delegated responsibility for their health to their physicians and hoped that medical science would be able to cure whatever ailed them. This approach to health care emphasized the role of medical technology and funneled billions of dollars into medical research. The net result of all this spending is the most technically advanced and expensive health care system in the world. Unfortunately, health care costs have risen so high that millions of Americans can no longer afford health care, and even those who can, have limited access to many of the new technologies because the cost is prohibitive. Despite all the technological advances, the medical community has been unable to reverse the damage associated with society's unhealthy lifestyle. This fact, coupled with rapidly rising health care costs, has prompted millions of individuals to assume a more active role in safeguarding their own health. Evidence of this change in attitude can be seen in the growing interest in nutrition, physical fitness, and stress management. If we as a nation are to capitalize on this new health consciousness, we must devote more time and energy to educating Americans in the health sciences so they will be better able to make informed choices about their health.

Health is such a complex and dynamic subject that it is practically impossible for anyone to stay abreast of all the current research findings. For this reason Americans have generally come to rely on the public press for information on major health issues. Unfortunately, the information presented in some health articles is questionable at best and, in many cases, it is totally inaccurate. If consumers are to make wise decisions about their health based on such information, they must have the skills necessary to sort out fact from conjecture. *Annual Editions: Health 97/98* was designed to aid in this task. It offers a sampling of quality articles that represent current thinking on a variety of health issues and serves as a tool for developing critical thinking skills.

The articles selected for this volume were carefully chosen on the basis of their quality and timeliness. Because this book is revised and updated annually, it contains information that is not currently available in any standard textbook. As such, it serves as a valuable resource for both teachers and students. In an attempt to stay current with the field of health education, this edition has been reorganized and expanded to include a chapter on health behavior and decision making. The content areas presented in this edition generally mirror those that are covered in introductory health courses. The 10 topic areas covered are: Health Behavior and Decision Making; Stress and Mental Health; Nutritional Health; Exercise and Weight Control; Drugs and Health; Human Sexuality; Current Killers; America's Health and the Health Care System; Consumer Health; and Contemporary Health Hazards. Because of the interdependence of the various elements that constitute health, the articles selected were written by naturalists, environmentalists, psychologists, economists, sociologists, nutritionists, consumer advocates, and traditional health practitioners. The diversity of these selections provides the reader with a variety of points of view regarding health and the complexity of the issues involved.

Annual Editions: Health 97/98 is one of the most useful and up-to-date publications currently available in the area of health. Please let us know what you think of it by filling out and returning the postage-paid article rating form on the last page of this book. Any anthology can be improved. This one will be—annually.

Richard Yarian
Editor

Contents

To the Reader iv
Topic Guide 2

UNIT 1

Health Behavior and Decision Making

Five articles examine how Americans make choices about controlling their health.

Overview 4

1. **A Picture of Health,** Consumer Reports on Health, January 1996. — 6
   In 1995 the *U.S. Public Health Service* gave a *midterm exam* to determine whether we as a nation are moving in the right direction when it comes to our *health behaviors*. How do you rate on this test?

2. **Healthy Habits: Why Bother?** Consumer Reports on Health, May 1995. — 10
   If you do not smoke, do not start, and if you do, stop! Cut your dietary fat intake to 30 percent or less of your total caloric intake! These and other *lifestyle recommendations* have been the backbone of the movement toward healthier lifestyles. However, there are reports suggesting that adherence to these recommendations may yield only minimal benefits. This article explains that the way statistics are calculated can minimize the *benefits of a prudent lifestyle*.

3. **Risk: What It Means to You,** Harvard Women's Health Watch, November 1995. — 13
   How do you interpret your risk level for various illnesses when reading reports of late-breaking news that could affect your health? This article offers tips about important factors to keep in mind that will facilitate informed judgments about such reports.

4. **"Just Do It" Isn't Enough: Change Comes in Stages,** Tufts University Diet & Nutrition Letter, September 1996. — 15
   Have you ever considered making a change in your behavior so as to improve your health? James Prochaska, a leading expert on behavior change, describes the *6 stages of change* that anyone who wants to achieve lasting success must go through. He also suggests strategies that will help with each stage of the process.

5. **Challenging America's Inverted Health Priorities,** Elizabeth M. Whelan, Priorities, Volume 8, Number 1, 1996. — 18
   Despite the known dangers of tobacco and alcohol use, Americans continue to focus on *minor and often speculative health risks* that account for few deaths and injuries by comparison. Why is this the case? Epidemiologist Elizabeth Whelan argues in this provocative article that five factors have inverted public health priorities. She urges the participation of scientists and physicians in health debates and the abandonment of *political correctness*.

UNIT 2

Stress and Mental Health

Five selections consider the impact of stress and emotions on mental health.

Overview 24

6. **Critical Life Events and the Onset of Illness,** Blair Justice, Comprehensive Therapy, Volume 20, Number 4, 1994. — 26
   Death and taxes are said to be the only two things we can be sure of, but stress should be added to this list. Despite the fact that everyone experiences stress, why is it that not everyone is as susceptible to its damaging effects? Blair Justice argues that the differences are largely the result of our *sense of support and acceptance*, coupled with our sense of *control over our own lives*.

7. **Can You Laugh Your Stress Away?** Mary Roach, Health, September 1996. — 33
   In 1976 Norman Cousins credited laughter with saving his life in a book titled *Anatomy of an Illness*. Since that time, research studies have found that *laughter* not only relieves emotional distress, but that it actually *strengthens* the functioning of the *immune system*.

8. **Good Mood Foods,** Shawna Vogel, Health, October 1996. — 37
   The sweet aroma of freshly baked cinnamon rolls conjures up pleasant memories for most people, but the association is more than just memories. Researchers have begun to identify tangible effects that certain foods have on our *moods* by *altering our brain chemistry*.

The concepts in bold italics are developed in the article. For further expansion please refer to the Topic Guide and the Index.

9. **Out of the Blues,** Kathleen McAuliffe, *Walking,* March/April 1994. — 41

For years health experts have told us that walking is good for the heart, muscles, and bones. Now researchers are discovering that *walking may also be an effective form of psychotherapy,* either alone or in conjunction with more traditional forms of treatment. Kathleen McAuliffe discusses how walking can be used to help beat *depression* and moodiness.

10. **Depression: Way beyond the Blues,** Sandra Arbetter, *Current Health 2,* December 1993. — 44

Everyone feels blue or depressed from time to time, but *clinical depression* is much more serious and lasts longer than a few days. Each year over 6,000 adolescents commit suicide, and depression is considered the biggest risk factor. Sandra Arbetter examines various facets of depression and offers ways to help a friend who is depressed.

Overview — 48

UNIT 3

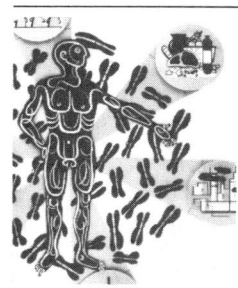

Nutritional Health

Five articles discuss the effects of diet and nutrition on a person's well-being. The topics include dietary supplements, the food pyramid, and the value of fast foods.

11. **Dietary Gospel—or Phony Baloney?** *Consumer Reports on Health,* June 1996. — 50

While dietary advice seems to change on a daily basis, some mistaken notions regarding nutrition die especially hard, despite substantial evidence that they are misleading. This article addresses nine of the *most common nutritional myths.*

12. **Food for Thought about Dietary Supplements,** Paul R. Thomas, *Nutrition Today,* March/April 1996. — 53

Interest in dietary supplements among Americans has never been higher. This interest has fueled numerous unsubstantiated claims by the health food industry, which would like to cash in on all the hype. Paul Thomas examines the issue of dietary supplements and discusses *when they are appropriate and when they are not.*

13. **The Food Pyramid: How to Make It Work for You,** *Consumer Reports on Health,* September 1996. — 61

Five years ago the U.S.D.A. introduced the Food Guide Pyramid to assist Americans in making food choices that lead to a *balanced diet.* While the Food Guide Pyramid has increased the public's awareness regarding the importance of vegetables, fruits, and grains, it falls short in advising consumers about *fiber and fat.* This article contains useful tips for boosting fiber intake and limiting fat content.

14. **Fast Food: Fatter than Ever,** *Consumer Reports on Health,* August 1996. — 64

Over the last few years, fast-food giants like McDonald's have introduced low-fat items in an attempt to attract nutrition-conscious customers. But now, according to Consumers Union research, the fast-food industry has dropped many of its low-fat offerings and replaced them with *high-fat choices.*

15. **Snack Attack,** Patricia Long, *Health,* July/August 1993. — 67

Americans love snack foods, to the tune of over $13.4 billion a year. Unfortunately, of the 60 top snack foods, only three are not extremely high in either sugar or fat. Patricia Long examines the issue of *eating snacks* and suggests that snacking itself is good—it is just the choices we make that are bad.

UNIT 4

Exercise and Weight Control

Six articles examine the influences of exercise and diet on health. Topics discussed include the value of working out, choosing the right exercise, and dieting myths.

Overview — 72

16. **Fitness Fiction: Working Out the Facts,** *Consumer Reports on Health,* October 1996. — 74

Each year millions of Americans start exercising, only to quit and rejoin the ranks of couch potatoes. Some quit because of injury, some from boredom, and some because they began exercising with misconceptions about what to expect. This article discusses the truth behind *10 common misconceptions regarding exercise.*

17. **Which Exercise Is Best for You?** *Consumer Reports on Health,* April 1994. — 76

Most people know that *exercise* reduces the risk of disease, increases stamina, builds strength, burns calories, and relieves stress, but they may not know how to choose the right exercise program. This article provides useful information for selecting exercises that best suit one's fitness needs and goals.

The concepts in bold italics are developed in the article. For further expansion please refer to the Topic Guide and the Index.

18. **Fat Times,** Philip Elmer-Dewitt, *Time,* January 16, 1995. 80
The 1980s were the beginning of the wellness movement. People began to take their health seriously, and health clubs popped up everywhere. Joggers, walkers, and bicyclists could be found exercising at all hours of the day and night. It was as though Americans had finally decided to shape up. Now 15 years after the *fitness craze* began, Americans are fatter than ever and stuffing themselves with junk food. What went wrong?

19. **Test Your Weight-Loss IQ,** Stephanie Wood, *Walking,* May/June 1996. 84
How much do you know about weight loss? Every day a new strategy or diet is published in an attempt to convince you that it is the secret to weight loss. According to Stephanie Wood, many of these claims are based on fiction and not fact. This article is packed with the *facts concerning weight control.*

20. **Gaining on Fat,** W. Wayt Gibbs, *Scientific American,* August 1996. 86
How weight conscious are Americans? At any point in time, half of all Americans are trying to lose weight, and we spend in excess of $33 billion dollars yearly on *weight-loss programs.* Unfortunately, says W. Wayt Gibbs, the only things that are getting lighter are our wallets. This article explains why is it so difficult to lose weight.

21. **Body Mania,** Judith Rodin, *Psychology Today,* January/February 1992. 92
Judith Rodin discusses the issue of *body image* and suggests that our preoccupation with our bodies is a manifestation of the chaos and uncertainty that we experience in our daily lives. She argues that our obsession with dieting and exercise provides us with a much-needed sense of control in our lives.

UNIT 5

Drugs and Health

Five articles examine how drugs affect our lives. Subjects discussed include the dangers of tobacco, alcohol, and the potential hazards of over-the-counter medications.

Overview 96

22. **How to Pick a Pain Reliever,** *Consumer Reports on Health,* March 1996. 98
The most commonly used *nonprescription drug* is classified as an *analgesic,* and today Americans have five different varieties to choose from. This article examines the differences among these five pain relievers and discusses how to choose the one that is right for you.

23. **OTC Drugs: Prescription for Danger?** *Consumer Reports on Health,* September 1994. 101
Nonprescription drugs can cause serious harm to the user if the manufacturer's recommendations regarding dosage and usage are not followed. This article examines several common over-the-counter (OTC) drugs and lists the *specific risks* associated with each of them.

24. **Kicking Butts,** Carl Sherman, *Psychology Today,* September/October 1994. 104
Over the last 20 years, smokers have received many clear messages that tobacco use is hazardous to their health. Why then do so many people still smoke? Carl Sherman examines the process of quitting and discusses some unique aspects of *nicotine addiction* that make quitting this *drug* so difficult for many users. An interesting observation made by the author is that smoking, like alcoholism, may have a *genetic component.*

25. **Alcohol and Tobacco: A Deadly Duo,** Kristine Napier, *Priorities,* Spring 1990. 109
If you smoke, do not drink! Studies investigating *the combined use of alcohol and tobacco* indicate that, among tobacco users, drinkers smoke more than nondrinkers. Researchers also found that alcohol and tobacco appear to be synergistic in increasing the *risk of cancer.*

26. **Alcohol: Spirit of Health?** *Consumer Reports on Health,* April 1996. 111
Over the last three years, numerous reports have surfaced attributing significant health benefits to daily consumption of *a moderate amount of alcohol.* Does this mean that we should all have a daily drink? The answer is a qualified no. This article examines the issues and discusses who stands to gain and who is likely to lose.

The concepts in bold italics are developed in the article. For further expansion please refer to the Topic Guide and the Index.

UNIT 6

Human Sexuality

Four articles discuss the most recent research on human reproduction and sexuality. The selections consider sex differences, birth control, and sexual myths.

Overview 114

27. **The Lessons of Love**, Beth Livermore, *Psychology Today*, March/April 1993. 116
    Do men and women feel differently about love? How important is sexual desire to feelings of love? This article examines love and discusses the *similarities and differences* that exist between *men and women* when it comes to love.

28. **The Indispensables: 10 Key Reasons Why Love Endures**, Catherine Houck, *Cosmopolitan*, May 1992. 122
    Despite numerous social changes, ours is still a couples' world. Today, as in the past, the majority of people still view a happy and *successful marriage* as an important ingredient in achieving a meaningful life. Unfortunately, for many, the grim reality is that happy and successful marriages are becoming rarer. This article examines 10 key elements that contribute to the success or failure of many marriages.

29. **Choosing a Contraceptive**, Joseph Anthony, *American Health*, April 1994. 126
    Which contraceptive is best for you? The choice is not always easy, as each has its strengths and drawbacks. Joseph Anthony discusses the *contraceptive methods* currently available in the United States, and he evaluates their effectiveness for preventing both pregnancy and the transmission of STDs.

30. **Preventing STDs**, Judith Levine Willis, *FDA Consumer*, June 1993. 129
    Most people know that *condoms* have been demonstrated to be effective in preventing the spread of AIDS and other *sexually transmitted diseases (STDs)*, but not all condoms are equally effective. Judith Willis offers advice on purchasing, storing, and using condoms to maximize their effectiveness as protection.

UNIT 7

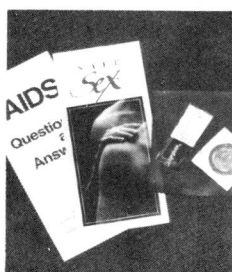

Current Killers

Eight selections examine the major causes of death in the Western world. Heart attack, cancer, and AIDS are discussed.

Overview 132

31. **Family History: What You Don't Know Can Kill You**, *Consumer Reports on Health*, September 1996. 134
    Among the risk factors for cancer, heart disease, and other disorders, one that you cannot change but should be aware of is your *family medical history*. This article describes how some *hereditary conditions* virtually ensure that disease will occur, while others are only *susceptibility* factors.

32. **Cholesterol**, *Mayo Clinic Health Letter*, June 1993. 137
    Most people know that a high blood cholesterol level is associated with an increased risk of developing *cardiovascular disease*, but they may not know that there are both good and bad types of cholesterol. This article discusses the various types of *serum cholesterol* and examines how various risk factors for cardiovascular disease can influence cholesterol level.

33. **Rating Your Risks for Heart Disease**, *University of California at Berkeley Wellness Letter*, May 1994. 141
    While the number of deaths due to heart attacks has dropped by over 50 percent since 1960, *cardiovascular disease* is still the number-one killer of Americans over 35 years of age. This reduction in the number of deaths due to heart attack is largely the result of *lifestyle modifications* that reduce risk factors.

34. **The Heart of the Matter**, Julia Califano, *American Health*, September 1995. 144
    Exercise not only helps you look better and feel better emotionally, but it appears to lower your risk of developing *cardiovascular disease, diabetes,* and some forms of *cancer*. This article presents the findings of several research studies indicating that *aerobic exercise* is a significant factor in preventing various diseases.

35. **Strategies for Minimizing Cancer Risk**, Walter C. Willett, Graham A. Colditz, and Nancy E. Mueller, *Scientific American*, September 1996. 148
    In 1996 alone, more than 550,000 Americans died of *cancer*. The number is even higher in Europe. According to this report, approximately 50 percent of these deaths might have been avoided through *primary prevention* and *early detection*.

The concepts in bold italics are developed in the article. For further expansion please refer to the Topic Guide and the Index.

36. **Cancer-Fighting Foods: Green Revolution,** *Harvard Health Letter,* April 1995.
Evidence is mounting that a diet high in fruits, vegetables, and grains may significantly lower one's risk of developing several types of cancer. Scientists have discovered a variety of *bioactive substances,* such as *phytochemicals* and *carotenoids,* that appear to interfere with the process of carcinogenesis. This article discusses their role in preventing or slowing the disease.

37. **Mutant Gene Can Slow AIDS Virus: Cancer Institute Study Indicates Some People May Be Impervious,** Rick Weiss, *Washington Post,* September 27, 1996.
In the 1980s health official predicted that AIDS would sweep through the U.S. population, and they also predicted that a vaccination to prevent it was just around the corner. They were wrong on both counts. Recent advances in their *understanding of AIDS* has prompted a *new optimism* among medical researchers.

38. **The Disease Detective,** Christine Gorman, *Time,* December 30, 1996 and January 6, 1997.
World-renowned scientist David Ho has developed a daring strategy for combating the virus that causes *AIDS.* In this essay on *Time's* Man of the Year, Christine Gorman describes the success Ho (and other doctors) are having using powerful new AIDS drugs called *protease inhibitors.* Many patients in the early stages of infection are experiencing encouraging results.

154

158

160

Overview

166

39. **Health Unlimited,** Willard Gaylin, *Wilson Quarterly,* Summer 1996.
No one can dispute the fact that health care costs have risen dramatically over the last 20 years, but most people place the blame on greedy physicians, unnecessary expenditures, and expensive medical technologies. Perhaps even more significant than all of these factors, according to Willard Gaylin, is the fact that *modern medicine* has expanded its boundaries to include conditions that previously were considered an inevitable *part of the human condition.*

40. **Medical Savings Accounts: A Solution to Financing Health Care?** Peter J. Ferrara, *USA Today Magazine (Society for the Advancement of Education),* May 1996.
In an effort to stem the rising costs of health care, several companies across the nation have decided to establish *Medical Savings Accounts* (MSAs) to finance their employees' health care costs. The MSAs confront the cost-control issues by providing direct incentives to consumers for limiting their expenditures.

41. **Can HMOs Help Solve the Health-Care Crisis?** *Consumer Reports on Health,* October 1996.
Since 1992 *managed care* has become a dominant player in the health care business, despite the fact that neither consumers nor Congress voted for it. The promise of managed care was lower health costs and extended health care for all. Unfortunately, according to this article, the direction managed care in general and *HMOs* in particular are heading will lead to neither. What we will have is *high costs without freedom of choice.*

42. **Examining the Routine Examination,** Marvin M. Lipman, *Consumer Reports on Health,* October 1995.
How often do you need a *medical exam,* and what tests should you receive in a typical check-up? This article discusses *tests that are unnecessary* and others that should be included in a routine physical examination.

43. **Your Hospital Stay: A Guide to Survival,** *Consumer Reports on Health,* August 1995.
America has some of the best health care in the world, but that does not mean that all health care services are risk-free. Recent studies suggest that over 1,000,000 Americans each year are injured due to *preventable mistakes* or the *hazards of hospitalization.* This article discusses what you as a patient can do to protect yourself.

168

172

177

185

187

UNIT 8

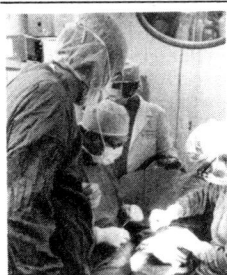

America's Health and the Health Care System

Six selections discuss the current state of health care in today's society by focusing on self-care, health care costs, and the health care industry.

The concepts in bold italics are developed in the article. For further expansion please refer to the Topic Guide and the Index.

UNIT 9

Consumer Health

Five selections examine how food labeling and food and drug interactions relate to consumer health.

UNIT 10

Contemporary Health Hazards

Eight articles examine hazards that affect our health and are encountered in today's world.

44. **The New Doctors of Natural Medicine,** Katherine Griffin, *Health,* October 1996. 191
Each year millions of Americans seek out alternative medical therapies as a way to cope with their health problems. This movement has propelled practitioners such as *naturopaths* into the spotlight, but what do they really have to offer someone who is truly in need of medical help? Katherine Griffin examines the *pros and cons* of several natural remedies currently being used by naturopaths.

Overview 198

45. **How Health Savvy Are You?** *Consumer Reports on Health,* January 1995. 200
Do you pride yourself on staying abreast of such health issues as exercise, nutrition, and medicine? This selection is a *quiz* that tests the reader's knowledge on a *variety of contemporary health issues.*

46. **Nutrition in the News: What the Headlines Don't Tell You,** *Environmental Nutrition,* September 1995. 205
You exercise regularly and take antioxidants daily because medical studies have shown that these practices will reduce your risk of developing premature cardiovascular disease and cancer. Then you read that antioxidants and exercise may not be as effective in preventing disease as once thought. What is a *consumer* to believe? This article discusses why there is so much *conflicting information* in the media, and it provides guidelines to help consumers make sense of it all.

47. **The Switch to OTC: No Prescription, No Protection?** *Consumer Reports on Health,* October 1996. 207
Over the past few years pharmaceutical companies have been successful in getting the FDA to reclassify several prescription medications for sale over the counter. This move has distinct *advantages for manufacturers.* The question is, does it also *benefit consumers*?

48. **The Doctor Is On,** Katie Hafner, *Newsweek,* May 27, 1996. 210
Last year alone, millions of Americans logged onto the *Internet* in search of information about *medical concerns and health issues.* The question is, How good is the information they are getting?

49. **Health Insurance Hazards: How to Spot Hidden Pitfalls in Your Plan,** Carolyn Hagan, *American Health,* November 1996. 212
America is rapidly moving to managed care, and as it does, consumers are being lulled into a false sense of medical security. Many unsuspecting patients have found that their *health care plans* had booby traps and *exclusions* buried deep in the fine print, or couched in the euphemistic and ambiguous language in which such policies are written. Carolyn Hagan offers ways to see how your policy stacks up.

Overview 214

50. **Are Your Shades Good Enough?** Patricia Long, *Health,* August 1995. 216
Sunglasses do more than make a fashion statement—they can protect your eyes from the damaging effects of *ultraviolet radiation* that cause cataracts. Beyond style, what factors should you consider when shopping for sunglasses? This article provides the reader with practical information to consider when purchasing sunglasses.

51. **Quiz: Are You Ready for the Sun?** Cynthia Moekle Pigott, *American Health,* May 1995. 218
Scientific studies linking skin cancer to sunburn have prompted millions of Americans to lather themselves up with *sunscreen lotions.* But do sunscreens really work? Which ones are best? Who really needs them? This selection tests the reader's knowledge regarding these and other questions concerning *UV radiation* and provides answers based on the most current information available.

The concepts in bold italics are developed in the article. For further expansion please refer to the Topic Guide and the Index.

52. **The Bad News Bugs,** Peter Radetsky, *American Health,* September 1995. 220

Movies like *The Andromeda Strain* and *Outbreak* dramatize the potential dangers that new *viruses* can pose to mankind, despite the sophisticated medical technology available today. In this article, Peter Radetsky discusses where viruses such as *Ebola, Hanta,* and *Dengue* came from and assesses the risk that they pose to the American public.

53. **'Wonder Drugs' Losing Healing Aura,** David Brown, *Washington Post,* June 26, 1995. 223

In April 1994 the Centers for Disease Control and Prevention warned that America has entered an era when the spectrum of infectious diseases is expanding and those once thought to be controlled are becoming drug resistant. This article examines the issue of *drug-resistant bacteria.*

54. **Prevent Sexually Transmitted Diseases,** Lauren Picker, *American Health,* October 1995. 228

While the term *safe sex* has primarily been used in discussions concerning *AIDS,* it is equally relevant for six other *sexually transmitted diseases (STDs)* spreading at a rate of 12 million new cases each year in the United States, with two-thirds of the victims under the age of 25. This article discusses the six most common STDs and provides information regarding their incidence, symptoms, and medical complications.

55. **How Much Are Pesticides Hurting Your Health?** *Tufts University Diet & Nutrition Letter,* April 1996. 233

Want to reduce your risk of cancer and other chronic illnesses? While nutrition experts are urging us to consume *increasing quantities of fruits and vegetables* as a hedge against disease, media headlines report stories warning against the *risk of pesticides* contaminating our food supply. This article examines common beliefs and the facts regarding such contamination.

56. **Why Is Date Rape So Hard to Prove?** Sheila Weller, *Health,* July/August 1992. 236

The National Victim Center estimates that one in every eight women in the United States has been raped, in most cases by someone she knew. Of all these rapes, only about 16 percent are even reported, and the majority of the *cases are dropped* by the prosecution prior to a trial. This article examines the issue of *acquaintance rape* and discusses why it is so hard to make the charge of rape stick. The author also discusses what a woman can do to enhance her chances of successful prosecution.

57. **What Every Woman Needs to Know about Personal Safety,** Lauren David Peden, *McCall's,* May 1992. 239

Clearly, one of the major health hazards facing Americans is violent crime. Current statistics indicate that a violent crime is committed every 17 seconds, and the majority of the victims are women. This article discusses *safety measures women can take* to reduce their risk of becoming victims of *date rape or other violent crimes.*

Index 241
Article Review Form 244
Article Rating Form 245

Topic Guide

This topic guide suggests how the selections in this book relate to topics of traditional concern to health students and professionals. It is useful for locating articles that relate to each other for reading and research. The guide is arranged alphabetically according to topic. Articles may, of course, treat topics that do not appear in the topic guide. In turn, entries in the topic guide do not necessarily constitute a comprehensive listing of all the contents of each selection.

TOPIC AREA	TREATED IN	TOPIC AREA	TREATED IN
Addiction	24. Kicking Butts 25. Alcohol and Tobacco: A Deadly Duo	Consumer Health (continued)	48. Doctor Is On 49. Health Insurance Hazards 50. Are Your Shades Good Enough? 51. Quiz: Are You Ready for the Sun? 54. Prevent Sexually Transmitted Diseases 55. How Much Are Pesticides Hurting Your Health?
AIDS (Acquired Immune Deficiency Syndrome)	6. Critical Life Events and the Onset of Illness 37. Mutant Gene Can Slow AIDS Virus 38. Disease Detective 54. Prevent Sexually Transmitted Diseases		
		Depression	9. Out of the Blues 10. Depression: Way beyond the Blues 24. Kicking Butts
Alcohol	25. Alcohol and Tobacco: A Deadly Duo 26. Alcohol: Spirit of Health? 33. Rating Your Risks for Heart Disease 35. Strategies for Minimizing Cancer Risk	Dietary Fat	2. Healthy Habits: Why Bother? 11. Dietary Gospel—or Phony Baloney? 13. Food Pyramid 14. Fast Food: Fatter than Ever 15. Snack Attack 19. Test Your Weight-Loss IQ 20. Gaining on Fat 32. Cholesterol 45. How Health Savvy Are You?
Birth Control/ Contraception	29. Choosing a Contraceptive 30. Preventing STDs 35. Strategies for Minimizing Cancer Risk		
Cancer	6. Critical Life Events and the Onset of Illness 12. Food for Thought about Dietary Supplements 13. Food Pyramid 25. Alcohol and Tobacco: A Deadly Duo 26. Alcohol: Spirit of Health? 31. Family History 34. Heart of the Matter 35. Strategies for Minimizing Cancer Risk 36. Cancer-Fighting Foods 42. Examining the Routine Examination 45. How Health Savvy Are You? 51. Quiz: Are You Ready for the Sun?	Dietary Fiber	12. Food for Thought about Dietary Supplements 13. Food Pyramid
		Dietary Minerals	12. Food for Thought about Dietary Supplements 36. Cancer-Fighting Foods
		Drugs	10. Depression: Way beyond the Blues 20. Gaining on Fat 22. How to Pick a Pain Reliever 23. OTC Drugs 24. Kicking Butts 25. Alcohol and Tobacco: A Deadly Duo 47. Switch to OTC 53. 'Wonder Drugs'
Cardiovascular Disease	6. Critical Life Events and the Onset of Illness 11. Dietary Gospel—or Phony Baloney? 12. Food for Thought about Dietary Supplements 14. Fast Food: Fatter than Ever 16. Fitness Fiction 18. Fat Times 26. Alcohol: Spirit of Health? 32. Cholesterol 33. Rating Your Risks for Heart Disease 34. Heart of the Matter 42. Examining the Routine Examination	Environmental Health Hazards	35. Strategies for Minimizing Cancer Risk 51. Quiz: Are You Ready for the Sun? 52. Bad News Bugs 53. 'Wonder Drugs' 55. How Much Are Pesticides Hurting Your Health?
		Exercise and Fitness	16. Fitness Fiction 17. Which Exercise Is Best for You? 18. Fat Times 19. Test Your Weight-Loss IQ 32. Cholesterol 33. Rating Your Risks for Heart Disease 34. Heart of the Matter 35. Strategies for Minimizing Cancer Risk 45. How Health Savvy Are You?
Consumer Health	12. Food for Thought about Dietary Supplements 18. Fat Times 22. How To Pick a Pain Reliever 23. OTC Drugs: Prescription for Danger? 30. Preventing STDs 40. Medical Savings Accounts 41. Can HMOs Help Solve Health-Care Crisis? 42. Examining the Routine Examination 43. Your Hospital Stay 44. New Doctors of Natural Medicine 45. How Health Savvy Are You? 46. Nutrition in the News 47. Switch to OTC	Food and Disease Prevention	12. Food for Thought about Dietary Supplements 32. Cholesterol 35. Strategies for Minimizing Cancer Risk 36. Cancer-Fighting Foods

TOPIC AREA	TREATED IN	TOPIC AREA	TREATED IN
Genetics	3. Risk: What It Means to You 10. Depression: Way beyond the Blues 12. Food for Thought about Dietary Supplements 18. Fat Times 19. Test Your Weight-Loss IQ 20. Gaining on Fat 31. Family History 33. Rating Your Risks for Heart Disease 35. Strategies for Minimizing Cancer Risk 37. Mutant Gene Can Slow AIDS Virus	Nutrition	11. Dietary Gospel—or Phony Baloney? 12. Food for Thought about Dietary Supplements 13. Food Pyramid 14. Fast Food: Fatter than Ever 15. Snack Attack 18. Fat Times 32. Cholesterol 35. Strategies for Minimizing Cancer Risk 36. Cancer-Fighting Foods 45. How Health Savvy Are You? 46. Nutrition in the News
Health Care Issues	39. Health Unlimited 40. Medical Savings Accounts 41. Can HMOs Help Solve Health-Care Crisis? 42. Examining the Routine Examination 44. New Doctors of Natural Medicine 49. Health Insurance Hazards	Osteoporosis	12. Food for Thought about Dietary Supplements 17. Which Exercise Is Best for You? 34. Heart of the Matter 45. How Health Savvy Are You?
Health Risk Analysis	2. Healthy Habits: Why Bother? 3. Risk: What It Means to You 5. Challenging America's Inverted Health Priorities 31. Family History 33. Rating Your Risks for Heart Disease 55. How Much Are Pesticides Hurting Your Health?	Personality and Disease	6. Critical Life Events and the Onset of Illness 33. Rating Your Risks for Heart Disease
		Radiation	35. Strategies for Minimizing Cancer Risk 50. Are Your Shades Good Enough? 51. Quiz: Are You Ready for the Sun?
Hypertension	11. Dietary Gospel—or Phony Baloney? 17. Which Exercise Is Best for You? 26. Alcohol: Spirit of Health? 32. Cholesterol 33. Rating Your Risks for Heart Disease 45. How Health Savvy Are You?	Sexual Behavior	27. Lessons of Love 28. The Indispensables 30. Preventing STDs 35. Strategies for Minimizing Cancer Risk 54. Prevent Sexually Transmitted Diseases
		Sexually Transmitted Diseases (STDs)	29. Choosing a Contraceptive 54. Prevent Sexually Transmitted Diseases
Immunity	7. Can You Laugh Your Stress Away? 12. Food for Thought about Dietary Supplements 36. Cancer-Fighting Foods 34. Heart of the Matter 37. Mutant Gene Can Slow AIDS Virus 38. Disease Detective 53. 'Wonder Drugs'	Stress	6. Critical Life Events and the Onset of Illness 7. Can You Laugh Your Stress Away? 8. Good Mood Foods 17. Which Exercise Is Best for You? 21. Body Mania 32. Cholesterol 43. Your Hospital Stay
Infectious Illness	30. Preventing STDs 34. Heart of the Matter 37. Mutant Gene Can Slow AIDS Virus 38. Disease Detective 43. Your Hospital Stay 52. Bad News Bugs 53. 'Wonder Drugs' 54. Prevent Sexually Transmitted Diseases	Tobacco and Health	5. Challenging America's Inverted Health Priorities 24. Kicking Butts 25. Alcohol and Tobacco: A Deadly Duo 32. Cholesterol 33. Rating Your Risks for Heart Disease
		Violence and Rape	56. Why Is Date Rape So Hard to Prove? 57. What Every Woman Needs to Know about Personal Safety
Longevity	5. Challenging America's Inverted Health Priorities 31. Family History 35. Strategies for Minimizing Cancer Risk 37. Mutant Gene Can Slow AIDS Virus	Vitamins	12. Food for Thought about Dietary Supplements 32. Cholesterol
Medical Concerns and Ethics	23. OTC Drugs 39. Health Unlimited 43. Your Hospital Stay 47. Switch to OTC 48. The Doctor Is On 49. Health Insurance Hazards	Weight Control/Obesity	11. Dietary Gospel—or Phony Baloney? 15. Snack Attack 16. Fitness Fiction 17. Which Exercise Is Best for You? 18. Fat Times 19. Test Your Weight-Loss IQ 20. Gaining on Fat 21. Body Mania 32. Cholesterol 33. Rating Your Risks for Heart Disease 35. Strategies for Minimizing Cancer Risk
Mental Health and Depression	7. Can You Laugh Your Stress Away? 8. Good Mood Foods 9. Out of the Blues 10. Depression: Way beyond the Blues 24. Kicking Butts 49. Health Insurance Hazards		

Health Behavior and Decision Making

Those of us who protect our health daily and those of us who put our health in constant jeopardy have exactly the same mortality: 100 percent. The difference, of course, is the timing." This quote from Elizabeth M. Whelan reminds us that we must all face the fact that we are going to die sometime. This book, and especially this unit, are designed to assist students in the development of cognitive skills and knowledge that, when put to use, can postpone the moment of death as long as possible. While we cannot control all of the things that happen to us, we must all strive to make informed decisions about things we can control.

To consider the issue of decision making in the proper perspective, let us first address the issue of risk taking. Everything we do in life involves risk, from taking a bath to bungee jumping. The question we must all address is whether any specific behavior is worth the risk. Answering such questions requires accurate information and active choice. The goal of health education is to assist students in learning the skills necessary to make informed decisions. We cannot predict what knowledge the future will bring, but we can acquire skills that can be used to evaluate the validity and significance of new information as it becomes available. The article "Challenging America's Inverted Health Priorities" argues that we have a tendency to minimize the dangers of known hazards such as tobacco and alcohol and focus our attention on potentially minor health hazards. The author argues that this situation is the result of economic and political forces.

Health-related articles fill our newspapers, magazines, and television broadcasts. Rather than inform and enlighten the public on significant new medical discoveries, much of this coverage does little more than add to the level of public confusion. At least two major factors lead to such confusion. The first is that, along with keeping the public informed, these media have the additional goal of increasing circulation and viewership. That is, they are dedicated to selling copies and advertising space and time. In their quest to create interest, then, the media often try to capitalize on medical discoveries by overstating their significance before all the facts are known. The second factor that contributes to confusion is ignorance on behalf of the American public regarding how scientific investigations are conducted. If we as health educators and students wish to reduce the confusion and hyperbole surrounding health matters, we must identify criteria for consumers' use in assessing news stories. The article "Risk: What It Means to You" is included in this unit because it discusses the strengths and weaknesses of the scientific methods being used to study health problems. The report "Healthy Habits: Why Bother?" demonstrates how scientific investigations can come to faulty conclusions if the statistical analysis does not include relevant variables. That is, numbers can be manipulated so that they are misleading. This article also addresses the influence that our health behaviors can have on both our longevity and the quality of our lives.

While the scientific community is in general agreement that certain behaviors promote health and others are damaging, experience has taught us that information alone is not enough to bring about behavioral change in many people. A good example of such resistance is discussed in "A Picture of Health." How can health educators assist people to change their behavior? In " 'Just Do It' Isn't Enough: Change Comes in Stages," Dr. James Prochaska is interviewed about the stages of change that most people go through when they are successful in making a lasting behavior change.

While the goal of health education is to promote healthy lifestyles, this objective cannot be reached unless

UNIT 1

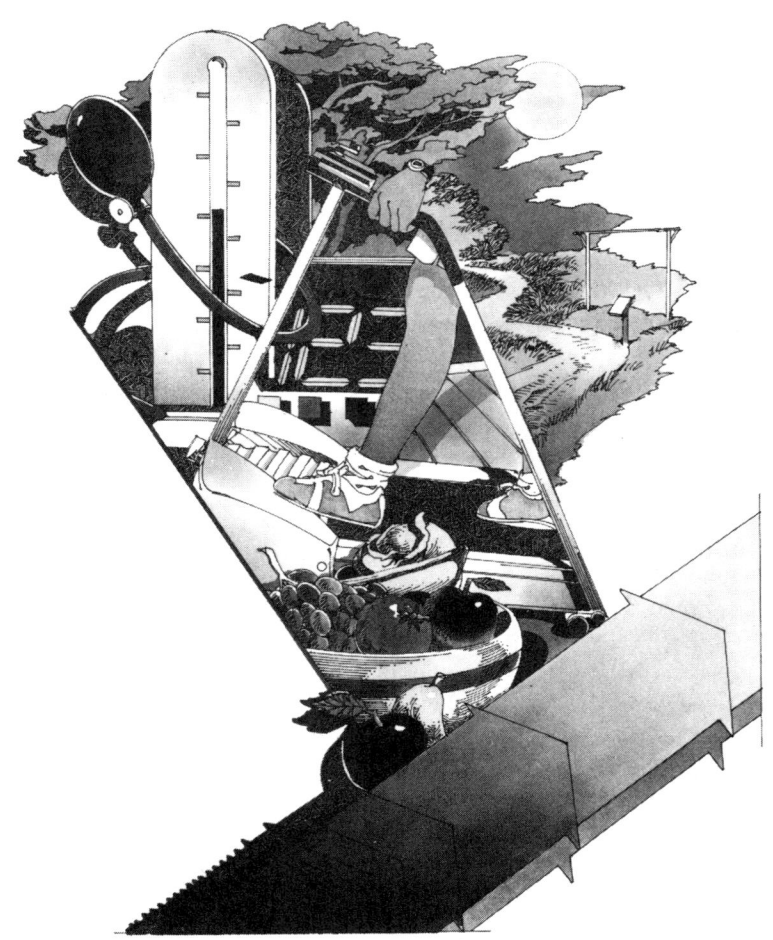

or until the public is armed with the knowledge and skills necessary to make informed decisions. Even then, the choice is, and must remain, up to each individual.

Looking Ahead: Challenge Questions

Why do people continue to engage in specific behaviors that they know will have a negative impact on their health?

How successfully are Americans moving toward the goals set forth by the "Healthy People 2000" initiative?

What is the difference between absolute risk and relative risk as it applies to the likelihood of developing a particular health problem? How are these statistics derived?

Explain how the improper use of statistical methods can yield misleading results to an otherwise sound research design.

Discuss the six stages of change and the role each plays in bringing about a permanent behavioral change.

Explain the statement that America has inverted its national health priorities.

Which of your health behaviors would you like to change? What prevents you from making these changes?

A PICTURE OF HEALTH

Here's a look at the health of the nation—and a chance to evaluate your own habits.

Last year, as part of its Healthy People 2000 program, the U.S. Public Health Service gave a "midterm exam" to see whether we're becoming a nation of healthier people. The results were mixed. Some trends are clearly headed in the right direction; in other areas, many Americans are losing ground. The table on page 8 lists baseline data collected mostly in the 1980s, midterm results mostly from the first half of the 1990s, and the goals for the year 2000. The final column shows how our readers stack up against the average American, based on the results of a random survey of some 900 subscribers.

Overall, our readers are a healthy lot—or at least a health-conscious lot, as you might expect. In most of the 19 areas covered by our quiz, they appear to have

> *There's room for improvement in several areas.*

quite a head start toward the national goals; in fact, they've surpassed many of those goals. But there's room for improvement in several other areas.

See how you compare—what you're doing right, and where you fall short.

Weight control

Your answer to **question #1**, body mass index, indicates whether you are officially overweight. A BMI of 27.8 or higher for men or 27.3 or higher for women qualifies.

The nation as a whole has put on quite a bit of weight since the Public Health Service set its objective of no more than 20 percent of all adults overweight by decade's end. But our readers seem to be on target for meeting that goal.

Maintaining a healthy weight is one of the most important things you can do to protect your overall health and longevity. In addition to the personal cost, overweight also costs society a bundle—as much as $52-billion a year, according to some estimates. (Note that the need to lose weight depends not just on your body mass index, but other factors as well. See *Consumer Reports on Health*'s September 1995 issue.)

Fitness

In response to **question #2**, roughly one-quarter of our readers reported getting physical activity at least as intense as sustained walking for at least half an hour a day. Another third said they "usually" did.

Such light-to-moderate exertion is what fitness authorities now recommend—having backed off from an earlier, more demanding prescription that probably scared away more people than it attracted. That change of heart came in response to studies showing that exercise's ability to prevent disease depends more on the total amount of activity people get than on how hard they work out. Best of all, you don't have to put in your half hour all at once; you can piece it together in brief bursts throughout the day.

Just because light exercise is good for you doesn't mean that more vigorous exercise isn't better. The traditional prescription of at least a 20-minute hard workout three times a week still gives the heart and lungs a boost you can't get from gentler exercise. Twenty percent of our readers report "always" getting that much exercise (**question #3**)—which exactly matches the national goal set for the year 2000.

On the other hand, our survey sample—and the rest of the nation—falls far short of the goal set for regular strength-training exercise (**question #4**), which includes weight lifting, resistance training, and other muscle-building activities. Even adding the 12 percent who "usually" perform strength training at least twice a week to the 15 percent who "always" do, our readers still don't approach the ambitious 40 percent participation level that the Public Health Service dreams of. That's unfortunate—since, as we reported last month, muscle-building exercise provides many important benefits, most of which you won't get from other types of exercise.

Diet

Reliable dietary data are notoriously difficult to collect. You really can't rely on off-hand self-reports of how much fat or how many servings of a particular food group are in the diet. That said, our readers' *impressions* of their typical diet make interesting reading.

Roughly one-third claimed that they "always" follow a diet that gets no more than 30 percent of its total calories from fat (**question #5**). Nearly as many believe their saturated-fat intake doesn't exceed the recommended maximum of 10 percent of calories (**question #6**). The latest Government data show that the average American's fat intake hovers around 34 percent of total calories, with saturated fat at about 12 percent.

Fewer readers put as much effort into getting at least six daily servings of grains, including bread, cereal, pasta, and rice (**question #7**). While the national average intake has nearly reached that Healthy People goal, the recommended intake is actually 6 to 11 servings of grains. That may sound like an awful lot, but it's actually quite doable when you consider what constitutes a single serving. Some examples:
- 1 slice of bread.
- 1/2 cup cooked cereal, rice, or pasta.
- 1/2 bagel, muffin, or bun.
- 1 small tortilla.
- 5 saltine crackers.
- 1 ounce, by weight, of ready-to-eat cereal.

Whenever possible, choose whole-grain products, which retain the nutrient-rich bran and germ. (Look for the words "100 percent whole grain" on the label, or check to see that "whole wheat flour" is the first ingredient listed.)

If it's true that 28 percent of our readers always eat at least five daily servings of fruits and vegetables (**question #8**), they are to be commended. The national average is about four servings—but at least one of those servings comes from white potatoes, half the time in the form of french fries. As we have reported many times, nothing beats the health benefits of a diet rich in produce. (But french fries don't count as a healthy vegetable.)

Compared with the national average, our readers report a somewhat higher intake of calcium-rich foods (**question #9**): 27 percent "always" eat at least two servings a day, versus 21 percent nationally. (Pregnant and lactating women should have at least three daily servings.) But that's still nowhere near the Healthy People goal of 50 percent.

It's worth noting that, on each of the above dietary questions, an additional 41 to 48 percent of our survey respondents reported that they "usually" achieved the goal.

Safety, stress, smoking, and shots

Thanks to legislation as well as education, the proportion of the motoring public that wears seat belts has increased substantially in recent years—from 42 percent to 67 percent. According to our survey (**question #10**), our readers have already reached the national goal of 85 percent compliance (93 percent, if you count the "usually's").

Half our readers "always" observe safe-sun practices to prevent sunburn, wrinkles, and skin cancer. **Question #11** notes the main strategies: Minimize your sun exposure, wear protective clothing, and use sunscreen. In tests of 38 sunscreens published last May, Consumer Reports found three brands that offer sufficient protection for well under a dollar an ounce: *Solace Sunblock* (from Kmart), *Eckerd Sunblock*, and *Rite Aid Sunblock*. If you need extended waterproofing, consider *Bain de Soleil All Day Waterproof*, which provides good "broad-spectrum" ultra-

> *French fries don't count as a healthy vegetable.*

violet protection, or *Vaseline Intensive Care Moisturizing*, the least expensive brand in this category at about $1.75 an ounce.

Considerable research has shown that unchecked stress can wreak havoc with emotional and physical health. In fact, as we reported last July, chronic stress can be deadly. Recognizing those hazards, the Public Health Service hopes that virtually all people who experience "significant" stress will take steps to reduce or control it. According to the response to **question #12**, some four out of five stressed-out readers currently take such steps. Meanwhile, the general public has been more or less holding steady at about three out of four.

The response to **question #13** shows that no one who subscribes to a health newsletter needs to be told not to smoke. Only 6 percent of our readers are smokers—and more than half of them have recently tried to quit. The total number of American smokers, though not yet down to the goal of 15 percent, continues to shrink and now stands at about 25 percent.

Apparently, the vast majority of our older readers have heeded public-health exhortations—including ours—to get an annual flu shot (**question #14**). Fully 80 percent of those aged 65 and older got one last year, which tops the national goal of 60 percent. New research shows that even healthy young adults can benefit from the vaccination. But it's critically important for older people and others at high risk

1. HEALTH BEHAVIOR AND DECISION MAKING

(and their caregivers), since influenza can lead to deadly pneumonia in those people. People at high risk should also be vaccinated against pneumonia directly; a single shot should last a lifetime in healthy people, but some high-risk people will need to be revaccinated. Most of our older readers have had the pneumonia vaccine, though not as many as have had an annual flu shot. Nationally, vaccination rates among older adults are considerably lower for both shots.

Blood cholesterol and blood pressure

If there's one word that best reflects the popular preoccupation with health these days, it's cholesterol. Probably not a single issue of Consumer Reports on Health has ever been entirely "cholesterol free." So it's no surprise that virtually all of our readers have had their cholesterol levels checked (**question 15**). Only 13 percent have highly elevated total-cholesterol levels of 240 mg/dl or more, and the nation as a whole has already achieved the goal of 20 percent. (An additional 32 percent of our respondents have moderately elevated cholesterol levels between 200 and 240 mg/dl.) Of those readers who do have dangerously high cholesterol levels, 87 percent are doing something about it (diet, drugs, or both), well above the national goal of 60 percent.

HEALTHY PEOPLE 2000

Objective	Public Health Service data			Our readers
	Baseline	Midterm	Goal	
WEIGHT CONTROL				
Overweight (Q1)	26%	34%	20%	23%
FITNESS				
Regular light-to-moderate physical activity (Q2)	22%	24%	30%	27%
Regular vigorous physical activity (Q3)	12%	14%	20%	20%
Regular strength-training activities (Q4)	11%	16%	40%	15%
DIET				
Low-fat diet (Q5)	36% [1]	34% [1]	≤30% [1]	34% [2]
Low-saturated-fat diet (Q6)	13% [1]	12% [1]	<10% [1]	30% [2]
Diet rich in grains (Q7)	3.5 [3]	5.8 [3]	≥6 [3]	20% [2]
Fruit- and vegetable-rich diet (Q8)	3.0 [3]	4.1 [3]	≥5 [3]	28% [2]
Calcium-rich diet (Q9)	19% [4]	21% [4]	50% [4]	27% [2]
SAFETY, STRESS, SMOKING, AND SHOTS				
Motor-vehicle safety restraints (Q10)	42%	67%	85%	85%
Safe sun exposure (Q11)	[5]	NA	60%	50%
Stress management (Q12)	76%	72%	95%	80%
Smokers (Q13)	29%	25%	15%	6%
Tried to quit in past year (Q13a)	34%	38%	50%	54%
Men and women aged 65 and older				
Annual flu shot (Q14a)	30%	52%	60%	80%
Pneumonia vaccine (Q14b)	14%	28%	60%	56%
BLOOD CHOLESTEROL AND BLOOD PRESSURE				
Blood cholesterol checked in past five years (Q15)	55%	60%	75%	94%
High total cholesterol of ≥240 mg/dl (Q15a)	27%	20%	20%	13%
Diet or drug therapy for high total cholesterol of ≥240 mg/dl (Q15b)	NA	NA	60%	87%
HEART DISEASE AND STROKE PREVENTION				
Blood pressure measured in past two years (Q16)	61%	76%	90%	98%
High blood pressure diagnosed (Q16a)	NA	NA	NA	22%
Drug/nondrug therapy for high blood pressure (Q16b)	79%	80%	90%	95%
High blood pressure under control (Q16c)	11%	21%	50%	83%
CANCER SCREENING				
All women				
Pap test in past three years (Q17)	75%	78%	85%	88%
Women aged 50 and older				
Professional breast exam and mammogram in past two years (Q18)	25%	55%	60%	89%
Men and women aged 50 and older				
Fecal occult-blood test in past two years (Q19a)	27%	30%	50%	62%
Sigmoidoscopy (Q19b)	25%	33%	40%	67%

[1] Percentage of total calories from fat or from saturated fat in average U.S. adult diet.
[2] Percentage of our survey respondents whose diet "always" meets the goal for that dietary habit.
[3] Number of servings of each type of food in the average U.S. adult diet.
[4] Percentage of U.S. adults who eat two or more daily servings of calcium-rich foods.
[5] Baseline data available only for individual safe-sun behaviors (31% limit sun exposure, 28% use sunscreen, 28% wear protective clothing); national goal and reader survey combine all three behaviors.

Last year, a widely publicized study suggested that cholesterol levels don't matter much in older people. We disputed that notion in a report last August and we follow up this month.

Our readers also appear to be fully aware of the importance of controlling blood pressure (**question #16**); 98 percent have had their blood pressure measured in the past two years. Among the 22 percent who have been diagnosed with hypertension (defined as 140/90 mm Hg or higher), 95 percent are treating their condition, through drug or nondrug therapy. And 83 percent of those readers have their high blood pressure under control, compared with the national goal of 50 percent and the national reality of just 21 percent. (For a complete guide to treatment of hypertension, see *CR on Health*'s May 1995 issue.)

Cancer screening

If all women had regular Pap smears, almost all of the nearly 5000 deaths from cervical cancer in the U.S. each year could be prevented. According to their response to **question #17**, almost 9 out of 10 of our female readers have had a Pap test within the past three years. (However, a study published last year in the Journal of the American Medical Association suggests that self-reported rates of such cancer screening tests may greatly exaggerate the true number.)

An equally high proportion of our female readers aged 40 and older report having a professional breast exam and a mammogram within the past two years (**question #18**). The Public Health Service goal of 60 percent kicks in only at age 50, but Consumers Union's medical consultants, like most public-health authorities, recommend mammography every one to two years from age 40 to 50, and annually thereafter.

Two other screening tests—sigmoidoscopy, in which the physician examines the rectum and lower intestine with a flexible lighted tube, and the fecal occult-blood test, which involves checking stool samples for hidden blood—can save lives by detecting early signs of colorectal cancer, the second leading cause of cancer death. (Lung cancer is first.) Everyone aged 50 and older should have a sigmoidoscopy every three to five years, but only one in three Americans has ever had one (**question #19**). Twice as many of our readers in that age range report the same. Nearly as many say they've had the occult-blood test within the past two years; actually, everyone should have that test each year after age 40. Squeamishness is certainly not a good reason to skip either test. Neither is fear of pain during sigmoidoscopy; the five-minute procedure causes only mild discomfort.

Healthy habits: Why bother?

The payoff is far greater than some stories and studies suggest.

Frenchwoman Jeanne Calment, the oldest person alive, stopped smoking three years ago at age 117. Conversely, heart attacks killed health-diet enthusiast Euell Gibbons at age 64 and running guru Jim Fixx at 52.

Last summer, a widely publicized Canadian study seemed to confirm the generalization suggested by those incidents—that self-discipline is a waste of time, since it won't really change how long you live. The study, based on a computer model, estimated that cutting consumption of fat and cholesterol roughly in half would lengthen the average man's life by a measly four months.

Is it all just a matter of fate? Not really.

Better than average

Scattered tales of smokers who live a long life or of health buffs who die young should come as no surprise. Health habits, good or bad, change the likelihood of living a long time; they don't guarantee a short or a long life.

That helps explain why expressing the effect of health habits on longevity as an average, as the Canadian computer study did, understates their potential importance. A low-fat, low-cholesterol diet may not, in fact, significantly reduce the risk of a heart attack in people who have little risk of an attack in the first place. Averaging in those low-risk people shrinks the apparent effect of diet on longevity—and obscures its potentially dramatic impact on more vulnerable individuals. Someone who dies, say, at age 65 due to a heart attack that could have been prevented by cutting down on fat consumption has typically lost 15 to 20 years of life.

Even in terms of averages, the Canadian study greatly understated the likely benefit of healthy living. First, the researchers considered only the effect of consuming less fat and cholesterol on heart-attack risk. But cutting fat consumption also reduces the risk of developing other potentially deadly conditions: obesity and certain cancers. Further, people who cut their intake of fat and cholesterol often boost their intake of fruits, vegetables, grains, and beans, which may also help fend off coronary disease and cancer. Indeed, data collected from the ongoing Framingham Heart Study, based on people's actual diets rather than a narrow computer projection, suggest that—on average—those who eat little fat will live almost two years longer than other people.

Most important, individuals who watch their diet typically practice other healthy habits that can further lengthen their lives. Researchers at Northwestern University combed through data from five large studies, lasting an average of 20 years, to identify two groups with contrasting risk factors for disease. One group, containing more than 130,000 people, smoked moderately; they also had marginally elevated blood pressure and blood-cholesterol levels, both of which can often be prevented or eliminated by exercising, losing weight, or following a careful diet. The other group, containing more than 11,000 people, had none of those traits.

Extrapolating from death rates during the studies, the researchers calculated that the low-risk group, with its presumably healthier habits, would live an average of five to nine years longer than the other group. And again, such averages tend to understate the potential increase in longevity.

Other studies that looked mainly at habits, not risk factors, provide more direct evidence that a healthy lifestyle can lengthen life. Researchers at the University of California at Los Angeles studied some 7000 people for more than two decades. They looked at three clearly harmful habits—smoking, excessive drinking, and physical inactivity—as well as three habits thought to identify people who neglect their health: skipping breakfast, eating between meals, and sleeping fewer than seven or more than eight hours a night. They also included being overweight, which tends to reflect overeating and lack of exercise. The results indicated that a 45-year-old man who has fewer than four of those negative traits will live an average of 11 years longer than a similar man who has more than five traits. Women can expect to experience somewhat smaller but still substantial increases in longevity.

Another large, lengthy study did more than just compare people with different habits: It analyzed the effects of actually improving those habits. The researchers, from Stanford and Harvard Universities, calculated that starting to exercise and giving up cigarettes would each add an average of almost two years to the men's lives. The volunteers who started to improve their habits during their 30s or 40s benefited more than that. But those who did so in their 70s or 80s still lengthened their lives significantly.

A better life, too

Extending life wouldn't mean much if it simply meant living more years with more disease and more disability. But the same steps that can add years to your life can add life to your years. Healthy habits reduce the risk not only of fatal heart attacks and cancer but also of chronic ailments that can be physically, psychologically, and financially debilitating. Indeed, older people who have maintained such habits often possess the abilities and overall health of people years or even decades younger.

To document that benefit, researchers at the California Department of Health Services asked nearly 4000 people about the same seven unhealthy habits examined in the UCLA longevity study. Nine years later, the researchers assessed the volunteers' overall health, in part by simply counting their chronic disorders, including coronary disease, hypertension, arthritis, ulcers, and 11 other ailments. Those who started out with the fewest harmful habits ended up far healthier than those with the greatest number of bad habits.

In a second study of some 4300 people, the UCLA researchers found that only 12 percent of those who started out with few or no unhealthy habits became disabled over the next decade, compared with 19 percent of those who had many bad habits—nearly a 40 percent reduction in risk.

Exercise, the best medicine

Regular exercise and a sound diet can each reduce the risk of potentially debilitating conditions, including coronary disease, diabetes, obesity, and osteoporosis. But exercise can also help keep people active by maintaining their strength, aerobic capacity, endurance, and mobility, all of which tend to dwindle with advancing age.

Researchers at Stanford University followed some 450 runners and 330 nonrunners, aged 50 to 72, for eight years. After adjusting for the presence of disease or disability at the start of the study, the researchers found that those who didn't run developed three and a half times more disabling ailments than those who did run. Even those exercisers who ran the least—just one to five miles a week—reduced their risk of disability nearly as much as those who ran the most.

Exercise can further boost the quality of life by keeping people's spirits up as they age. It apparently does that not only by keeping them strong and healthy but also by improving mood directly. Another team of Stanford researchers randomly assigned some 360 people, aged 50 to 65, either to start working out or to remain inactive. After one year, the exercisers reported significantly less stress, anxiety, and depression than the inactive group. It didn't matter how hard they exercised, as long as they exercised regularly.

Sound habits, sharp mind

Good health habits may help older people preserve their mental faculties as well. A recently published 35-year study of some 5000 Seattle residents found that those who stayed physically healthy—in part, presumably, because they practiced healthy habits—were more likely to stay mentally sharp when they reached their 70s or 80s. One theory: Chronic conditions such as hypertension, coronary disease, and lung disease may reduce the delivery of oxygen to the brain or even cause tiny, unnoticed strokes.

But there's another possibility: People who feel sick may avoid mentally challenging activity. And mental exercise may help preserve the mind, just as physical exercise preserves the body. The Seattle study, for example, linked several signs of robust mental activity—ongoing education, an interesting job, extensive travel or reading, even being married to a smart spouse—with a sharper mind later in life.

Indeed, mental exercise may help reverse the mental decline that often accompanies aging. The same

1. HEALTH BEHAVIOR AND DECISION MAKING

researchers offered some 230 Seattle residents, aged 64 to 95, training in various mental skills, such as how to recognize and logically manipulate patterns of words, numbers, or shapes. Afterward, 40 percent of those whose mental abilities had declined regained the acuity they possessed 14 years earlier. And 47 percent of the rest, whose thinking had not slowed down, became sharper than ever. Seven years later, the researchers reinterviewed more than half the volunteers and found that they still solved mental problems better than similar people who had not been trained. One reason for that lasting improvement, the researchers concluded, is that the training encouraged the volunteers to keep using their mind.

How long will you live?

If you were born before 1930, you've already lived at least several years longer than scientists back then expected you to live. The average life expectancy of infants born in 1930 was 62 years for girls, 58 for boys. Today, those same girls and boys, now in their mid-60s, can anticipate living until ages 84 and 80, respectively.

Some of that increased longevity is due simply to statistics: As you get older, your life expectancy automatically expands, since the possibility of dying young, which drags the average down, no longer applies. But the increased longevity also reflects a dramatic reduction in the risk of death from chronic diseases associated with aging, particularly coronary disease, due mainly to reductions in smoking and consumption of saturated fat and cholesterol. More encouraging, there's still lots of room for improvement: Researchers at Duke University project that if everyone born today took the steps needed to control the major risk factors for coronary disease and cancer, the average life span might soar as high as 100 years.

Numbering your days

The table at right shows how long you can expect to live, depending on your current age. Those numbers are based on averages for the entire population. Good or bad health habits—as well as hereditary factors beyond your control—can change them by as much as a decade or more.

Each of the factors listed below tends to push your life expectancy higher than average. The more factors you have and, in most cases, the longer you've had them, the longer your life expectancy.

- Regular exercise routine.
- Diet low in fat and high in fruits and vegetables.
- Blood level of low-density-lipoprotein (LDL) cholesterol significantly lower than average before age 65 or so. (In women, the average LDL level rises steadily from 110 mg/dl during early adulthood to about 145 mg/dl by age 60 or so. In men it rises from 120 mg/dl among young adults to more than 140 mg/dl by around age 60.)
- Blood level of high-density lipoprotein (HDL) cholesterol significantly higher than average before age 65. (Women's average HDL level holds fairly steady at 56 mg/dl; men's HDL averages 46 mg/dl.)
- Hormone replacement therapy if you're a postmenopausal woman.
- Family history of living to an old age.

In contrast, the following factors tend to drag life expectancy below the average:

- LDL level that's significantly higher than average or HDL level that's lower than average before age 65.
- Hypertension in a young person or severe hypertension in an older person.
- Smoking cigarettes.
- Obesity.
- Family history of early coronary disease, cancer, diabetes, or other deadly disease.
- Excessive alcohol consumption (more than two drinks a day for men, one a day for women).

LIFE EXPECTANCY BY CURRENT AGE

If your age now is...	You can expect to live to age...	
	Men	Women
0	72	79
20	74	80
25	74	80
30	75	80
35	75	81
40	76	81
45	76	81
50	77	82
55	78	82
60	79	83
65	80	84
70	82	86
75	85	87
80	87	89
85	90	92

Source: U.S. Department of Health and Human Services, 1995.

Risk: What it Means to You

Life is a risky business. We're born with a genetic legacy that puts us at risk for certain medical conditions, and many of the things we do as we go along—including simply getting older—compound our risk of illness and death.

Lest we lose sight of our mortality, we are constantly reminded of it by the media. By now we're well aware that the average woman's lifetime risk of being diagnosed with breast cancer is 1 in 8 and that we stand a 1 in 2 chance of developing cardiovascular disease eventually. Moreover, we're continually hearing of new ways that we may be raising those risks further—most recently, that long-term hormone-replacement therapy can increase the likelihood of breast cancer by 40% and that putting on 20 pounds in adulthood can elevate the chance of heart attack by 60%.

Not only are our brains awash in statistics, the numbers often succeed in heightening our anxiety as well as our awareness. Although these reports may be somewhat scary, they can be quite helpful if, when we read them, we keep in mind the nature of the studies mentioned, the magnitude of the risk the studies suggest, and our own personal risk profile.

The basis of risk

Epidemiologists—the scientists who search out causes of disease—coined the term risk factor to describe a specific practice or physical characteristic that increases the likelihood of illness or injury. Once it became obvious that we could stave off many diseases by changing our ways (in medical parlance, "modifying our risk factors"), increasing numbers of studies have been directed at identifying risk factors so that we might do away with—or at least reduce—them. These investigations commonly take one of two shapes—as an observational study or a clinical trial.

Epidemiologic studies

Epidemiologists accumulate extensive repositories of information by tracking large groups of people for several years, usually through interviews and questionnaires. These data bases are consulted periodically in search of answers to questions. For example, the researchers conducting the Nurses' Health Study, whose records include all sorts of information from 115,000 women over a 20-year period, have looked at wide-ranging assortment of suspected risk factors—from hair dye to high-fat diets to hormones.

When the Nurse's Health Study investigators looked into the possibility of a link between postmenopausal estrogen use and breast cancer they scanned the data base to assemble a group of women who had reported that they had used estrogen. They then put together a comparison group that mirrored the first group—except that its members said that they hadn't taken estrogen. The researchers assumed that if estrogen has no effect on breast-cancer risk, the breast-cancer rate in both groups would be about the same; that if estrogen raises breast-cancer risk, the group taking it would have a significantly higher breast-cancer rate; and if it reduces risk, the estrogen-takers group would have a significantly lower rate.

In epidemiologic investigations, the larger the number of people studied, the more reliable the results are considered to be. Having big numbers reduces the statistical probability that the events that occur—be they lymphoma among women who dye their hair or breast cancer among estrogen users—are due only to chance. When tens of thousands of people are enrolled in a study, it is almost certain that a wide array of characteristics will be represented in the study population, making it easier for the investigator to assemble groups with similar profiles for comparison.

Even well designed and brilliantly executed epidemiologic studies have built-in limitations. Most of the information comes from reports by the participants or from medical records and death certificates. Because human memory is fallible and record-keeping isn't standardized from place to place, the researchers can't be certain that the data are correct. Moreover, there may be confounding factors they haven't taken into account. For example, some experts have challenged the epidemiologic evidence that estrogen

1. HEALTH BEHAVIOR AND DECISION MAKING

prevents heart attack on the basis that women on estrogen are more likely to be health-conscious and to have frequent medical exams. Therefore, they contend, such women would be less prone to heart attack even if they weren't taking estrogen.

Clinical trials

Clinical trials are often used to verify risk factors suggested by observational investigations. In these studies, two or more groups are randomly selected from a pool of people with similar characteristics. Each group is instructed to follow a different regimen, and all are monitored, usually by periodic physical examinations and tests, for several years. For example, women in the HRT arm of the Women's Health Initiative will be assigned to one of three groups —two of which will take different HRT regimens, and one of which will take a placebo. Each group will be followed for several years to determine which group has the highest rate of heart disease.

In many instances, controlled trials aren't feasible for ethical or economic reasons. For example, there have been no such studies of the relationship of cigarette smoking to lung cancer because it is considered unethical to ask nonsmokers to adopt a practice that is generally considered to be harmful just so they can be studied. Moreover, to keep people coming for periodic examinations and tests for as long as it takes to develop a disease — often several decades— is often prohibitively expensive as well as impractical. Thus, many risk factors are often accepted on the weight of epidemiologic evidence alone, just as smoking has been.

Types of risk

The results of both observational investigations and clinical trials are reported in terms of *relative risk*, which is derived by comparing the outcomes of each group in a study. One group, usually the group made up of people without the suspected risk factor, is used as a reference point. For example, the Nurses' Health Study investigators divided the breast-cancer rate of each of the groups of women who took estrogen by the breast-cancer rate of the group not taking estrogen. They emerged with 1.4 for women ages 50–64 who took estrogen for more than 5 years, and 1.7 for those ages 65–69 who did the same. Thus, they reported that hormone use increased breast-cancer risk by 40% for the former group and by 70% for the latter group.

To put relative risk in perspective, it helps to look at the *absolute* risk as well. Absolute risk is based on incidence rates — the percentage of the population who develop a disease in a given year. For a woman between the ages of 55 and 59, the incidence of breast cancer is less than 0.3% — or, more precisely, her chances of being diagnosed with breast-cancer are 1 in 386. If the Nurses' Health Study's findings are applicable to most women, the risk for the average 57-year old woman with more than five years of hormone-replacement therapy is 40% higher, or about 0.4% (1 case in every 292 women).

What do these numbers mean to you?

It's not necessary to pick up the pocket calculator the next time you hear the words "increased risk" on the news. Despite the precision implied by decimal points, percentage signs, and odds ratios, knowing risk statistics won't help you to calculate the exact probability that *you* will develop — or escape — disease. However, they can serve as a general guide to more healthful living if you keep the following in mind:

• *Heredity*. Our genetic makeup — the hand fate dealt us — is usually the strongest single determinant of risk. The Human Genome Project — the major effort to identify and locate each of our 50,000 to 100,000 genes within the next decade — may make it possible for each of us to have our own genetic risk profile one day. In the meantime, for most of us, the best indicator of hereditary risk is family history.

• *Magnitude*. A slight elevation — 10 to 30% — in the risk of a given disease has about the same effect on our health as a minor increase in the price of a box of cereal on our grocery bill; it doesn't make a lot of difference unless our risk — or cereal consumption — is high to begin with. However, a marked increase — 100% or more — should serve as an alarm to all of us.

• *Repetition*. Anything pinpointed as a risk factor in several independent investigations — for example, smoking, excessive alcohol consumption, obesity, sedentary lifestyles, or diets high in saturated fats—is worth taking seriously. Conversely, multiple studies can clear some practices—like caffeine consumption—that were once suspect.

In the past few decades, identifying risk factors has done more than jangle our nerves. It has helped to drive down the death rate from heart attack and stroke, and may one day have a similar effect on breast cancer.

UPDATE

Taking too much vitamin A before or during pregnancy can dramatically increase the risk of bearing a child with birth defects, according to a study of 22,000 women. Researchers at Boston University determined that risk increased steadily in doses above 10,000 international units (IU) a day; women who took 20,000 IU or more had 480% the risk of those taking 5,000 IU, the approximate dose in prenatal vitamins.

The advice to women: If you are taking a supplement, choose beta-carotene — which the body converts to vitamin A on demand and is safe at most doses.

"Just do it" isn't enough: change comes in stages

The release earlier this summer of the Surgeon General's report entitled *Physical Activity and Health* certainly was well intended. But its advice was far from ground-breaking. Americans had heard it before in countless other official reports: Get some exercise.

Perhaps because more than 60 percent of adults still are not heeding the call to engage in enough physical activity, the report tries to make "enough" sound simpler than ever. Walk, rake leaves, wax your car, wash windows—just do *something*.

Why won't people get off the couch and move their bodies? For that matter, why won't they eat less fat, make a salad, or have fruit for a snack when they know these things are good for them?

James Prochaska, PhD, a psychologist and head of the Health Promotion Partnership at the University of Rhode Island, says it's because change doesn't begin with action. Thus, whenever advice to change starts with the admonition to act—which is most of the time—it can backfire.

Fewer than 20 percent of a population that needs to make a change are prepared for action at any given time, Dr. Prochaska says in his book *Changing for Good* (William Morrow and Company, New York, 1994, $22). "Yet more than 90 percent of behavior change programs are designed with this 20 percent in mind." Everyone else falls through the cracks.

Dr. Prochaska says action is the fourth of 6 stages of change (see box). Apparently, he's onto something. His approach has been used successfully by, among others, the National Cancer Institute to help people stop smoking, by the National Institutes for Alcoholism and Alcohol Abuse to help people stop drinking, and by the Centers for Disease Control and Prevention to curb behavior that leads to HIV infection.

To find out more about the stages of change, we conducted an exclusive interview with Dr. Prochaska.

Q: Don't many people make changes cold turkey? After all, you hear so many people say, "I quit smoking once and for all on January 1st"; or "I woke up one day and said, 'That's it!' and began to exercise."

Dr. Prochaska: We haven't been able to find those folks. Sure, there are people who say that. But if you start to assess them further, you often find that this is not the first time they've taken action. Studies show that on average, New Year's resolutions are made 3 years in a row.

If it is the first time, you have to ask, "What got you doing it at this point?" And you'll see that over time, they have been reevaluating themselves and becoming more aware that their values about healthful living are in conflict with their behavior.

Let's use smoking as an example. People can say exactly when they quit and that it was cold turkey. They can tell you it was sheer willpower. But they may not recognize how their awareness had been increasing, because it's a continuous kind of thing—becoming more and more tuned into the disadvantages of the old behavior and the advantages of change. It's something that happens gradually over time. In other words, they've been going through a couple of the preaction stages of change—contemplation and preparation. And those are stages that, together, could last for years.

Q: You said that some people claim they make a behavior change because of willpower. Is willpower really the crux of it?

Dr. Prochaska: I think it's helpful to think of willpower as equalling commitment. But you have to recognize that commitment alone will not solve the problem. It's an important process, but not the only one.

Think of smokers who enter the hospital for surgery for cardiovascular disease. They may never have made any move to stop—no conscious gathering of information about the dangers of smoking, no self-reevaluation, no thinking about behaviors that can substitute for smoking. But now they're scared, and they make a commitment. What happens is that a year later, 78 percent of them are still smoking. And they lapse back to the precontemplation stage—the first stage of change—where they aren't even thinking about quitting.

Q: Why do they go backwards like that?

Dr. Prochaska: Because they're demoralized. They mistakenly think that because willpower alone didn't get them to stop, they're weak and shouldn't bother to try again. "I can't do it," they say. "I'm not strong

1. HEALTH BEHAVIOR AND DECISION MAKING

enough." They don't recognize that they have to *prepare* to use willpower.

Also, they are not aware that a linear progression through the stages of change, while possible, is rare. Most people lapse at some point. But action followed by relapse is better than no action. People who take action and fail within a month are twice as likely to succeed over the next 6 months as people who don't take any action at all.

But when people don't know that change isn't a smooth process and that willpower isn't the be-all and end-all, they get caught up in self-blame rather than use the experience to help themselves the next time around. And they get defensive. And what makes them even more defensive is other people—loved ones or associates—trying to push them to action. A lot of our defenses build up as a way of not being controlled by the outside world. So if the world is telling us to do something we're not ready to do, one of our reactions is to make sure we don't do it.

Q: What *is* a loved one supposed to do?

Dr. Prochaska: That's a good question, since helping relationships are important in every stage of change. But to avoid being a nag and instead to really do some good, the loved one has to provide the kind of support that matches where the other person is at. Most helpers think the only way to change is to take immediate action. But for somebody in the precontemplation stage, the help, rather than goading, may have to be something less pushy. Like leaving around some articles about the advantages, say, of regular exercise, or of eating more healthfully. A "just for your information" sort of thing.

Q: It seems that when you talk about the various stages of change, you're breaking down the change into small steps so it doesn't appear too overwhelming. But isn't there a point at which you have to take a leap of faith and move forward, even though it feels uncomfortable? Doesn't there have to be some juncture where no matter how well armed you are, you still feel anxious?

Dr. Prochaska: There definitely are points where the norm is going to be anxiety, particularly between the stages of preparation and action. You never know exactly what something is going to feel like until you're doing it. So for most people, there's a bit of "I'm not exactly sure of myself here," or "I feel anxious and uncomfortable about this, but I'm ready to take the step and move forward anyway."

I want to say, though, that historically there has been a lot more anxiety around change than there needs to be. Again, that's because there has been such pressure to go to action, whether or not people have been ready for it. Yet by consciously dealing with change in stages—and we've found that people really do go through change in 6 distinct stages—it's easier to apply appropriate strategies at the appropriate times [see *The 6 stages of change*].

Anxiety also arises because of fear of failure, and it's well-founded because the majority of people do "fail" before they succeed. But if they remind themselves, "Hey, I don't have just one chance. If I don't make it this time, I'm going to use it as a learning experience," it takes the pressure off. It's a way of recognizing that change is a process rather than an event.

Q: What about changes that aren't so cut and dry? With cigarettes or alcoholism, it's an all-or-nothing deal. But with, say, weight loss, the goal isn't to never eat something again. When the goal is less precise, isn't it harder to change the behavior?

Dr. Prochaska: The way around that is to be as specific about behavior change plans as possible. With weight loss, for instance, the ultimate goal is to shed excess pounds. But losing weight is an outcome, not a behavior. What's the specific behavior that's going to get you to that goal? For some people, it's exercising 5 times a week for 30 minutes at a stretch. For others, it's eating 5 servings of vegetables and fruits a day. Most will need a combination of behaviors.

Q: Could people use one set of behavior changes to reach more than one goal? For instance, when people decide to exercise, they're not just moving toward the goal of losing weight. They're also cutting down on their risk for heart disease and other potentially debilitating conditions.

Dr. Prochaska: Absolutely. In fact, looking at it that way increases motivation. There are 2 ways to get more motivated. One is to make a single motive extremely important. The other is to increase the number of motives. That tends to work better. In the case of weight loss, for instance, many people want to shed some extra pounds for the sole purpose of improving their appearance. That might not provide enough impetus in and of itself. But if they take into consideration all the health benefits of losing excess weight—lower blood pressure, more energy, reduced risk of disease—they'll be more inclined to make the necessary behavior changes.

It's the same with exercise. The biggest barrier to regular exercise is "I'm too busy." True, if you think only about the calorie-burning benefit of exercise, "too busy" does have much more sway. But if you recognize all the other benefits—better heart rate, reduced feelings of depression, stronger bones, more flexibility—all of a sudden, you're getting a lot more back for your 30 minutes a day.

Q: Should people set a date for action, or should they just finally decide that "tomorrow is it"?

SPECIAL REPORT

The 6 stages of change

There are 6 stages of change, according to behavioral psychologist James Prochaska, PhD. You need to know which stage you're in to move forward effectively, because each one requires different strategies. Below is a brief description of the stages, with strategies for progressing through them.

1. Precontemplation Precontemplators have no current intention of changing. They often feel a situation is hopeless (perhaps because they've tried to change before without success), and they use denial and defensiveness to keep from going forward. They feel "safe" in precontemplation because they can't "fail" there.

Strategies: Help is needed from others, perhaps in the form of simple observations or, in the case of a problem like alcoholism, confrontation. Such help allows precontemplators to see themselves as others do. Consciousness-raising is important, too. Sometimes it comes from a visit to the doctor or perhaps a stirring life event, such as the birth of a grandchild or a 50th birthday.

2. Contemplation Contemplators accept or realize that they have a problem and begin to think seriously about changing it. *Note:* It's easy to get stuck in the contemplation stage—for years. Traps include the search for absolute certainty (nothing in life is guaranteed); waiting for the magic moment (you need to *make* the moment); and wishful thinking (hoping for different consequences without changing behavior).

Strategies: Contemplators need more consciousness-raising, for example, by reading up on their problem behavior. That allows them to focus on the negatives of their current behavior and to imagine the consequences down the line if they don't do things differently. Emotional arousal, sometimes accomplished by watching a painful movie on the subject (such as *Save the Tiger* in the case of alcoholics), also helps. In addition, "social liberation" can play a big role. For a smoker, social liberation might be eating in the nonsmoking section of a restaurant as a way of experiencing social support for a different way of behaving.

3. Preparation Most people in this stage are planning to take action within a month. They think more about the future than about the past, more about the pros of a new behavior than about the cons of the old one. In other words, they pull themselves in a new direction more than they pull themselves away from an old one.

Strategies: Preparers develop a firm, detailed scheme for action. Many motivate themselves by making their intended change public rather than keeping it to themselves. Social liberation continues to play a role, as does self-reevaluation.

4. Action This is the overt modifying of behavior, and the busiest stage of change. It's also the stage most visible to others.

Strategies: People in the action stage need to apply their sense of commitment to the change. They should also reward themselves, perhaps by buying new clothing after reaching a particular exercise goal or by going out to dinner with money they otherwise would have spent on cigarettes or alcohol. "Countering" is extremely important at this stage—exercising instead of giving in to the desire to eat fatty foods, for instance. Making the environment more change-friendly—say, having cut-up fruit in the house rather than cake and cookies—is crucial, too. Helping relationships with people who support changers' goals and applaud their efforts provide more motivation.

5. Maintenance Often far more difficult to achieve than action, maintenance can last 6 months to a lifetime. Programs that promise easy change usually fail to acknowledge that maintenance is a long, ongoing process. Three common internal challenges to maintenance are overconfidence, daily temptation, and self-blame for lapses.

Strategies: People in maintenance should apply the same strategies as those in the action stage: commitment, reward, countering, modification of the environment, and helping relationships.

6. Termination The problem no longer presents any temptation. The cycle of change is exited. Some experts say termination never occurs, only that maintenance becomes less vigilant over time.

Dr. Prochaska: It's too easy to assume that the next day is going to be the "magic moment." One place people err is "tomorrow and tomorrow and tomorrow." But rarely do they err when they say, "I'm setting this date, and I'm going to go for it."

Q: How far in advance should the date be set?

Dr. Prochaska: If you're already in the preparation stage, a few weeks to a month. And the date doesn't have to be set in December in anticipation of New Year's. As for why you hear so much about people taking action on January 1, it may be that it's seen as an opportunity, if you will. But some people take action on a special birthday, like when they turn 40. Or Labor Day—summer's over; back to work. People tend to have that "new start" feeling in September, that feeling of shifting gears, even years after they have left school. That's why any time in September is excellent—the world is shifting into a new season, and there's a sense of new possibilities.

Challenging America's Inverted Health Priorities

Elizabeth M. Whelan

Elizabeth M. Whelan, Sc.D., M.P.H., co-founder and president of ACSH, is the recipient of the 1996 Ethics Award from the American Institute of Chemists (AIC). The award is given to persons who perform "duties dictated by ethical considerations, in the face of difficulties, for the benefit of the public and/or workers in chemistry and chemical engineering"; who display "leadership in an organization's ethical relationships with the public and/or employees in the field"; and who perform "effective advocacy of organizational and/or governmental policies relating to chemistry that encourage ethical treatment of individuals." Excerpts from her acceptance speech follow:

My organization—my duty—is the American Council on Science and Health. And I accept this award not only for myself but for my colleagues at ACSH—for all those people whose own work and love and, yes, high ethical standards—have made my success possible.

Of the hundreds of people who have been involved in ACSH over the years, I must make special mention of my mentor, Dr. Fredrick J. Stare, founder of the Harvard Department of Nutrition. Dr. Stare and I have worked together for almost two decades now—and together have withstood many attacks, particularly when we have the audacity to state that the American food supply is safe. We were sued for the very act of forming ACSH by the national trade association of health food manufacturers, who accused us of conspiring to undermine their business. But Dr. Stare and I prevailed in court, albeit many years and many thousands of dollars later.

The very public criticism that has been leveled at Dr. Stare and me—remarks meant to discredit and humiliate us—has actually solidified our relationship and strengthened our work.

A second person I would like to acknowledge today is AIC President Dr. Roger Maickel. Roger is an active member of ACSH's board of directors and a tireless fighter in what is always an uphill battle in pursuit of truth. If there is a misleading health claim in the media—about food, pharmaceuticals, the environment—Roger will pursue it until the matter is rectified. Purveyors of health fraud don't stand a chance in his presence.

Our top priority at ACSH is to help Americans distinguish between real and hypothetical health risks—to separate the leading causes of disease and death from the leading causes of unnecessary anxiety. At ACSH we try to ensure that both individual health decisions and public policies are based on sound scientific evidence.

> **Those of us who protect our health daily and those of us who put our health in constant jeopardy have exactly the same mortality: 100 percent. The difference, of course, is in the timing. I believe that epidemiologists should help people learn how to die young—at a very old age.**

Today I will approach the issue of America's inverted health priorities from my vantage point as an epidemiologist—a public health specialist. We epidemiologists have a basic premise, and it

5. Challenging America's Inverted Health Priorities

is also a basic premise of ACSH: That those of us who protect our health daily and those of us who put our health in constant jeopardy have exactly the same mortality: 100 percent. The difference, of course, is in the timing. I believe that epidemiologists should help people learn how to die young—at a very old age. To put that another way: We in public health and epidemiology should be giving people a good shot at avoiding premature disease and death.

Epidemiologists are interested in environmental factors as they relate to premature death. But we have a somewhat different definition of the word "environment" than the average person.

For an epidemiologist, the word "environmental" refers to any and all factors in the causation of disease that are not directly linked to genetic, inherited origins. Environmental factors in disease causation—and by causation here I refer to the concept of increased risk—thus include not only industrial-, air- or foodborne chemicals such as agricultural chemicals, radiation or other products of our technological age but also lifestyle factors. We epidemiologists give high priority to lifestyle factors in the avoidance of early disease and death in the 1990s.

I believe that the purpose—the only purpose—of public health measures, whether carried out at the EPA, at the FDA, in Congress or in the private sector, should be the prevention of premature disease and death. I do not believe that public health efforts should have hidden goals—goals that might include harassing industry, alarming people about nonrisks, banning useful substances or advancing other social and political agendas. The purpose of public health measures should be, quite simply, to protect public health. So what, then, are the leading causes of premature death in 1996?

Each year:

- Two million people die.

- One million people die prematurely (in the sense that these deaths can be postponed) before age 80.

- 500,000 premature deaths—that is, one death in four, or one in two premature deaths—are directly and causally related to the use of tobacco. I cannot emphasize enough how remarkable this number is—and how it so dramatically influences the whole public health scene today.

- 100,000 premature deaths are due to the abuse and misuse of alcohol.

Thus, two causes, tobacco use and alcohol abuse, account for nearly 60 percent of all premature deaths. Smaller but significant numbers of other premature deaths are linked with failure to use lifesaving technology such as seat belts and smoke detectors; with failure to screen for and treat life-threatening diseases, particularly hypertension and treatable malignancies; and with reckless recreation and the abuse of addictive substances. This last category includes those HIV infections that result from IV drug use and unsafe sexual practices.

These causes represent real, documented opportunities for us to make clear progress. They are the modern-day challenges facing epidemiologists and other public health professionals. But what alleged public health risks get the attention of the media, of legislators and of regulatory bodies? Let me give you a few examples:

Each summer for the past few years I have temporarily assumed the role of an "epidemiologist from Mars" who comes to Earth to find out the causes of disease and death. Each year I turn to the leading popular women's magazines as my sources of information—*Ladies' Home Journal*, *Glamour*, *Redbook*, *Self*, *Woman's Day* and the like.

Here's what I have learned: that food additives such as sodium nitrate, BHA and BHT cause cancer; that not eating sufficient carrots and spinach causes strokes; and that eating shark-fin soup combats cancer (sharks never get cancer, they said). Women's magazines have also warned that alarm clocks' electromagnetic fields can cause cancer and that the droppings of pet birds might play a role in the causation of lung cancer. And nearly every magazine takes as a given that pesticide residues in foods are a cancer hazard, particularly to children.

Yet these same wary, seemingly health-conscious magazines are chock full of ads for cigarettes—glamorous, fun, sexy, elegant and—oh, yes—slimming cigarettes.

I now ask you: Are these not inverted health priorities?

I could regale you with many other examples of magazine hype, but I would like to move on to legislation and policies that purport to promote public health.

- There's Superfund, which promises to reduce cancer risk by protecting us from chemical risks at toxic-waste sites, even though the science of epidemiology has never pointed to these sites as a source of risk for cancer, birth defects, miscarriage or any illness.

1. HEALTH BEHAVIOR AND DECISION MAKING

- There's California's Proposition 65, which requires a warning label—or a ban—on any consumer product containing even a trace level of a chemical that has caused cancer in a laboratory animal. For example, under Proposition 65, Liquid Paper—the familiar "white-out" found in every office—was designated a carcinogen (it contained trace levels of trichlorethylene as a solvent).

- There's the congressionally mandated warning label on saccharin, which says that saccharin causes cancer in animals and may pose a risk to us as well.

- And, perhaps most infamously, there was the substantial publicity given to the agricultural chemical Alar—specifically, to the claim that Alar posed an intolerable cancer risk.

These, then, are examples that underscore my dismay about the inverted health priorities in the United States today. When we at ACSH ask epidemiologists on our scientific advisory board to quantify the contribution of bird droppings, pesticide residues, exposure to chemicals at toxic-waste sites, food additives and the like to premature death, their answer is, "We don't know, but our best guess is zero."

Under a policy of inverted priorities, not only do we pursue public health goals by running rapidly in the wrong direction, but we also push purely hypothetical health issues to center stage and squander our limited public health resources—our time and our financial investment.

What are the implications and the consequences of policies based on these inverted health priorities? I think they are pretty obvious:

Under a policy of inverted priorities, not only do we pursue public health goals by running rapidly in the wrong direction, but we also push purely hypothetical health issues to center stage and squander our limited public health resources—our time and our financial investment.

The mother who worries about Alar in apple sauce may well be the same mother who doesn't worry about putting a helmet on the child perched on the back of her bike or about buckling up her seat belt in the back of a taxi. The father who worries about cellular telephones and electric blankets may be a smoker who doesn't have a working smoke detector at home. The sheer distraction of constantly reading about killer apples and toxic alarm clocks (or whatever happens to be the carcinogen of the week) is at the very least leading to a lack of perspective about what is important and what is not.

But there is at least one other downside risk. As we demand that big Government require American business to protect us from risks that simply do not exist, we all end up paying more for goods and services. A mindless pursuit aimed at controlling hypothetical risks carries an enormous price tag: It not only raises the cost of doing business, but also stifles innovative activity that could dramatically improve the quality of life for all of us.

Why are the public health priorities so inverted in our country? Why are hypothetical health risks given such big play as important causes of disease when mainstream scientists do not see them playing an etiologic role at all? And what are we going to do about it?

These are complex questions. I will briefly outline five reasons why the hyperbole about environment risk prevails and describe some possible, immediate solutions. The five factors I believe are most responsible for our inverted priorities are these:

- first, the highly emotional aspects of health issues;

- second, the enormous political and economic clout of the manufacturers of the leading cause of preventable death—cigarettes;

- third, the failure of most American scientists and physicians to participate in debates about relative health risks;

- fourth, the contamination of the public health profession by an ideologically fueled form of political correctness that chills open dialogue;

- and, finally, the devastating effects of the codification into law of a scientifically baseless, uncritical extrapolation of cancer risks from animal to man.

5. Challenging America's Inverted Health Priorities

First, issues relating to food, the environment and health are highly emotional, highly volatile issues. Psychiatrists tell us that people always fear things they cannot see—things that are unfamiliar, that they do not understand. And people have long projected their fears onto postulated, invisible, hostile agents. Food additives, pesticides and "chemical residues" are ideal targets for such projection.

Psychiatrists also point to a related theme: When it comes to the causes of ill health and other adversity, human beings reject introspection: It's better to blame an outside source—some big, bad industry—than to examine critically one's own lifestyle.

The solution? It must be long term, but we need to make a concerted effort to eliminate the scientific and technological illiteracy now rampant in the United States. We need to advance understanding of the controllable lifestyle factors that contribute to risk and promote the basic toxicological premise that "only the dose makes the poison."

Second, tobacco companies—the manufacturers of the leading cause of death—dominate the print media in this country and exert a tremendous influence on both the print and broadcast media's coverage of health issues.

The tobacco industry spends nearly six billion dollars in advertising and promotion each year. This clearly buys silence and diversion. Surely nothing could make this killer advertiser more content than seeing consumer cancer-prevention efforts focused on "cancer-causing apples" and having the word "carcinogen" used so often it loses all its meaning. Remember: When everything is dangerous, then nothing is.

Over and beyond its influence with the media, the tobacco industry's substantial economic clout—and its deep roots that run throughout corporate America—have served it well. Some day I plan to write a book about the number of times representatives from the food, chemical, pharmaceutical, paper, alcoholic-beverage and every other imaginable industry have made a concerted effort to silence the scientists of the American Council on Science and Health in our attempt to make the dangers of smoking well known.

Cigarette companies have metastasized, if you will, throughout corporate America, buying up everything from General Foods to Miller Beer and from Bulova watches to Saks Fifth Avenue. The number of American corporations that service the cigarette manufacturers—and thus owe them allegiance—is truly staggering. America's health priorities are inverted because the leading cause of death has enough clout to keep the legislative and publicity spotlights off the cigarette—and on the multitude of nonrisks around us.

The solution? We will not be able truly to realign our health priorities until Congress strips the cigarette industry of its privileged legal status and levels the playing field so that the manufacturers of the leading cause of death are forced to scrimmage on the same legal and regulatory turf as the rest of corporate America.

Third, our health priorities are inverted, and nonrisks continue to dominate, because American scientists and physicians essentially remain mute while hyperbole about risk is served up all around them. You might argue that there are few public health professionals who would want to join ranks with the likes of Jane Fonda and Meryl Streep in claiming that trace levels of environmental chemicals cause human disease—but silence is assent. Where are the professionals in toxicology, epidemiology and environmental science when the risks of dioxin, Alar, PCBs and cellular phones are exaggerated? Where are the scientists when their own profession is distorted as laws based on pseudoscience are proposed? Where are the true experts when we need to communicate the reality that we have the safest, most enviable food supply in the world?

Well, I know where they are. They are in their offices, in clinics, in classes and in laboratories. They say they don't want to get involved in what they perceive as a political process. Scientists today are highly specialized, and they feel uncomfortable in public forums. Most of all, scientists dread that four-letter word "safe." Scientists rarely talk in absolutes, yet in the everyday consumer world people need easily understandable concepts of relative risk.

The solution? Get the scientists involved! That is exactly what ACSH is doing. We now have over 250 scientists and physicians as advisors. We are encouraging them to write letters to the editor, to contribute op-ed pieces to major newspapers and to show up in television debates. Our nation's health priorities will remain inverted if the only visible spokesmen on public health issues come from the Chicken Little School of Environmental Hyperbole.

Fourth, our health priorities are inverted because the practice of preventive medicine and public health has become corrupted by a form of politically correct science that abandons the principles of epidemiology and instead advances ideological agendas and social aims. Politically correct science (PCS) is dogmatic and intolerant. Its ideology is anticapitalistic and anti–free enterprise. It sees man, industry and technology as the enemies of nature. It is an ideology that has abandoned science, reason and rationality in favor of intuition, inconsistency and a commitment to goals other than the goal of improved public health. Practitioners of PCS never address real, documented public health threats. Nature, always benign, is the new god; environmentalism and consumerism are the new religions.

The solution? A return to peer-reviewed, mainstream science and a rejection, once and for all, of what is perhaps the darkest side of PCS—the antiquated, destructive view that a growing industrial economy is the enemy of a clean environment and a healthier people. The continued march of PCS undermines our ability to achieve both economic and public health goals.

Now is the time for reason and rationality. It's the time for public health professionals to reclaim their profession—to take it back from Hollywood and the political activists.

Fifth and finally, our nation's health priorities are inverted by our dependence on animal-to-man extrapolation in predicting human cancer risk.

The mouse-is-a-little-man premise dates back to 1958, when Congressman James Delaney of New York proposed a law to ban from the food supply any food additive that caused cancer in any dose in any laboratory animal. The so-called Delaney clause promptly triggered the first major food scare—the great cranberry scare of November 1959. The Delaney clause later prompted the banning of cyclamates, the near banning of saccharin and other media extravaganzas.

The clause originally applied only to additives, but the Delaney concept of mouse to man has now spread to pesticides and to trace levels of environmental chemicals generally. Laws and regulatory definitions relying on rodent data abound at the EPA and elsewhere and are consuming billions upon billions of our limited preventive-medicine dollars—money that could be used on real public health problems.

I am not suggesting that we abandon animal testing, which is critical to biomedical research. I am, however, in favor of at least a little bit of common sense in interpreting these studies and accepting the reality that only the dose makes the poison. As far I know, this common-sense element is totally lacking in the EPA's definition of a "probable human carcinogen" based on one high-dose animal test.

I suggest that we apply the "dose makes the poison" principle to our regulation of pesticides and other environmental chemicals. Obviously, pesticides are inherently toxic: Their job is to kill bugs. We need to encourage agricultural workers to adhere meticulously to occupational protocols that limit workplace exposures. And, just to be extremely conservative about potential toxic levels of pesticides appearing in food, we need to comply with the tolerance levels now set by the EPA. But once that safety protocol is set and met, we should treat minuscule levels of synthetic chemicals in food in the same way that we do low levels of naturally occurring carcinogens and toxins.

For example, we regulate naturally occurring aflatoxin by acknowledging that it is there and monitoring it to ensure it stays within the tolerance levels. Then we stop worrying about it, because trace levels play no known role whatever in the causation of human cancer.

The aflatoxin regulatory approach makes sense. Aflatoxin causes cancer in a full spectrum of animal species and shows a distinct dose-response effect. Aflatoxin is a bad actor, and it is prudent to limit our exposure to it. Note that I said *limit*—not eliminate. Now contrast the common-sense approach for aflatoxin with the regulatory actions and designations made on Alar and saccharin: Consumers were led to believe that the only protection from these chemicals—which in high doses caused cancer in one species—was the exorcist approach: zero tolerable exposure.

I maintain that the fixation on rodent carcinogens—aminotriazole on cranberries in 1959, Alar on apples in 1989 and every pesticide and food additives scare in between—actually CAUSES more premature deaths, both by distracting people from real health risks and by potentially reducing the availability of and increasing the prices of the very fruits and vegetables that protect our health.

At the close of the Rio Summit in 1992, 425 members of the scientific and intellectual community formally objected to the politically correct agenda of those who dominated the conference. Those who objected rejected the theme that man was the enemy and that industry, technology and profits posed a worldwide hazard. They signed what is now known as the Heidelberg Appeal. Over 3,000 scientists have now signed this document.

5. Challenging America's Inverted Health Priorities

The Heidelberg Appeal pledges a dedication to the preservation of the Earth but raises concern about the emergence of what it calls an "irrational ideology" that opposes scientific and industrial progress. The appeal notes that "many essential human activities are carried out . . . by manipulation of hazardous substances. . . . [P]rogress and development have always involved increasing control over hostile forces to the benefit of mankind. The greatest evils which stalk our Earth are ignorance and oppression, not science, technology and industry."

One of my top professional priorities is to encourage our federal and local regulatory agencies to enable the philosophy of the Heidelberg Appeal—to reaffirm the principles of good science and the principles found in worldwide peer-reviewed scientific literature. Our federal and local agencies can do this:

- first, by abandoning all regulatory policies and definitions that designate a chemical as a "probable" or "possible" human carcinogen on the basis of limited animal data;

- second, by incorporating a broad understanding of dose of exposure in determination of potential human risk, thus dismissing concerns about trace levels of chemicals;

- third, by establishing closer ties with prominent academic scientists from universities around the world and by regularly drawing upon their expertise in toxicology, epidemiology and environmental sciences;

- fourth, by obtaining the concurrence and approval of experts on cancer causation at the National Cancer Institute before designating an environmental chemical as a "cancer risk" under conditions of current exposure. Such consultation and verification would avoid baseless cancer scares.

Until we return to mainstream science, our nation's health priorities will continue to be inverted. We must defend peer-reviewed, mainstream science in the public arena. We must stand up for reason and rationality; we all must fight, as I have fought, for the truth. We must stop dogmatic and intolerant politically correct science before it's too late and must reject, once and for all, its darkest side—the view that a growing industrial economy is the enemy of a clean environment and a healthier people. We must not yield to those who would abandon facts in pursuit of the hypothetical—to those who are motivated not out of reason but out of fear and a commitment to goals other than public health.

I will leave you with the wise counsel of a great American—a man who faced and made and stood fast by a harrowing series of life-and-death ethical decisions from which a lesser man might have fled. These words are posted on the door to my office. I see them every day, and every day they give me strength to carry on:

> *If I were to try to read, much less answer, all the attacks made on me, this shop might as well be closed for any other business. I do the best I can, and I mean to keep doing so until the end.*
>
> *If the end brings me out all right, what is said against me won't amount to anything. If the end brings me out wrong, ten angels swearing I was right would make no difference.*

The words are Abraham Lincoln's. He fought and won his good fight; let us not shirk in ours.

Stress and Mental Health

Years of medical research have significantly advanced our knowledge and understanding of the human body to a point where not only can organs be transplanted, but machines can be built to replicate their functions. The one organ that still mystifies and baffles the scientific community, however, is the brain. While more has been learned about this organ in the last five years than in all the rest of recorded history, our understanding is still in its infancy.

Traditionally, the medical community has viewed health problems as either physical or mental, treating each type separately. This dichotomy between the psyche (mind) and soma (body) is fading in light of scientific data revealing profound physiological changes associated with mood shifts. The discovery of the interaction between mind and body has stimulated intense research regarding the role of stress in health. The essay "Critical Life Events and the Onset of Illness" explores the psychophysiology of emotions and their impact on health.

Stress has been described as a nonspecific physiological response to anything that challenges the body, including both mental and physical stimuli. Some general characteristics of the response include increases in heart rate, muscle tension, blood pressure, blood sugar, blood fats, and blood coagulability. While these responses are adaptive during times of crisis, it has been found that the same mechanisms could provoke physiological dysfunction if they persisted for prolonged periods of time. These findings clearly suggested that stress could play a crucial role in the etiology of various diseases.

Today researchers are examining the role stress may play in a variety of illnesses, such as coronary heart disease, hypertension, obesity, diabetes, asthma, tension headaches, migraine headaches, ulcers, cancer, and a generally increased susceptibility to infectious illnesses. If stress is a generalized physiological response, why, then, are so many illnesses associated with it?

While this question has not been conclusively answered, most experts think the explanation may be "the weak organ theory." According to this theory, every individual has one organ system that is most susceptible to the damaging effects of prolonged stress. While there is no definitive test to validate this theory, it is consistent with the clinical observations that different individuals exposed to the same stressor develop different illnesses.

Mental illness, which is generally regarded as a major dysfunction of normal thought processes, has no identifiable etiology. One may speculate that this is due to the

complex nature of the brain. It may also be that many conditions labeled as mental illnesses are not really illnesses at all, but rather behaviors that society has deemed unacceptable. While the latter seems to be true for conditions and behaviors such as homosexuality, drug abuse, child abuse, and sexual dysfunction, there is mounting evidence to suggest an organic component to the more traditional forms of mental illness such as schizophrenia, chronic depression, and manic depression. As researchers identify specific neurochemical disturbances associated with these conditions, experts debate whether these findings represent the cause or the effect of the mental illness.

The fact that certain mental illnesses tend to occur within families has divided the mental health community into two camps: those who believe there is a genetic factor operating in mental illness, and those who see the family tendency as more of a learned behavior. Regardless of which side is correct, the evidence strongly supports mental illness as yet another example of the weak organ theory.

The reason one person is more susceptible to the damaging effects of stress than another is not clear, but evi-

UNIT 2

dence is mounting that an individual's perception and interpretation of stressors may be key factors. It may be reasonable to assume, then, that changing one's view or mind-set could alter one's response to any given stressor. In "Critical Life Events and the Onset of Illness," Blair Justice discusses how our perception of an event and not the event itself is the critical factor in establishing the degree to which it is regarded as stressful.

While the media has alerted the public to the dangers of stress, it has also created the belief that all stress is bad and should be avoided. Avoiding all stress is not only an impossible task, but an undesirable goal as well. Current thinking on this issue has changed the focus from the elimination of stress to an approach that views stress as an essential component of life and a potential source of health. The notion that stress could serve as a positive force in one's life was presented by Dr. Hans Selye in 1974 in his book *Stress without Distress*. Dr. Selye felt that there were three types of stress: negative stress (distress), normal stress, and positive stress (eustress). He maintained that positive stress not only increases a person's self-esteem, but inoculates him or her against the negative effects of distress. The distinction between these two types of stress is a subjective assessment based solely on the perception of the individual. If these assumptions are correct, then the most effective way to change distress into eustress is to work on changing the context or mind-set.

Recent studies in the area of occupational stress challenge the commonly held notion that executive jobs are the most stressful, due to the decision-making requirements of these jobs. Current findings suggest that while executive positions do entail a relatively high level of stress, it is in sharp contrast to the distress experienced by workers at the bottom of the job ladder. These jobs emphasize performance and provide little latitude for decision making or control. The importance of perceived control as well as social support are also addressed in "Critical Life Events and the Onset of Illness."

While researchers have made significant strides in their understanding of the mechanisms linking stress to physical ailments, they are less clear on the mechanisms involved when it comes to mental illness. Despite this fact, it is a commonly held assertion that perceived stress has a profound impact on one's mental health. According to a recent government document, the incidence of mental illness among adult Americans is approximately 19 percent and growing. This statistic is based on a broad definition of mental illness that includes some 230 separate categories, such as tobacco dependence, sexual dysfunction, and developmental defects. Reports such as this, coupled with increasing evidence that mental stress is a contributing factor to many health problems, is prompting researchers to develop therapeutic interventions that will protect individuals from the damaging effects of stress as well as treat those already experiencing some degree of dysfunction. While tranquilizers have been the traditional treatment of choice, a new branch of medicine termed behavioral medicine is utilizing such techniques as biofeedback, meditation, self-hypnosis, mental imagery, progressive relaxation, exercise, and nutrition counseling to control stress.

In addition to these techniques, many stress management programs include time management training, assertiveness training, goal setting, exercise, and nutrition counseling. While all may serve a valuable function, none is universally effective. Kathleen McAuliffe, in "Out of the Blues," discusses how exercise such as walking can provide therapeutic benefits to those suffering from depression. In fact, according to McAuliffe, walking ranks with the best talk therapies as a mode of treatment. "Good Mood Foods" by Shawna Vogel discusses how various foodstuffs alter our brain chemistry and thus our moods and emotions. "Depression: Way beyond the Blues" examines various aspects of depression and suggests things that you can do to help a friend who is depressed.

While significant gains have been made in our understanding of the relationship between body and mind, much remains to be learned. What is known suggests that the mind-set of an individual is the key factor in shaping one's response to stress.

Looking Ahead: Challenge Questions

How have humankind's stressors changed over the last 5,000 years?

What are the major stressors in your life? How do you manage stress?

Discuss how positive feelings and a sense of purpose in your life can help to reduce stress.

What can you do to help someone who is suffering from depression?

Why are such activities as walking effective in treating mood disorders? What is the mechanism by which they work?

What impact do our food choices have on our moods?

How does laughter help one to cope more effectively with stress?

CRITICAL LIFE EVENTS AND THE ONSET OF ILLNESS

Blair Justice, PhD

Professor of Psychology University of Texas School of Public Health, Houston, Texas

■ In 1925, when Hans Selye was a medical student at the ancient German University of Prague and observing his first clinical cases, he asked a question that was considered so naive or pointless that his professor dismissed it as unworthy of reply. The question was: What is the "general syndrome of just being sick?"[1] What young Selye—who over the next 50 years became the world's leading authority on stress and disease—wanted to know was, why do all sick people have certain signs and symptoms in common: fatigue, loss of appetite, aches, pains, and other shared features.

After migrating to Canada and joining the biochemistry department at McGill University in Montreal, Selye began the research that eventually answered, at least in part, his original question. People get sick from "diverse noxious agents,"[2] and the resultant stress on the body produces certain nonspecific effects that sick people share in common. Selye learned that these "noxious" influences may come not only from harmful physical agents (such as viruses, bacteria, excessive cholesterol), but from an individual's appraisal of "noxious" or painful stimuli—how one looks at events in life and the meaning one attaches to them.[3]

After many years of studying the physiological effects on the body of stressors of all kinds—from chemical to emotional—Selye formulated a philosophy of life that he considered essential to health and happiness. Since unfavorable events—failures, rejections, losses—occur in everyone's life avoiding such stressors is impossible. What is important physiologically. Selye noted, is not the event but the person's reaction to it. "It's not what happens that counts; it is how you take it,"[4] he was fond of saying.

Although Selye's own work did not establish this finding, other research, both during his time and since, supports his ideas. These studies carefully document that the level and duration of potentially damaging neurochemicals in the body—such as epinephrine, norephrinephrine and cortisol—are a function of how we appraise life events and circumstances.[5,6] If we interpret a "noxious" experience as meaning it is the end of the world, the heart and immune system, as well as the gastrointestinal system, are placed at increased risk of impairment or compromise.[7,8] If, instead, we view an event as being bad, but not something so bad that we "can't stand it," then the body reacts less intensely. Neurochemicals are elevated just enough to prod us into effective action rather than helpless floundering.

How we react to an event—whether it is an illness, a divorce, a nuclear power plant accident, a pregnancy or childbirth—is strongly influenced by our perceived sense of acceptance and affirmation by others, by our interpersonal relationships and by social circumstances. The emerging science of psychoneuroimmunology (PNI) recognizes the association of such psychosocial factors with changes in biological functioning.

Almost a century and a half ago, Rudolph Virchow recognized that our very resistance to disease is affected by social conditions.[9] This perceptive German pathologist and physician char-

---

*Reprint requests to Blair Justice, PhD, University of Texas School of Public Health, 1200 Herman Pressler, Houston, TX 77030.

acterized medicine as a "social science." He knew that physiological processes are affected profoundly by social factors. Investigating a typhus outbreak in Upper Silesia, Virchow reported that people would not have gotten the disease had they lived in a democratic system and enjoyed more favorable social conditions.[10]

A long-term epidemiological view of mortality and life span across populations suggests that people become more vulnerable to disease when they feel little control over their lives and when they lack nurturing communities and supportive families. Leonard Sagan, in *The Health of Nations*,[11] reports a reduction of mortality and extension of life span when two factors materialize—when community and family supports develop, and a sense of control over one's destiny emerges.

Today we can, at least partially, identify the mechanisms by which psychological and social factors impact biological processes, including the cardiovascular and immune systems. When people have little control in their lives, or when conditions interfere with meeting their basic needs for love or attachment, they become more vulnerable to disease and illness.[12,13] Feeling less in control and unsupported, life events are appraised more negatively giving rise to greater arousal over time of both the sympathetic-adrenal medullary system and hypothalamic-pituitary-adrenal cortical system.[14]

HOW SOCIAL SUPPORT WORKS

After two decades of research, a clearer understanding is emerging of the key features of social support that can help protect people from illness or disease and other effects of excessive stress. Sarason,[15] a pioneer in the field, showed that giving social or tangible "provisions" in the form of information, advice, companionship or money can help a stressed person; however, they are not the critical helping features. The core element, he found, is the person's sense of acceptance, a sense of affirmation and affection he or she feels from others. This is an acquired trait. It becomes part of one's personality and is retained no matter where one goes or what life events are encountered. According to Sarason without a sense of acceptance, a person is vulnerable to illness, disease, and lowered performance.

Marital discord and disruption demonstrate the profound impact that social support can have on health. For example, Somers[16] reports that disruption in a marriage can be the single most powerful sociodemographic predictor of physical and emotional illness. Indeed, poorer immune function has been found in divorced men and women who are lonely and continue to feel drawn to their ex-spouses.[17] Similarly, unhappiness in a marriage, as measured by poor marital quality, is associated with lowered immune functioning.[18] Unhappily married individuals report more illness than either divorced or happily married persons of the same sex, age, and race.[17] These findings suggest that no simple connection can be inferred between an experience, such as being married, and health or illness. Any outcome will be affected by how an individual evaluates his or her experience and reacts to it.

ILLNESS OR DISEASE?

Whether illness or disease emerges from our reaction to life events is an important variable in the new understanding of why—and how—people get sick. Eisenberg,[9] among others, distinguishes between "disease" and "illness." Physicians think in terms of diseases and conceptualize them as abnormalities in the structure and function of individual body organs and tissues. Patients think in terms of how they feel and function as whole human beings, not as separate parts.[19] Eisenberg[9] describes illnesses as "experiences of disvalued changes in states of being and social function." Illness may occur in the absence of disease, just as disease may occur in the absence of illness. The patient is concerned with subjective signs and symptoms that may signal disease. The doctor looks for objective evidence. If none is found, no disease may be present, but an illness may still exist. Nonetheless, disease and illness are equally real to the patient. Whether the evidence is subjective or objective, psychosocial factors influence both the onset and outcome of the problem.

SUPPORT, CONTROL AND HEART ATTACKS

The influence of perceived control and support can be seen in the alternative outcomes of people who experience a heart attack. The critical life event here is myocardial infarction. Both disease and illness are present. The question is: In a group of people with the same tissue pathology receiving equally good treatment, why do some recover much better and faster than others? And, why does illness persist in some patients even when objective measures of pathology show successful treatment of the disease?

One answer involves the patient's opportunity to participate in his or her own treatment. In one study, a group of hospitalized heart attack patients received explanations about the causes, effects and treatment of myocardial infarctions. They learned how they could join in their own treatment.[20] With access to cardiac monitors, they could obtain an EKG tracing whenever they experienced symptoms. They also were taught mild isometric and foot-pedaling exercises which they did under supervision. Compared with a similar group receiving only routine information and no chance to take part in their own recovery, these patients had shorter hospital stays. Whatever greater sense of control and support the first group acquired may have affected how they continued to view their life event. This in turn would impact their cardiovascular system.

Because the cardiovascular system is particularly influenced by strong emotions, which in turn generate stress chemicals, the heart cannot be regarded simply as a mechanical pump if optimal functioning is desired. Payer[10] has observed that "in the United States the heart is viewed as a pump, and the major cause of heart pathology is considered to be due to a physical blockage in the plumbing serving the pump." She adds that "for Germans the heart is not just a pump, but an organ that has a life of its own, one that pulsates in response to a number of stimuli including the emotions."

Research in the United States and elsewhere shows that acute myocardial infarction and angina pectoris—indicating insufficient blood and oxygen supply to the heart muscle—may occur not only because of congested vessels but also because of spasm in coronary arteries, which are not simply inflexible pipes connected to a mechanical pump.[21] Cognitions can give rise to high levels of catecholamines and testosterone. Consequently, they are a key part of the mechanisms underlying arterial spasms and platelet clumping, both of which can lead to myocardial ischemic.[22] Norepinephrine and epinephrine can also stimulate release of thromboxane A2.[23] Both thromboxane A2 and the catecholamines are potent constrictors of smooth arterial muscle and strong stimulators of platelet aggregation.[24]

Given these factors, how well people recover from a heart attack, or whether they ever will ever encounter such a critical event, might therefore depend on their primary care physician's concept of the heart, a pump or an organ with a life of its own, as well as the prescribed treatment or prevention regimen. On patients' part, an increased perception of control and support plays an important role in the effectiveness of both their treatment and prevention programs.

INFLUENCE OF MEANING AND CONFIDING

The effects of trauma, even severe trauma, such as incest or a Holocaust experience, varies according to the meaning ascribed to the event by the survivors and the amount of support they perceive in their lives. Both Frankl[25] and Dimsdale[26] report how survival in concentration camps was deeply affected by whether the prisoner could find meaning in the experience. Even if meaning was expressed in a vow to live in order to seek revenge or to bear testimony, survival was enhanced and a fatal sense of hopelessness and despair averted. The ability to cling to memories of support from loved ones also was a powerful sustaining influence.

More recently, when a Jewish, Russian "refusnik" was released after 10 years of Soviet confinement, he reported that his strength to endure in prison came from knowing that a community of love supported him from the outside.[15] He maintained a strong sense of support even though he was allowed no contact with his family or the outside world for 10 years. As Sarason[15] has indicated, this political prisoner carried in his head a strong feeling that he was accepted, affirmed and loved by those he had left behind. He never doubted that they were thinking of him and working for his release. His sense of support gave him confidence in dealing with his captors. It lowered his anxiety and facilitated positive coping.

Children who recover with the least damage from years of incest or physical abuse are those who find some loving figure in their lives—a teacher, a neighbor or, in adulthood, an understanding spouse—who will listen to them and support them.[27] The most resilient children also perceived some sense of control by turning to God or becoming absorbed in the mastery of a skill.

People who have close ties to others may also benefit from confiding in them during or after a traumatic experience. In a series of recent studies Pennebaker[28] showed that after traumatic events, both psychological and physiological symptoms are relieved by systematically disclosing one's deepest thoughts and feelings either orally or in writing for 15 minutes on each of 4 consecutive days, repeating the cycle as needed. Where there is no one with whom to share painful memories, writing about one's deep feelings can bring significant benefit.[29]

Spiegel et al.[30] found that women with metastatic breast cancer live twice as long if they participate in group therapy, sharing and expressing feelings, and supporting each other in dealing with their disease. Recent studies at UCLA suggest that when people allow themselves to feel and express grief, immune proliferative response increases over time while repression of feelings and depression are associated with a decrease.[31]

PRENATAL INFLUENCES AND CHILDBIRTH

Happy events, as well as traumatic ones, can be critical in one's life. Their effects on health and illness have been well studied. For example, antibody levels are known to fluctuate with mood and happiness, with high mood being associated with high levels and low mood with low levels.[31] Holmes and Rahe,[32] first to demonstrate a correlation between life experiences and illness, argued that adjustment to change, not an event's undesirability, makes an event stressful.[33] Since then, numerous studies have established this. Events that are perceived as undesirable are more strongly correlated with risk of illness than are desirable experiences.[34] Pregnancy and birth are often viewed as happy events, but the mother may not . . . perceive them in this way. Pregnant women who feel that they have little interpersonal support and little control over life's problems may dread having a baby. These women are at higher risk for bearing low-birth weight babies and babies with complications.[35,36,37] Women under equally high stress, measured by the number of changes occurring in their lives, but who have high social support seem to be protected against these problems.[35]

Maternal attitudes toward a pregnancy and having a child have profound effects on the infant, both at birth and later. Studies in the 1970s in Germany, Austria and the United States confirmed that when a baby is unwanted, complications in pregnancy or at birth are more likely to occur.[36,38,39] High levels of catecholamines have been found in the bloodstreams of pregnant women who feel unsupported, without control or are distressed about the prospects of having a baby.[40] Passing the placental barrier, these chemicals impact the embryo and fetus.[41]

This is not the case for women whose pregnancy is welcomed, and who feel supported. What the unborn child reacts to, not only in the mother but in her environment, has increasingly come under investigation. Verny[41] reports that in the 1920s, a German doctor was told by several of his pregnant patients that they felt they should give up going to concerts because their unborn children reacted so stormily to the music. A half century later, research established that from the 25th week on, a fetus will jump in rhythm to the beat of an orchestra drum.[42] Music by both Vivaldi and Mozart seems to calm the unborn, as measured by fetal heart rate and kicking,[43] whereas music by Beethoven and Brahms has the opposite effect. All forms of rock music tend to create internal storms.[43]

SYMPTOMS AFTER NUCLEAR POWER ACCIDENTS

Pregnancy and birth have been the subject of study and speculation since the dawn of humankind. Two new life events equally as profound, however, are so recent that they have become known only in this century—in fact, only in the last decade. One of these new phenomena comes out of today's technology—the creation of nuclear power plants. The other is acquired immune deficiency syndrome (AIDS). The outcomes of people exposed to a nuclear power plant accident or infected with the AIDS virus are influenced by the individual's sense of support and control.

In March 1979 an accident occurred at the Three Mile Island (TMI) nuclear power station near Harrisburg, Pennsylvania. Although the mishap was less disastrous than the later accident at Chernobyl in the former Soviet Union, it took 11 years until the radioactive wreckage was cleared from the site.[44] Damage to the nuclear reactor produced a continued threat of radiation exposure to thousands of people living in the area. Twenty-eight months following the accident, area residents continued to exhibit higher levels of stress than did people in comparison areas who were less affected by the disaster.[45] Psychological, behavioral and biochemical measurements of 103 subjects were taken at intervals of 17 months, 22 months and 28 months after the accident. Residents with the lowest perceived control in their lives experienced the highest somatic distress and depression.[45]

In another study, heightened symptomatology after the accident was associated with a prior history of poorer social support in 312 young mothers living in the TMI area and 161 nuclear power plant workers.[46]

Compared with natural disasters, such as earthquakes, hurricanes or volcanic eruptions, technological disasters seem to have longer-lasting effects on perceived control. The difference, some researchers suggest, may be that technological disasters reflect a *loss* of control while natural disasters are associated with a *lack* of control.[45] People may accept that they lack control over the forces of nature, but believe that they can control technological power. When something goes wrong as in the case of nuclear accidents, the unexpected loss of control can be more profound. In either case, possessing a sense of control and support in one's life generally demonstrates the importance of faith and/or social affirmation for buffering the effects of stress and protecting against illness.[47,48]

PSYCHOSOCIAL EFFECTS, AIDS, AND CANCER

Control and support have an equally significant influence on patients with AIDS, affecting both the onset and course of the disease. Solomon et al. note that "while the prevalent belief among the general public, among persons with AIDS and even the professional community, is that AIDS is invariably fatal, there is a small but growing number of individuals who are alive and well 3, and even 5 years after diagnosis."[49] In Los Angeles, UCLA researchers are studying a group of men who were diagnosed with AIDS as long as 11 years ago.[50] Other investigators are finding that fatalism among those diagnosed with AIDS significantly compromises the immune system and powerfully predicts survival time.[31] Cognitive-behavioral group therapy, in early results, show improvement in immune functioning for HIV-positive persons.[31]

The San Francisco study found that psychological "hardiness" distinguishes long-term AIDS survivors from those who succumb to the disease.[49] "Hardiness" is measured by how much control, commitment and challenge a person reports.[51] Control, on this measure, means the opposite of a helpless-hopeless attitude toward bad events in life. Commitment is the opposite of alienation. People who score high on this dimension find meaning in their work, values and personal relationships. Challenge describes a person's ability to interpret stressful events as changes to be explored and successfully met rather than threats to be dreaded and feared.

Solomon and colleagues also found that one kind of social support seems to distinguish exceptional AIDS survivors who have *Pneumocystitis carinii pneumonia,* a life-threatening complication of AIDS.[49] Those who followed suggestions or took advice from people in their social network lived longer. The San Francisco researchers caution that the number of subjects in their study was small (N=21) and that their results are preliminary. They note, however, that the results are consistent with findings on the effects of control and support in other diseases. For example, Temoshok, Solomon's associate, has reported that a "Type C" coping style is associated with an unfavorable prognosis for cutaneous malignant melanoma.[52] Type C characteristics include being passive, appeasing, helpless and unexpressing of emotion. The San Francisco research group currently is investigating whether Type C in men infected with the AIDS virus is associated with greater risk of developing Kaposi's sarcoma, another serious complication of immune deficiency.

Because the asymptomatic phase of HIV-1 infection can be as long as 10 to 15 years,[53] helping people remain free of symptoms and slowing down the progression of the disease is a matter of top priority. At the Center for the Biopsychosocial Study of AIDS at the University of Miami, researchers report that aerobic exercise training has improved the immunological functioning and psychological health of a group of both HIV-1 seropositive and seronegative men.[54] They note that the exercising not only seems to have direct physiological benefits, but it also results in a greater sense of control. The researchers also are investigating the effects of a program that includes cognitive restructuring, assertiveness training, mental imagery, social support enrichment and progressive muscle relaxation. Preliminary results seem promising, but need further replication.[55]

Similar psychological intervention has been effective in improving affective state and immune function in a group of postsurgical patients with malignant melanoma.[56,57] Thirty-five patients in a 6-week program received stress management, enhancement of problem-solving skills, relaxation training, and group support. Compared to 26 controls, assessment at a 6-month followup showed significant increases in natural killer cells, NK cytotoxic activity, and percent of large granular lymphocytes. The experimental group also showed significantly less depression, fatigue and mood disturbance. They also used significantly more active-behavioral and active-cognitive coping than did the controls.[56,57]

SUMMARY

What can we conclude from these studies? One fact seems certain: there is no simple connection between life events and illness. Whether we get sick from an infection or a negative life experience depends on more than a germ or stress. All disease is multifactorial, and the resources that help protect us have much to do with our sense of support and control over our lives. What happens in our endocrine system and to our immune response is a function of what is going on inside our heads and hearts—the meanings we give to events and the feelings we have about them.

Skeptics have long doubted these tenets.[7,8] However, emerging evidence increasingly dispels these doubts and has replaced them with a biopsychosocial model based on psychoneuroimmunology (PNI). Indeed, Cousins[50] described PNI as "the new science of medicine." To date, more than a dozen academic medical centers in the United States have PNI research programs and the list is growing.

With expanded scientific study of the mind-body connection, people in general will come to recognize that whether they become ill is not always a matter of chance, but to a considerable extent something under their own control.

REFERENCES

1. Selye H: *The Stress of Life.* New York: McGraw-Hill; 1956.
2. Selye H: A syndrome produced by diverse nocuous agents. *Nature* 1936; 138: 32.
3. Selye H: *Selye's Guide to Stress Research.* New York: Van Nostrand Reinhold; 1980.
4. Selye H: *Stress Without Distress.* New York: Signet; 1975.
5. Lazarus RS: *Psychological Stress and the Coping Process.* New York: McGraw-Hill; 1966.
6. Lazarus RS, Launier R: Stress-related transactions between persons and environment. In: Pervin LA & Lewis M ed. *Perspectives in Interactional Psychology.* New York: Plenum; 1978.
7. Justice B: *Who Gets Sick: How Beliefs, Moods and Thoughts Affect Health.* Los Angeles: Tarcher; 1988.
8. Justice B: *Wer Wird Krank?* (A. Pott, trans.). Hamburg, Germany: Goldmann Verlag; 1991.
9. Eisenberg L: Science in medicine: Too much and too limited in scope? In: White KL ed. *The Task of Medicine.* Menlo Park, CA: Henry J. Kaiser Family Foundation; 1988; 290–217.
10. Payer L: *Medicine & culture.* New York: Henry Holt; 1988.
11. Sagan L: *The Health of Nations: True Causes of Sickness and Well-being.* New York: Basic Books; 1987.
12. Leighton AH: *My Name is Legion.* New York: Basic Books; 1959.

13. Leighton AH: Conceptual perspectives. In: Kaplan RN, Wilson AH and Leighton AH ed. *Further Explorations in Social Psychiatry*. New York: Basic Books; 1976.
14. Rodin J: Managing the stress of aging: The role of control and coping. In: Levine B and Holger U ed. *Coping and Health*. New York: Plenum 1979; 171–202.
15. Sarason IG: Sense of social support. Paper presented at the annual meeting of the American Psychological Association, Atlanta, GA; August 1988.
16. Somers AR: Marital Status, Health, and Use of Health Services. *JAMA* 1979; 241: 1818–1822.
17. Kiecolt-Glaser JK, Kennedy S, Malkoff S, Fisher L, Speicher CE, and Glasser R: Marital discord and immunity in males. *Psychosomatic Med* 1988; 50: 213–229.
18. Kiecolt-Glasser JK, Fisher L, Ogrocki P, Stout JC, Speicher EE, and Glaser R: Martial quality, marital disruption, and immune function. *Psychosomatic Med*, 1987; 49: 13–34.
19. Schwartz MA, Wiggins OP: Scientific and humanistic medicine: A theory of clinical methods. In: White KL ed. *The Task of Medicine*. Menlo Park, CA: Henry J. Kaiser Family Foundation; 1988: 137–171.
20. Cromwell RI, Butterfield EC, Brayfield FM, and Curry JJ: *Acute Myocardial Infarction: Reaction and Recovery*. St. Louis: Mosby; 1977.
21. Ornish D: *Stress, Diet and Your Heart*. New York: Signet; 1982.
22. Oliva PB: Pathophysiology of acute infarction. *Annals of Internal Medicine* 1981: 94: 236–250.
23. Hirsch PD, Hillis LD, Campbell WB, Firth BG, and Willerson JT: Release of prostaglandins and thromboxane into the coronary circulation in patients with ischemic heart disease. *NEJM* 1981; 304: 685–691.
24. Moncada S, Vane JR: Arachidonic acid metabolites and the interactions between Platelet and blood vessel walls. *NEJM* 1979; 300: 1142–1149.
25. Frankl VE: *Man's Search for Meaning*. 3rd ed. New York: Simon & Schuster; 1984.
26. Dimsdale JE: The Coping Behavior of Nazi Concentration Camp Survivors. *American Journal of Psychiatry* 1974; 131(7): 792–797.
27. Mrazek FJ, Mrazek DA: Resilience in child maltreatment victims: A conceptual exploration. *Child Abuse & Neglect* 1987; 11: 357–366.
28. Pennebaker J: *Opening Up: The Healing Powers of Confiding*. New York: Morrow; 1990.
29. Pennebaker J: Writing is healing. Presentation at the Hawthorne Training Conference, Houston, TX; March 1990.
30. Spiegel D, Bloom JR, Kraemer HC, Gottheil E: Effect of psychosocial treatment on survival of patients with metastatic breast cancer. *Lancet* 1989; Oct 14: 1888–891.
31. Kemeny M: Mind, emotions and the immune system. Presentation at annual conference of Institute of Noetic Sciences, Arlington, VA; June 1993.
32. Holmes TH, Rahe RH: The social readjustment rating scale. *J of Psychosomatic Res* 1976; 11: 213–218.
33. Holmes TH, Masuda M: Life Change and Illness Susceptibility. In: Dohrenwend BS Dohrewend BF eds. *Stressful Life Events: Their Nature and Effects*. New York: Wiley; 1974: 9–44.
34. Dohrenwend BB, Dohrenwend BP: Life Stress and Illness. In: Dohrenwend BB and Dohrenwend BP eds. *Stressful Life Events and Their Contexts*. New York, Prodist; 1981: 1–27.
35. Nuckolls KB, Cassel J, Kaplan BH: Psychosocial assets, life crisis, and the prognosis of pregnancy. *Am J Epi*, 1972; 95: 431–441.
36. Morris NM, Udry JR, Chase CL: Reduction of low birth weight birth rates by the prevention of unwanted pregnancies. *Am J Public Health* 1973; 3(11): 935–938.
37. Norbeck JS, Tilden VP: Life stress, social support, and emotional disequilibrium in complications of pregnancy: A prospective, multivariate study. *J of Health and Social Behavior* 1983; 24(3) 30–46.
38. Rottman G: Untersuchungen uber Einstellung zur Schwangerschaft und zur fotalen Entwiklung. In: Graber H ed. *Geist und Psyche* Munchen: Kindler Verlag; 1974.
39. Lukesch M: Psychologie Faktoren der Schwangershaft. Unpublished dissertation, University of Salzburg; 1975.
40. Kruse F: Nos souvenirs du corps maternal, *Psychologie Heute* 1978: 56.
41. Verny T, Kelly J: *The Secret Life of the Unborn Child*. New York: Summit Books; 1981.
42. Liley A: The fetus as a personality. *The Australian and New Zealand Journal of Psychiatry* 1972; 6: 99–105.
43. Clements M: Observations on certain aspects of neonatal behavior in response to auditory stimuli. Paper presented at the Fifth International Congress of Psychosomatic Obstetrics and Gynecology, Rome; 1977.
44. Wald M: After the meltdown, lessons from a clean-up. *New York Times* 1990; April 24: B5–B6.
45. Davidson LM, Baum A, Fleming, Gisriel MM: Toxic Exposure and Chronic Stress at Three Mile Island. In Lebovits AH, Baum A, and Singer JE eds. *Advances in Environmental Psychology*. Hillsdale, NJ: Erlbaum, 1986; 6: 35–46.
46. Bromet EV, Schulberg HC: The Three Mile Island Disaster: A Search for high-risk Groups. In Shore JH ed. *Disaster Stress Studies: New Methods and Findings*. Washington, DC: American Psychiatric Press; 1986: 2–19.

47. Levine JS, Schiller PL: Is there a religious factor in health? *J Religion & Health* 1987; 6: 9–36.
48. King DG: Religion and health relationships: A review. *Journal of Religion and Health* 1990; 29(2): 101–112.
49. Solomon GF, Temoshok L, O'Leary A, Zich J: An Intensive Psychoimmunologic study of long-surviving persons with AIDS. *Annals of the New York Academy of Sciences* 1987; 496: 647–655.
50. Cousins N: New dimensions in healing. Presentation at the Tenneco Distinguished Lecture Series, University of Houston, TX; March 1990.
51. Kobasa SCO, Maddi SR, Puccetti and Zola MA: Effectiveness of hardiness, exercise and social support as resources against illness. *J Psychosomatic Res* 1985; 29(5): 525–533.
52. Temoshok L, Heller BW, Sagebiel RW, Blois MS, Sweet DM, DiClemente RJ, and Gold ML: The relations of psychosocial factors to prognostic indicators in cutaneous malignant melanoma. *J Psychosomatic Med* 1985; 29: 139–153.
53. Munoz A, Wang MC, Good R, Detels H, Ginsberg L, Kingsley J, et al.: Estimation of the AIDS-free times after HIV-1 seroconversion. Paper presented at the Fourth Annual Meeting of the International Conference on AIDS, Stockholm, Sweden, June 1988.
54. Antoni MH, Schneiderman N, Fletcher MA, Goldstein DA: Psychoneuroimmunology and HIV-1. *J Consulting and Clinical Psychology* 1990; 58(1): 38–49.
55. Antoni M: Psychosocial stress management and immune functioning in an HIV-1 risk group. Paper presented at the annual meeting of the American Psychological Association, New Orleans, LA; August 1989.
56. Fawzy FW, Cousins N, Fawzy NW, Kemeny ME, Elashoff R, Morton D: A structured psychiatric intervention for cancer patients; I. Changes over time in methods of coping and affective disturbance. *Arch Gen Psychiatry* 1990; 47: 720–725.
57. Fawzy FI, Kemeny ME, Fawzy NW, Elashoff R, Morton D, Cousins N, et al.: A structured psychiatric intervention for cancer patients; II. Changes over time in immunological measures. *Arch Gen Psychiatry* 1990; 47: 729–735.

Can You Laugh Your Stress Away?

MEMBERS OF **the Laughing Clubs of India** SAY A DAILY DOSE OF GUFFAWS LOWERS THEIR BLOOD PRESSURE, REVS THEIR IMMUNE SYSTEM, AND HELPS THEM SLEEP BETTER AT NIGHT ⌒ THEY'VE GOT TO BE JOKING.

Mary Roach
Mary Roach is a contributing editor.

THE FOUNDER of Laughing Clubs International stands in his study in Bombay, cinching a canvas truss around his abdomen. I would like to be able to report that this is a man who laughs so much and so heartily that he has given himself a hernia. In fact, he has a bad back.

Madan Kataria is not a man you would describe as jolly. At 41, he has no laugh lines. Since coming to India to meet him, I have never seen him giggle or snicker or snort or pound the table and roar till tears run down his cheeks. His laugh is a monotone *huh-huh-huh,* somewhere between Beavis (or is it the other one?) and a quietly idling outboard motor.

Except at 7 A.M. Every day at dawn Kataria walks down the street to the local laughing club and cuts loose. His jaw drops halfway to his collarbone, and his usual low-key chortle becomes a slapstick of hoots and guffaws. Kataria founded the first laughing club in March 1995. Like *Saturday Review* editor Norman Cousins, who claimed he laughed away a life-threatening form of arthritis, Kataria believes that laughter is good medicine. He will tell you that it can lower your blood pressure, combat stress, boost your immune system, and give you energy. The clubs, he says, simply seemed like the best way to provide a regular dose of laughter to people who might not otherwise come into contact with anything funny. And the idea has caught on. In one year the total number of clubs in India has grown to 80, and Kataria hopes the movement will soon spread to other countries—"along the lines of the Rotary Club."

Unlike Cousins, who self-medicated with Marx Brothers movies and "Candid Camera" episodes, Kataria and his laughing club cohorts don't laugh at anything in particular. They just laugh: Fifty Indians stand around in the pink, polluted light of dawn, busting their guts for no apparent reason.

The 28 laughing clubs in Bombay meet in parks all around the city. The Jogger's Park Laughing Club, where we are going this morning, gathers in the parking lot outside the main gate. "The authorities have not yet permitted us inside," Kataria says a bit sorrowfully. Residents of a nearby apartment complex have filed formal noise pollution complaints.

This morning's laughers number around 40. Most of them are dressed in a mix of traditional Indian garb and Western casual wear—saris with Keds, sweatshirts with turbans and Gandhi-style dhoti pants.

Kataria tells me that the session will begin with a warm-up exercise in which everyone shouts, "Ho-ho, ha-ha!" in unison, over and over. "It is called the Ho-Ho, Ha-Ha Exercise," he says, with somewhat more gravity than the statement demands.

"Another instruction that is given to the laughing members is to put their hands up in the sky. This takes away the inhibitions. Laughing becomes easier. Like this." He demonstrates, and I follow suit. I don't feel like I'm about to laugh; I feel like I'm about to be frisked against a squad car. Why don't they just find something funny to laugh at?

"At first we did take the help of jokes," says Kataria. "But the stock of good jokes was over after about 15 days. After that, stale and silly jokes came. Camel jokes, vulgar jokes. It was no good."

He excuses himself to begin the warm-up. "Ho-ho, ha-ha, ho-ho, ha-ha..." On Kataria's cue, the members raise their arms and laugh. They look joyous and enthused and just slightly nuts, like hockey fans or people in a Sure commercial. Whether it's the absurdity of the situation or the infectious quality of laughter, I don't know, but soon I'm laughing along with them.

Twenty seconds of all-out hilarity is followed by deep breathing "to improve the vital capacity of the lungs." Then the group moves on to Silent Laughter With Mouth Closed, a sort of giggles-in-the-back-row affair, more deep breathing, Silent Laughter With Mouth Open, and a final round of guffaws.

Kataria introduces me to the group's

2. STRESS AND MENTAL HEALTH

PERCENTAGE OF LISTENERS WHO LAUGH UPON HEARING THE FIRST BURST ON A CANNED LAUGHTER TAPE 50

PERCENTAGE WHO LAUGH AFTER THE TENTH LAUGHTER BURST 2.5

members and tells them I want to know why they joined a laughing club.

"Why not join? It's free," says an effervescent little man with a persistent grin. "Even a poison you don't get free! Ha-ha-ha-ha-ha!"

I ask him if he feels healthier since he joined the laughing club. "Yes, definitely! I reduce my weight about 15 kilogram."

I give him two seconds of Silent Skepticism With Eyebrows Raised. He insists he's not the only one. "There, see that gentleman." He gestures at a man in rumpled, white dhotis, a huge unmade bed of a man. "He also has reduced his weight."

The gentleman's name is Manohar. He begins his tale. "Some weight I lost it, yes." He regards his mountainous midsection and sighs like a monsoon. "But, most places, I gain it. No matter. I am not bothered about my weight. I am not coming for that thing. I am coming with my friends to laugh. This is my pleasure, which I can't buy in the market. I am a rich man. I am rich with my friends."

This turns out to be a common sentiment among the laughers. "When I come here, I meet so many people, make new friends," says a woman named Laksmi, whose smile competes with her *Bindi*—her sparkling rhinestone forehead dot. "Otherwise I am sitting at home, sad, oh, so many problems, you know?"

The woman beside her nods. "It makes you more friendly. People are so shy here, they don't want to laugh. Then they come here in the morning for laughing.

friendship that's made the members healthier and happier, helped them sleep better at night, and lowered their blood pressure? Simply having a network of close, caring friends, research shows, is a tonic all by itself.

The laughers drift from the parking lot, joking among themselves. Many head toward the park. "They are going for a walk now," says Kataria. "That's another reason the laughing clubs are good. It gets them out, and they exercise afterward. This I call double benefit."

This I call confounding factors. Again, who's to say it's the laughter and not the exercise that's making these people feel better? Or the companionship? Or the deep breathing?

To FIND OUT exactly what laughing does for the human body, you need to take laughers out of the park and into the laboratory. That is what laughter researcher Lee Berk has done. In a series of studies at Loma Linda University in California, Berk measured the effects of laughter on the immune system. Subjects were divided into two groups and hooked up to IVs. Half were shown a video of stand-up comic Richard Gallagher (their choice, not Berk's); the other half sat quietly in a room. During the video and for a half hour afterward, blood samples were drawn every ten minutes. While the control group showed no physiological change, the video watchers had significant increases in various measures of

emotions such as grief and anger can suppress the immune system, positive emotions such as mirth, he says, can strengthen it. In other words, laughter creates its own unique physiological state, with changes in the immune system opposite to those caused by stress.

Opposite and, one study suggests, even stronger. Using a group of 96 men over a three-month period, psychiatrist Arthur Stone, at the State University of New York at Stony Brook Medical School, measured levels of an antibody thought to be the body's first defense against cold and flu viruses. The men also kept track of their daily emotional ups and downs during that time. Stone reports that positive social interactions, such as entertaining friends or playing with children, affected the men's antibody levels—in this case, raising them—to a greater extent and for a longer period than did negative events, such as arguments or being criticized at work.

As support for the eustress theory, Berk cites the work of Peter Derks, a psychologist at the College of William and Mary in Williamsburg, Virginia. Derks and his colleagues conducted a study in which they decked subjects with electrodes and mapped their brain activity while they listened to jokes. Rather than pinpointing a localized response—"a funny bone in the brain," as Derks puts it—the researchers found that the entire cerebral cortex (the outer layer of the brain) is involved when people laugh. Mirth, Derks reasoned, stimulates the

PERCENTAGE BY WHICH THE SPEAKER OUTLAUGHS THE LISTENER DURING AN AVERAGE CONVERSATION 46

PERCENTAGE BY WHICH THE AVERAGE FEMALE SPEAKER OUTLAUGHS A MALE LISTENER 127

Oh, they are so bold now! They can laugh a river!"

She lets loose her own little tributary of glee, which is joined by Laksmi's giggles and the chortles of the spry grinning man until a Class V torrent of laughter washes over me.

I begin to suspect that the Jogger's Park Laughing Club is a kind of social center, a lonely hearts' club for singles and widows and home-alone housewives. In which case, is it the laughter or the

immune function: activated T cells, primed to battle infection; natural killer cells, which attack tumors and microbes; immunoglobulin A antibodies, which patrol the respiratory tract; and gamma interferon, a key immune system messenger. Their levels of cortisol, a hormone that suppresses the immune system, were significantly lower.

Berk believes that laughter is a state of "eustress," which is psychology-speak for the opposite of distress. Just as stressful

brain's pleasure centers, and that could in turn boost the immune system, resulting in the therapeutic effects of humor suggested by Norman Cousins.

The emphasis rests on *could*. "At the moment," says Derks, "no one can say with any certainty exactly what's going on when people laugh."

Even if someone could, that's still several steps away from being able to say that laughter benefits health. How much of a difference do these transient boosts

7. Can You Laugh Your Stress Away?

to the immune system make? Do people who laugh more get sick less often or actually live longer?

So far, findings are mixed. At Oberlin College in Ohio, psychologist Albert Porterfield gave 220 students two questionnaires, one to assess their sense of humor and a second called the Physical Symptom Scale. He found that those with better humor scores had no fewer symptoms of disease.

A study of humor's effect on longevity, however, yielded more encouraging data. Psychologists Mark Yoder and Richard Haude, at the University of Akron in Ohio, asked a group of senior citizens who had outlived their siblings by an average of seven years to rate their own sense of humor against their sibling's. According to the scores, the living siblings generally believed they had a better sense of humor than the brother or sister who had died.

If a good sense of humor can somehow help people live longer, you'd expect comedians to live longest of all. But they don't. Psychologist James Rotton, at the Florida International University in Miami, sifted through ten years of *Time* and *Newsweek* obituaries. Taking into account gender and cause of death, Rotton compared the life spans of three groups: humorous entertainers, nonhumorous entertainers, and people whose fame had nothing to do with entertaining or humor.

Contrary to expectations, Rotton discovered that the humorists, as a group, died youngest. (He dismisses the popular notion that comics are unhappy, neurotic people who use humor as a defense or to mask depression; their suicide rate, he found, was no higher than average.) It also appears that being a successful entertainer of any variety takes its toll: Those who had no performing skills, humorous or otherwise, lived longest.

Good news for Madan Kataria. He has just told me a monumentally dumb joke about a flatulent Indian on an airplane. We are back in his office, a simple room with little decoration other than some peacock feathers and a wall clock. The clock's face is a photograph of Kataria's mother-in-law. This is not a humorous item, or not to Kataria, anyway. I already made the mistake of laughing at the clock. Yesterday I made a similar mistake regarding the Have a Nice Day coaster set on his desk. Kataria looks like he wants to pummel me. Laughter is not always good for your health.

TO UNDERSTAND the real long-term benefits of laughter—and why laughing clubs are so popular in India—you have only to walk down a street in Bombay. From the moment you step outside, stress is all over you. Noise, traffic, crowds, a cataclysm of diesel and potholes and horns. Children beg at the traffic lights. Cows jaywalk. Men in shirtsleeves sort through heaps of rubble, diligent and methodical, as if it were a desk job. Rather than watching the passersby, people at sidewalk cafés turn their backs to the street, trying to ignore the insanity that surrounds them. It doesn't take a Ph.D. to know that a few good laughs would ease people's nerves.

Suppose it were as straightforward as this: You can't laugh and be tense at the same time. In other words, laughing is a coping mechanism, a buffer between your immune system and the situation that's causing stress. A jovial moment pulls you out of your funk, distracts you from your troubling thoughts and feelings, creating a respite from the stress that hampers your immune system.

In this case, the health-sustaining element wouldn't be laughter itself, but the ability to laugh under stressful circumstances. In the early eighties researchers Rod Martin and Herbert Lefcourt, then of the University of Waterloo in Ontario, decided to investigate this notion. They showed subjects an unsettling video (ye olde gruesome aborigine initiation rite) and asked them to describe what they'd witnessed in a humorous way. As expected, subjects who managed to make light of the bloody scene were also those who experienced less stress in their lives.

This may explain why professional comics don't live any longer than the rest of us: What matters is not the ability to make other people laugh but the ability

Get in the Humor Habit

- **Turn off the TV and be sociable** According to laughter researcher Robert Provine, at the University of Maryland Baltimore County, people laugh 30 times more often in a social setting than they do alone. So get together with friends. Play a game with your family. Invite the neighbors over.
- **Learn something new** Try an activity you may not excel at, preferably with someone you like. A friend's art-class attempts to draw a cube in proper perspective or your first time on in-line skates may generate more hysterics than back-to-back episodes of "Friends" and "Seinfeld."
- **Choose your friends carefully** A friend with whom you always laugh is a treasure. Unload the duds and cultivate the gems.
- **Don't be lazy** Too many people don't bother with humor; it's so much easier to be dull. Make the extra effort. When you're talking to friends or coworkers, don't just get to the point: Noodle a bit along the way. Make wisecracks and blurt out non sequiturs. To keep your comic juices flowing, make yourself a reminder—something silly on your desk or tacked to your bulletin board.
- **Cultivate running jokes** When you find yourself in a moment of shared hilarity, milk it. Work it into a conversation or an E-mail message the next day.
- **Master the art of comic complaining** It's all in the presentation. Exaggerate and overstate. Poke fun at yourself. Many a stand-up comedian has based his or her career on well-worded griping.
- **Share the joke** When you hear or read something funny, pass it along and laugh all over again. And again and again.
- **Get a pet** Stupid Pet Tricks helped launch David Letterman's career. Why? Dogs and cats crack people up. And you don't even have to train them. Ever watch a dog with peanut butter on its nose, or a cat with its head stuck in a paper bag, backing around the room?
- **Start the day with a laugh** Swap the A.M. talk show for a lively dose of the Roadrunner. Fifteen minutes of looniness can set your mood on silly for the rest of the day.

—M.R.

2. STRESS AND MENTAL HEALTH

to make yourself laugh. Michelle Newman, an assistant professor of psychology at Pennsylvania State University, recently tested this idea. She divided subjects into two groups based on whether they scored high or low on a sense-of-humor questionnaire. Like Martin and Lefcourt's subjects, the groups were asked to narrate a disturbing video (ye olde gruesome industrial accident). Newman had half of each group's members do it seriously; the other half tried to do it humorously. Meanwhile she monitored heart rate, skin conductivity, and other measures of stress. Both groups registered lower stress levels when they de-

end of a lawn to the other and back, turning when she reaches the edge, like a swimmer doing laps.

I approach a laughing club member in a wool cap and scarf and ask him about his day-to-day life. Does he experience a lot of stress? How has laughing helped?

"Well, I'll tell you," he begins. "We human beings have small, small irritations. You perhaps do not like my mustache, maybe it irritates you. I used to feel this—so irritated. But this laughter gave me more and more relaxation. And that took away the irritations." Abruptly he steps away. "We are starting."

"Ho-ho, ha-ha, ho-ho . . ." Today's

among the laughers, Joy Mukherjee, a "film star of yesteryear." Mukherjee says that the morning laughing session frees him from tension. "In the morning, if you laugh, your whole mood gets in the proper shape." As he speaks, he cracks his knuckles so loudly it sounds like he could be cracking walnuts. "You are happy the whole day."

I believe this. I used to watch Woody Woodpecker cartoons in the morning before I went to work. It somehow set the mood for the rest of the morning. The more you laugh, the more you laugh. The happier you are, the healthier.

The laughing session over, Kataria is

AVERAGE NUMBER OF TIMES PER DAY A PRESCHOOLER LAUGHS 400

AVERAGE NUMBER OF TIMES PER DAY AN ADULT LAUGHS 15

scribed the scene with humor. When they amused themselves, they were able to cope better with their unease.

I DECIDE TO BRING UP the topic of laughter and stress at the second laughing club I visit with Kataria, which meets in Lokhandwala Garden, down the road from his office. It's a pleasant park, marred only by a mild sewer smell and the groundskeeper's predilection for painting the rocks gaudy colors. At 6:45 A.M. the lawns are crowded with health-conscious Indians, jogging and doing yoga. A man stands on his head by an azalea bush. A woman in a maraschino-colored sari strides from one

group has 20 more people than yesterday's, and the laughter seems exponentially louder and more contagious. By the time the session is over, everyone looks flushed and relaxed. They have that happy, noodly exhaustion that comes after a good, long bout of helpless hysterics. You can almost believe what laughter researcher William Fry, an emeritus professor at Stanford University, says: that 100 laughs is the aerobic equivalent of ten minutes on a rowing machine. (Fry did the calculations himself, comparing the heart rates of study subjects during laughter with his own heart rate during exercise, measured on the rowing machine in his home.)

Kataria introduces me to a celebrity

standing by the park entrance with several club members, eating cloves of raw garlic. (To the mild misfortune of his family and friends, Kataria believes in garlic almost as vigorously as he believes in laughter.)

I ask him why he believes laughter is such a wonder tonic. Without solid scientific evidence, how can he be sure?

Kataria regards me with curiosity. "You question whether laughter is good for you?"

"Not exactly . . ."

"You are perhaps concerned about an overdose? Some kind of laughter toxicity?" I shake my head. "Then just laugh! Too many hows and whys make you a tense person."

Good Mood Foods

The research is becoming clearer: Certain foods really can calm you down—and cheer you up

SHAWNA VOGEL

Shawna Vogel is a freelance writer in Boston.

Standing in line at a Cinnabon bakery the other day, I watched a man behind the counter preparing the delicacy of the house. He placed two cups of softened butter on a sheet of dough and began spreading the goo as if it were icing. Hey, isn't this much fat against the law? Then he started sprinkling cinnamon across the buttery surface. The cloud of spice wafted toward me, and all of a sudden I was a kid again, back in my grandmother's kitchen. Her cinnamon rolls were the perfect antidote to any bad mood. No wonder I'm still a sucker for these concoctions.

Forget sweet nothings whispered into a willing ear; food is the most powerful seducement of all. When a friend of mine put her house on the market, she dropped a stick of cinnamon into a pot of boiling water for her first open house. The aroma was enough to trigger sentimental reveries in the most heartless prospective buyer poking through her closets. Freshly baked cinnamon rolls! Apple pie! Call it coincidence, but the house sold that day.

Yet there is more to the emotional power of some foods than associations with things past, or even things forbidden. During the past two decades, researchers have identified tangible effects that certain foods have on our brain chemistry. The undisputed leader of the food and mood movement is Judith Wurtman of the Massachusetts Institute of Technology. A respected research scientist who was involved in the early studies in the field, Wurtman was also the first to seek and find an audience for these ideas far from academia: women in search of ways to feel better day to day.

Standing today at the front of a packed auditorium in Boston, Wurtman is a compact, vibrant presence in a cherry red suit. "On the face of it, it doesn't *seem* like there would be any relationship at all between whether you eat four ounces of chicken or a potato and what your mood is going to be like," she says, "unless maybe the chicken is dry or the potato is cold and tasteless."

However, she tells the audience, she's convinced that a potato eaten by itself can calm jumpy nerves, simply because it's almost pure carbohydrate. Meanwhile, she says, choosing a protein such as chicken at lunch will keep you fresh for your afternoon job interview.

It's a formula that Wurtman has elaborated on in five books and hundreds of speeches—an idea that led this year to the test-marketing of the first food product designed solely to help someone deal with emotional ups and downs: PMS Escape, a prepackaged, pure-carbohydrate drink mix for women suffering from premenstrual syndrome. (The drink is currently available only in drugstores in New England.) "If a woman really has emotional pain," she tells the gathering, "this drink will help her decrease her pain in 15 to 20 minutes."

Surprisingly, such infomercial-like claims do not produce derisive laughter from Wurtman's colleagues. Other scientists also have turned up tantalizing signs that eating pure carbohydrate can cause a shift in a person's mood. No, her colleagues' major reaction to Wurtman's declarations is that, in real life, following her advice is both hard to do and promises small returns.

Wurtman will acknowledge that other substances—a cup of coffee or a glass of wine—pack more mood-altering power. "It's clearly not the same as taking a Prozac," she says. "And it doesn't last long—only a few hours." Still, she challenges any woman who's interested to see for herself if the adjustments in attitude warrant an adjustment in eating habits. "It *does* work," she says.

Can eating carbohydrates calm you down?

TWENTY-FIVE YEARS AGO Wurtman's husband, Richard, a neuroscientist at MIT, was the first scientist to catch on to the idea that carbohydrates affect brain chemistry. Feeding rats mostly starch and sugar, he found, elevated their levels of serotonin, the brain chemical most associated with good moods. Carbohydrates, the Wurtmans discovered, increase serotonin levels by starting a chain of events that results in more tryptophan entering the brain.

Tryptophan, you may remember, is an amino acid—one of the building blocks of protein. A synthetic version used to be sold as a sleeping aid until impurities in some supplements caused dozens of deaths and the pills were yanked off drugstore shelves. The compound helps people relax—even nod off—because once it gets into the brain it is converted into soothing serotonin.

Carbohydrates help tryptophan get into the brain in a roundabout way. Normally tryptophan must compete with five other amino acids in the blood for transport across the blood-brain barrier, a complicated mesh of capillaries that keeps many substances out of the brain. Carbohydrates trigger the pancreas to release insulin, which ferries the other amino acids out of the bloodstream and into the body's tissues. For some reason, insulin leaves tryptophan behind, free to flood the brain. When that happens, your mood improves.

At least that's how it works in theory. Because researchers can't actually measure serotonin levels in the human brain, they have to rely on asking people how they feel after eating carbohydrates. Which is exactly what Wurtman did. She had 32 women, some with severe premenstrual symptoms, rate their energy level and emotional state before a high-carbohydrate meal and an hour later. Those suffering PMS symptoms felt far less tense, angry, and tired after the meal.

But even women with no PMS symptoms felt slightly less tense and tired.

"We know that people who are stressed reach for cookies, potatoes, pasta, pretzels, popcorn, or candy," Wurtman says, kindly not mentioning cinnamon rolls. "We now think that they are trying to medicate themselves with carbohydrates, to increase serotonin levels in order to feel better."

Trying, unfortunately, is not achieving. To obtain the serotonin increase, researchers say, you have to eat an *all-carbohydrate* snack on an empty stomach. Because fat slows digestion, buttering your toast or dribbling oil on your pasta will dampen and delay the effect. And putting any protein in your system within four hours of your dose will disarm the mood shift completely.

What's more, not all high-carbohydrate foods work. Fruit doesn't, Wurtman says, because its sugar, fructose, causes insulin to be released too slowly to trigger a serotonin boost. Muffins or brownies are so high in slow-digesting fat that they probably don't increase serotonin levels at all.

What does that leave you? Starch. Here's Wurtman's advice: Let's say you're nervous about a presentation you will have to give at 1 P.M. Don't eat anything after 9 A.M. Then, a half-hour or an hour before the meeting, have a small snack of a low-calorie, starchy food. "About 30 grams is enough," Wurtman says. "That's a cup and a half of dry breakfast cereal. An english muffin with jam. Two cups of pasta is more than enough." Best of all is a potato. Our bodies digest potato starch quickly, inducing a fast insulin response.

"So if you're at home and the world is falling apart," Wurtman says, "just pop a potato in the microwave." Then wait 30 minutes—without eating anything else—and you should be feeling better.

Will eating protein really perk you up?

IF YOU LISTEN TO WURTMAN long enough, you'll become convinced that eating a meal that's mostly protein—red snapper, say, or steak—will improve your brainpower. Just as tryptophan is the precursor to serotonin, another amino acid, called tyrosine, is the precursor for norepinephrine and dopamine—brain chemicals that aid reaction time and mental acuity. And protein—from animal sources like chicken and fish or plant sources like beans—is known to boost the body's levels of tyrosine.

"If you're doing something very mentally taxing, putting together some type of argument if you're a lawyer, or writing something complicated, then

8. Good Mood Foods

Medical School who has done several studies on food and mood, "you simply don't have that effect."

Still, if a chunk of lean ham won't help you master the theory of relativity, it *will* keep carbohydrates from zonking you out. That's right: As they relax you, carbohydrates can also make you feel downright drowsy. Researchers think this soporific effect helps explain the traditional post-spaghetti energy dip. People who complement their carbohydrates with protein, experts agree, avoid this drop in alertness.

This jibes with biochemistry. When you eat a ham sandwich for lunch, the ham introduces amino acids that compete with tryptophan for entry to the brain. With tryptophan outnumbered, the rise in serotonin never materializes—so you don't get sleepy.

What does this mean in real life? If you notice that your morning pancakes or lunchtime bowl of rice leaves you lethargic, balance out the meal with some protein. Then again, if you're really looking for a pick-me-up, you're probably already in line for a hot fudge sundae.

SNACKS THAT HELP YOU RELAX

Eating one of these low-protein, fat-free carbohydrate snacks, says researcher Judith Wurtman, author of *Managing Your Mind & Mood Through Food*, can help you wind down by raising levels of serotonin, the feel-good chemical in your brain. The caveats: Don't eat anything else for four hours before or 30 minutes after the snack—and don't add butter or milk. If you manage that, she says, you should start to feel more relaxed within a half hour.

BAKED POTATO WITH SALSA
BAGEL WITH JAM
OATMEAL WITH BROWN SUGAR
PASTA WITH TOMATO SAUCE
PRETZELS

FOODS THAT FIGHT DROWSINESS

If you tend to get *too* relaxed after eating a high-carbohydrate meal, next time add in protein-rich foods, which limit the post-meal energy dip. Some options:

COTTAGE CHEESE
BEANS OR LENTILS
LOW-FAT YOGURT
HARD-BOILED EGG
TUNA OR OTHER FISH

BONBONS FOR A QUICK BUZZ

As long as they don't ruin your appetite for healthier fare, no foods can lift your mood as fast as goodies high in sugar or fat.

M & Ms
CARAMEL POPCORN
ICE CREAM
LEMON DROPS
SOFT DRINK

---

you're using up these chemicals in your brain," Wurtman says. "And the only way you can replace them is by supplying the amino acid tyrosine. In other words, by gnawing on a chicken drumstick.

But Harris Lieberman, a psychologist at the U.S. Army Research Institute of Environmental Medicine in Natick, Massachusetts, has researched tyrosine's psychological effects extensively, and he doesn't see it that way. For someone's brain to exhaust its supply of these brain chemicals and depend on tyrosine to make more, Lieberman says, he or she would have to endure truly extreme stress—arctic cold or military combat.

"Under ordinary, everyday circumstances," says Bonnie Spring, a psychologist at the Chicago

Do sweets bring the biggest lift of all?

YOU BET, SAYS ADAM DREWNOWSKI, director of the Human Nutrition Program at the University of Michigan School of Public Health in Ann Arbor. He thinks the link between food and mood has more to do with sugar and fat than with carbohydrates. Though he concedes that a dose of carbohydrates can leave people calmer an hour later, he doesn't believe that explains why people go weak in the knees at the first taste of ice cream, chocolate, or cheesecake. "Wurtman uses sweet, high-fat foods like chocolate and doughnuts in her tests, except she calls them carbohydrates," he says. The real power in these foods, Drewnowski believes, resides not in the carbohydrates they contain but in their hefty proportions of sugar and fat.

Certainly, eating sugar can bring anxious people quick relief. Among newborns having blood drawn from their heels, those given a teaspoon of sugar water just before being struck cry (and presumably hurt) far less than those given plain water. Studies in animals suggest that high-fat foods have a similar soothing effect. Says the author of the best-seller *Food & Mood*, nutritionist Elizabeth Somer, "Sweet and creamy is the dynamic duo—fat makes the food desirable, and sugar makes the fat invisible."

2. STRESS AND MENTAL HEALTH

In Drewnowski's view, humans hunger for fat and sugar because the substances trigger the brain to release endorphins, morphinelike chemicals that send pleasure signals throughout the body, including the mouth. In one study, he gave people a drug that disarmed their endorphins, then fed them goodies from Snickers to Oreo cookies. Without the endorphin reward, the normally irresistible morsels gave the volunteers no more joy than a stick of celery.

Of course, one risk of turning to a sweet snack when you're anxious or blue is that you may not be able to stop at one scoop or cookie. And even if you don't go overboard, sweets may leave a sour taste. "Women in particular often feel guilty or angry with themselves when they give in to a craving," Somer says.

If you aren't susceptible to binges or self-reproach, however, there's no safer route to pure pleasure than nibbling on forbidden foods. The queen, of course, is chocolate, which not only boosts endorphins but probably packs enough sugar to trigger Wurtman's serotonin effect. (Though the fat content, which slows digestion, is likely to delay the onset.) Chocolate also contains caffeine and a similar substance called theobromine. Many researchers believe these compounds give chocolate-lovers a coffeelike buzz.

But if something low-cal is called for, you're better off experimenting with Wurtman's carbohydrates. Slather your potato with salsa, savor every bite, then sit back in an easy chair and let your mind drift to a white sand beach: You are lying on a chaise lounge beneath a warm Tahitian sunset. The waiter from the seaside bar is bringing you a tall, tropical drink. What's that in his other hand? Could it be a cinnamon roll?

Out of the Blues

Walking regularly is turning out to be your best medicine for bad moods and bad days. Why? The answer is all in your head.

Kathleen McAuliffe

KATHLEEN MCAULIFFE *is a freelance writer based in Miami. Her work has appeared in* Omni, U.S. News & World Report, *and* The New York Times Magazine.

Laura G. had been feeling depressed, lonely, blah, so a psychiatrist suggested she try the antidepressant Prozac. After months of sessions and no luck with the wonder drug, she turned to another psychotherapist, Austin "Ozzie" Gontang. Therapy sessions were scheduled for sunrise. Almost miraculously, Laura's moods brightened; her lethargy went away.

What caused Laura to feel so much better? The catalyst wasn't a drug or talking about her childhood. Hardly. The cure was walking.

Surprisingly, perhaps, Laura's psychological experience isn't that far out. There's convincing clinical—and anecdotal—evidence that regular exercise improves self-esteem, reduces anxiety and hostility, and can even lift clinical depression.

How can something as simple as walking have such a profound effect on how you feel? Here's what researchers have to say.

TAKE TWO WALKS AND CALL ME

Scientists are finding out that walking affects your brain chemistry—and ultimately your moods—in two ways: by making you feel good and by keeping you from feeling bad.

An expert on this phenomenon is Keith Johnsgard, a clinical psychologist and professor at San Jose State University and the author of *The Exercise Prescription for Depression and Anxiety* (Plenum Press). According to Johnsgard, exercise is a mind-altering technique that brings about changes—sometimes for days at a time—in numerous chemical systems in the brain. There is ample evidence, for instance, that physical activity unleashes beta-endorphin, the natural opiate widely credited as the secret to "runner's high." But endorphin is only part of the story behind the psychological benefits of exercise—and perhaps only a small part at that.

Despite all the media hoopla surrounding endorphin, physical activity triggers a cascade of neuro-chemical events. Specifically, Johnsgard reports, researchers have found laboratory rats that exercise on a treadmill produce significantly higher levels of dopamine, norepinephrine, and serotonin. These, he notes, are the very brain compounds that antidepressant drugs are known to impact.

While most people report an immediate boost of spirit after working out, it usually takes three to five weeks of regular physical activity to lift a clinical depression. This is roughly the same amount of time it takes an antidepressant drug to begin to lift a clinical depression. Johnsgard believes this is more than a coincidence: He suspects that exercise mimics the neuro-chemical action of antidepressants.

Walk vs. Talk

Brisk walking ranks with the best talk therapies as a treatment for depression. Some studies even suggest that the long-term benefits of exercise may surpass the traditional tell-your-life-story cures.

In a landmark study conducted at the University of Wisconsin by psychiatrist John Greist, now at the Dean Foundation in Madison, exercise was compared to psychotherapy in the treatment of clinically depressed patients.

Although both groups were significantly improved by the end of the three-month study, they differed sharply a year later. A full 80% of the exercisers were symptom-free, whereas half of those who had received psychotherapy had returned for further treatment within the year.

2. STRESS AND MENTAL HEALTH

Signs of Depression

Depression affects mood, thoughts, body, and behavior. The American Psychiatric Association recommends that you see your physician if you experience four or more of the following symptoms for more than two weeks:

- Significant loss or gain in weight
- Sleeping too much or too little
- Loss of interest in activities you once enjoyed
- Fatigue and loss of memory
- Inability to concentrate
- Recurring thoughts of death or suicide
- Overwhelming feelings of sadness or grief
- Headaches or stomach aches

In addition to juicing up our systems with all these "feel good" chemicals, regular exercise helps the body burn off stress hormones such as cortisol, which is found in abnormally high levels in stressed individuals.

In a recent survey, 98% of Walking *readers said that a primary reason for walking was to feel good afterward.*

"Regular exercise produces an antidote against stress even before it occurs," says University of Nebraska psychologist and exercise physiologist Wes Sime. He bases this claim on an ongoing study that compares how exercisers and non-exercisers react to a series of traumatic stimuli. Sime shows his subjects films of gruesome events such as the Holocaust and then gives them difficult cognitive tasks to perform in a hostile, competitive atmosphere. Early results appear to suggest that among the 50 people tested so far, regular exercisers who took part in the test produced less cortisol and other stress hormones than did their inactive counterparts.

"What this demonstrates is a conditioning effect," explains Sime. "The body uses the same system to deal with both physical and emotional stress. So, when we get ourselves in physical shape, it has a carryover effect in the mental realm."

AMERICA NEEDS TO WALK

Tonya C., a 24-year-old student, started walking briskly to help herself quit smoking. She kicked the habit—and much more. An unexpected benefit of her new exercise regimen is that her moods no longer control her life; she controls them. "People used to call me moody and ultra-sensitive. I was on an emotional roller coaster," she reports. "Now I don't have any more mood swings, and I'm a lot more confident around people."

Cathy L., a 26-year-old student from San Jose, Calif., experienced the same "mental transformation" when she started outrigger canoeing. "I was in therapy for a year and a half, but once I started paddling, I stopped going to therapy," she says. "I found the tool I needed to deal with my anxiety and confidence problems."

Why did three bright women—Laura, Tonya, Cathy—seek professional help to feel better? Why is the popularity of mood-lifting drugs increasing? Some say it's the curse of the couch potato. In our national effort to make life easy, we're making ourselves depressed and anxious.

According to the government's latest count, 12.6% of Americans are ridden with anxiety, and another 9.5% suffer from debilitating depression. Although we take this epidemic of malaise for granted today, Johnsgard insists that it is a comparatively new phenomenon that arose with the "good life"—arrival of automobiles, dishwashers, TVs, and all those other conveniences that have turned us into a nation of inert couch potatoes. As evidence, he cites several studies that show a gradual ten- to twentyfold increase in depression in the U.S. during this century—a trend that directly parallels the shift away from labor-intensive occupations to an increasingly mechanized, sedentary society.

"Americans," Johnsgard argues, "have become unnaturally depressed and anxious as a result of turning our backs on the active lifestyle which characterized all but our most recent past."

USE IT OR LOSE IT

To experience the mood-elevating impact of exercise, experts now believe that the frequency—rather than the type—of activ-

---

Therapy on the Move

"Talking it out" is now being paired with "walking it out" by a handful of energetic psychotherapists such as Ozzie Gontang and Keith Johnsgard, who practice therapy during walks or runs with their clients. Stress management and improvement of the self-concept of their clients are common goals cited by these pioneers. Also, they find that exercise is cathartic. "Feelings and creative thoughts come to mind a lot more easily while participating in exercise involving rhythmic flow of the body," reports University of Nebraska psychologist and exercise physiologist Wes Sime, who takes clients on a walk for a "good portion of the clinical hour, weather permitting."

Kate Hays, a clinical psychologist in private practice specializing in sports psychology in Concord, N.H., concurs: "Individuals who are extremely agitated or withdrawn will often open up while walking."

Your local hospital or athletic clinic may know of a walking therapist in your area.

ity is the most important factor. As little as 40 minutes of exercise three times a week has been demonstrated to lift depression.

But don't expect to maintain the gain for long if you revert back to your sedentary ways. A study by Sime at the University of Nebraska tracked patients whose depression had been alleviated through exercise almost a year earlier. Only those who remained active were still free of symptoms.

Those who make the effort to fit exercise into their schedule may find it a small price to pay for peace of mind. Indeed, exercise compares favorably with traditional therapy or drugs when you consider cost, convenience, and the exhilarating process of mastering a sport, which leaves little room for the feelings of helplessness and hopelessness that breed depression. As Johnsgard emphasizes, "Strenuous exercise is not something you can purchase and not something an expert does to you, for you, or with you. It is your very own virtually cost-free, self-administered, guaranteed intervention."

WORKING IT OUT

Even extreme phobic reactions may yield to exercise if it is creatively combined with other behavior-modification techniques. Johnsgard tells the dramatic story of a female patient who was debilitated by panic attacks that first struck when she was in a shopping mall and eventually confined her to her home. Her treatment consisted of running across a huge parking lot toward the entrance of the mall until she was completely breathless. The physical exhaustion she felt upon arrival at the feared target—no doubt coupled with the sedative effects of endorphin—made it impossible for her to experience a panic attack. This strategy also enabled her to reinterpret symptoms normally associated with a panic attack in a more positive light. Her elevated heart rate and strained breathing, for example, could now be attributed to the healthful effects of running. By repeating this routine over a number of days, she ultimately gained the confidence to return to public places unescorted.

Johnsgard credits the British psychologist Arnold Orwin with pioneering this approach, and notes that Orwin has used variations of it to successfully treat more than 100 patients hospitalized with agoraphobia (fear of open spaces) and other disorders.

To be sure, some phobias and depressions are so severe that exercise alone will not be sufficient to bring relief. In such intractable cases, Johnsgard would be the first to admit that all the tools of modern medicine may need to be brought to bear. But for most of us, walking may be enough to ward off the periodic stresses and strains of life. "To be blessed," says Johnsgard, "all we have to do is behave the way we were designed to work the best."

Depression
Way Beyond the Blues

Sandra Arbetter

Maria hasn't smiled in a month. Not even when her terrier rushes around in circles trying to bite his tail. Not even when her boyfriend lip-synchs to the Spin Doctors. Either of those things used to set her to howling, but lately she just wants to stay in her room and sleep, and it's a struggle for her to get up in the morning and go to school.

Andy, on the other hand, is always smiling. He talks nonstop, and his energy is endless. He jumps into things without a second thought—he drives too fast, drinks alcohol, and can't wait to bungee jump. At night his mind races over the next day's activities, until he finally falls into a restless sleep.

Which of these two may be depressed? If you say Maria, you're right. And if you say Andy, you're right, too. Even though they act very differently, they both are in the midst of a long period of depression. If you say that's confusing, you're right again. Depression is a murky pool of feelings and actions that scientists have been trying to plumb since the days of Hippocrates, who called it a "black bile."

To further muddy the waters, feelings of depression come and go in most of us from time to time. But short periods of sadness or hyperactivity don't mean clinical depression.

Clinical depression is severe enough to require treatment. It lasts a longer time than the blues—at least two weeks—and it interferes with daily life—school, friends, family. It's considered a medical disorder and can affect thoughts, feelings, physical health, and behaviors. Here's what it's not: It's NOT a personality weakness or a moral lapse. And it's NOT the fault of the person who is depressed.

Diagnosing depression in a teenager is not easy, says Dr. Richard Marohn, past president of the American Society of Adolescent Psychiatry. That's because it's normal for teens to have mood swings—within limits.

It's a confusing time of life, says Marohn. For one thing, the teen's body is changing. Teenagers have little control over those changes. Secondly, their relationship with parents is changing, and teens are pulled between

---

Science Whips Up a Moral Dilemma

Ron was a pleasant, quiet boy who liked to spend time by himself, mostly with his computer. His mother said he "moved at his own pace," which was a bit slower than the rest of the family.

When Ron was 17, he withdrew further from others, stopped showering and shampooing, and even lost his interest in computers. His parents arranged for him to see a psychiatrist, who prescribed an antidepressant medication.

To say he responded well would be an understatement. He was peppier than ever before, moved faster, laughed more readily, liked being with people, went from being a B to an A student, and got a girlfriend.

His doctor was pleased—but puzzled. Now that Ron was no longer depressed, should he go off medication and return to his former quiet self? Or should he stay on medication and retain his livelier, more confident personality? Did the medication uncover the "real" Ron who had lived a lifetime beneath a cover of chronic, mild depression? Or did it create a false self?

Antidepressants are designed to relieve the symptoms of depression. But is it OK to use them as what one doctor called "mood brighteners"? That's the question posed by author Peter Kramer, M.D.

Mental health experts express the concern that we will look to a pill to make us feel better and we'll ignore the external problems in our world. Some fear that antidepressants interfere with reality by making things look more positive. Or could it be that depression distorts reality by making things look more grim?

the security of home and the challenge of testing out their own beliefs.

So how do you tell if it's depression? Time tells, says Marohn. If your feelings affect your schoolwork, your activities, your relationship with family and friends, then it's beyond normal.

Suicidal urges and plans are also a warning sign. But even that's not surefire, because lots of teens have transient thoughts of suicide.

Finally, adolescent depression is difficult to diagnose because adolescents don't necessarily look sad and depressed. To be a teen means to externalize feelings and deal with the world through action. So depression may show up as truancy, running away, violent behavior, or substance abuse. Teens may self-medicate with alcohol or other drugs to try to feel better.

WHAT IS DEPRESSION?

Lots of people assume they know what depression is because they've had at least a touch of it. It's natural to feel sad when you're hit by one of life's inevitable losses. It's a loss when you start kindergarten and give up the safety of home. It's a loss when you move to a new house and leave the old one behind. It's a loss to break up with a boyfriend or girlfriend, and it's even worse when he or she is doing the breaking up.

The sadness that comes with events like these can be intense at first, but usually mellows in a short while. If you get back to a relatively normal state in a week or so, there's nothing to worry about. But if feelings of great sadness or agitation last for much more than two weeks, it may be depression.

Depressed feelings after a major loss, such as the death of a loved one, last much longer, and no one expects recovery in a week or two. Experts won't make a diagnosis of depression (at least, not right away) if a person has had a recent major loss. They'll also hold off if a person is taking certain medications or has certain illnesses that bring on depression-like symptoms.

How Antidepressants Work

Antidepressants help people feel better by affecting neurotransmitters and, in turn, brain function. Neurotransmitters are brain chemicals that help nerve cells communicate with each other. Certain ones are thought to control feelings of security and alertness.

Although the specific effects have not been worked out, it is though that antidepressants work by helping to regulate the dysfunction in the brain that is causing a person to feel depressed.

CHECK THESE SYMPTOMS

Changes in habits and personality are clues to depression. Here are some specifics:
1. There's no interest in school and grades fall.
2. Being with friends holds absolutely no appeal.
3. Sleep problems are common—either not being able to fall asleep at night or wanting to sleep all day.
4. Appetite is out of whack. There's either no desire for food, or the person seems to be eating all the time.
5. The person is obsessed with thoughts of death, maybe suicide. It's estimated that 15 percent of people with major depression commit suicide, and many more attempt it. There are 6,000 suicides by adolescents each year, and depression is the biggest risk factor.
6. Everything seems hopeless, and there's the feeling it will never get better.
7. Headaches, stomachaches, or other aches and pains appear.
8. It's impossible to concentrate or make a decision.

WHAT IT FEELS LIKE

Anyone who's ever felt sad has only the barest clue as to what major depression is like, according to one 16-year-old who recently spent three weeks in a hospital after taking an overdose of pills.

"I had this buzzing in my head all the time," says Emmy, a small, dark-haired girl with large brown eyes. "And I felt tired. I didn't want to do anything except lie on my bed and listen to tapes. When my friends called, I didn't feel like talking to them. I knew they were getting mad, and sometimes I'd try to talk on the phone, but I couldn't push the words up out of my throat."

Emmy had always been a good student and had managed a B+ average while holding a job at a discount store and swimming in competition. Her father was a building contractor, and her mother was a secretary.

"My mother never liked her job, and she kept telling me that I needed to get into a good college so I could be a lawyer and have a happier life than she had. I know now that she was struggling with her own problems, but I used to worry all the time that I was disappointing her. I wanted so badly to be an A student, but no matter how hard I studied, I couldn't pull it off.

"Then I just started not caring. Nothing special happened; I just shut down. I felt so alone, like I was living in a bubble and couldn't punch my way out. I felt like screaming so someone would notice me.

"And I was so tired all the time. Nobody can understand that. I wasn't tired physically like after a swim meet or staying up late. I was tired in every cell of my body, so that I couldn't think straight, and it was too much of an effort to eat. Finally, one day I decided it was too much of an effort to live. That's when I took the pills."

2. STRESS AND MENTAL HEALTH

The doctor prescribed an antidepressant drug for Emmy for about six months, and she and her parents were in family therapy for more than a year. She's a junior now and planning to go to college to study environmental sciences. Her mother is in law school.

DEPRESSION IS A MIXED BAG

For a long time, people who were feeling depressed were told to "snap out of it," and, if they didn't, people said they had a flaw in their personality. That's simply not true and only added guilt to the heavy burden these people were already carrying.

Research in the last decade or two has shown, first of all, that there are several kinds of depression and a multitude of causes.

- Major depression: More than one episode of clinical depression is considered major depression, an illness marked by hopeless feelings, inability to feel pleasure, physical changes or complaints, thoughts of death and suicide. The Public Health Service estimates that 11 million people in this country have episodes of major depression, women outnumbering men more than 2 to 1.
- Bipolar disorder (also known as manic-depressive disorder): A person with this illness alternates between periods of high activity, or mania, and periods of hopelessness or depression.

In the manic phase, people may talk a lot—and fast. They have feelings of greatness and think nothing is beyond them. They've been known to go days without sleeping. They've got lots of thoughts racing through their mind at once. They often act on these thoughts and get into trouble because of their behaviors. So, if you have a friend who is in the manic phase of this illness, don't be surprised if you get a call at three in the morning about his or her plans to save the earth.

Bipolar disorder occurs in about 1 percent of the population, or about 2 million people, equally in men and women. Bipolar disorder can take years to develop into its classic form. When a bipolar disorder emerges during adolescence, it's sometimes hard to distinguish it from the normal emotional ups and downs associated with that age.

- Seasonal Affective Disorder, or SAD: It's not exactly a news flash that most people feel better when the weather is sunny and bright than when it's gloomy. But for some people, wintry weather brings on feelings of depression. Here's one explanation: Many of the body's functions operate on circadian cycles, which are about 24 hours in length. Lack of light puts these cycles out of whack. One treatment is to have patients sit under bright lights for a few hours each day.
- Dysthymia: This is low-level chronic depression. It's usually not severe enough to put someone in the hospital, or to prompt suicide, but it robs a person of the capacity to take pleasure in living.

WHY, OH, WHY?

Experts don't completely understand the causes of depression, but there seems to be an important interplay of two factors: environmental and biological.

Environmental factors include such events as death of a parent, parents' divorce, physical or emotional abuse, family violence, and other difficult family relationships. A depressive episode can be triggered by moving, graduating, losing a job, winning an award, or a hundred other life changes. It can be related to emotional conflicts within the person, such as a past experience that was not resolved. It's been described as "anger turned inward." Or it can come on for no apparent reason.

Biological factors, primarily changes in brain function, are an important aspect of depression. It is not known whether the observed changes in the function cause depression, or whether depression from some other cause accounts for the changes in brain function.

There seems to be a genetic factor involved, too. A child whose parent has suffered from depression has a greater chance of developing the illness than a child with no family history of depression.

TREATMENT

Major approaches to helping depression are medication and psychotherapy, or counseling. Experts say upward of 80 percent of people with depression can be helped.

Medications affect brain function and reduce the symptoms of depression but do not provide a cure. All antidepressants have side effects. Experts worry that people will think of them as magic potions and not accept responsibility for their own behaviors. (See "Science Whips Up a Moral Dilemma".) Finally, parents are cautious about allowing medications for their children.

Psychiatrist Richard Marohn says that many experts view adolescent depression as short-lived and say treatment should deal with underlying issues rather than the symptoms themselves. Therefore, "talk therapy" is preferable and "most of us working with adolescents tend to stay away from medication." Exceptions are suicidal behaviors and depression that's been going on since childhood.

Dr. Marohn says he is concerned about the increasing lack of mental health services. "Kids wind up in prison," he says, rather than in hospitals where treatment is available and they may get some help.

TALKING IT OUT

Some experts say the most effective treatment for severe depression is a combination of medication and counseling. Counseling can help by making people aware of negative thought patterns, such as: "If I'm not perfect, people will think less of me." Or, "If I fail this test, it means I'll always be a failure." It can improve a person's ability to get along with others and to understand him- or herself better. It can bolster self-esteem.

What's more, there are lots of things people can do on their own to help themselves feel better. Michael Maloney and Rachel Kranz, authors of *Straight Talk About Anxiety and Depression*, suggest these:
- Try to focus on the positives about yourself rather than the negatives.
- Accept the fact that others aren't perfect. Then you won't be disappointed when they act human.
- Accept that you aren't perfect, either.
- Enjoy the present moment. Stop regretting the past and worrying about the future.
- Take care of yourself physically. Eat well, exercise, get plenty of sleep.
- Do something nice for yourself.
- Improve your surroundings. Clean your closet. Get a new poster. Surround yourself with things you like to look at.
- Talk to someone. Call up a friend you trust, or start a conversation with a neighbor to prove you *can* connect.
- Indulge your feelings. Let yourself cry and wallow in sad songs. But only for a little while.

Depression is one of the most common mental illnesses of our era and responds well to treatment. So while people don't do anything to make themselves feel bad, they *can* do something to make themselves feel better. A generation ago, there was a comic strip character named Arthur, who walked everywhere with a cloud over his head. If he knew then what you know now, he'd reach up and pull out a silver lining.

FOR MORE INFORMATION

American Psychiatric Association
1400 K St. NW
Washington, DC 20005
   Pamphlets: "Depression," Manic-Depressive Disorder," "Teen Suicide," *single copy of each free. Booklet:* "Let's Talk About It," *$1 per copy. Also available in Spanish.*

S. James
Consumer Information Center-3C
P.O. Box 100
Pueblo, CO 81002
   Pamphlets: #564z "What To Do When A Friend Is Depressed—A Guide For Teenagers," #566z "You Are Not Alone," *single copy of each free.*

National Mental Health Association
1021 Prince St.
Alexandria, VA 22314-2971
   Pamphlets: "Adolescent Depression," "Adolescent Suicide," *single copy of each free with self-addressed, stamped business-size envelope.*

American Academy of Pediatrics
Dept. C-Depression
P.O. Box 927
Elk Grove Village, IL 60009-0927
   Pamphlet: "Surviving: Coping With Adolescent Depression/Suicide," *single copy free with self-addressed, stamped business-size envelope.*

How to Help a Friend Who Is Depressed

Sometimes it's more difficult to help others than to help yourself. But here are some things to think about if a friend seems depressed.

1. Make an effort to be with your friend, even though it might not be easy. Depressed people tend to feel isolated.
2. Don't use false cheerfulness. Your friend may feel you aren't taking the problem seriously.
3. Don't blame. Depression is no one's fault.
4. Don't get angry. It's nothing personal if your friend doesn't respond to your help.
5. Express your own feelings. If you don't want to listen to your friend's woes again, just say so. Go out and have fun and don't feel guilty.
6. Get adult help. If your friend talks about suicide, or you're worried for any other reason, talk to your parents, your friend's parents, your school counselor. It's not a breach of loyalty to save a friend's life.

Nutritional Health

Skyrocketing health care costs, coupled with a plethora of studies implicating lifestyle patterns as a major cause of disease and infirmity, appear to have motivated the American public to assume more personal responsibility for safeguarding their health. Exercise and nutrition are two areas that seem to have generated the most interest. While both are extremely important to overall health, Americans are more likely to make dietary changes than to alter their activity levels. This is probably because they require less effort and involve a behavior that most people enjoy doing—eating. Despite the widespread interest in nutrition, Americans continue to make poor dietary choices and are confused about several nutritional issues. At least part of the blame may be attributed to conflicting reports in the mass media. Another reason for confusion is the nature of nutritional science. Compared to the sciences of biology, chemistry, and physics, nutritional science is still in its infancy, and many unanswered questions remain. This unit will provide the most current information available on issues ranging from how to make dietary changes to who needs dietary supplements, which ones, and how much.

To better understand why the American consumer is so confused about nutritional issues, all one has to do is look at how nutritional recommendations have vacillated over the last 5 years. A case in point is the issue of dietary cholesterol. For more than 20 years, nutrition experts warned Americans of the dangers of dietary cholesterol. Now these same experts are telling us that it is instead the saturated fat in our diet that threatens our arteries. To further confuse the issue, consider the following facts: (1) In 1989 the National Academy of Sciences cut in half the Recommended Dietary Allowances (RDA) for folic acid from 400 micrograms to 200 micrograms because it was felt that the recommended level was unnecessarily high; (2) In 1990 a number of research studies found that low blood levels of folic acid could cause a dramatic rise in the level of homocysteine, a substance that thickens the blood and damages arteries. The net result of these changes is an increased risk of both heart attack and stroke. It should be noted that individuals that consumed at least 400 micrograms of folic acid daily did not demonstrate these destructive vascular changes; (3) Studies have also found that, based on the current RDA of 200 micrograms, women are at increased risk for giving birth to a child with spina bifida or anencephaly. These findings have prompted the Food and Drug Administration (FDA) to consider requiring food manufacturers to fortify refined-grain products with folic acid; (4) Studies have also shown a link between low blood levels of folic acid and colon cancer, depression, and a weakened immune system. Given all of this evidence in support of increasing the RDA for folic acid back to 400 milligrams a day, one can only wonder what the FDA is waiting for.

For years the majority of Americans paid little attention to nutrition, other than to eat three meals a day and, perhaps, take a vitamin supplement. While this dietary style was generally adequate for the prevention of major nutritional deficiencies, medical evidence began to accumulate linking the American diet to a variety of chronic illnesses. The most ominous finding was the link between dietary fat and coronary heart disease. The exact nature of this connection has been the focus of numerous studies, and, as a result, the role that dietary fats play in the process of atherosclerosis has been well documented. Recommendations based on these studies strongly suggest that Americans should reduce their intake of saturated fats and substitute monounsaturated or polyunsaturated fats whenever possible. This appears to be particularly true for individuals under stress.

As a result of all the bad press that dietary fats have gotten, millions of Americans are making a concerted effort to cut the fat content of their diets. The area where consumers have had the least success in reducing fat consumption has been snack foods. Americans currently spend over $13.4 billion dollars a year on snack foods and are eager to try low-fat alternatives to the most popular ones. The food industry has responded by introducing the production of low-fat potato chips and candy bars that retain the flavor and texture of the originals. It is too early to tell how well these low-fat versions will be accepted by consumers, but the food industry is banking on the belief that consumers will settle for less crunch and flavor if the trade-off means significantly less fat. However, the fast food industry is rapidly moving in the other direction. This reversal appears to be the result of a lack of consumer acceptance of the low-fat entrees that quick-service restaurants had introduced over the last few years. "Fast Food: Fatter than Ever" discusses how such restaurants as McDonalds and Taco Bell have pruned their low-fat menu choices in favor of high-fat alternatives.

Another way in which food companies have attempted to maintain their market share in the face of negative press regarding dietary fat has been to substitute monounsaturated and polyunsaturated fats for tropical oils and animal fats. "Snack Attack" examines the fat content of various snack foods and suggests that the problem is not with eating between meals but with the food choices made. The author explains which snack foods would be good choices any time as compared to those that should be eaten only once a day.

Unlike fats, carbohydrates have been given high ratings for health. Nutritionists generally agree that Americans should eat more carbohydrates, particularly the complex type, as they are good sources of vitamins, minerals, and fiber. While complex carbohydrates generally receive high

UNIT 3

marks for their nutritional value, highly refined forms, such as sugar, do not fare nearly as well. For example, the American public has been sold the idea that while sugar is bad, fruit sweeteners are good. The fact is that fruit sweeteners are also simple sugars, and while they may contain trace amounts of vitamins and minerals, they do not contain enough of them to warrant their use instead of table sugar. This nutritional myth as well as several others are discussed in "Dietary Gospel—or Phony Baloney?"

Dietary fiber has become a hot issue in nutrition circles. Several studies report that individuals eating high-fiber diets demonstrate a lower incidence of colon cancer and lower blood cholesterol levels. In response to these findings, noted health authorities have encouraged Americans to increase their consumption of dietary fiber. The "Food Pyramid: How to Make It Work for You" advises ways to add fiber to your diet and to limit fat. The food industry also responded by marketing several new high-fiber products and emphasizing the fiber content of their other products. Researchers have recently reinterpreted the data from several earlier studies and have come to some interesting conclusions. While it is true that the individuals who ate high-fiber diets did have lower rates of both colon cancer and cardiovascular disease, these health benefits could also be explained by the fact that individuals filling up on high-fiber foods would naturally eat less foods high in dietary fat. Another variable that confounds the accurate assessment of the impact of dietary fiber is the fact that most of the foods that are high in dietary fiber are also high in a variety of other important nutrients, including the much-touted antioxidant vitamins.

The use of dietary supplements is another highly controversial topic in the area of nutrition. Today, approximately 33 percent of Americans take some form of dietary supplement regularly. For some, this consists of a simple multiple-vitamin; others, however, rely on megadosing. Most nutritional experts agree that eating a varied and balanced diet is the single best way to meet all your nutritional needs, but not everyone eats a balanced diet, and for those who do not, supplements may be necessary.

Of all the dietary supplements, vitamins consistently receive the most attention and attract the most consumer dollars. While specific recommendations regarding vitamin supplements are lacking, the National Academy of Sciences (NAS) does provide the consumer with RDAs. Over the last few years, the NAS has been criticized for using nutritional deficiencies as a basis for setting the RDAs. These critics contend that the RDAs should be raised to levels that would maximize health rather than merely prevent deficiencies. At the present time, there is no definitive evidence to demonstrate that vitamins can actually bolster one's health, but a group of vitamins known as antioxidants has generated considerable interest in this regard. Over the last couple of years, vegetables that include broccoli, brussels sprouts, cabbage, and cauliflower have received publicity because they appear to contain potent anticancer compounds. The net result of all the hype and publicity is a new megavitamin craze in which supplement makers are claiming to pack several servings worth of these vegetables in a single pill. Do not believe it! Stick with the real thing! The essay "Food for Thought about Dietary Supplements" by Paul Thomas examines the use of dietary supplements and addresses several key issues surrounding the use of these products.

Another nutritional concern that has received considerable attention in the last few years is the problem of osteoporosis, particularly in women. Currently, most authorities agree that many Americans do not get sufficient amounts of dietary calcium. There is, however, considerable debate on how this deficit is best corrected. While there are several calcium supplements on the market, there is little evidence that these supplements will be as effective in preventing the development of osteoporosis as the calcium derived from food (dietary calcium).

If after reading some of the current literature on nutrition you decide to make some dietary changes, where should you begin? The food pyramid guide is a good place to start, but it provides little guidance as to which food choices within each group constitute good choices. The article "The Food Pyramid: How to Make It Work for You" examines the guidelines set forth by the food pyramid, and makes specific recommendations as to how this guideline can best be used to ensure a nutritionally balanced diet.

Of all the topical areas in health, nutrition is certainly one of the most interesting, if for no other reason than the rate at which dietary recommendations change. Despite all the controversy and conflict, the one message that seems to remain constant is the importance of balance and moderation in everything we eat.

Looking Ahead: Challenge Questions

Given the controversies that abound in the area of nutrition, what guidelines should an individual use to make dietary decisions?

How would you advise someone who needed to reduce the fat content of his or her diet?

What advice would you give someone who is considering making significant dietary changes?

What dietary changes could you make to improve your diet? What is keeping you from making those changes?

How would you advise someone who was considering using dietary supplements?

Dietary gospel—or phony baloney?

Mistaken notions about diet and health are tough to shake. Here's the truth behind nine enduring nutrition myths.

Nutrition wisdom sometimes seems to be a moving target. Witness the apparent flip-flops in recent years on such high-profile dietary items as oat bran, fish oil, margarine, and beta-carotene, to name a few. But such reversals of fortune are to be expected; dietary influences on health are notoriously difficult to pin down. And while the latest study may appear to prove or disprove a point, more often than not, it's just one more piece of information to add to the puzzle.

Sometimes, however, mistaken notions persist long past the time they're disproved. The belief that sugar makes children hyperactive, for instance, has been thoroughly discredited by scientists, yet it's still widely held by parents, teachers, and children. Going without a cupcake or candy bar, of course, won't hurt anyone. But other nutrition myths can have more serious consequences, leading you to neglect an important element of a healthy diet or perhaps to trade a wise practice for a foolish one. Here are nine persistent nutrition myths—and the facts.

❶ Myth: A high-protein diet helps you lose weight.

Truth: The old notion that substituting protein for carbohydrates in the diet will magically melt away fat has enjoyed a renaissance with the release of several new protein-promoting diet books. But that theory is based largely on anecdotes; there's no good scientific support for it. Protein and carbohydrates both contain 4 calories per gram, and the body socks away unused calories from both sources equally efficiently.

Pro-protein myths like this one perpetuate the philosophy that makes protein the crux of a balanced diet. But, if anything, Americans get too much protein in their diet. Although a certain amount of protein is critical for bones, muscles, organs, skin, immune function, and much more, protein overload can produce serious side effects, including dehydration, diarrhea, calcium loss, and even kidney or liver damage. Some evidence suggests that a high protein intake may increase the risk of cancer and coronary heart disease.

An optimal diet gets roughly 12 to 15 percent of its total daily calories from protein, no more than 30 percent from fat, and the remaining 55 percent or so from carbohydrates. But no matter what your diet, you can lose weight only if you burn more calories than you consume, from whatever source.

❷ Myth: Starchy foods are fattening.

Truth: It's not the bread, pasta, potatoes, and other carbohydrate-rich foods that are fattening, it's the fatty company they keep—the butter, margarine, mayonnaise, sour cream, gravies, and cream sauces. A gram of fat packs 9 calories—more than twice the caloric density of carbohydrates. Moreover, unadorned carbohydrates are the best source for most of your calories, because they also supply many other nutrients without the baggage of saturated fat or excess protein. As with any food, just watch your serving sizes.

One reason why carbohydrates are unfairly blamed for weight gain is confusion abut "insulin resistance," a common metabolic abnormality.

Carbohydrates are converted to glucose in the body, and insulin helps cells use the glucose for energy. When a person with insulin resistance eats a lot of carbohydrates, insulin production jumps. Some self-styled diet gurus say that the excess insulin stimulates appetite and the production of body fat. That's false. Being overweight is a *cause* of insulin resistance, not the result.

> **Sodium has little or no effect on the great majority of people with normal blood pressure.**

❸ Myth: Fruit sweeteners are better than refined sugar.

Truth: The boom in fruit-juice-sweetened cookies and similar "all natural" confections is testimony to the widespread belief that fruit sugar, or fructose, gives you something you don't get from ordinary table sugar, or sucrose. It doesn't. While fruit juices do contain many vitamins and minerals, there's just not enough juice in juice-sweetened products to provide any significant benefit. And fructose, like sucrose, offers only calories. The same goes for other sweeteners, including brown sugar, honey, corn syrup, and maple syrup. (The one exception is blackstrap molasses, which contains some calcium, iron, and other nutrients.)

❹ Myth: Beef and pork spoil a low-fat diet.

Truth: While beef and pork are generally far more fatty than chicken, several studies have shown that small, lean cuts of red meat can work just as well in a cholesterol-lowering diet. Moreover, new breeding and feeding methods, plus closer trimming of fat, have produced some truly lean cuts of red meat. A 3-ounce serving of roasted top-round beef or pork tenderloin, for example, is almost as lean as a serving of roasted, skinless chicken breast (see chart at right).

Of course, the key to making any sort of meat fit in a low-fat diet lies in the size of the serving. The recommended 3-ounce portion is about the size of a deck of cards—far less than most Americans are accustomed to seeing on a plate, especially in a restaurant. It helps to think of meat as the side dish to a meal, rather than the centerpiece. And consider skipping meat altogether on some days.

❺ Myth: Most people need to cut back on salt to prevent or control high blood pressure.

Truth: Sodium has little or no effect on the great majority of people with normal blood pressure. So if your blood pressure is fine, there's no need to reduce your present salt consumption. If you've been holding back out of caution, you might even be able to consume more salt, so long as you monitor your blood pressure for any sign of an increase.

Among people with hypertension, fewer than half react to sodium. Unfortunately, those people can't tell if they're in the salt-sensitive minority without conducting a complex, month-long experiment under close medical supervision. So people with hypertension are usually advised to restrict the salt in their diet just to play it safe.

❻ Myth: "Lactose intolerance" is a common problem that makes many people unable to digest dairy products.

Truth: About one in nine Americans has low levels of lactase, the enzyme that breaks down milk sugar, or lactose. That fact has been aggressively publicized by the makers of reduced-lactose milk and enzyme supplements—such as *Dairy Ease*, *Lactaid*, and *Lactrase*—intended to prevent the indigestion that supposedly occurs when those people eat dairy foods. But such indigestion often doesn't occur. Recent research suggests that most "lactose intolerant" people can tolerate quite a bit, such as a glass of milk with breakfast, without discomfort.

If you think you're lactose intolerant, test your sensitivity. First eliminate all dairy products for a week. Then drink the amount of milk you would like to consume at one time, and have it with food if that's what you would normally do. Even if symptoms such as bloating, diarrhea, gas, or pain do develop, you still may not need special products. You might, for example, try having dairy foods more often but in smaller amounts.

❼ Myth: Milk thickens mucus, so people with respiratory problems should avoid it.

Truth: Another bum rap against milk. Many people with asthma or even just a cold shun milk for fear

---

Lean and mean Beef, pork, and poultry alike can make or break a low-fat diet.

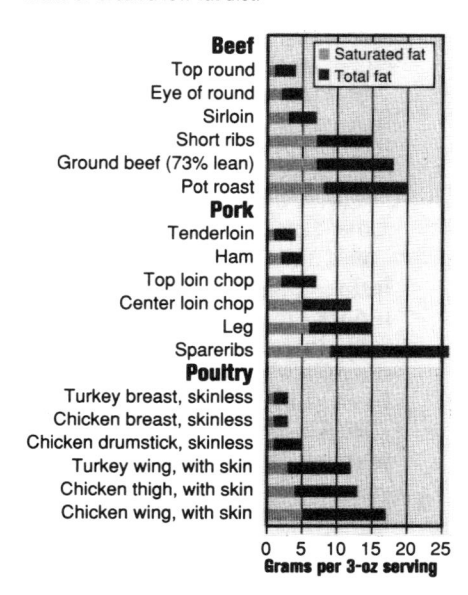

that it will increase mucus production and restrict breathing. But studies have shown that drinking milk has no effect on mucus production or airflow. And excluding milk from your diet deprives you of an important source of calcium and other nutrients.

8 Myth: What you eat can affect your looks.

Truth: Food doesn't cause acne, strengthen fingernails, or make hair look better. Acne is usually brought on by hormonal changes, not by chocolate, greasy foods, or nuts. The main cause of weak fingernails is repeated immersion in water; nothing you ingest will help—not calcium, gelatin, or vitamins. And there's no evidence that any food or dietary supplement will make hair grow. Only gross nutritional deficiencies can cause temporary nail changes and hair loss.

9 Myth: Many people need more iron to stay healthy.

Truth: Only about 10 percent of premenopausal women, 6 percent of post-menopausal women, and fewer than 2 percent of men are short on iron. Most older people who become deficient do so not because they consume too little iron, but because of chronic internal bleeding, caused by anti-inflammatory drugs, ulcers, polyps, or tumors. In those cases, the solution is to treat the underlying problem, not just take iron supplements.

When there's no internal bleeding, the only people who need to take iron supplements regularly are those with no teeth who have trouble eating a balanced diet, and women who menstruate heavily—provided they first make sure that menstruation is the sole cause of their deficiency. (Pregnant women should also take iron supplements, to help nourish the developing fetus.)

Taking iron supplements when there's no need can be harmful. Extra iron won't relieve fatigue, and it can mask signs of internal bleeding by turning stools black. It can also damage the heart, liver, and pancreas in people with hemochromatosis, a genetic disease that makes the body absorb too much iron. (Because of that risk, everyone should be screened for iron overload at least once by middle age.) Some evidence suggests that high iron stores may raise the risk of cancer and coronary heart disease in healthy people, but that link has not been proved.

Ironed out? Iron deficiency is uncommon and usually reflects an underlying disorder.

More myths to dismiss

Here are some other common nutrition myths that persist against all odds—and all evidence to the contrary.

Vitamins and minerals

■ **Vitamins can boost your energy.** Energy comes from calories burned. Vitamins provide no calories.

■ **Vitamins can help you cope with routine daily stress.** There's no evidence that stress uses up vitamin stores, or that taking vitamins can lessen stress.

■ **Magnesium helps the body absorb calcium.** The only nutrient that's known to help the body absorb calcium is vitamin D—easily obtained by minimal sun exposure and from dietary sources.

Low-fat diet

■ **Cholesterol in food is the most important factor influencing cholesterol in the blood.** Dietary cholesterol is not nearly as important as saturated fat.

■ **Buttermilk is especially fatty.** Not any fattier than the milk it's made from—and it's usually made from low-fat or skim milk.

■ **Air-popped popcorn is lower in fat than oil-popped.** Most commercial brands of "air popped" popcorn are actually soaked in oil after popping, raising their fat content above even oil-popped brands.

■ **Dry-roasted nuts have less fat than oil-roasted nuts.** Oil-roasted nuts are not immersed in the boiling oil long enough to absorb any of it, and the excess oil is drained off afterward.

■ **Low-fat yogurt has fewer calories than regular yogurt.** Not necessarily—due to the added milk solids that make up for the lost fat.

Vegetarian diet

■ **Vegetarians—especially those who eat no eggs or dairy products—need extra protein.** Plant sources alone can provide plenty of protein.

■ **Every meatless meal should include complementary foods, such as rice and beans, to provide a "complete" protein source.** There's no need to consume complementary foods at each meal, so long as you follow a varied diet each day.

Foods and disease

■ **Spicy foods can cause ulcers.** While certain foods and beverages may aggravate an ulcer, none has been shown to *cause* an ulcer.

■ **Too much sugar commonly causes hypoglycemia.** Sugar consumption rarely pushes blood-sugar levels low enough to lead to hypoglycemic symptoms such as sweating, trembling, rapid heartbeat, and hunger.

■ **Sugar can cause diabetes.** The real culprits are problems with the body's production of and sensitivity to insulin.

Leftovers

■ **Oil-packed tuna has more fish oil than tuna packed in water.** That's vegetable oil, not fish oil. Water-packed tuna is just as high in potentially beneficial omega-3 fatty acids, but much lower in fat and calories.

■ **Plastic cutting boards are safer than wooden boards.** Either material can be rendered free of bacteria by washing the board in hot soapy water.

■ **Frozen vegetables are less nutritious than fresh ones.** That's generally true only if you buy your vegetables fresh off the farm—or if you grow your own.

Food for Thought about Dietary Supplements

The surge of public interest in nutrition supplements has been fired by the recently enacted federal regulations governing health claims, which permits the health food industry to make claims about the function of nutrients not permitted for food products. This article provides healthy skepticism about the common rationales for the use of supplements.

PAUL R. THOMAS, ED.D., R.D.

Paul Thomas, currently a Fellow at the Georgetown Center for Food and Nutrition Policy, Georgetown University, previously served as a staff scientist for the Food and Nutrition Board, Institute of Medicine, National Academy of Sciences. He is a registered dietitian who received an Ed.D. degree in nutrition education from Columbia University. He is an author and editor of several books on contemporary nutrition issues. Correspondence can be directed to him at the Georgetown Center for Food and Nutrition Policy, 3240 Prospect Street, N.W., Washington, DC 20007.

The dietary supplements industry is very healthy. Sales of vitamins, minerals, and other food concentrates are roughly $4 billion per year. Although at least one quarter of American adults swallow these pills, powders, and potions daily,[1] probably the majority of us take them at least occasionally. What are we getting in return?

I've asked myself this question since the 1960s when, as a teenager, I began taking dozens of supplements after reading about their magical powers in *Prevention* and *Let's Live* magazines, and books by Adelle Davis. Surely they would help cure my adolescent acne; I just needed to find the right combination. But my pizza face only improved when I took tetracycline and topical retinoic acid (the drug, not the vitamin) prescribed by a dermatologist. Growing out of adolescence also helped.

My education about dietary supplements became more comprehensive when I discovered the medical library during my college education as a biology ("pre-med") major. I learned that the hype surrounding them in the popular press was rarely supported by studies in the journals. Dietary supplements have benefited me in that they developed my interest in nutrition to the point where I chose to make a career in this discipline. But over time, and despite the growing popularity of supplements even among nutrition professionals, I have gone from being an enthusiastic vitamin promoter to a skeptic.

Most of us would agree that it's best to meet our nutritional needs with food, which means that everyone should eat a healthy, balanced diet. I believe that, short of that, dietary supplements are at best a poor and inadequate substitute. Supplements are appropriate for some people for specific purposes. But should they be taken every day, by everybody? I don't think so, and I make my case with the following eight points.

POINT 1: NO EXPERT BODY OF NUTRITION EXPERTS RECOMMENDS THE ROUTINE USE OF SUPPLEMENTS

A small number of nutritionists support regular supplement use. But no scientific body of nutrition experts recommends that everyone take supplements on a routine basis as dietary insurance or for optimal health. Expert bodies are by nature conservative and unlikely to recommend a practice until the evidence is convincing and perhaps even overwhelming. That's the point, since dietary guidance for most people should be based on strong evidence.

In 1989, the Food and Nutrition Board of the National Academy of Sciences issued a comprehensive review of the relationships between diet and health.[2] The report stated that dietary supplements should be avoided at levels above the Recommended Dietary Allowances (RDAs). Finally, however, a group of nutrition experts was not warning people to stay away from supplements with pronouncements of dire risks from their use. The recommendation was not to stay away from supplements, but to take them in no more than RDA amounts. The Food and Nutrition Board acknowledged that the long-term potential risks and benefits of supplements had not been adequately studied and called for more research.

The latest pronouncements on supplements are found in the new (4th) edition of *Dietary Guidelines for Americans*, which was released in January.[3] The report states that "diets that meet RDAs are almost certain to ensure intake of enough essential nutrients by most healthy people," and that people with average requirements are likely to have adequate diets even if they don't meet RDAs.

About supplements, the report states: "Daily vitamin and mineral supplements at or below the Recommended Dietary Allowances are considered safe, but are usually not needed by people who eat the variety of foods depicted in the Food Guide Pyramid." It acknowledged, however, that some people might benefit from supplements. These include older people and others with little exposure to sunlight who may need extra vitamin D. Women of childbearing age might reduce the risk of neural-tube de-

3. NUTRITIONAL HEALTH

fects in their infants with folate-rich foods or folic acid supplements. Pregnant women usually benefit from iron supplements. And vegans, who avoid animal products, might need some nutrients in pill form. The report urges the public not to rely on supplements.

Surveys show that most supplementers take a one-a-day multiple-vitamin-mineral product. But some take large doses of single nutrients or nutrient combinations as self-prescribed medication for disease or to try to reach a more optimal state of health, the latter fueled most recently by the enthusiasm for antioxidants. The practices of these aggressive supplementers merit some concern.

POINT 2: NUTRITION IS ONLY ONE FACTOR THAT INFLUENCES HEALTH, WELL-BEING, AND RESISTANCE TO DISEASE

The major chronic diseases that prematurely maim and kill most Americans have multiple causes. However, just as the advent of antibiotics and vaccines led many to think that the cure of diseases awaited specific "magic bullets," some proponents of supplements seem to think that these products are nutritional magic bullets for cancer, heart disease, and other maladies.

Health reporter Jane Brody calls us "a nation hungry for simple nutritional solutions to complex health problems."[4] Edward Golub, in his recent book, *The Limits of Medicine*, warns us against "thinking in penicillin mode."[5] It can be easy to do in nutrition because the first identified nutrient-related diseases (*eg*, scurvy and beriberi) were caused by dietary deficiencies. Anyone who doesn't get enough of the proper nutrient will eventually succumb to the relevant deficiency disease. No matter how much you exercise, who your parents are, or whether or not you smoke, you will become scorbutic without sufficient vitamin C.

Unfortunately, there is no such simple cause-effect relationship for diseases such as cardiovascular disease, cancer, stroke, and diabetes. Large doses of vitamin E, for example, may or may not influence the risk of developing heart disease. For some people, it may potentially be important. For most, however, it is at best one factor, and probably not a major one.

A primary contributor to chronic disease risk is our genetic heritage. Nutritionist Elizabeth Hiser writes, "Genes have a powerful influence over body size and disease risk, and though diet helps temper unwanted tendencies, *who* you are is often more important than *what* you eat.... Because of genetics, diet helps some people a lot, some people a little, and a very few people not at all."[6] Genetic endowment accounts in large measure for why some people get heart disease when young, for example, no matter how well they care for themselves, and why others live long lives even when they violate many of the commandments of healthy living.

Chronic disease risk is also affected by whether or not we exercise, refrain from smoking, avoid drinking to excess, limit exposure to unproductive stressors, and have sufficient rest, relaxation, and fun—and, of course, eating a diet that meets dietary guidelines and the RDAs. In our enthusiasm for supplements, however, we run the risk of reducing the importance of these factors.

One example of "thinking in penicillin mode" is linking calcium with the treatment, and especially prevention, of osteoporosis. However, bone health is influenced by many factors, including smoking, alcohol consumption, exercise, and intake of nutrients such as phosphorus, protein, and boron that affect calcium absorption, utilization, and excretion. In fact, osteoporosis is uncommon in several countries with relatively low calcium intakes.

Social commentator H. L. Mencken said, "For every complicated problem there is a simple solution—and it is wrong."[7] Supplements are not the answer to health and disease for the vast majority of people. Who our parents are, how we live our lives, and the food we put into our mouths several times a day affect our health more profoundly.

POINT 3: FOOD IS MORE THAN THE SUM OF ITS NUTRIENTS

Nutritionists used to think that macro- and micronutrients made a food nutritious and good for health. Other food constituents, such as fiber, were seen as nonessential, and therefore unimportant, since death is not directly associated with fiber deficiency. However, we have learned that, while fiber is not essential in the traditional sense, its presence in the diet makes it much easier to defecate and influences blood cholesterol levels and risk of diseases such as diverticulosis and certain cancers.

Many compounds in food that are not classical nutrients can apparently influence health and risk of disease. Several hundred studies show that heavy fruit and vegetable eaters have approximately half the risk of cancer compared with those who don't eat these foods, but the results are not consistently related to one or several nutrients. New biologically active constituents found mostly in plant foods—phytochemicals (or "phytomins" as *Prevention* magazine calls them)—are being discovered regularly. They include flavonoids, monoterpenes, phenolics, indoles, allylic sulfides, and isothiocyanates. Phytochemicals became a "hot item" in 1994 when they were the subject of a cover story in *Newsweek* that April.[8] The title: "Better than Vitamins: The Search for the Magic Pill." (There's that word too often linked with supplements: magic! So is "miracle.")

Whole natural foods, to quote *Newsweek*, "harbor a whole ratatouille of compounds that have never seen the inside of a vitamin bottle for the simple reason that scientists have not, until very recently, even known they existed, let alone brewed them into pills." Even when phytochemicals can reliably be found in supplements, it will never be appropriate to swallow pills (or consume specially fortified processed foods) instead of eating recommended amounts of the foods that contain them, such as vegetables, fruits, whole grains, and legumes. To do so would be to inappropriately rely on preliminary science, when the future will bring the discovery of new phytochemicals that have always been available from today's natural foods. Determining whether and how isolated food constituents with biologic activity may improve health, treat disease, or extend life is a daunting task that will occupy researchers for decades or longer.

Scientists continue to learn more about the complexity of foods and the myriad of biologically active constituents they contain that can influence health and disease risk. How ironic, then, that the calls this research generates for renewed efforts to persuade people to eat healthier diets—the tried and true—often seems to be drowned out by the acclaim for dietary supplements.

POINT 4: DEVELOPING RDAs AND OPTIMAL NUTRIENT RECOMMENDATIONS IS VERY DIFFICULT

As a staff scientist with the Food and Nutrition Board, I worked with the subcommittee that developed the most recent (10th) edition of the RDAs. I was surprised to learn that the research base for the RDAs is quite limited. There are not as many studies as one would like to determine minimum and average nutrient requirements for each age-sex group, estimate the population variability in need, and to feel more comfortable about the judgments made to derive nutrient allowances. Setting RDAs is tough work!

Now there is substantial discussion about so-called optimal intakes of nutrients, levels of intake that might allow people to be healthy and fit for a longer time. Some nutrition scientists believe optimal nutrient intakes will typically exceed RDA levels and may require supplements in some cases to achieve. Still, no one doubts that developing optimal nutrient intakes will be orders of magnitude more complex than developing RDAs.

The optimal intake of any nutrient will probably vary substantially among individuals and even throughout one person's life from infancy to old age. It will probably also depend on the parameter of interest. For example, an optimal intake of a nutrient to reduce the risk of heart disease might not be optimal to decrease cancer risk and might actually increase it. Defining, understanding, and assessing optimal nutrition is becoming one of the most exciting challenges for investigators in the nutrition and food sciences.

POINT 5: TAKING SUPPLEMENTS OF SINGLE NUTRIENTS IN LARGE DOSES MAY HAVE DETRIMENTAL EFFECTS ON NUTRITIONAL STATUS AND HEALTH

On April 14, 1994, the *New England Journal of Medicine* published the infamous Finnish study.[9] In this clinical trial, 29,000 male smokers in Finland were randomly divided into four groups, receiving either a placebo, 20 mg beta-carotene (approximately four to five times the amount in five servings of fruits and vegetables), 50 IU of vitamin E (about three to four times average dietary intakes, but still a small dose as a supplement), or both the beta-carotene and vitamin E. After 5 to 8 years, the beta-carotene takers had an 18% *higher* incidence of lung cancer, with hints that this carotenoid might also have raised their risk of heart disease. Vitamin E seemed to reduce the risk of prostate cancer but increased the risk of hemorrhagic stroke.

This study is noteworthy, both because of its surprising findings and the fact that it is one of the few large clinical trials on supplements and disease risk. The majority of studies investigating this relationship are epidemiologic in nature. Clinical trials in which subjects are randomly assigned to treatment or control groups help to identify cause-and-effect relationships. Epidemiologic studies, in contrast, can only identify whether the variables under study are related in some way.

The Finnish study showed that antioxidant nutrients might harm rather than help male smokers, so it has been scrutinized intensely. Blumberg, for example, noted that those with the highest plasma concentrations of vitamin E and beta-carotene at the start of the study had the lowest risk of developing lung cancer[10]; therefore, these nutrients may have provided some protection to some smokers. But for those who would suggest that the subjects should not have expected any benefits from supplements, given their deadly habit, two points should be made. First, several epidemiologic studies show that fruit and vegetable consumption reduces the risk of lung cancer in smokers—again, foods (containing beta-carotene and many other carotenoids and phytochemicals), not supplements. Second, dietary supplements are often promoted to smokers and those who are not eating or taking care of themselves as well as they should with claims that the products protect health.

The Center for Science in the Public Interest, a consumer advocacy group that had recommended antioxidants to its readers, changed its position after the Finnish study.[11] "Shelve the beta-carotene," it said, or take no more than about 3 mg per day, the amount found in many multivitamins. It also advised people to "reconsider taking vitamin E." *New York Times* medical writer Nicholas Wade, commenting on the Finnish study, said: "The vitamin supplement industry... would like everyone to believe the issue of benefits is settled.... For all who assumed the answer was already known, the Finnish trial offers two lessons. One is that science can't be rushed. The other is not to put all your bets on those convenient little bottles: back to broccoli and bicycles."[12]

Time shows the wisdom of Wade's advice. Two large clinical trials were completed in January of this year that further debunk beta-carotene as a magic bullet. After 12 years of taking either 50 mg beta-carotene or a placebo every other day, 22,071 physicians learned that the phytochemical provided no protection against cancer or heart disease. In the second trial, 18,314 men and women at risk for lung cancer due to smoking or exposure to asbestos were given supplements of beta-carotene (30 mg/day), vitamin A (25,000 IU/day), or a placebo. Those receiving the supplements had a *higher* rate of death from lung cancer and heart disease; although the results were not statistically significant, the study was halted. Dr. Richard Klausner, the director of the National Cancer Institute, which financed both trials, concluded, "With clearly no benefit and even a hint of possible harm, I can see no reason that an individual should take beta-carotene."

A major concern with supplements is potential toxicity. Fat-soluble vitamins like A and D, which are stored in the body, are obviously harmful in excess, but so are some water-soluble nutrients. Large doses of vitamin B6, for example, can produce neuropathy in the arms and legs, leading to partial paralysis. Some people taking tryptophan have developed and died from eosinophilia-myalgia syndrome, a connective tissue disease characterized by high levels of eosinophils, severe muscle pain, and skin and neuromuscular problems. (It is not yet certain whether the syndrome was caused by the tryptophan itself, by a contaminant produced in the manufacturing process, or by the two in combination.) High-dose niacin supplements, especially in the time-released form, have caused liver damage. Large amounts of beta-carotene can be dangerous to alcoholics with liver disorders. And antioxidant nutrients can act as prooxidants under certain conditions, generating cell-damaging free radicals.[13]

Another concern with supplements is the possibility of adverse nutrient interactions. Calcium, for example, affects the absorption of iron and vice versa. Various amino acids compete with each other for absorption from the small intestine and to cross the blood-brain barrier. Large doses of one nutrient or phytochemical can adversely affect nutritional status in relation to another. In one study, for example, very large doses of beta-carotene, 100 mg/day given for 6 days, decreased the concentration of another important carotenoid, lycopene, in the low-density lipoproteins by 12 to 25%.[14] Beta carotene is not the only carotenoid of benefit to health, or perhaps even the most important one. I am reminded of Walter Mertz, the renowned nutrition and trace mineral expert, who was asked if he took beta-carotene as a supplement. He replied he would be "afraid" to take it, not knowing how extra beta-carotene would affect the balance of all the other carotenoids in his body that he obtained from food.

Little information is available to demonstrate that the long-term and possibly lifetime intake of large doses of nutrients is completely safe. Studies on the consequences of large nutrient intakes in humans rarely have a large sample size and go beyond several months. If high levels of iron in the body, for example, really increase the risk of heart disease, as at least one study suggests,[15] the chances are remote that a physician will think that a patient who died of a heart attack possibly did so because of supplemental iron. In other words, nutrient toxicity may be a cause of more illness and death than suspected, because the problems will not be linked (or even thought to have a possible link) to use of supplements.

POINT 6: DIETARY SUPPLEMENTS VARY SUBSTANTIALLY IN QUALITY

Few federal manufacturing and formulation standards exist for supplements, in part because they fall into a regulatory gray area between foods and drugs.[16] A decade ago, investigators discovered that many calcium supplements did not disintegrate or dissolve in the digestive tract; the calcium was simply excreted. These results prompted the development of disintegration and dissolution standards for some types of supplements by the US Pharmacopoeia, the scientific organization that establishes drug standards. Some supplement labels now carry a statement that the products meet these standards. Unfortunately, expiration dates on the labels of some supplements provide no consistent mark of quality, since they can be chosen arbitrarily. At some point, the Food and Drug Administration (FDA) will propose basic quality control standards for supplements.

Supplements are highly processed products whose manufacture can be compared to the refining of sugar. The purpose of the processing in both cases is to concentrate the desired ingredient (the nutrients or the sucrose), typically using heat, solvents, and distillation. The processing removes most of the compounds in the raw material, be it sugar cane or deodorizer sludge from edible oils in the case of vitamin E. Some believe that "natural" vitamins are better than synthetic ones, because the former contain unidentified factors said to enhance nutrient utilization. However, one cannot know whether these factors survived the extensive processing, assuming they exist and were present in the raw material.

Garlic supplements provide an example of not necessarily getting what you think you paid for. They have become popular because several studies suggest that garlic may help to lower blood cholesterol and reduce the risk of cancers of the breast, colon, and other organs. Attention has focused on two compounds that may be responsible for these effects: allicin and s-allyl cysteine. The Center for Science in the Public Interest analyzed garlic powder and various garlic pills and found major differences by brand in their content of these two compounds.[17] Plain garlic powder was best and least expensive, whereas the most popular brand of garlic supplement contained no allicin (Table 1). Similarly, Consumers Union recently found that ginseng products varied greatly in their content of ginsenosides, the root's supposed active ingredients.[18]

It is difficult to find a comprehensive, one-a-day type of supplement that supplies nutrients at RDA levels. Most products are not well balanced. They contain, for example, many times the recommended amount of inexpensive B vitamins like thiamin and riboflavin but only small amounts of calcium and magnesium, because recommended amounts of these minerals can add substantially to the size of the pill. Some supplements contain superfluous ingredients such as bee pollen, hesperidin complex, and PABA, which do little more than boost the price (see Refs. 19 and 20 for good advice on choosing a supplement).

POINT 7: SUPPLEMENTS ARE PROMOTED BY COMMERCIAL AND OTHER FORCES ON THE BASIS OF INCOMPLETE OR PRELIMINARY SCIENCE

I stated earlier that the bulk of evidence linking supplements to reduced risks of heart disease, cancer, and other diseases is epidemiologic in nature, or based on *in vitro*, mechanistic, or biochemical studies. They show correlations and indicate the possibility of protective effects, but do not prove cause and effect. So we do not know whether most of these suggestive data are of practical importance to people over the long run as they eat good or bad diets, smoke or refrain from smoking, live in polluted or clean environments, and are either exercisers or couch potatoes.

The scientific community tends to blame journalists for distorted reporting about nutrition. True, there are both good and mediocre reporters on the subject. And too often the reporting is bad, incomplete, prepared from press releases, or focused on one study without placing it in perspective–a poor foundation for people to make intelligent decisions.

A recent study illustrates this point. Houn and colleagues examined popular press coverage of research on the association between alcohol consumption and breast cancer.[21] Of the 58 published journal papers on this topic over 7 years, only 11 were cited by the press. Three studies published in the *New England Journal of Medicine* and the *Journal of the Medical Association* were featured in more than three quarters of the news stories. And almost two thirds of the stories gave recommendations to women on alcohol consumption based on one study. Reporters ignored the published review articles and editorials that would have provided a better basis for advice. This highlighting of a few studies, which seems to occur in many other nutrition areas, tends to confuse people and lead them to think that a new study will undoubtedly contradict the findings of the previous one. It's the new math of media nutrition coverage: $1+1 = 0$. As syndicated columnist Ellen Goodman puts it, "Fresh research has a sell-by date that is shorter than the one on the cereal box."[22]

Responsibility for distorted reporting of nutrition does not rest with the media alone. Increasingly, it involves nutrition scientists. Although they tend not to make exaggerated claims when reporting their work at scientific meetings, some are more bold when they speak to reporters or the public. Sometimes their institution's press office encourages this boldness. As research funds become harder to secure, scientists and their employers are learning that being in the news raises their visibility, which can help to raise money.

Now, major journals like the *New England Journal of Medicine* and *Journal of the American Medical Association* reach reporters before they reach biomedical professionals. And because a growing amount of research is financed by industry, a company might seek publicity about a new finding to enhance the value of its stock or draw attention to itself. A good book on the changing nature of reporting scientific advances is *Selling Science*, by sociologist Dorothy Nelkin.[23]

The dietary supplements industry is busy making bold claims for its products on the labels, in advertising, and in product literature using preliminary science. The 1990 Nutrition Labeling and Education Act, which resulted in the new nutrition labels on packaged foods, allows supplement manufacturers to present the same health claims that are allowed on foods—claims supported by "significant scientific

Table 1
Comparison of Garlic Supplements

Name of Supplement	Cost per Tablet* (cents)	Allicin (μg)†	SAC (μg)‡
McCormick Garlic Powder§	6	5,660	590
KAL Beyond Garlic	18	4,800	270
Garlique	33	3,840	130
Garlicin	18	2,165	145
Nature's Way	8	1,530	140
Kwai	11	815	60
Quintessence	9	535	185
Natural Brand (GNC)	10	300	45
P. Leiner (private label)||	5	115	45
Kyolic¶	11	0	255

© 1995, CSPI. Adapted from *Nutrition Action Healthletter* (1875 Connecticut Ave., N.W., Suite 300, Washington DC 20009-5728. $24.00 for 10 issues).
* Based on list price when available or average price paid.
† One large clove of fresh garlic supplies about 5,000 μg allicin.
‡ S-allyl cysteine.
§ One third teaspoon.
|| Product usually carries the name of the drugstore or other chain where it is sold.
¶ The best-selling garlic supplement.

3. NUTRITIONAL HEALTH

agreement" and preapproved by FDA. Two of the authorized health claims are relevant to supplements: the links between calcium and osteoporosis and between folate and neural tube defects.

However, the Dietary Supplement Health and Education Act passed in 1994 allows the industry to make claims pertaining to the structure and function of a nutrient. For example, a supplement could not claim that it helps cure AIDS; but it might be possible to state that the product "boosts the immune system." The legal basis for a claim is that (1) some substantiation exist, (2) FDA be notified of the claim within 30 days of its presence on the label, and (3) two additional sentences be added to such claims: "This statement has not been evaluated by FDA. This product is not intended to diagnose, treat, cure, or prevent any disease." Along with these so-called "structure-function" claims, a retailer may now provide literature on supplements, although it is supposed to be balanced scientifically and not be misleading. Some members of the dietary supplements industry are fighting even these limitations, arguing that their absolute freedom of speech to provide whatever information they think is appropriate is being threatened.

An advertisement in *Time* magazine last October for Bayer Corporation's One-A-Day Brand Vitamins suggests the growing boldness of claims for even mainstream dietary supplements. The copy states: "It's been all over the news. Findings on folic acid studies were announced recently at a medical conference in Bar Harbor, Maine, suggesting that adequate intake of folic acid may significantly lower elevated homocysteine levels, one of the risk factors for heart attacks and strokes in men. One-A-Day Men's Formula contains 100% of the US RDA of folic acid. Why not start taking your One-A-Day today?"

Public health may benefit from the promotion of supplements by increasing the public's awareness of nutrient, diet, and disease relationships. But I fear the risks outweigh the benefits. The promotional copy typically fails to give information on food-related alternatives to supplements. In addition, the public rarely has the expertise to evaluate the information in the promotion. Furthermore, consumers' expectations of a product's effectiveness may be heightened by the hype and lead to irrational use of the product.

There can be a great difference between *a* truth and *the* truth. A truthful statement may inevitably be misleading. This lesson was made clear in the plethora of ridiculous health claims on foods back in the late 80s and early 90s. Some high-fat products, for example, were truthfully labeled as being cholesterol free, because manufacturers knew many people would think the product was more healthful.

Supplements supplying nutrients at levels beyond what can reasonably be obtained from food should be viewed as nonprescription drugs. High-potency products should not be used without careful thought and perhaps expert help.

POINT 8: FOCUSING ON NUTRIENTS AND SUPPLEMENTS CAN TAKE ATTENTION AND CONVICTION AWAY FROM IMPROVING ONE'S LIFESTYLE

Nationally representative surveys of American adults show that approximately one third are interested in nutrition and think they are on the right track to healthy eating. In contrast, another third couldn't care less about meeting dietary guidelines. Those in the middle third claim they are trying to eat better, but find it difficult.

So, the good news is that two thirds of adult Americans say they care about their nutrition. But the bad news is that perhaps only 5 to 10% of the US population meets dietary recommendations regularly, such as eating five or more servings of fruits and vegetables per day and limiting fat to no more than 30% of calories. Furthermore, obesity is a growing epidemic in this country, now affecting one third of adults and one quarter of children. The irony is that people who eat well are most likely to take supplements, whereas those most likely to benefit from higher nutrient intakes are least likely to take them.

My greatest concern about dietary supplements is the false sense of security it provides some people, those who use supplements to an extent as substitutes for a good diet. It is natural for us to want an easier way or, ideally, some magic bullet, to achieve health short of being vigilant or saintly all the time. We're especially likely to cut corners when we are short of time and feeling stressed, such as by choosing foods on the basis of convenience and ease of preparation and by not exercising. Taking a basic supplement as one small part of a health-promoting lifestyle may be reasonable and perhaps even prudent. But taking supplements is a problem for people, probably the majority, who are not making the lifestyle changes they know they should. A recent advertisement by Hoffman-La Roche, Inc. for vitamin E states ... "Many doctors ... believe taking supplements or eating fortified foods containing vitamins and minerals is a sound health measure, particularly for people who don't eat a good diet.... " Unfortunately, some people use supplements as a deliberate or unconscious excuse for not trying to improve their diets and lifestyles.

A reporter called me some time ago to ask how people could use vitamins to stay healthy. I replied that people should pay more attention to their diets. He told me to be realistic and used himself as an example. He said he leads a very busy life, has little time to shop for food and prepare it, and there are few places near work that serve nutritious lunches. So what supplements would help him cope more productively with his situation? Here is an example where supplements may harm more than help, by being used as a surrogate for tackling the hard things that would really improve his nutritional status, such as preparing lunches the night before, convincing nearby restaurants to offer more nutritious fare, and making sure he eats a very nutritious breakfast and dinner. This reporter was looking for what he acknowledged to be a sec-

12. Food for Thought about Dietary Supplements

ond-best solution, but taking a supplement will make him even less likely to attempt the best but more difficult solution.

As the debate over the merits of supplements continues, we health professionals should not forget that we have committed many errors of overconfidence in our dietary advice. Examples include cream and milk diets for ulcers, low-carbohydrate diets for diabetes, fiber-poor diets for digestive diseases, and diets low only in cholesterol for hypercholesterolemics. We are still very ignorant of how food, with its thousands of constituents, affects health. The public seems to comprehend this better than many of us. Supermarket shoppers have limited faith in nutrition experts, according to a recent survey by the Food Marketing Institute.[24] Approximately 40% of shoppers thought it "very likely the experts will have a completely different idea about which foods are healthful and which are not within the next 5 years." An additional 38% thought this is "somewhat likely" to happen. So more than three out of four people think that our dietary advice to them may be wrong!

There is a tendency to think we have failed at nutrition education, because we cannot get many people to really improve their diets. So perhaps we should simply try to make the foods they eat somewhat healthier and encourage them to take supplements in the hope that both actions will limit the harm from their unbalanced nutrition. Nutrition educator Joan Gussow, however, points out that nutrition education has not failed, "It hasn't really been tried. As a nation we spend less on nutrition education than is spent selling us one brand of soft drink [or dietary supplement] ... very few people change their diets because they learn about nutrients. We need to show and tell them about food, how to make it a wonderful, fulfilling part of their lives."[25]

One of the most sobering articles I read on the challenges of nutritionally educating the public was written by nutritionist Sandra Shepherd, who points out that "we'll have to fight to cut through the din of information that crowds the consumer's world."[26] Yet, at the same time, "consumers have less and less time to receive and absorb consumer information." Fewer people even keep up with the daily news as they "pursue tighter schedules and more rigorous routines" given their "fast-paced and rapidly changing lifestyle." To get people to hear your nutrition messages, she advises, "keep the information practical—making it simpler, briefer *and* more useful." Also, keep it entertaining. Shepherd touts *People* magazine as "an excellent example of this strategy in action."

The prospect of teaching nutrition by glitzy soundbite depresses me! More fundamentally, though, the expanding knowledge of nutrition does not translate easily into such soundbites, except for messages like "Balance, moderation, and variety in food selection" and, perhaps, "Take a supplement every day." These messages give the illusion of being practical. I am no proponent of teaching nutrition by focusing on individual food constituents (*eg*, saturated fat, beta-carotene, *trans* fatty acids, and phytochemicals) as we and the media tend to do and which people find confusing. However, I do believe that culinary literacy, and teaching people how to make healthful meals that are both delicious and convenient, needs to become an integral component of nutrition education.

We should be concerned about the impact of our nutrition messages on the public, especially since we tend to link our dietary advice more with medicine than with cuisine. Columnist Ellen Goodman warns that even an advance such as the new nutrition labels on food provides unintended messages: "Like many Americans, I spend more time in the supermarket studying than actually shopping. In the past decade, I have certainly read more cans than books.... So the news that we're going to get some E-Z reading in the food chain nourishes my consumer soul.... Nevertheless, ... I can read the fine print of a social message in this change of labels. It may be crammed in as densely as the new nutritional lesson on a tiny tuna can, but it's there: BEWARE OF FOOD.... The reason for the revision is, essentially, to slap a warning label on what we eat... Once food was love. Now it's just as likely to be fear. Fear of fat. Fear of heart disease, cancer, stroke, you name it. Eating is less of a hedonistic experience and more of a health experience. If we are what we eat, we're nervous.... The *New England Journal of Medicine* has become more of a guide to our menu planning than *Gourmet*. Even 'good foods' we praise are extolled for their medicinal purposes today. Increasingly we serve them because they are prescribed: fiber for breakfast and broccoli for lunch.... So I greet the new and legible labels with approval. Somehow, though, I wish they'd find room for two more words: Bon Appetit."[27]

Michelle Stacey, in her important book, *Consumed: Why Americans Love, Hate, and Fear Food* expands on Goodman's point: "If we are to truly eat better ... we must first give up this predilection for utter convenience and scientific certainty when it comes to food.... Perhaps eating well ... ought to mean eating fresh, well-prepared foods that are varied and satisfying, served in an appealing way, eaten at leisure.... That might also end the driving anxiety about our food—the idea that what we eat is killing us, and that we must do something drastic and painful to repair the damage. The name for this philosophy might be Enlightened Hedonism: a balance between information and pleasure, an educated hedging of bets."[28]

CONCLUDING THOUGHTS

I credit dietary supplements with generating my interest in nutrition. However, as I learn more about them, and despite the growing commercialism of supplements and support from health professionals, the more I believe that our genetically inherited capacity for health, resistance to disease, and longevity result from a diet of min-

3. NUTRITIONAL HEALTH

imally processed natural foods along with regular exercise and avoidance of smoking and negative stressors. I am not convinced that adding dietary supplements to this mix is necessary for most people or can even partially replace any of these essentials.

Those who recommend that healthy people supplement their diets with extra vitamins and minerals often call it a form of dietary insurance, as essential to have as car or home insurance. I disagree. When you purchase insurance, the benefits and costs of the policy are detailed and you choose a specific level of protection. The terms of a dietary insurance policy, though, can never be known, much less specified. Taking supplements without a clear need is more analogous to playing the lottery. You hope to win some money, and ideally the jackpot, by buying lottery tickets. You won't hurt yourself unless you buy more tickets over time than you can afford, but you are not likely to win anything either, especially the big prize.

Even comprehensive dietary supplements are, at best, poor substitutes for nutrient-rich foods. Foods, about which we know little, are more than the sum of their parts, about which we have some knowledge. Furthermore, it's harder to hurt yourself with foods than with supplements. Concentrating anything in the food chain—be it vitamin C, beta-carotene, salt, or fat—increases the likelihood of mistakes. Nutrients and other nonnutrient substances relevant to health are readily available in familiar and attractive packages called fruits, vegetables, legumes, grains, and animal products. And they come in concentrations and in combinations with which humans have had long cultural familiarity.[29]

It is much easier to become familiar with some useful generalities about food and save pharmacologic nutrition for the experts and for when it might be needed.

REFERENCES

1. Slesinski MJ, Subar AF, Kahle LL. Trends in use of vitamin and mineral supplements in the United States: The 1987 and 1992 National Health Interview Surveys. *J Am Diet Assoc* 1995;95:921–3.
2. National Research Council. *Diet and Health: Implications for Reducing Chronic Disease Risk.* Washington, DC: National Academy Press, 1989.
3. US Department of Agriculture, Department of Health and Human Services. *Nutrition and Your Health: Dietary Guidelines for Americans,* 4th ed. Washington, DC: Government Printing Office, 1995.
4. Brody J. Personal health: Sorting out the benefits of taking extra vitamin E. *New York Times,* July 26, 1995:C8.
5. Golub E. *The Limits of Medicine: How Science Shapes Our Hope for the Cure.* New York: Times Books, 1994.
6. Hiser E. Getting into your genes. *Eating Well* 1995;6(1):48–9.
7. Herbert V, Kasdan TS. Misleading nutrition claims and their gurus. *Nutr Today* 29(3):28–35, 1994.
8. Begley S. Beyond vitamins: The search for the magic pill. *Newsweek,* April 25, 1994:45–9.
9. The Alpha-Tocopherol, Beta-Carotene Cancer Prevention Study Group. The effect of vitamin E and beta carotene on the incidence of lung cancer and other cancers in male smokers. *N Engl J Med* 1994;330:1029–35.
10. Blumberg JB. Considerations of the scientific substantiation for antioxidant vitamins and β-carotene in disease prevention. *Am J Clin Nutr* 1995;62:1521S–1526S.
11. Liebman B. Antioxidants: Surprise, surprise. *Nutr Action Healthletter* 1994;21(5):4.
12. Wade N. Method and madness: Believing in vitamins. *New York Times Magazine,* May 22, 1994:20.
13. Herbert V. The antioxidant supplement myth. *Am J Clin Nutr* 1994;60:157–8.
14. Graziano JM, Johnson EJ, Russell RM, Manson JE, Stampfer MJ, Ridker PM, Frei B, Hennekens CH, Krinsky NI. Discrimination in absorption or transport of β-carotene isomers after oral supplementation with either all-*trans*- or 9-*cis*-β-carotene. *Am J Clin Nutr* 1995;61:1248–52.
15. McCord JM. Free radicals and prooxidants in health and nutrition. *Food Tech* 1994;48(5):106–11.
16. Anon. Buying vitamins: what's worth the price? *Consumer Rep* 1994;59:565–9.
17. Schardt D, Schmidt S. Garlic: Clove at first sight? *Nutr Action Healthletter* 1995;22(6)3–5.
18. Anon. Herbal roulette. *Consumer Rep* 1995;60:698–705.
19. Anon. A 9-point guide to choosing the right supplement. *Tufts Univ Diet & Nutr Letter* 1993;11(7)3–6.
20. Liebman B, Schardt D. Vitamin smarts. *Nutr Action Healthletter* 1995;22(9):1,6–10.
21. Houn F, Bober MA, Huerta EE, Hursting SD, Lemon S, Weed DL. The association between alcohol and breast cancer: Popular press coverage of research. *Am J Publ Health* 1995;85:1082–6.
22. Goodman E. To swallow or not to swallow. *Liberal Opinion Week,* April 24, 1994.
23. Nelkin D. *Selling Science: How the Press Covers Science and Technology,* revised edition. New York: WH Freeman and Company, 1995.
24. Anon. Many shoppers not yet aware of nutrition facts label. *Food Labeling News* 1995;3(32):21–3.
25. Gussow JD. *A Word on Behalf of Food.* Presentation at the Alumni Advances Conference of the dietetic internship program at Oregon Health Sciences University, Portland, OR, May 1995.
26. Shepherd SK. Nutrition and the consumer: Meeting the challenge of nutrition education in the 1990s. *Food & Consumer News* 1990;62(1):1–3.
27. Goodman E. Food literacy. *Liberal Opinion Week,* December 14, 1992.
28. Stacey M. *Consumed: Why Americans Love, Hate, and Fear Food.* New York: Touchstone Books, 1994.
29. Gussow JD, Thomas PR. *The Nutrition Debate: Sorting Out Some Answers.* Palo Alto, CA: Bull Publishing Co., 1986.

The views expressed in this article are those of the author and do not reflect the position of the Center for Food and Nutrition Policy.

The Food Pyramid: How to make it work for you

The Government's nutritional tool can lead you toward a healthy diet—but you need to know more than it tells you.

Five years ago, the U.S. Department of Agriculture introduced the Food Guide Pyramid, designed to convey a simple, graphic message: Grains, fruits, and vegetables are the cornerstone of a healthy diet. That message, reinforced by specific recommendations on how many servings per day to get from each food group, has increased many Americans' awareness of the need to eat lots of plant foods. But the pyramid offers no specific recommendations about which items to choose *within* each food group. So it's quite possible to get the appropriate number of servings for each group and still end up with an unbalanced, unhealthy diet.

Cracks in the pyramid

The pyramid falls short in two areas: fiber and fat. First, nutrition experts recommend you consume 20 to 35 grams of fiber per day. But the pyramid makes no distinction between refined-grain products such as white rice and white bread, which contain little fiber, and whole-grain foods like brown rice and whole-wheat bread, which pack a lot of fiber.

The tip of the pyramid advises people to use fats, oils, and sweets sparingly. But that advice apparently lumps together two very different groups of fat. The first includes the nontropical oils, such as olive or corn oil, which are harmless unless you're watching your waistline. The second includes items that are bad for both the waistline and the heart: butter, cream, lard, and tropical oils, rich in artery-clogging saturated fat; plus margarine and shortening, which are rich in artery-clogging trans fat.

The pyramid uses tiny circles and triangles as symbols to suggest that each of the other five food groups may also contain fats (and sweets). But it offers no explicit advice about how to limit fat consumption in those groups. For example, it doesn't distinguish between high- and low-fat dairy products. And it doesn't exclude from the grain group fatty items like fried rice, fettucini Alfredo, or garlic bread; or, from the vegetable group, such items as cauliflower au gratin, creamed spinach, or even french fries.

The group containing meat and meat substitutes (eggs, nuts, and beans) fails to separate typically lean foods like beans, fish, and skinless poultry breast from fatty items like hot dogs and hamburgers. And the recommendation to eat two to three servings per day works for meat but not for the meat substitutes. A better standard, mentioned in the seldom-read brochure that accompanies the pyramid, is a daily maximum of 5 to 7 ounces of either meat, an equivalent quantity of meat substitutes, or both combined. (One egg, 1/2 cup of cooked dried peas or beans, 2 tablespoons of peanut butter, and 1/3 cup of nuts are each considered the equivalent of 1 ounce of meat).

Fixing the flaws

To help you meet the pyramid's requirements in a healthy way, we've prepared the detailed table on the next page. It not only lists the recommended number of servings for each food group but also breaks each group down into three categories:

■ Foods you should choose **often**, since they're nutritious, lean, and, where applicable, high in fiber.

■ Those you should choose **sometimes**, since they're either somewhat fattier, less nutritious, lower in fiber, or, in the case of some seafood, higher in potentially hazardous chemicals than foods in the "often" category. For example, canned vegetables are listed as "sometimes" because they contain fewer nutrients than fresh or frozen vegetables. And several kinds of fish are listed there because they often contain significant amounts of such chemicals as mercury or PCBs—and, in most cases, are also fairly fatty.

■ Those you should **seldom** choose, since they're either high in fat or low in nutrients and fiber. Coconut, for example, is loaded with saturated fat. And regular biscuits, crackers, and sweetened muffins typically offer an undesirable combination of low fiber, mediocre nutrient levels, and moderately high fat.

If you eat many foods more or less often than the table recommends, you're probably eating too much fat and possibly too little fiber. Try to adjust your diet gradually, choosing more foods from the often column and fewer from the seldom column.

How to get more

Our table leaves one important aspect of the pyramid virtually unchanged: the recommended number

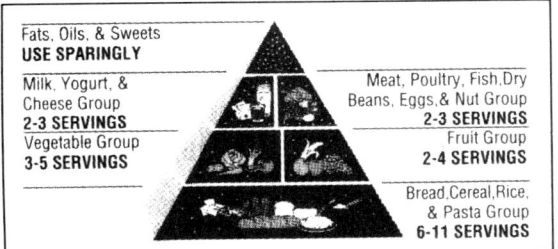

USDA's Food Guide Pyramid The pyramid shows how many servings to eat from each food group, but it offers no specific guidance on which foods to eat within each group.

For more information
■ "The M *FIT* Grocery Shopping Guide," University of Michigan, 1995. Extensive listings of brand-name and other foods, according to their overall nutritional value. $18.95. Call 313-998-7645.

3. NUTRITIONAL HEALTH

Beyond the pyramid: Healthy choices for a healthy diet

Choose often	Choose sometimes	Choose seldom
Fats, oils, and sweets: Use sparingly		
While all regular fats and oils should be used sparingly, some alternatives to those items, such as nonfat spreads or salad dressings, can be used often.	Fruit-snack candies, fruit drinks (not juices), hard candies (particularly sugarless), honey, jelly, molasses, soda, sorbet, refined sugar, syrups. Nonfat or low-fat cookies, cakes, and other desserts. Mayonnaise. Light margarine; other reduced-fat spreads with less than 2 grams of saturated fat per serving. Nontropical vegetable oils, such as olive and canola. Salad dressing.	Candy bars; chocolate; regular cakes, cookies, and pies; and other rich desserts. Butter, lard, stick margarine. Coconut, palm, and other tropical oils.
Dairy: 2 to 3 servings per day		
Milk, buttermilk, and cottage cheese: skim or 1% fat. Nonfat or low-fat yogurt. Nonfat cheese. Nonfat or low-fat frozen dairy desserts.	Milk, buttermilk, and cottage cheese: 2% fat. Low-fat cheese. Reduced-fat dairy desserts.	Whole milk, whole-milk yogurt. Regular cheese; cottage cheese: 4% fat. Regular frozen dairy desserts.
Meat and meat substitutes: 5 to 7 ounces per day		
Any unground meats labeled "extra lean." **Beef:** Eye of round, top round. **Veal:** All kinds not listed in next two columns. **Pork:** Tenderloin, 95% lean ham. **Lamb:** Foreshank. **Chicken:** Skinless breast. **Turkey:** Breast, drumstick, or wing without skin. **Fish:** Lean varieties such as bass, cod, flounder, halibut, monkfish, pollack, trout. **Shellfish.** **Nonfat or low-fat lunch meats or hot dogs,** with up to 3 grams of fat per serving. **Meat substitutes:** Beans, peas, and lentils; tofu; eggs [2] or egg substitutes.	Any unground meats labeled "lean." **Beef:** Tip or bottom round, sirloin, chuck pot roast, top loin, tenderloin, flank, T-bone, ground sirloin, extra-lean ground. **Veal:** Loin, loin chop, ground. **Pork:** Sirloin chop, top or center loin chop, rib chop, ham, Canadian bacon. **Lamb:** Shank, leg, loin chop, sirloin. **Chicken:** Skinless drumstick, thigh, or wing; breast with skin. **Turkey:** Any piece with skin; thigh without skin; extra-lean ground. **Fish:** Bluefish, catfish, herring (including sardines), mackerel, pompano, salmon, shad, swordfish, tuna.[1] **Reduced-fat lunch meats or hot dogs,** with 4 to 5 grams of fat per serving. **Meat substitutes:** Nuts; nut butters.[3]	**Beef:** All cuts not listed in first two columns (such as brisket, rib roast, chuck blade roast, lean and regular ground). **Veal:** Rib roast. **Pork:** All kinds not listed in first two columns (such as spareribs, sausage, ground). **Lamb:** All kinds not listed in first two columns (such as rib chop, arm, blade, shoulder, ground). **Chicken:** Drumstick, thigh, or wing with skin; liver. **Turkey:** Lean or regular ground. **Duck, goose.** **Regular lunch meats or hot dogs,** with more than 5 grams of fat per serving.
Vegetables: 3 to 5 servings per day [4]		
Fresh or frozen vegetables not listed in third column. Vegetable juice [5] (except canned).	Canned vegetables. Canned vegetable juice.	Vegetables in cheese, cream, or other fatty sauces. French fries, onion rings, other deep-fried vegetables.
Fruit: 2 to 4 servings per day		
Fresh or frozen fruit not listed in next two columns. Fruit juice. [5]	Canned fruit; dried fruit. Avocado, olives. [3]	Coconut.
Grains: 6 to 11 servings per day		
Higher-fiber foods: Amaranth, barley, brown or wild rice, cracked or bulgur wheat, kasha, quinoa. Low-fat popcorn or unbuttered air-popped popcorn. Rice cakes, corn or whole-wheat tortillas. **Higher-fiber versions** (Any of the following items that are labeled "whole wheat" or "100% whole grain"; that make a claim about fiber, such as "high fiber" or "good source of fiber"; or that contain at least 2 grams of fiber per serving): Bread, bagels, English muffins, rolls. Pasta, couscous. Cereals with up to 3 grams of fat per serving. Bread sticks, pretzels. Nonfat or low-fat biscuits, crackers, or sweetened muffins.	Any item in the first column, under "higher-fiber versions," that does not bear those labels, make those claims, or contain that much fiber. White rice. Regular popcorn flavored with or popped in nontropical oils. Wheat tortillas. Whole-wheat biscuits, crackers, or sweetened muffins that are not low-fat or nonfat. Whole-wheat pancakes, waffles, or French toast. Higher-fiber cereals with more than 3 grams of fat per serving, such as granola or muesli.	Fried rice; any grain dish with fatty sauce. Regular popcorn flavored with butter or popped in tropical oils. Biscuits, crackers, or sweetened muffins that are not high-fiber, low-fat, or nonfat. Croissants, Danish, donuts. Regular pancakes, waffles, or French toast.

---

[1] Young children and women who are or may become pregnant should avoid bluefish, salmon, swordfish, tuna, and probably other large predatory fish, which may contain high levels of hazardous chemicals and heavy metals. Other people should eat those fish no more than once a week.

[2] These are high in cholesterol, which can raise blood-cholesterol levels in some people. Eat eggs only sometimes—no more than four yolks per week—if you have borderline or high cholesterol.

[3] Although these foods contain little saturated fat, the artery-clogging kind, they do contain a significant amount of other fats and, in turn, calories. People who are watching their weight may want to eat these foods seldom rather than sometimes.

[4] Includes beans and potatoes. Note that beans are included in both the meat and vegetable groups. (But count each serving only once.)

[5] Count as only one serving per day. You still need to eat lots of whole fruits and vegetables, since whole produce, unlike juice, supplies lots of fiber.

of servings. Americans typically have the most trouble meeting those recommendations for fruits and vegetables, which call for a combined total of 5 to 9 daily servings. Many people also find it hard to get the recommended 6 to 11 servings of grains. (Where you fit within those ranges depends on your caloric needs; the low ends, for example, are appropriate for most inactive women and older people, the high ends mainly for active younger men.)

But getting enough servings may be easier than you think, since standard serving sizes are typically small. For example, one slice of bread, half a muffin, a half-cup of cooked or chopped vegetables or fruit, and a small glass of fruit or vegetable juice each equal one serving. (For more details on serving size, see the series in "A Picture of Health" in *CR on Health*'s April through July issues.)

Here are some strategies that can help you meet your daily quotas:

Produce

- Get two servings of fruit at breakfast by drinking a small glass of orange juice and finishing the meal with, say, a nectarine. (But count only one serving of juice per day.)
- Add fruits and vegetables to other foods—berries in pancakes, peaches in yogurt, peppers and onions in omelets, shredded carrots in sandwiches.
- Take double servings of vegetables.
- Snack on raw vegetables or fruit.
- Thicken soups with pureed vegetables.

Grains (preferably whole wheat or whole grain)

- Eat cereal for breakfast and add bread or rolls to any meal.
- Cook whole grains in soup stock and season with herbs. Toss with cooked vegetables and beans.
- Make cold salads from cooked grains plus chopped raw vegetables.
- Add cereals to yogurt.
- Add cooked grains or wheat germ to soup.

Summing up

To get the most benefit from the food pyramid, you need to know more than just the number of servings in each food group.

What to do:

- Consult our table, which shows the ideal balance among various foods in each category, based on their fat, fiber, and nutritional content.
- If your diet doesn't conform to that ideal, try to eat more of the "often" foods and fewer of the "seldom" items. More generally, aim to boost your intake of lean, high-fiber foods, and to eat fewer fatty, highly refined, or processed foods.
- If your diet doesn't include enough servings of produce or grains, look for creative ways to get more, such as adding chopped fruits or vegetables to other dishes.

Fast food: Fatter than ever

The chains are beefing up their menus, leaving health-conscious patrons in a pickle.

A few years ago, the fast-food industry attempted to trim its image, in the hope that salads, seaweed-laced burgers, and other low-fat fare would attract nutrition-conscious customers. But the public didn't bite. Now the fast-food chains are heading fast in the opposite direction, unabashedly pushing fattier fare than ever.

In May, McDonald's ditched its side salads and replaced its low-fat *McLean Deluxe* burger with the high-fat *Arch Deluxe*, a quarter pound of beef topped with cheese and optional bacon. The chain is also expected to boost the size of its basic patty by 25 percent. Meanwhile, Burger King has already increased the size of its regular burger by nearly 60 percent. And Taco Bell has pruned its *Border Light* line of reduced-fat foods and introduced a new line of fattier items, such as the *Big Border Taco*, which packs twice the meat and cheese of a regular taco.

Is it time for people who care about their health to bid fast food a hasty farewell?

Fast food's fatty toll

A recent study, funded by McDonald's, showed that it's possible to eat a diet that gets just 30 percent of its calories from fat—the maximum recommended amount—while dining at McDonald's five times a week. But it sure wasn't easy. The volunteers had to eat small meals at McDonald's, featuring the few relatively lean options. Outside McDonald's, they had to curtail their fat intake to substantially less than 30 percent of calories to make up the difference.

Even a single fast-food meal can supply so many calories and so much fat that you'd have to fast for an entire day and avoid all fat for a second day to compensate. Worse, some evidence suggests that an extremely fatty meal might trigger a heart attack in people with coronary heart disease, in theory because fat pouring into the bloodstream stimulates clotting.

Those findings don't mean you should never set foot in a fast-food restaurant again. But they do mean that it's best to exercise some restraint on even an occasional fast-food foray—and a lot of restraint if you eat fast food regularly.

Fast and lean

Here are four guidelines on how to choose lean meals from fast-food menus that are glutted with fat.

■ **Think small.** Something about fast-food restaurants seems to trigger a primal urge to pig out. The chains feed that frenzy with signs like Burger King's "Go large" or McDonald's "Super size it," for just a little more money. But thinking big in a fast-food restaurant is a bad deal for both your waistline and your heart (see chart below). The smallest burgers are often especially lean—just 33 percent of calories from fat in a Wendy's *Junior*, for example—because they're not only small but plain.

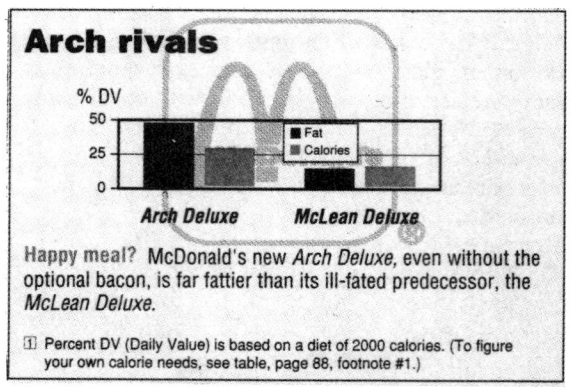

Arch rivals

Happy meal? McDonald's new *Arch Deluxe*, even without the optional bacon, is far fattier than its ill-fated predecessor, the *McLean Deluxe*.

Percent DV (Daily Value) is based on a diet of 2000 calories. (To figure your own calorie needs, see table, page 88, footnote #1.)

Size counts

Large: Double Whopper, Large fries, Large Coke
Medium: Whopper, Medium fries, Medium Coke
Small: Whopper Jr., Small fries, Small Coke

■ **Hold the toppings.** Salad vegetables and baked potatoes have no fat, and roast beef can be quite lean. So why is the first meal in the next chart—salad, potato, and beef sandwich—loaded with well over a day's worth of fat? Because it's loaded with toppings. The sour cream, cheese, butter, and bacon bits on the potato alone add 16 grams of artery-clogging saturated fat, four-fifths of the recommended daily maximum for the average person. The blue-cheese dressing on that salad supplies nearly half a day's worth of total fat—and many people add a second packet. Salads that contain cheese can be fattier still. But if you hold the toppings or switch to low-fat alternatives (see chart), those same dishes can provide a much leaner meal.

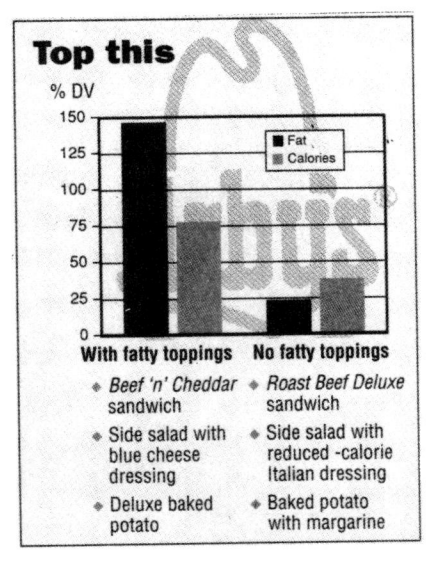

14. Fast Food

Top this

- With fatty toppings
  - Beef 'n' Cheddar sandwich
  - Side salad with blue cheese dressing
  - Deluxe baked potato
- No fatty toppings
  - Roast Beef Deluxe sandwich
  - Side salad with reduced-calorie Italian dressing
  - Baked potato with margarine

Toppings have loads of salt, too, so they're particularly bad for people who are on a low-sodium diet. The biggest offenders are often the reduced-calorie dressings, since the chains often add salt to compensate for the loss of palate-pleasing fat. Two packets of Arby's reduced-calorie Italian, for example, provide 2000 mg of sodium—nearly a full day's ration.

■ **Don't get fried.** Frying can bloat the leanest foods. The cod or pollack in Burger King's *Big Fish Sandwich*, for example, gets just 7 to 10 percent of its calories from fat. But those figures jump to an average of 37 percent after the fish has been breaded and deep fried. Add tartar sauce, and the sandwich gets more than half its calories from fat and supplies more than two-thirds the daily dose of fat.

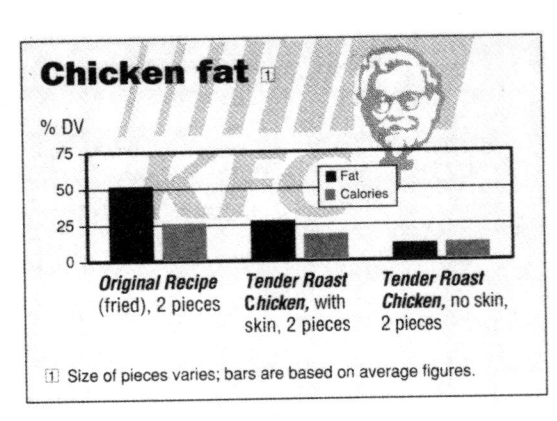

Chicken fat [1]

- Original Recipe (fried), 2 pieces
- Tender Roast Chicken, with skin, 2 pieces
- Tender Roast Chicken, no skin, 2 pieces

[1] Size of pieces varies; bars are based on average figures.

While there's no lean version of fast-food fish, there are good alternatives to other fried foods. In some restaurants, you can get a baked potato, topped with just a pat of margarine or butter, instead of french fries. Or you can order roasted or grilled chicken, rather than fried chicken pieces or sandwiches, which typically supply as much or more total fat—though less saturated fat—than a regular burger. For still leaner chicken, order it roasted without the skin if possible (see the bar chart above).

■ **Watch the drinks and desserts.** Regular soda adds lots of calories but no other nutrients. Shakes are more nutritious, and they're usually low in fat, since they're usually made with at least some skim milk. But they're still full of calories—up to a quarter of a day's worth for the average adult—since they're full of sugar. Better choices include diet soda, juice, or low-fat milk.

Don't expect anything healthful from fast-food fruit pies, which get nearly half their calories from fat. Sundaes, like shakes, are usually leaner than the pies, but they're still high in calories. McDonald's offers low-fat frozen yogurt; elsewhere, you might decide to skip dessert.

Best and worst

So despite the trend toward fattier fare, it's still possible to order a low-fat, reasonably low-calorie fast-food meal, such as the "lean meal" platter shown in the bar chart below. But it's usually not possible to construct a thoroughly healthful meal—one high in whole grains, fruit, and significant amounts of any vegetable other than iceburg lettuce, which contains insignificant amounts of vitamins, minerals, and fiber. (Only Wendy's offers a salad bar containing nutritious produce.) And if you break all the rules, you could end up with a belly-bloating, artery-clogging meal like the "fatty meal" shown in the chart below.

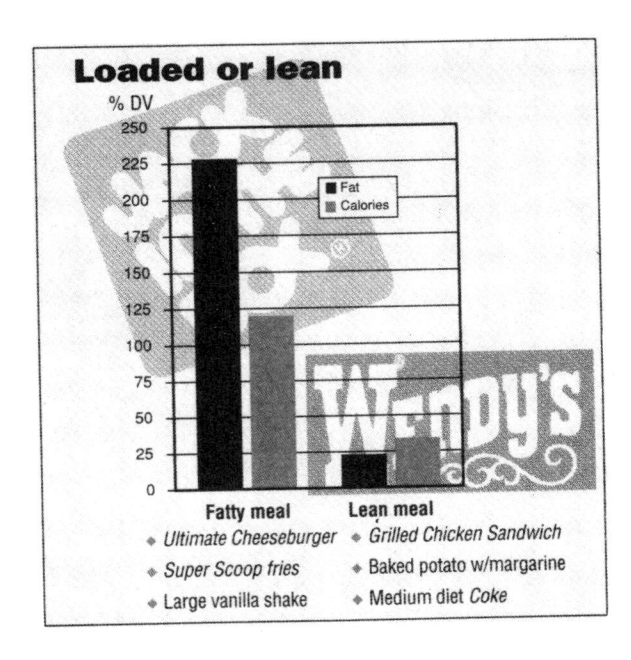

Loaded or lean

- Fatty meal
  - Ultimate Cheeseburger
  - Super Scoop fries
  - Large vanilla shake
- Lean meal
  - Grilled Chicken Sandwich
  - Baked potato w/margarine
  - Medium diet *Coke*

Summing up

If you want to help squeeze an occasional fast-food meal into an otherwise healthful diet, follow these guidelines:

■ Choose modest portions; go easy on the top-

3. NUTRITIONAL HEALTH

pings; avoid fried foods; choose diet soda, juice or low-fat milk; and skip the fruit pies and other fatty desserts.

■ To identify the leaner options, see the table below, or check the brochures or wall posters found at many major fast-food chains.

Fast-food nutritional profile

	Calories	% Calories from fat	Total fat (% DV) [1]	Saturated fat (% DV) [1]	Sodium (% DV) [1]
BURGERS					
McDonald's Hamburger	270	33%	5%	18%	22%
Wendy's Jr. Hamburger	270	33	15	15	23
McDonald's Cheeseburger	320	41	22	30	31
Wendy's Plain Single w/ Everything	420	43	31	35	34
McDonald's Quarter Pounder	420	45	32	40	29
McDonald's Big Mac	530	47	43	50	40
Hardee's Quarter Pound Cheeseburger	420	48	34	55	36
McDonald's Arch Deluxe	570	49	48	55	46
Burger King Whopper Jr.	420	52	37	40	22
Jack in the Box Jumbo Jack	560	52	49	50	31
Burger King Whopper	640	55	60	55	36
Burger King Double Whopper	870	57	86	95	39
Jack in the Box Ultimate Cheeseburger	1030	69	122	130	50
CHICKEN / TURKEY					
McDonald's McGrilled Chicken Classic	260	13%	6%	5%	21%
Wendy's Grilled Chicken Sandwich	310	23	12	8	33
Arby's Roast Turkey Deluxe	260	24	11	10	53
Hardee's Chicken Fillet Sandwich	420	31	23	15	50
KFC Tender Roast Chicken, no skin [2]	114	32	6	6	19
Arby's Turkey Sub	550	44	42	35	87
Jack in the Box Chicken Caesar Sandwich	520	44	40	30	44
KFC Tender Roast Chicken, with skin [2]	185	47	14	15	22
Burger King BK Broiler Chicken Sandwich	550	47	45	30	20
McDonald's McChicken Sandwich	510	53	46	25	34
Burger King Chicken Sandwich	710	55	66	45	58
KFC Original Recipe [2]	263	61	26	21	32
ROAST BEEF					
Arby's Roast Beef Deluxe (Light menu)	296	30%	15%	15%	34%
Hardee's Regular Roast Beef	270	37	17	25	32
Hardee's Big Roast Beef	410	51	35	45	48
Arby's Beef 'n Cheddar	487	52	43	45	51
FISH					
Hardee's Fisherman's Fillet	450	40%	31%	30%	46%
McDonald's Filet-O-Fish	360	42	25	20	29
Arby's Fish Fillet	529	46	42	35	36
Burger King BK Big Fish Sandwich	700	53	63	30	41

[1] Data for percent of Daily Value (% DV) based on a diet of 2000 calories per day. To determine your own caloric needs (for maintaining current weight), multiply your weight in pounds by one of the following factors, depending on your activity level: 11, if you're nearly sedentary; 13, if moderately active; 15, if a moderate exerciser or physical laborer; 18, if an extremely active exerciser or physical laborer.

[2] Data for this item represent an average of one chicken breast, one leg, and one thigh.

Snack Attack

Patricia Long

Patricia Long is a contributing editor.

SITTING IN BAR 234, a windowless, fluorescent-lit room, it's difficult to tell day from night, lunchtime from dinnertime. But the place fairly well shouts snack. The walls are lined with 22 mechanical dispensers that disgorge everything from Care Free gum to Famous Amos cookies, from pickles to Lay's potato chips, from Ultra Slim-Fast to the latest vending triumph, French fries cooked with hot air.

A uniformed U.S. Army major walks in the door and heads toward a machine. He presses his face up against the glass and plunks in a few quarters. I sidle up.

"Fritos, eh?"

"Excuse me?"

"Fritos. Kinda high in fat and salt, aren't they?"

Maybe I shouldn't be so confrontational with a guy trained in combat techniques. But orders are orders, and mine are to explore the workaday snacking habits that cost Americans $13.4 billion a year. Find out why we shove $2.5 billion of that into vending machines, yet of our 60 favorite selections, only three of them aren't extremely heavy in sugar or fat—Snak-Ens party mix, Snyder's hard pretzels, and Fig Newtons (and they're numbers 12, 42, and 43 in the ranking). I'm after the answer to perhaps America's most intriguing dietary question: Is there some way for even the stuff in vending machines to improve our national diet, rather than ruin it?

Bar 234 is named for its location on the second floor at the junction of corridors three and four in the world's largest office building: the Pentagon, situated outside Washington, D.C. The Pentagon is a perfect test environment, because offices—along with schools and factories—are where the nation's snacking culture truly thrives. While a visitor could easily get lost in the nearly 18 miles of corridors and among the 23,000 employees, there's little hazard of starving. At almost every turn sits a vending machine. Les Barnett, the Pentagon's snack vendor, figures that between the machines in the halls, in Bar 234, and in one other snack bar, every week he sells about 5,000 candy bars, 2,900 packages of cookies, crackers, and nuts, and 7,000 bags of chips, pretzels, and pastries.

One of those bags of chips is now being torn open by the major, a polite man.

"I tend to snack if I'm edgy," he says. "I feel guilty only when I get on the scale in the morning and weigh too much. Then I skip my snack that day." He hesitates, figuring how to upgrade his image from a Fritos-only type. "Once in a while I get a granola bar."

I haven't the heart to point out that regular granola bars aren't much better than Fritos. They're loaded with sugar and get between 38 and 55 percent of their calories from fat. But otherwise the major has the right idea. When his weight rises, he cuts back on snacking for a while. That's one good thing about being in the military: Twice yearly mandatory weight checks keep most personnel from letting themselves go to pot.

An army lieutenant colonel whom I corner at the burrito machine confirms this. "Because we're military," he says, "we're theoretically healthier than the rest of the drone population." He pauses as the smell of buttered popcorn—more than half its calories from fat—wafts over us. He shakes his head. "Someone convinced someone in this building that popcorn consumed in industrial-size bags will not make you pudgy."

Here's a man, I think, who's not deceived by marketing, who understands that while plain air-popped popcorn boasts less than 10 percent of calories from fat, the microwave kind we're smelling is in the same fat league as fried chicken. I ask him what he snacks on.

"Diet Coke and doughnuts."

He notes my surprise. "Put it this way," he says, backpedaling. "Working in this building is like attending one continuous meeting. I don't get regular meal breaks, so I just have to lay my hands on whatever's not moving."

No matter how you figure it, combining a diet soda with a greasy doughnut is living by a weird credo: "Sugar is bad, fat isn't." True, sugar offers little more than calories, but it's not the demon fat is. Too much fat is linked to cancer, obesity, and heart disease. That's why we're advised to hold fat to under 30 percent of calories.

That's also why one look at the way we snack will tell you we're in big trouble.

AMERICANS ARE VERY concerned about nutrition. Just ask them. Fifty-eight percent of those surveyed by the Food Marketing Institute believe fat in food is a "serious health hazard." But how many are doing anything about it? According to one food industry survey, some 86 percent of adults admit to eating between meals. As for what they're eating—well, the overall top-selling snack food in America is potato chips. From vending machines it's the Snickers bar.

"Everybody says, 'Boy, we'd really like to see some healthier snacks in vending machines,'" says Tim Sanford, executive editor of the trade magazine *Vending Times*. "And that's exactly what they mean. They don't want to buy them, they just want to see them."

Consider what happened to Ruth Ward-Gross, vice president of Vendmark Inc. in Eagan, Minnesota. To celebrate "nutrition week" in a local health center, she replaced all the vending snacks with healthier ones such as raisins and trail mix, leaving only one exception—a slot

3. NUTRITIONAL HEALTH

The Vending Machine Top 30

SOME WE GREW UP ON; others only recently hit the popularity chart. Either way, these classic snack foods aren't going to disappear from machines anytime soon, despite the fact that (or maybe *because*) most are heavy in fat and sugar. Still, say nutritionists, it's okay to eat them every once in a while, if you follow the advice on these pages.

In the meantime, see how your tastes match up with those of America's other snackers, and then take a look at the real price of your favorite vending machine pick.

	% of calories from fat	calories
1. **Snickers bar** *(2.07 oz)*	42	280
2. **M & M's peanut candies** *(1.74 oz)*	47	250
3. **Reese's peanut butter cups** *(1.6 oz)*	54	250
4. **M & M's plain chocolate candies** *(1.69 oz)*	39	230
5. **Butterfinger bar** *(2.1 oz)*	39	280
6. **Baby Ruth bar** *(2.1 oz)*	43	290
7. **Pay Day bar** *(1.85 oz)*	43	250
8. **3 Musketeers bar** *(2.13 oz)*	28	260
9. **Hershey's almond bar** *(1.45 oz)*	55	230
10. **Cheetos** *(1 oz)*	54	150
11. **Twix caramel cookie bar** *(2 oz)*	45	140
12. **Snak-Ens snack mix** *(1 oz)*	17	133
13. **Milky Way bar** *(2.15 oz)*	32	280
14. **Famous Amos Chocolate Chip cookies** *(1 oz or 3 cookies)*	36	150
15. **Act II Microwave Popcorn** *(3 cups popped)*	51	140
16. **Fritos corn chips** *(1 oz)*	60	150
17. **Almond Joy bar** *(1.76 oz)*	50	250
18. **Nestlé Crunch bar** *(1.55 oz)*	47	230
19. **Oreo cookies** *(1 oz or 3 cookies)*	36	150
20. **Lay's potato chips** *(1 oz)*	60	150
21. **Planters peanuts** *(1 oz)*	74	170
22. **Doritos Nacho Cheese tortilla chips** *(1 oz)*	45	140
23. **Kit Kat bar** *(1.4 oz)*	47	220
24. **Mr. Goodbar** *(1.65 oz)*	55	260
25. **Planters cheese peanut butter sandwiches** *(1.4 oz or 6 sandwiches)*	45	200
26. **Nature Valley Oats 'N Honey granola bar** *(.83 oz)*	36	120
27. **Milky Way Dark bar** *(1.76 oz)*	33	220
28. **Cheez-It crackers** *(.5 oz or 12 crackers)*	51	70
29. **Starburst Original Fruit Chews** *(2.07 oz)*	19	240
30. **M & M's peanut butter candies** *(1.63 oz)*	45	240

Excludes gum. Based on vendors' dollar purchases for the year ending June 1992. Ranking source: DEBS, Ann Arbor, Michigan. Vended samples vary in size.

full of Snickers. Within two days she got a call for more Snickers. "That's the reality," she says.

And we're ashamed about it. Fully one in three snackers confess to feelings of guilt, according to a 1990 survey. Of those, nearly half say they feel worse about snacking than they do about lying about their weight or age or letting the answering machine take a call when they're home. A third think it's worse than breaking a date, taking a phony sick day, or cheating on taxes.

"I'll see someone in front of a machine," says Barnett, the Pentagon's vendor, "and I'll ask if something's wrong. 'No, I'm just looking,' they'll say. They'll stand there, and you can almost hear them thinking, *I really should get something healthy, but I really want such-and-such. I had a late lunch, I'm having an early dinner, I'm too fat. It just goes on and on.*"

But, really, is all this guilt warranted?

Not in theory. Studies on both animals and humans show that snacks—if complementary to regular meals—can help you feel more alert, lose weight, and lower your levels of "bad" cholesterol.

For one thing, standard mealtimes aren't always in synch with the body's rhythms. "After lunchtime your circadian performance rhythms are on a downswing," says Bonnie Spring, a psychologist at The Chicago Medical School. "Fatigue will peak around one to three in the afternoon." Reports Robin Kanarek, a psychologist at Tufts University in Medford, Massachusetts, "Somebody looking at a computer screen—at letters or numbers or whatever—does worse after lunch than before." British researcher Andrew Smith describes the feeling archly: "Lethargic, feeble, clumsy, and muzzy."

Kanarek's research confirms that a snack can reverse the letdown. In two experiments, she asked 18 men to either skip or eat a moderate lunch. Hours later some got no snack (actually, a diet soda), while others got a snack (in one, a chocolate bar, in the other, a yogurt). Then the men took tests measuring memory, math reasoning, reading speed, and attention span. It didn't matter much whether the men had lunched or not. Those eating calories at snacktime scored higher than those who didn't.

If we could manage it, eating tiny meals all day long—a meal pattern researchers refer to, not surprisingly, as nibbling—would actually cut more than our muzziness. For instance, our weight and our heart disease rates. Lab animals fed two large daily meals—known as gorging

15. Snack Attack

No-Guilt Everyday Snacks

NUTRITIONISTS WHO understand human nature agree that a once-every-week-or-so splurge on your snack of illicit choice (*Oh, Lorna!*) can actually help you manage your cravings and diet. But how are you supposed to satisfy your desires the *other* days?

These 21 snacks are low in fat or high in nutritional value (some are both), not too caloric, and tasty to many. (In other words, tofu didn't make the list.)

ANYTIME

Low in fat and filled with vitamins, minerals, or fiber

	% of calories from fat	calories
Nonfat yogurt with fruit (8 oz)	0	100
Baby carrots (3 oz)	4	40
Fresh fruit (pear)	6	98
Bagel (1)	6	152
Raisin bran (1.4-oz box)	6	111
Fig bar (1)	15	60
Graham crackers (.5 oz or 2 crackers)	15	60
Instant oatmeal (1-oz package)	18	100

ONCE A DAY

Low to moderate in fat

	% of calories from fat	calories
Hard candy (1 piece)	0	22
Nonfat pudding (4 oz)	0	100
Rice cakes (2)	8	70
Pretzel twists (10)	8	229
Air-popped popcorn (1 cup)	9	31
Animal crackers (.5 oz or 5 crackers)	26	70
Gingersnaps (.5 oz or 3 cookies)	30	60
Saltines (5)	30	60
Whole wheat crackers (.5 oz or 3 crackers)	30	60

WHEN YOU'RE ACTIVE

Fatty, but high in vitamins and minerals

	% of calories from fat	calories
Trail mix (1 oz)	57	131
Roasted pumpkin seeds (1 oz)	73	148
Roasted peanuts (1 oz)	76	163
Sunflower seeds (1 oz)	82	176

All of the above items have no cholesterol or only moderate amounts; people on low-salt diets should always check labels for sodium content.

—experience large surges in insulin. Some studies show that because insulin converts glucose into body fat, big-meal eaters have more weight problems than the critters who eat the same amount, but spread out over the day.

Weight-conscious people especially should eat something every four or six hours, say diet experts. Anything less, and the body thinks it's starving so slows down its metabolism (not exactly what a weight-watcher wants). It also grows famished; the liver stores only about 340 calories' worth of fuel to maintain steady blood sugar levels. In other words, the I-didn't-eat-anything-all-day diet is bound to fail, explains Evelyn Tribole, a Beverly Hills, California, dietitian and author of *Eating on the Run.* "If you have a light meal at lunch and no snack, then work out and don't eat dinner until seven o'clock, you are too hungry to exercise any self-control."

Such big meals lead to higher levels of cholesterol. In one study, David Jenkins, a nutrition researcher at the University of Toronto, fed two groups of men identical food. One group polished it off as three meals, the other as 17 snacks. Sure enough, snackers experienced drops in "bad" cholesterol levels, lowering their risk of heart disease. Researchers believe the insulin surges that follow big meals prompt the liver to generate more of the cholesterol that helps cause heart disease.

But before you start nibbling, look at what happens when lab animals are given *unlimited* access to either wholesome Purina rat chow or an assortment of tasty chocolate cookies, peanut butter, and marshmallows. They turn up their little noses at the boring chow, gorge on the snacks, and grow very, very fat.

You don't need a research study to know humans do the same thing. Big lunch at noon, candy at two, potato chips at four, and so on into the evening. "The downside to nibbling in real life is that most people don't have any self-control," says Jenkins. "They gain weight."

SO WHAT'S A snack lover to do? Here's what the experts advise:

THINK OF SNACKS AS MINI-MEALS

The way nutritionists see it, we'd be healthier if we skipped candy, chips, cookies, and other typical snack foods altogether or ate them only occasionally. Instead, we'd snack on "meal-type" foods, such as fruit salad, instant oatmeal,

3. NUTRITIONAL HEALTH

New and Improved

STROLL THE SNACK aisle of any grocery store these days and you might think you've blundered into the health-food section. Cookies are sweetened with fruit juice, while tortilla chips sport ingredients like beets, carrots, and flax seed.

If you eat any of the four C's—cookies, cakes, chips, chocolate bars—it can't hurt to see if you like the lighter alternatives. Though some still have loads of sugar or salt, all of the newcomers are a *lot* lower in fat.

CHIPS

Some chip makers now bake instead of fry. But a "baked-not-fried" claim isn't the same as "fat free." For taste, some companies spike their dough with shortening; others spray fat on after baking.

	% of calories from fat	calories
OLD-TECH		
Regular tortilla chips	47	142
Regular potato chips	62	158
NEW-TECH		
Guiltless Gourmet Baked Tortilla Chips	11	110
Childers Oven Toasted Potato Chips	0	98
Mr. Phipps Tater Crisps	30	120

COOKIES AND CAKES

Commercial bakers are replacing fat with fruit pectin or vegetable gums—xanthan gum, for example, or cellulose gel—which help keep the products moist.

	% of calories from fat	calories
OLD-TECH		
Regular blueberry muffin	34	210
Regular oatmeal raisin cookie	41	44
Regular granola bar	38	134
NEW-TECH		
Entenmann's Fat Free Blueberry Muffin	0	150
R.W. Frookie Oatmeal Raisin Fat Free Cookie	0	45
Health Valley Fat Free Granola Bar	0	140

CHOCOLATE BARS

Bars are now being made with two new ingredients. Caprenin, a manufactured fat, provides about half the calories per gram of most fats. Polydextrose, a lower-calorie bulking agent, replaces some of the candies' carbohydrates.

	% of calories from fat	calories
OLD-TECH		
Milky Way *(2.15 oz)*	32	280
Hershey's *(1.55 oz)*	54	240
NEW-TECH		
Milky Way II *(2.05 oz)*	24	190
Hershey's Reduced Calorie and Fat *(1.37 oz; in test marketing)*	30	150

strawberry yogurt, snack-size cans of tuna, and bagels.

At the very least, we should avoid having our snacks make matters worse. Deep inside the Pentagon I meet an air force senior airman whose regular meals are high in fat and cholesterol. For breakfast, he says, he eats ham and cheese omelettes, bacon, toast, juice, and vitamins; for lunch, pizza; and for dinner, fried chicken, mixed vegetables, and rice.

In between? He consumes two Cokes and two bags of Fritos.

While this man looks fit enough, there's no telling what's happening to his arteries. And it wouldn't take a visit to a health food store every afternoon for snacks to become his healthiest meals. Pretzels, gingersnaps, animal crackers, popcorn (unbuttered, that is), bread sticks, and hard candy are *far* less fatty than what he eats all day. Fresh fruit would be even better. Instead of the soda, he could drink fruit juice (not fruit punch or fruit ade, which are mostly sugar water). Instead of the Fritos, he could eat fig bars, graham crackers, or oatmeal raisin cookies, which all have fiber.

COMPENSATE FOR SNACKS IN YOUR WORKOUT OR NEXT MEAL

"If I want a candy bar," says a senior master sergeant in the air force, "I'll flip it over, look at the grams of fat, and figure out how many miles I have to run to work it off." By that measure, after eating a 250-calorie Reese's peanut butter cup he would run 2.5 miles. (In general, you burn about 100 calories for every mile you walk or run.) His other choice? At dinner he could skip the caloric equivalent of a Reese's: an order of French fries or a cup of ice cream.

Here's one way to handle this internal bargaining: Pretend you're carrying around a grocery bag filled with all your day's food—the perfect number of calories (for the average man and woman, 2,200 and 1,600 respectively). You can eat whenever and however much you want until the bag is empty, but that's all you get. If you use up your allotment with high-calorie candy bars and potato chips, you won't need a very big sack. Fill it with lower-calorie fruits, vegetables, whole grain cereals and crackers, and you'll get to eat a lot more before your hand scrapes bottom.

AVOID MINDLESS SPEED-EATING

Perhaps the sole advantage of vending machines is that they force you to consciously get out of your chair, walk to a machine, and pay money for a single item (provided you don't stock up on *several* candy bars).

Less measured eating styles invite disaster. An air force captain cheerfully pulls out the second drawer of his desk to reveal a stash of Brach's mints and Gummy Bears. He tells me he eats them throughout the day for an "energy high." I tell him he's a candidate for "eating amnesia," what happens when your hand goes to your mouth repeatedly without your brain kicking in.

It's a particular problem with itty-bitty snacks. On the Ritz Bits label, for example, a serving is listed as 22 pieces totaling 70 calories. Three calories per bit seems like nothing, and some out of control snackers will keep munching until the box is empty. That's almost as much food as the average woman needs in a day.

Eating too fast is another problem, because it takes 20 minutes from the start of eating before your body can tell your mind that it's had enough. "It's not like putting your hand on a hot stove, and you instantly know it's hot," says Captain Ellen Stoute, an army dietitian at Walter Reed Army Medical Center in Washington, D.C. "If our bodies worked that way, no one would overeat."

INDULGE YOUR DESIRES—
NOW AND THEN

"When I go to a vending machine, I'm usually thinking candy bar," says a woman air force technical sergeant who is a confessed lover of Mars bars. "Sometimes I can even feel my craving."

It's a feeling deep inside all of us. A newborn given a sweetened solution in place of an unsweetened one, say taste researchers, drinks more eagerly—and also looks more contented. So it can be with adults, says Evelyn Tribole. "Don't necessarily swear off all your favorite foods, because deprivation can lead to an overeating backlash. Instead, sit down and savor them."

Sounds reasonable to me. Back in Bar 234, despite the lack of windows, I can tell from my stomach that the day's getting on. I face the machines. Yogurt? (It's got calcium for bones.) Pretzels? (They're low in fat.) Orange juice? (I could use the vitamin C.) The choices seem tortuous.

Then again, maybe not. Smiling, I drop in the coins, remember the part about indulging every once in a while, and press the button . . . for a Reese's.

Exercise and Weight Control

The fitness movement that this country is experiencing began in the early 1970s in response to medical reports that linked Americans' sedentary lifestyle to the rising incidence of cardiovascular disease and obesity. The early advocates of this movement took up jogging and racquet sports as a way to trim off excess pounds and to reduce their risk of coronary heart disease. As the movement grew, so did the diversity of the exercise programs being offered. Many people found that jogging was painful and boring, and the popularity of racquet sports diminished in the face of rising costs and competition for facilities. These factors, coupled with a broadening interest in physical fitness, prompted the exploration and development of numerous fitness programs. With all the choices currently available, one of the biggest problems facing consumers is deciding which one is best. The best fitness program is the one that not only meets your fitness goals, but is enjoyable enough that you will stick with it. The article "Which Exercise Is Best for You?" discusses five of the most common fitness goals and provides a comparative analysis of 18 common fitness activities related to these goals.

We have all heard numerous claims as to the health benefits associated with exercise; however, we may be less clear on exactly how much exercise is necessary to achieve these benefits. For the last 20 years, fitness experts have promoted an exercise regime based on the "no pain, no gain" concept. The basic guidelines of this approach to fitness were as follows: frequency—3 to 5 days a week; duration—20 to 30 minutes of continuous exercise; intensity—60 to 90 percent of one's maximal heart rate. These guidelines, while scientifically valid, were based on studies investigating the impact of exercise on the athletic performance of college-age males. Following these guidelines will indeed yield a physically fit individual, but they have proved to be too demanding for most people to incorporate into their lives. Recently, a new set of guidelines, dubbed "Exercise Lite," has been issued by the U.S. Centers for Disease Control and Prevention in conjunction with the American College of Sports Medicine. These guidelines still call for 30 minutes of exercise 5 days a week, but there any similarity to the old guidelines ends. No mention is made of target heart rates, and the 20 to 30 minutes can be spread over the course of a day, rather than in consecutive minutes. The primary focus of this approach to exercise is improving one's health, not athletic performance. "Exercise Lite" will strengthen your heart and bones and, possibly, add years to your life. Examples of activities that qualify are walking your dog, playing tag with your kids, scrubbing your floors, washing your car, mowing your lawn, weeding your garden, and having sex. From a practical standpoint, this approach to fitness will likely motivate many more people to become active and stay active, because compliance can be accomplished without making substantial changes to one's daily routine. "Fitness Fiction: Working Out the Facts," discusses 10 common misconceptions about exercise that can sabotage your efforts to get into shape.

Everyone knows that exercise is good for you, but most people are not aware of the specific health benefits directly attributable to exercise. The following is a list of the top 10 benefits associated with exercising regularly: reduced risk of coronary heart disease; reduced blood pressure; improved blood cholesterol levels; improved cardiovascular function (increased energy and endurance); enhanced bone density; increased muscle mass (a trimmer physique); enhanced blood glucose regulation; improved flexibility and range of motion; reduced stress (better sleep and enhanced sense of well-being); and an enhancement in immunological function (increased resistance to infectious illnesses). Unfortunately, many of these benefits can take weeks or even months before they become apparent. It is very important, therefore, that an individual chooses an exercise program and sticks with it. While the health benefits associated with low levels of activity are not as great as with higher levels of activity, research now indicates that low to moderate levels of exercise seem to yield the greatest return for the time and energy invested in exercise.

For years researchers have studied the physiological benefits of exercise and have concluded that, in addition to promoting cardiovascular endurance, muscle strength, flexibility, and coordination, exercise can also improve one's outlook on life. While few controlled studies have been conducted regarding the psychological benefits of exercise, numerous individuals have reported enhanced self-esteem, greater self-reliance, decreased anxiety, and relief from mild depression as a result of exercising regularly. At a 1995 symposium in Chicago, several of the nation's top brain researchers met to discuss the effect of exercise on the brain. One conclusion they reached was that aerobic exercise enhances the biological functioning of the brain as measured by the number of neural connections and the richness of the brain's capillary network. These changes appear to translate into enhanced mental functioning as measured by one's capacity to learn and remember.

Even though exercise is widely recognized as an effective means for shedding unwanted body fat, it still rates a distant second to dieting as the method of choice for

UNIT 4

weight control. The obsession that Americans have about their weight is evidenced by statistics indicating that 90 percent of Americans think they should lose weight, and many of these individuals are either currently on a diet or have tried to diet at some point in their lives. Despite our obsession with weight, recent data suggest that for the first time in our history the average American is now overweight when judged according to standard height/weight tables. In addition, more than 25 percent of Americans are clinically obese, and the numbers appear to be growing. One can only wonder how this is possible, given the prevailing attitude that Americans have toward fat. One obvious explanation is that diets do not work and are, in fact, counterproductive. When asked why people go on diets, the predominant answer is for social reasons such as appearance and group acceptance, rather than concerns regarding health. "Fat Times" discusses how it is that Americans are getting fatter despite their apparent preoccupation with weight.

One of the most interesting aspects regarding our obsession with fat is that it is not limited to obese individuals but is shared by many with normal, and even low, body weight. Young women of normal body weight who feel they are fat are of particular concern, because some of them become so obsessed with their body weight that they turn to starvation as a way to control it. This approach to weight control may result in a medical condition known as anorexia nervosa. Still others with distorted body images resort to vomiting and purging their systems with laxatives in an attempt to control their weight. This condition is known as bulimia. Both anorexia and bulimia are serious eating disorders that may have deadly consequences. Judith Rodin, in "Body Mania," discusses the issue of body image and suggests that how we look has become a significant component of our self-worth. Rodin contends that we have become preoccupied with a quest for the perfect body, and in doing so have lost much of the joy and pleasure of life.

America's preoccupation with body weight has given rise to a billion-dollar industry. Unfortunately for most, the money spent on dieting has thinned their bank accounts more than it has their bodies, and the prognosis for keeping pounds off among those who do lose weight is poor. Current statistics indicate that approximately two-thirds of those who lose weight will gain back the pounds they lost, and sometimes more, within a few months or years. Many dieters do not fully understand the biological and behavioral aspects of weight loss, and, as a result, they have unrealistic expectations regarding the process. "Test Your Weight-Loss IQ" by Stephanie Wood addresses several common myths surrounding weight loss.

In 1993 the National Institutes of Health examined several of the leading diet programs in the United States and concluded that most of them were ineffective as long-term weight management programs. The problem with most of the diets is that they are promoted as quick ways to lose weight, and they are not designed to be used as a long-term method of weight control. Programs such as these should generally be avoided for the following reasons: they promote a rapid weight loss (usually water); they tend to be nutritionally unbalanced; unless they include an exercise component, most of the weight lost will be muscle mass and not fat; they provide no long-term approach to maintaining a weight loss; and repeatedly going on and off diets (the yo-yo effect) reduces one's lean muscle mass and not only makes it more difficult to lose weight in the future, but increases the likelihood that the dieter will regain the weight.

Being overweight not only causes health problems, it also carries a social stigma. Overweight people are often thought of as weak-willed individuals with little or no self-respect. The notion that weight-control problems are the result of personality defects is being challenged by new research findings. Evidence is mounting that physiological and hereditary factors may play as great a role in obesity as do behavioral and environmental factors. Researchers now believe that genetics dictate the number of fat cells an individual will have, as well as the location and distribution of these cells within the body. The study of fat metabolism has provided additional clues as to why weight control is so difficult. These metabolic studies have found that the body seems to have a "set point," or desired weight, which it will defend through alterations in basal metabolic rate and fat cell activity. "Gaining on Fat" by W. Wayt Gibbs examines current research regarding how our bodies regulate our weight.

As America strives to contain the high cost of health care, the role that preventive health practices play in the solution will continue to grow. To this end, we must all strive to become more physically active so that we may not only increase our resistance to various disease processes but enhance our capacity to enjoy life. "Exercise Lite" and the concept of achieving your natural ideal body weight suggest that we need to take a more realistic approach to both fitness and weight control and serve to remind us that a healthy lifestyle is based on the concepts of balance and moderation.

Looking Ahead: Challenge Questions

How important is regular exercise to optimal health?

Why should exercise be included in weight-control programs?

What advice would you give to someone who was considering going on a diet to lose weight?

Are Americans too weight-conscious? Explain your response.

How does American society encourage or contribute to weight-control problems? What changes would you suggest?

How do you feel about people who are overweight? Has weight control been a problem for you? If so, what have you done about it?

Fitness fiction: Working out the facts

Misconceptions about exercise can sabotage your efforts to get in shape. Here's the truth behind 10 common myths.

In a recent Op-Ed piece in The New York Times, Martina Navratilova decried one of sport's most persistent myths—that women lack stamina and endurance. That's why their tennis matches are limited to three sets, while men's matches can go five sets. Actually, the physiological differences that make men more muscular than women confer no edge in endurance. Women can exercise at least as hard and long as men can. And they recover from a grueling workout significantly faster than men do.

While scientists and female athletes are finally laying that myth to rest, other antiquated notions about exercise have stubbornly persisted—and new misconceptions keep popping up. Such incorrect notions can discourage you from exercising or lead you to waste time, effort, or money on workouts and products that don't really work. They can even harm your health. Here are the facts about 10 unfounded fears, negative notions, and false hopes about working out.

❶ Myth: While light exercise does yield some benefits, it's not nearly as beneficial as strenuous exercise.

Truth: Strenuous workouts do improve aerobic capacity far more than light or moderate workouts do. While that may improve athletic performance, it does not necessarily translate into a great health advantage.

The death rates from coronary heart disease, cancer, and all causes combined are much lower in moderate exercisers than in nonexercisers; but they're only a little lower in heavy exercisers than in moderate exercisers. The same holds true for the risk of developing type II diabetes, by far the most common kind.

In addition, nonstrenuous exercise seems to reduce stress, anxiety, and blood pressure as effectively as strenuous exercise does. And moderate exercise like walking can do just as much to control weight as vigorous exercise like jogging, since the number of calories burned depends mainly on how much ground you cover, not how fast you cover it. In fact, moderate exercise is potentially more effective than vigorous for most people, since they can walk much farther than they can run.

❷ Myth: You can lose fat from specific parts of your body by exercising those spots.

Truth: There's no such thing as "spot reduction." When you exercise, you use energy produced by burning fat in all parts of your body—not just around the muscles that are doing most of the work. In fact, your genes may dictate that fat disappears from, say, your face or arms before your belly, even if you do endless abdominal exercises. However, working a specific region like the belly can have one site-specific benefit: Strengthening the muscles can make you *look* thinner by helping you hold in your gut.

❸ Myth: The more you sweat during exercise, the more fat you lose.

Truth: The harder you work out, the more calories you'll burn within a given period and thus the more fat you stand to lose. But how much you sweat does not necessarily reflect how hard you're working. Some people tend to sweat profusely due to heavy body weight, poor conditioning, or heredity. And everyone sweats more in hot, dry weather or dense clothing than in cool, humid weather or porous clothing. (You may *feel* as if you're sweating more in humid weather; but that's because moist air slows the evaporation of sweat.)

Exercising in extremely hot weather or in a plastic "weight loss" suit will indeed make you sweat heavily and lose weight immediately. But that lost weight is almost entirely water; the pounds will return when you replenish your fluids by drinking after the workout. Further, you could develop heat exhaustion if you push yourself too hard in extreme heat or in plastic clothes, which prevent sweat from evaporating and, in turn, from cooling you off.

❹ Myth: Sports drinks can help you exercise more safely and effectively.

Truth: Sports drinks contain two main ingredients that are theoretically beneficial for exercisers: sodium, which helps the body retain water, and sugar, which the body burns for energy. But very few

Illustration by Karl Edwards

people exercise hard enough to sweat away much sodium or to use up their carbohydrate reserves, which the body converts to sugar. You'd have to jog for at least two hours, for example, before your carbohydrate stores would start to run low. So unless you're doing a marathon or other exhaustive exercise, plain water is all you need.

More important than finding the ideal drink is making sure you drink enough. The sense of thirst underestimates the need for fluids during and after exercise, particularly in older people. Whatever your age, try to drink two 8-ounce cups of water about two hours before a demanding workout, another cup every 20 minutes during the workout, and an additional cup or two within a half hour after the workout. Or simply drink enough water to make you weigh the same a few hours after the workout as you weighed before.

⑤ Myth: Aerobic exercise tends to make you hungry, so it can actually undermine your efforts to lose weight.

Truth: Aerobic exercise, such as jogging or brisk walking, may indeed increase your appetite—but only, it seems, if you need extra calories. Studies suggest that lean individuals do get hungrier after such exercise; that helps prevent them from getting too thin. In contrast, working out does not seem to boost appetite in obese individuals; so exercise should help them slim down.

⑥ Myth: Strength training won't help you get thinner, since it burns few calories and adds pounds of muscle.

Truth: Strength training, using either weights, machines, or elastic bands, can substantially increase the number of calories you burn. A typical session, in which you rest briefly after each muscle-building maneuver, uses up calories at least as fast as walking does. Circuit training, in which you move quickly from one strengthening maneuver to the next, burns calories faster than walking does. And your body continues to burn extra calories for hours after either type of strength training. More important, the muscle you build consumes calories rapidly, even when you're not exercising.

In one study, three months of strength training boosted the average calorie-burning rate by an average of 7 percent, burned off 4 pounds of fat, and added nearly that much muscle. Since muscle is denser than fat, the volunteers presumably did become thinner. Equally important, they burned off that fat despite a 15 percent increase in their calorie intake. If the researchers hadn't prodded them to maintain their weight by eating more than they felt like eating, the volunteers almost surely would have lost weight.

Strength training is particularly helpful as part of a comprehensive weight-loss program that includes both aerobic exercise—which burns lots of calories during the workout and some calories after the workout—and a moderately low-calorie diet. (Forget crash diets, which almost never work and can be dangerous.) A recent study found that women who ate a moderately restrictive diet and did either strength training or aerobic excercise lost more weight than those who only dieted. But those who split their workout time between strength training and aerobic exercise lost the most weight of all.

⑦ Myth: Strength training builds muscle and bone but does nothing for the heart.

Truth: Strength training plus aerobic exercise may be the ideal exercise regimen not only for the waistline but also for the heart. One analysis of 11 clinical trials found that strength training can reduce levels of LDL cholesterol, the artery-clogging kind (though it has little effect on HDL cholesterol, the artery-clearing kind). Aerobic exercise has a complementary benefit: It improves HDL but does little for LDL. Further, some studies suggest that strength training, like aerobic exercise, may help reduce blood pressure. (But check with your doctor for guidance before starting a muscle-building program if you have hypertension, since straining can temporarily *increase* blood pressure.) One final benefit: By fortifying the muscles, strength training reduces the likelihood that sudden or unaccustomed exertion, such as moving furniture or shoveling snow, will trigger a heart attack.

⑧ Myth: When you stop exercising, your muscles turn to fat.

Truth: Lack of exercise does make the muscles shrink, reducing the body's calorie-burning rate. The lack of activity itself further reduces the number of calories you burn. So people who stop working out are indeed in danger of getting flabby.

But that doesn't mean that muscle actually turns into fat—they're totally different types of tissue. Nor does it mean you're doomed to gain fat *around* the muscles after you stop exercising; you just need to cut back on the calories you consume. (Of course, the best way to stay slim is to eat a lean diet and continue to exercise regularly.)

⑨ Myth: Building muscles reduces flexibility.

Truth: If you strength train without moving your joints through their full range of motion, you can indeed lose flexibility. But strength training can actually improve flexibility if you do move your joints fully. Stretch after a muscle-building workout to help keep yourself limber. (Stretch before as well as after an aerobic workout. For more on stretching, see *CR on Health*'s August 1995 issue.)

⑩ Myth: Strength training tends to give women a bulky, masculine physique.

Truth: It's very difficult for most women to build large muscles. That's because women have relatively low levels of the hormone testosterone, which influences muscle growth. Both men and women can build firmer rather than bulkier muscles by working against lighter resistance more than about 25 times rather than heavier resistance fewer times.

WHICH EXERCISE IS BEST FOR YOU?

The wrong exercises can make you sweat in vain. Here's how to choose the right ones.

Most health-conscious people know the many benefits of exercise—that exercise reduces the risk of disease, increases stamina, builds strength, burns calories, and relieves stress. But they may not know which exercise best suits their particular goals.

An inappropriate exercise can wreck a budding exercise habit. An overweight person who plunges into a vigorous running program, for example, may end up sore—and sorely disappointed—when the exercise proves too hard on overburdened joints and fails to burn off more than a pound or two after a month of panting and sweating.

This report will help you identify the most effective workouts that can enable you to achieve each of the five most important goals of exercise.

1. Preventing disease

Any regular exercise that requires sustained movement, such as walking or bicycling, reduces the risk of several life-threatening diseases, including coronary heart disease, hypertension, diabetes, and possibly cancer. The harder you work out, the greater the reduction in risk. But the sharpest risk reduction occurs when previously inactive people start doing even a little exercise, not when moderately active people start exercising strenuously.

To get that modest, disease-preventing dose of exercise, you don't need to climb into exercise clothes or sweat through formal workouts. Gardening, dancing, even shopping expeditions are all moderately good exercise. You could even squeeze exercise into your daily routine—for example, by walking short distances instead of taking the car, bus, or elevator, or by attacking household chores vigorously. (For more ways to take the boredom and inconvenience out of exercise, see CRH, 7/93).

It's not clear whether strength training helps prevent all the diseases that aerobics do. But strength training may be the best exercise for cutting the risk of osteoporosis, the brittle-bone disease. Strengthening workouts exert much more pressure on the bones, particularly the spine, than nonweight-bearing exercises such as swimming or cycling, or even moderately weight-bearing exercises like walking or jogging. That pressure stimulates the flow of bone-hardening calcium into the skeleton. Indeed, one study, not yet published, found that weight lifters have 15 percent denser spinal bones than either runners or people who don't exercise. While runners had denser thigh bones than inactive people, the weight lifters' thigh bones were even denser than the runners', by an additional 11 percent.

2. Boosting aerobic fitness

Aerobic (or cardiovascular) fitness is the ability of the heart and the lungs to supply the muscles with enough oxygen, so you don't get winded or fatigued when you run for a bus, climb stairs, or walk more than a few blocks. To improve aerobic fitness, you need to work out more often—at least three times per week—than you would to reduce your risk of disease. You also need to exercise more intensely, enough to push your heart rate to between 60 and 90 percent of its maximum rate—a rate calculated by subtracting your age from 220. (Before regularly exercising close to your maximum heart rate, get an O.K. from your doctor.)

Jogging typically pushes the heart rate into that aerobic benefit zone, but it's too demanding for many people, and it puts considerable stress on the knees, shins, and feet. Listed below are some good, low-impact alternatives:

■ **Brisk walking, with arms swinging.** To increase the aerobic benefit, carry 1- to 3-pound hand or wrist weights or walk on hilly terrain rather than on flat roads.

■ **Low-impact aerobic dance.** You can boost the aerobic intensity by increasing the arm movements you make at or above shoulder level. Arm movements make the heart pump blood against the force of gravity.

■ **Swimming.** Note that overweight people may have to work harder to get a good aerobic workout in a swimming pool, since their extra body fat lets them float more easily.

■ **Step aerobics.** This exercise involves stepping on and off a low bench while moving your arms, usually in time to music. (For more information, see CRH, 10/92; or get an instructional video, available at many libraries and video stores.)

■ **Stair-stepping or cross-country-skiing machines.** Using a machine with movable bars that you pump with your hands increases the aerobic benefit of stair stepping. (Stationary cycling machines with movable bars can also provide a good aerobic workout without making you pedal uncomfortably fast.)

People who just want to maintain their current level of fitness can get by with somewhat less exercise than it would take to improve their stamina—say, two workouts per week instead of three or four, 20 minutes per session instead of 30, or 60 percent of the maximum heart rate instead of 70 to 90.

3. Building strength

After age 30 or so, people often begin to lose muscle. When they get older, they may start having trouble with everyday tasks such as opening windows or carrying grocery bags. Worse yet, they may eventually be unable to climb stairs or even walk normally, maintain their balance, or get up out of a chair.

Strength training—mainly weight lifting—can help prevent or reverse that deterioration, even among people in their 80s or 90s. (Weight lifting may even improve aerobic fitness in older people, particularly if they move rapidly from one maneuver to the next, an approach known as circuit training.)

The most effective way to build strength—the ability to lift a heavy suitcase, for example—is to pick a weight you can lift only about six to eight times. (**Warning:** People with high blood pressure should avoid such "power lifting.") To increase endurance—the ability to carry that suitcase for several blocks—pick a lighter weight that you can lift 15 to 20 times. Performing 8 to 12 repetitions of an intermediate weight builds both strength and endurance.

For fastest results, repeat each set of repetitions two or three times, three or four days per week. If you just want to maintain your current strength, you can get by with one set performed twice a week; even a single session per week will slow muscle loss substantially.

Weight machines, barbells, dumbbells, or any heavy object around the house, such as a plastic jug filled with water, can be used to provided resistance for strength training. However, older people, particularly if they're frail, may want to avoid barbells, since they're harder to control and more likely to fall on you.

Strengthening the upper body. For people who don't have much time for exercise, here's a streamlined strength-training regimen, involving just four exercises, that works the major upper-body muscles:

■ **Push-ups.** Lie face down with your palms on the floor beside your shoulders. Without arching your back, push up with your arms to raise your body from your toes. If that's too difficult, push up from your knees or do the exercise in a standing position, leaning forward with your hands against a wall. Stop just before your elbows lock. To make the push-ups harder, elevate your knees or feet.

■ **Biceps curl.** Hold a weight at your side in one hand, palm facing forward. Keeping your elbow stationary, raise the weight to your shoulder, then lower it again.

■ **Upright row.** Hold the weights in front of your thighs, with your palms facing your legs. Raise the weights to your armpits without rotating your wrists, them lower the weights.

■ **Partial sit-ups.** Lie on your back, with your arms at your sides. Bring your knees partway up, keeping your feet flat on the floor. Raise your head and shoulders until your shoulder blades come up off the floor, then return to the starting position. To increase the difficulty, lock your hands behind your head, lift your upper body farther off the ground, or do the sit-ups on an incline, with your buttocks higher than your head.

Strengthening the legs. Aerobic exercise that vigorously works the legs will prevent young and middle-aged people from losing muscle in their lower body. But most older people, as well as younger ones who don't exercise their legs, could benefit from lower-body strength training. Here's a simple, effective exercise for improving leg strength:

■ **Partial squats.** Stand with your back to a wall, with your feet about six inches from the wall and spread slightly beyond shoulder width. Keeping your back against the wall and your feet flat on the floor, slowly crouch down until your thighs are almost parallel to the floor, then return to the starting position.

After age 30, people often start to lose muscle.

4. EXERCISE AND WEIGHT CONTROL

To increase the difficulty, hold a weight in your hands or strapped to your waist. **Warning:** People with knee or back problems should not do partial squats. Taken together, these two exercises are a good alternative:

■ **Leg extension.** Sit in a chair, with your feet on the floor and weights strapped to your ankles. Keeping your thigh stationary, raise one foot by straightening your knee, then bring the foot back down to the floor.

■ **Hamstring curl.** Stand erect, holding the back of a chair and wearing ankle weights. Lift your foot behind you as high as possible by bending your knee, then lower your foot to the floor.

People who want to increase their strength dramatically will need to do more than just those four to six basic exercises. The book "Get in Shape, Stay in Shape," by F. Skip Latella, Winifred Conkling, and the editors of Consumer Reports Books, offers a wide range of muscle-building and other exercises. It's available at most libraries, or you can order it for $17.45 by calling 800-272-0722.

4. Losing weight

It takes two different kinds of exercise to help you shed pounds and keep them off: one to burn a lot of calories, the other to build muscle.

Burning calories. The more vigorously you exercise, the faster your body will burn calories. However, strenuous exercise is not the best way for the average person to lose weight. That's because most people can sustain regular exercise much longer at a moderate pace—and thus burn many more calories overall—than they could keep going at a strenuous pace. In addition, some evidence suggests that the body consumes mainly carbohydrates during intense workouts, while it relies more on fat to fuel prolonged, moderate exercise.

Building up to a program of workouts lasting at least 45 minutes to an hour, four to five times per week, is generally the most effective exercise strategy for slimming down. Bicycling, brisk walking, and even energetic dancing, for example, are good slimming exercises: They're vigorous enough to burn calories at a reasonable clip; at the same time, they're sufficiently moderate, interesting, and easy on the joints that the average person could do them for an extended period. Exercising on a stationary-cycling, stair-stepping, or cross-country-skiing machine set at a low resistance level also allows you to get a prolonged workout.

Swimming, on the other hand, is not a good way to lose fat, for reasons that aren't clear. Some researchers believe that swimming is simply too easy for overweight people, and doesn't burn enough calories; others speculate that the body responds to the cold water by altering its metabolism to preserve its insulating layer of fat. Aerobic dance routines that mainly feature hand and arm movements won't help you lose much weight either, since those muscles are too small to burn many calories.

More muscle, less weight. Muscle helps you stay slim, because it burns calories faster than fat does, even when you're resting. Lifting weights can

HEALTH BENEFITS OF SELECTED ACTIVITIES

	Disease prevention	Aerobic fitness	Muscular strength	Muscular endurance	Weight loss [1]
Gardening	◐	◐	○	◐	◐
Lawn mowing (power push)	◐	◐	○	○	○
Cleaning house	◐	◐	○	○	○
Raking leaves	◐	◐	◐	○	◐
Shopping	◐	●	○	○	○
Walking (leisurely, 2.5 mph)	◐	◐	●	◐	○
Walking (brisk, 4 mph)	◉	◉	◐	○	◉
Jogging (6 mph)	◉	◉	○	○	◐
Bicycling (10 mph)	◉	○	○	○	◉
Cross country skiing (slow)	◉	◉	○	◐	◉
Aerobic dance, low impact (moderate)	◉	◉	◐	○	◐
Step aerobics (moderate)	◉	◉	○	◐	◉
Tennis (doubles)	◐	◐	●	◐	○
Tennis (singles)	◉	○	○	○	◐
Golf (18 holes, with hand cart)	◐	◐	◐	◐	○
Strength training (high weight, few repetitions)	[2]	◐	◉	○	◐ [3]
Strength training (low weight, many repetitions)	[2]	○	◐	◉	◐ [3]
Circuit strength training	[2]	◐	◐	◐	◐ [3]

[1] Based on how effectively each exercise would help the average overweight person lose weight or keep it off.
[2] Studies have not determined whether strength training reduces the risk of diseases other than osteoporosis.
[3] These exercises help control weight mainly by building muscle and boosting metabolism.

◉ ◐ ○ ◐ ●
Better ←→ Worse

EXERCISES FOR SPECIAL AILMENTS

People who have a chronic disorder need a specially tailored exercise program that provides maximal benefit with minimal risk. Here's how to choose the right exercise—and, with your doctor's help, take the right precautions—if you have arthritis, diabetes, or hypertension, three of the most common chronic ailments.

Arthritis

People with arthritis, particularly rheumatoid arthritis, should stretch the affected joints every day, even when those joints are inflamed. It's also important to strengthen the joints: Start with isometric exercises, in which you tense the muscles without moving the joint; if possible, progress to isotonic exercises, such as weight lifting. When you have little or no pain and inflammation, work on improving stamina by doing low-impact aerobic exercises such as walking, cycling, swimming, or dancing.

Two particularly safe and effective workouts are calisthenics in a heated pool and t'ai chi, a relaxing exercise that features slow, sweeping movements. (For more information on exercise and arthritis, see CRH, 9/93; or contact your local chapter of the Arthritis Foundation, or call the national office at 800-283-7800.)

Diabetes

Aerobic exercise can help control diabetes directly, by improving the body's use of sugar, as well as indirectly, by facilitating weight loss. Exercise is safest and most effective for people with type II diabetes (once called "adult-onset" diabetes), the most common form of the disease. But certain precautions are still essential:

■ If you're over age 35, ask your doctor for an exercise stress test to check for coronary heart disease, a common complication of diabetes.

■ If you have eye or nerve damage, choose low-impact exercises such as cycling or swimming. Jarring exercises like jogging can burst weakened blood vessels in the eye or injure a nerve-damaged foot that no longer sends pain signals to warn of impending damage. Before and after workouts that put stress on your feet, check them for breaks in the skin, blisters, redness, or swelling.

■ Monitor your blood-sugar levels carefully before and after exercising.

■ Don't lift heavy weights. Straining raises blood pressure and can damage the blood vessels.

Hypertension

Regular aerobic exercise produces temporary and possibly lasting reductions in blood pressure. Moderately intense exercise, between 60 and 70 percent of your maximum heart rate (see story), actually lowers your blood pressure more effectively than intense exercise does. Moreover, strenuous exertion, either from aerobic exercise or from lifting heavy weights, can push blood pressure to dangerously high levels during the workout.

---

build muscle or at least counter the tendency of a low-calorie diet to shrink muscle along with the fat. And since muscle is denser than fat, you can trim your profile without even losing any weight simply by replacing a large amount of body fat with a smaller amount of muscle.

In addition to doing the strengthening exercises described above, overweight individuals may want to focus on two frequently neglected muscle groups—the gluteus maximus and the thigh adductors—that can help improve your appearance by firming up the buttocks and inner thighs:

■ **Gluteal lifts.** Crouch down on your hands and knees, with your back straight and your hands directly below your shoulders. Slide one knee straight back. Keeping that knee on the floor, bend it 90° to raise your foot. Now lift that leg as high as possible, keeping the knee bent; hold that position for several seconds, then return your knee to the floor. Repeat with the other leg. To increase the difficulty, wear ankle weights.

■ **Inner-thigh lifts.** Lie on your back with your arms by your sides. Lift both legs straight upwards, bending your knees, if necessary, and spread your legs to form roughly a 45° "V." Then separate your legs as wide as possible without discomfort, and slowly bring them back to the original V position. Again, ankle weights will increase the difficulty.

5. Easing stress

Numerous studies have shown that working out reduces anxiety, muscle tension, and blood pressure—three measures of stress—for at least several hours and possibly much longer. Other studies suggest that exercise may ease moderate depression and help people stay calm when they're under pressure.

Aerobic exercise improves mood and eases stress better than strength training and most other nonaerobic exercises. (Yoga and t'ai chi, a martial art that features slow sweeping movements, may also fight stress effectively.) Some people even report that aerobic exercise gives them an exhilarated feeling—the so-called runner's high.

But any exercise that gives you a sense of accomplishment, boosts your confidence, or simply diverts you from your everyday problems can help you feel better—provided you don't turn it into a distasteful chore by pushing yourself too hard. Since the emotional lift may start to fade after several hours, try to exercise often and to time your workouts for maximum impact. If you feel anxious at work, for example, try exercising in the morning; if you have trouble sleeping, exercise in the late afternoon or early evening (though not within three hours of bedtime, which can make it difficult to fall asleep).

Fat Times

What health craze? Thanks to too much food and too little sweat, Americans are heavier than ever

Philip Elmer-Dewitt

While they were happening, the '80s seemed so darned healthy. Joggers and bicyclists clogged the pathways. Exercise spas threw open their glass doors and mirrored chambers. Folks didn't just watch their weight, they also enrolled in diet movements, diet 12-step programs and diet franchises complete with celebrity TV endorsements and calorically correct prepackaged snacks, meals and desserts. Even the Christmas turkey seemed somehow leaner.

But when scientists finally put a representative sampling of Americans on the scale, the decade's secret scandal was uncovered: rather than getting healthy in the health-conscious '80s, Americans actually plumped out. It's not just that individuals got heavier as they got older, although they did: the average weight gain between ages 30 and 39 is 4 lbs. for men and 9 lbs. for women. It's that fortysomethings are now heavier than fortysomethings were 10 years ago, thirtysomethings now are heavier than thirtysomethings then, and so on down the demographic ladder.

In fact, the latest results from a long-term study conducted by the federal Centers for Disease Control and Prevention show that the number of Americans who are seriously overweight, after holding steady for 20 years at about a quarter of the population, jumped to one-third in the 1980s, an increase of more than 30%. According to a report in the *Journal of the American Medical Association*, some 58 million people in the U.S. weigh at least 20% more than their ideal body weight—making them, in the unforgiving terminology of dietary science, obese.

"All of us were stunned," says Dr. Albert Stunkard, a psychiatrist at the University of Pennsylvania and a leading expert on what makes people put on pounds. "It runs counter to what we as a nation seem to be doing." In a sharply worded *JAMA* editorial, Dr. F. Xavier Pi-Sunyer of New York City's St. Luke's–Roosevelt Hospital sounded the medical alarm, pointing out that the extra baggage is not just unsightly but unhealthy as well. Pi-Sunyer says the plumping of America will put millions of

> **7-ELEVEN**
> **Double Gulp**
> Size: 64 oz. Calories: 768
> Jump in size:
> 45% more than Super Big Gulp

people at an increased risk for diabetes, hypertension, heart disease, stroke, gout, arthritis and some forms of cancer. "If this were about tuberculosis," he observes, "it would be called an epidemic."

Moreover, there are alarming signs that the next generation may be in even worse shape by the time it comes of age. The percentage of teens who are overweight, which held steady at about 15% through the 1970s, rose to 21% by 1991. "The kids eat nothing but junk food," says Liam Hennessey, a special-ed teacher from San Francisco who watches students on school trips open the lunches their parents pack for them, gobble up the Oreos and Pop-Tarts and toss out the sandwiches.

These issues always seem particularly sobering in the wake of the holidays—after those Thanksgiving dinners, Christmas parties and New Year's revelries have conspired to undermine whatever remained of the previous year's resolutions. But this year the situation may be worse than ever. According to a CNN/*Prevention* magazine poll of 771 Americans taken just before the holidays, nearly 70% said they planned to go ahead and eat whatever they wanted. Most took it for granted that they would put on weight—nearly 5 lbs. on average. Fully 40% also said they expected to take it off in the New Year, but that may not be as easy as they think. As many a thickening boomer can attest, those pounds just get harder and harder to lose.

In 1990 the U.S. Department of Health unveiled the Healthy People 2000 Goals, as ambitious framework of 22 programs aimed at disease prevention. One goal was to reduce the percentage of overweight Americans from 25% to 20% by the turn of the century. It was, for the Bush Administration, an unusually activist experiment in preventive medicine, with the added purpose of helping curb health costs. Now the U.S. is not only unlikely to meet that target, says Robert Kuczmarski, lead author of the big CDC study, "but it's going in the opposite direction." Just when the country needs to reduce its health-care bills, its eating habits may be pushing costs higher.

Food is now dished out in **humongous** portions that would satisfy Godzilla

How could this happen? How could the health movement, which seemed to be chugging along so energetically, have backfired? There is no shortage of theories. Weight-loss tycoon Jenny Craig blames the news media. "They pushed one diet, then the other," she says. "Now they broadcast that diets don't work." Exercise guru Richard Simmons fingers TV advertising. "It's crazy," he says. "The ads say 'eat, eat, eat!' but show a girl who's so thin she clearly never eats." Julia Child, TV's French chef (no caloric slouch herself), cites sedentary life-styles. "Maybe they're not doing enough in the way of activity," she speculates. "Maybe they don't have jobs. Maybe they're not doing anything but sitting around eating."

And maybe it has something to do with what they're eating: those orders of fettuccine Alfredo that the Center for Science in the Public Interest calls "a heart attack on a plate," or those tubs of greasy movie-theater popcorn, which pack four days' worth of fat into a container nearly as big as a fire bucket, or those servings of extra-rich Häagen-Dazs Triple Brownie Overload, each of which contains 44 grams of fat—the artery clogging equivalent of half a stick of butter.

Nutritionists say it really boils down to this: despite all the fuss about diet and fitness, Americans in the '80s ate too much and exercised too little. In thermodynamic terms, they took in more calories than they burned, and they stored the excess as fat.

But why that is so, and why it finally hit home in the middle of what everybody thought was a fitness craze, is harder to explain. It's a complex story, experts say, one that pits a lucrative diet industry against an even bigger and more aggressive packaged-food industry. It pits a handful of exercise machines against a century of labor-saving devices. It pits a frenetic workaday pace against the understandable temptation to put one's feet up at the end of the day, turn on the tube and just veg out. It may even turn out that the best-intentioned resolutions made in the '80s—to lose weight, to eat "lite," to plunge headlong into heart-pounding aerobics—ended up doing more harm than good.

SATURDAY NIGHT AT THE CHEESECAKE FACtory in Atlanta: the restaurant is packed with customers waiting up to an hour and a half to stuff themselves with slices of fat-laden cheesecake so thick that most will be forced to take home a doggy bag. A half-pound slice of cheesecake may contain 700 calories—roughly a third of an adult's recommended daily allowance. Manager Michael Moore notes that the Factory's reduced-calorie cheesecakes languished on the shelves when they were introduced last year. "If people want cheesecake, they don't want 'lite,'" he says. "They come to our restaurant to mow."

Americans, it seems, have been mowing with abandon lately. A thesis about why so many have gained so much weight puts the blame squarely on America's huge, well-oiled, heavily advertised food industry. There may be salad bars at the local fast-food joints, but to find them customers have to run a gauntlet of starchy, beefy delights and breathe air perfumed with the scent of rendered lard. According to the Agriculture Department, the food and restaurant industries spend $36 billion a year on advertisements designed to entice hungry people to forgo fresh fruit and sliced vegetables for Ring Dings and Happy Meals. The average child, says psychologist Kelly Brownell, head of the Yale University Center for Eating and Weight Disorders, watches 10,000 food ads a year on TV. "And they're not seeing commercials for brussels sprouts," Brownell complains. "They're seeing soft drinks, candy bars, sugar-coated cereals and fast food."

McDONALD'S
Super-Size Fries
Size: 6.2 oz. Calories: 540
Jump in size:
20% bigger than large fries

Drive-through windows and 7-Elevens just make things worse. Takeout-food consumption climbed sharply in the 1980s—up about 13%, according to a Roper poll—as Americans found themselves with less and less time to prepare meals. That represents a triple whammy on the waistline: 1) takeout food tends to be high in fat, carbohydrates, sodium and calories; 2) it tends to be eaten quickly, which means more of it is consumed; and 3) it tends to get *eaten*, all of it, no matter how much of it there is. "I've found that people have no idea what they're eating," says Claudia Plaisted, a dietitian at Duke University's Center for Living, a health camp for adults. "They just eat until they clean their plates."

Given the size of the servings these days, that is an increasingly dangerous practice. Food that used to be delivered in modest quantities is now dished out in hu-

NESTLE
King-Size Butterfinger
Size: 3.8 oz. Calories: 510
Jump in size:
80% bigger than a regular bar

mongous portions that would satisfy Godzilla. Graphing the size of McDonald's largest burgers, from the Big Mac to the Double Quarter Pounder and the Triple Cheeseburger, is like watching America's appetite grow before your eyes. And yet that seems downright modest compared with the bloat at movie-theater concessions stands, where candy bars have tripled in size since the '70s. "It's a food and utensil explosion," says Gail Frank, a professor of nutrition at California State University at Long Beach. "For a thousand years we had one glass size—8 oz. Then in a decade it's quadrupled in size!"

How can the school nutritionist compete against BigFoot pizzas and Super-Size fries? The $50,000 the U.S. government allots each state annually to teach kids to eat right is lost next to the billions spent designing food and packaging that will ring the kids' Pavlovian bells. A telling statistic: Kellogg's in 1993 spent $32 million advertising a single product: Frosted Flakes. By comparison, last year the produce industry spent $55 million on an educational program to promote its entire product line, from asparagus to zucchini.

This kind of comparison, however, is too simplistic. The reasons people eat what they eat, and as much as they eat, go deeper than government programs, nutrition classes or even the ads on TV.

Look at it from a psychological point of view. According to Dr. Lawrence Cheskin, director of the Johns Hopkins Weight Management Center, "We eat out of emotional

4. EXERCISE AND WEIGHT CONTROL

Could all those diets have **backfired**?

needs. We eat when we're happy, we eat when we're sad. We've grown up in a way that food is a substitute for many other things." Or as an eating-disorder sufferer put it, "When I get depressed, I eat fat. It coats my nerves and numbs the pain."

The truth is that for many Americans, the '80s and '90s have been tough. Malaise. Recession. Unemployment. Double employment. The decline of the family. The rise of AIDS. The real epidemic, says Dr. Dean Ornish, author of the best-selling *Eat More, Weigh Less,* is not obesity but what he calls "emotional and spiritual heart disease." "There's been such a radical shift in our culture," he says. "People feel lonely, isolated and alienated."

But like the last recession (and, for that matter, the economic recovery), America's new heft is not evenly distributed. The bone-thin models in the fashion ads seem to live only in slivers of the U.S. along the two coasts—primarily in New York City and Los Angeles. The people in the country's midsection, points out Dr. Michael Jensen, who treats obese people at Minnesota's Mayo Clinic, tend to be beefier. "There's a lot less social pressure to maintain a lean weight in the Midwest," he says.

As anybody who travels widely in America will attest, there are deep pockets of obesity, especially in rural areas and among certain racial and ethnic groups. The CDC study found that the prevalence of obesity was nearly 50% for black and Mexican-American women—compared with 33.5% for white women. In some Native American communities, up to 70% of adults are dangerously overweight.

In all groups, genetic factors play a role. Scientists have known for years that twins separated at birth are far more likely to grow into the body types of their genetic kin than to resemble their adoptive parents. And last November researchers at Rockefeller University reported that they had discovered a defective gene that disrupts the body's "I've had enough to eat" signaling system and may be responsible for at least some types of obesity. But genetic traits alone cannot explain the American weight trend. As Dr. George Bray, editor of the journal *Obesity Research,* points out, "Our genes haven't changed in the past 10 years."

One thing that has changed is the cost of eating right. "Junk food is pretty cheap," notes San Francisco lawyer Peter Haley. A Burger King meal may be more expensive than one that is home cooked, but calorie for calorie, burgers are cheaper than the salad bar or the fare at fancier restaurants that serve vegetables. And eating out is a lot easier than chopping broccoli and cauliflower in your own kitchen.

"No woman can be too rich or too thin," goes the old saying. Pity, then, America's underclasses, who are not only poor but heavy—or at least they have been since 1965, when a landmark study showed that the rate of obesity among the lowest economic brackets was five times as great as among the highest.

In many other cultures it's just the reverse: the rich are fat and the poor are emaciated. Anthropologist George Armelagos of Emory University calls it the Henry the Eighth syndrome, referring to the corpulent King of England who lived so well off the labor of his peasantry. "Think about how many people had to work to make the King the size that he was," says Armelagos. Being rotund is still a sign of prosperity and prestige in Polynesia and parts of Africa.

Food was money for mankind's first million years or so. When it is plentiful, the body—for sound physiological reasons—stores the excess away as fat, biology's own energy reserve. It's no accident that fat adds taste to food; evolution reinforces the body's urge to eat the things it needs to survive. In peasant villages, people instinctively gain weight in the summer and burn it off in the winter. Laboratory animals will eat Crisco right out of the can.

The advent of agriculture upset the balance of nature, creating food surpluses.

LOEWS THEATERS
Large Popcorn
Size: 130 fl. oz. Calories: 864
Jump in size:
50% bigger than medium

And the practice of fattening animals for slaughter consolidated those surpluses into the dietary equivalent of a gold brick: the thick juicy steak, marbled with fat.

What You Should Aim For

WOMEN Height	Weight in lbs.* from — to	MEN Height	Weight in lbs.* from — to
4'9"	106 — 118	5'1"	126 — 136
4'10"	108 — 120	5'2"	128 — 138
4'11"	110 — 123	5'3"	130 — 140
5'0"	112 — 126	5'4"	132 — 143
5'1"	115 — 129	5'5"	134 — 146
5'2"	118 — 132	5'6"	137 — 149
5'3"	121 — 135	5'7"	140 — 152
5'4"	124 — 138	5'8"	143 — 155
5'5"	127 — 141	5'9"	146 — 158
5'6"	130 — 144	5'10"	149 — 161
5'7"	133 — 147	5'11"	152 — 165
5'8"	136 — 150	6'0"	155 — 169
5'9"	139 — 153	6'1"	159 — 173
5'10"	142 — 156	6'2"	162 — 177
		6'3"	166 — 182

*Medium build, without clothing
Source: Metropolitan Life Insurance Co.

Nowhere else are those steaks (served rare, chicken-fried, chopped or charbroiled) so affordable for so many as in the U.S., whose farms and slaughterhouses produce an average of 3,700 calories a day for every man, woman and child—a third more than the recommended daily allowance for men and twice that for women. With the price of beef falling, Americans last year ate nearly 64 lbs. per person—the highest consumption level in five years—and that number is expected to increase again this year. No wonder America has become the fat Polynesian prince of the world, the 20th century's answer to Henry the Eighth.

But all this talk of food ignores the other side of the weight-gain equation. Most Americans are bulging not just because they consume too many calories but also because they burn off too few. In fact, people are eating less now than their ancestors did at the turn of the century, when the rate of obesity was much lower than it is today. What has occurred, says Mayo's Jensen, is a century of invention and industrial development. Technology has taken the majority of people out of fields and factories and plopped them behind desks—and in front of computers. "With more and more conveniences," says Jensen, "we're doing less and less manual work."

THE AUTOMOBILE, OF COURSE, IS A culprit, along with an astonishing array of other inventions: elevators, escalators, garage-door openers, food processors, push-button telephones, drive-in windows and a drawerful of remote controls. "It used to be that when you'd watch TV, you'd at least have to use some energy to get up and change the channel," complains pediatrician Dr. William Dietz of the New England Medical Center in Boston.

If the so-called information highway ever gets built, things could get worse. "My husband has gained 10 lbs. since he got his laptop," says Maria McIntosh, a dietitian at the Pritikin Longevity Center in Santa Monica, California, who feels the highway has already arrived at her home. "We're all glued to machines. We're on information overload."

Americans who hold desk jobs and want to burn off extra calories have to do it the hard way: by willing themselves to play organized sports, to go to aerobics classes, to climb onto the StairMaster. But that willpower seems to be flagging. Despite the continued presence of joggers and Rollerbladers on the sidewalks and streets, trend watchers say the exercise movement peaked in the '80s and then headed south. "It's now a 'screw-it' attitude," says pop prognosticator Faith Popcorn. "Consumers are having a secret bacchanal. 'I'll eat,' they say. 'I'll have a drink. I won't exercise.'"

Indeed, the CDC reported that in 1991 58% of U.S. adults said they exercised sporadically or not at all. The inactivity was especially marked among blacks, Hispanics, low-income people and the unemployed, according to another CDC study. Even school gym classes, which for generations forced even the laziest students to huff and puff at least once or twice a week, are becoming a thing of the past. Only 36% of U.S. schools still offer daily phys-ed classes.

Meanwhile, many of the steps Americans have been taking to get in shape and lose weight seem to have backfired. Take dieting, for example. Each year an estimated 80 million Americans go on a diet, but no matter how much weight they lose, 95% gain it back within five years. A major problem, say nutrition experts, is that most people perceive their diets as temporary restrictions imposed from outside. As soon as the diet is over, they slip back into their old habits—putting on the weight they lost and more. "We've got to stop the dieting mentality," says Carolyn Bernardi, program director for the Outpatient Nutrition Center at the Georgetown University Medical Center. "The long-term track record of success for these weight-loss programs is abysmal."

The explosion of "lite" and "reduced-calorie" foods may also have raised the needle on the scale. People often forget that reduced-calorie foods are not calorie-free. Cathy DeThorne, a research director at the Leo Burnett advertising agency, ran a series of focus-group studies for the Beef Industry Council that suggest that when it comes to food, people show an almost infinite capacity for self-delusion. A woman believed she was eating a low-fat diet because she was pouring the fat off her pork chops. Others forsook meat for healthy salads, and then drowned those salads in dressings that contained more fat than the meat they gave up.

Exercise itself has come under attack. Penn's Stunkard suspects that the fitness movement was too narrowly focused, hitting mostly the upper and upper-middle classes and missing the rest of the population. Kathy Smith, a Hollywood fitness expert, thinks aerobics and weight lifting scared a lot of people away. "The exercise message of the 1980s was too strong, too high impact," says Smith. "We ended up with a select group of élite exercisers with hard bodies." The proper message, most health experts now agree, is to set aside time for regular, moderate exercise—bicycling, climbing steps, walking briskly to work.

The Surgeon General's campaign against cigarettes also seems to have contributed to the bulging of America. Millions of people have given up smoking, driving annual per capita cigarette consumption by adults from its peak of 4,345 in 1963 to 2,493 last year, according to the American Health Foundation. And when people quit smoking, they usually gain weight—4 to 6 lbs. on average. But health officials are quick to point out that while those extra pounds may harm your health, cigarettes are even more damaging. Most doctors advise patients that a bit of additional weight is a small price to pay for kicking the smoking habit.

"YOU'RE NOT FAT," SAYS NATalie Tolbert, 26, to a friend who has just ordered chicken nuggets, waffle fries, a soft drink and a brownie from an Atlanta fast-food joint. "You're pleasantly plump." More and more Americans are couching their excess in euphemism these days, and they're not necessarily ashamed of it. "Obviously I don't care," says Tolbert, gesturing to her ample figure and equally ample lunch. "I don't care because I find most men I go out with like a woman with some meat on her body."

So does Laura Eljaiek, program director for the National Association to Advance Fat Acceptance, a lobby group that fights weight discrimination. "Fat is a natural state for most women," says Eljaiek. "We feel people should accept their weight without shame or denial."

There is some truth to what NAAFA teaches. And it is certainly unfortunate that some teenage girls have taken to binging and purging and starving themselves to keep their weight in check. But health officials warn that drifting into obesity may be just as dangerous in the long run. The growing prevalence of both extremes suggests America is struggling with something akin to a national eating disorder. "The society is dysfunctional," says Robin Wes, founder of the Little Gym fitness centers for children. "We are eating out of whack."

The situation is not beyond hope. Americans have been persuaded to change their eating and drinking habits in the past, when the message was clear and the alternatives palatable and affordable. There is 4% less cholesterol in the U.S. diet today than there was 15 years ago. Illegal drug use by adults is down. People are even drinking less hard liquor than they used to, although alcohol still accounts for 5% to 7% of the daily caloric intake of American men.

But it's one thing to switch from martinis to white wine or from saturated fat to unsaturated fat, and quite another to adopt moderation as a permanent life-style. The hardest challenge, perhaps, is to eat and drink just what your body needs, and not one ounce more.

Restraint and self-awareness have never been America's strong suits. How can one teach people to listen to their body? To eat when they're hungry, to taste what they're eating, to eat appropriate portions, to leave food on the plate? Deep, lasting behavioral changes cannot be imposed from the outside. They are internal battles. Before they can be won externally, they will have to be fought internally—one unsightly, unhealthy bulge at a time. —*Reported by Janice M. Horowitz and Lawrence Mondi/New York, Ken Myers/Cleveland, Bonnie I. Rochman/Atlanta, Martha Smilgis/Los Angeles and Richard Woodbury/Houston*

Test Your Weight-Loss IQ

Are you sure you know the facts about how to lose weight? Here's a look at the myths—and realities—of weight loss.

Stephanie Wood

STEPHANIE WOOD *is a freelance writer and editor in Blauvelt, N.Y. She has written for* Child, McCall's, *and* Bridal Guide.

You hear it all the time. You've probably even said it yourself: "I'll do anything to lose weight!" That sentiment fuels researchers—both legitimate and shady—in their search for secrets to simple weight loss. It also leads to almost daily news flashes about gimmicks, gurus, and gadgets that guarantee to help you melt off pounds and give you the body you've always dreamed of—without effort.

Has your desperation to take off weight led you to believe some of the latest less-than-believable news reports? Don't feel ashamed. Weight loss is a $30 billion to $50 billion industry in the United States, so a lot of money is spent trying to win your trust and your dollars. And let's face it: We'd all like an easy fix, so when we hear no-effort weight loss promises, no matter how absurd they may be, our ears perk up.

But to lose weight successfully, you must be firmly grounded in reality—and with so many conflicting claims, that's not always easy. Not sure what to believe? The following reality check will help you separate weight-loss fact from fiction. Plus, these strategies for success will help you have the body you're after—without resorting to gimmicks.

Myth: If you have a slow metabolism, you can't lose weight.
Reality: While recent research has shown that certain people do have a more difficult time dropping excess pounds, almost everyone can succeed with a carefully controlled program of diet and exercise. "Those people who do have a slower metabolism just need to increase their exercise to make up the difference," emphasizes John Foreyt, Ph.D., director of the Behavioral Medicine Research Center at Baylor College of Medicine in Houston.
Strategy: Speed up your metabolism with exercise. The more active you are the more muscle you build, the more efficient your metabolism will become.

Myth: When you are walking for weight loss, you need to walk fast enough to pant and break a sweat.
Reality: "You will burn calories whether you walk moderately, mildly, or intensely," explains Arlette Perry, Ph.D., director of the Human Performance Lab at the University of Miami in Florida. True, the faster you walk, the more calories you burn. But what matters most is building an everyday exercise habit. It is better to take frequent slower walks if speedy walks will wear you out.
Strategy: Walk as quickly as is comfortable. If you walk slowly, take longer, more frequent walks in order to burn more calories. And try to walk every day, even if just for a few minutes.

Myth: If your parents are overweight, you're sure to be, too.
Reality: For an unfortunate 80% of children born into overweight families, this statement will become a reality. But it doesn't have to be, according to Ronette L. Kolotkin, Ph.D., director of the behavioral program at the Duke University Diet and Fitness Center in Durham, N.C. Part of the problem is that overweight parents pass on bad eating and exercise habits, as well as their genes. Chances are fairly good that you also have inherited your parents' bad habits, not their bad genes.
Strategy: Stop blaming Mom and Dad, and change your bad habits. Even if you are genetically inclined to be overweight, you can still be healthy if you eat right and exercise regularly.

Myth: The fewer calories you consume, the more weight you'll lose.
Reality: To a certain extent, this statement is true—but then it becomes false. According to Georgia Kostas, M.P.H., R.D., director of nutrition at the Cooper Clinic in Dallas and author of *The Balancing Act Nutrition & Weight Guide* (Balancing Act Nutrition Books, 1996), calorie-cutting quickly reaches a point

19. Test Your Weight-Loss IQ

of diminishing returns. "You won't lose weight if you keep cutting calories, because your body will go into a starvation mode, slowing your metabolism down," she notes.

Strategy: Never eat fewer than 1,200 calories a day.

Myth: Since muscle weighs more than fat, you shouldn't build muscle if you're trying to lose weight.

Reality: While muscle does weigh more than fat, it also requires your body to burn calories to maintain it—even when you're not exercising. "Building muscle speeds up your metabolism," says Kostas, so even long after your exercise session is over and you're lazing in a hammock with the latest Jackie Collins novel, you're body is still working and burning calories. Of course, you should also couple strength training with aerobic exercise for maximum fat-burning benefits, she adds. Building muscle gives another benefit, as well: A body with strong muscles looks good even if it's not particularly slim.

Strategy: Add strength training to your weekly fitness regimen. Even 15 minutes of weight training three or four times a week can build the calorie-burning muscle you need.

Myth: There are good foods and bad foods, and when you diet, you can only have good foods.

Reality: "There are no good foods or bad foods, only good diets and bad diets," notes Foreyt. "Any food can be worked into a healthy eating plan and should be. If you can't live without cookies, plan to have a few a week and make up for the calories somewhere else."

Strategy: Try to avoid foods that are high in fat and calories and low in nutrients. If you do indulge, cut fat and calories elsewhere.

Myth: Exercise makes you hungry, so you eat more and gain more when you work out.

Reality: You may eat a little more if you exercise, but you can still lose weight. Why? Exercise increases your metabolic rate, so you burn calories faster all the time, Perry says.

Strategy: If you feel hungry after exercising, fuel up with a high-carbohydrate snack such as a piece of fruit or some whole-wheat toast, and don't sweat a few extra calories.

Myth: Lowfat cookies are always a better choice than regular cookies.

Reality: Lowfat foods are often high in calories—especially dessert-type items —because they're loaded with sugar, says Foreyt. In fact, some lowfat sweets have nearly as many calories as their full-fat counterparts. Snacks that are low in fat save calories only when you eat them in moderation.

Strategy: Don't assume that because something is labeled "lowfat" it is a calorie bargain. Think—and read—before you eat.

Myth: If you crave a fattening food when you're trying to lose weight, try to distract yourself—the craving will eventually go away.

Reality: You can and should give in to cravings occasionally. Otherwise, feelings of deprivation will set in, and you'll want the food even more.

Strategy: If you crave something, eat a small amount of it, and the craving should subside.

Myth: It's easier for men to keep weight off than it is for women.

Reality: Men may have an edge when it comes to losing unwanted pounds, but they are no better than women at keeping those pounds off. "The literature suggests that men do drop more pounds in weight-control programs," says Foreyt, but that's because they are often bigger to begin with, and they tend to have a lower percentage of body fat and a greater percentage of muscle than women. "However, neither sex has an advantage when it comes to keeping weight off."

Strategy: Don't compare yourself to others. Find an exercise and eating plan that works for you, and do some strength training to build your own muscular advantage.

Myth: The best way to lose weight is to eat only three times a day.

Reality: Small frequent meals keep you from ever getting too hungry. "Unsuccessful dieters tend to starve themselves all day and then binge at night," says Foreyt. "Instead, some people need to eat often to reduce their feelings of hunger and deprivation." In addition, "if you eat regularly spaced meals, your blood sugar levels stabilize, and you won't crave foods like chocolate as a result of low blood sugar," Kostas says.

Strategy: Spread meals and snacks throughout the day. Snack on healthful foods such as nonfat yogurt, fresh fruit, raw vegetables, or unbuttered popcorn.

Myth: Over time, diet is more important than exercise in a weight-loss program.

Reality: Exercise can mean the difference between permanent weight loss and another flip of the weight-loss yo-yo. When you exercise, you not only get calorie-burning benefits, but you may also begin to eat more healthfully because you feel good about yourself, says Foreyt. He studied two groups of people who were trying to lose weight: One group only dieted, and the other only exercised. Foreyt found that while it takes longer to lose weight through an exercise-only plan, exercisers are far more likely to keep the weight off for a long period of time. "An important way to maintain weight loss is by exercising, and walking is one of the best exercises you can do," he adds.

Strategy: If you spend more time walking, you can spend less time obsessing over calories. Plus, you'll improve your cardiovascular fitness, reduce your risk of disease, and feel better about yourself.

Gaining on Fat

As a costly epidemic of obesity spreads through the industrial world, scientists are uncovering the biological roots of this complex disease. The work offers tantalizing hope of new ways to treat, and prevent, the health risks of excess weight

W. Wayt Gibbs, *staff writer*

Throughout most of human history, a wide girth has been viewed as a sign of health and prosperity. It seems both ironic and fitting, then, that corpulence now poses a growing threat to the health of many inhabitants of the richest nations. The measure of the hazard in the U.S. is well known: 59 percent of the adult population meets the current definition of clinical obesity, according to a 1995 report by the Institute of Medicine, easily qualifying the disease for epidemic status. Epidemiologists at Harvard University conservatively estimate that treating obesity and the diabetes, heart disease, high blood pressure and gallstones caused by it rang up $45.8 billion in health care costs in 1990, the latest year studied. Indirect costs because of missed work pitched another $23 billion onto the pile. That year, a congressional committee calculated, Americans spent about $33 billion on weight-loss products and services. Yet roughly 300,000 men and women were sent early to their graves by the damaging effects of eating too much and moving too little.

The problem is as frustrating as it is serious. Quick and easy solutions—liquid diets, support groups, acupressure, appetite-suppressing "aroma sticks" and even the best-intentioned attempts to eat less and exercise more—have all failed in well-controlled trials to reduce the weight of more than a small fraction of their obese adherents by at least 10 percent for five years—an achievement shown to increase life expectancy sharply.

The discovery last summer of leptin, a natural hormone that cures gross obesity when injected into mutant mice that lack it, raised hopes of a better quick fix. Those hopes have faded as subsequent studies have found no fat people who share the leptin-related mutations seen in mice. But the identification of leptin is only one of many important advances over the past several years that have opened a new chapter in the understanding of obesity.

Armed with powerful new tools in molecular biology and genetic engineering, scientists are seeking physiological explanations for some of the most puzzling aspects of the fattening of industrial society. Why is obesity on the rise, not just in the U.S. but in nearly all affluent countries? How is it that some individuals remain fat despite constant diets, whereas others eat what they want without gaining a pound? Why is it so hard to lose a significant amount of weight and nearly impossible to keep it off? Perhaps most important, what can be done to slow and eventually reverse this snowballing trend? The traditional notion that obesity is simply the well-deserved consequence of sloth and gluttony has led to unhelpful and sometimes incorrect answers to these questions. Science may at last offer better.

What Makes the World Go Round

Contrary to conventional wisdom, the U.S. is not the fattest nation on earth. Obesity is far more common on Western Samoa and several other Pacific islands. On Nauru, a mere dot of eight square miles once covered to overflowing with seabird guano, the 7,500 islanders have traded that valuable source of phosphate to fertilizer companies in exchange for one of the highest per capita incomes in the world. Many also traded their plows for lounge chairs and their traditional diet of fish and vegetables for Western staples such as canned meats, potato chips and beer. Within the course of a generation, the change has taken its toll on their bodies. By 1987 well over 65 percent of men and 70 percent of women on Nauru were obese, and one third suffered from diabetes.

Many countries, developed and developing, are heading in the same direction at an alarming pace. Changes in diet alone do not explain the trend. Surveys—some of which admittedly are of dubious accuracy—show that the proportion of calories Americans get from fat has dropped about eight points since the 1980s, to 34 percent. Yet the prevalence of obesity has risen by a similar amount in nearly the same period. Britons ate 10 percent fewer calories overall in 1991 than in 1980, according to government estimates, while the number of heavyweights doubled. Polls that show gasoline consumption and hours spent watching television rising about as quickly as the rate of obesity in some countries seem to explain part of the disparity.

Evolutionary biology may provide a deeper explanation, however. In 1962 James V. Neel of the University of Michigan proposed that natural selection pressured our distant ancestors to acquire "thrifty genes," which boosted the ability to store fat from each feast in order to sustain people through the next famine. In today's relative surfeit, Neel reasoned, this adaptation has become a liability. The theory is supported by the Nauruans' plight and also by studies of the Pima Indians, a tribe whose progenitors split into two groups sometime during the Middle Ages. One group settled in southern Arizona; the other moved into the Sierra Madre Mountains in Mexico. By the 1970s most of the Indians in Arizona had been forced out of farming and had switched to an American diet with 40 percent of its calories from fat. They now endure the highest incidence of obesity reported anywhere in the world—far higher than among their white neighbors. About half develop diabetes by age 35.

Eric Ravussin, a researcher with the National Institute of Diabetes and Digestive and Kidney Diseases (NIDDK), has compared Pimas in Arizona with their distant relatives in Maycoba, Mexico, who still live on subsistence farming and ranching. Although the groups share most of the same genes, Pimas in Maycoba are on average 57 pounds (26 kilograms) lighter and about one inch (2.5 centimeters) shorter. Few have diabetes. Maycobans also eat about half as much fat as their counterparts to the north, and they spend more than 40 hours a week engaged in physical work. The fact that Mexican Pimas remain lean provides strong evidence that the high rate of obesity among American Pimas is the result not of a genetic defect alone but of a genetic susceptibility—exceptionally thrifty genes—turned loose in an environment that offers easy access to high-energy food while requiring little hard labor.

Because all human populations seem to share this genetic susceptibility to varying degrees, "we are going to see a continuing increase in obesity over the next 25 years" as standards of living continue to rise, predicts F. Xavier Pi-Sunyer, director of the obesity research center at St. Luke's-Roosevelt Hospital in New York City. He warns that "some less developed countries are particularly at risk. It is projected that by 2025, more than 20 percent of the population of Mexico will have diabetes."

Studies of Pimas, islanders and migrants "all seem to indicate that among different populations, the prevalence of obesity is largely determined by environmental conditions," Ravussin concludes. A few doctors have proposed changing those conditions by levying a "fat tax" on high-calorie foods or raising insurance rates for those who fail to show up at a gym regularly.

But economic and legal punishments are unlikely to garner much popular support, and no one knows whether they would effectively combat obesity. So most researchers are turning back to factors they think they can control: the genetic and biological variables that make one person gain weight while others in the same circumstances stay lean.

Finding Genes That Fit

Doctors have long known that the tendency to gain weight runs in families—how strongly is still under debate. Numerous analyses of identical twins reared apart have shown that genetic factors alone control a large part of one's body mass index, an estimate of body fat commonly used to define obesity [see box, "A Shifting Scale"]. A few have found weight to be as dependent on genes as height: about 80 percent. But the majority have concluded that genetic influences are only about half that potent.

Investigators at the National Institutes of Health who examined more than 400 twins over a period of 43 years concluded that "cumulative genetic effects explain most of the tracking in obesity over time," including potbellies sprouting in middle age. Interestingly, the researchers also determined that "shared environmental effects were not significant" in influencing the twins' weight gain. That result is bolstered by five studies that compared the body mass indexes of adopted children with their biological and adoptive parents. All found that the family environment—the food in the refrigerator, the frequency of meals, the type of activities the family shares—plays little or no role in determining which children will grow fat. Apparently, only dramatic environmental differences, such as those between the mountains of Mexico and the plains of Arizona, have much effect on the mass of a people.

Just which genes influence our eating, metabolism and physical activity, and how they exert their power, remains a mystery. But geneticists do have some encouraging leads. Five genes that can cause rodents to balloon have now been pinpointed.

Obese, cloned by Jeffrey M. Friedman and others at the Rockefeller University, encodes a blueprint for leptin, a hormone produced by fat cells. Mice with a mutation in this gene produce either no leptin or a malformed version and quickly grow to three times normal weight. *Diabetes*, cloned last December by a team at Millennium Pharmaceuticals in Cambridge, Mass., codes for a receptor protein that responds to leptin by reducing appetite and turning up metabolism. Mice with a bad copy of this gene do not receive the leptin signal, and they, too, get very fat from infancy.

Within the past year scientists at Jackson Laboratory in Bar Harbor, Me., have cloned two other fat genes, named *fat* and *tubby*. Mice with a mutation in either of these genes put on weight gradually—more like humans do. The *fat* gene gets translated into an enzyme that processes insulin, the hormone that signals the body that it has been fed. But the protein produced by the *tubby* gene is unlike any ever seen. Researchers do not yet know why mice with errors in *fat*, *tubby* or *agouti yellow*, a fifth obesity gene discovered several years ago, put on extra ounces.

Although geneticists have located versions of all five genes within human DNA, "so far, when we have looked for human mutations on these genes, we haven't found them," reports L. Arthur Campfield, a research leader at Hoffmann–La Roche, the drug company that has bought the rights to Millennium's work on the leptin receptor. In fact, clinical studies by Friedman and others have shown that unlike *obese* and *diabetes* mice, heavy humans generally produce a normal amount of leptin given the amount of fat they are carrying. At least at first glance, there seems to be nothing wrong with their leptin systems.

All of which is no surprise to most obesity researchers, who have long maintained that there must be multiple genes that interact with one another and with economic and psychological pressures to set an individual's susceptibility to weight gain. Although identifying clusters of interrelated genes is considerably trickier than finding single mutations, some labs have made headway in mice. David West of the Pennington Biomedical Research Center in Baton Rouge, La., has been crossing one strain that fattens dramatically on a high-fat diet with a closely related strain that remains relatively lean on the same menu. By tracking the way the trait is passed from one generation to the next, West has proved that the fat sensitivity is carried by one to four dominant genes, and he has nar-

4. EXERCISE AND WEIGHT CONTROL

rowed down the chromosome segments on which they could lie. Interestingly, the *tubby* gene happens to rest within one of these segments.

Eventually the genes involved in human weight regulation should be found. But that is the simple part. To make a dent in obesity, physiologists will then have to figure out how all these genes work in real bodies outside the lab. The first step will be to resolve once and for all an old dieters' debate: Do we or do we not have set points—predetermined weights at which our bodies are happiest—and can they be changed?

Set up for Failure

A typical American adult gains about 20 pounds between the ages of 25 and 55. "If you figure that an adult ingests 900,000 to one million calories a year and you calculate the energy cost of those additional 20 pounds," observes Rudolph L. Leibel, co-director of the human metabolism laboratory at Rockefeller, you find that "just a few tenths of 1 percent of the calories ingested are in fact being stored. That degree of control or balance is extraordinary."

Multiple feedback loops maintain the body at a stable weight by shunting messages through the bloodstream and the autonomic nervous system between the brain, the digestive tract, muscle—and, it turns out, fat. Until recently, fat was generally considered just a passive storage tissue. In fact, says Ronald M. Evans of the Salk Institute in La Jolla, Calif., "it is a type of endocrine tissue. Fat secretes signals—hormones such as leptin—and also monitors and responds to signals from other cells."

Last December, Evans reported his discovery of a new hormone, with the catchy name of 15d-PGJ$_2$, that is produced inside fat cells and seems to trigger the formation of new ones, at least in children. Any drug that tried to interfere with the hormone to prevent new fat from forming would probably work only in children, Evans says, because fat cells in adults usually inflate in size rather than increase in number. But a synthetic molecule that mimics 15d–PGJ$_2$, called troglitazone, does appear to be an effective drug for the type II diabetes associated with obesity, because it also signals muscle cells to respond normally to insulin.

In mapping the maze of intertwined pathways that control short-term appetite as well as factors (such as fat and carbohydrate levels) that change over days or weeks, researchers are slowly working out how all these signals combine to hold weight steady. Two major theories vie for acceptance: set point and settling point.

The set-point hypothesis is the older and more deterministic. It asserts that the brain continuously adjusts our metabolism and subconsciously manipulates our behavior to maintain a target weight. Although the set point may change with age, it does so according to a fixed genetic program; diet or exercise can move you away from your set point, at least for a time, but the target itself cannot change—or so the theory goes. Last year Leibel and his colleagues Michael Rosenbaum and Jules Hirsch, who are three of the strongest proponents of the set-point theory, completed a study that seems to support their hypothesis.

The physicians admitted 66 people to the Rockefeller hospital. Some of the patients were obese, and some had never been overweight, but all had been at the same weight for at least six months. Over the next three months the subjects ate only precisely measured liquid meals. The doctors ran an extensive battery of tests on the volunteers and then increased the calories that some were fed and put the others on restricted diets. When the

---

A Shifting Scale

Obesity appears to be rising in most industrial nations, although comparisons are tricky because epidemiologists have never settled on consistent categories for measuring the disorder. Nearly all rely on the body mass index (BMI) [*see formula below*], because this figure is highly correlated with body fat. Still, studies have used a wide range of BMI levels, from below 27 to over 30, to categorize the obese.

The World Health Organization classifies obesity in three levels, with those having BMIs of 30 or higher considered at major risk. Doctors in the U.S. have conventionally used "ideal weight" tables assembled by the Metropolitan Life Insurance Company from actuarial data. Yet recent mortality studies, such as one published last year by Harvard University researchers who examined 115,195 nurses over 16 years, have found that the standard tables underestimate the risks of excess weight—primarily because they fail to account for smokers, who tend to be thin but unhealthy. These newer studies show risks increasing significantly at BMIs of 25 and higher. In 1995 the National Institutes of Health and the American Health Foundation issued new guidelines that define healthy weight as a BMI below 25. According to a recent report by the Institute of Medicine, 59 percent of American adults exceed that threshold.

Calculating Body Mass Index

$$BMI = \frac{w}{h^2}$$

w is weight in kilograms (pounds divided by 2.2)
h is height in meters (inches divided by 39.4)

Weighing the Risks
Percent increase in risk by level of obesity

	BODY MASS INDEX (BMI)
	26 27 28 29 30 31 32 33 34 35
Death/all causes (versus BMI < 19)	60% (28-30), 110% (31-32), 120% (33-35)
Death/heart disease (versus BMI < 19)	210% (28-29), 360% (30-32), 480% (33-35)
Death/cancer (versus BMI < 19)	80% (29-31), 110% (32-35)
Type II diabetes (versus BMI 22–23)	1,480% (28-29), 2,660% (30-31), 3,930% (32-33), 5,300% (34-35)
High blood pressure (versus BMI < 23)	180% (26-28), 260% (29-31), 350% (32-35)
Degenerative arthritis (versus BMI < 25)	400% (30-35)
Gallstones (versus BMI < 24)	150% (27-29), 270% (30-35)
Neural birth defects (versus BMI 19–27)	90% (28-35)

SOURCES: *New England Journal of Medicine; Annals of Internal Medicine; American Journal of Clinical Nutrition; Journal of the American Medical Association; Circulation*

A Spoonful of Medicine: Obesity Drugs under Development

TISSUES	DRUG	ACTION	DEVELOPER	STATUS
Brain	Dexfenfluramine	Increases the circulation of serotonin, a neurotransmitter that quells appetite	Interneuron with Wyeth-Ayerst Laboratories	Approved by the FDA in April
	Sibutramine	Boosts levels of both serotonin and noradrenaline in the brain, staving off hunger	Knoll Pharmaceutical	Submitted to the FDA for approval in August 1995
	Neuropeptide Y inhibitors	Inactivate NPY, an appetite stimulant that also signals the body to burn more sugars and less fat	Neurogen, Pfizer, Synaptic Pharmaceutical	Phase I trials* began in March
	Bromocriptine	Mimics the neurotransmitter dopamine. Given at certain times of day, may reduce blood sugar and fat production by the liver	Ergo Science	Phase III trials under way for diabetes, planned for obesity
	Leptin	Hormone produced by fat cells and received by receptors in the hypothalamus. Some obese people may be insensitive to leptin; supplemental injections may help	Amgen	Phase I trials began in May
Brain, digestive tract	CCK_A promoters	Increase availability of certain cellular receptors that reduce appetite when stimulated by cholecystokinin (CCK), a family of hormones and neurotransmitters	Astra Arcus USA; Glaxo Wellcome	Preclinical research
	Butabindide	Blocks an enzyme that restores appetite by breaking down CCK. In hungry mice, reduces food intake by 45 percent	INSERM (France)	Preclinical research
Digestive tract	Orlistat	Interferes with pancreatic lipase, one of the enzymes that breaks down fat, so that about one third of the fat eaten passes undigested through the body	Hoffmann–La Roche	Phase III trials complete; FDA application expected by late 1996
	Insulinotropin	Synthetic version of the hormone glucagonlike peptide-1, which may improve obesity-related diabetes by slowing stomach emptying and boosting insulin levels	Novo Nordisk (Denmark)	Phase II trials under way
Fat	Bta-243	Binds to $beta_3$-adrenergic receptor on fat cells, increasing the amount of fat in the blood and burned for energy	Wyeth-Ayerst Laboratories	Preclinical research
Fat, muscle	Troglitazone	Synthetic version of the hormone $15d-PGJ_2$, which is produced by fat cells and somehow signals muscle cells to burn fat rather than sugars. May help reverse insulin resistance in obese diabetics	Parke-Davis; Sankyo	Approved in Japan. Phase III trials concluding in U.S.; FDA application expected by late 1996
Entire body	Cytokine regulators	Change the activity of cytokines, hormonelike proteins that act as messengers among cells	Houghten Pharmaceuticals	Phase II trial under way for obesity-related diabetes

*Drugs generally must clear three types of clinical trials before the Food and Drug Administration will approve them for sale. Phase I trials test a drug's safety, and Phase II trials study its effectiveness, both on a small number of patients. Phase III trials must prove that the drug has acceptable side effects and benefits when given to a large group of subjects.

---

subjects had gained 10 percent or lost either 10 or 20 percent of their original weight, the tests were run again to see what had changed.

The investigation disproved some tidbits of weight-gain folklore, such as that thin people do not digest as much of their food as heavyweights. The study also found that "the idea that you will be fatter—or will require fewer calories to maintain your starting body weight—as a result of having yo-yoed down and back up again is wrong," Rosenbaum adds. Moreover, the research showed that obese people, when their weight is stable, do not eat significantly more than lean people with the same amount of muscle but less fat.

But the trial's real purpose was to determine how much of a fight the body puts up when people attempt to change the weight they have maintained for a long time—why, in other words, dieters tend to bounce back to where they started. When both lean and obese subjects dropped weight, "it seemed to set off a bunch of metabolic alarms," Leibel recalls. The subjects' bodies quickly started burning fewer calories—15 percent fewer, on average, than one would expect given their new weight. Surprisingly, the converse also seems to be true for weight gain. Even rotund people have to eat about 15 percent more than one would expect to stay very far above their set point.

That fact raises a major problem for set-point theory: How does it explain the rapid increase in the prevalence of obesity? "Clearly, set points have to be rising, just as we are getting taller in every generation," Rosenbaum says. "But set points are not changeable in adulthood, as far as we can tell. So there must be a window of opportunity sometime in childhood where the environment influences the set point," he speculates. "If you could figure out when and how that occurs, maybe you could modify the environment then, and you wouldn't have to worry about your kids getting fat 20 years down the line."

That will remain wishful thinking until set-point advocates demonstrate

4. EXERCISE AND WEIGHT CONTROL

how weight is centrally controlled. Their best guess now, explains Louis A. Tartaglia, a scientist at Millennium, is that "the body's set point is something like a thermostat"—a lipostat, some have called it—and leptin acts like the thermometer.

As you gain weight, Friedman elaborates, "you make more leptin. That shuts off appetite, increases energy expenditure and undoubtedly does other things to restore body weight to the set point. Conversely, if you get too thin, levels of leptin fall, and now you eat more, burn less, and again your weight returns to where it started. Now that we know what the gene and its product are, we can test that simpleminded theory."

Amgen, a biotechnology firm in Thousand Oaks, Calif., that has reportedly promised Rockefeller up to $100 million for the right to produce leptin, has begun injecting the hormone into obese people in clinical trials. "The goal," Rosenbaum says, "is to co-opt your body into working with you rather than against you to maintain an altered body weight" by tricking it into believing it is fatter than it is.

But the body may not be easily fooled. In May, scientists at the University of Washington reported that they had engineered mice that lack the gene for neuropeptide Y (NPY), the most powerful appetite stimulant known. Leptin curtails NPY production; this, it was thought, is how it quells hunger. But mice lacking NPY do not lose weight—something else compensates.

Critics of the set-point hypothesis also protest that it fails to explain the high rates of obesity seen in Nauruans and American Pimas. Moreover, if body fat is centrally controlled, they argue, the amount of fat in your diet should have little impact on your weight. Numerous studies have found the contrary. One recent survey of some 11,600 Scotsmen observed that obesity was up to three times more common among groups that ate the most fat than among those who relied on sugars for most of their energy.

Fat in the Balance

At a conference last year, researchers reviewed the evidence and judged that although the set-point hypothesis has not been disproved, there is more "biological merit" to the idea of a "settling point." This newer theory posits that we maintain weight when our various metabolic feedback loops, tuned by whatever susceptibility genes we carry, settle into a happy equilibrium with our environment. Economic and cultural changes are upsetting this equilibrium and propelling more people—those with more genetic risk factors—into obesity.

The prime culprit suspected in this trend is hardly surprising: it is the fat dripping off hamburgers, smoothing out ice cream and frying every meat imaginable. But biochemists are at last working out precisely why fat is bad. For years, they have known that people fed a high-fat meal will consume about the same amount as those given a high-carbohydrate meal. Because fat has more calories per bite, however, the subjects with greasy grins tend to ingest more energy than they can burn, a phenomenon known as passive overconsumption.

One reason for this, according to biopsychologist John E. Blundell of the University of Leeds, seems to be that the systems controlling hunger and satiety respond quickly to protein and carbohydrates but slowly to fat—too slowly to stop a high-fat meal before the body has had too much. Metabolic systems seem to favor carbohydrates (which include sugars and starches) as well. Knock down a soda or a plate of pasta, and your body will soon speed up its carbohydrate combustion. Polish off a bag of pork rinds, however, and your fat oxidation rate hardly budges, points out Jean-Pierre Flatt, a biochemist at the University of Massachusetts Medical School. Most incoming fat is shipped directly to storage, then burned later only if carbohydrate reserves dip below some threshold, which varies from person to person.

There is another way to increase the rate at which fat is burned for energy: pack on the pounds. More fat on the body yields more fatty acids circulating in the bloodstream. That in turn boosts fat oxidation, so that eventually a "fat balance" is reached where all the fat that is eaten is combusted, and weight stabilizes. Many genetic and biological factors can influence the fat oxidation rate and thus affect your settling point in a particular environment.

Olestra, an artificial fat approved earlier this year by the Food and Drug Administration, may change that rate as well. Olestra tastes more or less like an ordinary fat, but it flows undigested through the body. A preliminary study by George A. Bray, Pennington's executive director, suggests that the ingredient may short-circuit passive overconsumption. For two weeks, Bray replaced the natural fat in his subjects' meals with olestra. "They did not compensate at all by eating more food," he reports, adding that "it remains to be seen whether that holds up in longer-term studies."

The fat balance explains in part why settling points vary among people who overeat fat: some oxidize fat efficiently at normal weights; others burn too little until excess pounds force the oxidation rate up. But the model does not by itself explain why some do not overeat at all. To answer that, Flatt has proposed a "glycogen hypothesis."

The human body can store about a day's supply of carbohydrates in the form of glycogen, a simple starch. Glycogen reserves function somewhat like fuel tanks; we partially refill the stores with each meal but rarely top them off. In fact, the range between "empty" and "full" appears to be a matter of individual preference, influenced by such factors as the diversity and palatability of food at hand, social pressures and meal habits. People who are content with lower glycogen levels or who frequently deplete them through exercise burn fat more readily than those who like to keep their tanks full, Flatt suggests. But he concedes that the "crucial link from glycogen stores to appetite remains to be proven."

Researchers need more evidence before they can pronounce either set point or settling point—or neither—correct. James O. Hill of the University of Colorado Health Sciences Center has begun collecting some of those critical data. He is assembling a registry of the most precious resource in obesity research: the people who have lost a large amount of weight and kept it off for several years without relapse. Hill has already identified about 1,000 such individuals and has begun examining a handful for biochemical clues to their success.

Unfortunately, no current explanation of weight regulation leaves much room for voluntary control; all the metabolic cycles involved are governed subconsciously. Settling-point theory does at least suggest that sufficiently drastic changes in lifestyle might prod the body to resettle at a new weight. But without assistance, changes radical enough to make a difference are evidently uncomfortable enough to be infeasible—for millions of dieters have tried this strategy and failed.

Getting over the Hump

Increasingly, obesity researchers argue that the most effective assistance they can provide their patients will probably be pharmacological. "The treatment philosophy of the past 40 years, which has been to train patients to eat differently, is simply not going to cure the epidemic of obesity that we see worldwide," asserts Barbara C. Hansen, director of the obesity research center at the University of Maryland School of Medicine.

Untangling the biology beneath body fat has created a plethora of new drug targets that has drawn dozens of pharmaceutical firms off the sidelines [*see table on page 89*]. The potential market is enormous, not only because obesity is common and growing but also because even an ideal drug will have to be taken indefinitely, according to Hansen and others. "Obesity isn't curable," Bray says. "It's like high blood pressure. If you don't take the medication, your blood pressure won't stay down. And if you don't take drugs—or do something—to treat obesity, your weight won't stay down."

Part of the reason for the resurgence of commercial interest is a shift in policy at the FDA, which decided in May to allow the appetite suppressant dexfenfluramine to be prescribed for obesity in the U.S., as it already is in 65 other countries. It is the first weight-loss drug approved in the U.S. in 23 years, and nearly all obesity researchers agree it has been too long coming. The FDA also recently relaxed its guidelines for obesity-drug applications. "As our compromise right now, we're suggesting that a company can present us with two years of data—in some cases, one year if the data look good enough and the company gives us a firm commitment to do follow-up studies under tight controls," says Leo Lutwak, a medical officer with the FDA's Center for Drug Evaluation & Research.

Lutwak admits that with only two years of information, the FDA may approve drugs that turn out to have serious long-term side effects. "The best we can hope for is something like insulin for the treatment of diabetes," Leibel says. Insulin rescues a type I diabetic by replacing a hormone that is missing. "But after 15 years, you begin to have complications of our inability to perfectly mimic the biology," Leibel continues. "If we're lucky, that's the kind of problem we'll face in the treatment of obesity." Lutwak responds that "when that happens, the public will be informed, and they will have to make a decision about whether it is worth it."

If the long-term cost of treatment is unknown, the benefits are becoming clearer, thanks to studies on people who have an operation, called gastroplasty, that reduces the size of the stomach. Although infrequently used in the U.S., the procedure has proved remarkably effective in Sweden. A long-term study there of 1,150 obese patients who underwent gastric surgery found that they typically dropped 66 pounds over two years—88 pounds if a more severe procedure was used—whereas control subjects given standard dietary treatment lost nothing. The surgery cured more than two thirds of those with diabetes, compared with 16 percent cured in the control group. Likewise, twice as many (43 percent) of the hypertension cases were cured by the operation.

Gastroplasty has drawbacks in addition to the risks that always accompany major surgery—principally a high rate of digestive complications. Drug treatments might be better, but Hansen's work with rhesus monkeys suggests that prevention would be best. A decade ago her team began a trial on young adult monkeys, equivalent in maturity to 20-year-old men. The researchers adjusted the animals' food supply so that they neither gained nor lost weight. "In the past 10 years we have had 100 percent success preventing both obesity and type II diabetes," Hansen asserts. "In the control group, which was simply allowed to feed freely on the same diet, half are diabetic. Because everything we know about human obesity is also true of nonhuman primate obesity, that shows you the power of weight control."

It does not, unfortunately, demonstrate a feasible way to achieve it. The NIDDK has launched a program to educate Americans about ways to avoid weight gain, but Susan Z. Yanovski, the program's director, admits that so far it has had little perceptible impact. There is no major lobbying organization for the disease, notes Pi-Sunyer, and the NIH directs less than 1 percent of its research funding at obesity. "Many people seem to be unaware of how big a health problem this is now and how big it is going to grow, particularly when you look at the increasing obesity of children," Yanovski says. Because obese adolescents usually become fat adults, "we're really heading for trouble in another 20 to 30 years," she adds.

At least one grade school intervention has had modest success, knocking a few percentage points off the number of children who turn into overweight adolescents by taking fat out of the children's lunches, giving them more strenuous recreation and educating their parents about weight control. "We have to be very careful about putting children on restrictive diets," Yanovski warns. "That is inappropriate. But we can be more proactive in getting our kids away from the television set, more physically active, riding their bikes instead of being driven everywhere. If people recognize that this is a serious public health problem affecting their children, then maybe they will start taking some action." If not, economists should start adjusting their models now to account for the tremendous health care cost increases that lie ahead.

Further Reading

WEIGHING THE OPTIONS: CRITERIA FOR EVALUATING WEIGHT-MANAGEMENT PROGRAMS. Edited by Paul R. Thomas. National Academy Press, 1995.

REGULATION OF BODY WEIGHT: BIOLOGICAL AND BEHAVIORAL MECHANISMS. Edited by C. Bouchard and G. A. Bray. John Wiley & Sons, 1996.

Additional information, including an extensive bibliography, is available on the *Scientific American* World Wide Web site at http://www.sciam.com

Body Mania

After a lifetime of work on the body-image front, one of the country's leading experts reveals her insights into the dilemma—and offers a way out

Judith Rodin, Ph.D.

Judith Rodin, a professor of psychology, medicine, and psychiatry at Yale University, is the author of more than 200 articles and papers as well as Breaking the Body Traps *(William Morrow, 1992). She is codirector of the Yale Center for Eating and Weight Disorders and past president of the Society for Behavioral Medicine.*

If *Pygmalion* were written today it would not be a story about changing Eliza Doolittle's speech, clothing, or manners, but rather about changing her face and body. Using methods from face-lifts to miracle diets to liposuction, women in increasing numbers are striving—with a degree of panic and, more often than not, to their own detriment—to match the ultimate template of beauty.

Has the situation worsened in the past few decades? The answer is undeniably yes. Since beginning this research 20 years ago, I have witnessed growing concern with appearance, body, and weight among women of all ages. Men, too, no longer seem immune.

In 1987, PSYCHOLOGY TODAY published the results of a survey of readers' feelings about appearance and weight. Only 12 percent of those polled indicated little concern about their appearance and said they didn't do much to improve it. The results of this survey are similar to those of many studies where the participants are selected at random: People feel intense pressure to look good.

An earlier survey on body image was published in PSYCHOLOGY TODAY in 1972. The 1970s respondents were considerably more satisfied with their bodies than were the 1980s respondents. The pressure to look good has intensified for both sexes in the last two decades. As the table below shows, our dissatisfaction has grown for every area of our bodies.

Unhappy Bodies

THE SURVEY ALSO SHOWS HOW IMPORTANT weight has become to body image; it is the focus of dissatisfaction in both studies and the area showing the greatest increase. I recently evaluated a survey for *USA Today* which also showed identical results. People today are far more critical of themselves for not attaining the right weight and look.

Body preoccupation has become a societal mania. We've become a nation of appearance junkies and fitness zealots, pioneers driven to think, talk, strategize, and worry about our bodies with the same fanatical devotion we applied to putting a man on the moon. Abroad, we strive for global peace. At home, we have declared war on our bodies.

It is a mistake to think that concern with appearance and weight is simply an aberration of contemporary Western culture. Generations of ancient Chinese women hobbled themselves by binding their feet in order to match the beauty ideal of the time. And we all remember Scarlett O'Hara in search of the 17-inch waist. What *Gone With The Wind* did not show us was that tight corseting induced shortness of breath, constipation, and, occasionally, uterine prolapse. But if we moderns are following a tradition hallowed by our forebears, the industrialization of fitness and beauty is conspiring with other trends to raise the stakes to their highest point in history.

Of all the industrial achievements of the 20th century that influence how we feel about our bodies, none has had a more profound effect than the rise of the mass media. Through movies, magazines, and TV, we see beautiful people as often as we see our own family members; the net effect is

People Dissatisfied With Body Areas or Dimensions

1972	MEN	WOMEN	1987	MEN	WOMEN
Height	13%	13%	Height	20%	17%
Weight	35	48	Weight	41	55
Muscle Tone	25	30	Muscle Tone	32	45
Overall Face	8	11	Face	20	20
Breast/Chest	18	26	Upper Torso	28	32
Abdomen	36	50	Mid Torso	50	57
Hips and Upper Thighs	12	49	Lower Torso	21	50
Overall	15	25	"Looks As They Are"	34	38

to make exceptional beauty appear real and attainable. Narcissus was lucky: He had only to find a lake. The modern woman has television, in which she doesn't see herself reflected.

In my experience as a researcher and clinician, I have found that many women avoid the mirror altogether; those who do look may scrutinize, yet still fail to see themselves objectively. Most of us see only painful flaws in exquisite detail. Others still see the fat and blemishes that used to be there in the teenage years, even if they're no longer there.

Like a perverse Narcissus, a woman today looks at her reflection in a mirror and finds it wanting—and then is consumed by a quest to make herself fit the reflection the media has conditioned her to expect is possible. She works harder and harder to attain what is, as I will explain, most likely impossible. Ignoring the hours movie stars spend on makeup and hair, forgetting how easily and well the camera can lie, she aspires to a synthetic composite of what she thinks her reflection should be.

It is also likely that she is unaware of what other research shows: Such detailed attention has a negative influence on self-esteem. It makes us feel that many features of ourself are flawed, even those having little to do with weight or appearance.

Many of us have traveled through the looking glass with Alice into a world where what is and what might be blur and confuse us. We may be thin and think we are not. We may be heavy and think that life isn't worth living because we do not match our culture's physical ideal. Our self-image has become far too plastic, too malleable. It depends too much on transitory moods, on what we feel is expected of us and how we feel we are lacking. It is not dependent enough upon a stable internal sense of ourself. We grow larger or smaller, in our mind's eye, in response to the image of woman modern society has encouraged us to idealize.

Unlike Alice, however, we have not returned. We are stuck there in a world of obsessional self-criticism, where what we see is not at all what we really are. The mirror is woman's modern nemesis.

Some call such obsession with appearance vanity—but that misses the point. We are responding to the deep psychological significance of the body. Appearance does indeed affect our sense of self and how people respond to us; it always has, always will. What's different today is that the body and how it looks has become a significant component of our self-worth.

Why Now?

WHY DO WEIGHT AND APPEARANCE MATTER so much? And why now? What is occurring at this particular moment in time?

Our society has changed dramatically in this century. There are few remaining hierarchies or social structures based on religion, parentage, money, or education. Society has become more egalitarian, but intrinsic to human nature is the desire to judge, evaluate, and compare ourselves to others. If class and lineage no longer provide the tools for measuring ourselves against our neighbors, what are the new social standards? It is my premise that they are the more visible, tangible, observable aspects—first among these, the physical self.

Our bodies have become the premier coin of the realm. Appearance, good looks, and fitness are now the measure of one's social worth. How closely we can approximate a perfect body has also unfortunately become a sign of how well we're doing in life.

Not only is how we look suddenly of the utmost importance, but we have also come to accept and idealize a single image of beauty—slim but fit. The media now expose us to this single "right" look, and the beauty industry promises it is attainable by all. When the prescription for how we should look is so well-defined, deviations are all the more noticeable.

What's more, our culture holds out the lure of an easy fix for all corporeal dissatisfactions. The goal of looking good is attainable by anyone, as long as he or she works out hard enough, exercises long enough, and eats little enough.

Beauty, health, diet, and fitness have become very big businesses. But they weren't always. During the late 1950s and early '60s—when models and Miss Americas wore girdles, did a little exercise just for their thighs and hips, and wore a size 10—only overweight women dieted. A survey of *Ladies Home Journal* issues from the 1960s showed an average of only one diet article every six months. But by the mid-'70s almost every woman in America had tried some kind of diet, and losing weight was a national obsession.

Because we sincerely believe that the perfect body is attainable by anyone, Americans spend more on beauty and fitness aids than they do on social services or education. Such distribution of a primary resource is a shocking revelation of our true priorities.

Yet another reason appearance is everything today hinges on the blurring of traditional definitions of female and male. Our view of the differences between the sexes is in flux, as women move into such traditionally male domains as the office and men become more involved in the household. In many ways our bodies remain our most visible means of expressing the differences between the sexes. Having the right body may be a way for women who have moved into male occupations to declare their feminine identity without compromising their professional persona.

Asked to make it in a man's world, they are, like the rest of society, still confused about women's roles. Internalizing society's ambivalence, they succeed in one domain and fall back in the other, reverting to the traditionally feminine arena of competition over thinness and beauty.

In addition, the fitness movement, taken to extremes, has fostered the notion that a "good" physique not only equals a healthy body but a healthy soul. Getting in shape has become the new moral imperative—an alluring substitute for altruism and good work, the desire to look good replacing the desire to do good. In this new secular morality, values and ideals of beauty and appearance supplement moral and religious standards.

Today's moral transgressions involve eating something we feel we shouldn't have or feeling we don't look good enough or haven't tried hard enough to look good.

If our current self-absorption has its reasons, it also has its comforts. The quest for physical perfection is the up-to-date way we barter with the uncertainty of life. Like a set of worry beads, we always have our calories to count, our minutes of aerobics to execute. If everything else in our lives seems out of control, we at least have our diet and exercise regimens. In the chaos called modern life, ordering the body to do what we want it to may give us a much-needed illusion of control.

Where we differ, too, from our forebears is that the body today is no longer considered a finished product, a fait accompli. It is strictly a work in progress. And we devote ourselves to perfecting it with the dedication of the true artist. According to the American Society of Plastic and Reconstructive Surgeons, "aesthetic" surgeries are up 61 percent over the past decade. A marketing research firm in New York calculates that Americans spent $33 billion on diets and

4. EXERCISE AND WEIGHT CONTROL

diet-related services in 1990, up from $29 billion in 1989. By the turn of the century we will be spending $77 billion to lose weight—just slightly less than the entire gross national product of Belgium.

The Limits of the Body

THERE IS AN OVERRIDING FALLACY IN THIS view of ourselves. The body is not infinitely malleable in the way that advertisers with a product to sell would have us believe. Despite wide dissemination of news about great advances in science and medicine, the individual American remains virtually unaware of the role that physiology plays in body weight, in determining how quickly we lose or gain weight and in how our general health and appearance respond to exercise and diet. Most of us are exposed to and accept a staggering amount of misinformation.

Genes play a major role in setting metabolism as well as body shape and size; they determine how much fat we burn, how much we can store easily, and where it's distributed on our bodies. One of our clinic patients came from a family where everyone had thick, solid legs and big thighs. For years she tried every diet that became popular. No matter how much she lost, no matter how thin she became, she couldn't change the size of her legs and thighs nearly as much as the rest of her body. "My greatest goal in life," she admitted, "is to have thin legs....I know why women have liposuction. It's the ultimate solution. I used to dream about a big vacuum cleaner sucking out the fat—it was my constant childhood wish—but I just can't afford it yet."

The Pursuit Is Costly

THE QUEST FOR THE PERFECT BODY IS, LIKE most wars, a costly one—emotionally and physically, to say nothing of financially. It leaves most of us feeling frustrated, ashamed, and defeated. Yet we keep at it, wearing down our bodies and our optimism while narrowing the focus of our lives.

In addition, as a society obsessed with a set standard of beauty, we have become intolerant of and sometimes cruel to those who do not meet it, especially the overweight. We learn early in life that there is something shameful about obesity. And the obese are painfully stigmatized. Even children with a life-threatening chronic illness would rather be sick than fat.

We learn these antifat attitudes in childhood, and they figure strongly into why normal-weight people greatly fear becoming overweight. In our research, we hear many people state that they would kill themselves if they were fat. While this is just a figure of speech, some overweight people are so unhappy about their appearance that they *do* contemplate suicide. A few follow through.

The accompanying test will give you an idea of how much you subscribe to society's standards of beauty.

Social Attitudes Scale

Please read the following statements and indicate how strongly you agree or disagree with each.

1. A man would always prefer to go out with a thin woman than one who is heavy.
Strongly Agree | Agree Somewhat | Agree | Neither Agree nor Disagree | Disagree | Disagree Somewhat | Strongly Disagree

2. Clothes are made today so that only thin people can look good.
Strongly Agree | Agree Somewhat | Agree | Neither Agree nor Disagree | Disagree | Disagree Somewhat | Strongly Disagree

3. Fat people are often unhappy.
Strongly Agree | Agree Somewhat | Agree | Neither Agree nor Disagree | Disagree | Disagree Somewhat | Strongly Disagree

4. It is not true that attractive people are more interesting, poised, and socially outgoing than unattractive people.
Strongly Agree | Agree Somewhat | Agree | Neither Agree nor Disagree | Disagree | Disagree Somewhat | Strongly Disagree

5. A pretty face will not get you very far without a slim body.
Strongly Agree | Agree Somewhat | Agree | Neither Agree nor Disagree | Disagree | Disagree Somewhat | Strongly Disagree

6. It is more important that a woman be attractive than a man.
Strongly Agree | Agree Somewhat | Agree | Neither Agree nor Disagree | Disagree | Disagree Somewhat | Strongly Disagree

7. Attractive people lead more fulfilling lives than unattractive people.
Strongly Agree | Agree Somewhat | Agree | Neither Agree nor Disagree | Disagree | Disagree Somewhat | Strongly Disagree

8. The thinner a woman is, the more attractive she is.
Strongly Agree | Agree Somewhat | Agree | Neither Agree nor Disagree | Disagree | Disagree Somewhat | Strongly Disagree

9. Attractiveness decreases the likelihood of professional success.
Strongly Agree | Agree Somewhat | Agree | Neither Agree nor Disagree | Disagree | Disagree Somewhat | Strongly Disagree

These items test how much you believe that appearance matters. Score your responses as follows:

For items 1, 2, 3, 5, 7, and 8, give yourself a zero if you said "strongly disagree"; a 2 for "disagree"; up to a 6 for "strongly agree."

Items 4, 6, and 9 are scored in reverse. In other words, give yourself a zero for "strongly agree" and a 6 for "strongly disagree."

Add together your points for all nine questions. A score of 46 or higher means that you are vulnerable to being influenced by the great importance that current society places on appearance.

The vast majority of American women have accepted at face value the message we have been continually exposed to: that beauty and physical perfection are merely a matter of personal effort and that failure to attain those goals is the result of not doing enough. Consequently, we are now subjecting ourselves and even our children to an ever more complicated regimen of diet, exercise, and beauty. We have come to believe in what I see as the "techno-body," shaped by dieting and surgical techniques.

Humans appear to be the only animals who decline to eat when hungry, who willingly starve the body. Occasionally they do it to feed the soul. Many religions have institutionalized fasting as a way of asking for redemption. But in the more modern version of these self-denial rituals, people fast and starve, purge and renew in search of a better self.

It has become fashionable, even politically correct, to worry about the environment. We rally to plant trees to save the Earth without even realizing that at the very same moment in history we are defacing and dehumanizing our bodies by using chemical peels, dermabrasion, hair dye, synthetic diet foods, and fake fats and sweeteners. Where is our concern for the human part of our environment?

What Is the Problem?

MY STUDIES SHOW THAT SURGERY, DIET, and exercise are only symptoms of the real problem: body preoccupation and an obsessive concern with body image. In accepting the quick fix as a solution, we are overlooking the depth and complexity of the problem we are facing. Shedding pounds, counting calories, and pumping iron—manifestations of body preoccupation—are only a reflection of the fact that we now believe the body is the window to the self, perhaps even the soul.

The psychological self is fundamental to our preoccupation with the physical self. Of all the ways we experience ourselves, none is so primal as the sense of our own bodies. Our body image is at the very core of our identity. Our feelings about our bodies are woven into practically every aspect of our behavior. Our bodies shape our identity because they are the form and substance of our persona to the outside world. Appearance will always be important because we are social beings. How we look sends messages, whether we want it to or not, and people respond to us accordingly.

The old saw cites death and taxes, but in fact we have one other nonnegotiable contract in life: to live in and with our bodies for the duration. People must learn to treat the issue of body image seriously and validate their concerns about their bodies. In my clinical experience, people find that hard to do because admitting how deeply we anguish about our bodies often leads to a profound sense of shame.

In an era of acid rain, AIDS, nuclear disaster, and poverty, we are embarrassed by our body preoccupation—but that, of course, does not stop it.

Getting Out of the Body Trap

RECOGNIZING THE PROBLEM IS THE FIRST step to solving it. Our work has shown that people do better when they are nonjudgmental about their concerns with body, diet, and exercise patterns. These are not trivial worries and complaints, but painful experiences and issues deserving attention. It is crucial to acknowledge the scope and depth of what you are feeling. No one is alone in their body concerns. All women share them to some extent—as do many men these days, as well.

If you treat your body with more respect, you will like it better. What your body really needs is moderate exercise, healthy foods, sensual pleasures, and relaxation. Give it those, and it will respond by treating you better. Not everyone can afford expensive trinkets or clothes, but everyone can afford small indulgences—a long, warm bath, a half-hour of time off, a new haircut. Some of you will be amazed at how hard it is to do something nice for yourself. But treating your body better will make you feel better about yourself.

To break the body-image barrier, we must bring self-image into focus. When people worry about how they look, they are worrying about who they are. That's not necessarily good, but we need to acknowledge that there is a deep connection between the two. In my work with patients, I strive to help them overcome the feeling that their happiness rises or falls depending on what the scale said that morning.

We must also look at what we really want and need from our lives and pursue those goals; it is not wise to continue expending so much of our creative energy on thinness and appearance. Since our bodies are not infinitely plastic, it may be easier to add other joys to life than to subtract pounds. Increasing and nurturing self-complexity by expanding the number of roles we value may boost health in many ways. Current research suggests that multiple roles are typically health enhancing. Varying our routines and adding new interests to our lives will help broaden our horizons so that how we look is not the sum of what we are.

As a character in Henry Jaglom's movie *Eating* says, "Twenty or thirty years ago, sex was the secret subject of women. Now it's food." In fact, sex and food have become interchangeable. "I like the feel of food. I don't like knives and forks because I like to touch it all over," says one woman. Another: "I think it is erotic. It's the safest sex you can have, eating." Food. It is comfort, balm for a trying day in a trying world, sometimes even more. Moderation is the best advice. It is the key to body sanity.

Whether we want to value, accept, or change our bodies, we need first to change our minds. We have to relearn how we observe ourselves. Instead of searching for flaws, we must attempt to see ourselves objectively. We must scrutinize our appearance less.

Caring about our bodies is normal, but how we look has become far too significant. Women have become martyrs to their appearance, slaves of that impossible master, perfection. Men go through life judged mostly on their achievements; women bear the burden of society's image. Although the effort is exhausting and painful, the deep, psychological significance of the body has made it seem worthwhile.

The burden of maintaining a perfect body image is far too costly. Women are crippled by a tragic degree of self-consciousness that limits other aspects of their lives—friendships, careers, even families.

One of the most important steps toward changing your body image is to have compassion for the millions of women struggling with their own body-image problems—especially for yourself. It is time to face the person you see in the mirror with profound new insight: She hasn't been worrying about nothing. In fact, she hasn't been taking the real problem, body preoccupation, seriously enough. Neither has society. It's time to understand the price she has been paying and help her shed that burden.

Drugs and Health

As a culture, Americans have come to rely on drugs not only as treatments for disease but as an aid for living normal, productive lives. This view of drugs has fostered both a casual attitude regarding their use and a tremendous drug abuse problem. The term "drug abuse" conjures up visions of derelicts, dark alleys, and wasted lives. In reality, this description is accurate for only a small minority of drug users. This is not to say that drugs are not responsible for destroying many lives, but rather that drug abuse has become so widespread that there is no way to describe the typical drug abuser, except to say that he or she could be anyone. What constitutes abuse varies, depending on the drug used and the circumstances in which it is used. Based on current trends, it seems likely that the problems of drug abuse will remain as long as attitudes toward drugs remain so casual.

What accounts for this attitude? There is no simple explanation for why America has become a drug-taking culture, but there is evidence to suggest some of the factors involved. From the time that we are children, we are constantly bombarded by advertisements about how certain drugs can make us feel and look better. Growing up, most of us probably had medicine cabinets full of over-the-counter (OTC) drugs, freely dispensed to family members to treat a variety of ailments. Coupled with rising health care costs, this familiarity has prompted many people to diagnose and dose themselves with OTC medications without sufficient knowledge of their possible side effects. While most of these preparations have little potential for abuse, that does not mean they are innocuous. The risk of dangerous side effects rises sharply, for example, when people exceed the recommended dosage. Another potential danger is the drug interactions that can occur when OTC drugs are taken in conjunction with prescription medications. The gravest danger of OTC drugs is that an individual may use them to control symptoms of an underlying disease and thus prevent its timely diagnosis and treatment. "OTC Drugs: Prescription for Danger?" discusses these hazards. The essay "How To Pick a Pain Reliever" examines the most frequently used OTCs, the analgesics, and discusses how to decide which one is right for you.

Many people question why coffee, cigarettes, and alcohol are included under the topic of drugs, since we frequently observe people drinking coffee, smoking cigarettes, and having an occasional alcoholic beverage. Despite the casual nature of our exposure to these substances, each contains a potent drug. Alcohol, nicotine, and caffeine are the most widely used and abused drugs in America, but they do not get nearly as much media coverage as do the more exotic and illicit drugs, such as cocaine, crack, PCP, and marijuana. Does this mean that these drugs are not as dangerous? When it comes to tobacco and alcohol, the answer is a resounding "no." Clearly alcohol and tobacco are far and away the leading causes of death and disability related to drug usage. How can we as a society expect to significantly curtail drug usage in general if we sanction the use of two drugs with such a deadly track record?

Of the drug problems facing this nation, alcohol use is clearly one of the most complex. This complexity stems from the ambivalence we feel regarding its use. While we deplore alcohol for the countless deaths and disabilities it causes each year, we openly sanction its moderate use in a variety of social situations.

Ambivalence regarding alcohol use permeates even the scientific community. While it is clear that heavy alcohol use results in significant damage to a variety of organ systems, the same cannot be said of moderate use. In fact, the scientific community is currently wrestling with this issue regarding cancer and coronary artery disease. Several recent studies have reported that moderate alcohol use increases a woman's risk of breast cancer, and, at the same time, several studies have suggested that moderate alcohol use may help prevent coronary artery disease. What is the public to think in response to reports such as these? "Alcohol: Spirit of Health?" examines both the positive and negative aspects of alcohol use and discusses important issues that need to be considered before making a decision to drink for health reasons.

At issue here is not just alcohol but the meaning of the term moderation. What constitutes moderate alcohol use? Is it the same amount for all people and at all ages? Given the conflictual feelings we have as a culture regarding the use of alcohol, a reasonable approach to our alcohol problem would be an educational program that teaches the responsible use of alcohol rather than one that merely condemns it.

By contrast, few people continue to harbor any misconceptions about the health hazards caused by the prolonged use of tobacco. Most realize that this drug is associated with emphysema, lung cancer, strokes, and heart disease, but they may not be aware that smoking can cause retinal damage, impotence, cold fingers, and

UNIT 5

One cancer you can give yourself.

Horrible isn't it?

AMERICAN CANCER SOCIETY

low back pains. "Alcohol and Tobacco: A Deadly Duo" is particularly interesting because, in addition to presenting the health hazards of this dual addiction, it discusses why drinkers are heavier smokers. Given the amount of bad press that tobacco has had over the last few years, why is it that so many Americans continue to smoke? Perhaps the answer is nicotine. Recent studies indicate that nicotine is as addictive as heroin; thus, smoking is an addiction rather than merely a habit. Carl Sherman, in "Kicking Butts," discusses the process of quitting smoking and suggests that for many smokers, nicotine not only gives pleasure but eases pain. For some smokers, the addiction to nicotine is so strong that even if they do stop smoking they will always need nicotine from some source to feel normal.

While many nonsmokers feel sympathetic to the needs of the addicted smoker, they also feel that they deserve to breathe clean, smoke-free air. This conflict between the needs of the smoker and the nonsmoker has pushed the issue of smoking in public places to the forefront. As one might expect, the tobacco industry, fearing passage of legislation that would severely restrict the use of tobacco products in public places, is once again waging a propaganda war. This time the target is the hazards of second-hand and side-stream smoke. Another area of concern regarding tobacco use has to do with a form of smokeless tobacco called snuff. The popularity of snuff is largely due to the fact that many famous professional athletes use it, leading their admiring young fans to believe that it is relatively harmless. The sad truth is that smokeless tobacco also poses a real health threat to the user.

For years we have heard our political leaders declare that we are in the midst of a drug war, but we must ask who the enemy is. As a culture, we have grown up believing that there is, or should be, a drug to treat any malady or discomfort that befalls us. The pharmaceutical industry, driven by profits, has responded to this demand, as have illicit drug dealers. Would we have a drug problem if there were no demand for drugs? We have seen the enemy and it is us!

Looking Ahead: Challenge Questions

Do you think America has a drug problem? If so, why?

How might a person decide when drug use has become drug abuse?

What responsibility does the U.S. government have in preventing drug abuse? Local communities?

Should insurance companies pay medical costs incurred as a result of drug abuse?

What factors should a person consider before making the decision to use alcohol to safeguard health?

What restrictions, if any, should be placed on the use of tobacco products?

Some states are considering passing laws that would make it a crime to abuse drugs during pregnancy. How do you feel about this?

HOW TO PICK A PAIN RELIEVER

Despite the clutter on the shelves—and the nonsense in the ads—choosing the right product needn't be a headache.

"There are basically just three over-the-counter pain-relieving ingredients on the market: aspirin, acetaminophen, and ibuprofen." That's how we began our last report on pain relievers in November 1993. Since then, that basic selection has nearly doubled with the addition of two more ingredients previously available only by prescription: naproxen sodium, which hit the shelves under the brand name *Aleve* in 1994, and ketoprofen, which arrived as *Orudis KT* last fall and was joined this year by *Actron*.

The newest choices are still limited to those brand names—but not for long: Exclusive marketing rights for naproxen and ketoprofen will soon expire, opening the door to other brands and generic knockoffs. The original three ingredients, meanwhile, long ago spread to countless products, from national brands to local drugstore and supermarket labels.

Yet it needn't be that hard to choose the drug that's right for you. It just takes shutting out the promotional clamor long enough to concentrate on two things: your pain and your medical profile. All five basic ingredients can relieve garden-variety aches and pains and reduce fever; some are a bit better than others for particular types of pain. The drugs vary slightly in how long they work. And they vary in the kind and degree of side effects they can produce.

Here's a close look at some of the latest pain-reliever promotions—and the facts behind the promises.

Effectiveness

The claim: "*Actron*. It's so small because it's so powerful."

The claim: "New *Orudis KT*. The potent medicine for pain."

The facts: The ads go on to compare the standard dose of ketoprofen with other pain relievers—"just 12½ mg [of *Actron*] are as effective as 200 mg of *Advil* or 650 mg of *Tylenol*," "just 25 mg [of *Orudis KT*] is as effective as 400 mg of *Motrin IB*, 440 mg of *Aleve*, or 1000 mg of *Extra Strength Tylenol*"—highlighting what appears to be an impressive edge.

It's true that ketoprofen is more powerful than the others on a milligram-for-milligram basis. But that's a meaningless comparison; people take pills, not milligrams. So what if one active ingredient requires fewer milligrams to have the same effect as another? One possible "so what" might be that you can fit the drug into a smaller pill, and *Actron* capitalizes on that opportunity: Each pill measures 7 millimeters in diameter (about one-quarter inch), compared with 10 to 12 mm (roughly one-third to one-half inch) for the others—including its chemical twin, *Orudis KT*. That's a plus for people who have trouble swallowing something the size of the average aspirin tablet, but a minus for those who have trouble handling tiny pills.

Both brands of ketoprofen are indeed more "powerful" and "potent" than at least one competitor—acetaminophen (*Tylenol*)—in one regard: They reduce inflammation, though no better than the others. That's because ketoprofen, ibuprofen, and naproxen are all "nonsteroidal anti-inflammatory drugs," or NSAIDs, which makes them better for muscle sprains, pain after dental procedures, and some types of arthritis pain. NSAIDs are also particularly effective against menstrual pain. (Though aspirin is an NSAID, it's usually not best for those purposes since it can promote bleeding and cause other side effects.)

Duration

The claim: "All day long. All day strong. *Aleve*."

The counterclaim: "Nothing has been shown to last longer than *Advil*. And that includes *Aleve*."

The facts: Sorry, *Advil*, that doesn't include *Aleve*. In a recent U.S. District Court case, American Home Products, the maker of *Advil*, lost an attempt to bar Procter-Syntex from claiming *Aleve* lasts longer. The judge noted that the U.S. Food and Drug Administration, in approving naproxen's over-the-counter switch, had itself found a trend toward longer duration of action in *Aleve* over *Advil* (ibuprofen).

Ibuprofen, ketoprofen, acetaminophen, and aspirin all work for roughly four to six hours—at which time you can take another dose, if needed. Naproxen lasts

COMPARING PAIN RELIEF

Here's a quick reference for the particular strengths and weaknesses of the five over-the-counter pain relievers. (See story for details; for brand names, see table, facing page.)

Purpose	Aspirin	Acetaminophen	Ibuprofen	Ketoprofen	Naproxen
Occasional headaches, garden-variety pain	★	✔	✔	✔	✔
Fever	✔	★	✔	✔	✔
Pain in people with certain medical conditions [1]	✘	★	✘	✘	✘
Children's pain relief	✘	★	✔	✘	✘
Osteoarthritis pain	✔	★	✔	✔	✔
Inflammation (muscle sprains, dental pain, some arthritis [2])	✔	✘	★	✔	✔
Menstrual cramps	✔	✔	★	✔	✔

★ Best choice (except when contraindicated).
✔ Equally effective for that purpose, though not first choice—due to cost, side effects, or other factors.
✘ Not appropriate or not safe for that purpose.

[1] Includes ulcer, other stomach or intestinal problems, high blood pressure, clotting problems, and kidney disease. (People with liver disease or who have three or more alcoholic drinks a day should consult their physician before using pain relievers.)

[2] For arthritis pain not relieved by acetaminophen.

up to seven or eight hours in most people, and sometimes longer. However, naproxen's longer dosing schedule is not necessarily a plus. For one thing, a typical headache, once relieved, often won't return after a single dose wears off, no matter which pain reliever you use. And while the standard dosage for naproxen permits a repeat dose as frequently as every eight hours, older adults are advised not to take the drug more often than once every 12 hours.

The makers of *Aleve* have tried to turn that restriction into an advantage, with ads saying, "If you're over 65, just take two *Aleve* for the entire day"—as if the drug were particularly effective in older people. In fact, it's just particularly risky for them; more frequent doses pose a risk of ulcers and kidney damage. *Aleve* is the only over-the-counter pain reliever with a dosage restriction for people over age 65.

Stomach upset

The claim: "*Aleve* is . . . gentler to your stomach lining than aspirin."

The facts: Naproxen is less likely than aspirin to cause stomach upset and gastrointestinal bleeding—but other pain relievers are milder than either of those. Acetaminophen is the hands-down winner, followed by ibuprofen. Naproxen is more likely to cause such side effects, and some evidence suggests that ketoprofen may be even harsher. For healthy, occasional users of pain relievers, the stomach and intestinal risks aren't big concerns. But if you're a regular user, particularly if you have an ulcer, they can be.

The likelihood of stomach irritation from any pain reliever can be reduced by taking it with a full glass of water. "Buffered" aspirin products containing antacids (*Ascriptin, Bufferin*) may ease stomach upset from an occasional dose, but may not be gentler over long-term use. Enteric-coated aspirin (*Ecotrin*), which should dissolve only after leaving the stomach, may also cause less irritation, but it takes that much longer to relieve pain. Anyone concerned about stomach upset should avoid pain relievers that contain caffeine (*Anacin, Excedrin*), which can boost pain relief somewhat but can also irritate the stomach.

Arthritis pain

The claim: "For minor arthritis pain, more doctors recommend *Advil* than any other pain reliever."

The counterclaim: "Doctors recommend *Tylenol* twice as often as aspirin and ibuprofen for anyone with common arthritis."

The counter-counterclaim: "*Extra Strength Bayer*. The pure power to safely relieve the arthritis inflammation *Tylenol* can't touch."

The facts: The standard drug therapy for osteoarthritis, the most common form of arthritis, used to be prescription-strength NSAIDs. But in many cases, osteoarthritis pain doesn't stem from inflammation. So acetaminophen, which eases pain but not inflammation, works just as well in those cases. And recent studies have shown that acetaminophen can often do the trick even when the joint is inflamed, so the drug is now the best first choice for osteoarthritis pain. If acetaminophen fails, aspirin or some other over-the-counter anti-inflammatory may help.

People who continually take repeated doses of acetaminophen for osteoarthritis pain might be tempted to consider *Tylenol Extended Relief*, *Tylenol's* answer to long-lasting *Aleve*. Rather than the usual four-to-six hour dosing schedule, the time-release product delivers the same amount of active ingredient when taken every eight hours. (There's also a time-release aspirin product, *Extended-release Bayer 8-Hour*, but due to aspirin's chemical properties, it works no better than just doubling the usual dose of

Continued on next page

OVER-THE-COUNTER PAIN RELIEVERS

Brands [1]	Cost per maximum daily dose [2]	
ACETAMINOPHEN		
REGULAR STRENGTH		
Actamin	Tylenol:	$0.75
Genapap	Generic:	$0.37
Tylenol	Saving:	51%
Valorin		
EXTRA STRENGTH		
Aspirin Free Anacin Maximum Strength	Tylenol Extra Strength:	$0.57
Arthritis Foundation Pain Reliever,	Generic:	$0.35
Aspirin Free	Saving:	38%
Panadol Maximum Strength		
Tylenol Extended Relief		
Tylenol Extra Strength		
ASPIRIN		
REGULAR STRENGTH		
Bayer	Bayer:	$0.65
Ecotrin	Generic:	$0.25
Empirin	Saving:	61%
Norwich		
EXTRA STRENGTH		
Maximum Strength Arthritis Foundation	Extra Strength Bayer:	$0.92
Extra Strength Bayer Arthritis Pain Formula	Generic:	$0.27
Extended-release Bayer 8-Hour	Saving:	70%
Ecotrin		
Norwich Extra-Strength		
IBUPROFEN		
Advil	Advil:	$0.49
Arthritis Foundation Ibuprofen	Generic:	$0.27
Motrin IB	Saving:	44%
Nuprin		
KETOPROFEN		
Actron	Orudis KT:	$0.53
Orudis KT	Generic:	[3]
NAPROXEN SODIUM		
Aleve	Aleve:	$0.24 [4]
	Generic:	[3]

[1] Table lists brand names of common products that contain the drug as the single active ingredient. Several other brands contain acetaminophen and/or aspirin in combination with other active ingredients: *Aspirin-Free Excedrin* and *Bayer Select Maximum Strength* (acetaminophen and caffeine); *Anacin* and *Anacin Maximum Strength* (aspirin and caffeine); *Excedrin Extra-Strength* (acetaminophen, aspirin, and caffeine); *Vanquish* (acetaminophen, aspirin, caffeine, and antacid); *Arthritis Pain Ascriptin, Bufferin,* and *Arthritis Strength Bufferin* (aspirin and antacid).

[2] Cost comparison based on typical drugstore price of leading brand and generic version for 100-tablet containers (except extra-strength aspirin, based on 50-tablet containers).

[3] Not yet available in generic form.

[4] Cost based on standard maximum dose of three 220-mg tablets per day; people over age 65 can take no more than two tablets per day.

ordinary aspirin.) However, a study by the University of Pittsburgh's Randy Juhl, Ph.D., who chairs the FDA's advisory committee on nonprescription drugs, found that most people with arthritis prefer shorter-acting pain medication, even if that means taking it more frequently. That might be, Juhl speculates, because more frequent dosing provides a greater sense of control over symptoms.

Extra-strength acetaminophen or aspirin offers no real advantage. People who regularly take the maximum dose of either drug can get the same amount of active ingredient just by taking three 325-mg pills rather than two 500-mg pills at each dose. And as an all-purpose pain reliever, extra-strength formulas are a bad idea: One pill may be too weak; two are often more than you'll need.

Safety

The claim: *"Tylenol is the safest type of pain reliever you can buy."*

The facts: That's true. Even in light of safety concerns raised last year (see *CR on Health*'s May 1995 issue), acetaminophen is still least likely to cause stomach upset, gastrointestinal bleeding, or kidney damage. And it won't boost blood pressure, the way chronic use of NSAIDs can. But that doesn't mean acetaminophen is risk-free. Even a modest overdose can be dangerous. That's especially true for older people, as well as people who have liver disease and those who down three or more alcoholic drinks a day. Before using *any* pain reliever regularly, it's important to check with your physician.

> ### *Summing up*
> Naproxen sodium (*Aleve*) and the latest entry, ketoprofen (*Actron, Orudis KT*), add little to the over-the-counter pain-reliever lineup. They're not more effective than ibuprofen (*Advil, Motrin IB*) or less risky than acetaminophen (*Panadol, Tylenol*).
>
> ### What to do
> ■ For occasional pain relief in healthy adults, aspirin is still a fine first choice.
> ■ For frequent use and for certain types of pain or certain medical conditions, either acetaminophen or ibuprofen may be best (see chart, "Comparing Pain Relief").
> ■ Consider naproxen or ketoprofen only as a fallback for ibuprofen.
> ■ Choose low-cost, generic versions.
> ■ Before using any pain reliever regularly, consult your doctor.

PRECAUTIONS ON PAIN RELIEVERS

To prevent dangerous side effects, consult a doctor about over-the-counter pain medications if you:

■ Have a painful chronic condition, such as arthritis, that requires high doses of pain relievers.
■ Have a history of stomach or intestinal irritation or bleeding.
■ Take anticoagulants or have a bleeding disorder.
■ Take medication for high blood pressure.
■ Have impaired kidney or liver function, or a condition that affects those organs, such as congestive heart failure.
■ Have a history of allergy to aspirin or other pain relievers.
■ Have more than three alcoholic drinks a day.

One final caution: Don't give aspirin to children or teenagers. If they have flu or chicken pox, which may not be obvious at first, aspirin can cause Reye's syndrome, a rare but often fatal disorder. Acetaminophen is the best option.

OTC DRUGS: PRESCRIPTION FOR DANGER?

"Soothing. Strong. Trustworthy." According to the maker of the new over-the-counter pain reliever *Aleve*, that's the message conveyed by the product's white and blue colors. But anti-inflammatory pain relievers like *Aleve* and aspirin are not so soothing to the stomach: Prolonged use of such drugs is one of the main causes of ulcers.

Indeed, nonprescription drugs can cause serious harm if you don't know—or don't follow—the appropriate precautions, not all of which are listed on the label. Taking these medications too often or in high doses can produce severe side effects, worsen the very symptoms you're trying to treat, or delay diagnosis of major diseases. Taking them with the wrong foods, drinks, or medications can spark dangerous reactions.

You can now buy some 450 over-the-counter drugs that would have required a prescription just 15 years ago. Naproxen (*Aleve*) is the latest to make the switch. That trend increases your ability to manage your own health—but it also increases the potential for overuse and misuse. Moreover, it means that people will now be getting much of their information about drugs from advertisements, such as an ad for the yeast-fighting drug *Monistat 7*, which printed a crucial warning in such tiny type that you could easily mistake it for a smudge at the bottom of the page. (That warning cautioned women not to treat an apparent yeast infection on their own unless their doctor had diagnosed the same kind of infection in the past.)

This report describes the kinds of trouble that nonprescription drugs can cause, lists the specific risks of the most common drugs (see table), and tells you how to get the information you need to use over-the-counter drugs safely.

A grab bag of risks

Although over-the-counter drugs taken at the recommended doses rarely cause dangerous side effects in healthy people, they can cause a number of unpleasant symptoms. Those include insomnia and irritability from oral decongestants, constipation from aluminum-containing antacids, diarrhea from magnesium-containing antacids, and indigestion from all pain relievers except acetaminophen (*Tylenol*). One common side effect—drowsiness from antihistamines, which are contained in all allergy drugs and some cold medications—could be more hazardous. In fact, the maximum recommended dose of some antihistamines can slow reaction time more than the amount of alcohol that would make driving illegal in most states.

The risk of side effects from over-the-counter drugs increases sharply when people take more than they should. For example, swallowing just three times more than the maximum recommended dose of phenylpropanolamine—contained in the oral decongestant *Propagest*, many cold remedies, and all diet pills—can cause severe and even life-threatening rises in blood pressure. Taking a drug continually without consulting a doctor also multiplies the risk of side effects, such as anemia from chronic use of aspirin or potassium depletion and bowel damage from excessive use of the laxative bisacodyl (*Carter's Little Pills, Dulcolax, Fleet Bisacodyl*).

Further, overuse of certain nonprescription drugs can lead to an insidious form of dependency. People who keep taking drugs to relieve headaches or nasal congestion will often get "rebound" symptoms—headaches or congestion worse than the original symptoms—as soon as the drug starts wearing off. That may lead to a vicious cycle of increasingly frequent use of the drug and worsening rebound. Similarly, prolonged use of laxatives can weaken the bowel muscles, causing renewed constipation as soon as the drug is discontinued.

The gravest danger from sustained use of over-the-counter medications is that you might be controlling symptoms while allowing an underlying disease to go untreated. For example, people with stomach pain sometimes take over-the-counter antacids or pain relievers for months without seeing a doctor. Those people may have ulcers or inflammation of the stomach, which can cause serious bleeding; or they may even have stomach cancer.

Drug interactions

Over-the-counter drugs can become more dangerous when they're taken with other medications—an all-too-common practice. According to a recent survey, one out of three people who take antihistamines for allergies take other drugs at the same time. But many common medications can make antihistamines even more sedating than they are when taken alone. The alcohol in a cough syrup such as *Comtrex Liquid, Tylenol Cough with Decongestant Liquid*, or *Vicks Formula 44 Multi-Symptom Cough Medicine* can combine with antihistamines to cause excessive drowsiness. In addition, you can get an unexpected double dose of antihistamines by taking an allergy drug along with a cold remedy such as *Alka-Seltzer Plus Cold* or *Contac Severe Cold Formula* or with a sleep aid such as *Nytol* or *Sominex*, all of which contain antihistamines.

Nonprescription drugs can also change the way other, more vital medications are supposed to work. Taking an antacid to prevent an antibiotic from upsetting your stomach may also prevent your body from absorbing the medicine, so it never reaches the infec-

Just because you can buy them without a doctor's okay doesn't mean they can't harm you.

tion. Conversely, taking a stool-softening laxative may ease constipation caused by the antihypertensive drug verapamil (*Isoptin, Calan*)—but it may also increase absorption of the drug, leading to an excessive reduction in blood pressure and, in turn, possibly to fainting.

Even ordinary foods can turn a seemingly innocuous drug into a hazardous one. For example, trying to calm your stomach by drinking large quantities of milk and taking antacids containing either calcium, magnesium, or sodium bicarbonate can eventually cause kidney failure.

People with certain chronic diseases are particularly vulnerable to the adverse effects of over-the-counter medications. But by far the most common condition that increases such vulnerability is simply old age.

Older people have more diseases and take more drugs than younger people, which increases all drug-related risks. In addition, the body becomes less efficient at breaking down and eliminating drugs as it ages. As a result, drugs may reach higher levels in the bloodstream and remain there longer. Even at normal levels, many medications have more pronounced effects on the brain and other parts of the aging body. Unfortunately, researchers rarely test new drugs on older people, so the recommended doses are often set too high for them.

The limits of labels

Labels for over-the-counter drugs do print certain crucial directions and precautions. Some packages also contain an insert, which may give more complete information. But neither labels nor inserts tell you everything you need to know about using these drugs, in part because the manufacturers don't want to scare people away.

The label or insert usually specifies how long you can safely use the medication—but it doesn't always. Some labels or inserts say nothing about possible side effects, interactions with food or other medications, or conditions that might make using the drug risky; those that do list such risks omit a good deal of potentially significant information. For example, neither the label nor the insert for *Aleve* mentions two relatively common side effects, dizziness and gastrointestinal bleeding. And neither label nor insert warns that the drug can harm people who have liver or kidney disease, or that it can neutralize the effect of antihypertensive medications.

Here's how to get more complete information about drugs than the manufacturer provides.

Ask the pharmacist

If you buy all your prescription and over-the-counter medications at one neighborhood pharmacy, rather than price shopping, make sure the pharmacist enters those medications—as well as any drug allergies you may have—in the pharmacy's computerized drug record. The computer will automatically alert the pharmacist to potential drug interactions and allergic reactions. If you're allergic to aspirin, for example, you might not realize that *Alka Seltzer Plus Nighttime Cold* contains aspirin, or that ibuprofen (*Advil, Motrin-IB*) and naproxen (*Aleve*) may each trigger similar reactions in aspirin-sensitive individuals. Even mail-order pharmacies typically provide a toll-free hotline staffed by pharmacists who will answer customer questions.

Read the package insert or label before you leave the store—or after you receive the drug in the mail—so you can ask the pharmacist to clarify anything that you don't understand or that the packaging doesn't specify, such as the following:

● What's the maximum length of time you should take the medication on your own without consulting your doctor?
● Does the drug interact with any of the other medications you might be taking or with any food or beverage?
● Are there any unlisted side effects you should know about?
● Should you take the drug with meals or on an empty stomach?
● Should you take the drug at bedtime?
● Can anything help you minimize minor side effects such as an upset stomach?
● How should you store the drug?

In addition to those questions, older people may want to ask the pharmacist whether the medication poses any increased risk for them.

Ask the doctor

Call your doctor before starting to take an over-the-counter drug if:

You have an unfamiliar symptom. It's safe to treat yourself with medication temporarily only if you have commonplace symptoms such as a runny nose, cough, headache, or upset stomach, or if your physician has diagnosed the same problem, such as an asthma attack or a vaginal yeast infection, on an earlier occasion.
● You have any chronic disorder.
● You are pregnant or nursing.
● The pharmacist says the drug may pose an increased risk for you. If so, your doctor can suggest solutions, such as reducing the dosage or trying a different medication.

Keep your doctor up to date on all the over-the-counter medications you're taking, including vitamins, minerals, or other supplements. If you're experiencing symptoms, those drugs or supplements may actually be the cause of the problem; or they may interact with prescribed medications or skew the results of laboratory tests. Even better, throw all your medications in a bag and bring them with you on your next office visit, so your physician can review your entire drug regimen.

In addition to talking with a pharmacist or doctor, consult a consumer drug-information book such as The Complete Drug Reference, available in most libraries or from Consumer Reports Books. (Send $39.95 to Box 10637, Des Moines, Iowa, 50336. Or call 515-237-4903.)

RISKS OF SOME COMMON OVER-THE-COUNTER DRUGS

Drug	Side effects	High-risk groups [1]	Interactions
PAIN RELIEVERS			
Aspirin Bayer Empirin Norwich	Common: Stomach upset [2], heartburn, gastrointestinal bleeding, nausea, vomiting, decreased clotting. Less common or rare: Bloody or tarry stools, bloody urine, ringing in the ears, loss of hearing, allergic reaction (skin rash, hives, itching, tightness in chest). Signs of overdose: Confusion, severe diarrhea, fast or deep breathing, severe drowsiness, convulsions.	People with allergies to aspirin or other nonsteroidal anti-inflammatory drugs, ulcers, anemia, bleeding disorders, overactive thyroid, asthma, high blood pressure, kidney or liver disease; children or teenagers with flu or chicken pox.	Can increase effect of anticoagulants. Can alter urine-sugar tests for diabetics.
Acetaminophen Actamin Tylenol Valadol	Common: None. Rare: Bloody or decreased urination, allergic reaction (skin rash, hives, tightness in chest). Signs of overdose: Diarrhea, increased sweating, loss of appetite, nausea, vomiting, or stomach pain.	People with kidney or liver disease; active alcoholics.	Can alter urine-sugar tests for diabetics.
Ibuprofen Advil Motrin-IB Nuprin	Common: Stomach upset [2], gastrointestinal bleeding, heartburn, nausea, vomiting, dizziness, drowsiness, lightheadedness, headache. Less common or rare: Bitter taste, gas, constipation, loss of appetite, allergic reaction (skin rash, hives, itching, tightness in chest). Signs of overdose: Lethargy, low blood pressure, irregular heartbeat, difficulty breathing.	People with diabetes, asthma, kidney or liver disease, colitis, ulcers, congestive heart failure, high blood pressure, epilepsy.	Can increase effect of anticoagulants. Side effects increase when taken with aspirin. Can decrease effect of antihypertensive drugs.
Naproxen Aleve	Generally same as ibuprofen. [2]	Generally same as ibuprofen. [3]	Same as ibuprofen.
ANTIHISTAMINES [4]			
Brompheniramine Dimetane **Chlorpheniramine** Aller-Chlor Chlor-Trimeton Pfeiffer's Allergy **Clemastine** Tavist-1 **Diphenhydramine** Benadryl 25 Benylin Cough Sominex	Common: Drowsiness, thickening of mucus. Less common or rare: Blurred vision, confusion, difficulty urinating, dizziness, dryness of mouth, nose, or throat, loss of appetite, nervousness, restlessness, irritability. Signs of overdose: Clumsiness or unsteadiness, facial flushing, difficulty breathing, severe drowsiness, seizures.	People with glaucoma, liver disease, enlarged prostate, difficulty urinating.	Increases sedative effect if taken with alcohol, narcotics, sleeping medications, or tranquilizers. Can cause increased drowsiness or dry mouth if taken with or up to two weeks after a monoamine oxidase inhibitor (antidepressant drugs). Can cause dry mouth if taken with anticholinergics (drugs for stomach cramps).
ORAL DECONGESTANTS			
Pseudoephedrine Efidac/24 Halofed Sudafed **Phenylpropanolamine** [5] Propagest	Common: Insomnia, nervousness, restlessness, irritability. Less common or rare: Difficulty urinating, dizziness, fast, slow, or irregular heartbeat, headache, sweating, nausea, vomiting. Signs of overdose: Convulsions, fast breathing, hallucinations, increase in blood pressure, irregular heartbeat, difficulty breathing.	People with diabetes, enlarged prostate, heart disease, high blood pressure, or overactive thyroid.	Can reduce effect of beta blockers. Can cause high blood pressure, fever, or seizures if taken with or up to two weeks after a monoamine oxidase inhibitor (antidepressant drugs). Can cause insomnia, irritability, irregular heartbeats, or seizures if taken with asthma medications, caffeine, or amphetamines.
TOPICAL DECONGESTANTS [6]			
Oxymetazoline Afrin 12-Hour Dristan 12-Hour Duration 12-Hour **Phenylephrine** Alconefrin Neo-Synephrine Vicks Sinex	Common: Prolonged use may cause rebound congestion. Less common or rare: Rapid heartbeat, lightheadedness, trembling, insomnia, nervousness.	People with diabetes, heart disease, high blood pressure, or overactive thyroid.	May increase risk of serious side effects if taken with or up to two weeks after a monoamine oxidase inhibitor (antidepressant drugs).

[1] People with these conditions should avoid drug or check with doctor.
[2] Aspirin causes the most stomach upset; naproxen causes somewhat less, but more than ibuprofen.
[3] People over age 65 must follow lower dosage instructions.
[4] Antihistamines vary in their sedative effects: Diphenhydramine is highly sedating, clemastine moderately sedating, and the others mildly sedating.
[5] More likely than pseudoephedrine to increase blood pressure sharply. Phenylpropanolamine is also found in all over-the-counter diet pills and in many cold medicines.
[6] Available in drops or sprays.

KICKING BUTTS

Nicotine is more powerfully addictive than most people realize. It will probably take several tries before you learn enough tricks to stay cigarette-free for good.

Carl Sherman

Carl Sherman writes on health, medicine, and psychology for national magazines and medical newspapers. He lives in New York City. He last wrote for Psychology Today *about sexual abuse in psychotherapy. He is the coauthor of a book on psychological aspects of skin disorders and his writings are anthologized in many collections.*

It may not be a "sin" anymore, but few would dispute that smoking is the devil to give up. Of the 46 million Americans who smoke—26 percent of the adult population—an estimated 80 percent would like to stop and one-third try each year. Two to 3 percent of them succeed. "There's an extraordinarily high rate of relapse among people who want to quit," says Michael Fiore, M.D., M.P.H., director of the Center for Tobacco Research and Intervention at the University of Wisconsin.

The tenacity of its grip can be matched by few other behaviors, most of which, like snorting cocaine and shooting up heroin, are illegal. Since 1988, nicotine dependence and withdrawal have been recognized as disorders by the American Psychiatric Association, legitimizing the experience of the millions who have tried, successfully and otherwise, to put smoking behind them while kibitzers told them to use more willpower.

It's not just a habit, the medical and scientific communities now fully agree, but an addiction, comparable in strength to hard drugs and alcohol.

In fact, the odds of "graduating" from experimentation to true dependence are far worse for cigarettes than for illicit drugs, which testifies to tobacco's one-two punch of addictiveness and availability: Crack and heroin aren't sold in vending machines and hawked from billboards. Alcohol is as legal and available as cigarettes are, and as big a business, but apparently easier to take or leave alone. The majority of people who drink are not dependent on alcohol, while as many as 90 percent of smokers are addicted.

If nothing else, the persistence of smoking in the face of a devastating rogue's gallery of bodily damage, little of which has been kept secret, attests to the fact that this is no rational lifestyle decision. "Take all the deaths in America caused by alcohol, illicit drugs, fires, car accidents, homicide, and suicide. Throw in AIDS. It's still only half the deaths every year from cigarettes," says Fiore.

The news, however, isn't all bad. For the last 20 years, the proportion of Americans who smoke has dropped continuously, for the first time in our history. In America today, there are nearly 45 million ex-smokers, about as many as are still puffing away.

These quitters, perhaps surprisingly, are for the most part the same folk who tried and failed before. The average person who successfully gives up smoking does so after five or six futile attempts, says Fiore. "It appears that many smokers need to go through a process of quitting and relapsing a number of times

TIPS FOR QUITTERS

• Nicotine addiction is powerful. Expect to struggle for a couple of months. It's an up-and down course.

• Don't despair. It may take six tries to learn enough skills to beat this addiction.

• Aim for absolute abstinence—even a single puff leads to relapse.

• Inventory those things that make you feel good and treat yourself to them—exercising, kissing, reading, taking a nap—instead of a smoke.

• Watch your coffee intake. Not only is it a trigger to smoke, your sensitivity to caffeine increases, mimicking nicotine-withdrawal symptoms.

• Change routines associated with smoking. Take a walk before your morning coffee. Drive to work a different way.

• Although most quitters succeed (eventually) on their own, programs that involve counseling improve the odds, especially for the depressed or anxious.

• Don't dismiss nicotine replacement with patch or gum. Gum allows you control over your blood nicotine level.

• Keep your guard up. Most lapses occur three or four weeks out, when you're feeling better.

• In the first weeks, avoid, or severely limit, alcohol.

before he or she can learn enough skills or maintain enough control to overcome this addiction."

> *'Evidence has mounted that a substantial number of smokers use cigarettes to regulate emotional states, particularly to reduce anxiety, sadness, or boredom.'*

Never underestimate the power of your enemy. Although nicotine may not give the taste of Nirvana that more notorious drugs do, its effects on the nervous system are profound and hard to resist. It increases levels of acetylcholine and norepinephrine, brain chemicals that regulate mood, attention, and memory. It also appears to stimulate the release of dopamine in the reward center of the brain, as opiates, cocaine, and alcohol do.

Addiction research has clearly established that drugs with a rapid onset—that hit the brain quickly—have the most potent psychological impact and are the most addictive. "With cigarettes, the smoker gets virtually immediate onset," says Jack Henningfield, Ph.D., chief of clinical pharmacology research for the National Institute on Drug Abuse. "The cigarette is the crack-cocaine of nicotine delivery."

Physiologically, smoking a drug, be it cocaine or nicotine, is the next best thing to injecting it. In fact, it's pretty much the same thing, says Henningfield. "Whether you inhale a drug in 15 seconds, which is pretty slow for an average smoker, or inject it in 15 seconds, the effects are identical in key respects," he says. The blood extracts nicotine from inhaled air just as efficiently as oxygen, and delivers it, within seconds, to the brain.

The cigarette also gives the smoker "something remarkable: the ability to get precise, fingertip dose control," says Henningfield. Achieving just the right blood level is a key to virtually all drug-induced gratification, and the seasoned smoker does this adeptly, by adjusting how rapidly and deeply he or she puffs. "If you get the dose just right after going without cigarettes for an hour or two, there's nothing like it," he says.

The impetus to smoke is indeed, as the tobacco companies put it, for pleasure. "But there's no evidence that smoke in the mouth provides much pleasure," says Henningfield. "We do know that nicotine in the brain does."

For many, nicotine not only gives pleasure, it eases pain. Evidence has mounted that a substantial number of smokers use cigarettes to regulate emotional states, particularly to reduce negative affect like anxiety, sadness, or boredom.

"People expect that having a cigarette will reduce bad feelings," says Thomas Brandon, Ph.D., assistant professor of psychology at the State University of New York at Binghamton. His research found this, in fact, to be one of the principal motivations for daily smokers.

Negative affect runs the gamut from the transitory down times we all have several times a day, to clinical depression. Smokers are about twice as likely to be depressed as nonsmokers, and people with a history of major depression are nearly 50 percent more likely than others to also have a history of smoking, according to Brandon.

Sadly, but not surprisingly, depression appears to cut your chance of quitting by as much as one-half, and the same apparently applies, to a lesser extent, to people who just have symptoms of depression.

According to Alexander Glassman, M.D., professor of psychiatry at the Columbia University College of Physicians and Surgeons, the act of quitting can trigger severe depression in some people. In one study, nine smokers in a group of 300 in a cessation program became so depressed—two were frankly suicidal—that the researchers advised them to give up the effort and try again later. All but one had a history of major depression.

"These weren't average smokers," Glassman points out. All were heavily dependent on nicotine, they smoked at least a pack and a half daily, had their first cigarette within a half hour of awakening, and had tried to quit, on average, five times before. It is possible, he suggests, that nicotine has an antidepressant effect on some.

More generally, suggests Brandon, the very effectiveness of cigarettes in improving affect is one thing that makes it so hard to quit. Not only does a dose of nicotine quell the symptoms of withdrawal (much more on this later), the neurotransmitters it releases in the brain are exactly those most likely to elevate mood.

For a person who often feels sad, anxious, or bored, smoking can easily become a dependable coping mechanism to be given up only with great difficulty. "Once people learn to use nicotine to regulate moods" says Brandon, "if you take it away without providing alternatives, they'll be much more vulnerable to negative affect states. To alleviate them, they'll be tempted to go back to what worked in the past."

In fact, negative affect is what precipitates relapse among would-be quitters 70 percent of the time, according to Saul Shiffman, Ph.D., professor of psychology at the University of Pittsburgh. "We invited people to call a relapse-prevention hot line, to find out what moments of crises were like; what was striking was how often they were in the grip of negative emotions just before relapses, strong temptations, and close calls." A more precise study using palm-top computers to track the state of mind of participants is getting similar results, Shiffman says.

Most relapses occur soon after quitting, some 50 percent within the first two weeks, and the vast majority by six months. But everyone knows of people who had a slip a year, two, or five after quitting, and were soon back to full-time puffing. And for each of them, there are countless others who have had to fight the occasional urge, desire, or outright craving months, even years after the habit has been, for all intents and purposes, left behind.

Acute withdrawal is over within four to six weeks for virtually all smokers. But the addiction is by no means *all* over. Like those who have been addicted to other drugs, ex-smokers apparently remain susceptible to "cues," suggests Brandon: Just

5. DRUGS AND HEALTH

as seeing a pile of sugar can arouse craving in the former cocaine user, being at a party or a club, particularly around smokers, can rekindle the lure of nicotine intensely. The same process may include "internal cues," says Brandon. "If you smoked in the past when under stress or depressed, the act of being depressed can serve as a cue to trigger the urge to smoke."

Like users of other drugs, Henningfield points out, addicted smokers don't just consume the offending substance to feel good (or not bad), but to feel "right." "The cigarette smoker's daily function becomes dependent on continued nicotine dosing: Not just mood, but the ability to maintain attention and concentration deteriorates very quickly in nicotine withdrawal."

Henningfield's studies have shown that in an addicted smoker, attention, memory, and reasoning ability start to decline measurably just four hours after the last cigarette. This reflects a real physiological impairment: a change in the electrical activity of the brain. Nine days after quitting, when some withdrawal symptoms, at least, have begun to ease, there has been no recovery in brain function.

How long does the impairment persist? No long-term studies have been done, but cravings and difficulties in cognitive function have been documented for as long as nine years in some ex-smokers. "There are clinical reports of people who have said that they still aren't functioning right, and eventually make the 'rational decision' to go back to smoking," Henningfield says.

The conclusion is inescapable that smoking causes changes in the nervous system that endure long after the physical addiction is history, and in some smokers, may never normalize.

The wealth of recent knowledge about smoking clarifies why it's hard to quit. But can it make it easier? If nothing else, it should help people take it seriously enough to gear up for the effort. "People think of quitting as something short term, but they should expect to struggle for a couple of months," says Shiffman.

What works? About 90 percent of people who give up smoking do so on their own, says Fiore. But the odds for success can be improved: Programs that involve counseling typically get better rates, and nicotine replacement can be a potent ally in whatever method you use.

In a metaanalysis of 17 placebo-controlled trials involving more than 5,000 people, Fiore found that the patch consistently doubled the success of quit attempts, whether or not antismoking counseling was used. After six months, 22 percent of the people who used the patch remained off cigarettes, compared to 9 percent who had a placebo. Of those who had the patch and a relatively intense counseling or support program, 27 percent were smoke-free.

More than 4 million Americans have tried the patch, which replaces the nicotine on which the smoker has become dependent, to ease such withdrawal symptoms as irritability, insomnia, inability to concentrate, and physical cravings that drive many back to tobacco.

'Smoking causes nervous system changes that endure after the physical addiction is history. Some people may never normalize.'

You're likely to profit from the patch if you have a real physical dependence on nicotine: that is, if you have your first cigarette within 30 minutes of waking up; smoke 20 or more a day; or experienced severe withdrawal symptoms during previous quit attempts.

Standard directions call for using the patches in decreasing doses for two to three months. Some researchers, however,

---

BORN TO SMOKE

Although the difference between smokers and nonsmokers appears to reflect complex environmental and social factors, genetics apparently plays a role comparable to that observed in alcoholism, responsible for about 30 percent of the propensity.

In particular, shared genetics appears to account for the link between smoking and depression, according to data collected on nearly 1,500 pairs of female twins. "The twin data show that whatever gene puts you at risk for depression, the same gene puts you at risk for smoking," says Alexander Glassman.

Further evidence for this conclusion comes from a prospective epidemiological study, in which 1,200 people in their twenties were surveyed twice, 18 months to two years apart. Nonsmokers who were depressed at the first interview were more likely to be smoking at the time of the second, while nondepressed smokers were more likely to have become depressed by then.

Genetics may even play a role in *how* you smoke. Shiffman studied a group of people who had smoked regularly but lightly, five cigarettes or less, four days or more a week, for several years at least. Says Saul Shiffman: "They had ample opportunity to become addicted—on average, they'd smoked 46,000 cigarettes, but we found not the slightest evidence of dependence: they showed no signs of withdrawal when abstinent. They really could casually take smoking or leave it."

Such nonaddicted users—"chippers," in drug culture parlance—are also seen among consumers of hard drugs. "We didn't delve deeply into what made these smokers different," says Shiffman. "But we did find evidence that they also had relatives who smoked with little dependence, who followed the same pattern. This makes it plausible, although it doesn't prove that these folks are biologically different." With rare exceptions, chippers have always smoked that way, he points out. For a once-addicted smoker to try to become a chipper is "a risky business" that's probably doomed to failure.—C.S.

suggest that for certain smokers, the patch may be necessary for years, or indefinitely.

"It's already happening," says Henningfield. "Some doctors have come to the conclusion that some patients are best able to get on with their life with nicotine maintenance." One such physician is David Peter Sachs, M.D., director of the Palo Alto Center for Pulmonary Disease Prevention. "I realized that with some of my patients, no matter how slowly I tried to taper them off nicotine replacement, they couldn't do it," says Sachs. "They were literally using it for years. Before you start tapering the dose, you should be cigarette-free for at least 30 days."

His clinical experience leads him to believe that 10 to 20 percent of smokers are *so* dependent that they may always need to get nicotine from somewhere. One study of people using the gum found that two years later, 20 percent of those who had successfully remained cigarette-free were still chewing. The idea of indefinite, even lifetime, nicotine maintenance sounds offensive to some. "Clearly, the goal to aim for is to be nicotine-free," says Sachs. "But if that can't be reached, being tobacco-free still represents a substantial gain for the patient, and for society." And getting nicotine via a patch or gum source means a far lower dose than you'd get from a cigarette. Plus, you're getting just nicotine, and not the 42 carcinogens in tobacco smoke.

Although the once-a-day patch has largely supplanted the gum first used in nicotine replacement, Sachs thinks that for some, the most effective treatment could involve one or both. The patch may be easier to use, but the gum is the only product that allows you control over blood nicotine level. Some people know they'll do better if they stay in control. And would-be quitters who do fine on the patch until they run into a stressful business meeting may stifle that urge to bum a cigarette if they boost their nicotine level in advance with a piece of gum, Sachs says.

However, nicotine replacement "is not a magic bullet," says Fiore. "It will take the edge off the tobacco-withdrawal syndrome, but it won't automatically transform any smoker into a nonsmoker." Other requisite needs vary from person to person. A standard approach teaches behavioral "coping skills," simple things like eating, chewing gum, or knitting to keep mouth or hands occupied, or leaving tempting situations. Ways people cope cognitively are as important as what they do, says Shiffman.

He advises would-be quitters at times of temptation to remind themselves just why they're quitting: "My children will be so proud of me," or "I want to live to see my grandchildren," for example. Think of a relaxing scene. Imagine how you'll feel tomorrow if you pass this crisis without smoking. Or simply tell yourself, "NO" or "Smoking is not an option."

Coping skills, however, are conspicuously unsuccessful for people who are high in negative affect. Supportive counseling works better. Depression or anxiety may interfere with the ability to use cognitive skills.

One exercise that Brandon teaches patients asks them to inventory—and treat themselves to—things that make them feel good, a substitute for the mood-elevating effect of a cigarette. These might include exercising, being with friends, going to concerts, reading, or taking a nap. "Positive life-style changes that improve mood level" are particularly useful if you use cigarettes to deal with negative emotional states, he says.

Depression treatment is particularly important for those trying to quit smoking. One study found that cognitive therapy significantly improved quit rates for people with a history of depression. Various antidepressants have been effective in small studies, and a large double-blind trial using the drug Zoloft is underway.

Fiore has found that having just one cigarette in the first two weeks of a cessation program predicted about 80 percent of

NICOTINE IN THE NINETIES

Smoking just doesn't have the cachet it once did. Instead of a mark of worldliness and *joie de vivre,* it's become something of a social disease, banned from airplanes, restaurants, and, in some localities, public parks. Except on billboards and in magazine ads, the smoker him- or herself is less likely to be the object of admiration than of pity and contempt.

The change in smoking's status is no doubt in part responsible for the 40 percent decline in its prevalence since 1964. And it would seem logical that those people who are still smoking in the face of such adversity are an increasingly hard-core, heavily addicted bunch, unable to quit.

Alexander Glassman conjectures that as the social environment grows more hostile to smoking, the genetic component of the behavior will become more evident. And as the number of smokers drops, an increasing percentage will have psychiatric problems, particularly depression.

But the change hasn't yet been documented. "Actually, I don't think the data support the idea that today's smokers are very different from years back," says Fiore. "The average number of cigarettes they smoke today isn't dramatically different from 20 years ago—about 22 per day."

One thing that has happened is a change in the sociodemographics of smoking. "More and more, it's a behavior predominantly exercised by disadvantaged members of society: 40 percent of high-school dropouts smoke, compared to 14 percent of college grads. Poor people are more likely to smoke than wealthy. It's getting marginalized," he says.

If nothing else, today's antismoking climate has eliminated much denial about the true nature of the cigarette habit. "Smokers are much more aware of being hooked," says Saul Shiffman. "You can't tell how dependent you are if access is easy. If you can smoke at your desk and at a restaurant, you can delude yourself, as people have for decades: 'I like to smoke but I can take it or leave it.' It's hard to say that when the only place you can smoke is outside when it's hailing and 20 degrees."—C.S.

5. DRUGS AND HEALTH

relapses at six months. Even when the withdrawal symptoms are gone, a single lapse can rekindle the urge as much as ever.

In the critical first weeks without cigarettes, a key to relapse prevention is avoiding, or severely limiting, alcohol, which not only blunts inhibitions, but is often powerfully bound to smoking as a habit. Up to one-half of people who try to quit have their first lapse with alcohol on board.

Watch your coffee intake, too. It can trigger the urge to smoke. And nicotine stimulates a liver enzyme that breaks down caffeine, so when you quit, you'll get more bang for each cup, leading to irritability, anxiety, and insomnia—the withdrawal symptoms that undermine quit efforts.

Try to change your routine to break patterns that strengthen addiction: drive to work a different way; don't linger at the table after a meal. And don't try to quit when you're under stress: vacation time might be a good occasion.

And if you do have a lapse? Don't trivialize it, because then you're more likely to have another, says Shiffman. But, "if you make it a catastrophe, you'll reconfirm fears that you'll never be able to quit," a low self-esteem position that could become a self-fulfilling prophecy. "Think of it as a warning, a mistake you'll have to overcome."

Try to learn from the lapse: examine the situation that led up to it, and plan to deal with it better in the future. "And take it as a sign you need to double your efforts," Shiffman says. "Looking back at a lapse, many people find they'd already begun to slack off; early on, they were avoiding situations where they were tempted to smoke, but later got careless."

Don't be discouraged by ups and downs. "It's normal to have it easy for a while, then all of a sudden you're under stress and for 10 minutes you have an intense craving," says Shiffman. "Consider the gain in frequency and duration: the urge to smoke is now coming back for 10 minutes, every two weeks, rather than all the time."

If lapse turns into relapse and you end up smoking regularly, the best antidote to despair is getting ready to try again. "Smoking is a chronic disease, and quitting is a process. Relapse and remission are part of the process," says Fiore. "As long as you're continuing to make progress toward the ultimate goal of being smoke-free, you should feel good about your achievement."

ALCOHOL and TOBACCO:
A Deadly Duo

Kristine Napier

Kristine Napier, M.P.H., R.D., is a Cleveland-based freelance writer. She studied alcohol/tobacco interactions during her graduate work.

Cancer of the upper respiratory and alimentary tracts claimed over 23,000 lives in 1989 and 57,000 additional cases were diagnosed. The majority of individuals who fall prey to this type of cancer are males who abuse both alcohol and tobacco.

THE RISK
The fact that the risk of developing cancer of the esophagus, lip, tongue, mouth, pharynx or larynx, increases dramatically in people who are heavy users of alcohol and tobacco is substantiated by 30 years of collective research. Studies demonstrate that the risk to individuals dually addicted far outweighs the risk to individuals who abuse only one substance. This confirmed link between alcohol and tobacco abuse and an increased risk in upper alimentary and respiratory tract cancer makes this type of disease among the most preventable.

THE CORRELATION BETWEEN SMOKING AND DRINKING
It has been observed that individuals who drink alcohol have a greater tendency to smoke than non-drinkers. One of the first studies to establish and quantify the degree of association between drinking and smoking was reported in 1972. The investigation compared 130 alcoholic men hospitalized for alcohol withdrawal to 100 non-alcoholic psychiatric outpatients. Ninety-four percent of the alcoholic men smoked one or more packs of cigarettes per day, as compared to only 46 percent of the non-alcoholics, who smoked one or more packs per day.

Another study, which compared male and female alcoholics enrolled in an army drug and alcohol rehabilitation program to non-alcoholic army personnel and their relatives, affirmed the smoking-drinking association. The report found that individuals who were alcoholics smoked an average of 49 cigarettes per day, but that the non-alcoholic subjects smoked only 13 cigarettes per day. In addition, the study established a high correlation between the number of cigarettes smoked and the grams of alcohol consumed by alcoholics, as opposed to a very weak association for the non-alcoholic control group.

In a similar report, 58 percent of the non-drinkers were non-smokers, but the individuals who were alcoholics did not abstain from smoking. The finding that smokers who did not drink smoked significantly less than smokers who did drink was further substantiated in additional studies.

WHY DO MANY DRINKERS SMOKE MORE?
Studies released in the late 1950s, correlating heavy coffee consumption with smoking and drinking, suggested that a strong oral drive caused drinkers to smoke more frequently. However, new evidence suggests that a strong oral drive is not the culprit.

In one study, alcoholics who had successfully stopped drinking demonstrated no appreciable increase in smoking. In fact, some even smoked less with alcohol abstinence. If a strong oral drive was responsible for the drinking-smoking association, one would expect an increase in smoking during periods of alcohol abstinence.

An alternative theory claimed that drinkers smoked more due to social pressure. However, a study showing that alcoholics who drank alone smoked just as much as alcoholics who drink in the company of other people

5. DRUGS AND HEALTH

dispelled this theory. The most plausible explanation is that drinkers smoke more than non-drinkers due to a greater physiological need for nicotine.

Nicotine, the main psychoactive component of tobacco, is a potent chemical. It has a stimulating effect on the nervous system, causing, among other things, increased heart rate and mental stimulation. Once addicted to **nicotine, a person may experience tremors or shakiness as** blood levels of nicotine decrease to critically low levels. The smoker will crave another cigarette as blood levels reach this threshold to avoid these uncomfortable symptoms. Alcohol apparently causes blood levels of nicotine to fall more rapidly in smokers by activating enzymes in tissues which metabolize drugs. For example, rats pretreated with ethanol cleared nicotine from their blood more rapidly than rats not receiving ethanol. This research, coupled with numerous independent observations, strongly suggests that drinkers must smoke more in order to maintain the blood nicotine levels upon which they have become dependent.

WHY IS THERE MORE CANCER AMONG ALCOHOL AND TOBACCO USERS?

Investigations are under way to find an answer to this question. Laboratory studies have shown that alcohol enhances the metabolism of several tobacco associated carcinogens, including nitrosamines. It is known that tobacco and its smoke contain many classes of chemical carcinogens which must be activated to react with DNA and initiate steps towards carcinogenesis. Important in this activation process are cytochrome P-450 enzymes, which are induced by alcohol in heavy drinkers. Thus, alcohol and smoking are synergistic in increasing cancer risk.

Since alcohol increases the metabolism and hence the need for nicotine, it follows that the success of smoking cessation programs will be improved if drinking habits of patients are controlled. Treatment of incipient alcoholism thus becomes a prerequisite for the ultimate success of behavior modification aimed at the elimination of smoking.

Alcohol: Spirit of health?
A little alcohol can be good for some people. Is it good for you?

Three years ago, we described the research showing that moderate drinking can protect the heart and help people live longer. Since then, researchers have uncovered evidence of a possibly major benefit: a reduced risk of diabetes. In its new Dietary Guidelines for Americans, released this January, the U.S. Government for the first time acknowledged the potential health benefits of alcohol.

But there's more to the story. New studies indicate that moderate drinking may raise the risk of breast cancer significantly more than previously believed. For that and other reasons, researchers are abandoning their blanket endorsement of moderate drinking; instead they're specifying who stands to gain—and who may actually be harmed.

How alcohol helps

Several large studies, involving a total of more than 600,000 people and lasting up to 12 years, have shown that people who drink moderately—no more than one drink a day for women, two for men—have 20 to 40 percent less risk of developing coronary disease than nondrinkers do. That reduction in risk is comparable to what you might gain from a strict low-fat diet.

Moderate drinking seems to protect the heart in three ways:

■ It boosts HDL. Studies have consistently shown that blood levels of HDL cholesterol (the "good" kind) are 10 to 15 percent higher in moderate drinkers than in nondrinkers. And several intervention trials have confirmed that drinking does raise HDL levels.

■ It inhibits potentially dangerous blood clots. As a result, the risk of heart attack drops significantly in the 24 hours after you take a drink.

■ It may increase the body's response to the hormone insulin. That can lead to decreased secretion of insulin. And lower insulin levels may be good for the heart, since insulin lowers HDL levels and increases both blood pressure and triglycerides, a fat that may raise coronary risk.

An improved insulin response also tends to lower blood-sugar levels. That may explain the latest apparent benefit of alcohol: a reduced risk of developing diabetes. Three large, lengthy studies, two of them published last year, have found that moderate drinkers are less likely to develop the disease than nondrinkers are.

Finally, the anti-clotting effect of moderate drinking increases the risk of hemorrhagic stroke, caused by bleeding in the brain; but it reduces the risk of thrombotic stroke, the more common though less deadly kind, caused by blood clots. The net result: a slight drop in the overall risk of having a stroke, though not of dying from one.

The sobering news

Until recently, research suggested that moderate drinking might marginally increase a woman's risk of breast cancer, by perhaps 10 percent. But two careful studies published last year have caused greater concern. One, a report on some 60,000 Dutch women, found that those who had just one drink a day faced a 30 percent increase in breast-cancer risk. The other, a study that compared some 6600 breast-cancer patients with 9200 other women, linked a single daily drink with a 40 percent increase and two drinks with a 70 percent increase. One possible explanation: Alcohol may boost blood levels of estrogen, which helps fuel the growth of breast cancer.

Other potential risks of moderate drinking include:

■ **Accidents.** A single drink in the average woman or two in the average man can disrupt coordination, cloud judgment, and weaken inhibitions. As a result, the risk of dying from accidents or violence is up to 40 percent higher in moderate drinkers than in abstainers.

5. DRUGS AND HEALTH

■ **Other cancers.** Some research suggests that moderate drinking may slightly increase the likelihood of cancer in regions exposed to high concentrations of alcohol, including the mouth, throat, larynx, esophagus, and liver.

■ **Cirrhosis of the liver.** Several studies have found that moderate drinkers are more likely to die of cirrhosis, or irreversible liver damage, than non-

> **Alcohol's impact on health depends partly on your gender. But the most important factor is age.**

drinkers are. But it's not clear whether those findings are accurate, since cirrhosis patients often misrepresent how much they actually drink.

Longer lives—for some

In theory, the ability of moderate drinking to help prevent coronary disease and possibly diabetes should outweigh the risks. And indeed, the overall death rate is roughly 10 percent lower in moderate drinkers than in nondrinkers.

But that doesn't mean all Americans should start stocking their medicine cabinet with spirits. For one thing, that 10 percent reduction comes from studies that looked mainly at people who have been drinking for some time. So it minimizes another potentially major risk: that new drinkers won't be able to keep their drinking moderate.

Immoderate drinking can harm rather than protect the heart, by raising blood pressure, weakening the heart muscle, and triggering abnormal cardiac rhythms. Excessive drinking increases the risk of breast cancer even more than moderate drinking does, and it clearly increases the chance of liver damage and of digestive-tract cancers. It can inflame the pancreas and the stomach lining, and increase susceptibility to osteoporosis. And it's the leading cause of deadly mishaps and mayhem.

Equally important, that 10 percent lower death rate is an overall average. That average obscures the fact that moderate drinking may have strikingly different effects in different groups of people.

Alcohol and age

The impact of alcohol on your health depends partly on whether you're a man or a woman. But the most important factor is how old you are.

Younger people. Accidents kill more men under age 40 than heart attacks and diabetes combined; accidents plus breast cancer similarly kill more women under age 50 than heart attacks and diabetes. So the increased risk of accidents and breast cancer due to moderate drinking should nullify or outweigh the reduction in the risk of coronary disease and possibly diabetes in those age groups. One other drawback of such drinking: The earlier you start, the greater your risk both of starting to drink heavily and of eventually developing an alcohol-related disease.

In a 12-year prospective study of 86,000 nurses, Harvard researchers found that women in their 30s who drank moderately died at a *faster* rate than those

---

What'll it be?

Five years ago, sales of red wine surged after Morley Safer announced on 60 Minutes that drinking the beverage protected the heart. Late last year, Safer touted wine again on 60 Minutes, citing a recent Danish study. Wine sales surged again—but wine's scientific stock remains flat.

Red wine and, to a lesser extent, white wine do contain flavonoids, which in theory may help protect the heart in two ways: They fight blood clots and they inhibit oxidation, chemical damage that may promote clogged arteries. In addition, red wine contains resveratrol, which also inhibits clotting. At least eight studies have found that either wine in general or red wine in particular cuts coronary risk or total mortality better than other alcoholic beverages.

But just as many studies have supported liquor or beer. In a recent review of the evidence, Harvard researchers concluded that no particular alcoholic beverage is any better for your health than the others. How you drink, they said, is far more important than what you drink.

The researchers noted that the seemingly superior drink in many studies was simply the one that people typically drank at mealtime—such as wine in France, beer in Hawaii, or cocktails in mainland America. Further, an Italian study on moderate drinkers linked wine with reduced risk only in those who drank while they ate.

Here are some possible reasons why alcohol may be safer or more healthful when it's consumed with food:

■ People who drink with meals typically consume less alcohol at one sitting than other drinkers do. So they're less likely to get drunk and have accidents. And food slows the absorption of alcohol, reducing that risk even more.

■ Drinking with meals—as opposed to just on social occasions—puts a little alcohol in your blood a lot of the time; that may maximize the benefit, much as time-release capsules maximize the effect of some medications.

■ Drinking with meals may provide the alcohol just when you need its anti-clotting ability the most. That's because the digested fat pouring into the blood after you eat makes it stickier and more likely to clot.

who didn't drink at all. Those in their 40s who drank moderately died at the same rate as the nondrinkers did. While there are no corresponding analyses for younger men, researchers anticipate similar trends.

> **Most middle-aged and older people who drink moderately can relax and enjoy the habit.**

A drink's a drink
One "drink" equals:
- 12 oz. of beer.
- 5 oz. of wine.
- 1½ oz. of 80-proof liquor.

▶ *Recommendation:* If you do drink, keep it light. That means a maximum of three drinks a week for premenopausal women, one drink a day for men under 40. (There are at least two reasons for the lower limit in women: They have a far greater breast-cancer risk, of course; and they typically have a smaller volume of fluids in their body to dilute the alcohol and less of the stomach enzyme that breaks the alcohol down.)

Older people. The risk of heart attack rises steadily after menopause in women and after age 40 in men, soon outstripping all the possible risks of moderate drinking. In the Harvard study, the nurses over age 50 who drank moderately had a 12 to 20 percent lower death rate than the nondrinkers did. In theory, moderate drinking should save even more lives in older men than in older women, given a man's generally higher coronary risk and much lower breast-cancer risk.

▶ *Recommendation:* Most middle-aged and older people who drink moderately can relax and enjoy the habit. Moderate drinking means no more than one drink a day if you're a woman, two if you're a man, until your mid-60s or so. After that, gradually reduce the size of your drinks, since the body can no longer handle as much alcohol as before, increasing the chance of accidents, confusion, and insomnia.

Safe to start?

Some older people, particularly those who face an increased risk for coronary heart disease, may wonder if they should start having, say, a glass of wine with dinner to help protect their heart—even if they don't really like the taste of alcoholic beverages. That decision should be made only after discussing the pros and cons thoroughly with your doctor. Don't even think about starting to drink—or even continuing to drink moderately—if you have a family history of alcoholism or depression; a personal history of anxiety, depression, or dependency on a medication or illicit drugs; or the slightest doubt about your own self-control.

Several medical factors can also make even moderate drinking potentially unsafe. Avoid alcohol or at least minimize your intake:

- If you have liver disease, abnormal heart rhythms, a previous hemorrhagic stroke, peptic ulcers, gout, pancreatitis, or high triglyceride levels.

- If you have either chronic insomnia or sleep apnea (spasmodic breathing during sleep).

- If you take certain medications. Alcohol can make certain common drugs dangerous, including antihistamines, aspirin or other nonsteroidal anti-inflammatory drugs such as ibuprofen (*Advil*) or diclofenac (*Voltaren*), nitrates (*ISMO, Nitrostat*), certain painkillers, sleeping pills, and tranquilizers. And alcohol can reduce the effectiveness of other drugs, including anticonvulsants and beta-blockers such as propranolol (*Inderal*) or metoprolol (*Lopressor*).

- If you may be pregnant, or are breast feeding. Some studies suggest that having as little as one drink a day during pregnancy may increase the chance of miscarriage, slightly low birth weight, cognitive and behavioral problems, or minor physical defects. In addition, one study found that breast-fed children of women who drank moderately had poorer motor development than the children of nondrinkers. While none of that evidence is conclusive, it's best to play it safe and avoid alcohol if you're either pregnant or breast feeding.

Of course, you should never drink before driving, boating, operating machinery, or doing anything else that requires good coordination and sharp reflexes.

Summing up

On average, moderate drinking reduces the overall death rate by about 10 percent. But middle-aged and older people may benefit more than that, while younger people may not benefit at all, or may even be harmed. Here's our advice:

- **Women:** Have no more than three drinks a week if you're premenopausal, one drink a day if you're postmenopausal. And don't drink at all if you're pregnant or breast feeding.

- **Men:** Have no more than one drink a day if you're under age 40, two a day if you're over 40.

- **For maximum benefit and minimum risk, drink mainly with meals** (see box, "What'll it be?").

- Don't start to drink for your health's sake unless you've discussed the pros and cons thoroughly with your doctor—and don't start at all if you have any susceptibility to alcoholism.

- Avoid alcohol if you take certain medications, have trouble sleeping, or have liver disease, certain heart problems, or any other medical reason for not drinking. And never drink before driving.

Human Sexuality

How sex differences affect the behavior of human beings is a topic that scientists and laypersons have been considering for quite some time. That women and men do differ, behaviorally, cognitively, and biologically, cannot be disputed. Why they differ and whether or not these differences matter are questions that remain unanswered. Beth Livermore, in "The Lessons of Love," examines the similarities and differences between men and women on this issue.

While sex is an important component of intimacy between a man and a woman, it is by no means the most significant or the best predictor of a lasting relationship. Most people acknowledge that love tops their wish list, but statistics indicate that nearly 50 percent of all marriages fail, and intimate relationships without marriage fare even worse. Studies suggest that certain factors are vital to the success of lasting relationships. While it may take some of the mystery and romance out of relationships, an instrument designed to measure the presence or absence of these factors might assist couples in making better choices of mates. "The Indispensables: 10 Key Reasons Why Love Endures" examines such factors.

Three topics in human sexuality that have received considerable media attention are teenage pregnancy, abortion, and AIDS. The standard approach to dealing with these problems has been to provide students with contraceptive-based sex education. Critics argue that not only has this approach failed to reduce teenage pregnancies, abortions, and the spread of AIDS, but it may actually be contributing to the problem by fostering the expectation that it is normal for teenagers to experiment sexually. This assertion is supported by a 1986 Harris poll that found teenagers who were receiving contraceptive-based education were 53 percent more likely to have intercourse than those whose sex education did not include information on contraceptives. Even more distressing is the fact that the majority of the teens choosing to become sexually active do not even use the contraceptives they have learned about. This poor showing on the part of contraceptive-based sex education has prompted a growing movement within this country to try abstinence-based sex education.

Birth control itself has been a source of controversy and confusion. In the 1970s one of the most popular contraceptive devices was the IUD. This form of birth control was very effective and convenient to use. This all changed rather abruptly in the 1980s as it fell victim to legal and medical issues. The IUD named the Dalkon Shield was linked to pelvic inflammatory disease, infertility, and sometimes death. The litigation that ensued prompted several other manufacturers to remove their IUDs from the market for fear of staggeringly expensive lawsuits. The impact of this incident had a chilling effect on the entire contraceptive industry. Research and development into new birth control technologies was put on hold, and some manufacturers abandoned the contraceptive market altogether. It now appears that the fallout from the Dalkon Shield controversyhas finally ended as new contraceptive choices are once again starting to appear in the marketplace. Depo-Provera, Norplant, and the female condom are the first wave of new contraceptive devices to enter the U.S. market in more than a decade. In addition to these newly approved products, several others are currently under development. They include contraceptive vaccines, a male birth control pill, male condoms that promise greater comfort, a two-capsule version of the Norplant device, creams and gels with anti-HIV and spermicidal properties, and barrier methods that release spermicides. "Choosing a Contraceptive" examines the contraceptive choices currently available and compares them on the basis of their cost, failure rate, and ability to prevent sexually transmitted diseases.

While the concept of "safe sex" is nothing new, the degree of public discussion regarding sexual behaviors is. With the emergence of AIDS as a disease of epidemic proportions and the spread of other sexually transmitted diseases (STDs), the surgeon general of the United States initiated an aggressive educational campaign based on the assumption that knowledge would change behavior. As has been the case with drug abuse and contraceptive-based sex education, this approach, while logical, appears to have had little impact on the problem. Why has education failed? Most experts agree that for education to succeed in changing personal behaviors, the following conditions must be met: (1) the recipients of the information must first perceive themselves as vulnerable and,

UNIT 6

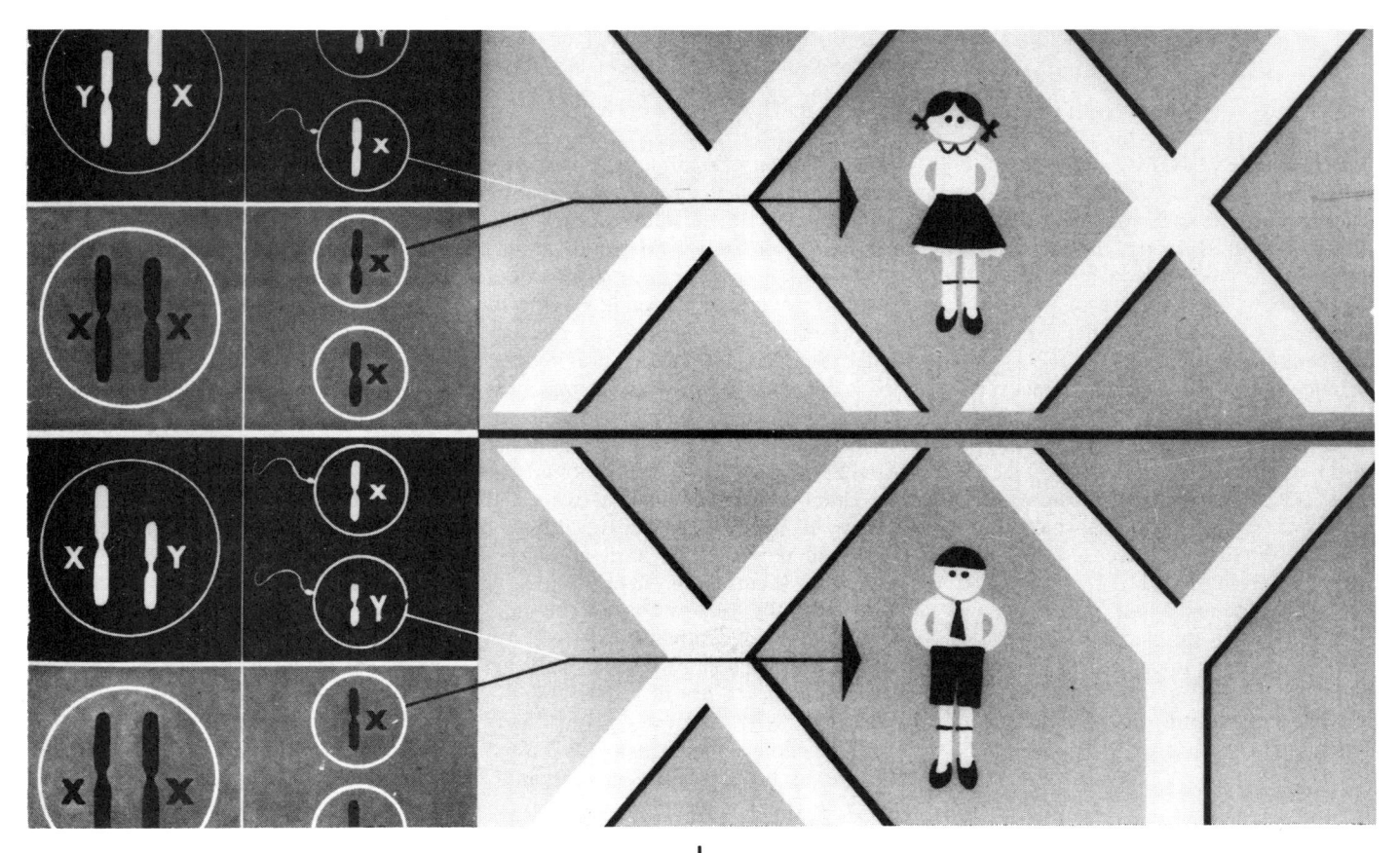

thus, be motivated to explore replacement behaviors; and (2) the replacement behaviors must satisfy the needs that were the basis of the problem behaviors. To date most education programs have failed to meet these criteria. Given all the information that we now have on the dangers associated with AIDS and STDs, why is it that people do not perceive themselves at risk? A major factor may be that when it comes to choosing sex partners, most people think that they use good judgment. Unfortunately, most decisions regarding sexual behavior are based on subjective criteria that bear little or no relationship to the actual risks of contracting AIDS or STDs. Even when individuals do view themselves as vulnerable to AIDS and STDs, there are currently only two viable options for reducing one's risk of contracting these diseases through sexual behavior: using a condom or practicing abstinence. "Preventing STDs" explains what you need to know about purchasing, storing, and using condoms to maximize their effectiveness as prophylactics.

Looking Ahead: Challenge Questions

Do you feel that contraceptives have contributed to increased promiscuity and the rapid spread of sexually transmitted diseases? Why or why not?

What approach to sex education do you think would be most effective in reducing teenage pregnancies, abortions, and the spread of AIDS and other STDs?

Are you at risk of contracting AIDS or other STDs? If not, why not? If so, what might you do to reduce your risk?

How important is beauty in selecting a mate? Explain your response.

Do you think compatibility assessment prior to marriage is a good idea? Why or why not?

How do men and women differ in their feelings about love?

What are the key factors that appear to serve as the glue that binds successful marriages?

THE LESSONS OF LOVE

Yes, we've learned a few things. We now know that it is the insecure rather than the confident who fall in love most readily. And men fall faster than women. And who ever said sex had anything to do with it?

Beth Livermore

As winter thaws, so too do icicles on cold hearts. For with spring, the sap rises—and resistance to love wanes. And though the flame will burn more of us than it warms, we will return to the fire—over and over again.

Indeed, love holds central in everybody's everyday. We spend years, sometimes lifetimes pursuing it, preparing for it, longing for it. Some of us even die for love. Still, only poets and songwriters, philosophers and playwrights have traditionally been granted license to sift this hallowed preserve. Until recently. Over the last decade and a half, scientists have finally taken on this most elusive entity. They have begun to parse out the intangibles, the *je ne sais quoi* of love. The word so far is—little we were sure of is proving to be true.

OUT OF THE LAB, INTO THE FIRE

True early greats, like Sigmund Freud and Carl Rogers, acknowledged love as important to the human experience. But not till the 1970s did anyone attempt to define it—and only now is it considered a respectable topic of study.

One reason for this hesitation has been public resistance. "Some people are afraid that if they look too close they will lose the mask," says Arthur Aron, Ph.D., professor of psychology at the University of California, Santa Cruz. "Others believe we know all that we need to know." But mostly, to systematically study love has been thought impossible, and therefore a waste of time and money.

No one did more to propagate this false notion than former United States Senator William Proxmire of Wisconsin, who in 1974 launched a very public campaign against the study of love. As a member of the Senate Finance Committee, he took it upon himself to ferret out waste in government spending. One of the first places he looked was the National Science Foundation, a federal body that both funds research and promotes scientific progress.

Upon inspection, Proxmire found that Ellen Berscheid, Ph.D., a psychologist at the University of Minnesota who had already broken new ground scrutinizing the social power of physical attractiveness, had secured an $84,000 federal grant to study relationships. The proposal mentioned romantic love. Proxmire loudly denounced such work as frivolous—tax dollars ill spent.

The publicity that was given Proxmire's pronouncements not only cast a pall over all behavioral science research, it set off an international firestorm around Berscheid that lasted the next two years. Colleagues were fired. Her office was swamped with hate mail. She even received death threats. But in the long run, the strategy backfired, much to Proxmire's chagrin. It generated increased scientific interest in the study of love, propelling it forward, and identified Berscheid as the keeper of the flame. Scholars and individuals from Alaska to then-darkest Cold War Albania sent her requests for information, along with letters of support.

Berscheid jettisoned her plans for very early retirement, buttoned up the country house, and, as she says, "became a clearinghouse" for North American love research. "It became eminently clear that there were people who really did want to learn more about love. And I had tenure."

PUTTING THE SOCIAL INTO PSYCHOLOGY

This incident was perfectly timed. For during the early 1970s, the field of social psychology was undergoing a revolution of sorts—a revolution that made the study of love newly possible.

For decades behaviorism, the school of psychology founded by John B. Watson, dominated the field. Watson argued that only overt actions capable of direct observation and measurement were worthy of study. However, by the early seventies, dissenters were openly calling this approach far too narrow. It excluded unobservable mental events such as ideas and emotions. Thus rose cognitive science, the study of the mind, or perception, thought, and memory.

Now psychologists were encouraged to ask human subjects what they thought and how they felt about things. Self-report questionnaires emerged as a legitimate research tool. Psychologists were encouraged to escape laboratory confines—to study real people in the real world. Once out there, they discovered that there was plenty to mine.

Throughout the seventies, soaring divorce rates, loneliness, and isolation began to dominate the emotional landscape of America. By the end of that decade, love had become a pathology. No longer was the question "What is love?" thought to be trivial. "People in our culture dissolve unions when love disappears, which has a lasting effect on society," says Berscheid. Besides, "we already understood the mating habits of the stickleback fish." It was time to turn to a new species.

Today there are hundreds of research papers on love. Topics range from romantic ideals to attachment styles of the young and unmarried. "There were maybe a half dozen when I wrote my dissertation on romantic attraction in 1969," reports Aron. These days, a national association and an international society bring "close relationship" researchers close together annually. Together or apart they are busy producing and sharing new theories, new questionnaires to use as research instruments, and new findings. Their unabashed aim: to improve the human condition by helping us to understand, to repair, and to perfect our love relationships.

SO WHAT *IS* LOVE?

"If there is anything that we have learned about love it is its variegated nature," says Clyde Hendrick, Ph.D., of Texas Tech University in Lubbock. "No one volume or theory or research program can capture love and transform it into a controlled bit of knowledge."

Instead, scholars are tackling specific questions about love in the hopes of nailing down a few facets at a time. The expectation is that every finding will be a building block in the base of knowledge, elevating understanding.

Elaine Hatfield, Ph.D., now of the University of Hawaii, has carved out the territory of passionate love. Along with Berscheid, Hatfield was at the University of Minnesota in 1964 when Stanley Schacter, formerly a professor there and still a great presence, proposed a new theory of emotion. It said that any emotional state requires two conditions: both physiological arousal and relevant situational cues. Already studying close relationships, Hatfield and Berscheid were intrigued. Could the theory help to explain the turbulent, all-consuming experience of passionate love?

Hatfield has spent a good chunk of her professional life examining passionate love, "a state of intense longing for union with another." In 1986, along with sociologist Susan Sprecher, she devised the Passionate Love Scale (PLS), a questionnaire that measures thoughts and feelings she previously identified as distinctive of this "emotional" state.

Lovers rate the applicability of a variety of descriptive statements. To be passionately in love is to be preoccupied with thoughts of your partner much of the time. Also, you likely idealize your partner. So those of you who are passionately in love would, for example, give "I yearn to know all about—" a score somewhere between "moderately true" and "definitely true" on the PLS.

True erotic love is intense and involves taking risks. It seems to demand a strong sense of self.

The quiz also asks subjects if they find themselves trying to determine the other's feelings, trying to please their lover, or making up excuses to be close to him or her—all hallmarks of passionate, erotic love. It canvasses for both positive and negative feelings. "Passionate lovers," explains Hatfield, "experience a roller coaster of feelings: euphoria, happiness, calm, tranquility, vulnerability, anxiety, panic, despair."

For a full 10 percent of lovers, previous romantic relationships proved so painful that they hope they will never love again.

Passionate love, she maintains, is kindled by "a sprinkle of hope and a large dollop of loneliness, mourning, jealousy, and terror." It is, in other words, fueled by a juxtaposition of pain and pleasure. According to psychologist Dorothy Tennov, who interviewed some 500 lovers, most of them expect their romantic experiences to be bittersweet. For a full 10 percent of them, previous romantic relationships proved so painful that they hope never to love again.

Contrary to myths that hold women responsible for romance, Hatfield finds that both males and females love with equal passion. But men fall in love faster. They are, thus, more romantic. Women are more apt to mix pragmatic concerns with their passion.

And people of all ages, even four-year-old children, are capable of "falling passionately in love." So are people of any ethnic group and socioeconomic stratum capable of passionate love.

Hatfield's most recent study, of love in three very different cultures, shows that romantic love is not simply a product of the Western mind. It exists among diverse cultures worldwide.

Taken together, Hatfield's findings support the idea that passionate love is an evolutionary adaptation. In this scheme, passionate love works as a bonding mechanism, a necessary kind of interpersonal glue that has existed since the start of the human race. It assures that procreation will take place, that the human species will be perpetuated.

UP FROM THE SWAMP

Recent anthropological work also supports this notion. In 1991, William Jankowiak, Ph.D., of the University of Nevada in Las Vegas, and Edward Fischer, Ph.D., of Tulane University published the first study systematically comparing romantic love across 166 cultures.

They looked at folklore, indigenous advice about love, tales about lovers, love potion recipes—anything related. They found "clear evidence" that romantic love is known in 147, or 89 percent, of cultures. Further, Jankowiak suspects that the lack of proof in the remaining 19 cultures is due more to field workers' oversights than to the absence of romance.

Unless prompted, few anthropologists recognize romantic love in the populations that they study, explains Jankowiak. Mostly because romance takes different shapes in different cultures, they do not know what to look for. They tend to recognize romance only in the form it takes in American culture—a progressive phenomenon leading from flirtation to marriage. Elsewhere, it may be a more fleeting fancy. Still, reports Jankowiak, "when I ask them specific questions about behavior, like 'Did couples run away from camp together?', almost all of them have a positive response."

For all that, there is a sizable claque of scholars who insist that romantic love is a cultural invention of the last 200 years or so. They point out that few cultures outside the West embrace romantic love with the vigor that we do. Fewer still build marriage, traditionally a social and economic institution, on the individualistic pillar of romance.

Romantic love, this thinking holds, consists of a learned set of behaviors; the phenomenon is culturally transmitted from one generation to the next by example, stories, imitation, and direct instruc-

LOVE ME TENDER

How To Make Love to a Man
(what men like, in order of importance)

taking walks together
kissing
candle-lit dinners
cuddling
hugging
flowers
holding hands
making love
love letters
sitting by the fireplace

How To Make Love to a Woman
(what women like, in order of importance)

taking walks together
flowers
kissing
candle-lit dinners
cuddling
declaring "I love you"
love letters
slow dancing
hugging
giving surprise gifts

---

tion. Therefore, it did not rise from the swamps with us, but rather evolved with culture.

THE ANXIOUS ARE ITS PREY

Regardless whether passionate, romantic love is universal or unique to us, there is considerable evidence that what renders people particularly vulnerable to it is anxiety. It whips up the wherewithal to love. And anxiety is not alone; in fact, there are a number of predictable precursors to love.

To test the idea that emotions such as fear, which produces anxiety, can amplify attraction, Santa Cruz's Arthur Aron recorded the responses of two sets of men to an attractive woman. But one group first had to cross a narrow 450-foot-long bridge that swayed in the wind over a 230-foot drop—a pure prescription for anxiety. The other group tromped confidently across a seemingly safe bridge. Both groups encountered Miss Lovely, a decoy, as they stepped back onto terra firm.

Aron's attractive confederate stopped each young man to explain that she was doing a class project and asked if he would complete a questionnaire. Once he finished, she handed him her telephone number, saying that she would be happy to explain her project in greater detail.

Who called? Nine of the 33 men on the suspension bridge telephoned, while only two of the men on the safe bridge called. It is not impossible that the callers simply wanted details on the project, but Aron suspects instead that a combustible mix of excitement and anxiety prompted the men to become interested in their attractive interviewee.

Along similar if less treacherous lines, Aron has most recently looked at eleven possible precursors to love. He compiled the list by conducting a comprehensive literature search for candidate items. If you have a lot in common with or live and work close to someone you find attractive, your chances of falling in love are good, the literature suggests.

Other general factors proposed at one time or another as good predictors include being liked by the other, a partner's positive social status, a partner's ability to fill your needs, your readiness for entering a relationship, your isolation from others, mystery, and exciting surroundings or circumstances. Then there are specific cues, like hair color, eye expression, and face shape.

Love depends as much on the perception of being liked as on the presence of a desirable partner. Love isn't possible without it.

To test the viability and relative importance of these eleven putative factors, Aron asked three different groups of people to give real-life accounts of falling in love. Predictably, desirable characteristics, such as good looks and personality, made the top of the list. But proximity, readiness to develop a relationship, and exciting surroundings and circumstances ranked close behind.

The big surprise: reciprocity. Love is at heart a two-way event. The perception of being liked ranked just as high as the presence of desirable characteristics in the partner. "The combination of the two appears to be very important," says Aron. In fact, love just may not be possible without it.

Sprecher and his colleagues got much the same results in a very recent cross-cultural survey. They and their colleagues interviewed 1,667 men and women in the U.S., Russia, and Japan. They asked the people to think about the last time they had fallen in love or been infatuated. Then they asked about the circumstance that surrounded the love experience.

Surprisingly, the rank ordering of the factors was quite similar in all three cultures. In all three, men and women consider reciprocal liking, personality, and physical appearance to be especially important. A partner's social status and the approval of family and friends are way down the list. The cross-cultural validation of predisposing influences suggests that reciprocal liking, desirable personality and physical features may be universal elements of love, among the *sine qua non* of love, part of its heart and soul.

FRIENDSHIP OVER PASSION

Another tack to the intangible of love is the "prototype" approach. This is the study of our conceptions of love, what we "think" love is.

In 1988, Beverly Fehr, Ph.D., of the University of Winnipeg in Canada conducted a series of six studies designed to determine what "love" and "commitment" have in common. Assorted theories suggested they could be anything from mutually inclusive to completely separate. Fehr asked subjects to list characteristics of love and to list features of commitment. Then she asked them to determine which qualities were central and which more peripheral to each.

People's concepts of the two were to some degree overlapping. Such elements as trust, caring, respect, honesty, devotion, sacrifice, and contentment were deemed attributes of both love and commitment. But such other factors as intimacy, happiness, and a desire to be with the other proved unique to love (while commitment alone demanded perseverance, mutual agreement, obligation, and even a feeling of being trapped).

The findings of Fehr's set of studies, as well as others', defy many expectations. Most subjects said they consider caring, trust, respect, and honesty central to love—while passion-related events like touching, sexual passion, and physical attraction are only peripheral. "They are not very central to our concept of love," Fehr shrugs.

Recently, Fehr explored gender differences in views of love—and found remarkably few. Both men and women put forth friendship as primary to love. Only in a second study, which asked subjects to match their personal ideal of love to various descriptions, did any differences show up. More so than women, men tended to rate erotic, romantic love closer to their personal conception of love.

Both men and women deem romance and passion far less important than support and warm fuzzies . . .

Still, Fehr is fair. On the whole, she says, "the essence, the core meaning of love differs little." Both genders deem romance and passion far less important than support and warm fuzzies. As even Nadine Crenshaw, creator of steamy romance novels, has remarked, "love gets you to the bathroom when you're sick."

LOVE ME TENDER

Since the intangible essence of love cannot be measured directly, many researchers settle for its reflection in what people do. They examine the behavior of lovers.

Clifford Swensen, Ph.D., professor of psychology at Purdue University, pioneered this approach by developing a scale with which to measure lovers' behavior. He produced it from statements people made when asked what they did for, said to, or felt about people they loved . . . and how these people behaved towards them.

Being supportive and providing encouragement are important behaviors to all love relationships—whether with a friend or mate, Swensen and colleagues found. Subjects also gave high ratings to self-disclosure, or talking about personal matters, and a sense of agreement on important topics.

But two categories of behaviors stood out as unique to romantic relationships. Lovers said that they expressed feelings of love verbally; they talked about how they enjoyed being together, how they missed one another when apart, and other such murmurings. They also showed their affection through physical acts like hugging and kissing.

Elaborating on the verbal and physical demonstrations of love, psychologist Raymond Tucker, Ph.D., of Bowling Green State University in Ohio probed 149 women and 48 men to determine "What constitutes a romantic act?" He asked subjects, average age of 21, to name common examples. There was little disagreement between the genders.

Both men and women most often cited "taking walks" together. For women, "sending or receiving flowers" and "kissing" followed close on its heels, then "candle-lit dinners" and "cuddling." Outright declarations of "I love you came in a distant sixth. (Advisory to men: The florists were right all along. Say it with flowers instead.)

. . . as one romance novelist confides, "love gets you to the bathroom when you're sick."

For men, kissing and "candle-lit dinners" came in second and third. If women preferred demonstrations of love to outright declarations of it, men did even more so; "hearing and saying 'I love you didn't even show up among their top ten preferences. Nor did "slow dancing or giving or receiving surprise gifts," although all three were on the women's top-ten list. Men likewise listed three kinds of activity women didn't even mention: "holding hands," "making love"—and "sitting by the fireplace." For both sexes, love is more tender than most of us imagined.

All in all, says Tucker, lovers consistently engage in a specific array of actions. "I see these items show up over and over and over again." They may very well be the bedrock behaviors of romantic love.

SIX COLORS OF LOVE

That is not to say that once in love we all behave alike. We do not. Each of us has a set of attitudes toward love that colors what we do. While yours need not match your mate's, you best understand your partner's approach. It underlies how your partner is likely to treat you.

There are six basic orientations toward love, Canadian sociologist John Allen Lee first suggested in 1973. They emerged from a series of studies in which subjects matched story cards, which contain statements projecting attitudes, to their own personal relationships. In 1990 Texas Tech's Clyde Hendrick, along with wife/colleague Susan Hendrick, Ph.D., produced a Love Attitude Scale to measure all six styles. You may embody more than one of these styles. You are also likely to change style with time and circumstance.

Both men and women prefer demonstrations of love to outright declarations of it.

You may, for example, have spent your freewheeling college years as an Eros lover, passionate and quick to get involved, setting store on physical attraction and sexual satisfaction. Yet today you may find yourself happy as a Storge lover, valuing friendship-based love, preferring a secure, trusting relationship with a partner of like values.

There are Ludus lovers, game-players who like to have several partners at one time. Their partners may be very different from one another, as Ludus does not act on romantic ideals. Mania-type lovers, by contrast, experience great emotional highs and lows. They are very possessive—and often jealous. They spend a lot of their time doubting their partner's sincerity.

Pragma lovers are, well, pragmatic. They get involved only with the "right" guy or gal—someone who fills their needs or meets other specifications. This group is happy to trade drama and excitement for a partner they can build a life with. In contrast, Agape, or altruistic, lovers form relationships because of what they may be able to give to their partner. Even sex is not an urgent concern of theirs. "Agape functions on a more spiritual level," Hendrick says.

The Hendricks have found some gender difference among love styles. In general, men are more ludic, or game-playing. Women tend to be more storgic,

THE COLORS OF LOVE

How do I love thee? At least six are the ways.

There is no one type of love; there are many equally valid ways of loving. Researchers have consistently identified six attitudes or styles of love that, to one degree or another, encompass our conceptions of love and color our romantic relationships. They reflect both fixed personality traits and more malleable attitudes. Your relative standing on these dimensions may vary over time—being in love NOW will intensify your responses in some dimensions. Nevertheless, studies show that for most people, one dimension of love predominates.

Answering the questions below will help you identify your own love style, one of several important factors contributing to the satisfaction you feel in relationships. You may wish to rate yourself on a separate sheet of paper. There are no right or wrong answers, nor is there any scoring system. The test is designed to help you examine your own feelings and to help you understand your own romantic experiences.

After you take the test, if you are currently in a relationship, you may want to ask your partner to take the test and then compare your responses. Better yet, try to predict your partner's love attitudes before giving the test to him or her.

Studies show that most partners are well-correlated in the areas of love passion and intensity (Eros), companionate or friendship love (Storge), dependency (Mania), and all-giving or selfless love (Agape). If you and your partner aren't a perfect match, don't worry. Knowing your styles can help you manage your relationship.

Directions: Listed below are several statements that reflect different attitudes about love. For each statement, fill in the response on an answer sheet that indicates how much you agree or disagree with that statement. The items refer to a specific love relationship. Whenever possible, answer the questions with your current partner in mind. If you are not currently dating anyone, answer the questions with your most recent partner in mind. If you have never been in love, answer in terms of what you think your responses would most likely be.

FOR EACH STATEMENT:
A = Strongly agree with the statement
B = Moderately agree with the statement
C = Neutral, neither agree nor disagree
D = Moderately disagree with the statement
E = Strongly disagree with the statement

Eros
Measures passionate love as well as intimacy and commitment. It is directly and strongly correlated with satisfaction in a relationship, a major ingredient in relationship success. Eros gives fully, intensely, and takes risks in love; it requires substantial ego strength. Probably reflects secure attachment style.

1. My partner and I were attracted to each other immediately after we first met.
2. My partner and I have the right physical "chemistry" between us.
3. Our lovemaking is very intense and satisfying.
4. I feel that my partner and I were meant for each other.
5. My partner and I became emotionally involved rather quickly.
6. My partner and I really understand each other.
7. My partner fits my ideal standards of physical beauty/handsomeness.

Ludus
Measures love as an interaction game to be played out with diverse partners. Relationships do not have great depth of feeling. Ludus is wary of emotional intensity from others, and has a manipulative or cynical quality to it. Ludus is negatively related to satisfaction in relationships. May reflect avoidant attachment style.

8. I try to keep my partner a little uncertain about my commitment to him/her.
9. I believe that what my partner doesn't know about me won't hurt him/her.
10. I have sometimes had to keep my partner from finding out about other partners.
11. I could get over my affair with my partner pretty easily and quickly.
12. My partner would get upset if he/she knew of some of the things I've done with other people.
13. When my partner gets too dependent on me, I want to back off a little.
14. I enjoy playing the "game of love" with my partner and a number of other partners.

Storge
Reflects an inclination to merge love and friendship. Storgic love is solid, down to earth, presumably enduring. It is evolutionary, not revolutionary, and may take time to develop. It is related to satisfaction in long-term relationships.

15. It is hard for me to say exactly when our friendship turned to love.
16. To be genuine, our love first required caring for a while.
17. I expect to always be friends with my partner.
18. Our love is the best kind because it grew out of a long friendship.
19. Our friendship merged gradually into love over time.
20. Our love is really a deep friendship, not a mysterious, mystical emotion.
21. Our love relationship is the most satisfying because it developed from a good friendship.

Pragma
Reflects logical, "shopping list" love, rational calculation with a focus on desired attributes of a lover. Suited to computer-matched dating. Related to satisfaction in long-term relationships.

22. I considered what my partner was going to become in life before I committed myself to him/her.
23. I tried to plan my life carefully before choosing my partner.
24. In choosing my partner, I believed it was best to love someone with a similar background.
25. A main consideration in choosing my partner was how he/she would reflect on my family.
26. An important factor in choosing my partner was whether or not he/she would be a good parent.
27. One consideration in choosing my partner was how he/she would reflect on my career.
28. Before getting very involved with my partner, I tried to figure out how compatible his/her hereditary background would be with mine in case we ever had children.

Mania
Measures possessive, dependent love. Associated with high emotional expressiveness and disclosure, but low self-esteem; reflects uncertainty of self in the relationship. Negatively associated with relationship satisfaction. May reflect anxious/ambivalent attachment style.

29. When things aren't right with my partner and me, my stomach gets upset.
30. If my partner and I break up, I would get so depressed that I would even think of suicide.
31. Sometimes I get so excited about being in love with my partner that I can't sleep.
32. When my partner doesn't pay attention to me, I feel sick all over.
33. Since I've been in love with my partner, I've had trouble concentrating on anything else.
34. I cannot relax if I suspect that my partner is with someone else.
35. If my partner ignores me for a while, I sometimes do stupid things to try to get his/her attention back.

Agape
Reflects all-giving, selfless, nondemanding love. Associated with altruistic, committed, sexually idealistic love. Like Eros, tends to flare up with "being in love now."

36. I try to always help my partner through difficult times.
37. I would rather suffer myself than let my partner suffer.
38. I cannot be happy unless I place my partner's happiness before my own.
39. I am usually willing to sacrifice my own wishes to let my partner achieve his/hers.
40. Whatever I won is my partner's to use as he/she chooses.
41. When my partner gets angry with me, I still love him/her fully and unconditionally.
42. I would endure all things for the sake of my partner.

Adapted from Hendrick, Love Attitudes Scale

more pragmatic—and more manic. However, men and women seem to be equally passionate and altruistic in their relationships. On the whole, say the Hendricks, the sexes are more similar than different in style.

Personality traits, at least one personality trait, is strongly correlated to love style, the Hendricks have discovered. People with high self-esteem are more apt to endorse eros, but less likely to endorse mania than other groups. "This finding fits with the image of a secure, confident eros lover who moves intensely but with mutuality into a new relationship," they maintain.

When they turned their attention to ongoing relationships, the Hendricks' found that couples who stayed together over the course of their months-long study were more passionate and less game-playing than couples who broke up. "A substantial amount of passionate love" and "a low dose of game-playing" love are key to the development of satisfying relationships—at least among the college kids studied.

YOUR MOTHER MADE YOU DO IT

The love style you embrace, how you treat your partner, may reflect the very first human relationship you ever had—probably with Mom. There is growing evidence supporting "attachment theory," which holds that the rhythms of response by a child's primary care giver affect the development of personality and influence later attachment processes, including adult love relationships.

First put forth by British psychiatrist John Bowlby in the 1960s and elaborated by American psychologist Mary Ainsworth, attachment theory is the culmination of years of painstaking observation of infants and their adult caregivers—and those separated from them—in both natural and experimental situations. Essentially it suggests that there are three major patterns of attachment; they develop within the first year of life and stick with us, all the while reflecting the responsiveness of the caregiver to our needs as helpless infants.

Those whose mothers, or caregivers, were unavailable or unresponsive may grow up to be detached and nonresponsive to others. Their behavior is Avoidant in relationships. A second group takes a more Anxious-Ambivalent approach to relationships, a response set in motion by having mothers they may not have been able to count on—sometimes responsive, other times not. The lucky among us are Secure in attachment, trusting and stable in relationships, probably the result of having had consistently responsive care.

While attachment theory is now driving a great deal of research on children's social, emotional, and cognitive development, University of Denver psychologists Cindy Hazan and Philip Shaver set out not long ago to investigate the possible effect of childhood relationships on adult attachments. First, they developed descriptive statements that reflect each of the three attachment styles. Then they asked people in their community, along with college kids, which statements best describe how they relate to others. They asked, for example, about trust and jealousy, about closeness and desire for reciprocation, about emotional extremes.

The distribution of the three attachment styles has proved to be about the same in grown-ups as in infants, the same among collegians as the fully fledged. More than half of adult respondents call themselves Secure; the rest are split between Avoidant and Ambivalent. Further, their adult attachment patterns predictably reflect the relationship they report with their parents. Secure people generally describe their parents as having been warm and supportive. What's more, these adults predictably differ in success at romantic love. Secure people reported happy, long-lasting relationships. Avoidants rarely found love.

Secure adults are more trusting of their romantic partners and more confident of a partner's love, report Australian psychologists Judith Feeney and Patricia Noller of the University of Queensland. The two surveyed nearly 400 college undergraduates with a questionnaire on family background and love relationships, along with items designed to reveal their personality and related traits.

In contrast to the Secure, Avoidants indicated an aversion to intimacy. The Anxious-Ambivalent participants were characterized by dependency and what Feeney and Noller describe as "a hunger" for commitment. Their approach resembles the Mania style of love. Each of the three groups reported differences in early childhood experience that could account for their adult approach to relationships. Avoidants, for example, were most likely to tell of separations from their mother.

It may be, Hazan and Shaver suggest, that the world's greatest love affairs are conducted by the Ambitious-Ambivalents—people desperately searching for a kind of security they never had.

THE MAGIC NEVER DIES

Not quite two decades into the look at love, it appears as though love will not always mystify us. For already we are beginning to define what we think about it, how it makes us feel, and what we do when we are in love. We now know that it is the insecure, rather than the confident, who fall in love more readily. We know that outside stimuli that alter our emotional state can affect our susceptibility to romance; it is not just the person. We now know that to a certain extent your love style is set by the parenting you received. And, oh yes, men are more quickly romantic than women.

The best news may well be that when it comes to love, men and women are more similar than different. In the face of continuing gender wars, it is comforting to think that men and women share an important, and peaceful, spot of turf. It is also clear that no matter how hard we look at love, we will always be amazed and mesmerized by it.

The Indispensables: 10 Key Reasons Why Love Endures

Why do some relationships self-destruct, while others stay solid—and sexy—for decades? Get ready for some surprising scientific findings . . .

Catherine Houck

Love tops everyone's wish list. We all want someone to hug a lot, somebody to go to the movies with, a person who *cares* that we just located a Pontiac Grand Am with only three thousand miles. Still, nearly half of all marriages go *poof,* while unmarried liaisons have an even higher mortality rate.

Until recently, we could only speculate why some relationships cool and collapse while others remain redhot *indefinitely.* Now, however, researchers looking into love are beginning to log in some basic truths about this elusive, chaotic emotion. Here, the latest *scientific* findings on what keeps love alive in the long run.

Although people often believe that important differences will go away with time, this is a myth. Marriage does not automatically bring lovers closer.

1. MAGNETS WE'RE NOT

"The belief that opposites attract explains magnets but misunderstands the nature of lasting love," says Atlanta psychiatrist Frank Pittman, author of *Private Lies: Infidelity and the Betrayal of Intimacy.* Instead, "mutuality"—similar values and attitudes, ethnic backgrounds, interests, IQs, religions, customs, life-styles—may be the single most important ingredient in successful relationships, Dr. Pittman and other researchers concluded.

In fact, a high level of mutuality is so vital for a couple's future happiness that, according to David H. Olson, professor of family social sciences at the University of Minnesota, Saint Paul, it's possible to predict as early as the day a couple becomes engaged whether that marriage will last. Questioning a cross section of 164 courting couples on their values, Olson identified more than 100 as seriously mismatched. Three years later, he found that 90 percent of these couples had not been able to produce successful marriages. Fifty-two never *got* married, while thirty-one of those who did had already separated. Another twenty-two described their union as unhappy.

On the other hand, the remaining lovebirds, who started off by sharing key characteristics, *did* settle down harmoniously. "Clearly, love seldom conquers all," says Olson. "Though people often believe that important differences will go away with time, we can now say with some certainty that this is a myth. Marriage does not automatically bring lovers closer."

2. HOW DO I LIKE THEE?

Though rock stars revel in finding new ways to croon "I love you," "I like you" seems to have more to do with lasting passion. Robert and Jeannette Lauer, authors of *Til Death Do Us Part,* found over 70 percent of the happily married couples they surveyed "strongly agreed" with the statement "I like my mate as a person, "while only 13.2 percent of the miserable twosome could say the same.

"A lover who is also a friend provides us with shored-up self-esteem, shared attitudes and interests, keeps us from feeling lonely, reduces our anxiety, and helps us get the things we want," observes psychologist Elaine Walster, a pioneer researcher on the dynamics of liking and loving. "I love my husband," said one wife of twenty-two years in the Lauers' study, "but it was the *liking* that helped us get through the times I wanted to wring his neck."

Many people think that "love" is simply a stronger form of "like" and that loving would be impossible without liking someone first. Not so, says Pittman. All too often, men and women choose partners who confer the most status, elicit the most envy, or horrify the most relatives. Others can be passionately, desperately in love yet consumed with distrust and rage at their mate.

The best indication of whether a man or women is capable of genuine friendship with a mate, claim social psychologists, is whether he or she has close, nonsexual friends of the opposite sex. Also important, says Pittman, is whether that person is friends with his parents, because a lover who is still at war with his parents is probably not ready for peace and friendship with a romantic partner.

3. INTIMACY: THE ESSENCE OF LOVE

"The need to feel close to another person is probably the most basic of all psychological needs," says psychologist Dan P. McAdams, whose national study of 1,208 men and women is the most intensive look at intimacy to date.

McAdams has found that emotional intimacy is of nearly equal importance for the happiness of both sexes, but its rewards tend to be different for men and women. For a women, feeling close to a man makes her feel happier; for a man, achieving intimacy not only bestows happiness, it seems to provide a springboard to confidence and resilience that encourages worldly achievements. "In relationships lacking intimacy, neither the man nor the women has a secure emotional base," says McAdams, who, along with other psychotherapists, reports seeing more couples than ever before who feel this essential relationship ingredient eludes them.

Perhaps that's because intimacy, once described by the late psychologist Abraham Maslow as "gentle, delicate, unintruding, undemanding, able to fit itself passively to the nature of things as water gently soaks into crevices," is not easily obtained through conscious effort. Instead, say researchers, the surest road to this meeting of two minds *and* hearts is good communication.

Couples who feel free to discuss whatever is deeply important to them—including their relationship—are both happier and more likely to bask in lasting love than less-chatty lovers. Honesty (accompanied by *plenty* of concern about the other person's feelings) is a necessity. "Even the smallest lie can be hopelessly disorienting," says Dr. Pittman. "Lovers usually know when they're being lied to. . . . They just don't know what the truth is. Intimacy seeps away, and the relationship soon follows."

In a study reported in the journal *Social Work,* couples married twenty-four years were asked to describe first their own interests, personality traits, characteristic feelings, and social needs, then those of their spouse. The happiest couples were uncannily able to portray their mates exactly as the mates portrayed themselves. "They were people who knew each other well," writes study author Nina S. Fields. "That sort of familiarity grows out of spending time together, and not only talking but *listening.*"

"Listening well requires a good deal of energy," say the Lauers. A mate "mustn't allow her mind to wander and must be prepared for some unpleasant feelings—she may not want to know about the frustrations or grievances of her lover, or it may be painful to acknowledge that the relationship is anything less than deeply satisfying." But accepting the risks and costs of both self-disclosure and listening are vital for intimacy—and happiness. Otherwise, issues are ignored and fester.

By listening requires more than just sitting quietly. When a mate confides his troubles, many lovers respond by freely sharing their thoughts on the matter. "They correct, judge, and give advice," says the Family Relations Institute's Lori Gordon. "This causes resentment, because it implies you think he isn't intelligent enough to solve his problems himself. Eventually, he may decide not to talk about problems—and good-bye, intimacy." According to Gordon, when your lover opens up, you must be sure to ask "Do you want my opinion, or should I just listen?"

In the movies the leading man and lady may hurl verbal missiles, then fall into each other's arms. But in real life, yelling or sobbing seldom helps solve problems.

Still another way happy couples encourage intimacy is through praise and mutual reinforcement. "Letting a partner know when he's done something that pleases, whether it's leaving a thoughtful phone message or successfully unclogging the pepper mill, helps make him feel loved and confident enough to share further expressions of love," says Robert J. Sternberg, IBM professor of psychology and education at Yale University.

4. BETTER ENEMIES

The difference between a relationship that gets better over time and one in which the lovers grow apart can often be traced to

6. HUMAN SEXUALITY

how conflicts are resolved, according to a study by John Gottman, a professor of psychology at the University of Washington, and Lowell Krokoff, a former assistant professor of psychology at the University of Wisconsin at Madison. When Gottman and Krokoff analyzed the actual emotional maneuvers of battling couples, then checked their status again three years later, they discovered that there are three particularly destructive ways certain couples deal with conflicts. In some cases, one or both partners simply refuse to listen to complaints by withdrawing ("I'm not going to argue with you about this"). Another devastating ploy is inaccurate "mind reading," in which the adversary claims to know what the other partner *really* thinks or feels ("You don't need anybody but your mother"). Still a third counterproductive pattern is making contemptuous or insulting remarks rather than asking for a specific behavior change "You know, you're really an exploitive person" instead of "I think you should take me out to dinner more, since I cook for us at home." Or "You're a slob" rather than "It bothers me that you leave your dirty underwear lying around the bathroom").

In a fruitful argument, each partner feels free to explain why he or she is mad while the other one listens—with respect. A particularly effective way some couples demonstrate that the explanation is getting through, the researchers have found, is by one partner's repeating, in his or her own words, the point that the other has just made.

Long-term happy couples also tend to argue calmly and in a normal voice. While in movies the leading man and lady may hurl verbal missiles and then fall into each other's arms, in real life, loss of control—yelling, quaking with fear, sobbing piteously—seldom helps a couple solve problems. "Couples whose relationship has improved over time usually have learned to keep the lid on arguments," says Gottman. "Rather than being swept away by anger, they know how to de-escalate by suggesting a compromise or solution."

5. THE LABOR OF LOVE

"To love somebody is not just a strong feeling—a feeling may come and it may go," wrote the late Erich Fromm in *The Art of Loving,* published several decades ago. "Rather, love is a decision, a judgment, a promise." Today we call this aspect of *l'amour* "commitment," and virtually all researchers report that it's the Elmer's glue of happy relationships. "To know your mate is committed to you—and you to him—is to have a sense of security in a turbulent world," say the Lauers.

"Successful couples view commitment as a task," says Yale's Robert Sternberg. "They don't take each other for granted but work constantly at rejuvenating their good feelings for each other. The most satisfied couples put the kind of thought and energy into their relationship that they put into their children or career."

This sort of commitment is being increasingly viewed as crucial for getting through marriage's most dangerous years: number four. Analyzing divorce data from fifty-eight different countries since 1947, anthropologist Helen Fisher found evidence in *all* societies of a "four-year itch" that made couples dramatically prone to divorce at that point. "Four years happens to be how long it took our ancestors to wean their young," Fisher explains. "It seems nature has a strong interest in keeping humans pair-bonded for four years but provides no similar incentive to keep couples bonded for life. That's why, after an initial period of grace, marriages must be worked on."

Today, more and more stable, loving couples credit professional help of some sort for keeping their marriage out of trouble—and divorce court. Some simply find a good family counselor, while others take courses, such as the sixteen-week program developed by Lori Gordon, director of the Family Relations Institute, in Falls Church, Virginia, which provides "skill training for relationships." There, couples attend seminars on how to share feelings, respond to a mate's criticisms, express affection, offer comfort, and work on problems with sensuality and sex. For still others, skill training has meant working with a therapist to understand the origins of destructive emotional patterns—and how to change them effectively.

6. A PINCH OF TOLERANCE . . .

"At the beginning of a romance, the other person's habits usually don't seem important and may even be endearing, but over the long term, his nightly snoring or her thing about never raising the window shades can begin to grate," says Sternberg. Yet the most successful couples, he finds, have developed a high tolerance for each other's imperfections. They've simply acknowledged that many problems are unsolvable—and learned to work around them.

After interviewing eighty-seven married couples for her book *Married People: Staying Together in the Age of Divorce,* Francine Klagsbrun found "an ability to forgo perfection" to be vital for relationship satisfaction. "Every relationship has sore spots," says Klagsbrun. "Successful lovers are usually able to accept these limitations and get on with life instead of wasting energy." One simple but effective ploy used by many devoted pairs, she found, is determinedly focusing on the relationship's strengths rather than its weaknesses. "With that outlook, they're able to enhance what's good so that it becomes the core of their relationship, while negatives become peripheral."

7. PASSION: LOVE'S SWEET POETRY

Virtually all serious researchers agree that sexual attraction normally peaks within the first year or two of a relationship. But they've also found that the happiest lovebirds still have plenty of sexy feelings left. Says psychologist Paul Pearsall, author of *Super Marital Sex,* "Staying at a peak isn't necessary for a happy union. An enduring attraction *is.* An ongoing sexual relationship with one person is the most intense, fulfilling experience any human can have."

Sternberg agrees but adds that an important component of continued ardor is the woman's appearance. "Men care about a woman's physical attractiveness. The more attractive a man feels his wife is, the more successful their relationship will be over time."

Among the thousands of couples he studied for his book, Pearsall found that those reporting the happiest marriages and sex lives put their relationship first. "Attending to each other came before the lawn, the kids, job, car, or leaky sink." Steven Carter and Julia Sokol, who interviewed 250 men and women for their book *What Really Happens in Bed,* reached much the same conclusion. "In happy marriages, both participants are deeply committed to making it work—and this includes working out a satisfactory sexual relationship," they say.

But research also demonstrates that even the most deliciously blissful couples seldom agree on how often to make love. One partner may feel amorous four times a week, the other once—and they compromise twice. As long as both partners enjoy the experience, couples who make love infrequently—even once a month—tend to be as happy as those who are more active.

One surprise: Though sex therapists have long lauded spontaneous sex, the most contented couples in all current surveys maintain that spontaneity gets less desirable the longer the relationship. "Women specifically mentioned that they prefer having time to mentally prepare themselves for sex as opposed to just being grabbed without warning," says Sokol. Many also report that making love on a familiar schedule provides something to look forward to.

8. LOVE RESPECTS EQUALITY

Q. Who's better off—the lover who loves more or the one who loves less? A. *Neither.* The lovers with the best chance for happiness are those who contribute more or less equally to a relationship, according to psychologist Elaine Walster, who, with colleague Jane Traupmann, interviewed more than six hundred people to find out what happens when one partner gives more than the other. "Lovers who knew they were getting far more than they really deserved felt uneasy and guilty, while those who felt they were getting less were angry and resentful," says Walster. "On the other hand, equitable relationships seem to be unusually solid."

Connell Cowan, coauthor of *Women Men Love, Women Men Leave,* also feels strongly that for a love relationship to flourish, the needs and desires of each partner must be *equally* important. "Healthy love has built-in constraints; it's conditional," he says. "Paradoxically, the happiest lovers are those willing to give up love if their sensitivities aren't respected.

"Women (or men) who give too freely inadvertently press all the wrong buttons in their partners," says Cowen. "Wishing only to please, they push their lovers away, making them determined to give less and less as the partner gives more and more. All chance for a mutually satisfying closeness vanishes, with lasting love soon to follow."

9. OLD-FASHIONED TRUST

"Feelings of love may wax and wane during a relationship, but trust is a constant," says Klagsbrun. Infidelity, of course, is the most devastating betrayal of that trust a couple can experience at *any* time in their relationship. In a survey of twelve thousand couples nationwide for their book *American Couples,* sociologists Philip Blumstein and Pepper Schwartz found that of all couples—whether married or living together, heterosexual or gay—those in which either partner had sex outside the relationship were more likely to break up than others. "Even a little bit of infidelity can set forces in motion that eventually wreck a marriage," says Schwartz.

Dr. Frank Pittman agrees. "It's commonplace for guilt-ridden people, after an infidelity, to distance their unsuspecting mate, whose love makes them feel even guiltier. At the same time, they seek out the only person who can assure them no wrong was done—the accomplice. Guilt therefore undermines the marriage and fuels the affair."

In addition, someone who is having an extramarital affair is clearly not trying to increase the degree of intimacy and mutual understanding in his or her marriage, which bodes badly for lasting love. Says Cowan, "Only when we trust our lover to be faithful and know that he or she can trust us do we feel comfortable and at peace with our own conduct and our relationship."

10. THE PATTER OF FOUR-LEGGED FEET

A recent Indiana University study has shown that adding dogs or cats to your household can make love more likely to endure. Researchers found that pets actually help ease marital conflicts. And their unconditional love for their owners also sets a good example. "Dogs relax people and reduce stress and anger," says Alan Beck, director of the University of Pennsylvania School of Veterinary Medicine's Center for the Interaction of Animals and Society. "A pet in the room makes people like each other better. When we get home and see the dog or cat curled up and content, we, too, relax our guard."

CHOOSING A CONTRACEPTIVE

What's Best for You?

Joseph Anthony

Joseph Anthony is a Contributing Editor at AMERICAN HEALTH.

If you've been frustrated by a lack of contraceptive choices, there's good news: In the last couple of years, several new forms of contraception specifically, the long-lasting, hormone-based products Depo-Provera and Norplant and the female condom have been approved for use in the U.S., which means that we're finally catching up with the rest of the world. Depo-Provera and Norplant have been in use in other countries for years. But much ballyhooed new methods, such as contraceptive "vaccines" and a male birth control pill, are still probably a decade or more away.

Why? Manufacturers worry about boycotts and other protests from the religious right and antiabortion activists. And, says Dr. Michael Policar, vice president for medical affairs at the Planned Parenthood Federation of America, "the threat of litigation has had an incredibly chilling effect on contraceptive development in the last 10 years."

What are in the pipeline are mostly variations on existing themes—a two-capsule Norplant (instead of today's six); redesigned, baggier male condoms that promise greater comfort; intrauterine devices (IUD's) that release hormones; barrier methods that release spermicides, creams or gels with anti-HIV as well as antisperm properties; and perhaps some new injectables. There has also been some movement toward making the Pill available over the counter (without a prescription), although the Food and Drug Administration (FDA) is not currently considering any formal proposals to do so.

Here's a rundown on newly available methods of birth control, followed by more-established and better-known alternatives.

THE FEMALE CONDOM: This device looks like a large, floppy tube closed at one end. Marketed by Wisconsin Pharmacal under the name Reality, the polyurethane barrier (thinner, stronger and a better conductor of heat than latex) was approved by the FDA last May. Like other barrier methods this one can take some time and patience to use correctly. The device has two rings, one around the outer rim and one inside. The inner ring is designed to fit over the cervix, anchored in place behind the pubic bone, like a diaphragm. The outer ring covers the labia and the base of the penis during intercourse. Some women have complained that the condom can rise into the vagina if not sufficiently lubricated; it can also twist around if not inserted properly.

The one-year failure rate with "typical use" is high, estimated at 21% to 26%, which means that about one in four women using it may become pregnant over the course of a year. (The pregnancy rate for "perfect use" would be much lower—about 5%.)

DEPO-PROVERA: This injectable prescription contraceptive, first available in New Zealand in 1969 and subsequently used by 30 million women in 90 countries, was finally approved in the U.S. in late 1992. One injection of this synthetic version of the female hormone progesterone every three months blocks ovulation.

The drug, which provides no protection against sexually transmitted diseases (STD's), may cause irregular periods, and women may not regain fertility until six to 12 months after they stop taking it.

Side effects of Depo-Provera are similar to those of other hormonal contraceptives and may include weight gain, headaches and fatigue. Women usually experience some irregular bleeding or spotting during the first months of use. On the plus side, studies by the World Health Organization have found a link between Depo-Provera use and a reduced risk of cancer of the endometrium (the lining of the uterus).

NORPLANT: This implant of six thin capsules, placed under the skin of a woman's arm, releases the hormone levonorgestrel, which keeps the body from producing the hormones necessary for ovulation. Norplant is effective for up to five years.

The implant was approved after two decades of testing on more than 50,000 women. More than 900,000 American women have received Norplant since it was introduced in February of 1991 by U.S. distributor Wyeth-Ayerst Laboratories. It's not appropriate for women who have liver disease,

29. Choosing a Contraceptive

blood clots, inflammation of the veins or a history of breast cancer, or for those who are breast-feeding in the first six weeks after delivery. Fertility returns soon after the implant is removed.

The most common side effect of Norplant is irregular menstrual bleeding during the first six months after implantation. Norplant provides no STD protection.

Wyeth-Ayerst Laboratories has been charging $365 for Norplant in the U.S. (With doctor's fees, Norplant generally costs between $500 and $800.) After congressional hearings last year revealed that the drug sells for as little as $23 in other countries, the company announced that the price to public clinics would be lowered in 1995. But company officials won't comment on what the new price will be.

STERILIZATION: Every year more than 600,000 women in the U.S. have their fallopian tubes surgically blocked or severed, thus preventing eggs from reaching the uterus. About 25% of all women at risk of pregnancy (sexually active, heterosexual and fertile) aged 15 to 50 have had this procedure, called a tubal ligation; among such women 35 to 44 the number soars to more than 60%, according to the Alan Guttmacher Institute, a nonprofit group studying contraceptive issues. In addition, each year about half a million American men have vasectomies, in which the tube that carries sperm from the testes is cut and sealed. Vasectomy, which is performed under local anesthesia, carries less surgical risk than tubal ligation, which requires general anesthesia.

Both forms of sterilization are more than 99% effective and virtually permanent. (Though surgical sterilizations can sometimes be reversed—the success rate for such procedures is better for vasectomies than for tubal ligations—but anyone contemplating surgical sterilization is generally advised to consider the operation irreversible.)

ORAL CONTRACEPTIVES: Commonly known as the Pill, oral contraceptives, which suppress ovulation, are the most popular form of birth control for women in the U.S. About 28% of American women at risk of pregnancy between 15 and 44 use oral contraceptives. Fewer than 1% of women using oral contraceptives properly will become pregnant in the course of a year.

Literally hundreds of studies over the past four decades have attempted to analyze the effect of the Pill on women's health. No solid connections between taking the Pill and getting breast cancer have been made. The Pill does appear to increase the risk of blood clots, heart attack and stroke for women over 35 who smoke. The authors of *Contraceptive Technology*, a leading reference manual in the field, characterize the risk for nonsmokers and smokers under 35 as relatively minor.

While the Pill has been linked to circulatory problems in women who have high cholesterol, hypertension or any heart or vascular disease, as well as those who have a family history of heart disease, oral contraceptives also have been associated with several health *benefits*. Some studies indicate that birth control pills can actually reduce a woman's chances of developing ovarian or endometrial cancer, as well as lower her risk of pelvic inflammatory disease. Women taking the Pill also have fewer ovarian cysts and benign breast tumors than other women.

There are more than a dozen side effects attributed to the Pill, including breast tenderness, fluid retention, weight gain and headaches.

BARRIER METHODS: Condoms, diaphragms, cervical caps, sponges and spermicides all operate on the same basic principle: preventing sperm from reaching an egg. Latex condoms have the added benefit of providing the most protection against STD's, although all barrier methods, even spermicides, are thought to provide some protection when used properly.

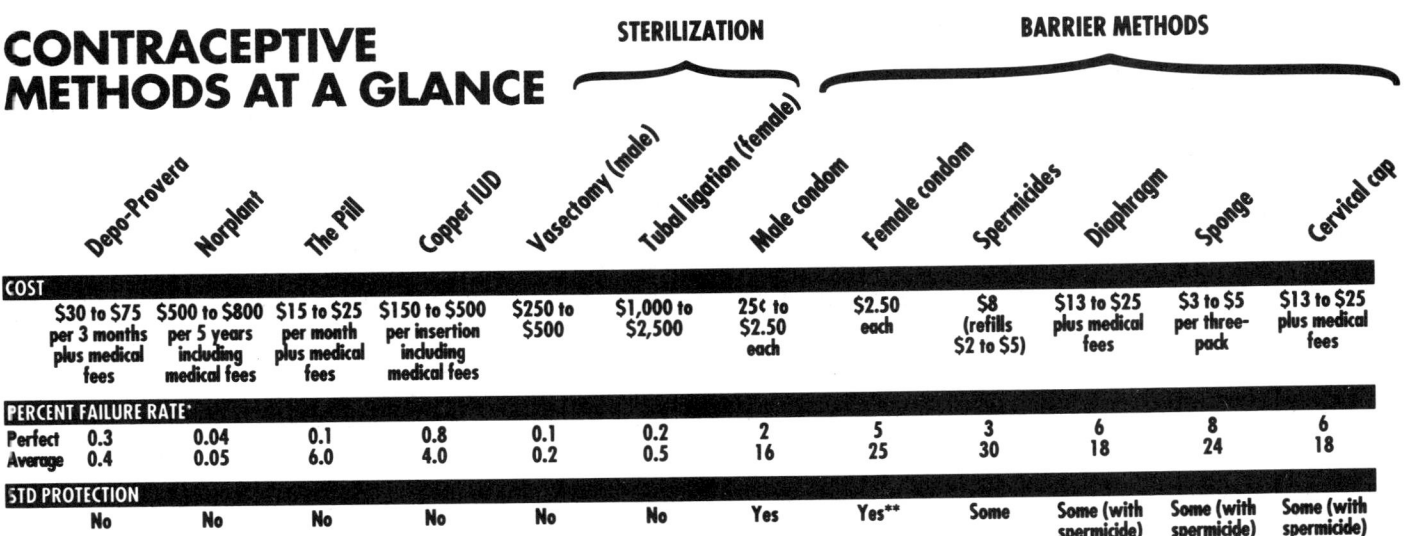

CONTRACEPTIVE METHODS AT A GLANCE

	Depo-Provera	Norplant	The Pill	Copper IUD	Vasectomy (male)	Tubal ligation (female)	Male condom	Female condom	Spermicides	Diaphragm	Sponge	Cervical cap
					STERILIZATION		**BARRIER METHODS**					
COST	$30 to $75 per 3 months plus medical fees	$500 to $800 per 5 years including medical fees	$15 to $25 per month plus medical fees	$150 to $500 per insertion including medical fees	$250 to $500	$1,000 to $2,500	25¢ to $2.50 each	$2.50 each	$8 (refills $2 to $5)	$13 to $25 plus medical fees	$3 to $5 per three-pack	$13 to $25 plus medical fees
PERCENT FAILURE RATE*												
Perfect	0.3	0.04	0.1	0.8	0.1	0.2	2	5	3	6	8	6
Average	0.4	0.05	6.0	4.0	0.2	0.5	16	25	30	18	24	18
STD PROTECTION	No	No	No	No	No	No	Yes	Yes**	Some	Some (with spermicide)	Some (with spermicide)	Some (with spermicide)

*Estimated percentage of women who get pregnant unintentionally in the first year of use. "Perfect use" is calculated from pregnancies occurring among couples who use the method correctly each time they have intercourse; "average use" combines perfect use figures with pregnancies occurring among couples who use the method sporadically or incorrectly.

**Although the female condom does provide protection against sexually transmitted diseases (STD's), its manufacturer is required by the Food and Drug Administration to note that for "highly effective protection" against STD's, including AIDS, it is important to use latex condoms for men.

FAILURE RATE DATA: ALAN GUTTMACHER INSTITUTE. FEMALE CONDOM FAILURE RATES: WISCONSIN PHARMACAL.

RU-486 and MORNING-AFTER TREATMENTS

Women who fear they may have become pregnant because they experienced condom rupture or otherwise engaged in unprotected intercourse have a little-publicized "morning-after," or postcoital, contraceptive option. Take what Dr. Felicia Stewart, director of research for the Sutter Medical Foundation in Sacramento, Calif., calls emergency contraceptive pills as soon as possible after the unprotected intercourse but no later than 72 hours afterward.

The "emergency pills" are regular birth control pills, but taken in two larger-than-usual doses (the second 12 hours after the first). The number of pills per dose depends on the brand: two Ovral, or four Lo/Ovral, Nordette, Levlen or yellow-colored Triphasil or Tri-Levlen (the yellow versions of both are the strongest formulas). By taking a larger-than-normal dose of birth control pills, you'll disrupt your body's natural hormone patterns, thereby reducing your chances of becoming pregnant by about 75%.

Obviously, the morning-after option shouldn't be looked at as a regular birth control method—it's a one-time emergency measure. And the procedure may not be suitable for women suffering from severe liver disease, blood clots or other circulation problems. Up to half of all women using this approach report short-term nausea or vomiting.

The drug RU-486, which prevents a fertilized egg from implanting itself in the uterine wall, might also find a secondary use as a morning-after contraceptive if it's approved for sale in the U.S. A University of Edinburgh study published in *The New England Journal of Medicine* found that if taken within 72 hours of unprotected sexual intercourse, RU-486 also prevents pregnancy. The women surveyed in the study reported much milder side effects than those taking birth control pills as morning-after measures.

Last year RU-486 manufacturer Roussel-Uclaf announced it would grant U.S. rights to the drug to the nonprofit research organization the Population Council, which would market and test the drug. As of the beginning of this year, however, the final details of the agreement had not been ironed out.

The main side effects of barrier methods are allergies or sensitivity to latex or spermicides. (The sponge is off-limits to women who have had toxic shock syndrome.)

INTRAUTERINE DEVICES (IUD's): IUD's are placed in a woman's uterus, where they prevent pregnancy by interfering with sperm transport and egg fertilization. The Dalkon Shield gave IUD's a terrible name in this country during the 1980s. After more than 10,000 lawsuits over pelvic inflammatory disease linked to the shield, IUD's have fallen out of favor. Fewer than 2% of women in the U.S. currently use them, a fact some experts regard as unfortunate.

"Compare that to around 30% of the women in Finland who choose an IUD," says Dr. Daniel Mishell, chairman of obstetrics and gynecology at the University of Southern California School of Medicine. "The IUD is effective and is one of the least expensive forms of long-term contraception, but it is also one of the least used in the U.S. because of the perception that it is dangerous." Recent studies have shown modern copper IUD's present little, if any risk of pelvic inflammatory disease.

The only IUD's currently sold in the U.S. are the Copper T-380A, which can be used for up to eight years, and the Progestasert, which releases progesterone and can be used for up to one year.

What form of contraception is right for you? People who have new or multiple partners have to be concerned about STD's as well as pregnancy. That means they should use condoms for maximum STD protection. A survey of 678 women receiving Norplant in Texas indicated that about half who had previously used condoms intended to keep doing so at least some of the time. "Until the last few years, nobody even *asked* questions about whether women using a hormonal contraceptive like Norplant would also continue to use barrier methods like condoms," says Margaret Frank, a contraceptive researcher at the University of New Haven in Connecticut and coauthor of the Texas study. People in monogamous, long-term relationships shouldn't have to worry about diseases and may focus instead on effective contraception.

But there's no way of saying that any one choice is "best." "Some women are going to get along really well with a particular method, and that's great," says *Contraceptive Technology* coauthor Dr. Felicia Stewart, director of research for the Sutter Medical Foundation, a managed-care organization in Sacramento, Calif. "If you have a method that is a comfortable fit with your hormonal makeup or your anatomy and your habits, then that method is fine for you. Trying, to say there's one best method is just ridiculous."

Preventing STDs

This article is part of a [continuing FDA Consumer*] series with important health information for teenagers. Unlike previous articles, however, it contains sexually explicit material in an effort to reduce the incidence of STDs among teens. Parents and teachers may want to review the article before giving it to teenagers.*

Judith Levine Willis

Judith Levine Willis is editor of FDA Consumer.

It's important to read the information printed on the package to make sure a condom's made of latex and labeled for disease prevention. The label may also give an expiration date and tell you if there is added spermicide or lubricant.

You don't have to be a genius to figure out that the only sure way to avoid getting sexually transmitted diseases (STDs) is to not have sex.

But in today's age of AIDS, it's smart to also know ways to lower the risk of getting STDs, including HIV, the virus that causes AIDS.

Infection with HIV, which stands for human immunodeficiency virus, is spreading among teenagers. From 1990 to 1992, the number of teens diagnosed with AIDS nearly doubled, according to the national Centers for Disease Control and Prevention. Today, people in their 20s account for 1 out of every 5 AIDS cases in the United States. Because HIV infection can take many years to develop into AIDS, many of these people were infected when they were teenagers.

You may have heard that birth control can also help prevent AIDS and other STDs. This is only partly true. The whole story is that *only one form of birth control—latex condoms* (thin rubber sheaths used to cover the penis)—is highly effective in reducing the transmission (spread) of HIV and many other STDs.

(When this *FDA Consumer* went to press, the Food and Drug Administration was preparing to approve Reality Female Condom, a form of birth control made of polyurethane. It may give limited protection against STDs, but it is not as effective as male latex condoms.)

So people who use other kinds of birth control, such as the pill, sponge, diaphragm, Norplant, Depo-Provera, cervical cap, or IUD, also need to use condoms to help prevent STDs.

Here's why: Latex condoms work against STDs by keeping blood, a man's semen, and a woman's vaginal fluids—all of which can carry bacteria and viruses—from passing from one person to another. For many years, scientists have known that male condoms (also called safes, rubbers, or prophylactics) can help prevent STDs transmitted by bacteria, such as syphilis and gonorrhea, because the bacteria can't get through the condom. More recently, researchers discovered that latex condoms can also reduce

6. HUMAN SEXUALITY

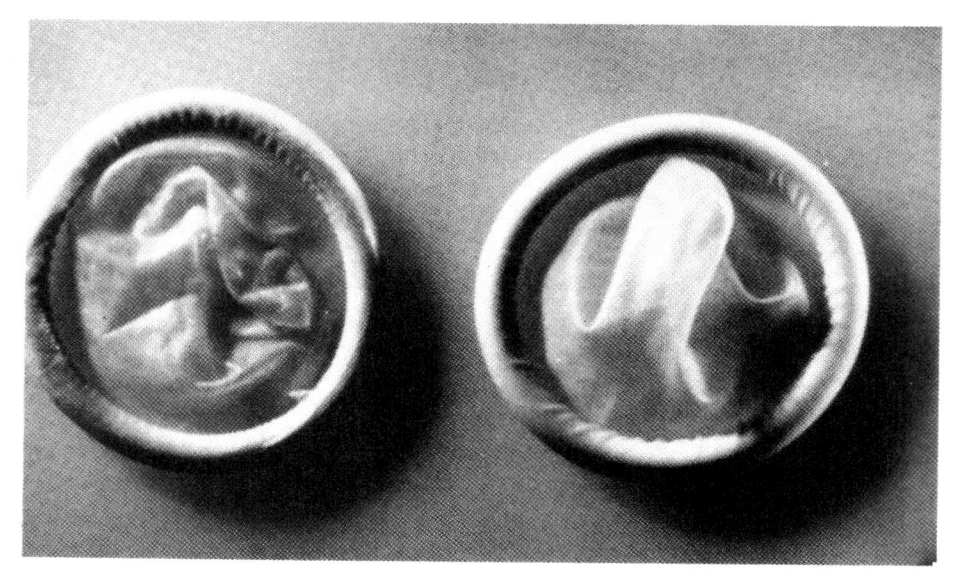

If a condom is sticking to itself, as is the one on the left, it's damaged and should not be used. The one on the right is undamaged and okay to use.

the risk of getting STDs caused by viruses, such as HIV, herpes, and hepatitis B, even though viruses are much smaller than bacteria or sperm.

After this discovery, FDA, which regulates condoms as medical devices, worked with manufacturers to develop labeling for latex condoms. The labeling tells consumers that although latex condoms cannot entirely eliminate the risk of STDs, when used properly and consistently they are highly effective in preventing STDs. FDA also provided a sample set of instructions and requested that all condoms include adequate instructions.

Make Sure It's Latex

Male condoms sold in the United States are made either of latex (rubber) or natural membrane, commonly called "lambskin" (but actually made of sheep intestine). Scientists found that natural skin condoms are not as effective as latex condoms in reducing the risk of STDs because natural skin condoms have naturally occurring tiny holes or pores that viruses may be able to get through. Only latex condoms labeled for protection against STDs should be used for disease protection.

Some condoms have lubricants added and some have spermicide (a chemical that kills sperm) added. The package labeling tells whether either of these has been added to the condom.

Lubricants may help prevent condoms from breaking and may help prevent irritation. But lubricants do not give any added disease protection. If an unlubricated condom is used, a water-based lubricant

New Information on Labels

Information about whether a birth control product also helps protect against sexually transmitted diseases (STDs), including HIV infection, is being given added emphasis on the labeling of these products.

"In spite of educational efforts, many adolescents and young adults, in particular, are continuing to engage in high-risk sexual behavior," said FDA Commissioner David A. Kessler, M.D., in announcing the label strengthening last April. "A product that is highly effective in preventing pregnancy will not necessarily protect against sexually transmitted diseases."

Labels on birth control pills, implants such as Norplant, injectable contraceptives such as Depo Provera, intrauterine devices (IUDs), and natural skin condoms will state that the products are intended to prevent pregnancy and do not protect against STDs, including HIV infection (which leads to AIDS). Labeling of natural skin condoms will also state that consumers should use a latex condom to help reduce risk of many STDs, including HIV infection.

Labeling for latex condoms, the only product currently allowed to make a claim of effectiveness against STDs, will state that if used properly, latex condoms help reduce risk of HIV transmission and many other STDs. This statement, a modification from previous labeling, will now appear on individual condom wrappers, on the box, and in consumer information.

Besides highlighting statements concerning sexually transmitted diseases and AIDS on the consumer packaging, manufacturers will add a similar statement to patient and physician leaflets provided with the products.

Consumers can expect to see the new labels by next fall. Some products already include this information in their labeling voluntarily. FDA may take action against any products that don't carry the new information.

FDA is currently reviewing whether similar action is necessary for the labeling of spermicide, cervical caps, diaphragms, and the Today brand contraceptive sponge.

Looking at a Condom Label

Like other drugs and medical devices, FDA requires condom packages to contain certain labeling information. When buying condoms, look on the package label to make sure the condoms are:
- made of latex
- labeled for disease prevention
- not past their expiration date (EXP followed by the date).

30. Preventing STDs

(such as K-Y Jelly), available over-the-counter (without prescription) in drugstores, can be used but is not required for the proper use of the condom. Do *not* use petroleum-based jelly (such as Vaseline), baby oil, lotions, cooking oils, or cold creams because these products can weaken latex and cause the condom to tear easily.

Condoms with added spermicide give added birth control protection. An active chemical in spermicides, nonoxynol-9, kills sperm. Although it has not been scientifically proven, it's possible that spermicides may reduce the transmission of HIV and other STDs. But spermicides alone (as sold in creams and jellies over-the-counter in drugstores) and spermicides used with the diaphragm or cervical cap do not give adequate protection against AIDS and other STDs. For the best disease protection, a latex condom should be used from start to finish every time a person has sex.

FDA requires condoms with spermicide to be labeled with an expiration date. Some condoms have an expiration date even though they don't contain spermicide. Condoms should not be used after the expiration date, usually abbreviated EXP and followed by the date.

Condoms are available in almost all drugstores, many supermarkets, and other stores. They are also available from vending machines. When purchasing condoms from vending machines, as from any source, be sure they are latex, labeled for disease prevention, and are not past their expiration date. Don't buy a condom from a vending machine located where it may be exposed to extreme heat or cold or to direct sunlight.

Condoms should be stored in a cool, dry place out of direct sunlight. Closets and drawers usually make good storage places. Because of possible exposure to extreme heat and cold, glove compartments of cars are *not* a good place to store condoms. For the same reason, condoms shouldn't be kept in a pocket, wallet or purse for more than a few hours at a time.

How to Use a Condom

- Use a new condom for every act of vaginal, anal and oral (penis-mouth contact) sex. Do not unroll the condom before placing it on the penis.

STD FACTS

- Sexually transmitted diseases affect more than 12 million Americans each year, many of whom are teenagers or young adults.
- Using drugs and alcohol increases your chances of getting STDs because these substances can interfere with your judgment and your ability to use a condom properly.
- Intravenous drug use puts a person at higher risk for HIV and hepatitis B because IV drug users usually share needles.
- The more partners you have, the higher your chance of being exposed to HIV or other STDs. This is because it is difficult to know whether a person is infected, or has had sex with people who are more likely to be infected due to intravenous drug use or other risk factors.
- Sometimes, early in infection, there may be no symptoms, or symptoms may be confused with other illnesses.
- You cannot tell by looking at someone whether he or she is infected with HIV or another STD.

STDs can cause:
- pelvic inflammatory disease (PID), which can damage a woman's fallopian tubes and result in pelvic pain and sterility
- tubal pregnancies (where the fetus grows in the fallopian tube instead of the womb), sometimes fatal to the mother and always fatal to the fetus
- cancer of the cervix in women
- sterility—the inability to have children—in both men and women
- damage to major organs, such as the heart, kidney and brain, if STDs go untreated
- death, especially with HIV infection.

See a doctor if you have any of these STD symptoms:
- discharge from vagina, penis or rectum
- pain or burning during urination or intercourse
- pain in the abdomen (women), testicles (men), or buttocks and legs (both)
- blisters, open sores, warts, rash, or swelling in the genital or anal areas or mouth
- persistent flu-like symptoms—including fever, headache, aching muscles, or swollen glands—which may precede STD symptoms.

- Put the condom on after the penis is erect and before *any* contact is made between the penis and any part of the partner's body.

- If the condom does not have a reservoir top, pinch the tip enough to leave a half-inch space for semen to collect. Always make sure to eliminate any air in the tip to help keep the condom from breaking.

- Holding the condom rim (and pinching a half inch space if necessary), place the condom on the top of the penis. Then, continuing to hold it by the rim, unroll it all the way to the base of the penis. If you are also using water-based lubricant, you can put more on the outside of the condom.

- If you feel the condom break, stop immediately, withdraw, and put on a new condom.

- After ejaculation and before the penis gets soft, grip the rim of the condom and carefully withdraw.

- To remove the condom, gently pull it off the penis, being careful that semen doesn't spill out.

- Wrap the condom in a tissue and throw it in the trash where others won't handle it. (Don't flush condoms down the toilet because they may cause sewer problems.) Afterwards, wash your hands with soap and water.

Latex condoms are the only form of contraception now available that human studies have shown to be highly effective in protecting against the transmission of HIV and other STDs. They give good disease protection for vaginal sex and should also reduce the risk of disease transmission in oral and anal sex. But latex condoms may not be 100 percent effective, and a lot depends on knowing the right way to buy, store and use them.

Current Killers

In the past 30 years, Americans have witnessed remarkable advances in medical technology. Today, not only are organ transplants a common occurrence, but human organs are being replaced with artificial substitutes. However, these medical marvels have done little to prevent the ravages of cardiovascular disease and cancer—the leading killers in this country. It is not always possible to prevent these illnesses, but your chances of success are much greater if you are aware of any genetic predisposition that you may have and can modify your lifestyle to compensate for it. The essay "Family History: What You Don't Know Can Kill You" identifies several diseases that have a strong genetic component and suggests how to go about constructing a family tree to find out if you are at risk.

Cardiovascular disease is this nation's number-one killer. The good news is that 7 of the 11 risk factors associated with it are controllable and, if controlled properly, can delay or prevent illness. The following recommendations serve as general guidelines for controlling these factors: (1) hypertension—have your blood pressure checked regularly, reduce your dietary consumption of salt or, perhaps, increase your dietary calcium intake, exercise regularly, and learn to relax; (2) high serum cholesterol levels—have your serum cholesterol checked regularly, reduce your dietary fat intake to less than 30 percent of your daily caloric intake, substitute monounsaturated and polyunsaturated fats for saturated fats, increase the amount of soluble dietary fiber in your diet, limit your use of foods high in cholesterol, and exercise regularly; (3) diabetes—monitor your blood sugar level regularly and maintain the proper insulin balance, and avoid both alcohol and foods high in refined sugars and fats; (4) obesity—reduce your percentage of body fat through a reasonable weight loss program that is nutritionally sound and includes some form of exercise; (5) homocysteine—reduce your consumption of animal protein and make sure you are meeting the RDA for the B vitamins, especially folic acid; (6) cigarette smoking—give it up and avoid or minimize your exposure to passive or secondhand smoke; (7) sedentary lifestyle—establish some type of exercise program and stay with it; and (8) stress—work on developing coping skills that will be useful during times of high stress and start an exercise program. While these guidelines are simplistic, they demonstrate the type of lifestyle modifications that are effective in reducing one's risk of developing coronary heart disease. The article "Rating Your Risks for Heart Disease" examines all the known risk factors and predictors of cardiovascular disease and presents a brief discussion of nine intervention strategies that can reduce one's risk of developing this deadly illness. "The Heart of the Matter" discusses how the physiological changes associated with exercise reduce one's risk of developing premature cardiovascular disease.

While the link between high serum cholesterol levels and premature cardiovascular disease is irrefutable, the connection between dietary fat and elevated serum cholesterol is embroiled in controversy. The issue is not whether dietary fat can raise one's serum cholesterol level, but what percentage of the population is susceptible to this cholesterol-elevating effect. The article "Cholesterol," published in the *Mayo Clinic Health Letter*, provides a comprehensive look at cholesterol by addressing questions such as: What is cholesterol? How can cholesterol be both bad and good? What does cholesterol do in your body? What constitutes an elevated cholesterol level? How do the other risk factors of coronary heart disease influence cholesterol levels? How can elevated cholesterol levels be reduced?

Cardiovascular disease may be America's number-one killer, but cancer takes top billing in terms of the "fear factor," which stems from an awareness of the degenerative and disfiguring nature of this deadly disease. A very disturbing aspect of this country's battle against cancer is the fact that millions of dollars are spent each year trying to advance the treatment of cancer, while funding for the technologies used to detect cancer in its early stages are quite limited. "Strategies for Minimizing Cancer Risk" addresses the importance of prevention and early detection as our best strategy for reducing the death toll from this illness.

Medical experts now believe that dietary factors contribute to one-third of the 500,000 yearly cancer deaths in this country. While the evidence is by no means conclusive, it appears that several foods may actually contain substances capable of blocking the cellular changes that lead to cancer. These cancer-blocking substances are called phytochemicals, and they have so excited the scientific community that the National Cancer Institute has launched a multi-million-dollar project to find, isolate, and study them. "Cancer-Fighting Foods: Green Revolution" addresses the concept of functional foods and discusses the role that phytochemicals, carotenoids, folic acid, and certain minerals may have in protecting one against various forms of cancer.

Of the three diseases discussed in this unit, AIDS has the potential to become the worst epidemic of this century. As medical researchers intensify their search for an effective AIDS vaccine, the disease continues to spread. Conservative estimates indicate that by the year 2000,

UNIT 7

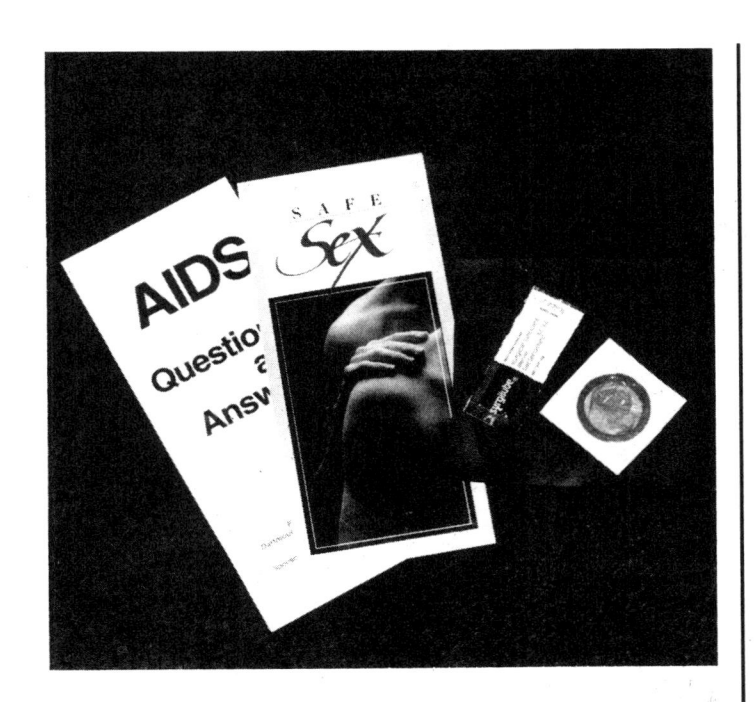

between 30 million to 110 million people will be infected with the AIDS virus. The World Health Organization estimates that there are already 5 million people carrying the virus with no apparent symptoms. One of the problems with trying to estimate the exact number of potential AIDS victims is the fact that this disease has an incubation period that may be as long as 10 years.

What is known about AIDS? Researchers have been able to identify the virus that causes AIDS. This virus, termed the HIV virus, has been found in both the blood and body fluids of infected persons, and case studies have documented that the disease can be transmitted through intimate sexual contact and the mixing of blood products. To date there have been no documented cases of AIDS being spread through casual social contact, and most experts do not believe that the viral content of saliva is sufficient to spread the disease. Currently there is no vaccine available to protect one from this dreaded disease, and there are no antiviral drugs available that can cure it. Despite the failure by the scientific community to produce an AIDS vaccine, there are however a couple of bright spots. (See "The Disease Detective.")

Many scientists now believe that with early treatment and close monitoring of HIV-infected patients, they may be able to use varying drug therapies to help these people live significantly longer once they are infected. This optimism is based on the belief that it may soon be possible to prevent many of the life-threatening complications that accompany this dreaded disease. While this may be good news for those that are HIV-infected, it does not address the issue of prevention. A recent discovery that appears to link a particular gene to a known HIV receptor site on the surface of cells has the scientific community very excited. It seems that within the population there are individuals who have a mutant gene for this particular receptor site, and as a result the HIV receptor site is absent. The net result is that these individuals are much more resistant to being infected with the HIV virus. Interestingly, this mutant gene is present in approximately 15 percent of all Caucasians of European descent, while only 1.7 percent of African Americans carry it. This finding is consistent with the data concerning the disproportionately high rate of HIV infection among African Americans. "Mutant Gene Can Slow AIDS Virus" discusses this new finding and speculates that it may provide scientists with the key to developing an effective vaccination against the HIV virus. One recent and hopeful treatment, involving the combining of protease inhibitors with standard antiviral medications, is reported in "The Disease Detective," highlighting the work of researcher Dr. David Ho.

While coronary heart disease, cancer, and AIDS are all deadly diseases, the good news is that many of the risk factors associated with each of them can be controlled through the lifestyle choices we make. This fact, coupled with our country's need to curb the high cost of health care, may be just what it takes to elevate the role of primary prevention to the forefront of health care, where it belongs.

Looking Ahead: Challenge Questions

What role can and should education play in combating the spread of AIDS?

What lifestyle changes could you make that would reduce your risk of developing cardiovascular disease, cancer, and AIDS?

How important is diet in terms of preventing both cardiovascular disease and cancer? Explain.

What dietary advice would you give someone to reduce his or her risk of cancer?

To what extent should the government be involved in promoting preventive medicine?

Which chronic disease do you think you are most likely to contract, based on your family history and your lifestyle?

Family history: What you don't know can kill you

Your risk of deadly disease can be influenced or even determined by hereditary factors.

Knowing that a specific disease runs in your family can save your life. Depending on the disease, it can allow you to watch for early warning signs, get more frequent screening tests, or change your health habits.

Unfortunately, most doctors pay scant attention to family background. One study of medical records for nearly 9000 patients found that physicians had noted family history in only 4 percent. The recent advances in genetic testing for hereditary disease may force many physicians—and their patients—to attend more closely to family matters. For the vast majority of people, however, there's no need for genetic tests; an old-fashioned family tree will be far more helpful.

Genetic mandate

For certain uncommon diseases, heredity is the primary cause: If your parents gave you the necessary genes, you're almost sure to get the disease. Such disorders include hemophilia, cystic fibrosis, sickle-cell anemia, at least some cases of Alzheimer's disease, certain cancers, and some 4000 other diseases, nearly all of them rare. It's impossible to prevent those disorders, but early detection can allow doctors to prevent or treat the complications that may develop.

In addition, some genetic disorders, while not harmful in and of themselves, can pave the way for disease. For example, familial hypercholesterolemia, an inherited elevation in blood cholesterol, is implicated in one of every five heart attacks that strike before age 60. And about 1 percent of all colorectal cancers evolve from polyps caused by a hereditary disorder known as familial polyposis. Detected early, those conditions can be treated before any disease develops.

Learn from history In one study, doctors noted family history on only 4 percent of all medical records. But virtually all families have some hereditary concerns.

If an uncommon disease appears somewhere in your family tree, you can get valuable information by looking it up in the medical section of your local library. A medical dictionary will usually tell you whether the disease is inherited directly and, if it is, which of the following types of genes transmits it:

■ **Dominant:** If one parent had a disease transmitted by a dominant gene, you have a 50/50 chance of getting the gene. If you carry the gene, you'll probably get the disease. Examples include familial hypercholesterolemia and familial polyposis of the colon.

■ **Recessive:** You'd get the disease only in the unlikely event that both parents carried the gene and both passed it on to you. The most common recessive diseases occur only in certain ethnic groups—such as Tay-Sachs disease, found primarily in Ashkenazic Jews.

■ **X-linked:** Only males get X-linked diseases, but only females transmit the gene. The son of a woman who carries the faulty gene has a 50/50 chance of inheriting the gene and almost as high a chance of getting the disease; daughters will not get the disease but have a 50/50 chance of being carriers. X-linked conditions include hemophilia and color blindness.

Genetic influence

Heredity plays a subtler role in many other diseases, which are caused at least in part by "environmental" influences such as infection, cancer-causing chemicals, or an artery-clogging diet. While your genes alone will not produce those diseases, they can determine how susceptible you are.

Researchers have found a genetic influence in most common disorders, including several major killers—coronary heart disease, diabetes, and cancer of the bladder, breast, colon, lung, ovaries, prostate, skin, or uterus. Heredity also influences susceptibility to many familiar, less deadly disorders, such as allergies, asthma, glaucoma, migraine, osteoporosis, and rheumatoid arthritis. Some psychological or behavioral problems, including depression, schizophrenia, and alcoholism, have a genetic link as well.

Fortunately, many of those diseases, unlike the purely genetic disorders, do have risk factors you can change. People whose relatives had coronary disease or type II diabetes, for example, may lower their risk by eating a low-fat, high-fiber diet, losing excess weight, and exercising regularly.

> **To gauge your true risk, you need to know something about your family's medical history.**

In general, the more relatives who had a genetically transmitted disease and the closer they are to you, the greater your risk. To gauge your true risk, however, you need to know something about your family's medical history. In some cases, nongenetic factors may have been more important than genetic ones in causing their diseases. As a general rule, however, signs of strong hereditary influence include:

■ Early onset of the disease. It generally takes decades for nongenetic factors to produce coronary disease, cancer, and many other disorders. So the earlier the disease strikes, the more likely it is that heredity played a role.

■ Appearance of the disease largely or exclusively on one side of the family.

■ Onset of the same disease at about the same age in more than one relative.

■ Tumors that cropped up independently in more than one place (as opposed to spreading from site to site). The daughter of a woman who had cancer in both breasts, for example, has three times the risk of getting the disease before menopause, compared with someone whose mother had cancer in one breast only.

■ Disease despite good health habits. Coronary disease in a physically fit vegetarian, for example, is more likely to have a genetic influence than the same disease in an unfit relative who ate lots of meat.

Constructing a family tree

You can put together a simple family tree by digging up a few key facts on your closest relatives: siblings, parents, aunts and uncles, and grandparents. Those facts include the date of birth, major diseases, and, for deceased relatives, the date and cause of death. (see the sample tree on the next page.)

Of course, the more you find out about each of your relatives, the more useful your tree will be. So you might want to try collecting at least some of these additional facts, particularly for your parents and grandparents.

■ Age when any disease first started. For cancer, ask whether tumors independently struck different sites.

■ Disabilities or major operations. (Asking may remind your relative of a disease he or she had.)

■ Allergies, including allergic reactions to drugs.

■ Other health-related conditions, notably obesity, hypertension, and high blood cholesterol.

■ Health-related habits, such as excessive consumption of alcohol, smoking, exercise, and general type of diet.

■ Miscarriages, abortions for medical reasons, stillbirths, infant deaths, and birth defects. Those are all possible signs of hereditary problems with the fetus or infant.

■ Psychological or behavioral problems, including alcoholism, anxiety, major depression, schizophrenia, psychiatric treatment or hospitalization, and suicide.

You can also expand your family tree by getting some basic medical information on some of your less-close relatives—your great-grandparents and any cousins, nieces, or nephews. While they're less genetically significant than your closest relatives, they can add weight to a pattern of, say, cancer or coronary disease. Casting a wider net may also allow you to identify a strictly genetic disease, since the genes for a great number of those diseases can be carried through many generations without actually causing the illness to develop. (Note that women can inherit the genes for diseases such as breast or ovarian cancer from their father.)

How to get the facts

Some relatives may be reluctant to divulge all that personal information about their health. So try to explain how important knowing a family health history can be, and promise to keep the information confidential if they wish.

Learn about a deceased relative from several family members, if possible, in order to corroborate their information. If you can't identify a disease from the

---

For more information
■ Alliance of Genetic Support Groups. Referrals to organizations providing peer support and education on specific inherited disorders. Call 800-336-GENE. (Internet: http://medhelp.org/www/agsg.htm)

7. CURRENT KILLERS

description, which may be vague, colloquial, or outdated—"consumption" instead of tuberculosis, for example—jot down the description and ask your physician to help decipher it.

You could also ask whether anyone has a copy of the death certificate. Or request a copy from the department of health in the state where your relative died. If a relative died fairly recently, see whether your doctor can contact the physician or the hospital that treated the person to learn the cause of death as well as any other diseases he or she may have had.

Once you've collected the information you want, plug it all into the tree format, using the example below as a guide. We've included a few basic symbols, which can help you see key facts at a glance.

Summing up

Armed with information about your family medical history, you'll be better able to take steps to safeguard your health—through early warnings, increased screening, or changes in health habits. To get the information you need:

■ Round up the medical facts on your closest relatives, at the very least including any diseases plus date of birth and, for deceased relatives, date and cause of death.

■ Plug all that data into a family tree and bring it to your doctor or a specialist for interpretation.

■ Plan ways to head off or prepare for any genetic risk you uncover.

■ Don't rush to have a genetic test. It often won't lead to actions any different from what would be suggested by family history alone, and testing poses a new set of problems.

How to create a family tree—and what to make of it

To get a full picture of what your family tree means, show it to your family doctor—and possibly to a physician or counselor specializing in genetics. You can also glean a lot of valuable information yourself, if you know what to look for.

In this family tree, the prostate cancer that killed this man's father means that he should be tested for a prostate tumor at a younger age and more frequently than usual. His sisters need to have earlier, more frequent mammograms because of their mother's breast cancer.

One grandmother and one uncle each died of a heart attack. There are several reasons not to worry too much about that: The two relatives were from different sides of the family; both had the attack at a relatively advanced age; both had two other major risk factors for coronary heart disease—smoking and either diabetes or obesity; and neither of the man's parents had any apparent heart trouble. Still, it would be worth checking further to see whether either relative had highly elevated cholesterol levels, which could be a sign of familial hypercholesterolemia.

The colon cancer that struck another grandmother and uncle is a different story. Two factors suggest a possible hereditary link: They were mother and son, and they both developed the disease at a comparatively young age. So the man should be screened early and often for colon cancer.

Finally, alcoholism seems to run in the family. The man should be aware that such a history could indicate a hereditary susceptibility to the problem, though the habit might simply have been passed down by example.

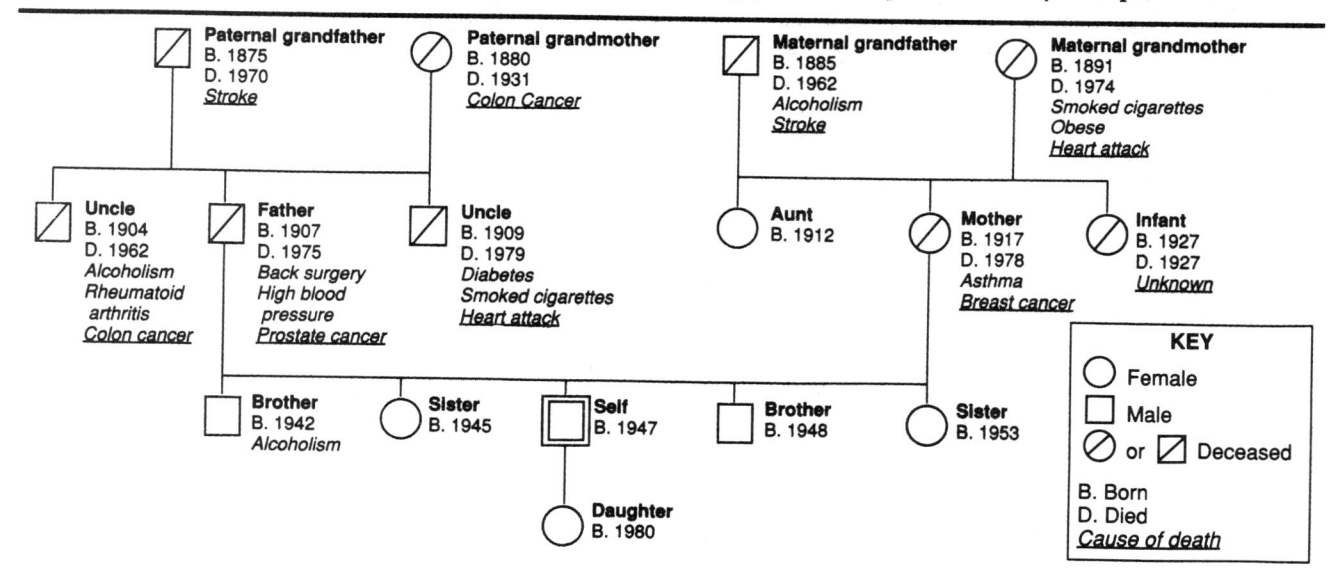

Paternal grandfather
B. 1875
D. 1970
Stroke

Paternal grandmother
B. 1880
D. 1931
Colon Cancer

Maternal grandfather
B. 1885
D. 1962
Alcoholism
Stroke

Maternal grandmother
B. 1891
D. 1974
Smoked cigarettes
Obese
Heart attack

Uncle
B. 1904
D. 1962
Alcoholism
Rheumatoid arthritis
Colon cancer

Father
B. 1907
D. 1975
Back surgery
High blood pressure
Prostate cancer

Uncle
B. 1909
D. 1979
Diabetes
Smoked cigarettes
Heart attack

Aunt
B. 1912

Mother
B. 1917
D. 1978
Asthma
Breast cancer

Infant
B. 1927
D. 1927
Unknown

Brother
B. 1942
Alcoholism

Sister
B. 1945

Self
B. 1947

Brother
B. 1948

Sister
B. 1953

Daughter
B. 1980

KEY
○ Female
□ Male
⊘ or ⊠ Deceased
B. Born
D. Died
Cause of death

Cholesterol

Put knowledge behind your numbers to lower your confusion level

"My doctor just gave me the results of my cholesterol test. He said, 'Your good cholesterol is low—that's bad, and your bad cholesterol is high—that's bad too. You need to raise your good and lower your bad—that would be good.'"

Confusing? You bet it is.

Chances are you know your cholesterol level is important and that it shouldn't be too high. But beyond that you may be unsure exactly how cholesterol fits into the cardiovascular disease puzzle.

Maybe you're too concerned about your cholesterol. Maybe you're not concerned enough.

In the following pages, we answer common questions, such as:
- What exactly is cholesterol?
- How can cholesterol be both good and bad?
- What does cholesterol do in your body?
- What is an elevated cholesterol level?
- When should you be concerned?
- What can you do about your concerns?

Why all the fuss about cholesterol?

Your blood cholesterol is important. Heart and blood vessel (cardiovascular) disease is the No. 1 killer of Americans, and study after study points to elevated cholesterol as a major contributor to the problem.

In general:
- The higher your cholesterol level, the greater your risk of cardiovascular disease.
- The higher your cholesterol level, the greater your chances of dying of cardiovascular disease.
- You can lower your risk of cardiovascular disease by lowering your cholesterol level.

Cholesterol and cardiovascular disease

The good news . . . Deaths from cardiovascular disease continue to fall. This encouraging trend is due to improved treatment and modification of cardiovascular disease risk factors, including cholesterol.

In 1980, heart attacks accounted for 163 deaths per 100,000 people. By 1990, this number had dropped to 112 people per 100,000.

The numbers for stroke are improving, too. In 1980, strokes claimed 41 people per 100,000. By 1990 this figure was down to 28.

The bad news . . . Far too many people still die from cardiovascular disease. The American Heart Association reports that cardiovascular disease still kills almost 1 million Americans each year. This is more than all cancer deaths combined.

Many of these deaths occur because of narrowed or blocked arteries (ath-

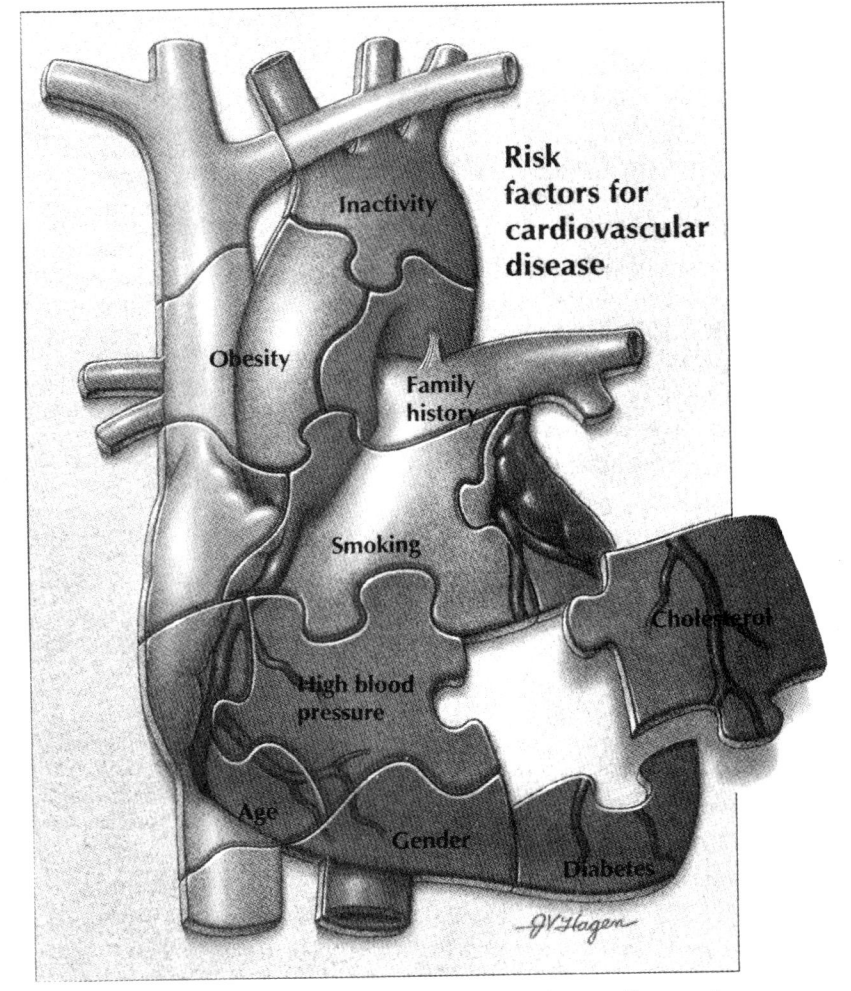

This puzzle includes nine major risk factors for cardiovascular disease, the nation's No. 1 killer. Cholesterol is among the most complex and important of all risk factors.

7. CURRENT KILLERS

erosclerosis). Cholesterol plays a significant role in this largely preventable condition.

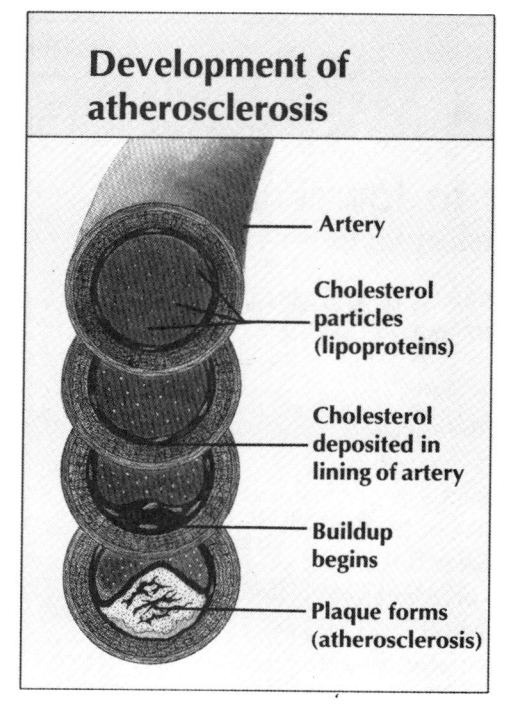

Development of atherosclerosis

A high number of cholesterol particles (lipoproteins) in your blood increases your risk for a buildup of cholesterol within the wall of your artery. Eventually, bumps called plaques may form, narrowing or even blocking your artery.

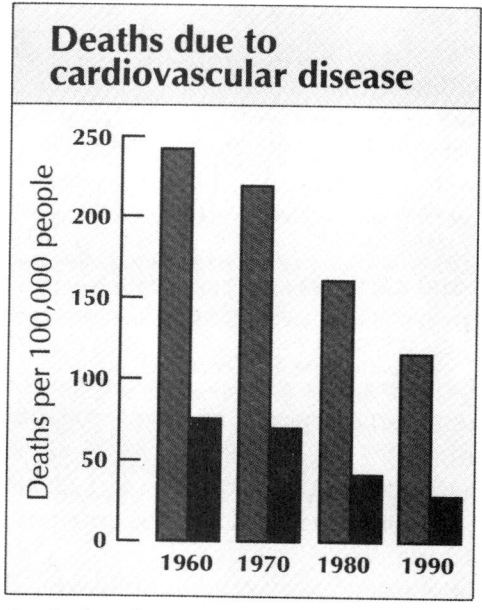

Deaths due to cardiovascular disease

Deaths from heart attacks (gray bars) and stroke (black bars) are declining. This encouraging trend is due to improved treatment and modification of cardiovascular disease risk factors, including cholesterol.
(Sources: National Center for Health Statistics and American Heart Association.)

Atherosclerosis (ATH-ro-scler-OH-sis) is a silent, painless process in which cholesterol-containing fatty deposits accumulate in the walls of your arteries. These accumulations occur as bumps called plaques. (See illustration.)

As plaque builds up, the interior of your artery narrows. This reduces the flow of blood. If reduced flow occurs in your coronary (heart) arteries, it can lead to a type of chest pain called angina pectoris.

As a plaque enlarges, the inner lining of your artery becomes roughened. A tear or rupture in the plaque may cause a blood clot to form. Such a clot can block the flow of blood or break free and plug an artery downstream.

If the flow of blood to a part of your heart is stopped, you'll have a heart attack. If blood flow to a part of your brain stops, you'll have a stroke.

Many factors influence the clogging of arteries. Cholesterol is important in the process, but it's not the only piece of the puzzle.

What is cholesterol?

Cholesterol is a waxy, fat-like substance (lipid). Although it's often discussed as if it were a poison, you can't live without it. Cholesterol is essential to your body's cell membranes, to the insulation of your nerves and to the production of certain hormones. It's used by your liver to make bile acids, which help digest your food.

The confusion that clouds cholesterol is partly due to the way some people use the word. "Cholesterol" is often a catch-all term for both the cholesterol you eat and the cholesterol in your blood.

■ *Your dietary cholesterol*—Cholesterol exists in your food as a dietary lipid. You'll find cholesterol only in animal products, such as meat and dairy foods.

■ *Your blood cholesterol*—Cholesterol also exists in a different way as a natural component of your blood lipids.

The cholesterol in your blood comes both from your liver and from the foods you eat. Your liver makes about 80 percent of your blood cholesterol. Only about 20 percent comes from your diet.

The amount of fat and cholesterol you eat may influence all levels of your blood lipids, including your blood cholesterol levels.

Blood cholesterol—the good, the bad and the ugly

To be carried in your blood, your body coats cholesterol with proteins called apoproteins (AP-oh-PRO-teens). Once coated, they form a package called lipoproteins (LIP-oh-PRO-teens).

Lipoproteins carry both cholesterol and triglycerides (another blood lipid) in your blood.

Some of your lipoproteins are called low-density lipoproteins (LDLs). They contain lots of cholesterol. Others are called high-density lipoproteins (HDLs). They contain mostly protein.

A third type of lipoprotein is called a very-low-density lipoprotein (VLDL). This type contains cholesterol, triglycerides and protein.

Some people call LDL "bad cholesterol" and HDL "good cholesterol." Here's why:

Cholesterol serves as a building material in cells throughout your body. LDL particles, which carry cholesterol, attach themselves to receptors on cell surfaces and are then received into your cells.

If there are too many LDL particles in your blood, if your liver cells (LDL receptors) do not receive LDL particles normally, or, if there are too few LDL receptors in your liver, your body's cells become saturated with cholesterol from the LDL particles. Cholesterol is then deposited in your artery walls.

At this point your high-density lipoproteins (HDLs) play their "good" role. They actually pick up cholesterol deposited in your artery walls and transport it to your liver for disposal.

The situation can turn ugly if too much cholesterol from LDL particles remains deposited in your artery walls. Your arteries will develop plaques and begin to narrow. This is atherosclerosis.

This is why a high HDL level relative to an LDL level is good. It can help protect you from developing atherosclerosis.

What's to blame?

Why do some people have high cholesterol? High levels result from genetic makeup or lifestyle choices, or both. Your genes can give you cells that don't remove LDL cholesterol from your blood efficiently, or a liver that produces too much cholesterol as VLDL particles, or too few HDL particles.

Lifestyle choices such as smoking, diet and inactivity can also cause or contribute to high cholesterol levels, leaving you at risk for atherosclerosis.

The cholesterol test

The only way to find out if your blood lipids are in a desirable range is to have them tested. The test is done by taking a blood sample after you have fasted overnight. You should have this test every three to five years—more often if

32. Cholesterol

you have a problem with your cholesterol level.

How much fat is that?

Limit fat to "30 percent of daily calories." Good advice. But what does it really mean?

This table converts this recommended guideline into the actual amount of fat you should limit yourself to daily.

If you eat . . .	Allow yourself this much fat daily . . .
1,400 calories	47 grams
1,600 calories	53 grams
1,800 calories	60 grams
2,000 calories	67 grams
2,200 calories	73 grams
2,400 calories	80 grams
2,600 calories	87 grams
2,800 calories	93 grams

Note: 1,400 calories is the minimum you should eat if you're trying to lose weight. 1,600 calories is about right for many inactive women and some older adults. 2,200 calories is about right for many sedentary men, most children, teenage girls and active women. 2,800 is about right for teenage boys, many active men and some very active women.

Calorie allowances are based on recommendations of the National Academy of Sciences and on calorie intakes reported by people in national food consumption surveys.

The test should measure your total cholesterol, HDL cholesterol and triglycerides. (Total cholesterol is made up of your LDL, HDL and other blood cholesterol particles.)

Some laboratories measure LDL directly, as part of the blood test. However, if your triglycerides are normal, your doctor can calculate your LDL level using the following formula:

$$\text{Total cholesterol} - \left(\text{HDL} + \frac{\text{triglycerides}}{5}\right) = \text{LDL}$$

In addition to your LDL level, your doctor might calculate the ratios between your LDL and HDL cholesterol, or between your total cholesterol and HDL.

Today, physicians pay more attention to your HDL number. Studies show that even with a desirable total cholesterol level, if you have a low HDL level, you may be at risk for cardiovascular disease.

It's critical to realize that numbers in the table on this page are only guidelines. If your numbers stray from the desirable ranges, your physician will counsel you.

Remember this too: Each number takes on greater meaning when you look at it in relation to the other numbers on your test and in relation to your other cardiovascular disease risk factors.

Other cardiovascular risk factors— the remaining puzzle pieces

To make the picture of your cardiovascular health more complete, you must consider your other risk factors for cardiovascular disease. (See illustration.) Each risk factor may influence your lipid levels.

The more risk factors you have, in combination with undesirable lipid levels, the greater your risk of developing cardiovascular disease. If you have several risk factors, their effects don't simply add up, they amplify each other.

For example, if you have high total cholesterol and you smoke, you're at much greater risk than a nonsmoker with the same cholesterol level.

However, you can make this amplifying effect work for you. Eating a diet low in fat, combined with exercise, can help you lose weight. At the same time, you can reduce your risk of high blood pressure, heart attack and stroke.

Risk factors for cardiovascular disease are divided into those you can change and those you can't. Consider

Your blood test: What do those numbers mean?

Your lipid levels can tell your doctor whether you're a candidate for cardiovascular disease. As you compare your numbers with these, remember: Numbers alone don't tell the whole story. Rely on your physician to interpret your test results.

Test	Your level (in mg/dl)*		
	Desirable	*Borderline*	*Undesirable*
Total cholesterol	Below 200	200-240	Above 240
HDL cholesterol	Above 45	35-45	Below 35
Triglycerides	Below 200	200-400	Above 400
LDL cholesterol	Below 130	130-160	Above 160
Cholesterol/HDL	Below 4.5	4.5-5.5	Above 5.5
LDL/HDL	Below 3	3-5	Above 5

* For people without known heart disease

Note: The numbers in this table represent a compilation of informed medical opinions from a variety of sources.

7. CURRENT KILLERS

how each risk factor affects your blood cholesterol and triglycerides.

Here are factors you can change:

■ *Smoking*—Smoking cigarettes damages the walls of your blood vessels, making them prone to accumulate fatty deposits. Smoking may also lower your HDL by as much as 15 percent. If you stop smoking, your HDL may return to its higher level.

■ *High blood pressure*—By damaging the walls of your arteries, high blood pressure can accelerate the development of atherosclerosis. Some medications for high blood pressure increase LDL and triglyceride levels and decrease HDL levels. Other medications don't.

■ *Inactivity*—Lack of physical exercise is associated with a decrease in HDL. Aerobic exercise is one way to increase your HDL. Aerobic activity is any exercise that requires continuous movement of your arms and legs and increases your breathing. Even 30 to 45 minutes of brisk walking every other day helps protect your cardiovascular system.

■ *Obesity*—Excess weight increases your triglycerides. It also lowers your HDL and increases your VLDL cholesterol. Losing just five or 10 pounds can improve your triglyceride and cholesterol levels.

■ *Diabetes*—Diabetes can increase triglycerides and decrease HDL in many people. Diabetes accelerates the development of atherosclerosis which, in turn, increases the risk for heart attack, stroke and reduced circulation to your feet.

If you have diabetes, have your total cholesterol, triglycerides and HDL tested at least annually. Keep your weight and blood sugar under control. Still, complications may develop. Diabetes is not a risk factor you can always change. (See *Mayo Clinic Health Letter* Medical Essay on diabetes, June 1992.)

These are risk factors you can't change:

■ *Age*—As you age, your level of LDL cholesterol usually increases. Researchers aren't sure why. The increase could be caused by aging or by an increase in your body fat.

■ *Gender*—Until age 45, men generally have higher total cholesterol levels than women. Also, up to about this age, women tend to have higher HDL levels. However, after menopause, women's total cholesterol rises and the protective HDL drops.

Caution: Don't think of cardiovascular disease as mainly a man's disease. Cardiovascular disease is also the No. 1 killer of women, claiming almost 500,000 women each year. Cancer kills fewer than 220,000 women. Women get cardiovascular disease as often as men; it just happens later in life.

■ *Family history*—If members of your family have undesirable lipid levels and cardiovascular problems, your risks for these problems are increased.

Your first lines of defense against high cholesterol

Diet and exercise are your first lines of defense against undesirable lipid levels. Changes in your diet, along with exercise, can reduce your blood cholesterol level by up to 15 percent. However, some people have genetically determined lipid problems (especially LDL) that don't respond to diet and require medication.

Making diet changes to improve your blood cholesterol levels involves three steps:

■ *Reduce your weight by reducing your total fat*—Limit all types of fat, saturated, polyunsaturated and monounsaturated, to no more than 30 percent of your total daily calories. Because all foods with fats contain a combination of these fats, it's important to reduce total fat.

Don't assume each food you eat must have less than 30 percent of its calories from fat. Use the guideline as a daily average. By balancing occasional high-fat foods with low-fat choices, your fat intake should average 30 percent of your daily calories.

■ *Reduce saturated fat*—No more than one-third of the fat you eat should be saturated. Major sources of saturated fat are butter, cheese, whole milk, cream, meat, poultry, chocolate, coconut, palm and palm kernel oil, lard and solid shortenings.

■ *Reduce dietary cholesterol*—Your daily limit for dietary cholesterol is 300 milligrams. A good way to accomplish this goal is to avoid dairy products made with whole milk and cream, and organ meats such as liver and tongue.

These limits on fat and cholesterol can also help you lose weight, which can improve your blood lipid levels. . . .

Exercise enhances the benefits of diet

A low-fat, low-cholesterol diet can improve your VLDL cholesterol level. If you also exercise and lose excess weight, you may see even greater improvements in your triglyceride and cholesterol levels.

Exercise helps you lose excess weight and reduces your chances of gaining weight as you get older.

For these benefits, set up your program using these guidelines and your doctor's advice:

■ *Choose aerobic activity*—Get involved in brisk walking, jogging, bicycling or cross-country skiing.

■ *Build up time and frequency*—Gradually work up to exercising for 30 to 45 minutes at least three times a week. If you're severely overweight or have been inactive for many years, take several months to gradually work up to this level. The higher the level of your activity, the greater your rate of weight loss.

■ *Keep it up*—Schedule a regular time for exercise. Make exercise fun. If it's not enjoyable you'll have difficulty exercising regularly, year in and year out.

Find a friend, or join an exercise group, to keep you motivated and committed to exercise. Or take up an activity that keeps you active.

Unless you stay with your program, you may not be able to keep off the pounds exercise helped you lose. Staying active also may prevent a gain in weight that often accompanies age. This, in turn, may help maintain lower levels of blood fats.

When are medications necessary?

Often changes in diet, exercise and smoking habits will improve your VLDL cholesterol and triglyceride levels. But if you've carried out these important lifestyle changes and your total cholesterol, especially your LDL level, remains high, your doctor may recommend a medication.

Before recommending a medication, your doctor will use careful judgment and weigh many variables—your changeable risk factors, your age, your current health, and the drug's side effects. If you need a medication to lower your cholesterol, chances are you will need it for many years.

Your LDL cholesterol level is usually the deciding factor. If you have no risk factors for cardiovascular disease, an LDL level over 190 generally requires medication. With two or more risk factors, an LDL level over 160 may require medication.

And remember . . .

The issue of cholesterol and cardiovascular health is important, but by no means simple. Just knowing your total cholesterol level is not enough. Understanding how your other blood fat levels and your cardiovascular disease risk factors influence this number is essential.

Only with this knowledge can cholesterol assume its proper place in the cardiovascular disease puzzle.

Rating your risks for heart disease

Since 1960, the mortality rate from heart attack in the U.S. has dropped by half, according to the National Center for Health Statistics—and since 1980 alone, by one-third. This success has been due not only to improved medical treatment of coronary artery disease (CAD), but also to preventive steps people have taken. Heart attack is still the leading killer of American men and women, however, accounting for about 500,000 deaths every year—about 20% in people under age 65. Most of these deaths, too, could be avoided or at least postponed if everyone paid attention to the risk factors for CAD and took preventive measures to counter them.

Just how far we have to go in preventing this disease can be seen in a recent report from the CDC that showed that only 18% of adults are free of the six major coronary risk factors. And among those over 50, only about 10% report that they are free of the major risk factors. Many people don't even know what these factors are, except perhaps high blood cholesterol. The other five proven risks—smoking, obesity, high blood pressure, diabetes, and being sedentary—are as bad, or even worse, for the heart.

The pillars of prevention

Scientists now know far more about the major controllable risk factors for CAD than for most other diseases. A risk factor merely increases the probability that you will develop CAD; it doesn't guarantee that you will develop it, nor does its absence (or even the absence of all risk factors) guarantee that you won't have a heart attack. If you have more than one CAD risk factor, the combined impact is greater than it would be if you added the individual risks together.

Most of the risk factors can be countered by relatively simple preventive measures. In 1992 Dr. JoAnn Manson and her colleagues from Harvard reviewed nearly 200 studies on CAD to evaluate the role of the known preventive measures; the results were published in the *New England Journal of Medicine (NEJM)*. Some of the details are as follows:

1. Quit smoking. This is perhaps the single most effective step you can take. Anywhere from 20 to 40% (100,000 to 200,000 every year) of all CAD deaths are still directly attributable to smoking. It more than doubles your chance of eventually having a heart attack and increases the chance of dying from it by 70%; it is also the leading cause of sudden cardiac death. Low-tar, low-nicotine cigarettes are not significantly safer for your heart than regular brands. Smoking even a few cigarettes a day can endanger your heart. In addition, it's estimated that more than 35,000 nonsmoking Americans die each year from heart disease because of long-term exposure to other people's smoke. The good news is that quitting smoking quickly reduces your CAD risk: within five to ten years, your risk of heart attack declines to a level similar to that of people who never smoked.

2. Reduce cholesterol. For every 1% reduction in blood cholesterol, there's a 2 to 3% decline in the risk of heart attack. Since 1960, the average blood cholesterol level in the U.S. has declined from 220 to 205 mg/dl (a "desirable" level is below 200), a 7% decline. That's a significant decline, but still leaves 20% of American adults with high cholesterol levels (above 240) and another 30% with borderline-high levels (200 to 239). For information on the government's new guidelines on cholesterol and for advice on how to lower total cholesterol and raise protective HDL cholesterol, see *Wellness Letter*, December 1993.

3. Avoid or control hypertension. About 50 million Americans have high blood pressure, which is a risk factor for stroke and heart attack. For every 1 point drop in diastolic blood pressure, there's a 2 to 3% drop in the risk of heart attack. If you can reduce your blood pressure by making the life-style changes—including limiting intake of sodium, calories, and alcohol—the coronary benefits are likely to be particularly great.

4. Stay active. Dozens of studies have shown that exercise protects against CAD. The *NEJM* report estimated that sedentary people who begin a regular program of exercise reduce their risk of a heart attack by 35 to 55%. And yet it is estimated that more than 60% of Americans are sedentary, and there has been little improvement in decades. Even low-intensity activities, such as

---

Risk factors you can't change

These should serve as an incentive to address the factors that *can* be changed.

Heredity. People with a parent or sibling who had a premature heart attack (before age 55 in a man or 65 in a woman) are at increased risk of CAD.

Race. African-Americans, for example, have an elevated risk of CAD, primarily because they have a higher risk of hypertension and diabetes than whites.

Increasing age. About 55% of all heart attacks, and more than 80% of fatal ones, occur after age 65.

Sex. Before age 55, men have a much higher rate of CAD than women. By the time they reach 60, women develop CAD at the same rate as men at 50—and this 10-year gap prevails until about the age of 75 or 80, when the differences disappear and the rates become similar. Women who have a heart attack, especially at older ages, are more likely to die from it than are men.

7. CURRENT KILLERS

gardening or walking, if done regularly and over the long term, can decrease the risk of heart attack. Exercise helps the heart work more efficiently, reduces blood pressure, decreases the tendency of blood to form clots, moderates stress, helps the body use insulin, helps people maintain a healthy weight, and may boost HDL ("good") cholesterol.

5. Maintain a healthy weight. About one in three American adults is seriously overweight or obese, which doubles the risk for CAD at a given age. And the more overweight you are, the greater the effect on CAD risk. Obesity also increases the risk for diabetes, hypertension, and high blood cholesterol, which further worsen CAD risk. How fat is distributed on the body also affects the risk. People who put weight on around the waist (apple-shaped or pot-bellied body) have a greater chance of CAD than those who accumulate weight on the hips (pear-shaped).

6. Avoid or control diabetes. Non-insulin-dependent diabetes (also called adult-onset diabetes), which afflicts about 12 million Americans, is an important risk factor for both CAD and hypertension. Diabetes increases the risk of CAD in men two- to three-fold, but in women three- to seven-fold. Even people who merely have slightly elevated blood sugar levels but no detectable diabetes are at increased risk. Weight control and exercise can improve the utilization of blood sugar and prevent or slow the onset of diabetes.

Additional steps

7. Consider hormone therapy after menopause. Estrogen therapy raises HDL cholesterol and also lowers the risk of heart attack in other ways. It also decreases the risk of osteoporosis and perhaps stroke. Today hormone replacement therapy, or HRT, usually includes progestin (a synthetic form of the hormone progesterone) along with estrogen. Recent studies suggest that the combined estrogen-progestin therapy also protects against heart disease. HRT is not appropriate for all women, so talk to your doctor about it.

8. Consider a drink a day. There's a growing consensus that light to moderate alcohol consumption—that is, two drinks or less a day for a man, one drink for a woman (a drink is defined as 12

Mind/body: stress and anger

Until recently, people with so-called Type A personality (aggressive, competitive, tense) were considered coronary-prone. But studies largely failed to confirm this notion. Some researchers therefore shifted their focus to various components of Type A—notably anger or hostility. Most studies have indeed found a link between anger or hostility and CAD risk. People who suppress their anger appear to be at greatest risk for CAD and other illness, though some studies have found that venting anger isn't necessarily better.

Some of the best research on stress has involved the workplace. A worker's sense of control, or lack thereof, is perhaps the major determinant of how he reacts to stress and of the effect stress has on health. Studies have consistently shown that people in high-strain jobs (heavy pressure to perform but little sense of control), such as bus drivers, have the highest rates of hypertension and heart attacks. Stereotypical "high-stress" jobs such as manager, engineer, and doctor tend to have the lowest rates, because these professionals have a greater sense of control. Even when such risk factors as age, race, education, and smoking are statistically eliminated from the equation, people in the bottom 10% of the job echelon have four to five times the risk of heart attack as those at the top 10% of the ladder.

Separating the wheat from the chaff

Frequent media reports of new risk factors for CAD and new potential protectors—often trivial and sometimes contradictory—may distract people from the truly significant risk factors. These scientific tidbits usually come from single studies or preliminary research and were never intended to guide personal behavior. Some are based on tenuous statistical associations; many will inevitably turn out to be false leads. Here are just four factors that have received much attention recently:

Baldness. Last February a study in the *Journal of the American Medical Association* claimed that white men under age 55 with a bald spot on top of the head are substantially more likely to suffer a heart attack than those with a full head of hair or a receding hairline. One theory: the male sex hormones that cause this type of baldness may also endanger the heart. But most researchers believe that if this type of baldness does pose a risk, it is minor when compared to, say, smoking or hypertension. In any case, if you're bald you can't do anything about the slightly increased risk, except to be diligent about controlling the known, modifiable risk factors.

Shortness. Several studies have found that women less than 5 feet tall and men less than 5 feet 6 inches have an elevated risk of heart attacks. But researchers have pointed out that the increased risk is comparatively minor. In addition, other researchers have suggested the shorter people in the studies may have been more likely to come from disadvantaged backgrounds (with poor childhood diets and health habits), which might account in part for their increased health risks.

Earlobe crease. As strange as it seems, most studies on the subject have found that men (and sometimes women) who have a crease across the earlobes are at increased risk for CAD.

Iron level in the body. In 1992 a Finnish study made headlines when it suggested that a high level of iron in the body dramatically increases the risk of a heart attack. At the time, we concluded that the study raised more questions than it answered (*Wellness Letter*, December 1992). Recently, three newer studies, which received far less media attention, disputed the results of the Finnish study. More research will need to be done. Meanwhile, continue to eat foods that supply your daily requirement of iron.

33. Rating Your Risks for Heart Disease

ounces of beer, four ounces of wine, or 1.5 ounces of 80-proof spirits) has a minor beneficial effect for the heart. However, drinking more than that is a good way to *increase* the risk of heart attack and stroke, as well as cirrhosis, cancer, and car crashes. As the *NEJM* report put it, "the difference between drinking small-to-moderate quantities of alcohol and drinking large amounts may mean the difference between preventing and causing disease."

9. Consider aspirin. Low-dose aspirin—usually half an aspirin (160 milligrams) a day—can lower the risk of heart attack by about one-third by reducing the ability of platelets in the blood to stick together and thus form a clot. Aspirin therapy is particularly advisable if you have an elevated risk of CAD. The research has focused mostly on men so far, but at least two encouraging studies have suggested that women benefit, too. Aspirin can have side effects and isn't right for everyone, so don't start aspirin therapy on your own—ask your doctor about it.

What about diet?

Although a healthful, low-fat diet is not generally considered a separate preventive measure against CAD, it clearly plays a role in many of the steps listed above, such as controlling cholesterol and body weight. In addition, there has been accumulating evidence that a high intake of antioxidant vitamins (usually supplements of C, E, and beta carotene) helps reduce the risk of CAD—see our January 1994 issue.

The Heart of the Matter

Aerobic exercise not only makes you look and feel better—it also cuts your risk of cancer and heart disease

Julia Califano

Julia Califano is a health and lifestyle writer in Hoboken, N.J.

Aerobic exercise has evolved since the days of high-impact classes and Jane Fonda videos. Today the term *aerobic* is likely to refer to almost any physical activity that gets your body moving and raises your heart rate for an extended period of time, from brisk walking to competing in a triathlon. (In contrast, activities that require sudden bursts of energy, such as sprinting or power lifting, are considered *anaerobic*.)

Lycra-clad fitness buffs may not care, but experts now know that the effects of aerobic exercise go far beyond what you see in the mirror: Working up a sweat on a regular basis is nearly as important to your health as kicking a longtime cigarette habit. You don't have to be an elite athlete to reap the benefits, either. Even moderate cardiovascular activities such as brisk walking can help ward off heart disease, diabetes and some types of cancer. Take up a more rigorous fitness regimen and you may add several years to your life.

What makes aerobic exercise so beneficial? Unlike strength training (which shores up skeletal muscles and bone), aerobic exercise has a significant impact on the heart. "People forget that the heart is a muscle," says Harvard University cardiologist Harvey Simon, author of *Conquering Heart Disease* (Little, Brown, 1994). "Like any other muscle, it gets bigger, stronger and more efficient with exercise."

After six to 10 weeks of thrice-weekly aerobic workouts, the heart muscle thickens, pumping more oxygenated blood with every beat. At the same time, the working muscles in the torso, arms and legs become more efficient at extracting oxygen from the bloodstream. Together, these changes increase exercise capacity tremendously. Circulation improves too, partly because exercise boosts the number of small blood vessels (capillaries) that deliver oxygen to tissues and carry waste away. (For more benefits, see "Athlete's Heart vs. Sloth's Heart.")

Aerobic exercise also reduces the major risk factors for heart disease. Besides lowering blood pressure, exercise also raises healthy HDL cholesterol levels, keeping blood vessels clear of plaque and reducing the risk of dangerous blood clots, a major cause of heart attacks. Finally, because aerobic exercise burns body fat, and raises metabolism to boot, it's one of the best weapons we have against obesity.

Physical activity benefits the rest of the body too. Any weight-bearing aerobic exercise, such as walking a mile or two a day, increases bone density and decreases the risk of bone-thinning osteoporosis. And because exercise helps regulate blood-sugar metabolism, it may ward off type II diabetes, the most common form of the disease.

Regular activity also revs up the immune system. "It improves the circulation of immune cells, which makes the body better able to fight off bacteria and viruses," says exercise physiologist David Nieman of Appalachian State University in Boone, N.C. In two studies of 66 women, Dr. Nieman found that those who walked 40 to 45 minutes five days a week for 15 weeks reported half as many cold and flu symptoms as a sedentary group.

Aerobic exercise also reduces the risk of colon and breast cancer. "Physical activity speeds the transport of waste through the intestinal tract, so it doesn't irritate the colon," explains Dr. Simon. A six-year Harvard study of 47,000 men found that the most active, who ran for at least four hours a week or played tennis for eight hours a week, had half the risk of colon cancer as sedentary men. Even less avid exercisers—those who ran for just two hours or walked for six hours a week—had two-thirds the risk of inactive men.

"Regular exercise also seems to put a

lid on estrogen production in women, which means it may protect against breast and other estrogen-sensitive cancers, including ovarian and endometrial cancer," says epidemiologist Leslie Bernstein of the University of Southern California School of Medicine in Los Angeles. In a USC study, Dr. Bernstein found that young women who regularly jogged, swam or played racket sports for at least three hours a week beginning in adolescence reduced their breast cancer risk 20% to 30%; those who worked out four or more hours a week cut their risk 60%.

Less quantifiable but perhaps even more important is the impact of aerobic activity on quality of life. Simply put, fit people tend to look and feel far younger than their age. Part of the reason is that sedentary people lose 9% of their cardiovascular fitness each decade after age 25; for active adults, the decline may be less than 5% a decade. And numerous studies suggest aerobic exercise reduces depression, eases anxiety and calms the mind. "We typically think of rest and relaxation as the best way to get energy, but exercise combats mental stress even more effectively," says Simon. "You may feel tired after working out, but if you do it regularly, you'll have more energy and sleep better in the long run."

What's less certain is exactly how much and what kind of aerobic exercise produces all these life-enhancing effects. For decades fitness experts thought only strenuous workouts did the trick. But recent long-term studies suggest that when done consistently, any kind of moderate physical activity can strengthen the heart, lower blood pressure and protect against a host of diseases. In fact, switching from a sedentary lifestyle to a slightly more active one provides the biggest health bang for your buck. Researchers at the Cooper Institute for Aerobics Research in Dallas ranked the fitness levels of 13,344 men and women according to how they did on a treadmill test, then followed them for more than eight years. Those in the fittest group had the lowest death rate, but the biggest drop in mortality (60% for men and nearly 50% for women) was found between the least fit volunteers and those who were just slightly more fit.

To get the health benefits of exercise, the American College of Sports Medicine, along with the Centers for Disease Control and Prevention, recommends that sedentary people put in at least 30 minutes of moderate physical activity (for example, a brisk walk) three to five days a week. (For specific exercises, see "A Workout for Life," below.) If you're strapped for time, the 30 minutes don't have to be consecutive, though it's unclear whether several short stints of activity are as protective as a single prolonged session.

What is clear is that you'll have to push yourself if you want to see a measurable gain in stamina—say, climbing stairs without panting. That means getting your heart rate into the training zone—specifically, 65% to 85% of your maximum heart rate—for 20 minutes to an hour three to five times a week. To find your target heart rate, first calculate your maximum heart rate by subtracting your age from 220. Multiply this number by .65 and .85 and keep your pulse in this range (117 to 153 beats per minute for a 40-year-old). An easier method: If you're huffing and puffing so hard you can't speak comfortably, you're beyond your training range; if

A Workout for Life

Beginners should start with 10 minutes of light to moderately strenuous exercise (pick something from the Moderate Activities list), three times a week. Warm up by walking or doing calisthenics for five minutes, then work in your target heart range for 10 minutes and finish with five minutes of stretching. Add about a minute of exercise—a 10% increase—a week.

To become more fit (as opposed to simply reducing your risk of disease), you'll need to work up to at least 20 minutes of moderate activity three times a week. For even greater benefits, and perhaps to prolong your life, build up to a regimen of more vigorous exercise (pick something from the Vigorous Activities list) and aim to do it for 45 minutes a day four to five times a week. (Note: Consult your doctor before starting any exercise program.)

Moderate Activities (raise oxygen consumption to three to six times the level burned by the body at rest):
- Walking briskly (three to four miles per hour)
- Cycling for pleasure or transportation (eight to 10 miles per hour)
- Swimming (moderate effort)
- Vigorous calisthenics
- Table tennis
- Golf (carrying clubs)
- Fishing (standing and casting)
- Canoeing leisurely (two to four miles per hour)
- Home care (such as general cleaning)
- Mowing the lawn (with a power mower)

Vigorous Activities (raise oxygen consumption to more than six times the level burned by the body at rest):
- Walking fast (four to five miles per hour)
- Cycling fast (11 to 12 miles per hour)
- Swimming (fast treading or crawl)
- Cardiovascular conditioning exercises (such as using a stair climber or cross-country ski machine)
- Singles tennis or racquetball
- Fishing (wading in a rushing stream)
- Canoeing fast (more than four miles per hour)
- Moving heavy furniture
- Mowing the lawn (with a manual mower)

Adapted from *The Journal of the American Medical Association*.

7. CURRENT KILLERS

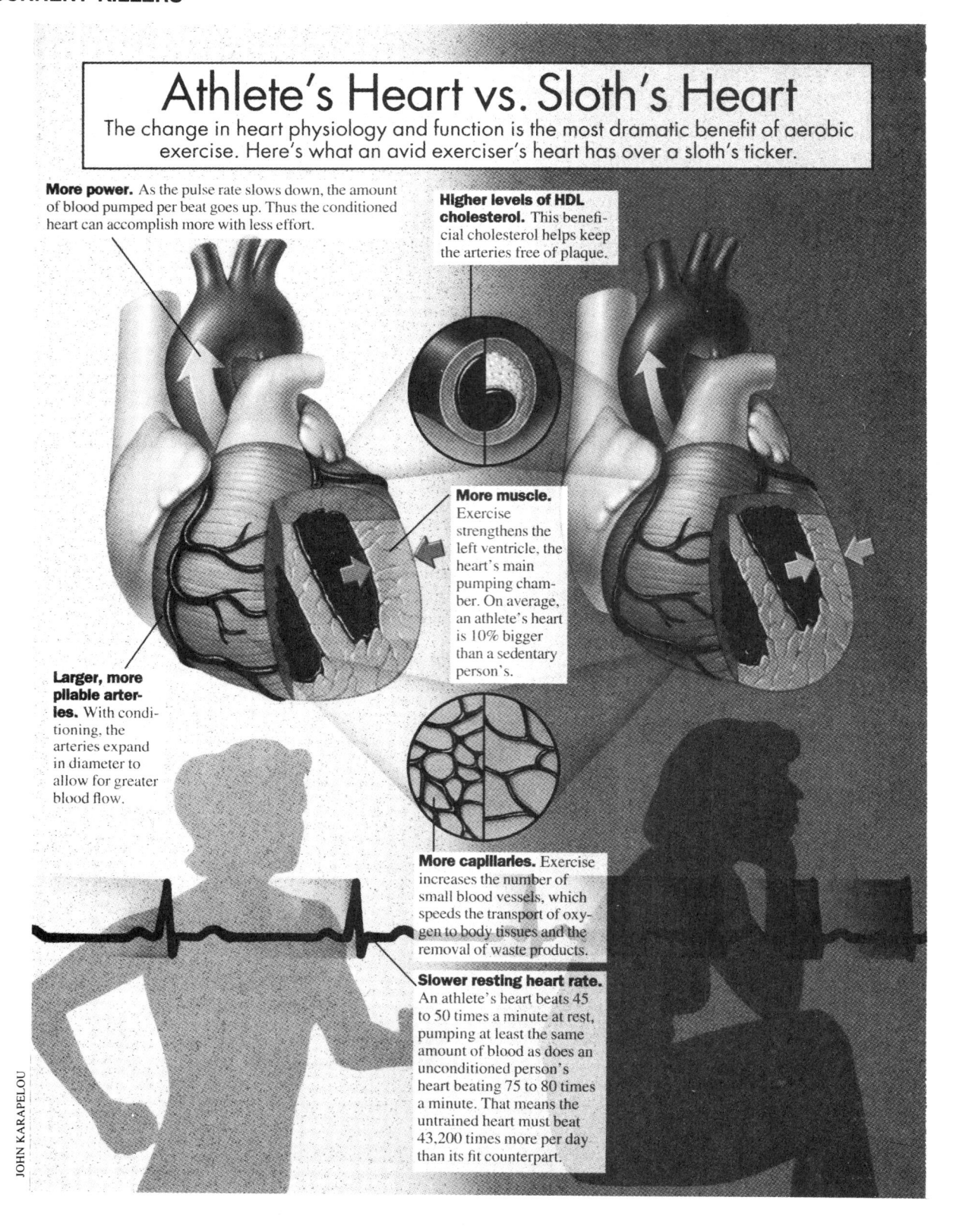

Athlete's Heart vs. Sloth's Heart
The change in heart physiology and function is the most dramatic benefit of aerobic exercise. Here's what an avid exerciser's heart has over a sloth's ticker.

More power. As the pulse rate slows down, the amount of blood pumped per beat goes up. Thus the conditioned heart can accomplish more with less effort.

Higher levels of HDL cholesterol. This beneficial cholesterol helps keep the arteries free of plaque.

More muscle. Exercise strengthens the left ventricle, the heart's main pumping chamber. On average, an athlete's heart is 10% bigger than a sedentary person's.

Larger, more pliable arteries. With conditioning, the arteries expand in diameter to allow for greater blood flow.

More capillaries. Exercise increases the number of small blood vessels, which speeds the transport of oxygen to body tissues and the removal of waste products.

Slower resting heart rate. An athlete's heart beats 45 to 50 times a minute at rest, pumping at least the same amount of blood as does an unconditioned person's heart beating 75 to 80 times a minute. That means the untrained heart must beat 43,200 times more per day than its fit counterpart.

JOHN KARAPELOU

you're able to sing, pick up the pace. Or follow Stanford epidemiologist Ralph Paffenbarger's fitness prescription: "Ideally," he says, "you should stay on your feet for at least an hour a day— chasing the kids, vacuuming or climbing stairs. On top of that, exercise hard enough so that you breathe deeply and break a light sweat for at least half an hour three or more times a week."

Is all that effort worth it? There's evidence that as you challenge yourself physically, the health benefits keep on accruing. A recent study of 7,000 male runners at the Lawrence Berkeley Laboratory in Berkeley, Calif., found that the more miles they logged a week, the higher their blood levels of beneficial HDL cholesterol.

Even more promising: The latest results from a study of 17,321 male Harvard alumni suggest that the more active you are, the longer you'll live. Men who expended 1,500 calories a week though vigorous exercise (the equivalent of five 45-minute sessions of brisk walking) had a 25% lower mortality rate during the 20-year study, compared with the least active men, who burned just 150 calories a week through exercise.

Unlike several other large-scale studies, however, the Harvard researchers found that men who did less vigorous activities (such as gardening or playing golf) did not live longer. "It may be that you need to improve your physical fitness in order to prolong your life, and vigorous activity is the most efficient way to do that," speculates study author Dr. I-Min Lee, a Harvard epidemiologist. But that doesn't mean light to moderate exercise is worthless. "Even mild workouts improve people's psychological well-being and functional capacity," says Lee. "Though they may not help you live longer, they certainly can help you live *better*."

Of course, too much exercise can be as harmful as too little. "As people approach two hours of vigorous activity a day, there's a huge increase in the output of so-called stress hormones—cortisol and epinephrine," says Appalachian State's Nieman. "This has a negative impact on the immune system, which can lead to getting sick more often." Studies have also shown that women who overdo exercise may stop menstruating, making them more vulnerable to osteoporosis. "And if you don't give your body time to recover after exercise, you risk a host of musculoskeletal injuries, including stress fractures and knee pain," Nieman adds.

For most of us, though, hitting that point of diminishing returns isn't a major concern. "The overwhelming majority of us simply haven't gotten the message," says Dr. Paffenbarger. "Everyone is looking for a magic pill to prevent disease. But you can't become aerobically fit with vitamins or by eating less. You need to go out there, rev up your heart and start sweating."

Strategies for Minimizing Cancer Risk

Simple, realistic preventive measures could save hundreds of thousands of lives every year in developed countries alone

Walter C. Willett, Graham A. Colditz and Nancy E. Mueller

During 1996, more than 550,000 people will die of cancer in the U.S. In Europe, there will be at least 840,000 cancer fatalities. Yet accumulating evidence indicates that in these two parts of the world, which have relatively high and closely tracked cancer mortality rates, more than half these deaths could theoretically have been prevented.

The notion that we can modify cancer risk emerges from decades of investigation. One laboratory experiment after another has demonstrated that a variety of chemicals and other environmental agents can cause cancer in animals, and studies of people have linked heavy exposure to certain substances in the workplace with high risks of specific types of cancer. Also, international studies of migrants repeatedly confirm that they tend to adopt the cancer pattern of their new country within a period that varies from about a decade (for cancer of the colon and rectum) to a few generations (for breast cancer)—a sign that something in the environment, such as changes in diet or exercise patterns, is implicated. If outside factors can increase cancer risk, avoiding those factors should decrease it.

How did we determine the extent to which mortality can be reduced? We began by identifying the lowest rates for various types of cancer among large international populations that keep reliable figures on death from cancer. The incidence of many of the most common cancers in the U.S. and Europe is much lower in Japan and China. To compile a list of estimated "baseline" cancer incidences, then, we chose the lowest rate for each type of cancer from among the data for the U.S., Japan and China. Then we calculated the difference between the highest rate and the baseline. From these comparisons, we conclude that it should be possible to reduce cancer mortality by approximately 60 percent in the U.S.—perhaps slightly less for black American women, because their incidence rate is already a bit lower. The figures for most Europeans would be similar.

Although we are confident that the death rates of most types of cancer could be substantially cut, there are two notable exceptions. For breast cancer in women and prostate cancer in men, there are no established preventive measures that are likely to have a major impact.

These figures are of interest to more than policy experts and actuaries. For millions of individuals, the results mean that changes in lifestyle can lengthen life—for several years, on average, but several decades for those who would have been stricken in midlife. For most of these people, minimizing the risk of cancer would require a good many changes to address a broad spectrum of causes. For the few people who have inherited mutant genes that dramatically increase the risk of particular types of cancer or for those who have been exposed to unusual occupational hazards, the strategies would be focused mainly on avoiding that specific cancer.

An Ounce of Prevention

A cancer death can be avoided through prevention of cancer, through detection of the disease early enough to treat it successfully, or through a combination of the two (trying to prevent the disease but being vigilant enough to catch it and treat it early if it develops). Examples of prevention strategies include never smoking and, if it is too late for that, giving up the practice. Kicking the habit enables a former smoker to enjoy a nonsmoker's lower risk for lung cancer after about a decade. Another prevention tactic is eating certain vegetables and other foods that counteract the activity of cancer-causing agents (carcinogens) in the body. In theory, vaccination against the various infectious agents that are known to cause cancer could help as well, although at the moment the only vaccine that can serve this purpose prevents hepatitis B infections.

Early detection relies on the diagnosis of disease at a more treatable stage, before the onset of symptoms that would bring the patient to medical attention. This approach has been applied to some cancers, such as cervical and colorectal cancer. Epidemiologic studies indicate that death rates from these

35. Minimizing Cancer Risk

two diseases could be reduced by at least 50 percent if screening were widely applied, making it possible to remove precancerous growth and to detect malignancies earlier. The test for cervical cancer is the well-known Pap smear; the most effective procedures for detecting cancer of the colon and rectum are sigmoidosocopy and colonoscopy.

No matter how effective they may be, early detection and treatment are less desirable than primary prevention, for many reasons. Most obviously, prevention avoids the shock and pain of being diagnosed and treated for cancer. In addition, many methods for cancer prevention, such as regular exercise and a sensible diet, have side benefits, such as reducing the risk of cardiovascular and other diseases—which makes them even more cost-effective in comparison with treatment. Moreover, the ability of medical science to treat many forms of cancer is limited by the disease's tendency to spread to other parts of the body, the phenomenon of metastasis. And of course, the failure of prevention still leaves treatment as a last resort.

These advantages notwithstanding, the power of prevention as a defense against cancer has never been fully appreciated by the public at large, if the widespread persistence of unhealthy habits is any indication. This disappointing observation is perhaps understandable. It is, after all, impossible to tell whether a healthy lifestyle warded off cancer in an individual. Conversely, successful treatment invariably becomes a landmark event. Moreover, the results of effective treatment become apparent quickly, whereas the impact of a prevention regime—quitting smoking, say—may take years to emerge.

As in our colleagues' article on causes of cancer, we focus here on fatal kinds of cancer rather than all cases to avoid distortions introduced by the large number of highly localized cancers and those forms of skin cancer that are seldom fatal. For each major cause, we estimate how much mortality could be reduced for people living in the U.S. or a similar developed country.

Potent Mix: Tobacco and Alcohol

Most cancer prevention campaigns rightly focus on controlling the tobacco smoking epidemic. But the goal has proved to be an elusive one. The decline of smoking in most developed countries has been more than offset in recent years by a rapid increase elsewhere in the world. Small-scale programs and traditional health education efforts are no match for the addictive power of nicotine and the marketing clout of the tobacco industry.

In democratic societies, three complementary approaches appear most promising: improved general education, taxation, and cultivation of an antismoking social ethos. The strong inverse association between educational achievement and smoking reinforces the importance of health education for all segments of society. High taxes on tobacco products, as well as social disapproval or regulation of smoking in office buildings, airplanes and public places, have been shown to reduce smoking rates.

Perhaps, too, we could do more to bring people's perceptions of risk in line with reality. It is not uncommon to meet heavy smokers who are genuinely concerned about the health effects of unproved or possibly trivial environmental agents, such as magnetic fields or chlorinated water.

Tobacco smoking cannot be completely eradicated; hardly any vices ever have been. But on the basis of the dramatic decline in smoking among the more educated adults in the U.S. over the past few decades and the increasingly pervasive sentiments against smoking, it would not be unrealistic to hope that tobacco smoking—and, eventually, deaths related to tobacco—can be reduced by about two thirds within a few

REALISTIC GOAL for reducing the chances of being stricken with any kind of cancer during a normal life span is, for white women, about one third (*right*). The corresponding goal for black women is less because their rates are already lower than those of white women. Men should be able to cut their risk at least in half (*next page*). Almost anyone can achieve such a reduction in cancer risk by adopting prudent habits, such as not smoking, exercising regularly, eating plenty of fruits, vegetables and whole grains and by avoiding animal fats, red meat, refined starches and alcohol. That such reductions in risk are realistic is supported by the fact that they have already been largely achieved by Seventh-Day Adventists, many of whom follow these practices. As the incidence of many cancers declines, the proportion of breast and prostate cancer cases will increase, because no established preventive measures are likely to have a major impact in the near future.

Women's Probability of Acquiring Cancer by Age 75

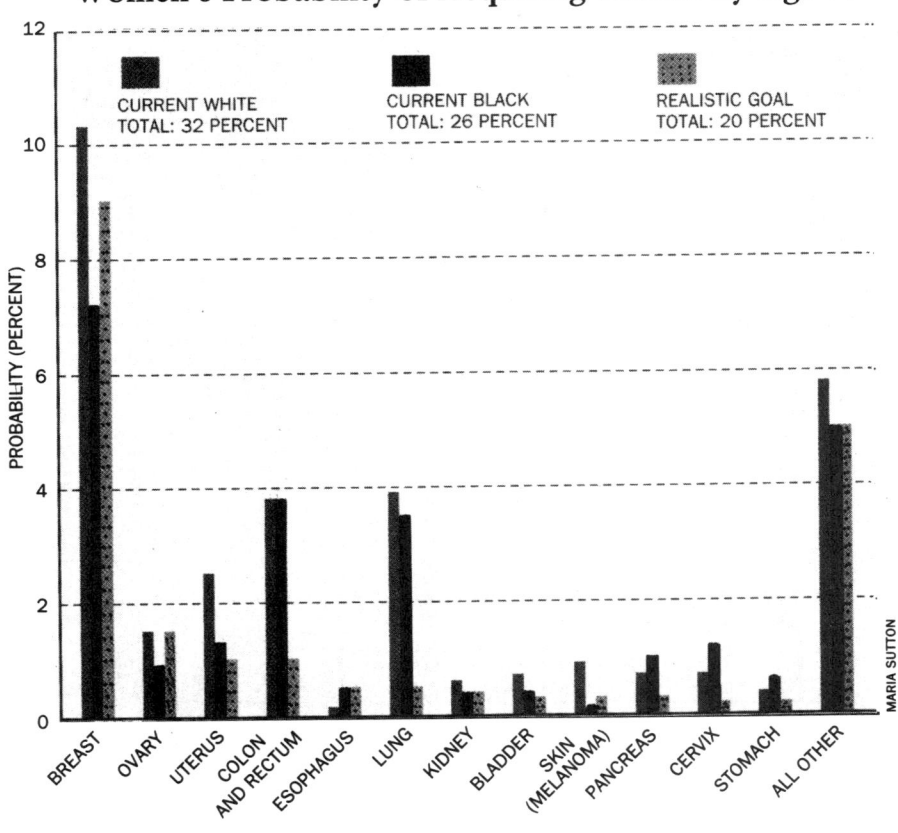

CURRENT WHITE TOTAL: 32 PERCENT
CURRENT BLACK TOTAL: 26 PERCENT
REALISTIC GOAL TOTAL: 20 PERCENT

(Bar chart showing probability percentages across: Breast, Ovary, Uterus, Colon and Rectum, Esophagus, Lung, Kidney, Bladder, Skin (Melanoma), Pancreas, Cervix, Stomach, All Other)

MARIA SUTTON

7. CURRENT KILLERS

decades. Such a reduction would of course require that the trend not only continue but also spread to less educated groups.

The moderate intake of alcoholic beverages, at about one or two a day, reduces mortality from cardiovascular causes. At the same time, alcohol has been linked with several forms of cancer. Effects of alcohol consumption and tobacco smoking are also believed to interact to cause cancer in the upper respiratory and gastrointestinal tracts.

Clearly, on many grounds, heavy alcohol consumption should be avoided. Anyone considering drinking moderately for the good of the heart should consult a physician and take into account any family history of alcoholism while weighing the risk of cancer against that of cardiovascular disease. Also, for women younger than 50 years, who are at relatively low risk of cardiovascular disease, there does not appear to be any reduction in mortality from moderate alcohol use. Overall, alcohol-related cancer mortality could probably be decreased by about one third if a realistically smaller number of people had more than two drinks a day.

Preventing Diet-Related Cancer

Although we know little about the specific beneficial or harmful constituents of food, we have a good idea of what people should eat if they want to improve their odds of avoiding cancer. Their diet should be high in vegetables, fruits and legumes (such as peas and beans) and low in red meat, saturated fat, salt and sugar. Carbohydrates should be consumed as whole grains—whole-wheat bread and brown rice as opposed to white bread and rice, for example. Added fats should come mainly from plants and should be unhydrogenated; olive oil, especially, appears potentially beneficial.

Everyone should work assiduously to avoid being overweight, ideally in part through physical activity. In addition to helping to control weight, exercise reduces the incidence of colon cancer and, perhaps, of other types as well. Regular physical activity during childhood and adolescence may also slow down excessive growth and avoid an early onset of menstrual cycles, both of which have been implicated in malignancy.

Some evidence links increased risk of breast and prostate cancer with high birth weight and other factors dating to around the time of birth. Although this information is of interest to scientists, it does not readily translate into practical means of prevention. This situation contrasts with that in most other forms of cancer, for which prevention strategies became apparent when causes were established. The implication is that in the near future, in developed countries, the incidence of cancers of the breast and prostate will prove more difficult to reduce—and that, therefore, these cancers could be responsible for an increasing percentage of all cancer mortality as deaths from many other kinds of cancer decline [see illustrations on this and previous pages].

Although the benefits of exercise and dietary moderation have been known for decades, the proportion of overweight Americans has been increasing. Between 1980 and 1991 the prevalence of obesity rose by 33 percent in the U.S. Nevertheless, many people, particularly those with higher education and income, have learned how to avoid age-related weight gain, so it is not unrealistic to hope for some improvement among other groups in the foreseeable future.

Similarly, modest shifts toward more healthy habits by the population as a whole should be possible. If a majority of people were to make two or more wise changes—exercising vigorously for 20 minutes a day, eating one more serving of leafy vegetables each day or consuming no more than one serving of red meat a week, for example—both diet-related and sedentary-life-related cancer mortality might be reduced by about one quarter. Taken together, such changes could prevent an estimated 40,000 premature cancer deaths annually in the U.S. The same measures would also lessen the incidence of cardiovascular disease, saving additional lives. Further knowledge of the specific cancer-fighting components of vegetables and fruits, which scientists are now striving to uncover, could allow more focused and effective dietary strategies

A great deal of evidence already suggests that most Americans do not get enough folic acid in their diets. Lack of this nutrient may contribute to colon cancer and heart disease, so multivitamins that include folic acid, also called folate, might prove beneficial. Regard-

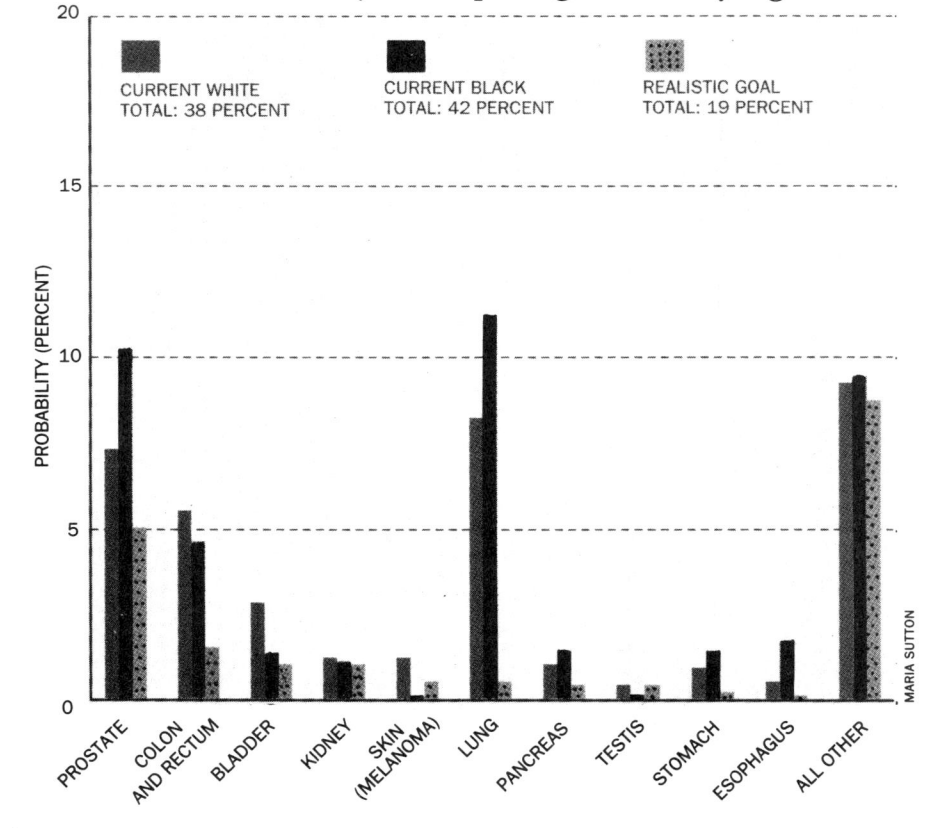

Men's Probability of Acquiring Cancer by Age 75

CURRENT WHITE TOTAL: 38 PERCENT
CURRENT BLACK TOTAL: 42 PERCENT
REALISTIC GOAL TOTAL: 19 PERCENT

(bar chart showing probability percent by cancer type: Prostate, Colon and Rectum, Bladder, Kidney, Skin (Melanoma), Lung, Pancreas, Testis, Stomach, Esophagus, All Other)

MARIA SUTTON

ing so-called megavitamins, little reliable research indicates that these highly concentrated supplements are any more protective against cancer than plain old multivitamins (and even for these, a benefit has not been established).

Avoiding Viruses

The human papillomavirus is the most common cancer-causing infection in the U.S. The sexually transmitted strains, which can lead to cervical cancer, are the most lethal. They can be combated, however, by the same measures directed against transmission of the AIDS-causing human immunodeficiency virus (HIV)—such as delaying initial sexual activity, reducing casual sexual contact and using latex condoms. More widespread application of these precautions could lead to a further modest decline in deaths from cervical cancer and from other genital tumors traceable to papillomavirus. Pap screening, which enables doctors to detect incipient tumors early enough to cure them, has contributed over the past few decades to the dramatic decline in deaths from cervical cancer. Greater use of this technique could enhance this decrease.

In the U.S., the hepatitis B and C viruses cause a minority of the cases of hepatocellular carcinoma, a form of liver cancer. The recently introduced vaccines against the hepatitis B virus, improved screening of blood and blood products and more pervasive use of disposable syringes and needles by intravenous drug abusers are all expected to help reduce the spread of the viruses. Although common, the Epstein-Barr virus causes relatively few American cancer deaths. No immunization for this large, complex virus is available yet.

Mortality from stomach cancer in the U.S. has been declining for the past half century. A partial explanation may be that improved sanitation has delayed infection by *Helicobacter pylori*, a bacterium causing chronic stomach inflammation that can become cancerous. Later infection by this prevalent microbe gives the disease less time to develop. Also, people now tend to consume less salt and more fruits and vegetables that contain vitamin C than was common years ago; these dietary improvements also seem to interfere with the infection's ability to induce cancer. Use of antibiotics to treat the infection may lead to further reductions.

Barring a breakdown of the measures and policies currently in force, mortality from cancers of infectious origin is likely to decline over the next few decades in the U.S., and most other advanced countries, probably by about one fifth. In less developed countries, however, infections are likely to continue causing substantial cancer deaths.

Reproductive Factors

Considerable evidence links certain reproductive behavior with cancer, particularly for cancer of the breast or ovaries in women. Unfortunately, as with many other findings about the causes of breast cancer, the insights have not led to effective prevention strategies. Part of the problem is that reproductive behavior is driven mainly by social and economic forces, so that modifying it to prevent cancer is for the most part unrealistic.

Birth-control pills cause a small increase in breast cancer rates while they are being used, but this excess risk declines rapidly after their use is discontinued. Use before 35 years of age, when the incidence of breast cancer is low, has minimal impact on breast cancer mortality. On the other hand, use of oral contraceptives for five or more years substantially reduces the lifetime risk of ovarian and endometrial cancer. Thus, the overall impact on cancer mortality—

Realistic Goals for Reducing Cancer Mortality

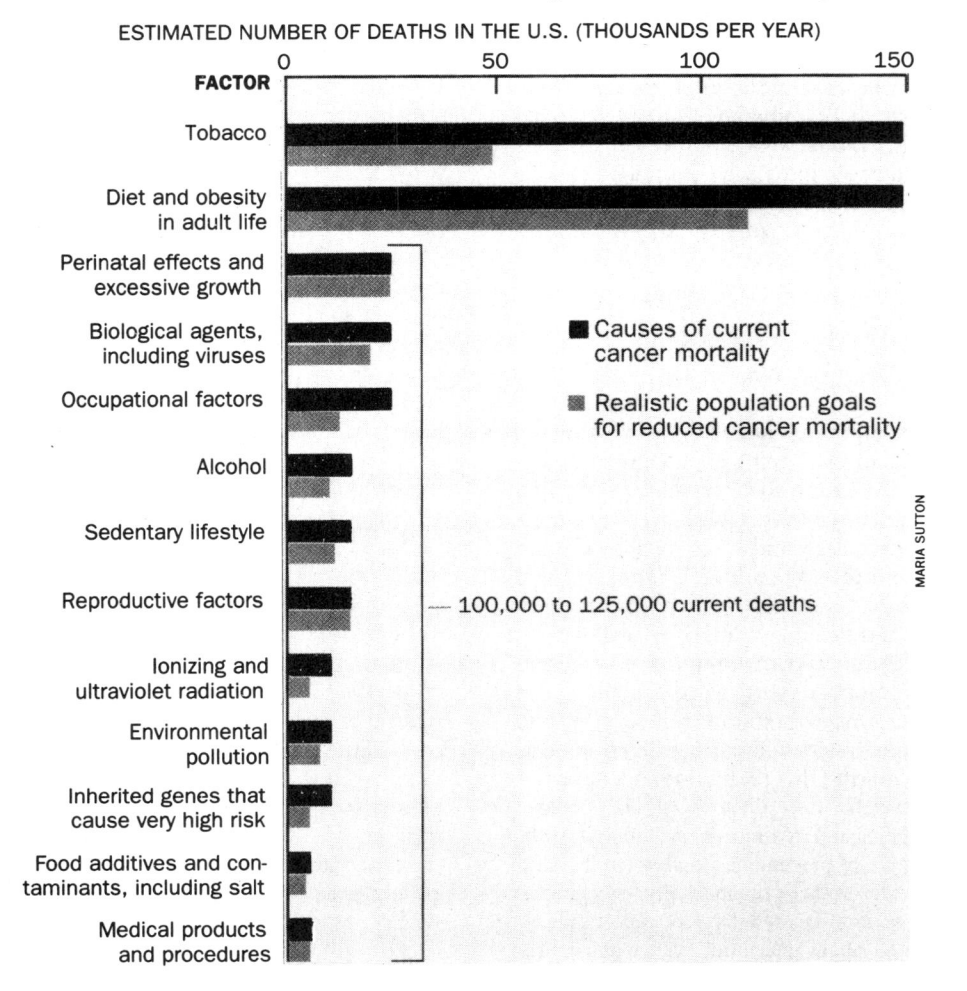

ESTIMATED NUMBER OF DEATHS IN THE U.S. (THOUSANDS PER YEAR)

FACTOR
- Tobacco
- Diet and obesity in adult life
- Perinatal effects and excessive growth
- Biological agents, including viruses
- Occupational factors
- Alcohol
- Sedentary lifestyle
- Reproductive factors
- Ionizing and ultraviolet radiation
- Environmental pollution
- Inherited genes that cause very high risk
- Food additives and contaminants, including salt
- Medical products and procedures

■ Causes of current cancer mortality
■ Realistic population goals for reduced cancer mortality

100,000 to 125,000 current deaths

TOBACCO AND DIET, including the latter's effects on obesity, account for about 300,000 cancer fatalities every year in the U.S.—or about 60 percent of the country's annual cancer mortality. Researchers hope these numbers, particularly those for tobacco-caused cancer deaths, can be significantly reduced. Other factors, however, such as those dating to around the time of birth (perinatal factors) or those related to reproduction, are expected to be much more resistant to improvement.

if pill use is limited to earlier reproductive life—is beneficial. Some evidence suggests that tubal ligation may also reduce ovarian cancer risk but that vasectomy may increase risk of prostate cancer in men.

Hormonal contraceptives that simulate early pregnancy in women in their teens or early twenties—or an early menopause in women in their thirties or forties—could potentially reduce the risks for breast cancer. A modest amount of research and development is being done on such contraceptives. Although the first early-menopause preparations may be available within a decade, another 10 years or more may be needed for investigators to assess their effects on breast cancer risk.

Environment and Pollution

Over the past 20 years, no field of cancer epidemiology has seen as many new hypotheses as that concerned with environmental pollution. The candidate carcinogens are diverse enough to include extremely low frequency magnetic fields from electric power lines, radio-frequency electromagnetic radiation used in cellular telephones, proximity to nuclear plants or chemical-waste dumps, water fluoridation and even unseen, unspecified sources responsible for "clusters" of cancer cases within small geographic regions. Few of these hypotheses have been corroborated. But they all serve an important function: preserving the necessary vigilance in the face of the exploding pace of technological change.

With respect to radiation from nuclear or x-ray sources and workplace carcinogens, all any one citizen can do is demand that the authorities enforce regulations. Technological progress resulting in a shift away from traditional industrial employment, fewer workers in relatively high cancer risk jobs, and the phasing out of asbestos use in buildings justify an expectation that deaths from job-related cancers can be cut by about one half over the next several decades.

In addition, greater awareness of the risks of being in the sun between 11 A.M. and 3 P.M. and more widespread use of sunscreens could reduce deaths from melanoma, the most lethal form of skin cancer, by one half. The reduction will be less, however, if the depletion of the earth's ozone layer continues, allowing more of the sun's ultraviolet rays through. Part of the ultraviolet spectrum is responsible for most skin cancers.

Air pollution has declined over the past 30 years in the U.S. Although the measures that brought about the reduction were mostly aimed at short-term goals, such as providing relief for those suffering from asthma, some drop in pollution-related cancer mortality may occur. Yet any such benefit will be as difficult to document as the existence of the original link itself. A decline of one quarter in pollution-related cancer, corresponding to less than 1 percent of all cancer deaths, may be possible.

Mammography, menopausal estrogens and tamoxifen for preventing breast cancer have also come under scrutiny as possible cancer-causing agents. It is now generally recognized that mammography conveys a negligible risk and a substantial benefit. Menopausal estrogens can cause cancer of the endometrium and the breast, although preparations that include progestin are safer in relation to endometrial cancer.

Tamoxifen, a valuable drug for treating breast cancer, is now being evaluated to determine whether it can prevent breast cancer among healthy women who are at high risk for the disease. The catch is that considerable evidence indicates that tamoxifen can cause endometrial cancer. No doubt, medical products and procedures will continue to cause a small proportion of all cancers, but in general, their substantial benefits outweigh their risks.

What to Do

In sum, anyone can reduce his or her chances of being afflicted with cancer by following some sensible guidelines: eat plenty of vegetables and fruits; exercise regularly and avoid weight gain; and avoid tobacco smoke, animal fats and red meats, excessive alcohol consumption, the midday sun, risky sexual practices and known carcinogens in the environment or workplace. Of course, not everyone will follow this advice, and many others will not heed it consistently. Taking this reality into account, we estimate [see illustration on previous page] that a reasonable medium-term objective of prevention programs in the U.S. or any other economically advantaged population is a reduction of cancer mortality by about one third, even without new discoveries or technological developments. This reduction is far less than the almost two thirds that is theoretically possible, but it is still considerable. With further research and new information about the causes of cancer, more reductions are likely.

For a small group of people, prevention strategies will be much more customized. Individuals born with mutant genes for various cancers, which greatly increase the probability that they will be afflicted, are commonly offered genetic counseling that focuses on preventing the kind of cancer they are facing. Assuming that such mutations are uncommon, that some high-risk births might be avoided and that prophylactic measures are taken in affected persons, it might be possible to reduce mortality from inherited cancer by about one half. Still, this is a very speculative estimate in a field that is rapidly changing and in which any impact would not be measurable for many years.

Because most of the actions to prevent cancer must be taken by individuals, the distribution of accurate information, together with peer support for the elimination of bad habits and for other behavioral changes, is critical. But effective cancer prevention requires activities at other levels, too, including counseling and screening by health care providers. At this level, dissemination of scientifically sound information to the providers themselves is crucial.

Another level involves regulation by government agencies to minimize the public's exposure to harmful agents, promote healthier products and ensure that industry provides safe working environments. In some cases, officials will have to deal with the displacement of workers whose livelihood depends on the production of toxic products. For example, the costs of subsidizing tobacco farmers to grow something other than tobacco may help avoid higher costs in the future if fewer people need to be treated for lung cancer. An additional level involves the implementation of policies to improve public health. Examples include providing community facilities for safe physical activity, such as bikeways for commuting and after-school gymnasium programs for children.

At the international level, the actions of developed countries affect cancer prevention worldwide. Unfortunately, tobacco exports are often promoted, and hazardous manufacturing processes are moved to unregulated Third World countries. Both trends will contribute to rising rates of cancers worldwide.

Most types of cancer are to a large extent preventable, even with today's knowledge and technologies. The "war on cancer," primarily fought by searching for improved cancer treatments, has met with limited success and should be better balanced by more extensive efforts in prevention.

The Authors

WALTER C. WILLETT, GRAHAM A. COLDITZ and NANCY E. MUELLER are colleagues at Harvard University. Willett is chairman of the department of nutrition and professor of epidemiology in the School of Public Health, professor in the Medical School and associate physician at Brigham and Women's Hospital in Boston. Colditz is associate professor in the Medical School and associate director for education at the Harvard Center for Cancer Prevention. Mueller is professor of epidemiology in the School of Public Health and a member of the board of scientific advisers for the National Cancer Institute.

Further Reading

THE TREATMENT OF DISEASES AND THE WAR AGAINST CANCER. John Cairns in *Scientific American*, Vol. 253, No. 5, pages 51–59; November 1985.
SMOKING AND HEALTH: A 25-YEAR EXPERIENCE. Kenneth Warner in *American Journal of Public Health*, Vol. 79, No. 2, pages 141–143; February 1989.
TOWARD THE PRIMARY PREVENTION OF CANCER. Brian E. Henderson, Ronald K. Ross and Malcolm C. Pike in *Science*, Vol. 254, pages 1131–1138; November 22, 1991.
THE CAUSES AND PREVENTION OF CANCER. Bruce N. Ames, Lois Swirsky Gold and Walter C. Willett in *Proceedings of the National Academy of Sciences*, Vol. 92, No. 12, pages 5258–5265; June 6, 1995.
AVOIDABLE CAUSES OF CANCER. Special issue of *Environmental Health Perspectives*, Vol. 103, Supplement 8; November 1995.

CANCER-FIGHTING FOODS

Green Revolution

No one wants to be one of the 1.2 million Americans diagnosed with cancer each year. In an effort to avoid this all too common fate, people may fill up on fiber, obsess about antioxidants, or shun red meat and fat. In recent years, however, scientists have realized that these dietary elements are only the tip of the iceberg when it comes to reducing cancer risk. A previously hidden world of natural chemicals in edible plants is unfolding, and the more researchers learn, the more certain they are that mom was right: we should eat our vegetables, and lots of them.

"There's an explosion of compelling and consistent data associating diets rich in fruits and vegetables with a lower cancer risk," said epidemiologist Tim Byers, who studies the relationship between diet and chronic disease at the Centers for Disease Control and Prevention in Atlanta. One analysis of data from 23 epidemiologic studies found that a diet rich in vegetables and grains slashed colon cancer risk by 40%. Another study found that women who ate few vegetables had an incidence of breast cancer that was about 25% higher than those who consumed more produce. All in all, at least 200 epidemiologic studies from around the world have found a link between a plant-rich diet and a lower risk for many types of tumors.

Findings such as these have inspired laboratory scientists to try and analyze just what it is about fruits and vegetables that might fend off cancer. "There's more to food than vitamins, minerals, fiber, calories, and protein," said cancer epidemiologist John D. Potter of Seattle's Fred Hutchinson Cancer Research Center. "We're discovering a plethora of bioactive substances in plant foods." Called *functional components,* these include a large class of naturally occurring compounds known as phytochemicals. Meanwhile, "many traditional nutrients, including folic acid and selenium, have functions that are becoming clearer — including an ability to fight cancer," said Dr. Potter.

This powerful epidemiological evidence is being bolstered by newer laboratory studies showing how functional components interfere with carcinogenesis. "These compounds seem to interact with every step in the cancer process, mostly slowing, stopping, or reversing them," Dr. Potter said. Most functional components appear to boost the production or activity of enzymes that act as

- *blocking agents,* detoxifying carcinogens or keeping them from reaching or penetrating cells, or
- *suppressing agents,* restraining malignant changes in cells that have been exposed to carcinogens.

Hotter than the Internet?
Anyone who hasn't yet heard about functional foods soon will — the term is well on its way to becoming the latest nutrition buzzword. Before settling on this appellation, researchers tossed around at least 20 different names, including "designer foods," "nutriceuticals," "pharmafoods," and "chemopreventers." But the functional foods label won out in 1994 when it was endorsed by the food and nutrition board of the Institute of Medicine. It simply means "foods with ingredients thought to prevent disease."

Although the conventional wisdom is that new trends take hold first on the coasts, in this case a midwestern institution appears to be out in front. The University of Illinois has the nation's first (and only) full-scale scientific program devoted to the study of phytochemicals and other functional components. The Functional Foods for Health Program (FFH) involves 63 faculty members from more than 20 disciplines and represents both the Chicago and Urbana-Champaign campuses of the university.

"The program combines expertise from agriculture and medicine to study how naturally occurring components in foods may protect people from disease," said FFH director Clare

Hasler. In related work, the department of medicinal chemistry and pharmacognosy on the Chicago campus maintains the world's largest database on the chemical constituents and pharmacology of plant extracts.

Phytochemicals

When life began, plants were *anaerobic* — they lived in a world devoid of oxygen. As they evolved and began turning carbon dioxide into oxygen, however, they gradually polluted their own environment. In order to survive, plants were forced to develop defenses against unstable forms of oxygen, explained researcher David Heber, head of the clinical nutrition research unit at the University of California-Los Angeles.

Phytochemicals, many of which are brightly colored and help give plants their vivid hues, are key parts of this antioxidant defense system. In addition to resisting oxidation, these substances guard against an array of adversities including viral attack, harsh weather, and the insults of handling.

Eons later, it appears that humans can now benefit from eating plants that contain these disease-fighting substances. Unlike other minor constituents in food, however, phytochemicals have no calories and no known nutritional value. In other words, they are not necessary for normal physiologic function.

There are literally hundreds of phytochemicals, only a sprinkling of which have been studied. They can be categorized in several ways: by chemical name, by primary food source, and by anti-cancer action. Many foods contain numerous phytochemicals, each acting via one or several mechanisms. And because new data are being published almost daily, constant updating is needed to keep any list of phytochemicals current. In this section, they are organized by chemical name.

As exciting as scientists find this area of inquiry, they don't pretend to have all the answers yet. "While there's no doubt that diets rich in fruits and vegetables are cancer-protective, much of what we know about individual phytochemicals is still speculative," cautioned nutrition researcher Phyllis Bowen, co-director of the University of Illinois' functional foods program.

Flavonoids are an array of chemicals widely found in fruits, vegetables, and wine. They may reduce cancer risk by acting as antioxidants: blocking the access of carcinogens to cells, suppressing malignant changes in cells, or a combination of these. "Flavonoids may also interfere with the binding of hormones to cells and thus may inhibit cancer development," said nutrition researcher Diane F. Birt of the University of Nebraska Medical Center's Eppley Institute.

Indoles and ***isothiocyanates*** (also called mustard oils) are largely responsible for putting broccoli on the cancer prevention map. Both account for some of the "bite" in the taste of cruciferous vegetables, and both are breakdown products of complex plant compounds called glucosinolates. They are formed when these compounds are altered by processing, cooking, or chewing. Scientists believe that indoles and isothiocyanates act mainly by blocking cancer-causing substances before they reach their cellular targets. Isothiocyanates may also suppress tumor growth. *(See box, "Beyond Broccoli.")*

Isoflavones are prominent in soy beans and everything that's made from them. Some scientists believe that differences in soy consumption explain why the incidence of breast cancer in Asian women is 5–8 times lower than in American women, as well as why prostate cancer is lower in Asian men. (See "Diet and the Prostate," *Harvard Health Letter*, July 1994.) Isoflavones can act as antioxidants, carcinogen blockers, or tumor suppressors. Plants contain many forms, including genistein, biochanin A, and daidzein.

Other cruciferous chemicals that are thought to have anti-cancer properties include dithiolthiones, chlorophylline (chlorophyll combined with sodium and copper), and organonitriles. In addition to these functional components, cruciferous vegetables are also rich in fiber and in vitamin C and selenium. "No doubt these substances work in some complex synergy to fight cancer," said Matthew A. Wallig, an investigator in functional-foods research at the University of Illinois.

Lignans occur in many foods, but are especially concentrated in linseed (which are seeds from flax, the same plant that is woven into linen cloth). Lignans may have an antioxidant effect and may block or suppress cancerous changes. "Although flax hasn't been used much in this country, an increasing number of health food stores and bakeries are adding it to bread products," said Dr. Bowen of the University of Illinois. This practice started because flax is also high in omega-3 fatty acids, which are thought to protect against colon cancer and heart disease.

Beyond Broccoli

There are a lot more cruciferous vegetables than most people realize. They include:

bok choy	collards
broccoli	kale
Brussels sprouts	kohlrabi
cabbage	mustard greens
cauliflower	rutabaga
	turnips

7. CURRENT KILLERS

Organosulfur compounds are found in plants from the genus *Allium* which includes garlic, onions, leeks, and shallots. Diallyl disulfide is the most potent of these chemicals, which may act as blocking or suppressing agents.

Monoterpenes occur naturally in citrus fruits (one variety is D-limonene) and in caraway seeds (in the form of D-carvone). Scientists think they act by interfering with the action of carcinogens.

Saponins are a large family of modified carbohydrates found in many vegetables and herbs. So far, researchers have identified 11 different saponins in soybeans alone. In addition to having anti-cancer activity, there is evidence that some of these substances break down red blood cells, deactivate sperm, or lower circulating levels of certain lipids.

Carotenoids

Although phytochemicals have been hogging the spotlight of late, the red and yellow plant pigments known collectively as *carotenoids* are also thought to be potent cancer fighters. This is still true, even though beta carotene supplements lost some of their luster after several large studies failed to demonstrate the kind of anti-cancer activity that many people had hoped for. (See "Second Thoughts About Antioxidants," *Harvard Health Letter,* February 1995.)

Researchers may have been too quick to assume that beta carotene by itself deserved credit for lower cancer rates, according to nutritional epidemiologist Regina G. Ziegler of the National Cancer Institute. People who ate diets rich in fruits and vegetables or who had high circulating levels of beta carotene showed a reduced risk of cancer. But, she pointed out, "blood levels of beta carotene may simply be a good marker for fruit and vegetable intake."

Beta carotene may be beneficial in its natural form, bound up with other constituents of food, but not when it is isolated as a supplement. It is also possible that other carotenoids may be the real cancer inhibitors, and that they may be more efficacious against some types of carcinogens and tumors than others.

In addition to having antioxidant properties, carotenoids may work in several other ways, Dr. Bowen said. They may enhance normal communication among healthy cells, a buzz of biochemical conversation that scientists think helps keep cancer cells from running amok. It's also possible that beta carotene is transformed into retinoic acid, a substance that some researchers say can turn on and off genes that may play a role in cancer development.

New roles for old nutrients

The phytochemicals and carotenoids are just two dietary defenses in the war against cancer. As scientists learn more about how cancer progresses, they are finding that some traditional vitamins and minerals also show protective promise.

Folate (also known as folic acid) is best known for its role in the formation of healthy red blood cells. Now there's compelling epidemiologic evidence that people with higher folic acid levels are less likely than others to develop colon cancer and precancerous colon polyps, according to researcher Joel B. Mason, an assistant professor of medicine and nutrition at Tufts University. "This relationship has been uncovered just in the last few years," said Dr. Mason, who is coordinating a multicenter trial probing folic acid's ability to modify colon cancer risk.

Other researchers have shown that folate contributes to normal tissue formation by guarding

> **"Much of what we know about individual phytochemicals is still speculative."**

the integrity of the genetic messages encoded in DNA, and Dr. Mason speculates that this protective effect may thwart carcinogens that would ordinarily cause colon cancer. But he isn't ready to recommend that people who are worried about colon cancer take large doses of folic acid. "It's definitely a good idea, though, to get the RDA of 200 micrograms (mcg), or perhaps up to 400 mcg, the level to which some experts recommend raising it." In his experiments, Dr. Mason uses doses 20–40 times greater than the RDA, which would not be safe for everyone. High folate intake can increase seizure risk for people with epilepsy, for example, or may mask B^{12} deficiency, which can lead to serious neurological troubles, especially in older people.

Calcium appears to have some preventive value where colon cancer is concerned. Researchers propose several mechanisms to explain how calcium acts as an anti-cancer warrior in the colon; these include inhibiting cell growth and/or disarming potential toxins by binding them to fatty acids.

Selenium is being actively studied by epidemiologists and basic scientists with mixed results. Interest was sparked by epidemiologic evidence that population groups with higher selenium intakes have less cancer than those who consume little of this trace mineral.

Although these findings were supported by results from animal experiments, further epidemiologic investigations have found little or no protective effect in humans. Some researchers believe that selenium may work best as an anti-cancer agent in concert with phytochemicals or antioxidants such as beta carotene and vitamin C. A large scale clinical trial now underway is expected eventually to shed more light on this mineral's possible benefits.

Conjugated linoleic acid's beneficial effects suggest that people cannot live by vegetables alone, and that a more varied diet may be best. "Substances that fight cancer may not always be in plants," said food and nutrition researcher Michael W. Pariza of the Food Research Institute at the University of Wisconsin-Madison.

In the 1970s, Dr. Pariza and his co-workers were investigating possible carcinogens formed by grilling meat when they stumbled across a substance that appeared to inhibit cancer instead of contributing to it. This was conjugated linoleic acid, a form of an essential fatty acid which is found in beef and in fat-containing dairy products.

When Dr. Pariza tested the substance in animals that spontaneously develop breast cancer, he found that the conjugated acid slows the growth of cells that give rise to cancer. There is some laboratory evidence that it does this by jump-starting the immune system, which repels cancerous changes. This does not mean that people should "chow down on dairy fat," he emphasized. But it does suggest that moderate consumption may be better than none at all.

Vitamin A is what the body produces when it metabolizes carotenoids; it's also found in dairy products and animal fat. Some studies indicate that vitamin A itself, either from food or supplements, may also offer some cancer protection.

Vitamin D's role is unsettled right now; early studies indicated that it might provide some protection against colon cancer, but subsequent ones weren't as promising.

Malignancy and Macrobiotics

Some people claim that the macrobiotic enthusiasts were on to something long before mainstream nutrition researchers discovered phytochemicals and other functional components in foods. Were they? Only to a certain extent, according to researcher Cheryl Rock, a University of Michigan expert on nutrition and cancer. "It's a big stretch to call the macrobiotic diet an anticancer diet. While the diet does call for a lot of vegetables, it's low in fruit and also low in calcium and vitamin D." It's also inadequate in many key nutrients and low in energy and protein, she noted. "Over time, protein and calorie deficits can harm the immune system, which may impair the body's ability to fight cancer."

But what to eat?

Will Americans soon be slurping down an elixir of lignans, flavonoids, saponins, and folic acid? Most likely not, agree the experts consulted for this article. "I don't condone emphasizing one or even several functional components," said Dr. Hasler from the University of Illinois. "Phytochemicals and other dietary substances no doubt work in concert to fight cancer and other diseases. In addition, isolated phytochemicals may actually be harmful at high doses."

"Simply put," said nutrition and cancer expert Cheryl Rock, an assistant professor at the University of Michigan, "the best advice is to eat real food instead of relying on supplements. If you just take supplements, you simply don't get all of the compounds in foods we're still learning about. We don't know yet if we should combine an indole with an isoflavone, or folic acid with selenium. Right now, only nature knows best."

Recommendations from the National Cancer Institute (NCI) and others emphasize the importance of eating at least five to nine servings of fruits and vegetables each day, aiming for a wide variety. This isn't as hard as it seems: try for one or two fruits at breakfast, one fruit and two vegetables at lunch and dinner, and a snack to make a total of nine.

Although the NCI doesn't fine-tune its advice about exactly what to eat, many experts believe that people can best attain a balance of beneficial substances by making sure that their diet includes foods from each of the following categories:

- cruciferous vegetables
- citrus fruits
- dark green leafy vegetables
- dark yellow/orange/red vegetables

A good rule of thumb is to eat at least three different colors of fruits and vegetables every day. "We know, for example, that the red pigment in tomatoes has completely different bioactive ingredients than the orange pigment in carrots; the same is true for the bioactive ingredients in citrus fruits versus those in the cruciferous vegetables," said Dr. Hasler.

And be sure to eat other plant foods as well, said Dr. Potter. "Grains, nuts, seeds, and legumes also contain a wide variety of bioactive compounds."

Humans got their start as gatherers, probably eating little bits of many different fruits and vegetables every day, and we should strive for such variety and quantity again, said Dr. Potter. "Vegetables and fruits contain the anticarcinogenic cocktail to which we are adapted. We abandon it at our peril," he said.

—*KRISTINE NAPIER, M.P.H, R.D.*

Mutant Gene Can Slow AIDS Virus

Cancer Institute Study Indicates Some People May Be Impervious

Rick Weiss

Washington Post Staff Writer

A genetic mutation common in U.S. whites slows the progression of AIDS in people infected with the AIDS-causing virus and, in some cases, protects individuals against the disease, according to a new study.

Scientists said the new information on the role played by the defective gene could lead to advances in the fight against AIDS by spurring the development of medicines or vaccines that mimic the protective mutation's effects.

"It's a beautiful study," said Robert C. Gallo, head of the University of Maryland's Institute of Human Virology in Baltimore, who in 1984 co-discovered the human immunodeficiency virus (HIV).

The new work shows that about 1 in 7 U.S. whites and about 1 in 59 U.S. blacks inherit the protective, mutant gene from one parent, along with a normal copy of the gene from the other parent. This harmless genetic condition naturally slows the progress of AIDS, giving an average of three extra years of life to those infected with HIV, according to the study in today's issue of Science.

The study also confirms previous hints that about 1 percent of American whites inherit a mutant version of the gene from both parents, a doubly protective dose that makes these individuals virtually impervious to infection even if they are repeatedly exposed to the virus.

The new research, led by the National Cancer Institute's Stephen J. O'Brien, Michael Dean and Mary Carrington, helps explain why some people exposed to HIV fare better than others. It also shows that the protective mutation is extremely rare in African blacks, which suggests that the genetic glitch may have arisen in an ancestral Caucasian some time after the two races diverged.

Researchers praised the findings as an example of the benefits that can accrue from the dogged and unglamorous work of community-based AIDS organizations, which have for more than a decade collected blood samples from thousands of HIV-infected people and kept track of each individual's fate. It was through the NCI team's genetic analysis of those samples that the naturally occurring protective factors were found.

"It's the extensive epidemiological data collected on these patients that made this work possible," said O'Brien, who directs NCI's laboratory of genomic diversity in Frederick, Md.

The work is the latest in a rapid-fire series of discoveries since June that has shifted AIDS researchers' attention away from the virus itself and onto a protein studding the surface of some human cells. The protein, known as CKR5 or CCR5, is part of a portal system that allows the AIDS virus to enter cells of the immune system. People with mutant CKR5 genes cannot make the crucial portal protein, and hence are protected to varying extents from viral invasion.

In collaboration with scientists in more than 20 U.S. cities, the NCI team analyzed genetic material, or DNA, from 1,955 people known to be at high risk of AIDS. Some participants already had full-blown AIDS, others were HIV-positive but not yet ill, and some were HIV-negative despite having been repeatedly exposed to the virus by having sexual intercourse with an infected person, sharing needles with an infected intravenous drug user, or receiving infusions of contaminated blood products used to treat hemophiliacs.

The researchers focused on the CKR5 gene, which carries instructions for making a protein on macrophages, the white blood cells that HIV initially infects. That protein serves as a docking site for an immune system hormone, but the AIDS virus can usurp the site to infect macrophages.

Everybody carries two copies of the CKR5 gene. The team found that 282 of the study participants shared a common mutation in one copy of that gene. In the mutated version, 32 of the gene's approximately 1,000 DNA coding units were missing, an absence that interferes with the docking site's construction. Since the other copy of the gene was intact in these people, HIV still had some doorways available. But the partial defect apparently slowed the virus's march through the immune system, lengthening the average time from infection to illness to 13 years, compared with the national average of 10 years.

Analysis showed that this slower rate of progression held true only for those who had become infected by sex, perhaps because the higher viral doses associated with blood product transfusions or use of injected drugs overwhelm the modest protection offered by having one copy of the mutated gene.

However, when the mutation occurred in both copies of the gene, docking site construction was completely blocked and protection from the virus was total. Among the 17 people in the study with dual mutations, none was infected with HIV, no matter what had put them at risk.

The team also found eight smaller mutations in the same gene that appear to offer some protection against AIDS. Yet, they note that 97 percent of 622 long-term nonprogressors studied—people infected with HIV whose health has not declined as expected—had none of the nine mutations. That suggests there are other protective mutations awaiting discovery.

Scientists said drug developers could now consider testing genetic therapies that interfere with the normal CKR5 gene's function, or drugs or vaccines that knock out the CKR5 protein. Since

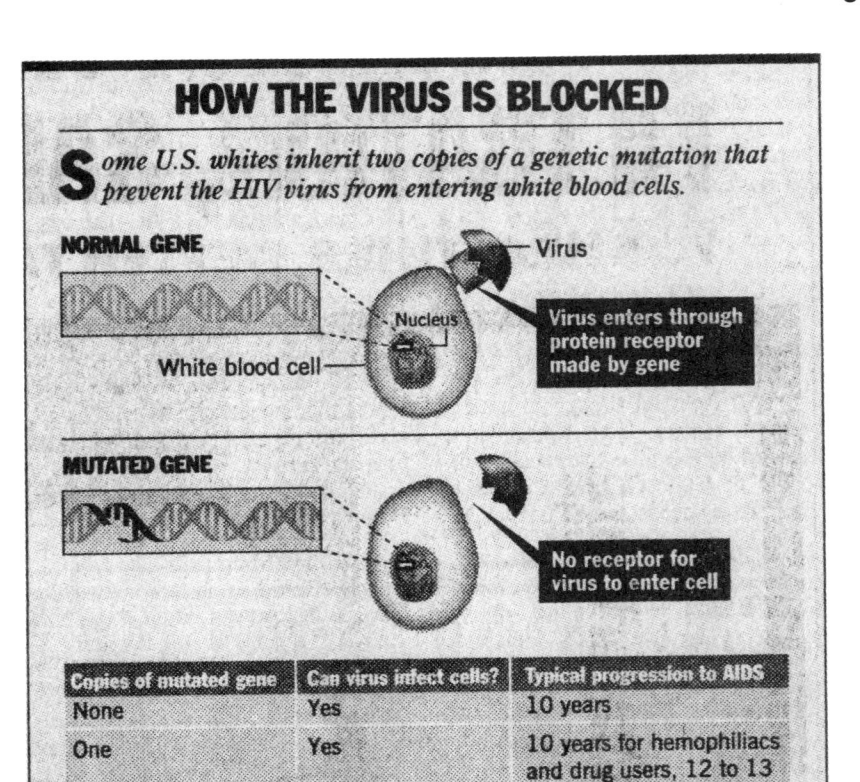

37. Mutant Gene Can Slow AIDS Virus

HOW THE VIRUS IS BLOCKED

Some U.S. whites inherit two copies of a genetic mutation that prevent the HIV virus from entering white blood cells.

NORMAL GENE
- White blood cell
- Nucleus
- Virus
- Virus enters through protein receptor made by gene

MUTATED GENE
- No receptor for virus to enter cell

Copies of mutated gene	Can virus infect cells?	Typical progression to AIDS
None	Yes	10 years
One	Yes	10 years for hemophiliacs and drug users, 12 to 13 years for those infected through sexual contact
Two	No	None

THE WASHINGTON POST

people with doubly mutated copies of the gene are apparently healthy, they said, it would appear that the CKR5 target is ideal: it is critical for the virus but unneeded by the patient.

Some suggested cautiously that bone marrow transplants from AIDS-resistant donors might prove useful. But they warned that transplants might be useless for recipients already infected with HIV, and unjustifiably expensive and risky for disease prevention.

"I'd rather use a condom than a bone marrow transplant" to prevent AIDS, said Anthony S. Fauci, chief of the National Institute of Allergy and Infectious Diseases, who otherwise praised the work.

The new report also holds interest for medical historians. Although about 15 percent of Caucasians of European descent carry one copy of the so-called delta-32 mutation, only 1.7 percent of African Americans do, according to the study. The mutation is essentially absent among native Africans, suggesting its existence in African Americans is the result of blood-line mixing in this country.

Those extreme differences in genetic frequencies suggest the mutation arose in the Caucasian lineage after it diverged from the African one some 150,000 to 200,000 years ago. O'Brien said scientists would not expect to find such a recently arising mutation in 15 percent of the U.S. white population unless it offered some benefit to those who acquired it.

O'Brien hypothesized that the world was once swept by an ancient epidemic caused by a virus that, like HIV, took advantage of the CKR5 protein. Because people who had the mutation were more likely to survive than those with the normal gene, the mutation's frequency in the population grew.

No one knows what that disease was, or whether it still exists. "It probably wasn't AIDS," O'Brien said. "But whatever it was, it probably had a high mortality."

Article 38

MAN OF THE YEAR

THE DISEASE DETECTIVE

As the AIDS epidemic unfolded, Dr. David Ho had a knack for asking just the right questions

CHRISTINE GORMAN

DR. DAVID HO DOESN'T LOOK LIKE A gambler. With his boyish face and slender build, he could more easily pass for a teenager than for a 44-year-old father of three—or, for that matter, for a world-renowned scientist. In fact, when he was an undergraduate at the California Institute of Technology back in the 1970s, Ho hung around the blackjack tables in Las Vegas, tilting the odds in his favor by memorizing each card as it was played. He got so good at counting cards that he was thrown out of several casinos.

Today Ho is still something of a gambler, though in a very different field and for much bigger stakes. The director of the Aaron Diamond AIDS Research Center in New York City, he has come up with a daring strategy for flushing out the virus that causes AIDS. As he explained at the 11th International Conference on AIDS in Vancouver, Canada, last summer, Ho (like more and more doctors) is using powerful new drugs called protease inhibitors in combination with standard antiviral medications. But unlike most doctors, he gives the so-called combination therapy to patients in the first few weeks of infection.

Already the HIV in his patients' blood has dropped so low it can no longer be measured. Because he is attacking early and not waiting for full-fledged AIDS to develop, Ho told the conference, there is a good chance that within two or three years the virus could be completely eliminated.

Eliminated. Just a few months ago, no one in the AIDS community and no reputable scientist would presume to imagine such a thing. Journalists, activists and researchers peppered Ho with questions at the podium. Had he found the cure? Could people stop worrying about AIDS? Could they throw away their condoms?

No, no and no. What he had done, Ho explained, was begin an experiment that might, under the right circumstances, eliminate the virus from a small group of men caught within three months of infection. He couldn't offer the same hope to the estimated 100,000 patients in later stages of infection who in the past year have begun taking the same antiviral "cocktails"—often with encouraging results—but whose AIDS is probably too far advanced for them to expect a long-term recovery.

Like so many promising HIV treatments, Ho's strategy could fail. It could even backfire if it is mistakenly touted as a kind of "morning after" treatment that allows people to relax their guard and engage in risky sexual behavior. By desensitizing the virus to medications, it could jeopardize a patient's ability to respond to future treatments. Worse yet, it could inadvertently create a mutant strain of virus resistant to all currently available drugs—a kind of super HIV—that could lead to a second, even more devastating AIDS epidemic.

There are other problems. Even if the treatment works, it isn't practical. HIV-positive patients would have to start taking the drugs immediately after infection, before they realize they're sick. And even if the drug cocktails can be made to work in the later stages of infection, they are far too expensive to do much good for the 20 million people in the developing world who are infected with HIV. In the long run, scientists believe, only an AIDS vaccine will stop the global epidemic.

Still, it's easy to understand the tentative sense of hope and excitement that has spread across the AIDS community in the months since the Vancouver conference.

THE BATTLE AGAINST AIDS

JUNE 1981
The U.S. Centers for Disease Control publishes the first report of a rare type of pneumonia, *Pneumocystis carinii*, in five gay men in Los Angeles.

JULY 1982
Faced with a growing number of cases—among homosexuals, intravenous drug users and hemophiliacs—in which the immune system collapses for no apparent reason, U.S. health officials coin the term AIDS (acquired immune deficiency syndrome) for the new disease.

DECEMBER 1982
The first documented case of AIDS resulting from a transfusion leads to a government warning that the blood supply might be contaminated.

JANUARY 1983
Heterosexuals are considered to be at risk after two women whose sexual partners had AIDS contract the disease.

MARCH 1983
Gay men, intravenous drug users and others considered at high risk of developing AIDS are urged to refrain from donating blood.

MAY 1983
Luc Montagnier's team at the Pasteur Institute in Paris reports that it has found a retrovirus that may cause AIDS.

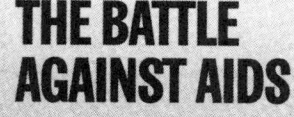

38. Disease Detective

Ho's speech, for all its caveats, provided the first concrete evidence that HIV is not insurmountable. After 15 years of horror, denial and disappointment, the pendulum may at long last be swinging against AIDS.

A TEAM EFFORT

David Ho would be the first to say that he cannot take all the credit. It was an immunologist from Los Angeles named Michael Gottlieb who in 1981 reported the first cases of what was then called gay pneumonia. It was the U.S. Centers for Disease Control that alerted doctors to the gathering epidemic and established that the infection was transmitted through blood transfusions, tainted needles and unprotected sex. It was Dr. Luc Montagnier's laboratory at the Pasteur Institute in Paris that first isolated the killer virus in 1983. It was Dr. Robert Gallo and his colleagues at the National Cancer Institute in Bethesda, Maryland, who made it grow in the lab, which allowed for the development of an antibody test. It was the National Institutes of Health that funded the basic research on HIV and AIDS. It was the big drug companies like Burroughs Wellcome and Merck that brought a growing list of anti-HIV drugs to market.

But Ho, working alone or in concert with others, fundamentally changed the way scientists looked at the AIDS virus. His breakthrough work in virology, beginning in the mid-1980s, revealed how HIV mounts its attack. His tenacious pursuit of the virus in the first weeks of infection helped show what the body does right in controlling HIV. His pioneering experiments with protease inhibitors helped clarify how the virus ultimately overwhelms the immune system. His work and his insights set the stage for an enormously productive shift in the treatment of AIDS away from the later stages of illness to the critical early days of infection.

Once, not so long ago, researchers believed that nothing much happened after HIV gained entry into the body. The virus simply hunkered down inside a few of the immune system's T cells—the linchpins of the body's defensive forces—for anywhere from three to 10 years. Then something, no one knew what, spurred the microbial invader to awaken. In this picture, the AIDS virus spent most of its life hibernating before starting its final, deadly assault.

In the past two years, Ho and his colleagues have demonstrated that this picture of the virus is wrong. There is no initial dormant phase of infection. Ho showed that the body and the virus are, in fact, locked in a pitched battle from the very beginning. At first many AIDS researchers found this hard to accept; it challenged some of their most cherished assumptions. If Ho was right, doctors would have to radically alter the way they treated AIDS.

It wasn't the first time that Ho had overturned conventional wisdom. During the past 15 years, he has demonstrated an uncanny ability to ask questions that seem obvious only in retrospect and to probe key issues others have overlooked. It's a trait that does not endear him to some of his rivals. A few have accused Ho of being a publicity seeker who is giving AIDS patients false hope. Upon examination, however, most of the accusations appear to spring from professional jealousy. "David is the type of individual whom I feel particularly good about when he achieves success," says Dr. George Shaw, one of Ho's strongest competitors, who runs a state-of-the-art AIDS research laboratory at the University of Alabama in Birmingham. "He is a stellar scientist."

Ho has an extraordinary knack for being in the right place at the right time. Two years after he received his M.D. from Harvard Medical School, Ho witnessed the birth of the AIDS epidemic.

LIFE CYCLE OF THE AIDS VIRUS AND HOW IT MIGHT BE STOPPED

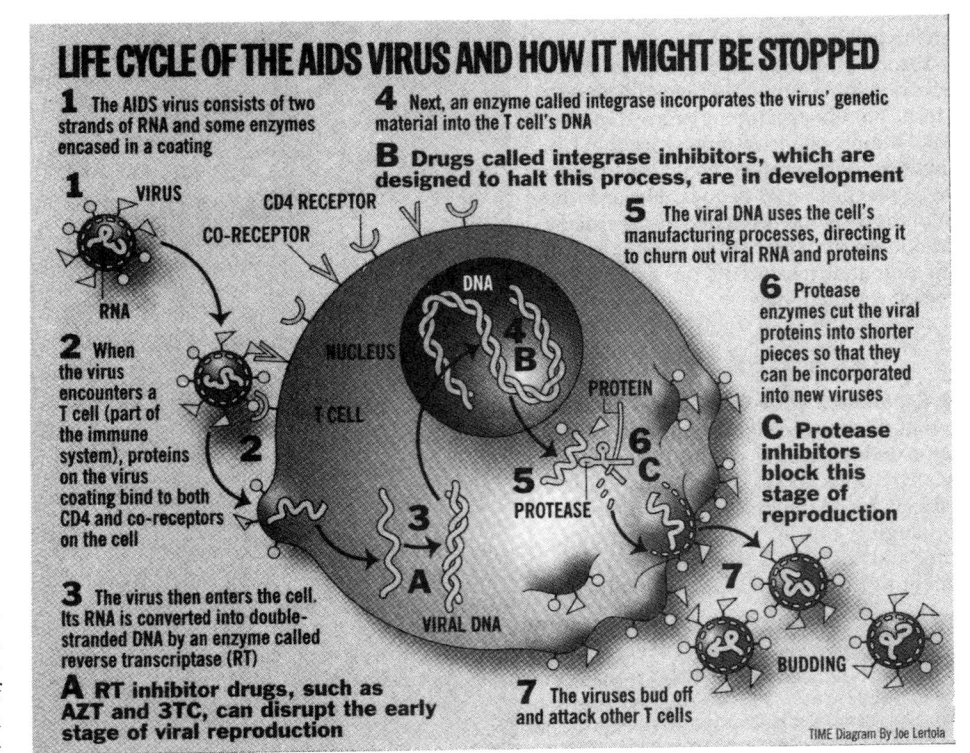

1. The AIDS virus consists of two strands of RNA and some enzymes encased in a coating

2. When the virus encounters a T cell (part of the immune system), proteins on the virus coating bind to both CD4 and co-receptors on the cell

3. The virus then enters the cell. Its RNA is converted into double-stranded DNA by an enzyme called reverse transcriptase (RT)

   A. RT inhibitor drugs, such as AZT and 3TC, can disrupt the early stage of viral reproduction

4. Next, an enzyme called integrase incorporates the virus' genetic material into the T cell's DNA

   B. Drugs called integrase inhibitors, which are designed to halt this process, are in development

5. The viral DNA uses the cell's manufacturing processes, directing it to churn out viral RNA and proteins

6. Protease enzymes cut the viral proteins into shorter pieces so that they can be incorporated into new viruses

   C. Protease inhibitors block this stage of reproduction

7. The viruses bud off and attack other T cells

TIME Diagram By Joe Lertola

APRIL 1984 — Dr. Robert Gallo, of the National Cancer Institute in Bethesda, Maryland, announces that his laboratory has also isolated the AIDS virus.

JANUARY 1985 — Montagnier, left, and Gallo each publish the genetic sequence of the AIDS viruses they have identified. A lawsuit resulting from their competing claims is settled in March 1987, with the U.S. and France agreeing to share patent royalties.

JULY 1985 — Journalists learn that actor Rock Hudson has AIDS.

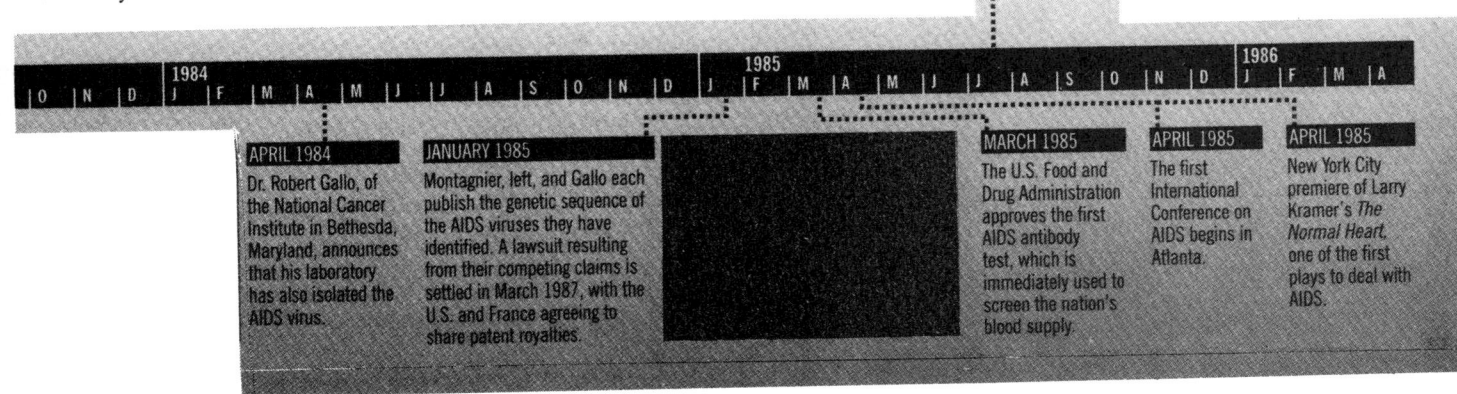

MARCH 1985 — The U.S. Food and Drug Administration approves the first AIDS antibody test, which is immediately used to screen the nation's blood supply.

APRIL 1985 — The first International Conference on AIDS begins in Atlanta.

APRIL 1985 — New York City premiere of Larry Kramer's *The Normal Heart*, one of the first plays to deal with AIDS.

7. CURRENT KILLERS

He remembers how baffling it seemed.

The year was 1981, and Ho was chief medical resident at Cedars Sinai Hospital in Los Angeles. Across town at UCLA, Gottlieb had identified a new syndrome that seemed to target gay men. Each of the cases was different, but all had one thing in common: whatever was making the men sick had singled out the T cells for destruction. Eventually the body's battered defenses couldn't shake off even the most innocuous microbial intruder. The men were dying from what doctors termed opportunistic infections, such as *Pneumocystis* pneumonia, which attacks the lungs, and toxoplasmosis, which often ravages the brain.

Ho began seeing more and more of these patients in the intensive-care units at Cedars Sinai. Some doctors thought that poppers and other recreational drugs triggered the immune collapse. Others believed it was a bizarre allergic reaction from having too many sex partners. But Ho fell into the camp that suspected a virus. He quickly decided to specialize in AIDS research. "David was clearly a big thinker even then," says Dr. Mark Ault, who was a resident at Cedars Sinai at the time. "But that didn't stop us from kidding him about how he was always looking for gay men."

Ho ignored the gibes and in 1982 landed in Martin Hirsch's virology laboratory at Massachusetts General Hospital in Boston. A prominent scientist in his own right, Hirsch is known for cultivating talented young researchers.

Like many other ambitious young scientists, Ho wanted to be the first to isolate the virus that causes AIDS. Luc Montagnier and Robert Gallo beat him to it. (Ho came in fourth, after Jay Levy of the University of California, San Francisco.) Still, while working in Hirsch's lab, Ho became expert at detecting HIV in places where few were able to find it. He was the first to show that it grows in long-lived immune cells called macrophages and among the first to isolate it in the nervous system and semen. Just as important, he showed that there isn't enough active virus in saliva for kissing to transmit the infection. "David had the Midas touch," Hirsch recalls. "Whatever he did worked."

Unfortunately, Hirsch was not Midas, and he couldn't afford to pay his postdocs more than the standard $18,000 yearly stipend. To support his family, Ho started moonlighting in Mass General's walk-in clinics. It turned out to be the right time to be in that place too. "The clinics are where you see the flus, the colds, the common illnesses," Ho says. In the mid-1980s, however, he started seeing gay men with what appeared to be an unusually severe flu. They always got over their illness without any of the hallmarks of AIDS. Still, he wondered, could there be a connection? Could these flu-like ailments be the signs of the men's very first exposure to HIV?

Sure enough, blood tests showed that the "flu" corresponded with the sudden appearance of HIV—and the total absence of any influenza viruses. Then, after a few weeks, the antibodies in the immune system would jump sharply while HIV disappeared from the circulation. It was the first evidence that HIV triggered an active infection. But not even Ho would recognize its significance until years later.

LEARNING FROM FAILURE

Despite rising casualties, Washington kept tight purse strings on funding for AIDS research for much of the 1980s. By 1987, though, even Ronald Reagan knew that AIDS was a serious threat. The plague had encircled the globe, stretching from Africa to Asia. The antibody test revealed the presence of HIV in the blood supplies of the U.S., France and Japan. The FDA approved use of the antiviral drug AZT in a record 14 weeks.

At that time, scientists across the U.S. were excited about a possible breakthrough treatment: soluble CD4. They knew that HIV does not infect T cells at random. It must first attach itself to a particular protein, called CD4, on the T cells' surface. Perhaps, researchers reasoned, if they flooded the bloodstream with free-floating CD4 molecules, the molecules would act as decoys and prevent HIV from infecting the T cells. Preliminary tests on viral samples grown under laboratory conditions showed that soluble CD4 worked beautifully.

Ho had taken a junior faculty position at UCLA and moved his family back to California. He contacted Dr. Robert Schooley of the University of Colorado Medical Center in Denver, and together they embarked on a clinical trial of soluble CD4 in two dozen patients, many of them in the later stages of AIDS. Unfortunately, Ho and Schooley wound up proving that soluble CD4 doesn't work. In the process, however, they discovered something very interesting—that there were tens of thousands of infectious viral particles in their patients' bodies, a lot more than anyone had expected.

It took Ho only a few weeks to figure out why soluble CD4 didn't work. The early tests on the treatment were done on weak strains of virus grown in the lab. Somehow wild viruses could tell which CD4 molecules were decoys. Ho and the rest of the AIDS scientists had just learned a valuable lesson. They would have to test all their potential treatments on viruses that infected real patients.

BACK TO BASICS

The experience with soluble CD4 showed Ho that there were significant gaps in science's understanding of the life cycle of HIV. He decided to revisit his earlier Boston work on the first stages of infection. By hanging out in hospital emergency rooms and talking to colleagues, he and his team at UCLA identified four young homosexual men suffering from the flu-like symptoms of a primary HIV infection. Ho

---

OCTOBER 1986
U.S. Surgeon General C. Everett Koop issues a landmark report on the AIDS epidemic that calls for public-health measures and sex education.

FEBRUARY 1987
Flamboyant entertainer Liberace, 67, who never admitted he was homosexual, dies of *Pneumocystis carinii*, a form of pneumonia triggered by AIDS.

MAY 1987
President Ronald Reagan, who took office in 1981, makes his first speech on the AIDS epidemic.

MARCH 1987
The FDA approves the antiretroviral compound AZT (zidovudine), the first AIDS drug.

JUNE 1987
Citing public-health concerns, the U.S. bars HIV-infected immigrants and travelers from entering the country.

JULY 1987
Broadway director Michael Bennett (*A Chorus Line, Dreamgirls*) dies of AIDS at 44.

OCTOBER 1987
U.S. scientists begin preliminary tests of the first experimental AIDS vaccine on non-HIV-infected volunteers.

OCTOBER 1987
Publication of *And the Band Played On*, Randy Shilts' definitive chronicle of the AIDS epidemic. In it, he identifies "Patient Zero," a Canadian airline steward named Gaetan Dugas. Dugas, right, who was one of the first people in North America infected with HIV, estimated that he had had as many as 2,500 homosexual encounters before he died in 1984.

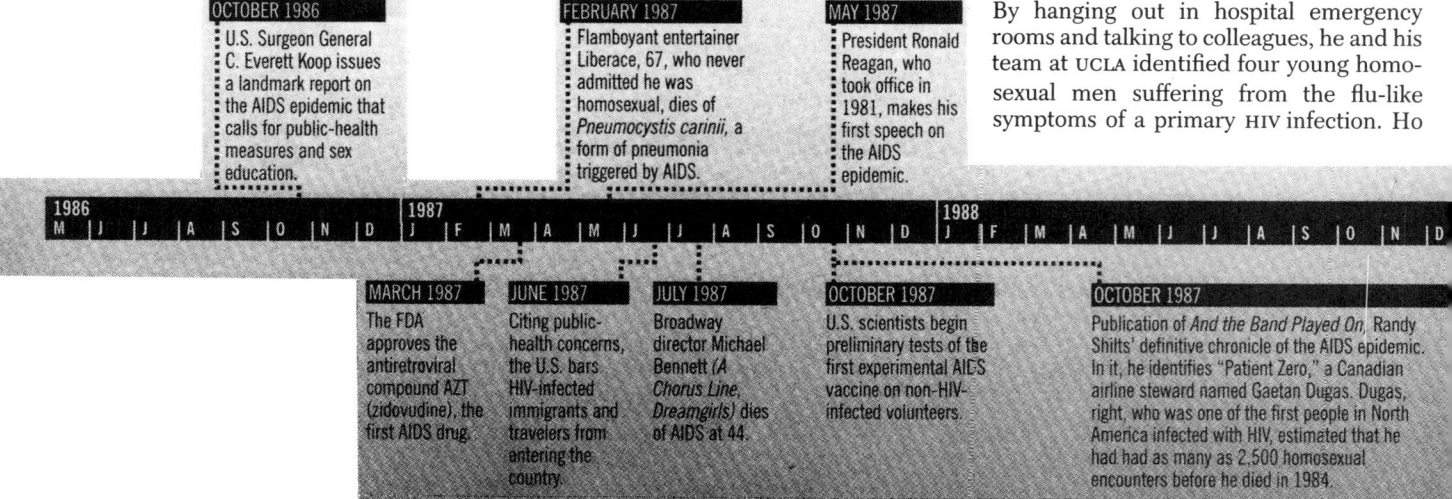

used a newly available tool of genetic engineering—the PCR test used most famously in the O.J. Simpson trial—to measure the amount of virus in the blood. Once again, he was astonished.

By this time, most researchers agreed that people in the later stages of AIDS had large quantities of HIV in their blood. But the PCR test showed that millions of viral particles were coursing through Ho's patients' blood in the earliest weeks of infection as well—as many as could be found in someone with a full-fledged case of AIDS. Within a few weeks, the viral load plunged to low and in some cases undetectable levels. The patients recovered and seemed healthy.

Ho wasn't the only scientist who had observed this. Another team, headed by George Shaw, had seen the same spike in HIV particles followed by a precipitous drop. The two researchers learned of each other's work and decided to co-publish their findings in a 1991 issue of the *New England Journal of Medicine*. It was the beginning of a friendly but no less keen competition between the scientists.

It was also the beginning of a new phase in Ho's career. Philanthropist Irene Diamond had decided to found an AIDS research center in New York City and had chosen Ho as its director. He was 37 years old. "I took a bit of flak because everybody said, 'He's so young, he's unknown.'" she recalls. "I said, 'I don't want a star, I want a wonderful scientist.'" For his part, Ho considered the benefits of having more lab space and secure financial backing. "It was still a risky venture," he remembers. "Marty Hirsch said, 'You're crazy. This is New York City. The politics will eat you up.'" But for Ho, the chance to do what he wanted, and to attract top-level scientists to join him, was too good to pass up.

Ho and Shaw had proved that there are high levels of virus in the first few weeks of infection. Ho and Schooley had already shown that there is a lot more virus in the end stages of AIDS than anyone had thought possible. The next question was obvious: What is going on during those middle years, when patients are still in relatively good health? Ho suspected that the answer could dramatically change the way doctors treated their HIV-positive patients.

All the blood tests indicated that the viral load was close to zero throughout the middle years, though it would gradually increase as time went by. Both Ho and Shaw realized, however, that zero doesn't always equal zero in the world of HIV. For one thing, the virus might be hiding out in the lymph nodes, where it could be producing thousands or even millions of copies of itself every day. As long as the immune system cleared those infectious particles as quickly as they formed, blood tests would show no change in viral load. "It's like a person running on a treadmill," Ho explains. It doesn't matter how fast they run. To an observer, they appear to be staying in place.

Not even the greatest marathoner could keep up that pace forever. If the virus reproduced very quickly, it would eventually exhaust the body's defenses. At least that's what Ho and Shaw thought. The trick to proving their idea was to find some way to suddenly stop the treadmill. If you did that to a jogger, he would lurch forward. Similarly, if you stopped HIV's cycle of reproduction in the blood, the immune system should suddenly rebound. By measuring that rebound, the scientists hoped to figure out just how rapidly the virus had been reproducing.

Great idea, in theory. There was just one problem: no one knew how to stop HIV that quickly. AZT wasn't powerful enough to do it. The pharmaceutical companies, however, had just started looking at a new class of substances, called protease inhibitors, that might fit the bill. As it turned out, it took several years of testing to come up with a formula for a protease inhibitor that was effective against HIV.

38. Disease Detective

REINFORCEMENTS

The year was 1994, and the new drugs were finally producing good results in the test tube. They worked against laboratory strains of the virus; they worked against viral samples taken from patients. Where AZT merely slowed viral reproduction, the protease inhibitors shut it down almost completely. Unfortunately, almost wasn't good enough. It often took less than a month for a few viral particles to mutate into a strain that was resistant to protease inhibitors. The new drugs were starting to look like another failure.

But a few weeks was all that Ho and Shaw needed to conduct their rebound experiments. The two laboratories raced to find the answer.

Ho chose 20 volunteers whose T cells had dropped from a normal level of about 1,000 cells per ml of blood to fewer than 500. The newest PCR tests showed that the viral load of these patients was holding steady at about 100,000 copies per ml of blood. Ho started treating his subjects with one of the new protease inhibitors being developed by Abbott Laboratories. As expected, the amount of virus that could be measured in the patients' blood practically disappeared. The treadmill had been stopped. But no one was ready for what happened next.

Preliminary calculations indicated that the immune system was rebounding faster than anyone had thought possible. The results showed that in every day of every year, in every infected person, HIV produced not thousands, not millions, but *billions* of copies of itself. And every day the body launched billions of immune cells to counter the threat. The wonder was not that the immune system eventually crashed. Given such intense fighting and heavy casualties, the wonder was that it lasted so long. Ho and Shaw came up with the answer at the same time and published

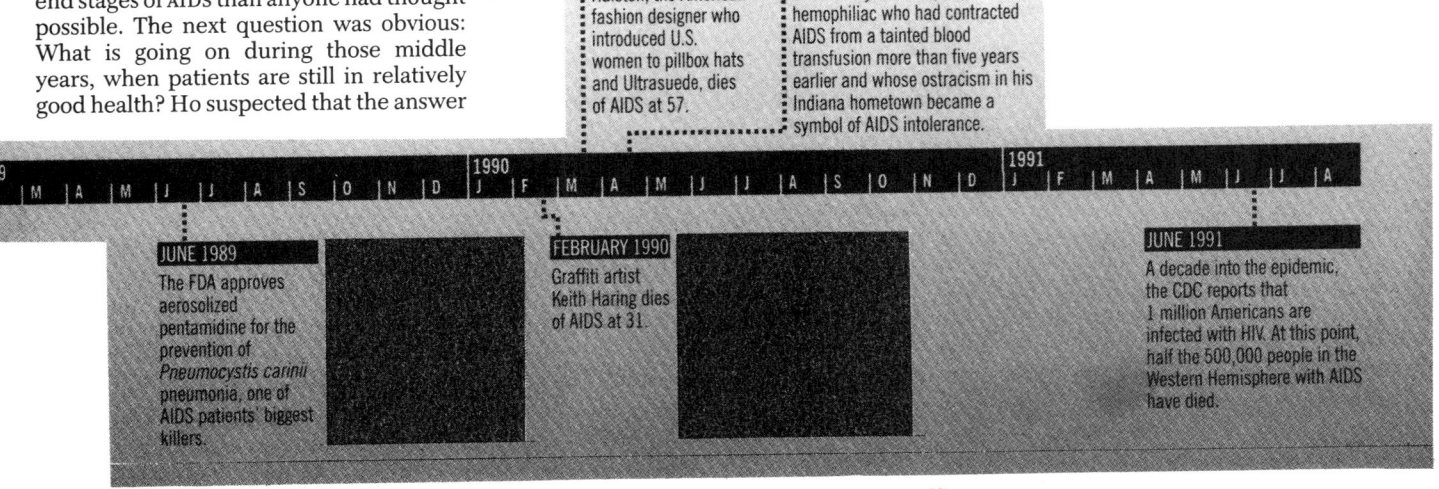

JUNE 1989
The FDA approves aerosolized pentamidine for the prevention of *Pneumocystis carinii* pneumonia, one of AIDS patients' biggest killers.

FEBRUARY 1990
Graffiti artist Keith Haring dies of AIDS at 31.

MARCH 1990
Halston, the American fashion designer who introduced U.S. women to pillbox hats and Ultrasuede, dies of AIDS at 57.

APRIL 1990
Death of Ryan White, 18, a hemophiliac who had contracted AIDS from a tainted blood transfusion more than five years earlier and whose ostracism in his Indiana hometown became a symbol of AIDS intolerance.

JUNE 1991
A decade into the epidemic, the CDC reports that 1 million Americans are infected with HIV. At this point, half the 500,000 people in the Western Hemisphere with AIDS have died.

7. CURRENT KILLERS

their results in back-to-back articles in a 1995 issue of *Nature*.

Suddenly the entire picture of AIDS had changed. As long as doctors thought that the virus was not very active through the early and middle years of infection, it made sense to conserve forces and delay treatment so they would be ready for the virus when it emerged from hibernation. Now it was becoming clear that the immune system needed all the help it could get right from the start.

But where would that help come from? Boston's Martin Hirsch and other virologists had already started looking to cancer research for inspiration. Oncologists have learned that it is often better to combine the firepower of several different chemotherapeutic drugs than to rely on any single medication to destroy cancer cells. Too often, they have found, the one-drug approach allows a few malignant cells to survive and blossom into an even more lethal tumor. The AIDS researchers faced a similar problem with HIV. Whenever they prescribed a single drug, such as AZT, for their patients, a few viral particles would survive and give rise to drug-resistant HIV.

Now that the protease inhibitors had become available, doctors were eager to combine them with the old standby AZT and a third drug called 3TC. A couple of mathematical models—created by one of Ho's collaborators, Alan Perelson of the Los Alamos National Laboratory—suggested that HIV would have a hard time simultaneously undergoing the minimum three mutations necessary to resist combination therapy. He placed the odds at 10 million to 1. It was at least worth a try.

HOPE AT LAST
For once in the history of HIV, a strategy that ought to work seemed in fact to succeed. Within weeks of starting combination therapy, 7 out of 10 men and women with AIDS begin to get better. Blood tests show that in many of them, the viral load has dropped below detectable levels. Relieved of the burden of fighting HIV, their long-suffering immune systems can finally tackle the deadly fungal and bacterial infections that have taken hold in their lungs, intestines and brains. Fevers break; lesions disappear; energy returns.

With the virus under control in at least some AIDS patients, doctors are considering how to rebuild their battered immune systems. After a decade of fighting HIV, many of the body's defensive reserves have been thoroughly depleted and cannot be regenerated from within. Researchers plan to grow replacement cells in the laboratory for transplant into recovering patients. Before the advent of combination therapy, no one would have considered such a rescue effort because the unchecked virus would have rapidly destroyed the new implants.

It all sounds so hopeful. Why don't scientists say at the very least that they're close to the cure? For the same reason that Ho did not promise the crowd in Vancouver that he could eliminate HIV from people in the later stages of the infection. Researchers know that after years of infection, there isn't a hiding place in the body that the virus hasn't penetrated. A cure must do much more than clear HIV from the bloodstream. It must remove the virus from the lymph nodes, the brain, the spinal fluid, the male's testes and everywhere else it may be hiding. Today's combination therapies work in the blood, but they don't reach into the brain or the testes very well.

Chances are that people in the later stages of the disease will have to stay on combination therapy the rest of their lives—assuming they can tolerate the often excruciating side effects, which range from diarrhea and fatigue to spasms, kidney stones and liver damage. They also have to bear in mind that they are probably still infectious and that eventually—perhaps in a few years, perhaps longer—their immune systems will probably once again collapse.

But what if you could avoid all those problems, Ho wondered. What if you didn't wait until the end stages of the disease but started combination therapy during the first few weeks of the infection, before too many billion viral particles had formed, before resistance became inevitable, before too many billion immune cells had died in the body's defense? Would you have tilted the odds enough in the immune system so that it could wipe out whatever stragglers might be left, wherever they were hiding?

To find out, Ho and one of his team, Dr. Martin Markowitz, recruited two dozen men in the earliest stages of infection and placed them on combination therapy. All the men appeared healthy before treatment. For them, ironically, the first signs of illness have been the side effects of the drugs they are taking, not the virus. Three have dropped out because they couldn't take the nausea and cramping.

Some of the men have been treated for more than a year. None of them show any trace of HIV in any of their blood. Ho has not forgotten, however, that zero does not always equal zero. He and Markowitz are looking for pockets of virus in the lymph tissue, the semen and the spinal fluid.

Ho believes that prospects for success are good. Assuming that nothing has been overlooked, combination therapy should burn the virus out of the body in two to three years, according to Perelson's latest mathematical models. Because treatment began so early, the men's immune systems should be able to replace any lost defen-

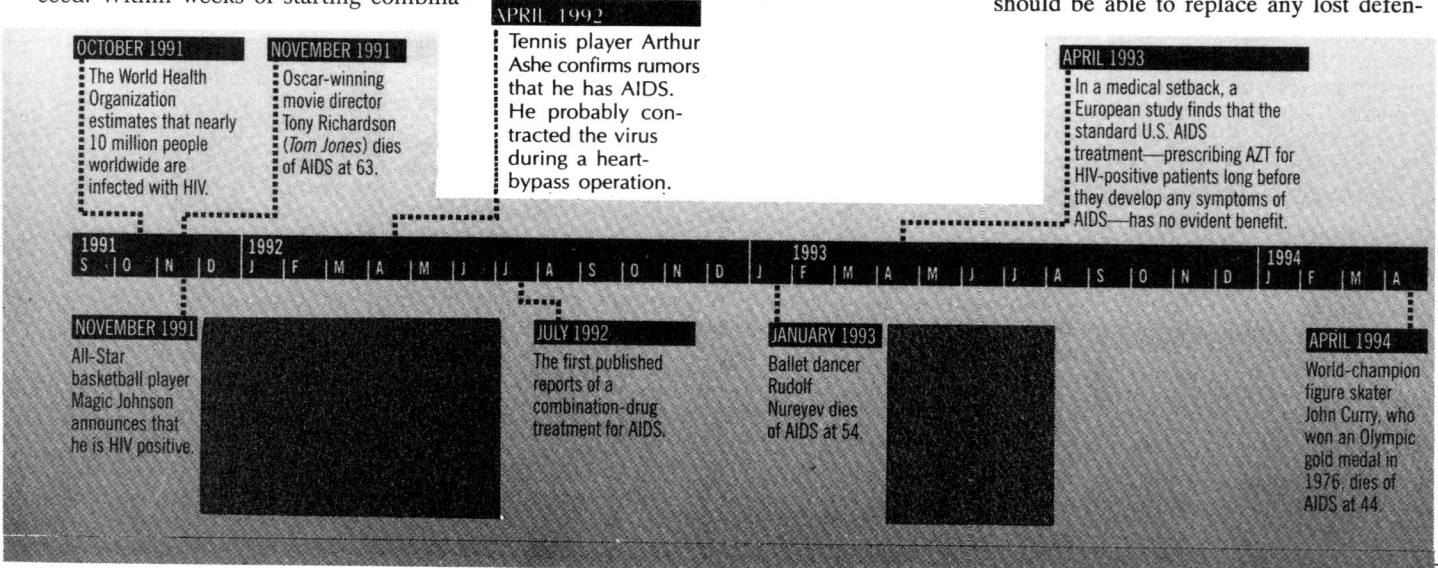

OCTOBER 1991
The World Health Organization estimates that nearly 10 million people worldwide are infected with HIV.

NOVEMBER 1991
Oscar-winning movie director Tony Richardson (*Tom Jones*) dies of AIDS at 63.

APRIL 1992
Tennis player Arthur Ashe confirms rumors that he has AIDS. He probably contracted the virus during a heart-bypass operation.

APRIL 1993
In a medical setback, a European study finds that the standard U.S. AIDS treatment—prescribing AZT for HIV-positive patients long before they develop any symptoms of AIDS—has no evident benefit.

NOVEMBER 1991
All-Star basketball player Magic Johnson announces that he is HIV positive.

JULY 1992
The first published reports of a combination-drug treatment for AIDS.

JANUARY 1993
Ballet dancer Rudolf Nureyev dies of AIDS at 54.

APRIL 1994
World-champion figure skater John Curry, who won an Olympic gold medal in 1976, dies of AIDS at 44.

38. Disease Detective

sive cells. There is still a chance that bits of the virus, called proviral DNA, are lodged in the chromosomes, beyond the reach of even the most powerful drugs. Ho has studied these vestigial snippets of genetic information and believes they are defective and cannot give rise to a new generation of HIV. Other scientists are not so sure. The only way to find out is to stop the medication and see if the virus comes back.

None of Ho's patients plan to take that step anytime soon. And he doesn't blame them. Just a few surviving viruses could manufacture enough copies to re-saturate a body in a matter of days, forcing the patient to start the long treatment process all over again. But at least one of Ho's patients has agreed to stop taking his drugs in another year or two—after his doctors assure him that tests show no evidence of HIV in his lymph, semen, spinal fluid or elsewhere in his body. When he does, we will know, probably within a few weeks, whether the virus has returned or whether it is gone for good.

Even if the virus stages a comeback, that doesn't necessarily mean that combination therapy has totally failed. It may be that additional ingredients could eliminate the virus completely. Ho has already started using a combination of four drugs in another early-intervention trial. And he has access to new, experimental medications that can better penetrate the brain and perhaps the testes. These drugs may help patients in later stages of the disease whose infections have become resistant to current treatments.

There is still a long way to go, both in the quest for an effective treatment and in the search for a way to prevent infection in the first place. In the flush of the new optimism, some scientists are more hopeful about the prospects for gene therapy, which could possibly make the immune system impervious to HIV attack. Another promising line of research centers on a group of molecules called chemokines, which may one day be used to shield cells from HIV. Other scientists, including Ho, are intensifying their search for a vaccine. Two weeks ago, the NIH increased its budget for AIDS-vaccine research 18%—to $129 million—and named Nobel-prize-winning molecular biologist David Baltimore to head the effort.

It has taken the collaborative work of thousands of scientists and physicians to get this far. It will take even greater cooperation and well-funded coordination to overcome the remaining hurdles. But the worst fear—the one that seeded a decade with despair, the foreboding sense that the AIDS virus might be invincible—has finally been subdued.—*Reported by Alice Park/New York and Dick Thompson/Washington*

For more information, visit our Man of the Year Website at **time.com/moy**

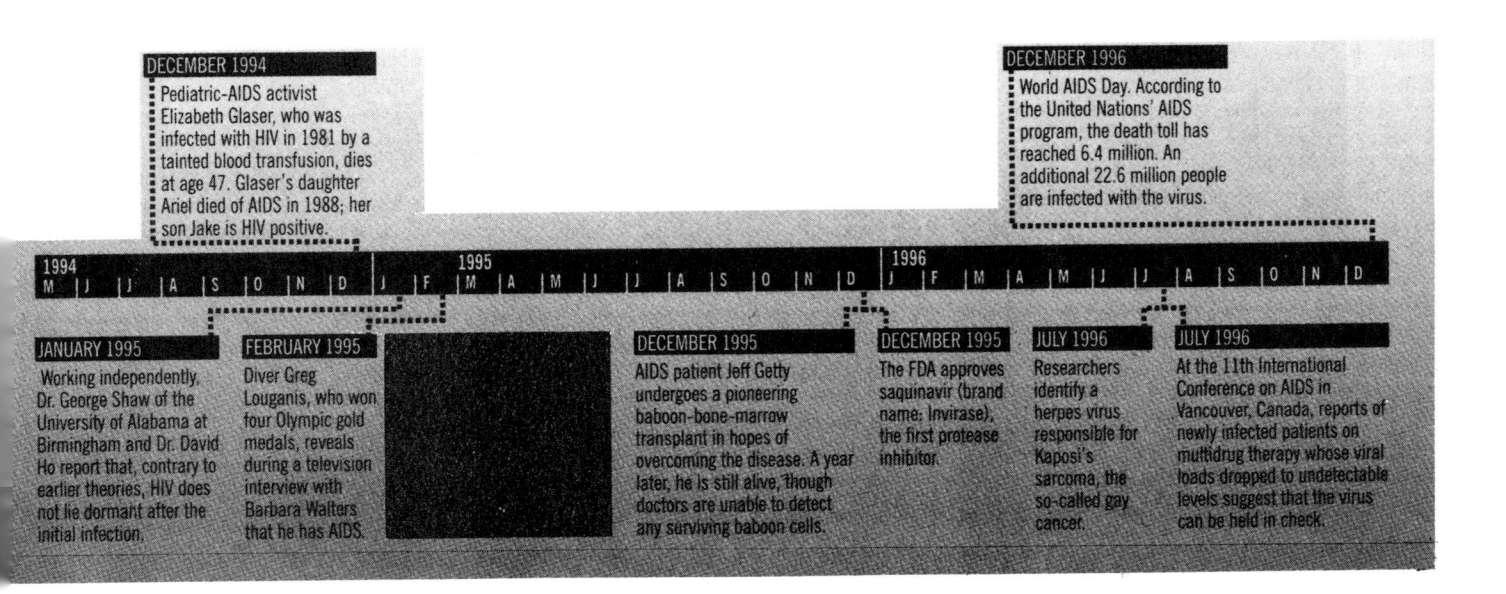

DECEMBER 1994
Pediatric-AIDS activist Elizabeth Glaser, who was infected with HIV in 1981 by a tainted blood transfusion, dies at age 47. Glaser's daughter Ariel died of AIDS in 1988; her son Jake is HIV positive.

DECEMBER 1996
World AIDS Day. According to the United Nations' AIDS program, the death toll has reached 6.4 million. An additional 22.6 million people are infected with the virus.

JANUARY 1995
Working independently, Dr. George Shaw of the University of Alabama at Birmingham and Dr. David Ho report that, contrary to earlier theories, HIV does not lie dormant after the initial infection.

FEBRUARY 1995
Diver Greg Louganis, who won four Olympic gold medals, reveals during a television interview with Barbara Walters that he has AIDS.

DECEMBER 1995
AIDS patient Jeff Getty undergoes a pioneering baboon-bone-marrow transplant in hopes of overcoming the disease. A year later, he is still alive, though doctors are unable to detect any surviving baboon cells.

DECEMBER 1995
The FDA approves saquinavir (brand name: Invirase), the first protease inhibitor.

JULY 1996
Researchers identify a herpes virus responsible for Kaposi's sarcoma, the so-called gay cancer.

JULY 1996
At the 11th International Conference on AIDS in Vancouver, Canada, reports of newly infected patients on multidrug therapy whose viral loads dropped to undetectable levels suggest that the virus can be held in check.

America's Health and the Health Care System

Americans are healthier today than at any time in this nation's history. Americans suffer more illness today than at any time in this nation's history. Which statement is true? They both are, depending on the statistics you quote. According to longevity statistics, Americans are living longer today and, therefore, must be healthier. Still other statistics indicate that Americans today report twice as many acute illnesses as did our parents and grandparents 60 years ago. They also report that their discomfort lasts longer. Unfortunately, this combination of living longer and feeling sicker places additional demands on a health care system that, according to experts, is already in a state of crisis. How severe is the health care crisis? What has caused it? Who is responsible? What can and should be done to solve it? This unit will explore these questions and present some possible solutions.

The American health care system is one of the best in the world. Nevertheless, each year over 1,000,000 Americans are injured or die due to preventable mistakes made by medical care professionals. In addition, countless unnecessary tests are performed that not only add to the expense of health care but may actually place patients at risk. "Your Hospital Stay: A Guide to Survival" discusses several steps that patients can take to protect themselves from the hazards of hospitalization.

One of the most distressing developments over the last several years has been the decline of the doctor-patient relationship. This relationship, once considered the cornerstone of medical care, has been subverted by a combination of economic forces, medical technology, and the restrictive nature of managed care. As the gap between the salaries of physicians and the public they serve has grown, so has public distrust of physicians. One measure of this distrust is the number of malpractice suits filed against physicians. The threat of malpractice has led many physicians to practice defensive medicine, in which physicians order unnecessary medical tests for their patients as a hedge against litigation. In addition to wasting billions of dollars, this approach to medicine subjects patients to unnecessary risks associated with the medical tests. Who is to blame? The answer is, "the system." And the focus seems to have shifted from the emotional and medical needs of patients to the financial concerns of doctors and the health care system.

Another indication of Americans' dissatisfaction with the current health care system is the number of visits made by individuals to unorthodox medical practitioners. Estimates suggest that patients make 425 million visits a year to massage therapists, homeopaths, herbalists, and other alternative healers. Are they legitimate, or are they just preying on people's ignorance and false hopes? Katherine Griffin's article, "The New Doctors of Natural Medicine," examines the growth of naturopaths in the Pacific Northwest region of the United States and discusses how they are being received by both the medical and social communities.

From the discovery of the smallpox vaccine and penicillin to the first heart transplant, the marriage of modern medicine and science has seemed a perfect match. Over the last 30 years, Americans have witnessed some remarkable scientific breakthroughs that have revolutionized the diagnosis and treatment of a variety of illnesses. While medical advances have served to establish America as the leader in medical technology, waste, inefficiency, and greed have so corrupted the system that millions of Americans can no longer afford basic health care. To better understand the gravity of the problem, consider that Americans spent over $817 billion dollars on health care in 1992, (which represents approximately 14 percent of the gross national product). If health care costs continue to grow at this rate for the next 40 years, they will account for 37 percent of the GNP by the year 2030. Simultaneously, the number of uninsured Americans has risen from 28 percent in 1992 to 40 percent in 1996. Although Americans spend more than twice as much per capita on health care as the average for industrialized nations, the United States ranks twenty-first in infant mortality, seventeenth in male life expectancy, and sixteenth in female life expectancy.

Why have health care costs risen so high? The answer includes physicians' fees, hospital costs, insurance costs, pharmaceutical costs, and health fraud. It could be argued that while these factors operate in any health care system, the lack of a meaningful form of outcomes assessment has permitted and encouraged waste and inefficiency in our system. Clearly ours is not the only health care system plagued by waste and inefficiency, but figures as high as 20 percent are outrageous and earn the United States the dubious distinction as the most wasteful and inefficient health care system among industrialized nations.

Ironically, one factor driving up the cost of health care is an ever-expanding aging population, which is the direct result of improved health care within this country. Yet another factor which is often overlooked as a major contributor to rising health care costs is the constantly expanding boundaries of the domain of health care. "Health Unlimited" by Willard Gaylin discusses how our success in treating various disorders has expanded health care

UNIT 8

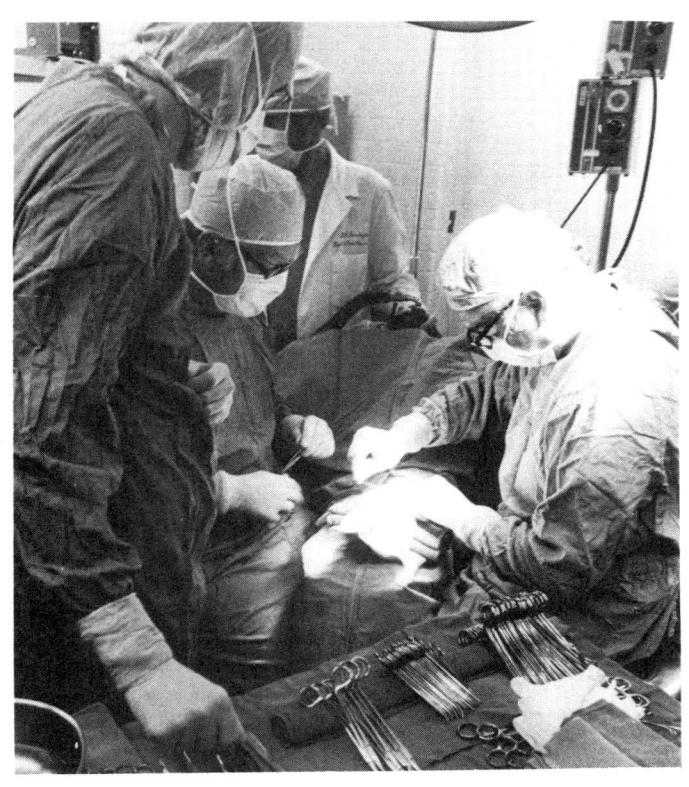

into areas where it once had little or no involvement. His discussion is both insightful and pragmatic in asking how far we should go and on what criteria we should base our rationing of health care.

The buzzword in health care over the last few years has been cost containment, but little has actually been done to cut costs. The primary strategy currently being employed is managed care. "Can HMO's Help Solve the Health-Care Crisis?" examines this issue in detail and discusses what we can realistically expect in the way of cost-cutting through managed care. Of the total health care bill, physicians' fees account for approximately 19 percent. Fees-for-service have risen steadily in response to reimbursement through third-party payors such as Medicare and private health insurance. Prior to this method of payment, doctors charged less because fees came directly out of their patients' pockets, which influenced physicians not to overcharge. It is ironic that the third-party payment plan that was introduced as a way to guarantee affordable health care for Americans has become a major factor fueling the rapid rise in the cost of health care. This form of reimbursement has not only reduced incentives to keep prices down but has triggered a monstrous paper shuffle that accounts for approximately 20 cents of every dollar spent on health care. Peter Ferrara's "Medical Savings Accounts: A Solution to Financing Health Care?" discusses how this concept reinstates market competition. Whether or not such accounts become a major force in health care, they do appear to be a viable alternative to third-party payments.

One area of health care costs that is often considered immutable is the cost of medical technology and pharmaceuticals. In fact, Americans pay substantially higher prices for pharmaceuticals and diagnostic tests than do citizens of any other industrialized country. Manufacturers argue that their prices are necessary if they are to continue to pour large sums of money into research and development in order to satisfy the stringent guidelines established by the Food and Drug Administration. It can also be argued that the reason technological advances have not resulted in lower health care costs is because our system does not include a means for evaluating outcomes and determining which medical procedures are most effective.

Additionally, Americans have exhibited an unhealthy dependence on providers to determine their state of health. We might all be better off if we accepted more personal responsibility for our health. At this time, the future of the American health care system is uncertain, but one thing is clear—change is coming.

Looking Ahead: Challenge Questions

Should health care be treated differently from other consumer services?

What role should alternative health practitioners have in our health care system? Would you consider going to one? On what basis would you make your decision?

Is quality health care a right or a privilege?

How have third-party payments contributed to the rising cost of health care in America?

How do medical savings accounts help to control health care costs?

What steps can you take to reduce your risk of injury during hospitalization?

How could outcomes assessment help reduce health care costs? Do you think there is likely to be much resistance to such efforts? Why?

What medical tests should a patient expect to undergo during a routine medical examination?

# Health Unlimited

Willard Gaylin

WILLARD GAYLIN, M.D., *is professor of psychiatry at Columbia University Medical School and cofounder and president of the Hastings Center, an institution devoted to bioethical research. His most recent book, with Bruce Jennings, is* The Perversion of Autonomy, *published by the Free Press.*

The debate over the current crisis in health care often seems to swirl like a dust storm, generating little but further obfuscation as it drearily goes around and around. And no wonder. Attempts to explain how we got into this mess—and it is a mess—seem invariably to begin in precisely the wrong place. Most experts have been focusing on the failures and deficiencies of modern medicine. The litany is familiar: greedy physicians, unnecessary procedures, expensive technologies, and so on. Each of these certainly adds its pennyweight to the scales. But even were we to make angels out of doctors and philanthropists out of insurance company executives, we would not stem the rise of healthcare costs. That is because this increase, far from being a symptom of modern medicine's failure, is a product of its success.

Good medicine keeps sick people alive. It increases the percentage of people in the population with illnesses. The fact that there are proportionally more people with arteriosclerotic heart disease, diabetes, essential hypertension, and other chronic—and expensive—diseases in the United States than there are in Iraq, Nigeria, or Colombia paradoxically signals the triumph of the American healthcare system.

There is another and perhaps even more important way in which modern medicine keeps costs rising: by altering our very definition of sickness and vastly expanding the boundaries of what is considered the domain of health care. This process is not entirely new. Consider this example. As I am writing now, I am using reading glasses, prescribed on the basis of an ophthalmologist's diagnosis of presbyopia, a loss of acuity in close range vision. Before the invention of the glass lens, there was no such disease as presbyopia. It simply was expected that old people wouldn't be able to read without difficulty, if indeed they could read at all. Declining eyesight, like diminished hearing, potency, and fertility, was regarded as an inevitable part of growing older. But once impairments are no longer perceived as inevitable, they become curable impediments to healthy functioning—illnesses in need of treatment.

To understand how the domain of health care has expanded, one must go back to the late 19th century, when modern medicine was born in the laboratories of Europe—mainly those of France and Germany. Through the genius of researchers such as Wilhelm Wundt, Rudolph Virchow, Robert Koch, and Louis Pasteur, a basic understanding of human physiology was established, the foundations of pathology were laid, and the first true understanding of the nature of disease—the germ theory—was developed. Researchers and physicians now had a much better understanding of what was going on in the human body, but there was still little they could do about it. As late as 1950, a distinguished physiologist could tell an incoming class of medical students that, until then, medical intervention had taken more lives than it had saved.

Even as this truth was being articulated, however, a second revolution in medicine was under way. It was only after breakthroughs in the late 1930s and during World War II that the age of therapeutic medicine began to emerge. With the discovery of the sulfonamides, and then of penicillin and a series of major antibiotics, medicine finally became what the laity in its ignorance had always assumed it to be: a lifesaving enterprise. We in the medical profession became very effective at treating sick people and saving lives—so effective, in fact, that until the advent of AIDS (acquired immune deficiency syndrome), we arrogantly assumed that we had conquered infectious diseases.

The control of infection and the development of new anesthetics permitted extraordinary medical interventions that previously had been inconceivable. As a result, the traditional quantitative methods of evaluating alternative procedures became outmoded. "Survival days," for example, was traditionally the one central measurement by which various treatments for a cancer were weighed. If one treatment averaged 100 survival days and another averaged 50 survival days, then the first treatment was considered, if not twice as good, at least superior. But today, the new antibiotics permit surgical procedures so extravagant and extreme that the old standard no longer makes sense. An oncologist once made this point using an example that remains indelibly imprinted on my mind: 100 days of survival without a face, he observed, may not be superior to 50 days of survival with a face.

Introducing considerations of the nature or quality of survival adds a whole new dimension to the definitions of sickness and health. Increasingly, to be "healthy," one must not only be free of disease but enjoy a good "quality of life." Happiness, self-fulfillment, and enrichment have been added to the criteria for medical treatment. This has set the stage for a profound expansion of the concept of health and a changed perception of the ends of medicine.

I can illustrate how this process works by casting stones at my own glass house, psychiatry, even though it is not the most extreme example. The patients I deal with in my daily practice would not have been considered mentally ill in the 19th century. The concept of mental illness then described a clear and limited set of conditions. The leading causes of mental illness were tertiary syphilis and schizophrenia. Those who were mentally ill were confined to asylums. They were insane; they were different from you and me.

Let me offer a brief (and necessarily crude) history of psychiatry since then. At the turn of the century, psychiatry's first true genius, Sigmund Freud, decided that craziness was not necessarily confined to those who are completely out of touch with reality, that a normal person, like himself or people he knew, could be partly crazy. These "normal" people had in their psyches isolated areas of irrationality, with symptoms that demonstrated the same "crazy" distortions that one saw in the insane. Freud invented a new category of mental diseases that we now call the "neuroses," thereby vastly increasing the population of the mentally ill. The neuroses were characterized by such symptoms as phobias, compulsions, anxiety attacks, and hysterical conversions.

In the 1930s, Wilhelm Reich went further. He decided that one does not even have to exhibit a neurosis to be mentally ill, that one can suffer from "character disorders." An individual could be totally without symptoms of any illness, yet the nature of his character might so limit his productivity or his pleasure in life that we might justifiably (or not) label him "neurotic."

Still later, in the 1940s and '50s, medicine "discovered" the psychosomatic disorders. There are people who have no evidence of mental illness or impairment but have physical conditions with psychic roots, such as peptic ulcers, ulcerative colitis, migraine headache, and allergy. They, too, were now classifiable as mentally ill. By such imaginative expansions, we eventually managed to get some 60 to 70 percent of the population (as one study of the residents of Manhattan's Upper East Side did) into the realm of the mentally ill.

But we still were short about 30 percent. The mental hygiene movement and preventive medicine solved that problem. When one takes a preventive approach, encompassing both the mentally ill and the potentially mentally ill, the universe expands to include the entire population.

Thus, by progressively expanding the definition of mental illness, we took in more and more of the populace. The same sort of growth has happened with health in general, as can be readily demonstrated in surgery, orthopedics, gynecology, and virtually all other fields of medicine. Until recently, for example, infertility was not considered a disease. It was a God-given condition. With the advances in modern medicine—in vitro fertilization, artificial insemination, and surrogate mothering—a whole new array of cures was discovered for "illnesses" that had to be invented. And this, of course, meant new demands for dollars to be spent on health care.

One might question the necessity of some of these expenditures. Many knee operations, for instance, are performed so that the individual can continue to play golf or to ski, and many elbow operations are done for tennis buffs. Are these things for which anyone other than the amateur athlete himself should pay? If a person is free of pain except when playing tennis, should not the only insurable prescription be—much as the old

8. AMERICA'S HEALTH AND THE HEALTH CARE SYSTEM

joke has it—to stop playing tennis? How much "quality of life" is an American entitled to have?

New technologies also exert strong pressure to expand the domain of health. Consider the seemingly rather undramatic development of the electronic fetal monitor. It used to be that when a pregnant woman in labor came to a hospital—if she came at all—she was "observed" by a nurse, who at frequent intervals checked the fetal heartbeat with a stethoscope. If it became more rapid, suggesting fetal distress, a Caesarean section was considered. But once the electronic fetal monitor came into common use in the 1970s, continuous monitoring by the device became standard. As a result, there was a huge increase in the number of Caesareans performed in major teaching hospitals across the country, to the point that 30 to 32 percent of the pregnant women in those hospitals were giving birth through surgery. It is ridiculous to suggest that one out of three pregnancies requires surgical intervention. Yet technology, or rather the seductiveness of technology, has caused that to happen.

Linked to the national enthusiasm for high technology is the archetypically American reluctance to acknowledge that there are limits, not just limits to health care but limits to anything. The American character is different. Why this is so was suggested some years ago by historian William Leuchtenberg in a lecture on the meaning of the frontier. To Europeans, he explained, the frontier *meant* limits. You sowed seed up to the border and then you had to stop; you cut timber up to the border and then you had to stop; you journeyed across your country to the border and then you had to stop. In America, the frontier had exactly the opposite connotation: it was where things began. If you ran out of timber, you went to the frontier, where there was more; if you ran out of land, again, you went to the frontier for more. Whatever it was that you ran out of, you would find more if you kept pushing forward. That is our historical experience, and it is a key to the American character. We simply refuse to accept limits. Why should the provision of health care be an exception?

To see that it isn't, all one need do is consider Americans' infatuation with such notions as "death with dignity," which translates into death without dying, and "growing old gracefully," which on close inspection turns out to mean living a long time without aging. The only "death with dignity" that most American men seem willing to accept is to die in one's sleep at the age of 92 after winning three sets of tennis from one's 40-year-old grandson in the afternoon and making passionate love to one's wife twice in the evening. This does indeed sound like a wonderful way to go—but it may not be entirely realistic to think that that is what lies in store for most of us.

During the past 25 years, health-care costs in the United States have risen from six percent of the gross national product to about 14 percent. If spending continues on its current trajectory, it will bankrupt the country. To my knowledge, there is no way to alter that trajectory except by limiting access to health care and by limiting the incessant expansion of the concept of health. There is absolutely no evidence that the costs of health-care services can be brought under control through improved management techniques alone. So-called managed care saves money, for the most part, by offering less—by covert allocation. Expensive, unprofitable operations such as burn centers, neonatal intensive care units, and emergency rooms are curtailed or eliminated (with the comforting, if perhaps unrealistic, thought that municipal and university hospitals will make up the difference).

Rationing, when done, should not be hidden; nor should it be left to the discretion of a relative handful of health-care managers. It requires open discussion and wide participation. When that which we are rationing is life itself, the decisions as to how, what, and when must be made by a consensus of the public at large through its elected and other representatives, in open debate.

What factors ought to be considered in weighing claims on scarce and expensive services? An obvious one is age. This suggestion is often met with violent abuse and accusations of "age-ism," or worse. But age *is* a factor. Surely, most of us would agree that, *all other things being equal*, a 75-year-old man (never mind a 92-year-old man) has less claim on certain scarce resources, such as an organ transplant, than a 32-year-old mother or a 16-year-old boy. But, of course, other things often are not equal. Suppose the 75-year-old man is president of the United States and the 32-year-old mother is a drug addict, or the 16-year-old boy is a high school dropout. We need, in as dispassionate and disinterested a way as possible, to consider what other factors besides age should be taken into account. Should political position count? Character? General health? Marital status? Number of dependents?

Rationing is already being done through market mechanisms, with access to kidney or liver transplants and other scarce and expensive procedures determined by such factors as how much money one has or how close one lives to a major healthcare center. Power and celebrity can also play a role—which explains why politicians and professional athletes suddenly turn up at the top of waiting lists for donated organs. A fairer system is needed.

The painful but necessary decisions involved in explicit rationing are, obviously, not just medical matters—and they must not be left to physicians or health-care managers. Nor should they be left to philosophers designated as "bioethicists," though these may be helpful. The population at large will have to reach a consensus, through the messy—but noble—devices of democratic government. This will require legislation, as well as litigation and case law.

In the late 1980s, the state of Oregon began to face up to the necessity of rationing. The state legislature decided to extend Medicaid coverage to more poor people but to pay for the change by curbing Medicaid costs by explicitly rationing benefits. (Eventually, rationing was to be extended to virtually all Oregonians, but that part of the plan later ran afoul of federal regulations.) After hundreds of public hearings, a priority list of services was drawn up to guide the allocation of funds. As a result, dozens of services became difficult (but not impossible) for the poor to obtain through Medicaid. These range from psychotherapy for sexual dysfunctions and severe conduct disorder to medical therapy for chronic bronchitis and splints for TMJ Disorder, a painful jaw condition. Although the idea of explicit rationing created a furor at first, most Oregonians came to accept it. Most other Americans will have to do the same.

Our nation has a health-care crisis, and rationing is the only solution. There is no honorable way that we Americans can duck this responsibility. Despite our historical reluctance to accept limits, we must finally acknowledge that they exist, in health care, as in life itself.

Medical $avings
A Solution to Financing

Companies across the nation are replacing traditional third-party insurance, controlling costs without rationing services.

by Peter J. Ferrara

IN OFFERING his health care reform plan in 1994, Pres. Clinton indicated that one of his primary goals, in addition to universal coverage, was to rein in rapidly rising health costs. Ironically, his proposal, and similar ones by both Democrats and Republicans, only would have made the fundamental problem worse.

By expanding traditional third-party insurance to everyone and covering more services, with minimal deductibles, the reform proposal would have maximized the perverse, cost-increasing incentives of third-party coverage. With a third party guaranteeing payment of all medical bills, neither patients nor doctors significantly are concerned about costs. The result is the cost explosion the nation has seen over the past 30 years.

Medical savings accounts (MSAs) are the one reform proposal designed precisely to counter the fundamental cost-control issue. They restore direct incentives to consumers to rein in costs, which stimulates true market cost-control competition.

Moreover, they are the only plan that is consistent with maintaining quality and consumer choice. All other proposals involve shifting more power and control to some third-party bureaucracy, either the government or insurance companies, that then would limit and ration care to reduce costs. MSAs put individual consumers in control of their own health care decisions. Consumers—not the government or insurance companies—decide whether a procedure or treatment is worth the expense.

MSAs are far more than a theory. Despite the heavy discrimination against them in the current Federal income tax code, employers and workers across the country have begun establishing and using MSAs in place of traditional third-party insurance. They have proved highly effective at trimming costs, as well as popular among workers.

Economists from across the political spectrum understand that one of the major factors driving health care costs is the third-party payment system that insulates consumers from the cost of their health care decisions. A third party—a private insurance company or the government through Medicare and Medicaid—usually is paying the physician and hospital bills for the patient. As a result, the patient lacks market incentives to hold down costs. He or she is not concerned with avoiding unnecessary care or tests or shopping for the best-priced care.

Because consumers lack market incentives to control costs, physicians and hospitals do not compete to reduce them. Because a third party is paying the bills, patients do not choose doctors and hospitals on the basis of cost-effectiveness. Rather, they seek to maximize quality without regard to expense. If an extra procedure or test is of even the most marginal value, they will demand it, leading to runaway expenses.

The incentive to ignore the cost of even marginal increases in quality can be seen particularly in the development and purchase of new medical technology and equipment. In most other markets, new technological advances operate to reduce costs. In health care, however, such breakthroughs often seem only to increase costs sharply. Health care providers generally are looking not for new technological advances that would reduce costs to consumers, but primarily for those that will improve quality regardless of expense, because that is what patients are looking for.

The result has been a "medical arms race" with providers adding ever more expensive technology, even if it produces only minimal improvements in quality. Attempts to control the growth of medical technology outside a functioning market have resulted in arbitrary regulatory procedures and requirements, such as certificates of need, that limit consumer choice and have had an adverse impact on the quality of care without significantly affecting costs.

Third-party payment increases health costs in at least two other important ways. First, the degree of third-party payment varies greatly among different types of health services. That often leads patients and physicians to choose services with greater insurance coverage, even though alternative services with less coverage may be at least as effective and less expensive over all. For example, a patient and doctor may choose hospitalization and surgery, which are covered completely by insurance, to treat a condition, even though it could be treated at least as well with far less expensive drug therapy, for which there is little or no insurance coverage. A 1994 study by the National Center for Policy Analysis estimates

Mr. Ferrara is senior fellow, National Center for Policy Analysis, Washington, D.C. This article is based on a Cato Institute Policy Analysis.

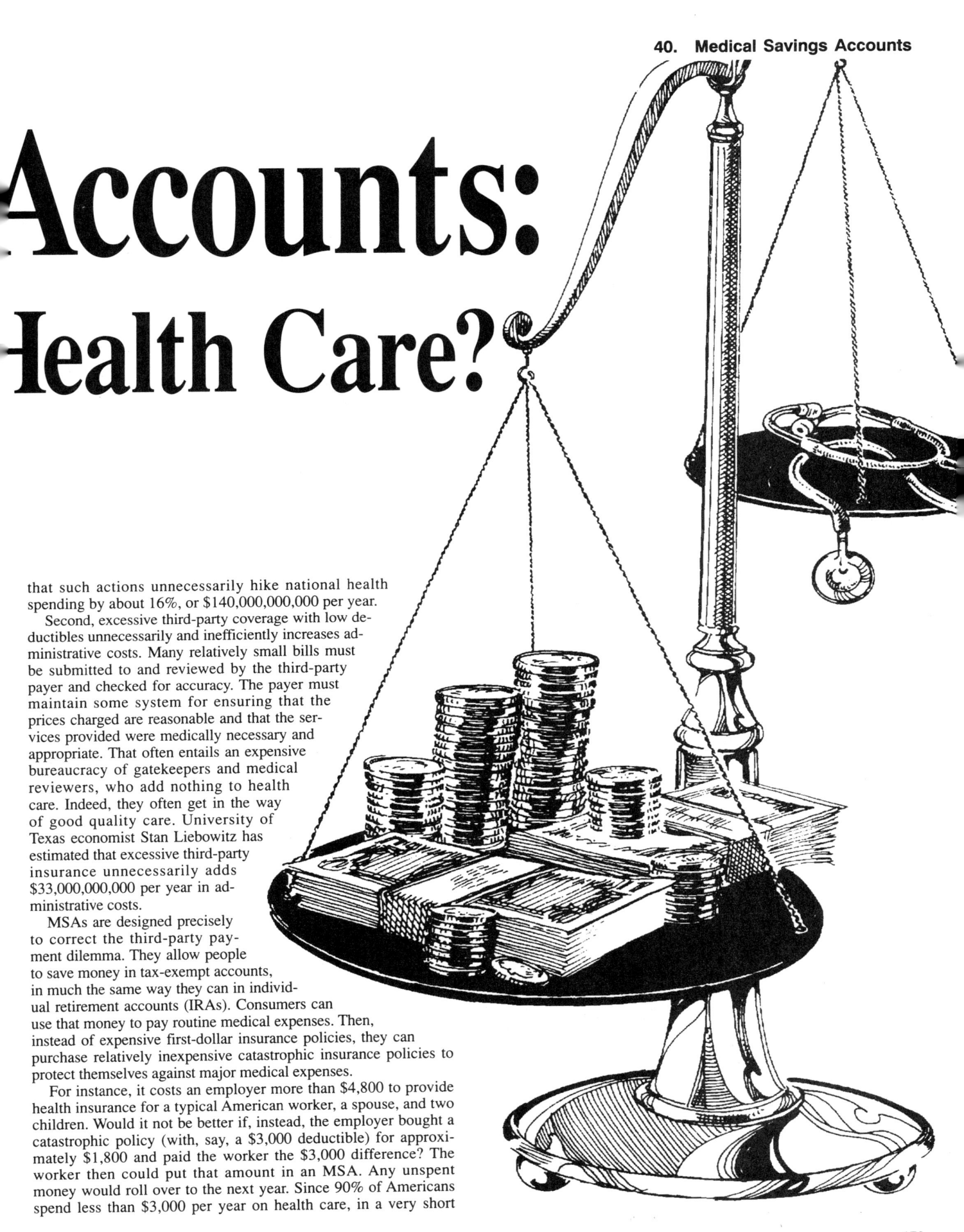

Accounts: Health Care?

40. Medical Savings Accounts

that such actions unnecessarily hike national health spending by about 16%, or $140,000,000,000 per year.

Second, excessive third-party coverage with low deductibles unnecessarily and inefficiently increases administrative costs. Many relatively small bills must be submitted to and reviewed by the third-party payer and checked for accuracy. The payer must maintain some system for ensuring that the prices charged are reasonable and that the services provided were medically necessary and appropriate. That often entails an expensive bureaucracy of gatekeepers and medical reviewers, who add nothing to health care. Indeed, they often get in the way of good quality care. University of Texas economist Stan Liebowitz has estimated that excessive third-party insurance unnecessarily adds $33,000,000,000 per year in administrative costs.

MSAs are designed precisely to correct the third-party payment dilemma. They allow people to save money in tax-exempt accounts, in much the same way they can in individual retirement accounts (IRAs). Consumers can use that money to pay routine medical expenses. Then, instead of expensive first-dollar insurance policies, they can purchase relatively inexpensive catastrophic insurance policies to protect themselves against major medical expenses.

For instance, it costs an employer more than $4,800 to provide health insurance for a typical American worker, a spouse, and two children. Would it not be better if, instead, the employer bought a catastrophic policy (with, say, a $3,000 deductible) for approximately $1,800 and paid the worker the $3,000 difference? The worker then could put that amount in an MSA. Any unspent money would roll over to the next year. Since 90% of Americans spend less than $3,000 per year on health care, in a very short time that worker probably would have a tidy pool of money available to use in the future. When the balance reached a certain level, he or she could transfer the funds to an IRA or other retirement fund.

With MSAs, therefore, workers effectively would be spending their own funds for noncatastrophic health care. As a result, they would have full market incentives to control the costs of such care. They would seek to avoid unnecessary care or tests and look for physicians and hospitals which would provide good quality care at the best prices. That, in turn, would stimulate true cost competition among physicians and hospitals. Since consumers would be choosing on the basis of cost as well as quality, providers would compete to minimize bills as well as maximize quality, as in a normal market. Accordingly, developers of innovations and new equipment would compete vigorously to produce new items that cut cost as well as improved quality.

People [that] paid for health care out of their own MSAs would eliminate the excessive third-party interference in the doctor-patient relationship.

The amount saved in premiums by switching to a policy with a $3,000 deductible would be almost enough in the first year alone to cover costs below the deductible with no greater out-of-pocket payments by the insured than under a traditional policy. In addition, the distorting effect of varying third-party coverage for different services would be eliminated, because funds in an MSA would be equally available for all health care services. Finally, administrative overhead would be reduced sharply. About half of all health expenses no longer would have to be submitted to and processed by third-party payers. They, in turn, no longer would have to monitor and check payments to determine whether they were accurate, the price charged was reasonable, and the service was medically necessary and appropriate.

That would add up to an enormous reduction in spiraling health costs. MSAs are the sole means of controlling them consistent with consumer choice and people's control over their own health care. Other proposed reforms, such as managed competition, would force people into health maintenance organizations (HMOs), in which a bureaucracy working for the insurer ultimately decides what care patients will get, or include global budgets, under which the government dictates how much may be spent on health care, reducing resources and ultimately services for the middle class and the elderly.

The public proved in the 1994 health care debates that it will not accept such rationing and third-party control. MSAs not only are the most economical means of controlling costs, they are the only politically feasible reform.

In addition to controlling costs, MSAs would provide several other advantages. First, they would improve the quality of health care. Patients paying for their own health care out of MSAs would not have to worry about obtaining permission or approval from third-party gatekeepers or whether the insurer would pay for the services or treatment that would be best for them. Increasingly, patients are being given lower quality drugs, pacemakers, joint replacements, hearing aids, and other items because the third-party payer refuses to approve the more expensive higher quality ones. That no longer would be the case with MSAs. To the extent that people paid for health care out of their own MSAs, they would eliminate the excessive third-party interference, which is increasing today, in the doctor-patient relationship.

Second, MSAs would help to reduce the number of uninsured. Those without employer-provided coverage would be able to get the same tax advantages that are provided today only to those who do have such coverage. That would lower the net cost to the uninsured of purchasing coverage. MSAs also would enable the uninsured to rely on low-cost catastrophic coverage and reap the benefits of avoiding unnecessary expenses, through end-of-year rebates of unspent MSA funds. With MSAs, the uninsured would escape most of the cost of the many unnecessary benefits state governments require be included in insurance policies, as such mandates would have just a small impact on the price of a high-deductible catastrophic policy. In addition, MSA funds could be used to pay premiums for catastrophic insurance during periods of unemployment, enabling workers to maintain coverage during such periods.

Third, MSAs would be completely portable. Employees could take their MSAs with them from job to job. Consequently, workers could avoid "job lock"—being tied to their current positions to keep the health insurance they provide. Moreover, MSAs would provide funds that could be used in the future for long-term care, long-term-care insurance, or other post-retirement medical needs not covered by Medicare.

Successful programs

Perhaps the leading example of MSAs at work is Golden Rule Insurance Co., Indianapolis, Ind. Its 1,300 workers have the option of choosing either traditional insurance coverage or an MSA. Traditional coverage includes a $500 annual deductible and 20% co-payment on the next $5,000 in expenses, for maximum out-of-pocket payments of $1,500 per year.

Alternatively, each employee can choose an MSA. For family coverage under this option, the employer purchases a catastrophic policy that pays all expenses over $3,000 annually, then deposits $2,000 in a personal MSA for the worker's family. Those funds can be withdrawn for health expenses below the deductible, leaving a maximum potential out-of-pocket expense of $1,000. For individual coverage, the employer purchases catastrophic insurance covering all expenses over $2,000 annually, then deposits $1,000 in the worker's MSA that can be used for medical expenses, again leaving a maximum out-of-pocket expense of $1,000. Whether coverage is individual or family, the employee can withdraw remaining MSA funds at the end of the year for any use.

Golden Rule first offered the MSA option to its workers in 1993. Approximately 80% chose MSAs that year. They each withdrew an average of $600 in remaining MSA funds at the end of the year to use however they chose. In 1994, about 90% elected MSAs.

Health care costs dropped precipitously for those employees. In addition to the $600 average remaining funds for each worker, health costs above the $3,000 deductible fell 40% from previous projections in 1993. Those who saved on costs below the deductible ended up not using the substantial amounts over the $3,000 deductible that they would have spent with traditional insurance.

At the same time, Golden Rule employees increased their use of preventive care. About 20% reported that they used their MSA funds to pay for a medical service they would not have bought under the traditional health insurance policy. That is because the MSA provided funds at hand that they could use to pay for such services, whereas the traditional policy imposed deductible and coinsurance fees that actually discouraged the use of such services. Moreover, the traditional policy might not cover some services, and the uncertainty alone discouraged workers from obtaining preventive care.

Even the sickest employees were better off under the MSAs at Golden Rule. Those workers faced a maximum out-of-pocket cost of $1,000 every year with the MSA. Under traditional insurance, those workers could incur annual maximum out-of-pocket expenses of $1,500.

Thompson and Associates, a health insurance marketing firm in Kansas, is offering another MSA-type plan. They combine the funding of employer-provided health care and retirement benefits in one fund for each employee so that retirement funds for the workers automatically increase as the workers' health expenses decline. Under that approach, the employer purchases catastrophic health insurance that pays all expenses over $3,000 or $4,000 per year for each employee, then puts an amount equal to the insurance deductible into an individual health and retirement account for each worker. Those funds can be used to pay for medical expenses below the deductible. Any unspent funds at the end of the year automatically go to support higher retirement benefits. The unspent funds also can be used to reimburse day-care expenses or for medical costs that may not be covered by the insurance, such as eye examinations and glasses, dental care, and prescription drugs.

A health benefits consulting firm in the Washington, D.C., area, Plan 3 Insurance, is selling still another version of MSAs. Under this approach, the employer self-insures health benefits for workers, but buys a catastrophic policy with a high deductible covering all of the company's health expenses above the deductible. For instance, a firm with 20 workers might buy a policy covering all expenses above $100,000 for the workers as a group. Such a policy would cost a small fraction of traditional first-dollar insurance coverage. The employer then would place the huge premium savings in a health fund reserve to pay for employee medical expenses below the deductible limit.

The employer covers all employee health expenses with no out-of-pocket costs for the worker. The employer sets a reference amount equivalent to a high deductible, perhaps $3,000 per year, and allows employees who incur less in covered health costs to withdraw the difference from the health fund reserve after a waiting period of three years.

The three-year waiting period allows the funds in the reserve to grow. That allows the employer to set the reference deductible at higher and higher levels over time, covering a greater proportion of total health spending with the cash rebates. Additionally, while funds are in the employer's health fund reserve, investment returns on the funds are tax-free.

Progress Sharing, an insurance-marketing firm in Saco, Maine, sells an MSA plan called Health Wealth. Workers are offered a high-deductible policy, and premium savings are placed in a mutual fund account for each worker. The funds can be used to pay out-of-pocket health expenses or withdrawn for any purpose at the end of the year.

Current Federal tax law discriminates heavily against MSAs and in favor of traditional third-party insurance coverage provided by employers.

The demonstrated success of MSAs led the United Mine Workers to negotiate successfully for them in its most recent contract. Under an agreement with the Bituminous Coal Operators Association, covering about 15,000 employees, coal mine operators now provide insurance with a $1,000 deductible replacing a zero deductible under the old health plan. The employees are given a $1,000 cash bonus at the beginning of the year that they can use for health care expenses below the deductible. At the end of the year, workers can keep for any use whatsoever any portion of the bonus they do not use for health care. The mine workers still have first-dollar coverage, but also have incentives to reduce costs and can gain directly by doing so.

State MSAs

Seven states have enacted legislation providing for MSAs in their income tax codes. Although states can not reverse the Federal tax discrimination against MSAs, they can eliminate any state tax discrimination, putting MSAs on an equal playing field under state law with traditional insurance and HMO coverage.

Arizona. Workers and employers receive tax deductions for MSA contributions of up to $2,000 for each worker, plus $1,000 apiece for as many as two dependents. Those maximum contribution limits are indexed to grow with inflation. Investment returns are tax-free, but all withdrawals, even those for health care, are included in taxable income. Funds deposited in an MSA may not be withdrawn during the year for anything but health care. Funds withdrawn for other purposes are subject to an additional 10% penalty, similar to that on premature withdrawals from IRAs. At the end of the year, all funds remaining in an MSA may be withdrawn without any penalty.

Colorado. Employer contributions to an MSA of up to $3,000 for each employee are deductible. Investment returns are tax-free, but all withdrawals are fully taxable, even those for health care. Remaining funds at the end of the year may be withdrawn for any use without additional penalty.

Idaho. Employer and worker contributions of up to $3,000 to an MSA are deductible. The contribution limit is indexed to increase with inflation each year. Investment returns are tax-free, but all withdrawals, including those for health care, are fully taxable. MSAs must be established through an employer, so the uninsured can not start them on their own to obtain coverage. Remaining funds at the end of the year can be withdrawn for any use without additional penalty.

Illinois. Employer and worker MSA contributions of up to $3,000 for each worker are deductible. The contribution limit is indexed to inflation. All investment returns are tax-free, but all withdrawals are taxable. The MSAs must be established through an employer. Any funds remaining in the MSA at year-end can be withdrawn without additional penalty.

Michigan. Employers and workers can receive a tax credit for up to $3,000 in contributions to an MSA for each worker. The credit is equal to 3.3% of contributions, the equivalent of a deduction at a 3.3% income tax rate. The contribution limit is indexed to inflation. Workers can establish MSAs independent of employers, thus helping to expand coverage.

Mississippi. Employers and individuals can establish MSAs. Contributions are tax-deductible, and the interest is tax-exempt. The maximum limit on contributions is $2,250 for individuals and $3,500 for families, but contributions may be no higher than the deductible in an accompanying catastrophic health insurance policy. Funds withdrawn for health care are tax-free, but funds withdrawn for any other purpose are subject to the regular income tax. Only funds in excess of the deductible of an accompanying catastrophic health insurance policy may be withdrawn for nonmedical purposes.

Missouri. Employers may establish MSAs for their workers, but individuals may not establish them independently.

8. AMERICA'S HEALTH AND THE HEALTH CARE SYSTEM

Contributions are not tax-deductible, but returns on MSA savings are tax-exempt. Withdrawals for medical expenses are tax-free, but any other withdrawals are subject to regular income tax. MSA funds may be withdrawn for nonmedical expenses to the extent they exceed a minimum balance established each year by state regulations.

If MSAs are so successful, why have they not been implemented more widely? The problem is that current Federal tax law discriminates heavily against MSAs and in favor of traditional third-party insurance coverage provided by employers. All that is needed is to remove that powerful bias and tax MSAs and traditional insurance equally.

If an employer pays for traditional third-party insurance for an employee, the employer receives a full tax deduction for the premiums. None of the premiums are included in employee income. All health insurance benefits also are tax-free to the worker. Any returns on health insurance reserves are not taxed, unless retained by the insurance company as profit.

In contrast, if an employer contributes to an MSA, although the employer still receives a deduction for the payments, the total of those payments is included in the employee's taxable income. While the funds are in the MSA, any returns are subject to triple taxation—the corporate income tax, capital gains tax, and individual income tax. That cripples private savings as an alternative to full third-party insurance coverage. Finally, any withdrawals from an MSA not previously taxed are included in employee income and fully taxed, even if the withdrawals are used for entirely legitimate medical expenses. Moreover, if an individual contributes to an MSA on his own, he or she receives absolutely no deduction for those contributions.

Because tax rates are so high, tax discrimination makes a big difference. For even a moderate-income worker, MSA funds included in taxable income would be subject to a 15% income tax and, effectively, the full 15.3% employer and employee shares of the Social Security and Medicare payroll tax. If the worker is subject to a common six percent state and local income tax as well, MSAs are effectively subject to a 36.3% tax in comparison with traditional employer-provided insurance, on which the employer pays none.

For higher-income workers, the tax penalty is even worse. Their MSA funds would be subject to at least a 28% Federal income tax, a 15.3% payroll tax, and, most commonly, at least a six percent state income tax, for a tax penalty of nearly 50% on MSAs. If MSAs ever are to be fully effective in reducing costs and providing the other benefits discussed above, the heavy tax discrimination must be removed.

Can HMOs help solve the health-care crisis?

MANAGED CARE HAS BECOME A HIGHLY COMPETITIVE, MULTI-BILLION-DOLLAR BUSINESS. BUT WHAT'S GOOD FOR HMOS MAY NOT BE GOOD FOR CONSUMERS.

In Part 1 of this series on managed health care, published in August, we told you how to choose a health maintenance organization that's likely to give you the best care. We rated 37 of the country's largest HMOs, with information from our survey of more than 20,000 readers and the HMOs themselves. Although people were generally satisfied with all the plans we rated, we found some significant problems and big differences among them. This month, we look at the business of HMOs. We also analyze the HMO policies available to individuals who have no health insurance, and examine the pros and cons of Medicare HMOs for the elderly.

The public didn't vote for managed care. Nor did its representatives in Congress. Yet HMOs are swiftly reshaping the way Americans get their health care. As we showed in Part 1 of this series,* many HMOs do offer high-quality medical treatment. But many people who join an HMO give up a lot: the ability to choose where and how they are treated; longstanding relationships with their doctors, who may not be part of the HMO; convenient access to care; and sometimes, care that is essential to their health.

In the aftermath of the failed Clinton health-care plan, HMOs became the vehicle for reform by default. Employers saw that they could save money by pressuring employees to join HMOs, and health-plan executives saw that they could make money by selling managed care to employers and investors. Managed care was a profit-driven, marketplace response to the health-care crisis.

In 1992, CONSUMER REPORTS argued in a series on health care that the old-fashioned system—based on traditional indemnity insurance and fee-for-service medicine—was in need of change. The system was wasteful and costly, and left too many people without coverage. Then, 37 million people had no insurance; today, 40 million people have none.

But managed care—at least in its current form—does not solve the problems we described. While managed care has had some immediate success in reducing costs, there are reasons to expect that any cost savings may be short-lived. And it has done little to extend coverage to the uninsured (see page 183). That's not surprising, since neither HMOs nor traditional insurance can solve the problem of the uninsured without a coherent, national program.

So far, the health-care system is changing without such a plan. Instead, changes have been driven by the ability of health-care companies to market themselves profitably, not by a national strategy that balances the profit motive with a commitment to serve the public.

Increasingly, HMOs are shifting from a not-for-profit to a for-profit model, which means they are under pressure to boost their stockholders' equity, perhaps at the expense of patient care. Our investigation shows that for-profit HMOs generally spent a lower percentage of the premiums they collect on actual patient care, and they offered care and service that was less satisfactory to their members.

Some of the money saved on medical care is going to the byproducts of competition—not only to stockholder equity, but to marketing, sales, information systems, and the acquisition of other HMOs. All those carry a high price tag. Their costs are being built into the system, have little to do with care, and are not likely to disappear.

Can HMOs control costs?

In the short run, HMOs have had some impact by lowering the price of the medical services. As we described in Part 1, HMOs try to cut costs by limiting the medical care their members receive. They also lower costs by slashing the fees they pay to doctors and hospitals. HMOs typically are paying doctors about one-half to one-third of what they would receive from fee-for-service patients.

For example, last fall, a New York City pediatrician charged our reporter $370 for a back-to-school checkup for her 10-year-old daughter. That sum included a $90 fee for the office visit, and separate charges for four lab tests and two vaccinations. If she had been a member of Oxford Health Plan, the doctor would have received $170 for the same bundle of services. If she had been a member of Chubb's HMO, he would have received $275, and if she had been part of Aetna's plan, he would have been paid $173.50.

Managed care has helped slow the pace of medical inflation, as measured by the Consumer Price Index. In 1990, the cost of medical care services was rising almost 10 percent a year; last year it went up about 4.5 percent.

It is also taking a toll on physicians' incomes and hospitals' revenues. For 1994, the American Medical Association recorded the first drop ever in physicians' income. Median net income fell nearly 4 percent, and for some specialists, like those who treat cardiovascular disease, the decline was as much as 12 percent. Hospital revenues increased only 3.8 percent between January 1995 and January 1996, the lowest increase the American Hospital Association has documented since it began tracking data in 1963.

Health-care providers are now beginning to fight back—much as they did in the 1980s, when they thwarted attempts by the Government and insurers to control costs.

Doctors and hospitals are organizing to increase their bargaining power with HMOs. More than 20 percent of all hospitals have formed physician-hospital organizations to negotiate contracts with HMOs. Some of those groups even act like HMOs themselves, contracting directly with employers and physicians. Doctors are selling their practices to physician management companies to gain negotiating leverage and obtain the capital they need to comply with the rules of managed care.

"In California, the industry has gone as far as it can go in reducing prices to providers," says Arnold Hebert, a senior vice president at PacifiCare. "Doctors are at the breaking point. If we pressed more to lower rates, it will break the system. We'll go out of business. It will be a lose-lose situation."

"The pendulum will swing back to providers," predicts John Erb, a principal at Foster Higgins, an employee benefits consulting firm. But if the pendulum swings too far, doctors and hospitals might once again set the price of care, fueling yet another spiral of cost escalation.

Premium increases may not be far off. Michael Close, senior vice president for sales at Health Net, predicts that premiums charged to employers may rise by the end of the year—largely because HMOs can't cut provider payments any further.

A rise in premiums would reverse the trend of the last few years, during which managed care has helped stabilize the premiums paid by employees and employers. In 1988, when employers were paying premiums mostly for traditional insurance plans, their premiums rose at a rate of more than 18 percent. In 1995, when many employers had switched to managed care, premiums went up only 2 percent, and that was after a 1 percent decline the previous year.

Despite those statistics, however, HMOs don't appear to have lowered premiums as much as they could. Although HMOs have always charged lower premiums than traditional insurance plans, the difference between the two doesn't reflect the price reductions HMOs have squeezed out of providers. Foster Higgins has found that the average premium employers paid in 1995 for traditional indemnity insurance, the most expensive option, was $3650; for HMO coverage, it was $3255, only about 11 percent less. "If that's the best we can do," says Erb, "one year of 20 percent rate increases will wipe out the difference, and we will be back on a par with fee-for-service plans."

The long-term picture

It's not clear how well managed care can really reduce health-care costs in the long term. "All of the research I'm familiar with shows that HMOs do reduce hospital costs by reducing use, and they achieve some savings through negotiated prices with providers. But the decline in hospital use is offset by increased use of physicians' services, other benefits, and by administrative costs," says Kathy Langwell, a health economist who has stud-

In their annual reports, HMOs like to boast about their financial performance. Oxford had a lot to crow about in 1994.

ied medical costs for the Barents Group, a subsidiary of KPMG Peat Marwick. "We don't have a good understanding of whether HMOs can control costs," she adds.

HMOs are now serving a younger and healthier population than they may eventually have to care for. The HMOs in our survey told us that about 75 percent of their members today are under age 45—a group that, on the whole, does not require a lot of medical services. In fact, many plans may be targeting that group by portraying happy, healthy, young people in their advertising. As those members begin to age and require more medical treatments, it's anyone's guess what will happen to costs—or to care.

It's also hard to gauge the cost-saving potential of managed care because so much of what the U.S. spends on health care—about two-thirds—still goes to fee-for-service medicine and is hardly touched by managed care. Some people go outside their HMO to obtain what they feel is

Medicare HMOs
Luring the elderly

At a recent gathering in El Cerrito, Calif., a representative of Secure Horizons, the country's largest HMO for seniors, tried to persuade Medicare beneficiaries to switch to his plan. The sales rep boasted that Secure Horizons was accredited by the National Committee for Quality Assurance. The NCQA is "a private organization run by the Government," he told the assembled seniors. "The number one thing they look at is how fast you can see the doctor. If it took one week to see a doctor, we wouldn't pass." Accreditation, he said, "almost assures quality of care." But the NCQA has no connection to the Government, it evaluates many aspects of a plan—and, as we pointed out in Part 1 of this series, its accreditation is no assurance of high-quality medicine.

At a New York City coffee shop over morning coffee and Danish, a representative from Oxford Health Plan told seniors why they should give up traditional Medicare benefits and join the HMO. Among them: the emergency-room benefit. "How do you define an emergency?" someone asked. "We leave that up to the person who is having an emergency," she replied. That would be news to Oxford, whose official literature says an emergency is "a sudden or unexpected onset of a condition requiring medical or surgical care." It clearly notes that the plan, not the member determines which conditions are emergencies.

At a presentation for Health Net in Walnut Creek, Calif., the sales agent faced a skeptical crowd. One woman asked, "What if someone goes outside the system?" The salesperson sidestepped the major point—the lock-in feature of the Medicare HMO, which means that once you join, you must get all your care from the plan. If you go outside, you have no Medicare benefits and will have to pay any bills yourself.

All over the country, presentations like those are luring seniors to Medicare HMOs. Partly because of such misrepresentations—which we've found are typical of sales presentations for all kinds of insurance—Medicare beneficiaries are signing up at an unprecedented rate, drawn in by the prospect of paying no monthly premium or a very low one for their HMO coverage. By contrast, insurance to cover the gaps in Medicare—commonly called Medigap policies—can cost $1000 a year or more. Seniors have also been attracted by the availability of extras—eyeglasses, hearing tests, some prescription drugs, and visits to podiatrists—which may be unavailable from Medicare or a Medigap policy.

To seniors worried about their future health, it may all sound too good to be true—and indeed it may be.

Right now, HMOs can offer seniors a generous amount of care plus the extras because of the Government's payment system. Medicare now pays HMOs more than enough to provide the same benefits someone would get outside the HMO. Medicare pays a flat fee every month to the plans for each beneficiary they enroll. That payment covers all the services a beneficiary is likely to need—although people in a Medicare plan, like those under 65 in a regular HMO, face certain restrictions on care.

Because of quirks in the payment formula—which is based on the price of health care in an HMO's service area—payments to Medicare HMOs operating in high-priced locations are also high. They're so high, in fact, that they more than cover the cost of services in many parts of the country. (An estimated 90 percent of beneficiaries use about $1300 worth of services during the year, but a Medicare HMO may get an average of $4700 for each senior in the plan.) That leaves plenty of money for a tidy profit, even after the HMO pays for eyeglasses and podiatry visits. The Medicare business is so lucrative that it has become a major profit center at many plans.

Medicare may not continue those over-generous payments indefinitely, however. If payments are reduced, HMOs may try to preserve their profits by charging seniors monthly premiums—perhaps substantial ones—and may even cut back on the free extras.

To make matters worse, some seniors in Medicare HMOs may find that they've become virtually trapped in their plan. Today, it's not hard to leave an HMO you're unhappy with and return to traditional Medicare; you can disenroll and be back on Medicare the first day of the following month. But even if you can get back your Medicare benefits, you may in the meantime have given up your Medigap policy and be unable to buy a new one.

The best time to buy Medigap insurance is within six months after you turn 65 and apply for Medicare; during that period, you can buy a policy without meeting an insurer's health requirements. But after that "window" of protection is gone, you could be out of luck if you're sick. So people in poor health who want to leave a Medicare HMO and buy a new Medigap

(continued)

8. AMERICA'S HEALTH AND THE HEALTH CARE SYSTEM

necessary treatment—18 percent of our readers who belong to HMOs did. Others simply have no choice but to use unmanaged care and pay whatever the doctors charge. Demand for services, especially costly extras, continues to increase, in part stimulated by providers.

But even if the country keeps shifting to managed care, health-care spending is still expected to rise. It is projected to hit 16 percent of the gross domestic product, or GDP, by the year 2000, and per capita spending is expected to increase by some 36 percent. For the foreseeable future, the U.S. will continue to have the costliest health-care system in the world. And unless the system changes dramatically, much of the money will be going toward expenses that have little or nothing to do with actual medical treatment.

The high cost of competition

Today, HMOs generally spend about 17 percent of the premiums they col-

---

policy may find that no insurance company will sell them one. That can pose a frightening choice: Go without Medigap insurance, or stay in an HMO that may not meet your medical needs.

Some seniors have soured on Medicare HMOs when they've had trouble getting adequate care. "We don't know how the really sick people are treated," says Bruce Vladeck, administrator of the Health Care Financing Administration, which oversees Medicare. And therein lies a big unknown for seniors considering a managed-care plan. Some satisfaction surveys have shown that most Medicare beneficiaries are happy with HMOs—but most of those beneficiaries are relatively healthy. These surveys, like those of people under 65, say little about what the plan will do when you are seriously ill.

We do, however, have an inkling of how HMOs are likely to treat some services seniors need—home care or treatment at a costly skilled-nursing facility. A study done for the Health Care Financing Administration found that HMOs may indeed skimp on home-health benefits that beneficiaries are entitled to under Medicare. "We've learned not to ask for visits," says Kate Simpson, director of operations support for the VNA & Hospice of Northern California. Home-health aides are far less common in managed care, she says. If a person gets these services, it may be only for a few weeks and then taper off.

Some people have had difficulty getting skilled-nursing care from HMOs and disenroll to get this care directly from Medicare.

Consider what happened to Miriam Hemy, a Medicare beneficiary in New York City. Attracted by the extras and lack of a monthly premium, Hemy's husband had just signed up the couple for U.S. Healthcare's Medicare HMO. Shortly afterward, Hemy fell and suffered traumatic brain injury; she required an emergency procedure to drain fluid from her brain. Afterward, she required rehabilitation, and her doctors recommended a facility specializing in injuries like hers.

According to her daughter, U.S. Healthcare first denied benefits for treatment at that facility, and instead suggested that she go to a skilled-nursing home where rehabilitation could be given. But the HMO eventually decided against that, too. U.S. Healthcare said she needed only oral medications and assistance with daily activities, which it does not pay for.

Medicare's appeal process upheld the HMO, which it does in about 55 percent of the cases. Hemy's family disenrolled her from U.S. Healthcare and put her back on Medicare. She is now at the rehabilitation center her doctors originally recommended. Medicare and Medicaid are paying the bills. Ironically, U.S. Healthcare recently sent the family a letter saying that Hemy now qualified for skilled-nursing care.

Unless money is a very big consideration and the cost of a Medigap policy is completely out of reach, most people are better off staying in traditional Medicare. If you have chronic care needs—for example, if you require a home-health aide, or you foresee a future need for skilled-nursing care—HMOs are clearly not the place to be.

On the other hand, if you have high prescription-drug costs, then an HMO that covers a portion of those costs might be worth your consideration. Understand how the plan's drug program works. Some have caps or count copayments in different ways, and you may end up with a smaller benefit than you think. Some also restrict the drugs your doctor can prescribe in a way that may make it hard to stay on your current regimen. You'll have to weigh the benefits of the HMO's drug program against buying a Medicare-supplement policy offering prescription drug coverage, which could cost $2000 or more each year.

If you decide on a Medicare HMO, the Ratings we published in August are a place to start. Consider first the plans our readers rated highly and those that had fewer readers who reported difficulty getting care they felt they needed.

Remember, though, that you will be subject to the same restrictions on services that affect members under 65. A specialist you've been seeing may be on a plan's list of physicians, but you first have to go through a primary-care doctor who could decide not to refer you to that specialist.

Medicare HMOs may yet develop into a good alternative for seniors. But right now, for most people, the risks outweigh the benefits. Says Vladeck: "Anyone satisfied in a fee-for-service system shouldn't change for an eyeglass benefit or $10 a month in savings."

lect on what they call marketing, general, and administrative expenses. That covers a lot of territory and includes:

Marketing expenses. HMOs spend millions on billboards, prime-time TV, slick brochures, and folksy newsletters.

Michael Close of Health Net says his company spends some "$40-million plus" on sales and marketing to project a glowing image of itself—an image that many of our readers did not share. (Our survey of the HMO's members put Health Net near the bottom.) Marketing has become so important that even Health Net's better-liked rival, Kaiser of Southern California, which had never found it necessary to advertise before, added some $20-million in advertising expenses to its budget in 1995.

"The jury is out on whether not-for-profits can stay not for profit."

Expenses for managing care. PacifiCare, for example, has 175 people who act as case managers, utilization review personnel, disease management specialists, data-management specialists, directors of wellness programs, and the like. Those activities cost the plan between $15-million and $20-million a year. U.S. Healthcare has a staff of 34 full-time and 60 part-time medical directors who make annual visits to doctors' offices.

Administrative costs are more burdensome for health-care providers as well. "It takes longer and longer to amass the information HMOs require," says Dr. Murray Goodman, an orthopedist in Salem, Mass. Consider the additional burden managed care has placed on the VNA & Hospice of Northern California. The organization used to submit most of its claims electronically to Medicare. Now the VNA does business with 80 to 90 different payers, including medical groups, health plans, and subcontractors. Employees must match the right primary-care doctor with the right payer, then generate a paper claim form with pages of documentation. "This unfortunately has turned into a very complicated business," says Kate Simpson, director of operations support.

Salaries. Compensation paid to HMO executives would not be exceptional in other industries, but their salaries raise eyebrows at a time when HMOs are cutting back on care to lower costs. "We want top managers," says David Olson, vice president for investor relations at Health Net. "These guys are expensive." Health Net's CEO, Dr. Malik Hasan, got more than $3 million in annual and long-term compensation in 1994.

Measuring quality. The biggest and most successful HMOs were first in line to secure accreditation from the National Committee for Quality Assurance (NCQA), which is being promoted as a seal of approval that they can use to attract members. Large plans can pay $100,000 or more in fees to the NCQA to go through the initial accreditation process.

Those costs are small, however, compared to the cost of collecting data known as the Health Employer Data and Information Set (HEDIS), which measures such things as immunization and mammography rates. Only the large HMOs with deep pockets can do it effectively, leaving smaller, less well-heeled plans at a competitive disadvantage.

The systems needed to collect HEDIS data require a huge investment. U.S. Healthcare says it has spent between $300-million and $350-million on computer systems, and a significant portion of those systems is used to capture HEDIS data. "Many plans are struggling because they don't have the systems to do it," says Dr. Neil Schlackman, a corporate medical director for U.S. Healthcare. "Unless you can extract information, you don't know what you can do to improve quality."

Fewer, bigger HMOs

All those new expenses have stimulated a huge appetite for capital. One way HMOs can get it is to add new members, which brings more revenue and gives plans more clout in negotiating discounts with providers. And one way to find additional members, short of convincing more employers to buy your plan, is to take over other plans or merge with them.

No merger has been bigger than the one earlier this year between U.S. Healthcare and Aetna. Aetna paid U.S. Healthcare nearly $9-billion for its expertise in running HMOs. In return, U.S. Healthcare got the capacity to move into new areas. By 1998, U.S. Healthcare hopes to establish a plan in nearly every state by setting up networks of doctors and hospitals and driving down the price of services. "In an oversupplied marketplace, physicians are willing to do more for less," says Joseph Sebastianelli, a co-president of the new organization.

The transformation in health-care economics follows a classic script. Mergers and acquisitions result in bigger organizations that can afford to drive down prices in order to eliminate competition. Eventually, however, an industry made up of a few big players can raise prices at will. "Over time you're talking about the creation of oligopolies and monopolies, and you'll have less competition," admits Geoffrey Harris, a managing director at Smith Barney, an investment firm that helps HMOs go public.

Many think the market will boil down to five or six national firms controlling almost all the health care in the U.S., with a sprinkling of local plans that manage to survive. "In many industries it makes sense to consolidate; in HMOs I'm not so sure," says Nancy Kane, a lecturer in management at the Harvard School of Public Health. "There's no proof that size makes a better HMO, or that being multi-state makes a better HMO from the patients' point of view."

It's hard to say how members will like the gigantic HMOs and the care and service they will deliver. We do know that our readers weren't thrilled with either U.S. Healthcare or Aetna before the merger. They rated U.S. Healthcare's New Jersey and Pennsylvania plans no better than average and ranked its New York plan close to the bottom. Aetna's PPO (a less restrictive form of managed care) ranked below average compared with other PPOs.

Patients vs. stockholders

On the cover of its 1994 annual report, Oxford Health Plan, an HMO whose earnings per share have been rising steadily, describes what's important to investors: "Membership up 122%—revenues up 131%—earnings up 87%—stockholders' equity increased 40%."

Investors also like plans that spend less on medical services. An HMO's efforts to cut fees and reduce services are reflected in a statistic known as the medical loss ratio—a measure of an HMO's medical expenditures as a percentage of the premiums it collects. From 1992 to 1994, that ratio declined for many plans in our survey, especially those in business to make a profit. At Keystone Health Plan East, for example, the loss ratio went down nearly 15 percent; at U.S. Healthcare, New Jersey, 14 percent.

An HMO with a low medical loss ratio looks good to investors but not necessarily to members. The plan with the lowest average medical loss ratio of any in our study over that period, Oxford, was only average in our readers' eyes. U.S. Healthcare's New York and New Jersey plans were among the HMOs in our study reporting the lowest average medical loss ratios from 1992 to 1994; as we noted above, they earned low to average marks from our readers.

Members may become less satisfied as more HMOs turn to Wall Street as a source of capital—capital that they say they need to compete. Today, 65 percent of all HMOs are for-profit enterprises; many big plans, such as Health Net and Blue Cross of California, have become for-profit HMOs in recent years.

(Consumers Union's advocates are working to prevent nonprofit plans from using assets—accumulated as a result of their nonprofit status—as seed money for for-profit expenses or as windfalls for executives.)

The nonprofit HMOs left behind may become an endangered species, and the kind of care they give could disappear. "The large publicly traded HMOs will move in with predatory

Not-for-profit plans spent 91 cents of every dollar for medical care; for-profits spent 79 cents.

prices and use pressure to drive down reimbursement to providers," says Richard Hallworth, the chief financial officer for Tufts health plan. "You don't want market forces to drive down reimbursement so that it affects quality of medical care." Hallworth worries what such practices might mean to Tufts, which our readers ranked highly. "The jury is out on whether not-for-profits can stay not for profit," he says.

As we reported in August, our readers were clearly happier with not-for-profit HMOs than with profit-making ones. For the most part, readers in profit-making plans were more likely to report that their plans discouraged care they felt they needed.

The for-profit plans also had lower medical loss ratios. For-profit plans in our survey spent on average 79 cents of every dollar collected in premiums on medical care from 1992 to 1994, while the not-for-profits spent 91 cents, or 15 percent more. Even the not-for-profits, however, are starting to spend less. At Tufts and Kaiser of Southern California, the loss ratio declined by 5.5 percent from 1992 to 1994.

What's to be done?

Managed care doesn't look like it can meet the country's health-care needs. CONSUMER REPORTS has long favored a single-payer system, like that in Canada, and we believe that option, among others, should still be considered. But if managed care is to dominate—at least in the near future—it must work better. These changes would help:

Make HMOs accountable. The health-care systems of other countries are ultimately accountable to the public they serve through the government that monitors them. Except for Medicare and Medicaid, there is no comparable accountability and oversight for managed care.

In the absence of a Federal role, some states are stepping in to fill the void and are beginning to enact legislation that deals with everything from one-day maternity stays to appeal rights. But the HMO industry is fighting such legislation and wants Congress to exempt it from state laws it considers anti managed care.

Strengthen the grievance process. Except for Medicare beneficiaries, HMO members have no effective way to appeal adverse treatment decisions, except by going through the plans' internal grievance procedures and ultimately to court. Consumers can complain to their state insurance departments (and should), but often those agencies are understaffed and uninterested in helping members who are having trouble with their HMOs.

Ensure that health plans are solvent. While most states have solvency standards for HMOs, there must also be standards for the medical and hospital groups that are assuming more of the financial risk of providing care.

Collect data on health plans. While health plans are beginning to collect data on the quality of care and member satisfaction, there is no way to make sure the data from different plans are comparable, usable, or even accurate, or to disseminate it fairly and impartially. The NCQA is trying to fill that function and has launched a "Quality Compass" project, which is attempting to collect HEDIS data for public dissemination. But however well-intentioned the NCQA's efforts are, it can't compel plans to participate. Only a government agency with the power to collect, monitor, and analyze data from plans can do that.

Even if managed care becomes accountable to the public and members receive the protections they need, it fails to address the major questions still facing the health-care system: How are costs to be controlled while assuring quality care, and how will health care be funded to extend coverage to the 40 million people who are still uninsured? Those issues are still on the table; no one in the health-care industry or in the political sphere has so far been willing to confront them head on.

See next page for listing of HMO policies for individuals.

41. Can HMOs Help Solve the Health-Care Crisis?

Can HMOs help you if you're uninsured?

HMOs may be eager to woo new members, but one group they are not courting is the uninsured. There's no gold to mine from uninsured people who may be sick, need medical services, and will cost the plan money.

Unless a state requires plans to insure everyone regardless of their health, HMOs sell individual coverage only to the healthy—and sometimes only to the very healthy. Most HMOs in our survey offer some sort of individual coverage, and most underwrite—that is, they scrutinize an applicant's health conditions and weed out those who are likely to rack up costs. Most plans described their underwriting as "strict" or "very strict." (HMOs, of course, are no different from traditional insurers when it comes to judging the health conditions of the uninsured.)

While HMOs tout their preventive-care programs for members who are part of employer groups, keeping the uninsured healthy is not their business. For instance, they heavily promote prenatal care for employee members, but when uninsured pregnant women apply for coverage, HMOs turn them down flat. Other restrictions abound:

- Foundation Health refuses to insure men who have relationships with women who are pregnant, whether or not those women want coverage. Foundation Health will also decline someone with chronic bronchitis or asthma if the disease has required emergency-room treatment in the last two years, and the HMO won't cover a baby with a cleft palate if surgery is required.
- PacifiCare declines people with cataracts that haven't been removed.
- Intergroup of Arizona rejects people with glaucoma and those with gallstones that have been treated within the past two years.

Some plans, like Kaiser of Northern California and Kaiser of Colorado, refused to disclose anything to us about their underwriting, simply saying that that information was "proprietary."

If you do clear the underwriting hurdles, the next challenge is to find a plan that offers comprehensive benefits. Benefits vary tremendously among plans. We reviewed 38 policies HMOs sell to individuals who are not part of an employer group. For each policy, we constructed a coverage index showing the proportion of medical services a

▶ Individual HMO policies *Listed in order of coverage index*

Annual rates: Where policies are age rated, individual premiums are based on a 45-year-old member; family coverage reflects a member, spouse, and two children. In southern California, rates are for Orange County; for northern California, Sacramento; for Arizona, Maricopa County; for Pennsylvania, Philadelphia County. **Coverage index:** Index reflects how completely a plan covers average health expenses: hospitalization, surgery, doctor visits, mental health/substance abuse, and prescription drugs. The index does not reflect durable medical equipment or dental benefits, nor is it a measure of quality. **Maximum cost sharing:** Maximum charges a member would pay for three common services. **Hospital stay** reflects the copayment for an inpatient hospital visit; **Prenatal & delivery** reflects copayments for 13 visits and hospital and obstetrical charges for delivery. Does not take into account lab charges that might be extra at some plans. **Outpatient surgery** reflects facility, doctor, and outpatient anesthesia copayments. **Mental health:** "OK" means plan covers at least 30 days of inpatient care for acute mental conditions with no more than $1500 of cost sharing and at least 20 outpatient mental-health visits with no more than 50 percent copayments. Plans substantially exceeding this level are "Better"; those with some significant coverage for acute mental-health services but failing to meet the minimum coverage standards are "Poor." Plans that do not offer coverage for institutional mental-health services are labeled as "No inpatient."

Name of plan and policy	Annual rates Individual	Annual rates Family	Coverage index	Maximum cost sharing Hospital stay	Maximum cost sharing Prenatal & delivery	Maximum cost sharing Outpatient surgery	Mental health
Kaiser North Calif. Personal Adv. $5 copay	$1392	$3840	93%	$0	$65	$0	Better
Kaiser South Calif. Plan II	1524	4116	91	0	0	0	OK
Intergroup of Arizona Value Plus	1284 (m) 1764 (fem)	4680	89	200	265	0	No inpatient
Kaiser Colo. Standard	1824	5198	89	100	230	10	Poor
Kaiser North Calif. Personal Adv. $15 copay	1008	2772	89	0	65	0	Better
Foundation Health Shasta 7	2220	5592	88	100	191	0	No inpatient
Health Alliance Plan (Mich.)	1907	4864	88	0	65	0	OK
Group Health f Puget Sound Plan A	2156	6670	88	500	0	10	Poor
U.S. Healthcare NJ $10 option	3120	9181	87	500	525	10	OK
Kaiser MidAtlantic DC	1704	4932	87	500	500	50	Better
Kaiser MidAtlantic Md.	1704	4944	87	500	500	50	Better
Kaiser MidAtlantic Va.	1692	4896	86	500	500	50	OK
CaliforniaCare Personal CaliforniaCare	1980	5160	86	0	1000	0	No inpatient
U.S. Healthcare Pa. Superior Plan	2035	5942	86	240	265	0	OK
Harvard Comm. Health Plan Personal Plan	1915	5170	85	250	250	50	Better
HealthPartners	1638	4805	85	[1]	[1]	10	Better
PruCare of California Plan 10	1800	4836	85	500	630	0	No inpatient
Oxford NJ HMO Plan $15 copay	3038	9114	84	750	775	15	OK
PacifiCare HMO 10	1620	4584	84	250	1130	250	No inpatient
U.S. Healthcare N.J. $15 option	2706	7963	84	750	775	15	Ok
Foundation Health Shasta 15	1920	4860	82	500	695	0	No inpatient
Intergroup of Arizona Value Option	1140 (m) 1536 (fem)	4200	82	500	695	100	No inpatient
Kaiser Northwest	1382	4146	82	0	250	10	Poor
U.S. Healthcare Pa. Standard	1831	5348	82	500	525	200	OK
Independent Health Encompass I-2	1980	5543	81	500	700	290	OK
Oxford NJ HMO Plan $20 copay	2659	7977	81	1250	1275	20	OK
Pilgrim Pilgrim Direct	Not yet approved	—	81	500	695	100 [2]	Better
U.S. Healthcare N.J. $20 option	2436	7169	81	1250	1275	20	OK
U.S. Healthcare N.Y.	2430	7222	81	500	700	275	OK
Blue Cross Blue Shield of Rochester, N.Y.	1534	4066	79	500	700 [3]	290	OK
CIGNA HealthCare of California	1370	4493	78	[1]	[1]	75	No inpatient
Oxford N.Y. Personal Plan	2654	7963	78	500	700	290	OK
Kaiser Colo. Basic	1536	4377	77	[4]	[4]	150	Poor
Tufts Associated Health Plans	"Proprietary"	—	75	500	695	500	Better
PacifiCare HMO 15	1476	4152	75	[1]	[1]	[1]	No inpatient
PruCare of California Plan 20	1728	4644	75	1250	[1]	[1]	No inpatient
Foundation Health Shasta Classic	1656	4164	67	[1]	760	[1]	No inpatient
Group Health Northwest	1740	4848	64	[1]	[5]	100	No inpatient

[1] *No specific maximum due to 20% coinsurance on some expensive services. Overall cap may apply.*
[2] *Assumes outpatient surgery is completed in one day.*
[3] *Includes surgical copayment for cesarean section.*
[4] *No specific maximum due to $300 per day charges. Overall cap may apply.*
[5] *No specific maximum; patient pays hospital charges over $800, unless delivery is "complicated." Overall cap may apply.*

8. AMERICA'S HEALTH AND THE HEALTH CARE SYSTEM

policy will pay for compared to a generous package of benefits a large employer might offer.(This index takes into account both the actual services covered and the amount that consumers would have to pay in deductibles, coinsurance and copayments.) The table ["Individual HMO policies"] shows that the most generous policy, from Kaiser of Northern California, provided 93 percent of the benefits; the skimpiest one, from Group Health Northwest, provided only 64 percent.

Some plans impose copayments—fixed amounts, such as $10 per office visit or $500 per hospital admission. Others require policyholders to pay 20 percent of the bills until a certain level is reached. Taking cost-sharing into consideration, the table also shows the maximum amount a policyholder would pay for a hospital stay, outpatient surgery, and maternity care (assuming, of course, a woman becomes pregnant after securing a policy). Plans with the lowest indexes usually leave policyholders with the greatest out-of-pocket expense.

The biggest holes in coverage are for prescription drugs (sometimes not covered) and for mental health and substance-abuse services. Many plans offer only minimal protection for the latter. Group Health Northwest, for example, provides no coverage for inpatient mental-health services, no coverage for inpatient or outpatient drug and alcohol services, and only 10 visits per year for outpatient mental-health care. Harvard Community Health Plan provides benefits that are far more generous—up to 60 days' coverage for inpatient mental-health services and up to 20 visits for outpatient care for mental health and substance abuse.

Comprehensive benefits for those conditions may be important even if you don't think you can use them now. The need for such coverage can arise unexpectedly, leaving you with an uncovered catastrophic expense. Remember, though, that just because a plan appears to offer generous benefits doesn't mean that you'll actually receive them. Policyholders are subject to the same restrictions on tests, treatments, and services that other plan members are. And as we noted in Part 1 of this series, mental-health services are one place HMOs tightly control care.

In making your choices, you should also look at our Ratings in Part 1 and consider how the HMOs treated their members on several aspects of care and service. Also keep in mind that the premiums for many policies are "age rated"—the price is higher the older you are when you buy. Premiums for someone over age 50 are generally twice as high as those for someone under 30. A 55-year-old man buying the more comprehensive policy from Kaiser of Southern California would pay $1824 a year; a man age 25 would pay $924.

We also found that premiums may bear little relationship to coverage. At some HMOs, choosing the least expensive plan, known as the low-option plan, is best; at others, the high-option plan is. The table shows low-and high-option plans. For example, Kaiser of Northern California charges 39 percent more for its high-option policy with a low copayment, but the average benefits offered by that plan are only 4 percent more. Thus its low-option plan with a higher copayment is the better choice. Other plans do the opposite, making their high-option policy more attractive. PruCare's high-option plan is better than its low-option plan; it charges only 4 percent more and provides 14 percent more benefits.

But although price shopping sounds good in theory, the reality is that the plan you want may not take you. In the end, you may have little choice.

The case of Norman Burns is all too typical. Burns, a 61-year-old self-employed machine-shop owner, has mild, noninsulin dependent diabetes that disqualifies him from most HMO plans in California. But in California—which has 20 percent of its population, or about 6.2 million people, without health insurance—Blue Cross offers options for people with health problems; so does the state's high-risk pool, which insures people other carriers reject. Burns has coverage through a preferred provider organization (PPO), a loose form of managed care, sold by Blue Cross.

The company just informed Burns that his premiums will increase by 12 percent and the reimbursement level will go down from 80 percent to 70 percent. In other words, he will be paying more for less.

The PPO coverage is far less comprehensive than that provided by CaliforniaCare, the Blue Cross HMO. Burns will have to pay 30 percent of most doctor bills after meeting a $500 deductible. If he had HMO coverage, his out-of-pocket expenditures would be capped at $2000. With the PPO, he could be liable for up to $10,000 in addition to the deductible.

The dilemma Burns faces is the same one confronted by individuals all over the country. If they want health insurance and are ill, they have few options. After the collapse of health-care reform, the uninsured were again left to fend for themselves in a marketplace that sees no way to profit from insuring them.

"We're not in the business of giving away health services," says Dr. William Roper, senior vice president at Prudential HealthCare. "The problem of the uninsured can only be solved by Government."

[*See *Consumer Reports on Health*, August 1996.]

Examining the Routine Examination

Marvin M. Lipman, M.D.

Marvin M. Lipman, M.D., has been Consumers Union's chief medical adviser since 1967. He is a diplomate of the American Board of Internal Medicine (certified in endocrinology and metabolism) and is clinical professor of medicine emeritus at New York Medical College.

On March 27, 1991, President Bush was given a clean bill of health after a complete physical exam. Within six weeks, an irregular heart rhythm that can cause stroke landed him in the hospital. The problem was an overactive thyroid, diagnosed by a simple blood test—a test omitted from his physical. In contrast, President Clinton's "routine" exam this year lasted four hours and seemed to omit nothing. It included a treadmill test, a chest X-ray, and an electrocardiogram—three tests known to be of virtually no value in evaluating an apparently healthy 48-year-old man.

If presidents can get too little of a routine examination or too much of one, just imagine how less-illustrious patients make out. Some physicians give an extensive and expensive battery of tests and procedures; others, not much more than a cursory thump on the chest and a pat on the back. So it's up to the health-care consumer to watch out for what should and shouldn't be done.

Tests that get results

Variation in routine checkups among physicians is especially great when it comes to the use of cancer-screening tests. There's genuine disagreement over the usefulness of some of those tests. Others, however, may be omitted simply out of neglect. Here are the most important ones:

■ **Mammography:** Annual X-rays of breast tissue can unquestionably save lives by catching cancer at a very early stage—at least in women over 50. What's still debated is whether the procedure is worthwhile in younger women. Last year, the National Cancer Institute broke ranks with other public-health organizations and recommended against mammography for women in their 40s. But the data behind that decision were flawed. I side with the American Cancer Society and the American College of Obstetricians and Gynecologists, which still recommend mammography every one to two years from age 40 to 50.

Even after 50, too many women don't have a regular mammogram. While it's true that some physicians fail to recommend the test, women often avoid it—out of denial, ignorance, or fear of discomfort, or because of the expense. But none of those reasons should stand in the way.

■ **Pap smear:** By examining cells gently scraped from the cervix, a laboratory technician can spot precancerous changes. Many women, especially older women, get Pap smears too seldom or not at all. With the exception of gynecologists, doctors often don't push the test aggressively enough, perhaps because of the extra time and expertise required. But if all women had regular Pap smears, almost all of the nearly 5000 deaths from cervical cancer in the U.S. each year could be prevented. Women should have regular Pap smears starting at age 18, or sooner if they're sexually active.

■ **PSA blood test:** The prostate-specific antigen test can detect prostate cancer early. The catch is, it's not always clear what to do with the information. Prostate tumors can grow very slowly and may never cause harm, especially in older men; meanwhile, treatment can cause serious complications, including incontinence and impotence. For those reasons, some physicians reserve the PSA test for those with a strong family history of the disease or for African-American men, who are at special risk.

Because we can't say for sure that what you don't know won't hurt you, I believe that all men should have an annual PSA test (along with a digital rectal exam) beginning at age 50—or 40, if they're at high risk. The decision about whether or not to treat early prostate cancer is one the patient must make for himself, after having the facts and options explained by his physician.

■ **Sigmoidoscopy:** In this procedure, a flexible lighted tube is guided into the rectum and lower intestine to look for cancer or precancerous polyps. Many doctors fail to recommend sigmoidoscopy, perhaps in part because they aren't trained in the technique and must therefore refer the patient to a specialist. For their part, patients often shy away from the procedure out of embarrassment or fear of pain. But the test is well worth the five minutes or so of mild discomfort: Sigmoidoscopy has been shown to prevent deaths from colorectal cancer. Men and women over age 50 should have the procedure done every three to five years.

■ **Fecal occult-blood test:** In this very simple test, the patient applies stool samples to special testing cards. Each card is then tested for hidden blood, which can indicate colon cancer. Doctors usually suggest the test and provide the testing cards, but patients often fail to follow through—perhaps because they're squeamish about collecting the necessary fecal sample. Yet the occult-blood test, like sigmoidoscopy, can save lives by leading to the detection of cancer while it's still curable. Everyone should have the test annually after age 40.

Tests that miss the mark

Sometimes physicians do tests that aren't needed. Unnecessary tests, even if innocuous, can lead to a cascade of more invasive, even risky, tests and treatments. At the very least, such tests add unnecessary time and expense. Be wary of these:

■ **Electrocardiograms:** In people who have no

8. AMERICA'S HEALTH AND THE HEALTH CARE SYSTEM

heart-related complaints and who aren't at risk for coronary heart disease, routine measurement of the heart's electrical activity is virtually useless. The test almost never reveals an unsuspected problem. All that most people need is a single baseline EKG for future comparison should symptoms occur.

■ **Treadmill tests:** Similarly, an exercise stress test (an EKG taken during exertion) shouldn't be done without good reason. The test can indicate heart trouble when nothing's really wrong.

■ **Chest X-rays:** Among nonsmokers, the chances of spotting lung disease in someone without symptoms are practically nil. Even in smokers and ex-smokers, a routine chest X-ray is unlikely to detect lung cancer early enough to cure the disease—though those patients may still want the procedure despite the long odds.

■ **Blood tests:** Many routine blood tests are useful and appropriate. The trouble is, some superfluous ones are also included in the automated testing process, and you have to take the bad with the good. More tests means more chance of spurious findings, especially "false positives." So you have to be cautious about abnormal test results—especially if those same tests were normal in the past. Before moving on to any further testing or treatment, you should have the original test repeated.

A time for plain talk

As important as the appropriate screening tests and procedures are, perhaps an even more important part of the routine exam is the chance to talk with your doctor, especially about preventive health strategies. It's the ideal time to discuss your medical concerns and health habits. Potential topics on the agenda include medication regimens, smoking, drinking, occupational hazards, recreational drugs, safe sex, and sun exposure. Ask for help starting or improving a fitness program, or about following a healthy diet. You stand to benefit more from frank discussions about those lifestyle practices than from tests that infrequently detect hidden disease.

The table below shows general guidelines for a complete exam. Exactly how often you'll need such an exam depends on your risk factors. And particular health problems may require additional tests.

THE ROUTINE ADULT CHECKUP [1]

PHYSICAL EXAMINATIONS	
Procedure	**To detect**
All adults	
Abdomen	Enlarged liver or spleen; also aortic aneurysm in men age 60 and over
Blood pressure	Hypertension
Breasts	Cancer (although breast cancer is uncommon in men)
Heart	Murmur, irregular heart beat
Height and weight	Obesity; also osteoporosis in women age 50 and over
Lymph nodes in neck, underarms, and groin	Early lymphoma, various other disorders
Mouth	Oral cancer
Neck	Thyroid nodules; also narrowed carotid arteries in people age 60 and over
Skin	Cancer, including melanoma
Adults age 40 and over	
Rectal [2]	Colorectal cancer; also prostate cancer in men age 40 and over
All women	
Pelvic	Cancer and other abnormalities in bladder, ovaries, rectum, uterus, and vagina
All men	
Groin	Inguinal hernia
Men ages 20 to 35	
Testicles	Tumors

LABORATORY TESTS	
Procedure	**To detect**
All adults	
Chemical profile of blood chemistries [3]	Diabetes, gout, thyroid or parathyroid problems, impaired kidney or liver function, risk factors for coronary heart disease
Complete blood count	Anemia, white-blood-cell disorders (such as leukemia), bleeding disorders
Urinalysis	Diabetes, infections, urinary-tract disorders
Men age 50 and over	
Prostate-specific antigen test [2]	Prostate cancer

DIAGNOSTIC PROCEDURES	
Procedure	**To detect**
Adults age 40 and over	
Fecal occult-blood test [2]	Intestinal polyps, cancer
Adults age 45 and over	
Tonometry	Glaucoma
Adults age 50 and over	
Flexible sigmoidoscopy [4]	Colorectal cancer
All women	
Pap smear [5]	Cervical cancer
Women age 40 and over	
Mammography [6]	Breast cancer

[1] All procedures recommended every one to three years, unless otherwise specified. Ages and intervals may vary, depending on risk of disease. Other procedures may be appropriate for certain individuals.
[2] Rectal exam, prostate-specific antigen (PSA) test, and fecal occult-blood test should each be performed annually.
[3] Chemical profile is an automated analysis of up to 22 blood chemistries, including calcium, cholesterol (total, LDL, and HDL), glucose, thyroid-stimulating hormone (TSH), triglycerides, uric acid, and kidney- and liver-function tests.
[4] Flexible sigmoidoscopy should be performed every three to five years.
[5] Pap smears should be performed annually until three consecutive normal results are obtained, and every one to three years thereafter.
[6] Mammography should be performed every one to two years from age 40 to 50, and annually thereafter.

Your hospital stay: A guide to survival

A hospital stay can be as perilous as the illness that sends you there. Here's how to protect yourself.

Early this year, the perils of hospitalization made headlines when a surgeon at University Community Hospital in Tampa amputated the wrong foot of a patient with diabetes. In the wake of that fiasco, some medical experts seriously suggested that surgery patients ask their doctor to mark the surgery site with a pen or even write "no" on the limbs they hoped to keep.

Since then, such blunders have been much in the news. In March, for example, investigators learned that a Boston Globe health columnist who died at the renowned Dana-Farber Cancer Institute had actually been killed by a chemotherapy overdose, which had been overlooked by at least a dozen doctors, nurses, and pharmacists. In May, surgeons at the equally renowned Memorial Sloan-Kettering Cancer Institute in New York City operated on the wrong half of a cancer patient's brain.

Potentially dangerous hospital errors are indeed alarmingly common. One Harvard study of some 30,000 hospital charts found that nearly 3 percent of patients are injured by some preventable mistake. Another 1 percent are harmed by the inevitable hazards of hospitalization, such as infection and adverse reactions to anesthesia or medications. Nationwide, those rates translate into more than a million injuries each year.

This report describes what you can do to prevent mistakes and minimize the risks.

Make surgery safer

To protect yourself when you're scheduled to go under the knife:

■ **Check out the surgeon.** If you or a friend knows someone who works at the hospital of a surgeon you're considering, ask about his or her reputation. If you can't do that, at least check the hospital's reputation (see box, page 189), since better hospitals tend to have better surgeons. And find out whether the surgeon teaches at the hospital or at a medical school, an indication that he or she probably keeps up with the latest practices.

The American Board of Medical Specialties (800-776-CERT) will tell you whether a physician is board certified; certification means that the surgeon has completed an approved residency program and passed a detailed written exam. In addition, find out whether the surgeon belongs to a professional organization, such as the American College of Surgeons, by calling the county medical society or consulting the medical directories in the library. (Note that none of those sources verifies all the information provided by physicians.) While requirements for joining professional groups vary, membership at least suggests that the surgeon has some interest in keeping up with the latest research. Finally, check the surgeon's experience by asking how many of the operations he or she has performed and what the success and complication rates have been.

■ **Limit preoperative tests.** Surgery patients often undergo a smorgasbord of standard preoperative tests, many of them unnecessary. Those procedures, while generally harmless in themselves, can not only create needless costs but also yield falsely positive results that can trigger other, sometimes hazardous, tests.

Adults younger than age 40 generally need nothing more than a simple blood count and, for sexually active women, a pregnancy test. Healthy people older than 40 may need only a few additional tests, such as an electrocardiogram plus blood tests for diabetes, liver disease, and kidney disease. Ask your doctor which preoperative tests, if any, you truly need. And ask your doctor to check whether you've had any of those tests recently enough to skip them.

■ **Bank your blood.** If you're likely to need a blood transfusion during an upcoming operation, ask your surgeon about banking your own blood supply ahead of time, to eliminate the slight risk of receiving tainted blood.

8. AMERICA'S HEALTH AND THE HEALTH CARE SYSTEM

KNOW YOUR RIGHTS

When you check into a hospital, you should receive a copy of the Patient's Bill of Rights, a nationally recognized code of conduct published by the American Hospital Association. The code expresses firmly established law on patients' rights in all states. Here are six of your most important rights:

■ To receive complete, understandable information about your diagnosis, treatment, and expected outcome.

■ To review your medical records. Such records can be difficult to decipher, so don't hesitate to ask your physician to explain anything you can't make out.

■ To refuse any treatment or test. All procedures require your consent, unless you're unconscious or require emergency care. Major procedures require your informed, written consent—doctors must explain the benefits and risks to your satisfaction before you sign on the dotted line.

■ To refuse to let anyone stay in your room who is not directly involved in your care (except, of course, your roommate and anyone seeing your roommate). For example, you don't have to allow medical students to watch while doctors examine you.

■ To have the details of your condition, treatment, and medical records kept confidential from anyone in the hospital who is not directly involved in your care.

■ To receive reasonable responses to your reasonable requests for the services of doctors, nurses, and other staff members.

Your right to nursing care

As hospitals cut costs by cutting staff, it's becoming increasingly difficult to get those reasonable responses to your requests, particularly from the overworked nursing staff. Indeed, minor delays and other inconveniences are practically inevitable during a hospital stay. Complaining or calling for help too often or too aggressively may only make things worse, by convincing the hospital staff that you're a malcontent.

But that doesn't mean you have to tolerate rudeness, consistently burnt, uncooked, or cold food, or long waits for pain killers or a bedpan. If your nurse ignores your reasonable requests, speak to the head floor nurse or to your doctor. If that doesn't work, ask to see the patient advocate, a specially trained person who will intervene on behalf of patients whose legitimate complaints—about nurses, doctors, or any other hospital employee—are being ignored. Hospitals that don't have a patient advocate often have social workers who can help you get what you need.

■ **Get antibiotics on time.** Taking antibiotics at the right time—no more than two hours before major surgery—can slash the risk of developing a wound infection. But surgery patients often receive those drugs too early or too late. Make sure your doctor gives the necessary orders and that your nurse carries them out. (And make sure the nurse checks your wound and changes the dressing regularly after the operation.)

■ **Prepare for anesthesia.** In rare cases, general anesthesia can cause devastating complications, including brain damage and death. One cause of such catastrophes is vomiting while you're unconscious. To reduce the risk, refuse any food or drink that the hospital staff may mistakenly offer you in the eight hours before surgery. If anesthesia has nauseated you in the past, ask for antinausea medication before the operation.

Having weak lungs sharply increases the risks from anesthesia. People who smoke, who are older than age 65 or so, or who have recently had a debilitating illness should ask their doctor to check their lungs before surgery and, if necessary, teach them deep-breathing exercises to strengthen their lungs. Smokers should stop smoking for as long as possible before surgery; even stopping for as little as 24 hours can help.

■ **Ease the pain.** Postoperative pain can keep you from moving around in bed, breathing deeply, moving your bowels, or even coughing; that can delay recovery and increase the risk of complications. Many physicians and nurses are still reluctant to give morphine, the most potent pain killer, even though the chance of addiction during a hospital stay is minuscule. And they dole out even the weaker pain killers "as needed," which means you get a dose only when you complain.

Ask to receive intravenous morphine after major surgery, at least at first. Better yet, ask whether the hospital offers patient-controlled intravenous analgesia, which lets you administer your own medication by pushing a button on a computerized pump.

■ **Fend off complications.** Surgery patients can help reduce their risk of three common postoperative complications:

Pneumonia. The bacteria that cause pneumonia are so abundant in hospitals that an estimated 4 percent of all patients develop the infection. The risk is particularly high following chest, back, or abdominal surgery, since weakness and pain may discourage the deep breathing that ordinarily helps clear the lungs of harmful bacteria. The same breathing exercises that can strengthen the lungs before surgery can reduce the risk of pneumonia after surgery.

Phlebitis. Lying in bed for long periods can lead to inflammation of the leg veins, usually accompanied by potentially dangerous blood clots. To cut the risk, ask the nurse to help you walk as soon as possible after surgery. If you're overweight or have varicose veins, wear special elastic stockings.

Urinary tract infections. These infections often develop because a doctor or nurse failed to remove a catheter soon enough. If 48 hours have passed since your operation and you're still using a catheter, find out whether it's there by design or neglect.

Get the right drugs

Hospital patients receive an average of 10 different drugs. Each patient is typically seen by several different physicians, who may order medications without knowing what other doctors have ordered. And both the pharmacists and the nurses have to decipher the doctors' handwriting and follow their prescriptions accurately.

A study published in July in the Journal of the American Medical Association found that about 7 percent of hospital patients experience some adverse drug reaction. Other studies have found adverse-reaction rates as high as 15 percent, up to half of them caused by errors—giving the wrong drug or the wrong dose, overlooking an allergy, or failing to spot a potentially dangerous interaction with another medication.

The following precautions can help prevent those potential errors:

■ **Check your drugs.** Bring to the hospital a list of all the medications you've been taking at home, including the dosages, so the physician who admits you can order those drugs. Further, ask your doctor whether there will be any additions, deletions, or other changes in your usual drug regimen. The doctor should add that information to your list, including the name, purpose, dosage instructions, and, if possible, the color and shape of any new pills. Use that list to check all the drugs your nurse brings. (If you don't feel well enough, have a friend or relative check for you.) In addition, have your doctor review all your medications at least once every 72 hours.

One other precaution: Ask your doctor to leave standing orders for medications to treat insomnia or constipation. Otherwise, you may face a long, uncomfortable wait for the appropriate order to be written and filled if the need arises.

■ **Check your IV.** Many drugs are started intravenously, then switched to an oral version. If you're getting IV drugs, ask your doctor when you'll start getting pills instead. If you're eating solid foods and drinking fluids but are still receiving drugs intravenously, a doctor or nurse may have forgotten to make the change.

HOW GOOD IS YOUR HOSPITAL?

Long before you need hospital care, you should investigate the hospitals located near you. Then try to choose doctors who have admitting privileges at one or more desirable hospitals in your area.

First, make sure the hospital is accredited by the Joint Commission on Accreditation of Healthcare Organizations (JCAHO), which monitors the nation's hospitals. About 80 percent of all hospitals apply for accreditation. While the JCAHO approves nearly all of them, it has recently started to issue detailed rating reports on all hospitals that have applied. The reports are already available for about one-third of those hospitals, and the rest should be ready by the end of next year. You may be able to get a report by calling a hospital's office of public information. Alternatively, the JCAHO will mail you a copy for $30. (Write to One Renaissance Blvd., Oakbrook Terrace, Ill. 60181, or call 708-916-5600.)

Next, check the quality of the medical staff. The hospital's public relations department or medical-staff office should be willing to answer the following questions over the phone:

■ **Is it a teaching hospital?** Such hospitals, affiliated with a medical school, tend to attract better doctors and to offer the most advanced and widest range of services.

■ **What percentage of the staff physicians are board certified?** Nationally, about 65 percent of all physicians are certified. At a good hospital in a large urban center, that figure may reach 80 percent or more. Smaller, more rural communities typically have fewer certified physicians.

■ **Are there doctors available in most specialties and subspecialties?** The more serious the ailment or the more complex the operation, the greater the need to have a full range of physicians on hand who can treat any unexpected problems.

■ **Do the major clinical departments have full-time chiefs?** Full-time status allows the chiefs to spend more of their time overseeing the department. It also reduces their financial dependence on referrals from other doctors in the department, leaving them freer to discipline the doctors when that becomes necessary.

■ **What percentage of the nurses are RNs?** Registered nurses have substantially more training than the other main type, licensed practical nurses (LPNs). About 70 percent of the nurses in the average hospital are RNs.

■ **How many patients does each RN care for?** Ideally, there should be one RN for every one or two patients in an intensive-care unit and for every six patients or so in most other areas of the hospital.

Does the hospital care?

Hospitals that follow a progressive philosophy that's strongly concerned with satisfying the patient tend to:

■ Use primary nursing, in which nurses are assigned to particular patients rather than to particular tasks (such as giving medications or examining patients).

■ Offer self-administered pain medication (see story).

■ Employ a full-time patient advocate and provide full information on patients' rights (see box, facing page).

■ Employ social workers who counsel patients or who help them obtain various rehabilitative, social, or financial services.

■ Have a hospice program for dying patients and encourage the use of living wills.

■ Have a birthing center, allow a woman to deliver and recuperate in the same room, and employ midwives.

■ Run community-outreach programs, such as support groups for breast-cancer or diabetes patients.

■ Have reasonable, flexible visiting hours.

■ Allow friends and relatives to bring food to patients who aren't on a special diet, or have kitchens where those patients can prepare their own food.

■ **Check your wristband.** Make sure the wristband correctly lists your name and any drug allergies you have. And make sure the nurse checks the band each time he or she brings you any drugs.

> ### Summing up
> On average, you face a 4 percent chance of being injured during a hospital stay. Keeping alert and being assertive—or having someone do that for you—can substantially reduce the likelihood of harm.
>
> **What to do**
> ■ Check the credentials and reputation of the surgeon and the hospital.
> ■ Make sure your personal physician is overseeing your care.
> ■ Keep track of your medications and tests.
> ■ Get ready for the anesthesia.
> ■ Demand adequate pain control.
> ■ Become active as soon as you can after surgery.
> ■ Know your rights and stand up for them.

Testing: Don't just take it

Hospitalized patients may sometimes be given tests that are unnecessary or even meant for someone else. To reduce the risk of that happening to you:

■ **Question the tests.** Medical tests are sometimes risky, painful, or expensive. The following questions can help you determine whether a test ordered for you is really necessary: What are the odds that the test will actually find something wrong? What would happen if you waited, and took it only if the condition got worse? Will the test actually affect treatment? How likely are inconclusive or falsely positive results, and would such results lead to further tests or treatment?

■ **Know what's coming.** Find out what tests your doctor plans for you while you're in the hospital. Refuse to be wheeled off to unexpected or unexplained tests.

In addition, patients often spend extra time in the hospital because staff members failed to withhold food, administer an enema or laxative, or make other preparations for a scheduled test. To avoid needless delays, find out what preparations you'll need, and see that they get done on time.

The New Doctors of NATURAL MEDICINE

If you're tantalized by alternative therapies but don't know where to start, a **naturopath** may be just what you're looking for.

KATHERINE GRIFFIN

IN SEATTLE PLENTY OF PEOPLE DREAD THE ONSET OF WINTER for the endless gray gloom it brings. But for Mia Jacobson, the dampness at the beginning of each rainy season signaled more than just months of cabin fever. A car accident years before had left her with arthritis and bone spurs, and for the past 15 winters she'd endured frequent episodes of severe pain in her neck and upper back. "Sometimes I couldn't change lanes in my car because I couldn't turn my head," she says. "There were days when I would just sit at my desk and cry."

Jacobson's doctors prescribed the standard trio of medications—muscle relaxants, painkillers, and anti-inflammatory drugs—plus physical therapy. Yet she was still in pain, and side effects were harsh. The anti-inflammatories, for one thing, triggered bleeding in her stomach. "I had pretty much resigned myself to feeling crummy every winter," Jacobson says. "I was getting kind of angry about it."

Then, a year ago, a friend prodded her to see a naturopath, a type of alternative health practitioner who believes that illness is rooted in disharmony with nature. Naturopathy's primary tools are herbs, homeopathy, dietary advice, and hands-on techniques such as massage. According to practitioners, these treatments can stimulate the body's natural healing mechanisms and strengthen its resistance to future illnesses.

Jacobson had never dabbled in alternative medicine—she didn't even take vitamins—but having pretty much exhausted the options that her doctors could offer, she decided to

8. AMERICA'S HEALTH AND THE HEALTH CARE SYSTEM

Natural Remedies

Naturopaths use a grab bag of therapies to address the physical, mental, and spiritual roots of an illness. The core techniques are herbal supplements, nutritional advice, homeopathy, water therapy, body work, and counseling. A practitioner may combine these with other treatments, such as aromatherapy or acupuncture, or even home remedies such as wearing ice water–chilled socks to rev up a flagging immune system.

You might be advised to replace your morning coffee with meditation to temper a stress-related affliction like migraine; to pop a magnesium supplement with the goal of strengthening your body's connective tissues after an injury; or to dissolve a homeopathic remedy under your tongue for seasonal sniffles and itchy eyes.

But how much is known about treatments like these? For a primer, check out this chart. —*Karmen Butterer*

HERBAL AND BOTANICAL REMEDIES

The leaves, berries, flowers, bark, and roots of plants have long been used for medicinal purposes. Today herbal and botanical remedies are sold in most drugstores in the form of capsules, teas, tablets, extracts, tinctures, or salves.

WHAT WORKS: Approximately 600 botanical remedies are sold in the United States, and the Food and Drug Administration allows manufacturers of 16 of these to make claims of druglike efficacy. Slippery elm bark, for instance, has been shown to soothe sore throats. Other botanicals supported by sketchier research or a long history of use include ginger to quell nausea, feverfew for migraines, echinacea to fend off colds, saw palmetto to shrink an enlarged prostate, milk thistle for jaundice and cirrhosis, and Saint-John's-wort to ease depression.

WHAT TO WATCH OUT FOR: The FDA lists nine herbs that can cause serious problems, including kidney failure and stroke: chaparral, comfrey, germander, jin bu huan, lobelia, magnolia, ma huang, stephania, and yohimbe. A well-trained naturopath will steer you away from risky botanicals. Dosing is less exact than with synthetic drugs because the potency of a botanical remedy can vary, depending on how it was prepared and even on the particular plant used as a source.

BODY WORK

A wide variety of physical techniques, including massage and posture work, are used to align the spine, muscles, ligaments, and joints, and to improve the flow of energy. Naturopaths also counsel clients on ways to work exercise into daily life. In some cases, a practitioner may suggest going to a specialist such as a massage therapist, a licensed chiropractor, or a physical therapist.

WHAT WORKS: Recent studies show that massage forces muscles to relax, which sends a message to the brain to produce fewer stress hormones; the result is a feeling of relaxed alertness. Just one session can temporarily reduce stress and improve sleep. Regular massages can boost the immune system, improve mental function, and ease chronic pain, as well as speed recovery from overuse injuries. Physical therapy, routinely prescribed to hasten recovery from injury, has a solid reputation in both conventional and alternative worlds. And many studies have established the sizable benefits of regular exercise.

WHAT TO WATCH OUT FOR: Anyone with heart disease, circulatory problems, high blood pressure, an infection from a cut or injury, inflammation from a sprain or strain, or a contagious skin condition should check with a doctor or naturopath before getting a massage.

FOOD THERAPY

Abundant research shows that a good diet can fend off disease. Naturopaths provide nutritional advice, test for and treat food allergies, and may prescribe a detoxifying diet or fast. Training in nutrition at accredited naturopathy schools is similar to that for registered dietitians and exceeds that of medical doctors.

WHAT WORKS: Eating five to seven servings a day of deeply colored fruits and vegetables can help stave off a variety of cancers. Cruciferous vegetables, broccoli for example, are packed with chemicals that flush carcinogens out of the body. Citrus fruits are loaded with antioxidants that can snag free radicals before they cause mutations in DNA. Adding garlic to your meals at least once a week may reduce your risk of colon cancer. And a couple of daily servings of soy—a glass of soy milk and a half cup of firm tofu, perhaps—is probably enough to lower cholesterol, cut cancer risk, and ease symptoms of menopause.

WHAT TO WATCH OUT FOR: There is no evidence that any fast or diet speeds the removal of toxins from the body. And while food allergies do exist, the American Academy of Allergy and Immunology says no research shows they're as prevalent as naturopaths say, nor that such allergies cause many of the disorders naturopaths pin on them.

44. New Doctors of Natural Medicine

What do they have to offer?

HOMEOPATHY

Homeopathy uses infinitesimal doses of herbs, minerals, or even poisons to stimulate the body's curative powers. The theory, called the law of similars, is that if large doses of a substance can cause a problem, minute doses can trigger healing of that same problem.

WHAT WORKS: Widely accepted in Europe, homeopathy is the leading alternative therapy in France, where the national health care system pays for the medicines. But evidence that the more than 1,200 homeopathic remedies work is primarily anecdotal, and mainstream researchers reject the discipline's theoretical underpinnings. A few small studies have shown homeopathy to be at least marginally effective when used to treat hay fever, diarrhea, and flu symptoms, but researchers in the scientific world call the studies flawed or preliminary.

WHAT TO WATCH OUT FOR: Even when a homeopathic remedy is based on a poison, such as arsenic, the chance of a toxic dose is vanishingly small, since remedies are supposed to be so dilute that not even a molecule of the original ingredients remain. Critics say that any homeopathic success is due to the placebo effect, but so long as a patient doesn't use this treatment in place of conventional therapy for a serious or life-threatening illness, it's unlikely to cause harm.

VITAMINS AND MINERALS

Naturopaths prescribe vitamin or mineral supplements to complement a healthy diet; to help fill temporary, extraordinary needs; or as part of the treatment for a specific disease.

WHAT WORKS: Research has established that vitamins and minerals can help prevent assorted ills. (And the body absorbs some nutrients, such as folic acid, more easily from supplements than from foods.) Studies have shown that vitamin A lowers the risk of macular degeneration, a leading cause of blindness; that vitamin C reduces the duration and severity of cold symptoms; and that high doses of niacin lower cholesterol. Researchers believe vitamin E and folic acid protect against heart disease as well. There is a wealth of suggestive but not definitive evidence that many other vitamins and minerals also have beneficial effects.

WHAT TO WATCH OUT FOR: If some is good, more is not necessarily better. Excessive amounts of fat-soluble vitamins such as A and D can be toxic, and doses of niacin high enough to lower cholesterol can cause liver damage and other problems. In addition, some minerals, including iron, can pose risks when levels get too high. Finally, scientists have done relatively little investigation of supplements as treatments for disorders or diseases.

WATER THERAPY

Water is used in all its forms, from ice to steam, to promote health. Baths, packs, compresses, sprays, douches, and colonic enemas are prescribed to improve circulation, reduce inflammation, hydrate the system, and flush toxins from the body.

WHAT WORKS: A few water-based remedies are well accepted in conventional as well as alternative medicine. Cold compresses reduce swelling by constricting blood vessels, which helps control minor internal bleeding; they also can bring down fever. Both conventional and alternative therapists often recommend hot baths and whirlpools to alleviate muscle soreness and joint pain.

WHAT TO WATCH OUT FOR: Some therapies are unsupported by research or conventionally accepted theory. There is no proof that sweating purges your body of anything other than water and salt, for instance. Medical doctors view most colonics as unnecessary, and they can be dangerous because they deplete important electrolytes. Pregnant women, the elderly, young children, and people with heart disease or high blood pressure should avoid intense-heat treatments like steam baths. Diabetics should not put hot compresses on their feet or legs or take hot baths or whirlpools, as these treatments can exacerbate circulatory problems.

RELAXATION THERAPY

Since nervous tension, fatigue, or emotional conflict may trigger or worsen a physical ailment, naturopaths counsel patients and teach stress management techniques, sometimes including biofeedback methods. (Stress and stress-related conditions, such as chronic pain, insomnia, and depression, prompt an estimated 60 to 90 percent of doctor visits.) Practitioners may also advise lifestyle changes to remove sources of stress or minimize their impact.

WHAT WORKS: Mainstream scientists have come to accept that the mind affects the body: Stress decreases the activity of immune cells, for instance, while relaxation through meditation or deep breathing may dampen the body's response to stress hormones. Short but regular sessions of meditation can lower blood pressure by as much as 10 percent and alleviate insomnia, headaches, backaches, and other chronic pain, as well as the symptoms of severe premenstrual syndrome.

WHAT TO WATCH OUT FOR: People who meditate occasionally experience adverse reactions, such as fear, anxiety, or confusion, during sessions. Researchers speculate that these feelings may be responses to the unaccustomed sensation of relaxation or to uninhibited and unwelcome thoughts that may surface during meditation.

follow her friend's advice. The first visit lasted an hour and a half; the naturopath asked about her diet, sleep patterns, and mental outlook, as well as the arthritis pain. Jacobson began taking the herbs and supplements the naturopath prescribed, and every few days, for progressively longer periods, she lay head-down on a slant board to loosen her neck and back. "I felt better last winter than I have in years," she says. In February she was able to drop the last of the drugs her conventional doctor had prescribed. Free of pain, she's been exercising more and has made dietary changes—cutting out caffeine, for example—that she credits with giving her more energy year-round.

Jacobson's predicament is familiar enough that her solution is tantalizing. People with chronic illnesses often run up against the limits of conventional medicine, finding that if they take the drugs that are supposed to help them, they merely trade symptoms for side effects. As for the rest of us, many of our ailments are preventable, caused or worsened by too little exercise and too much junk food and stress. Yet medical schools teach doctors to cure disease, not prevent it. Few physicians have the time, the inclination, or the skills to work closely with patients trying to make lifestyle changes to improve their health.

Dissatisfaction with this state of affairs has led millions outside the bounds of conventional medicine. In a 1990 Harvard survey, one-third of respondents said they had used some form of alternative medicine; researchers estimate that Americans make 425 million visits a year to homeopaths, massage therapists, herbalists, and other alternative healers.

But once beyond the territory marked by medical degrees and doctors' referrals, how do you find your way? Might homeopathy take care of what ails you, for instance, or would herbs be a better bet? More crucially—since a sympathetic ear does not guarantee a discerning brain—how do you find a practitioner who knows what he or she is talking about? The ideal would be someone who straddles two worlds, someone well trained in biology and medicine but with enough knowledge of alternative techniques to be able to pick and choose among them. Many residents of Seattle think they've found that exemplary alternative doctor in the form of a naturopath.

Stories like Jacobson's are as common as raincoats here. The city is home to Bastyr University, the largest naturopathic school in the country, with a clinic that logs about 2,000 appointments each month. Washington is one of 11 states in which licensed naturopaths can legally practice medicine, as primary care physicians, and a new state law requires insurance companies to cover their services. The discipline has achieved such prominence in the Seattle area that county officials—many of whom see naturopaths themselves—have voted to open the nation's first publicly funded natural medicine clinic this month, staffed with naturopaths and other alternative therapists as well as conventional doctors.

As Bastyr president Joseph Pizzorno sees it, Seattle's surge of interest in naturopathy is only the first sign of a much bigger trend. "The family doctor of the future will be the naturopathic doctor," Pizzorno says. "We help people understand why they get sick and teach them to become healthier."

Balderdash, says William Jarvis, a professor of public health and preventive medicine at Loma Linda University in California. By embracing naturopathy, the citizens of Seattle aren't out in front of the rest of us—they're out on a limb, says Jarvis, who's also president of the National Council Against Health Fraud. "Naturopathic ideas have almost no science behind them," he says, speaking for many in medicine. "To compare naturopathy with modern, scientific medicine is like comparing the space program with someone who meditates and thinks he's on the moon."

Prospective patients trying to make sense of naturopathy are left to wander the no-man's-land between Pizzorno's rosy projections and Jarvis's dark skepticism. Figuring out which assessment is closer to the truth requires addressing a few basic yet crucial questions: Do naturopathic treatments work? Are they safe? Just what might naturopathy have to offer that conventional medicine lacks?

THE CORE of naturopathic philosophy is what Hippocrates called *vis medicatrix naturae*, or the healing power of nature. Naturopaths believe that when the body is in sync with the mind and properly cared for—given a healthy diet, adequate rest, and minimal stress—its own vital forces are sufficient to ward off disease. Getting rid of an ailment, they say, is merely the first step toward correcting the underlying imbalance that allowed illness to take hold in the first place. Such an imbalance might be as simple as the shortage of a particular nutrient or as complex as overlong work hours combined with a run-down immune system and an inability to digest certain foods.

Naturopaths came to this country in the late 19th century and gained an enthusiastic following by promoting the "nature cures" of European health spas. They rejected the patent medications widely used at the time; instead, their simple prescriptions emphasized water treatments, a vegetarian diet, fresh air, and exercise. By mid-century, with the growing power of the medical system and its spectacular discoveries of antibiotics and other drugs, the approach had fallen out of favor. But in the 1970s naturopathy began a comeback in the Pacific Northwest, spurred by the back-to-nature ideas of the counterculture.

Naturopathy proved to be well suited to those times. Always something of a hodgepodge of ideas, the discipline had no trouble absorbing Eastern techniques like meditation as they became popular. By the 1980s this eclecticism had added still another element: a trend toward greater professionalism.

Today's licensed naturopaths use most of the same diagnostic tools as conventional physicians—X-rays, blood and urine tests, and so forth. They take Pap smears, listen to lungs, and examine breasts for lumps. Depending on the state, they may be able to perform minor surgery, such as stitching up cuts or removing skin tags. In most states they can prescribe antibiotics and a smattering of other drugs.

Like Jacobson, patients are usually treated with dietary advice, vitamins, and herbs. If Jacobson had complained of asthma instead of back pain, for example, her naturopath probably wouldn't have told her to stop using the inhaled drugs that are the preferred mainstream therapy. But he might have tried to strengthen Jacobson's lungs—and lessen her reliance on the drugs—by prescribing high doses of vitamin C, which research has suggested helps clear the lungs of cell-damaging free radicals. The treatment might also have included a plant chemical called quercetin, which some researchers believe helps prevent lung inflammation.

If all this sounds more medically grounded than you might have expected, it's because naturopathic training these days is similar in many ways to that of traditional physicians. Students applying to either of the country's two accredited naturopathic medical schools—Bastyr or the National College of Naturopathic Medicine in Portland, Oregon—must have completed standard premed courses. Once accepted, students take many of the same subjects as conventional medical students: about 4,500 course-hours of pathology, physiology, biochemistry, and other basic sciences, taught mainly by people with doctorates in those specialties. (Traditional U.S. medical schools include roughly the same number of hours on those topics.) In the third and fourth years of school, naturopaths study more or less the same array of specialties that mainstream doctors do—pediatrics, dermatology, gynecology, ophthalmology—but spend about one-third less time on them.

In place of the conventional studies they miss, naturopathic students take, among other things, some 140 hours of clinical nutrition, as well as herbal medicine, physical medicine (which includes massage as well as physical therapy techniques), and counseling.

"Naturopaths' training is generally good, particularly in the areas of nutrition and herbal medicine," says Andrew Weil, a physician at the University of Arizona in Tucson and author of six books on alternative medicine.

It's not just those well-disposed to alternative medicine who give naturopathic education high marks. The American Dietetic Association, for instance, recently certified one of Bastyr's nutrition programs as acceptable preparation for registered dietitians. After reviewing Oregon's naturopathic licensing exam, professors from Oregon Health Sciences University, a respected medical school, concluded that it required a biomedical education of similar breadth and depth as that received by any freshly graduated primary care physician. (The Oregon exam has since been superseded by an equally rigorous national test.) It's true that a newly minted naturopath doesn't have as much hands-on training as his M.D. counterpart—only Utah requires residency training for naturopaths, while it's a must for all M.D.s. Schools hope to make residency a standard part of education, Pizzorno says, although the change may take years.

Still, naturopathic education is *not* identical to that found in traditional medical schools. Nor is any patient likely to confuse conventional therapies with naturopathic treatments, some of which are unproven or just plain wiggy. For example, the World Wide Web site for the American Association of Naturopathic Physicians tells practitioners about "color therapy" for recovering stroke victims: The patient should wear purple to lower blood pressure, it suggests, or yellow to prevent another stroke.

Then there's the "natural allergy elimination technique," as described by the patient of one Seattle naturopath: You hold a vial of the substance that prompts an allergic response while your naturopath stimulates acupuncture points on your back. For the next 24 hours you must keep the substance away from your "electromagnetic field," not seeing, smelling, or touching it. "It takes 24 hours for the message to run through all the meridians," the patient explains. Naturopaths are also trained in the unproven field of homeopathy—prescribing infinitesimal doses of herbs or other substances that, in larger amounts, would provoke an ailment's symptoms.

Without question, naturopaths are more inclined than medical doctors to try treatments that have little or no scientific backing. Sure, controlled studies have shown that garlic can lower cholesterol; research indicates that the herb echinacea can ward off colds and viruses; and French scientists have found that another herb, ginkgo, reduces tinnitus (ringing in the ears). Indeed, a book that

Some naturopathic treatments have been well researched. Others are unproven. A few are just plain wiggy— like wearing yellow to prevent a stroke.

Pizzorno cowrote, *A Textbook of Natural Medicine*, carried 10,000 citations from the scientific literature that document one aspect or another of naturopathy. But many of these studies examined the way a single herb or vitamin affects a particular body function. The effort to study naturopathic *protocols*—the combination of treatments applied to particular conditions—is a recent one, and results so far have been mixed.

Of course, it's worth considering that many conventional medical practices have not been exhaustively studied either. A 1978 report by the federal Office of Technology Assessment found that only 10 to 20 percent of the treatments used by doctors had been evaluated in controlled clinical trials, the most reliable method of research. While drugs undergo rigorous testing before approval by the Food and Drug Administration, many surgical therapies have found their way into common practice without benefit of such trials. The same goes for off-label uses of drugs—that is, any use other than the one approved by the FDA. Many drugs used to treat certain cancers, for instance, have not been approved for that particular purpose.

And it's worth considering, too, that open-mindedness is precisely what many people are seeking from alternative prac-

8. AMERICA'S HEALTH AND THE HEALTH CARE SYSTEM

titioners. A patient may be willing to take the chance of wasting some time and money, so long as there are no big risks in doing so.

But the potential dangers of unproven therapies are what critics like Jarvis find most alarming. He says that some naturopathic practices and beliefs are hazardous, either inherently or because they may keep a patient from getting treatments that are proven to work.

Jarvis points to chelation therapy, a widely accepted treatment for lead poisoning, as an example. Some naturopaths say the therapy, which involves injections of chemicals, can remove plaque from clogged arteries. But this use has never been studied; the American Heart Association has warned that it can cause kidney failure and death. And Jarvis points to the belief of some naturopaths in the virtues of colonic irrigation, in which a machine delivers a powerful enema. The treatment is purported to improve the health of the bowels but has caused a handful of deaths, though none occurred under the care of a naturopath.

That all sounds scary. But under scrutiny, the red flags fall quickly. The vast majority of naturopaths practice neither chelation therapy nor colonic irrigation. Indeed, most naturopathic treatments are noninvasive and have few side effects, according to Ze'ev Young, a Seattle family physician who has reviewed naturopathic treatments for King County Medical Blue Shield, where he is associate medical director. As a group, licensed naturopaths have a good track record on safety issues. They are rarely sued for malpractice, and state licensing boards seldom receive complaints about them.

In the interests of safety, though, patients ought to make sure that a naturopath has a license or, in states that don't issue licenses, has attended one of the two accredited naturopathic medical schools. (In states without licensing laws, self-styled naturopaths who have merely taken a correspondence course can hang out a shingle.) And according to Weil, a wise patient will be skeptical if a practitioner strays outside the low-tech traditions of the profession.

Other concerns are subtler. Naturopaths may downplay the benefits of childhood vaccinations out of a belief that the occasional side effects of some vaccines pose a greater threat than the diseases they prevent. Where state laws require certain vaccinations for children, it's a moot point. But in cases where the

The Best of Both Worlds

So you're interested in alternative medicine but wary of hopping from homeopath to herbalist to hypnotist—and you don't want to give up the benefits of mainstream medical care. What should you do? Here are three options.

FIND AN M.D. WHO IS OPEN TO ALTERNATIVES

Medical doctors who have studied a broad range of nontraditional techniques— or taken up an alternative specialty, such as acupuncture or homeopathy—are sometimes called alternative physicians. One advantage of choosing an alternative physician as a caregiver is that insurers are likely to cover his or her services.

To find such a doctor, ask at the dean's office at a medical school in your area whether any faculty members are interested in alternative medicine; these professors may know of like-minded physicians in the community. Or contact the American Holistic Medical Association for a list of members (the association includes alternative physicians, doctors of osteopathy, chiropractors, and other therapists). Send a check or money order for $8 to 4101 Lake Boone Trail, Suite 201, Raleigh, NC 27607.

SEE A NATUROPATH IN ADDITION TO YOUR REGULAR DOCTOR

Most states don't license naturopaths as medical practitioners, so they can't legally diagnose or treat illness. That means they can't act as your primary care physician. They can, however, serve as your one-stop doc of the alternative world. Naturopaths who have graduated from one of the country's two accredited schools have studied virtually every alternative technique, from herbal medicine to massage. In this role, a naturopath might work with you on managing stress better or improving your diet. You might also call in a naturopath if you have a persistent condition—like premenstrual syndrome or chronic fatigue syndrome— for which the conventional treatments are few or ineffectual.

You're likely to find naturopaths listed in the yellow pages as specialists in nutritional or herbal therapies. To ensure you're in the hands of someone with a grounding in biology and medicine, as well as in alternative techniques, choose a practitioner who graduated from one of the two accredited naturopathic schools: Bastyr University in Seattle or the National College of Naturopathic Medicine in Portland, Oregon. (Correspondence-course naturopaths receive far less training.) Finally, don't settle for too recent a grad. Because naturopathy schools provide less hands-on training than do medical schools, you'll want to make sure the person you see has been in practice for several years.

CHOOSE A NATUROPATH AS YOUR PRIMARY CARE PHYSICIAN

If you live in one of the 11 states that license naturopaths, you can use one as your regular doctor. (The 11 licensing states are Alaska, Arizona, Connecticut, Florida, Hawaii, Maine, Montana, New Hampshire, Oregon, Utah, and Washington.) In those states naturopaths can treat earaches, allergies, and any of the other garden-variety complaints generally taken to a family practitioner or an internist. They can also refer you to a specialist for any complicated ailment.

The American Association of Naturopathic Physicians offers state directories of qualified naturopaths. Send $5 to 2366 Eastlake Avenue E., Suite 322, Seattle, WA 98102. In Connecticut and Washington, which have passed insurance equity laws, most policies will reimburse for naturopathic services. Elsewhere it depends on the company, but 90 insurers nationwide have covered naturopathic services for one ailment or another. —K.G.

decision rests with parents, most naturopaths would paint a somewhat ominous picture of childhood vaccines, making parents less likely to get the full battery of recommended shots for their children.

"That's an area that has to be ironed out," says Weil. "The benefits of immunization clearly outweigh the risks."

Then there's the fact that practitioners often caution patients not to expect quick results, explaining that many naturopathic therapies take effect gradually. As a consequence, gravely ill patients could delay too long before going for medical help. However, many physicians who have worked with naturopaths say this doesn't seem to be a big problem; naturopaths generally have a healthy respect for the limits of their medicine.

"One of my patients with ovarian cancer had just completely opted out of medical care," says David Aboulafia, a Seattle hematologist and oncologist who treats many patients who also see naturopaths. "It was her naturopath who was instrumental in getting her to come back to me. Rather than saying, 'Just take these herbs,' the naturopath said, 'Look, there's only so much I can do for you. You've got to see the specialist.'"

IF THE RISKS of naturopathy seem to be mostly theoretical, to a patient like Michael Lawrence its benefits appear substantial. Chronic, severe stomach pain had plagued Lawrence, a 45-year-old banker, for 20 years. Eminent gastroenterologists in Los Angeles, San Francisco, and Seattle had treated him, each time with limited success. They all ran the same tests and prescribed ulcer medication that helped for only a week or two and ultimately left him feeling no better.

Last year Lawrence's pain got worse, sapping his energy so he could barely drag himself to work and back. Meanwhile, after surviving several downsizings, he found himself putting in 12-hour days at work. He spent his weekends resting in bed and put himself on a bland, nearly liquid diet when his upset stomach made eating unbearable.

Compounding the pain was his sense that his physicians were indifferent to his suffering, interested in his stomach but not the person attached to it. Like many patients of naturopaths, Lawrence gets angry when he talks about his experiences with what he calls "AMA doctors."

"My last doctor treated me like part of an assembly line," he says. "He would come in, and in five minutes he would have 'diagnosed' my problem."

In desperation, Lawrence turned to Seattle naturopath Patrick Donovan. "He listened to me talk," Lawrence says. "It

Naturopaths give the kind of comforting care that doctors used to dispense more liberally, back in the days of fewer drugs and more time.

was a totally different experience." The first visit lasted nearly two hours, and the conversation covered not just Lawrence's symptoms but how he felt about his life. Later Donovan ordered stool and blood tests, and told Lawrence, for starters, that he was severely allergic to wheat and dairy products, as well as citrus fruits.

"He said, 'You've got to stop eating these foods.' I did, and within one month the chronic pain had stopped," Lawrence says. "No other doctor had ever talked to me about nutrition or tested me for allergies."

Over the months they worked together, Lawrence took advice from Donovan on other matters as well. The recommendations went beyond the commonly defined parameters of medicine.

"Dr. Donovan was very blunt with me," Lawrence says. "He said, 'Your health is in trouble. You need to find another job.'" Lawrence's other doctors had also recommended reducing stress; now the advice hit home. Since switching to a less harried position, Lawrence says, he's been healthier and happier.

There are many ways to think about Lawrence's success story. One is to suppose his naturopath discovered a medical solution that the conventional doctors had overlooked. Certainly, some alternative therapies have passed muster in scientific studies. In a study scheduled for publication later this year, for instance, a five-herb combination given to menopausal women relieved symptoms like hot flashes, insomnia, and mood swings. But in Lawrence's case, it's impossible to be certain he really has food allergies. Naturopaths frequently diagnose them as the source of all kinds of ills, but conventional doctors say they are rare and unlikely to cause the kinds of problems that Lawrence experienced. Food allergies, at least as many naturopaths define them—or food sensitivities, as a conventional doctor might put it in some cases—have not been researched thoroughly.

Another possibility is to decide that Lawrence was already getting better on his own, and the naturopath just came along at the same time. As Voltaire said, "The art of medicine consists in amusing the patient while nature cures the disease."

Still another is to chalk his recovery up to the placebo effect, the mysterious process by which a patient can get well after taking sugar pills or receiving some other bogus treatment. Researchers have identified some 30 elements that may contribute to the placebo effect, including how suggestible a person is, the patient's faith in the therapy and the caregiver, and the caregiver's confidence in the treatment. A combination of convictions can somehow trigger lasting physical changes.

But does it matter which explanation is closest to the truth? Any good clinician will tell you that medicine is as much an art as a science, and that the relationship between doctor and patient is a primary color on the palette. Today conventional doctors too often are rushed, and powerful treatments too often bring pain. Perhaps just as important as naturopaths' treatments is the listening they offer, and the reassurance. It's the kind of comforting care that doctors used to dispense more liberally, back in the days when they had fewer drugs and more time.

Just ask oncologist Aboulafia, who spends his days wielding some of the most potent medical tools ever devised. "There is a reason why people are seeing naturopaths so much more these days," he says. "Naturopathy captures something that Western medicine misses."

Katherine Griffin is a staff writer.

Consumer Health

For many people the term "consumer health" conjures up images of selecting health care services and paying medical bills. Actually, the term encompasses all consumer products and services that influence people's health and welfare. This broad definition suggests that almost everything we see or do may be construed as a consumer health issue. Such is the case with media coverage of medical investigations. In the last several years, millions of Americans have added food products that contain oat bran to their diets. Many of these individuals are now considering dropping oat bran from their diets. Why? First they read reports claiming that oat bran could reduce blood cholesterol levels. When reports began to question the value of oat bran as a cholesterol reducer, many people stopped using it. This scenario is typical of the way American consumers respond to media reports on health issues. "Nutrition in the News: What the Headlines Don't Tell You" discusses the impact that media coverage of health issues has on our health behavior and provides useful information to consider as part of your decision-making process as you sort through the health-related articles vying for your attention.

A number of federal government agencies in the United States serve to protect Americans from consumer health fraud. These organizations include the Food and Drug Administration, the Federal Trade Commission, the U.S. Postal Service, the Office of Consumer Education, the Office of Consumer Affairs, the Public Health Service, the National Institutes of Health, the Health Services Administration, and the Consumer Protection Agency. While they play an important role in protecting the health of consumers, they are unable to keep pace with the number

UNIT 9

of products and services being marketed and sold. Consumers need to understand, then, that if an advertised claim sounds too good to be true, it probably is.

Suppose that you read the newspaper every day and watch the nightly news religiously. You also subscribe to several magazines, one of which covers health. Health issues may still seem as variable as the weather, and any consumer can be ill-informed. "How Health Savvy Are You?" examines 20 questions to test your knowledge of nutrition, fitness, and medicine.

In the search for information about health, millions of Americans are turning to the World Wide Web. While it can be a wonderful resource for information on a wide variety of topics, the Internet has limitations. On the positive side, there are newsgroups that people can visit for emotional support and advice from others afflicted with similar illnesses. And there are home pages that deal with almost any known disease. These pages provide a virtual medical library of the most current information available. Many sites even have search facilities that allow visitors free access to the specific information they desire. But the downside of this wealth of information is that not all of it is accurate and reliable. The Web has become fertile ground for charlatans and purveyors of fraudulent claims. Given free access to all this information, how is a consumer to judge its quality? The best answer is probably that information is only as good as its provider. "The Doctor Is On" discusses the pros and cons of seeking health information from the World Wide Web.

Have you ever wished that you could get the medication you want without seeing your physician? Each year the number of medications available without prescription is growing. The main reason for this shift of drugs from prescription to nonprescription is economic. When the patent on a prescription medication will soon expire, it can be extended for an additional three years if the medication is sold over the counter. While that procedure is good for pharmaceutical companies, it can be bad for consumers, because it removes the safeguards that were deemed necessary when the drug was originally approved for use. The potential consumer hazards associated with such changes are discussed in "The Switch to OTC: No Prescription, No Protection?" Another consumer health issue covered in this unit includes advice on spotting hidden pitfalls in your health care plan. The unit is by no means exhaustive, but it demonstrates the diversity of topics that are consumer health issues.

Looking Ahead: Challenge Questions

Why should one question the validity of health-related information reported by the media?

Is the government doing enough to protect consumers? If not, what recommendations would you make for changes?

What are some of the potential pitfalls that one should be aware of when selecting a health care plan?

Is the switch from prescription to OTC good or bad? Why?

What are the pros and cons of going on-line in search of health-related information?

What suggestions would you make to someone who was about to search on-line for health information?

HOW HEALTH SAVVY ARE YOU?

20 questions to test your knowledge of nutrition, fitness, and medicine.

In our five-plus years of publishing Consumer Reports on Health, we've covered some varied—and changing—ground. When we published our first issue back in September 1989, oat bran (remember oat bran?) was the nutritional wonder of the day; now it's beta-carotene (or is it?). Exercise authorities still demanded a vigorous workout every other day for at least 20 minutes a pop; now it almost seems that just getting up to change the channel is a healthful improvement over using the remote.

Since our first issue, we've seen a wide range of genuine medical breakthroughs, including a blood test to detect early prostate cancer, antibiotic treatment to cure ulcers, life-saving therapy for diabetes, and improved drug treatment for heart failure, among many others. And we've witnessed a fair share of medical charades—such as the introduction of several "new" over-the-counter pain relievers no better than the old ones.

It's hard for a health-conscious consumer to keep up. To help you assess your grasp of the field, here are 20 questions on a variety of topics that we've explored over the past five years. You'll find the answers, along with a brief discussion of each topic, on the following pages. We surveyed some 400 readers at random last summer on the same questions, so you'll see how many of your peers knew the right answers.

This isn't an easy quiz. None of the readers we tested got all the answers right. So if you miss a lot of questions, don't get discouraged; just wait five years and check again. Maybe an answer that's wrong now will be right then.

Multiple choice: Take your best guess

1. Which of the following factors can increase your risk of catching cold?
   a. Exposure to cold, wet weather.
   b. Lack of rest.
   c. Psychological stress.
   d. All of the above.

2. Studies suggest that vitamin C:
   a. Can ease cold symptoms.
   b. Can help prevent a cold.
   c. Can cure the common cold.
   d. None of the above.

3. Which of the following can harm your eyesight?
   a. Wearing contact lenses overnight.
   b. Reading in dim light.
   c. Wearing off-the-rack reading glasses.
   d. All of the above.

4. Eating sugar can:
   a. Make children hyperactive.
   b. Cause tooth decay.
   c. Increase the risk of diabetes.
   d. All of the above.

Continued on next page

45. Health Savvy

HEALTH QUIZ *Continued*

5. Which can raise your level of "good" HDL cholesterol?
   a. Aerobic exercise.
   b. Strength training.
   c. Low-fat diet.
   d. Eating eggs.

6. Fish may be good for the heart because:
   a. It is low in saturated fat.
   b. It contains omega-3 fatty acids.
   c. It replaces fatty meals in the diet.
   d. All of the above.

7. The strongest evidence on dietary measures to prevent cancer is on:
   a. Beta-carotene.
   b. Fruits and vegetables.
   c. Low-fat diet.
   d. Vitamin E.

8. Vitamin E is plentiful in which foods?
   a. Fruits and vegetables.
   b. Plant fats such as vegetable oils.
   c. Dairy products.
   d. All of the above.

9. The single most powerful measure for preventing osteoporosis in women is:
   a. Calcium supplements.
   b. Estrogen replacement therapy.
   c. Weight-bearing exercise.
   d. Vitamin-D supplements.

10. The single most important thing to do for a muscle sprain is:
    a. Elevate the injury.
    b. Rest the joint.
    c. Apply ice.
    d. Compress the injured area.

True or false: A 50/50 shot

11. Frozen vegetables are usually less nutritious than fresh vegetables.
    True ___ False ___

12. Most people should cut back on salt to ward off hypertension.
    True ___ False ___

13. Exercise and diet are usually enough to control mild hypertension.
    True ___ False ___

14. You should brush your teeth after every meal.
    True ___ False ___

15. Total impotence (erectile dysfunction) usually reflects a psychological problem.
    True ___ False ___

16. Dry-roasted nuts have less fat than oil-roasted nuts.
    True ___ False ___

17. One way to reduce the fat in ground meat is to rinse the meat after cooking.
    True ___ False ___

18. Dark sunglasses help prevent cataracts better than lighter lenses do.
    True ___ False ___

19. Snoring may signal coronary heart disease.
    True ___ False ___

20. Sit-ups are dangerous.
    True ___ False ___

Here are the correct answers to our 20 questions—and a look at how many readers guessed right.

1. Which of the following factors can increase your risk of catching cold?
☑ **c. Psychological stress.** (10% of the readers we tested answered correctly.)

Apparently, not many readers realize that exposure to the elements and lack of rest don't boost your odds of getting sick—despite what your mother told you. Studies have shown that getting chilly or damp doesn't even increase the severity or duration of a cold. Colds are probably more common in cool weather because people spend more time together indoors, where viruses can spread more easily. In addition, the heated indoor air is drier, which leaves the nasal membranes more susceptible to infection. As for lack of rest, that may make you feel worse when you have a cold, but it won't make you more likely to catch cold in the first place.

Psychological stress, on the other hand, may indeed weaken a person's defenses against the common cold. In a recent study of volunteers deliberately infected with a cold virus, stress level made the difference between those who got sick in response to the infection and those who shook it off without developing symptoms.

2. Studies suggest that vitamin C:
☑ **a. Can ease cold symptoms.** (38% correct)

The most enduring legacy of Linus Pauling, who died last year at the age of 93, may be the unflagging popular enthusiasm for vitamin C to ward off the common cold. Unfortunately, there's no convincing scientific support for that practice—although a few studies have suggested that taking extra vitamin C regularly may *slightly* diminish the severity of symptoms after a cold develops.

3. Which of the following can harm your eyesight?
☑ **a. Wearing contacts overnight.** (41% correct)

Half of our readers believe that reading in dim light or using cheap, off-the-rack reading glasses can also damage vision. They can't. Reading in dim light is no more injurious to the eyes than straining to hear a

9. CONSUMER HEALTH

whisper is to the ears. Store-bought reading glasses are perfectly safe and work fine for most people with presbyopia (farsightedness due to aging eyes). The fact is, poor lighting and the wrong lenses—whether off-the-rack or prescription—can cause eyestrain, but they won't harm your eyesight.

Wearing "extended-wear" contact lenses overnight, on the other hand, does threaten eyesight. Even a single night increases the risk of a potentially blinding corneal infection. Closely following the manufacturer's sterilizing regimen doesn't eliminate that risk.

4. Eating sugar can:
☑ **b. Cause tooth decay.** (34% correct)

Nine out of 10 readers know that sugar can cause tooth decay. But 6 of those 9 also believe that sugar makes kids hyper and promotes diabetes. Trust us; it doesn't (see CRH, 10/94). To minimize the cavity risk from sugar, wait for mealtime to eat carbohydrates, including sweets and starchy foods (which contain complex sugars). That way, the other foods will boost saliva, which neutralizes the tooth-dissolving acids that stem from sugar and helps to clear food particles and sugar from the mouth.

Don't fall for the notion that "natural" sweeteners like fruit sugar, honey, and molasses are somehow gentler on the teeth. They all contain fructose, glucose, sucrose, or other sugars that can cause decay. In fact, because syrupy sweeteners like honey tend to stick to the teeth, they may actually be more harmful than refined sugar.

5. Which can raise your level of "good" HDL cholesterol?
☑ **a. Aerobic exercise.** (62% correct)

A low-fat diet tends to lower the "good" along with the "bad" (LDL) cholesterol, so other steps must be taken to boost HDL. The most effective nondrug measure is aerobic exercise. Strength-training exercise doesn't do much for HDL—though unlike aerobics, it does reduce LDL. Other ways to boost HDL without resorting to drugs include losing excess weight and quitting smoking.

6. Fish may be good for the heart because:
☑ **d. All of the above.** (59% correct)

Back in September 1989, the lead story in our first issue asked, "Is fish oil more than snake oil with gills?" At the time, the answer was an unequivocal "maybe." Mixed evidence suggested that the omega-3 fatty acids in fish oil might have cardiovascular benefits. So we recommended "fish, the food" over "fish oil, the capsule." Since then, further research has shifted that "maybe" closer to a tentative "yes." But we still favor fish over fish oil—because those apparent benefits of fish go beyond its omega-3 fatty acids: Low in saturated fat and calories, fish is a healthful alternative to red meat and other fatty meals. We recommend eating fish at least twice a week. (For ways to minimize the risk from potentially contaminated fish, see CRH, 6/94.)

7. The strongest evidence on dietary measures to prevent cancer is on:
☑ **b. Fruits and vegetables.** (47% correct)

About a third of our readers chose c, a low-fat diet. As we noted back in June 1990, however, "Many believe the link is solid, but enthusiasm may have outrun the evidence." Then as now, the closest thing to a clear fat-cancer connection involved colon cancer. Some studies also implicate fat in the progression of prostate cancer. Meanwhile, any link between fat and breast cancer looks increasingly less likely.

Antioxidant nutrients like beta-carotene and vitamin E have been much in the news for their supposed cancer-fighting abilities. In our reader survey, votes of confidence for beta-carotene topped vitamin E by a margin of 20 to 1. But the strength of the actual anti-cancer evidence on the two nutrients is comparable. The jury is still out on those nutrients and other individual antioxidants, such as vitamin C. However, as nearly half of our readers know, there's a clear verdict in support of fruits and vegetables. (Mom got that one right.) Numerous studies have found a connection between a produce-rich diet and reduced rates of various cancers, including cancers of the bladder, breast, colon, lung, mouth, stomach, throat, and prostate.

8. Vitamin E is plentiful in which foods?
☑ **b. Plant fats like vegetable oils.** (32% correct)

About half our readers believe that a low-fat diet rich in fruits and vegetables provides lots of vitamin E—as it does the other two main antioxidant nutrients, beta-carotene and vitamin C. But vitamin E is different from those nutrients. The foods that are highest in E are concentrated plant fats like vegetable and seed oils, as well as vegetable-oil products such as margarine and salad dressing.

Since it's hard to get large quantities of vitamin E through diet alone, many people hedge their bets with supplements. That appears to be safe enough, if you stay within a modest range. The usual multivitamin provides 30 mg of vitamin E (sometimes listed as 45 IU, or International Units). If you choose a supplement containing only vitamin E, stick with a relatively low dosage of 65 to 260 mg (100 to 400 IU).

9. The single most powerful measure for preventing osteoporosis in women is:
☑ **b. Estrogen replacement.** (15% correct)

For maintaining healthy bones after menopause, when the risk of osteoporosis is highest, nothing is more effective than replacing lost estrogen. An adequate intake of calcium (including calcium supplements, if necessary) is also essential—especially when estrogen replacement therapy is not an option. All adults should consume at least 1000 mg of calcium a day. Postmenopausal women who are not on estrogen and men over 65 should get at least 1500 mg. (Vitamin D helps the body absorb calcium, but most people get enough vitamin D from exposure to sunlight and from their diet.)

Regular weight-bearing exercise helps preserve bone, too. Recent research suggests that strength-training workouts may provide the maximum benefit—and without the jarring of high-impact exercise, such as running.

10. The single most important thing to do for a muscle sprain is:
☑ **c. Apply ice.** (59% correct)
All four strategies help heal a sprain, as summed up by the acronym RICE: Rest, Ice, Compression, Elevation. But the most important step to minimize the damage and speed recovery is to apply ice immediately. Cold constricts blood vessels and thus helps limit bleeding and prevent swelling. If you don't have a flexible ice pack, use a bag of frozen vegetables. (Crushed ice soon turns into a solid block.) Ice the injury for 10 to 20 minutes every hour or two for the first 6 to 12 hours—at least until the swelling is no longer increasing. If swelling resumes, apply ice again. After a day or two of RICE, gently stretch the muscle throughout the day for several days.

11. Frozen vegetables are usually less nutritious than fresh vegetables.
☑ **False.** (18% correct)
That's generally true only if you buy your vegetables fresh off the farm—or if you grow your own. Most people eat "fresh" vegetables that have been hauled across the country and displayed for a few days in the supermarket. That leaves plenty of time for air, heat, and light to break down vitamins. Frozen vegetables are especially likely to beat fresh vegetables that are out of season or that sit in the refrigerator for more than a couple of days. For maximum nutrition, don't thaw frozen vegetables before cooking. (Vegetables clumped together in the bag indicate thawing somewhere along the line.)

Canned vegetables don't stack up to fresh or frozen vegetables. Much of the vitamin content (not to mention taste) is destroyed by high processing temperatures or lost to water in the can.

12. Most people should cut back on salt to ward off hypertension.
☑ **False.** (28% correct)
Some people with hypertension do need to restrict their sodium intake to keep their blood pressure under control. But for everyone else, salt is simply not the health threat it's made out to be. To find out if you're in the salt-sensitive minority, see our April 1994 report for a dietary test you can take at home.

13. Exercise and diet are usually enough to control mild hypertension.
☑ **False.** (8% correct)
Those "lifestyle" measures are a good place to start, but they're usually not enough, even for mild hypertension—typically defined as a systolic reading (the upper number) of 140 to 160 mm Hg or a diastolic reading (the lower number) of 90 to 105 mm Hg. And there's now strong evidence that reducing even such borderline elevations in blood pressure helps prevent more serious disease.

Of course, nondrug measures to lower blood pressure are still valuable. Even if such therapy doesn't eliminate the need for medication altogether, it can enable many patients to use lower drug doses, thereby cutting down on possible side effects. Before starting on medication, people with mild hypertension should at least give nondrug therapy a fair trial. That means getting regular exercise (especially aerobic exercise), losing weight, reducing stress, and cutting down on alcohol and (possibly) sodium. If blood pressure does not decline after six months, antihypertensive medication may well be necessary—particularly if you have other risk factors for coronary heart disease.

14. You should brush your teeth after every meal.
☑ **False.** (19% correct)
There's really no need to brush every time you eat. It takes 16 to 24 hours for the bacteria fueled by food residues left on the teeth to produce plaque, which can eventually cause cavities and gum disease. If you brush properly in the morning and in the evening, and floss on one of those occasions, there won't be time for the bacteria to cause a problem. In fact, it's possible to get too much of a good thing: Brushing too often or too vigorously can irritate or even damage the gums.

15. Total impotence (erectile dysfunction) usually reflects a psychological problem.
☑ **False.** (61% correct)
Until recently, impotence was almost always blamed on psychological factors, such as stress, anxiety, or depression. Although such factors can contribute to impotence, they're usually not the primary cause. (Occasional difficulty achieving or maintaining an erection, which becomes increasingly frequent with age, is not considered true impotence.) The problem is much more likely to stem from medical factors, such as drug side effects, impaired circulation, neurological problems, or hormonal imbalance. If psychological factors really are to blame, counseling by a sex therapist or treatment for depression may help. When physiological or psychological treatment fails to correct the underlying problem, men can try a number of mechanical techniques for creating an erection, including drug injections, vacuum pumps, and surgical implants.

16. Dry-roasted nuts have less fat than oil-roasted nuts.
☑ **False.** (26% correct)
You'll save virtually no fat at all by choosing dry-roasted nuts over the usual oil-roasted kind. That's because oil-roasted nuts are not immersed in the boiling oil long enough to absorb any of it. And the excess oil is drained off afterward.

9. CONSUMER HEALTH

17. One way to reduce the fat in ground meat is to rinse the meat after cooking.

☑ **True.** (21% correct)

Here's the simplest technique: Brown ground meat in a nonstick pan, drain off the fat, pour hot water over the meat, and drain it again. That can rinse away as much as three-quarters of the fat. Of course, some of the flavor gets drained off with it. And the meat doesn't hold together well. So rinsed meat is best reserved for spaghetti sauce, casseroles, chili, and other seasoned dishes.

18. Dark sunglasses help prevent cataracts better than lighter lenses do.

☑ **False.** (57% correct)

Darkening the lenses blocks visible light, but has no effect on ultraviolet light, the end of the spectrum that contributes to cataracts. Plastic lenses—even clear ones—block most UV light, and glass lenses block some. Special coatings increase UV absorption. Darker lenses may help protect against a potential though unproved hazard from visible light: There's some evidence that lifetime exposure may damage the part of the retina that distinguishes fine detail.

19. Snoring may signal coronary heart disease.

☑ **True.** (50% correct)

Not all snorers have coronary disease, but the disease is more common among people who snore than among those who don't. More important, snoring may do more that just *signal* coronary disease; that's because the irregular airflow may actually *contribute* to the development of the disease. Those at greatest risk have a severe condition known as sleep apnea, in which the snorer actually stops breathing repeatedly throughout the night. There are various ways to help remedy snoring and apnea, ranging from changes in sleep position to surgery. A sleep specialist can help diagnose the problem and recommend a solution. . . .

20. Sit-ups are dangerous.

☑ **True.** (45% correct)

Done in the traditional fashion—lifting the upper body into the sitting position with hands clasped behind the head, and legs straight or bent at the knee—sit-ups strain the back. That's especially a problem for older exercisers and people with a history of back trouble (which includes most adults). Moreover, much of the sit-up motion is unnecessary, since the abdominal muscles are used to lift the upper body just the first few inches off the floor.

Partial sit-ups, a modified version of the original, are safer and more efficient for strengthening the abdominal muscles: Lying on your back with knees bent and with your arms crossed in front of your chest or hands clasped loosely behind your head, lift your head, shoulders, and upper back (not your entire upper body) off the floor.

RATING YOURSELF

The scoring guide below is based on the performance of the 400 readers who took the quiz as part of our monthly survey of randomly selected subscribers.

18 - 20 correct: Are you sure you didn't cheat?
15 - 17 correct: We have a staff opening for you.
10 - 14 correct: More than respectable.
5 - 9 correct: Graded on a curve, you should give yourself a solid "B."
0 - 4 correct: Start boning up on those back issues. But don't despair. You have lots of company.

Nutrition In The News: What The Headlines Don't Tell You

It just doesn't make sense. For years, you've been told that to live a long, healthy life, you've got to eat right and take care of yourself. So you cut down on fat, take vitamins and exercise regularly. Then one morning you glance at the headlines and learn that antioxidants may not be so effective in preventing cancer after all. Later, you hear that a low-fat diet may not be as heart-healthy as you were led to believe. How can nutrition experts change their minds so suddenly and so often? Frustrated and confused, you throw your hands in the air and race to the nearest fast-food joint for a cheeseburger and fries.

But before you take that first bite, there are some things you should know about nutrition research and how it is reported in the media. It's seldom as simple and straightforward as it seems.

At Cross Purposes. Much of the confusion exists because researchers and reporters speak different languages. Reporters spotlight unique or unusual findings of scientific studies in order to grab your attention. Scientists, on the other hand, prefer to wait for consensus opinions that are built slowly but surely over time.

"First-time findings are not the most interesting, nor are they necessarily true," says Jo Freudenheim, Ph.D., nutritional epidemiologist at the State University of New York at Buffalo. But they make great headlines.

The media often report on studies published in medical journals as the latest thinking. But scientists look at published studies as "works in progress" that serve either to support or refute existing research. Before a finding becomes fact, it must be confirmed repeatedly. That's why researchers are almost always ultraconservative about recommending changes in diet or lifestyle on the basis of a single study. "More research is needed" is a virtual mantra in scientific circles.

Limited By Design. Scientists conduct studies using a variety of methods, each with its own advantages and limitations. Only when results from all types of studies are viewed collectively can scientists put the pieces of the puzzle together to form a clearer picture of the link between diet and disease.

Epidemiological studies, or population studies, observe large numbers of people to see if there's a link between specific dietary or lifestyle habits and disease in a population. Since these studies observe people's behavior—say, how much fish Eskimo eat per week—it's always possible that unknown factors, like unreported foods or genetics, can influence findings.

For example, many epidemiological studies have found that people who eat diets rich in fruits and vegetables have lower cancer rates. But, people who eat fruits and vegetables may have other healthy habits—like not smoking or not drinking alcohol—that protect them from cancer. Since epidemiological studies do not provide proof of a direct cause and effect relationship, scientists turn to experimental studies with animals or humans to build a stronger case.

Such experiments allow researchers to manipulate the effect of a specific factor (what researchers call a variable), like a vitamin or drug, under tightly controlled conditions. But even experiments have limitations. For example, findings from *animal studies,* while one step beyond epidemiological studies, will not necessarily produce the same results when tested in people.

Human clinical trials offer strongest proof of cause and effect, especially if

9. CONSUMER HEALTH

the studies are *randomized, placebo-controlled* and *double blind*. This means that participants are randomly assigned to a treatment group. One group receives, for example, a vitamin under study. A control group receives a placebo, or dummy pill, and neither subject nor researcher knows who got what until the results are in. However, clinical trials also have shortcomings.

> "It is the totality of evidence, not the latest headlines, that should influence you."

Take last year's highly publicized study showing beta-carotene and vitamin E did not reduce lung cancer in male Finnish smokers. The study was criticized for being too short, providing insufficient amounts of vitamins to show any positive effect and applying only to smokers. It was also suggested that the unexpected results could have been a fluke, due purely to chance.

Since these results went against the accumulating body of evidence, it became a classic example of why you should not change your dietary habits on the basis of a single study. As researchers like to point out, it is the totality of evidence, not the latest headlines, that should influence you.

Risky Business. Understanding risk also helps keep research results in perspective. Since nothing in life is risk-free, changing your lifestyle or eating habits almost always means trading one risk for another. It's important to consider how risky something is and question whether the alternative is actually better. For example, you give up snacking on fruit to avoid pesticides, but you replace it with fat-free cookies. Not only do you lose out on the health benefits of fruit, you've added what is probably a high-calorie, low-nutrient food to your diet—a potentially bigger risk than a small pesticide residue.

That's why it's important to look at the bigger picture and decide how relevant the findings of a study are to you.

Ask yourself if the condition being studied is a rare or common occurrence. How likely is it to affect you? If a study on women showed that eating food X increased the risk of breast cancer by 10%, and eating food Y increased the risk of bladder cancer by 50%, should you give up food Y? Food X? Both? There's no way to know how you personally will be affected, but women in general would probably benefit more by dropping food X from their menus first. That's because breast cancer is so much more common in women than bladder cancer, that even a small increase in risk affects more women. Men should be more concerned about food Y since bladder cancer is three times more common in men than in women.

The point? Getting a sense of the potential risk prevents overreacting to frightening headlines.

Making Sense of It All. Keep these tips in mind when you're alerted to "breaking nutrition news."

❖ Read beyond the headlines. You'll often find practical advice and a broader perspective on the study near the end of an article or TV report.

❖ Consider the source. View industry-funded reports with some caution; corporate profits may be riding on the results. However, much solid research has been funded by industry. Research published in scientific journals like the *Journal of the American Medical Association* and *The New England Journal of Medicine,* which depend on experts to critically review research before publication, are safe bets.

❖ Look at the bigger picture. It makes more sense to stop smoking, lose weight and exercise than to rely primarily on the latest antioxidant research to reduce heart disease risk.

❖ Remember that there are few true breakthroughs in nutrition research. Be skeptical of claims to the contrary.

—*Adrienne Forman, M.S., R.D.*

The switch to OTC: No prescription, no protection?

More and more drugs are going over the counter. That increases your control—but it also increases your risk.

In the past 18 months, the U.S. Food and Drug Administration has approved the over-the-counter sale of four heartburn drugs formerly available by prescription only. Since receiving approval, the drug makers have poured roughly half a billion dollars into dueling ads, each claiming that their cure acts faster, lasts longer, or provides more protection than the others.

Actually, none of the four drugs—cimetidine (*Tagamet HB*), famotidine (*Pepcid AC*), nizatidine (*Axid AR*), and ranitidine (*Zantac 75*)—works any better than the others. In many cases, ordinary antacids are preferable to any of the new drugs (see box "Heartburn: How to quench the flames"). A federal judge, unable to stomach the ads, has ordered two of the combatants to stifle several of their claims and stick to the facts.

The heartburn slugfest highlights the potential problems created by the growing trend toward over-the-counter drugs. While direct access to those drugs increases your ability to manage your own health, it also increases the risk of misuse—a risk compounded by the marketers' claims.

Why the switch?

The FDA must approve the shift of a drug to over-the-counter status. But it's the drug maker, not the agency, that initiates the process. Most companies apply because their patent on a prescription drug is about to expire; going over the counter typically extends patent protection for another three years. Other companies apply simply because they think the drug will sell better without a prescription.

A drug's switch to OTC status sometimes offers little or no benefit to the consumer. The recently switched pain relievers naproxen (*Aleve*) and ketoprofen (*Actron, Orudis KT*) for example, are neither safer nor more effective than the related drug ibuprofen (*Advil, Motrin IB*), long available in cheaper, generic form without a prescription. More important, eliminating the need for a prescription eliminates two major safeguards—the guidance provided by a physician and a pharmacist.

Buyer beware

Here are some of the potential pitfalls you face when you use drugs on your own:

■ **Misdiagnosis.** Proper self-treatment starts with proper self-diagnosis, which can sometimes be dauntingly difficult. Consider vaginal yeast infections. Several antiyeast drugs formerly available only by prescription are now available over the counter. Those include butoconazole (*Femstat 3*), clotrimazole (*Gyne-Lotrimin, Mycelex-7*), and miconazole (*Monistat 3; Monistat 7*). Recent studies have shown that many women who treat themselves with such medications actually have a more serious bacterial infection, such as vaginosis or gonorrhea.

Misdiagnosis can be especially unfortunate if a drug controls symptoms for weeks or months on end while the underlying disease goes untreated. Pain that you think is heartburn, for example, may actually stem from ulcers or even esophageal cancer.

■ **Side effects.** FDA approval for over-the-counter sale simply means that the agency believes the benefits of increased accessibility outweigh the risks of unsupervised use; it doesn't mean the drug is harmless. For one thing, OTC drugs can cause unpleasant or, in rare cases, potentially dangerous side effects, even at the recommended doses. For example, the newly nonprescription versions of ketoprofen and naproxen, like all OTC pain killers except acetaminophen (*Actamin, Tylenol*), can upset the stomach. The decongestant pseudoephedrine, contained in several products, such as *Efidac/24* and *Sudafed*, can cause insomnia and irritability. And the maximum recommended dose of certain formerly prescription antihistamines, contained in all sleeping aids and some cold or allergy medications, can slow reaction time as sharply as the amount of alcohol that would make driving illegal in many states.

■ **Drug interactions.** Without professional supervision, you're more likely to take drugs that can interact adversely. Recommended doses of the heartburn drug *Tagamet HB* can cause potentially dangerous increases in the potency of the asthma medicine theophylline (*Theo-Dur*), the blood-thinner warfarin

9. CONSUMER HEALTH

Heartburn: How to quench the flames

Advertising campaigns for the four heartburn drugs that have recently gone over the counter—cimetidine (*Tagamet HB*), famotidine (*Pepcid AC*), nizatidine (*Axid AR*), and ranitidine (*Zantac 75*)—have confused an already confusing situation for people trying to figure out when to stick with a traditional heartburn drug, when to choose a new one, and which particular drug to choose.

Something old, something new

Heartburn, a burning pain under the breastbone, develops when acid from the stomach backs up into the esophagus, the tube leading down from the throat. The traditional OTC remedies—antacids such as *Alka-Seltzer*, *Maalox*, *Rolaids*, and *Tums*—relieve the pain by neutralizing the acid. The new OTC drugs, called H2 blockers, fight the pain by suppressing production of the acid.

Antacids can have certain advantages over H2 blockers. They start working within a few minutes, while the blockers take at least half an hour, often longer. And while the cost per hour is usually about the same—5 to 6 cents—a single dose of an H2 blocker works for at least eight hours, a dose of an antacid for just one to three hours. So antacids are cheaper if you need relief for fewer than eight hours.

However, the longer action of H2 blockers is an advantage if you need prolonged relief. Equally important, antacids can only relieve heartburn, while blockers can prevent the pain if you take them shortly before you eat.

Blocker versus blocker

Despite what the ads say, no H2 blocker works any better than the others. Both *Pepcid AC* and *Tagamet HB*, for example, claim to relieve and prevent heartburn, while *Zantac 75* claims only to relieve it, and *Axid AR* claims only to prevent it. But those differences stem merely from differences in what the marketers thought would sell the most pills, not in what the drugs can actually do.

The makers of *Tagamet HB* have also insisted that their drug works faster than *Pepcid AC*. The initial FDA-approved directions did recommend taking *Pepcid AC* an hour before a meal, *Tagamet HB* only 30 minutes before, to prevent heartburn. But that distinction simply reflected the design of the studies originally submitted to the FDA. Since then, the makers of *Pepcid AC* have submitted new studies showing that it too can start working in just 30 minutes.

There are, however, a few potential differences in safety between *Tagamet HB* and the other H2 blockers. *Tagamet HB* is more likely to interact with the asthma drug theophylline (*Theo-Dur*), the blood-thinner warfarin (*Coumadin*), and the seizure drug phenytoin (*Dilantin*). If you're taking any of those medications along with *Tagamet HB*, your doctor should monitor blood levels of the medication. Or you could simply choose a different H2 blocker. Further, taking excessive doses of *Tagamet HB* for a long time can cause impotence or breast enlargement, although both problems disappear if you discontinue the drug.

What to do

The major advantage of H2 blockers is their ability to prevent rather than just relieve heartburn. People who often experience such pain after eating could try taking an H2 blocker 30 to 60 minutes before eating.

For relief rather than prevention, stick with a traditional antacid, unless you experience prolonged attacks and don't want to keep taking antacids every hour or two. For maximum effectiveness, you could even take both drugs at the same time—an antacid for immediate relief, an H2 blocker for relief once the antacid wears off.

Of course, if you can figure out what triggers the attacks, you may be able to avoid drugs entirely. Common dietary triggers include alcohol, caffeine, carbonated drinks, chocolate, fat, hot spices, and peppermint. Other steps that can help prevent heartburn include losing weight, eating slowly, avoiding clothes with a tight waistband, stopping smoking, and staying upright after eating, rather than lying down.

(*Coumadin*), and the seizure medicine phenytoin (*Dilantin*). Many common medications can make antihistamines even more sedating than they are when taken alone. Even food or drink can complicate the use of a drug. Acidic beverages like coffee or orange juice, for example, can interfere with the absorption of OTC nicotine gum.

■ **Overuse.** The only safeguard against excessive use of OTC drugs is the warning on the label and the package insert specifying how long you can safely use the drug without seeing a physician. People who overlook or ignore that warning on, say, naproxen, ketoprofen, or even ibuprofen can develop gastrointestinal bleeding, ulcers, increased blood pressure, or liver or kidney damage. (Prolonged aspirin use can have the same effects, though not on blood pressure; overuse of acetaminophen is even more likely to damage the liver and may harm the kidneys as well.)

Frequent, repeated use of other drugs that have switched—drugs for headaches, insomnia, nasal congestion, or eye inflammation—can lead to dependency. After the drug wears off, you develop "rebound" symptoms, even worse than the original ones. That can create a vicious cycle of increasingly frequent drug use and worsening symptoms.

■ **Overdoses.** Some people are tempted to take more than the recommended dose of an OTC drug, either because they think such readily available drugs must be harmless, or because they want the potency of a prescription dose without the bother of getting a prescription. But even moderately excessive doses, like moderately excessive use, can turn a reasonably safe remedy into a hazardous substance. The recently switched heartburn drugs, for example, can trigger headaches, lethargy, and confusion if you take too much. With a few drugs, modest overdoses can have disastrous results. Swallowing just three times more than the maximum recommended amount of phenylpropanolamine, a decongestant contained in all diet pills and some cold medicines, such as *Tavist-D*, can trigger a severe, potentially fatal rise in blood pressure.

Rx-to-OTC switch hitters

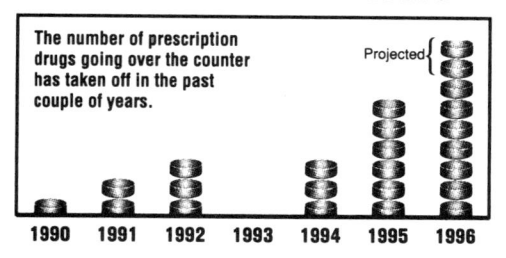

The number of prescription drugs going over the counter has taken off in the past couple of years.

1990 1991 1992 1993 1994 1995 1996 (Projected)

Where to get the facts

To learn how to safely use drugs that have gone over the counter, start by reading the label and the package insert, which give certain essential directions and warnings. However, those sources may be incomplete, omitting duration of use or certain side effects, drug interactions, or reasons to avoid the drug. So seek more complete information:

■ **Ask the pharmacist.** If possible, read the insert before leaving the store. Then ask the pharmacist any questions you still have. You should know how long you can take the drug without consulting a doctor; whether there are any unlisted side effects or drug interactions; how and when to take the drug; how to store it; and, if you're older, whether you face any special risks. (Drugs tend to reach higher blood levels in older people; even at normal levels, many drugs have stronger effects on the aging body.)

If you buy all your prescription and OTC drugs at one pharmacy, have the druggist enter those medications, as well as any drug allergies you have, in the drugstore's computer. The computer will then alert the pharmacist to potential drug interactions and allergic reactions.

■ **Ask your doctor.** If the pharmacist says the medication may pose an increased risk for you, ask your physician what to do. And call the physician before starting to take an OTC drug if you have a chronic disorder, are pregnant or nursing, or have an unfamiliar symptom. It's reasonably safe to treat yourself only if you have a highly familiar symptom, such as a runny nose or a cough, or if your physician has previously diagnosed the same problem, such as acne or athlete's foot. (But it may take more than just one previous diagnosis before a woman can safely treat a vaginal yeast infection on her own.)

Tell your doctor about all the OTC preparations you're taking, including drugs, herbs, and supplements. Those products may interact with prescribed medications or skew the results of laboratory tests; they may even be the cause of your symptoms.

■ **Check the books.** Consult a drug-information book, such as "The Complete Drug Reference," published by Consumer Reports Books and available in most libraries or bookstores.

Summing up

The growing number of drugs available without a prescription places more responsibility on you to make sure you use them wisely and safely.

What to do

■ Read the label and the package insert, and ask the pharmacist for additional information.

■ If possible, have the druggist enter in the computer all your over-the-counter drugs as well as any prescription medications and drug allergies.

■ Ask your doctor about the drug if you have unfamiliar symptoms, are pregnant or nursing, or have a chronic disease.

■ Consult a reference book on drugs.

The Doctor Is On

Patients are finding a treasure trove of medical information, emotional support—and even doctors with time to talk to them—on the Internet

KATIE HAFNER

WHEN ANDY BEAVER, A 42-year-old computer specialist in Toronto, began to experience a persistent twitch in his left hand last year, his doctor sent him to a neurologist. After some tests, Beaver was told he had ALS, or Lou Gehrig's disease, and had three to five years to live. The neurologist told him to go home and put his affairs in order, then scribbled down a telephone number with a reference for a second opinion. Then he shook Beaver's hand and wished him luck. "I was in his office for a total of about three minutes," Beaver recalls. "I stumbled back to work with a Post-it note in my hand, saying 'ALS? Lou Gehrig? Three to five years?'"

So that night, Beaver logged on to the Internet. He began subscribing to an electronic mailing list—part newsletter, part online discussion group—for ALS patients. Beaver quickly found state-of-the-art medical information, an instant support group and a chance to discover just what he was in for: feeding tubes and ventilators. "It scared the bejeebers out of my wife and me," he says. But Beaver gradually came to depend on the group as a source of information and inspiration. He was reassured to find that some 15 percent of its 1,700 participants were health professionals.

Electronic mailing lists, online support forums and World Wide Web sites devoted to every conceivable disease have turned the Internet into a trove of medical information. For the newly diagnosed, and for those with chronic conditions, the information and emotional support found online can be invaluable. And the fact that cyberspace renders geography irrelevant is a boon to those with debilitating illnesses who would otherwise feel hopelessly isolated.

Perhaps the most unexpected development is that more and more doctors are coming online as volunteer consultants. Clinicians and medical researchers are taking to cyberspace to advise online support groups, get an unfiltered view of patients' experiences and do what many of them entered the medical profession for in the first place: help people. "Being online is good for physicians because they get to see what's hot before it's even in the journals," says John R. Mangiardi, chief of neurosurgery at Lenox Hill Hospital in New York City and a participant in a popular mailing list devoted to brain tumors. "It's good for patients because they get interactive information." It was certainly good for San Diegan Bob Thomas and his 12-year-old daughter, Megan. Thomas posted a question about the nature of Megan's brain tumor to the mailing list. Within a day he had heard from six different specialists.

The time saved by getting answers online can be critical when patients are faced with what can amount to life-and-death decisions. When Monica Frydman, a 42-year-old language interpreter, was diagnosed with breast cancer last June, her surgeon recommended an immediate double mastectomy within two weeks, along with an extreme course of chemotherapy and the removal of adjacent lymph nodes. Frydman and her husband found the breast-cancer mailing list. Within a day, after hearing from a doctor and a prominent radiation specialist, they sought a second opinion from a doctor who agreed with the onliners that far less extreme treatment was needed.

Many physicians "lurk," which is cyberese for reading a discussion but not participating in it. By reading what patients say to one another in online forums, doctors say, they learn things about how patients are coping with an illness that would never be disclosed during an office visit. Although patients rarely discuss cosmetics with him personally, neurosurgeon Mangiardi saw people complain to one another on the brain-tumor list about unsightly scars left in their scalp following surgery. In response, he started using tiny metal meshes to conceal the disfigurement. As a rule, Mangiardi now avoids making large incisions. "If necessary, I'll go through someone's eyebrow to take out a giant tumor," he says.

Online eavesdropping can lead to specific help as well. When Carvel Gipson, a neurologist specializing in headaches, noticed that one of the participants in a headache and migraine discussion group was taking a medication for an unusual form of migraine, he warned her against taking it. Taken for the particular migraine she suffered from, the medication could cause paralysis, a fact the physician who prescribed the drug was unaware of.

Doctors in general have been slow to adopt online communications, and when they do go online, it's rarely to talk to patients. "Some doctors have freaked out when patients want to send them e-mail, or bring in medical reports that the doctors haven't even seen yet," says Tom Ferguson, a senior associate at Harvard Medical School's Center for Clinical Computing and author of "Health Online" (Addison-Wesley). "It doesn't fit the model they were trained in." Some doctors warn that online forums can stir false hopes. Two years ago, when a few ALS patients in the Boston area began an experimental treatment with Neurontin, a drug used for epilepsy, word spread throughout the online community and ALS patients everywhere began demanding the drug from their physicians. Before long, thousands of ALS sufferers were on Neurontin, hoping to slow the deterioration of their muscle strength. In formal studies conducted so far, a positive difference has been noted, but the effect is extremely slight and tests are inconclusive.

The Neurontin episode, though harmless in the end, highlights the speed with which information both good and bad can spread online. Not surprisingly, the Internet has

Getting Medical Help Online

FINDING THE RIGHT SPOT ON THE INTERNET FOR YOUR health concerns isn't as easy as you might think. There are more than 10,000 health-related web sites alone, and thousands more online support communities. For Web surfers, an excellent place to start is Yahoo's Health section (http://www.yahoo.com/Health), where you'll find a wealth of information on more than 2,000 sites. The Big Three commercial online service providers, America Online, CompuServe and Prodigy, are well known for their extensive health forums. Here are some other good places to go for medical information:

Web Sites
- Medaccess: http://www.medaccess.com
- OncoLink: http://www.oncolink.upenn.edu/
- National Cancer Institute: http://www.nci.nih.gov/
- HealthWorld (provides free access to MedLine): http://healthy.net/
- Psych Central: http://www.coil.com/~grohol/
- Medinfo: http://www.medinfo.org

Mailing Lists
- Breast cancer: Send the message "subscribe breast-cancer" followed by your real name to listserv@morgan.ucs.mun.ca
- Brain tumor: Send the message "subscribe braintmr" followed by your real name to listserv@mitvma.mit.edu
- ALS (Lou Gehrig's disease): Send e-mail to bro@huey.met.fsu.edu
- Depression: Send the message "subscribe walkers-in-darkness" to majordomo @world.std.com. Another list: send the message "subscribe depress" to listserv @soundprint.brandywine.american.edu

become ripe territory for quackery. Purveyors of magic elixirs pop up everywhere, feeding on people's desperation. But the groups with a heavy presence of health professionals guard well against fradulent claims. "My usual reply is 'That's very interesting, could you show me some data'," says Loren Buhle, a former professor of radiation oncology at the University of Pennsylvania who created OncoLink, a popular cancer-related Web site. The father of an ALS patient in Florida recently asked forum members whether his daughter should have her dental fillings removed (at $1,000 each) after hearing claims that the mercury in the fillings caused ALS. Researchers on the list gently counseled him against it.

The credibility of online information can often be gauged by who's providing it. Web sites sponsored by universities and government agencies, and those where information has obviously been pooled and reviewed by a variety of people, are usually the most reliable. While careful not to prescribe drugs or treatment for fear of liability, or offer definitive diagnoses over the Net, doctors who go on the Net say they find a particular satisfaction in doing online what they often don't have the time to do when they see patients in person: answer people's questions and help them understand what's wrong with them.

Health Insurance Hazards: How to Spot Hidden Pitfalls in Your Plan

CAROLYN HAGAN

Contributing Editor Carolyn Hagan is a health writer in Northampton, MA.

If you're like most Americans, you're enrolled in a managed-care plan. And if you're like most people, you're easily bored by instruction manuals. Admit it: You've only skimmed your health plan policy book. You searched for benefits you value—say, free Pap smears or low-cost prescription drugs—and your eyes glazed over at the rest.

Look again. Even if you're satisfied with your care thus far, loopholes may lie buried in the fine print. "Let the buyer beware: Not all plans are created equally," says Charlotte Yeh, M.D., physician-in-chief in emergency medicine at New England Medical Center in Boston. For every helpful benefit spelled out, there could be a catch couched in euphemism or ambiguity. Trouble is, you probably won't discover these booby traps until a crisis forces you to dig deeper into your plan's services. That's why it pays to learn the ins and outs of your benefits before you really need them. This lexicon of loaded phrases and tricky terms will help you spot a disaster in the making.

"TRUE MEDICAL EMERGENCY" Your plan says you can visit the emergency room (ER) only for a bona fide medical emergency. Sound obvious? Here's the rub: Many plans call a condition an emergency only *after* it's been diagnosed as such. In other words, the insurance company can withhold payment if it rules—after the fact—that whatever sent you running to the hospital wasn't a matter of life or death. "Many managed-care companies are creating a form of Russian roulette for patients who seek emergency care," says Worcester, MA, physician Richard Aghababian, M.D., past president of the American College of Emergency Physicians in Dallas. "No matter how serious their symptoms may be, patients have no way of knowing if an emergency visit will be covered until they are diagnosed."

To define an emergency after the fact is easy—and unrealistic. For example, the burning sensation caused by a heart attack can be mistaken for indigestion if it strikes without the classic chest pain. And one of the first signs of stroke may be a sudden, severe headache. Yet Aetna's plan book, like many others, deems nausea and headaches unworthy of an ER visit.

"PREAUTHORIZATION" Some plans, such as Health Insurance Plan (HIP) of Greater New York, HMO Blue and U.S. Healthcare, advise you to call for authorization from a gatekeeper (a plan representative or your primary-care physician) before heading to the hospital in an emergency. This wastes valuable time. It can also be risky for other reasons. For one, the person manning the phone is physically removed from the situation. On top of that, he or she is often an administrative person working from a rigid set of guidelines, not a doctor. A study done at the University of California at Davis found that gatekeepers denied care to about 11% of patients, some of whom were later found to have serious medical conditions. The ultimate injustice: Even patients who receive phone authorization still risk being denied reimbursement.

When in doubt, it's best to go straight to the hospital and worry about coverage later, advises Dr. Yeh. By law, ER physicians in hospitals that receive Medicare or Medicaid funding must evaluate and treat you in an emergency—no matter what. If your insurer denies payment, you can always appeal the decision later. . . .

"AMBULANCE AUTHORIZATION" What if you need to take an ambulance to the hospital? The same plans that specify preauthorization for emergency care may also want to approve a call to 911. This procedure often is not spelled out in plan books, so it pays to check with your insurer before an emergency strikes. Watch out for companies that instruct you to call a privately contracted ambulance service instead of 911. According to Dr. Yeh, some ambulances contracted by HMO's may not have the same level of training or equipment as those dispatched by a 911 operator, and they may not be held to such standards as a required response time. Fortunately insurers can only *encourage* patients to call a private contractor; they can't *require* it. The pending Access to Emergency Medical Services Act includes a provision that prohibits plans from discouraging the use of 911.

49. Health Insurance Hazards

"PRIMARY-CARE PHYSICIAN" This all-knowing doctor appreciates every facet of your health and coordinates your care. That's the promise. But the reality may fall short. It's true that a PCP, typically an internist or a family physician, provides a continuity of care that was long overdue in more fragmented fee-for-service medicine. These doctors also emphasize preventive medicine, including regular mammograms and Pap smears. But what your plan book *doesn't* tell you is that your PCP is paid a set amount for each patient, regardless of how much time the doctor spends with the patient, a practice called "capitation." On top of this, many insurers, including Oxford Health Plans and Choice Care, withhold a percentage of a doctor's monthly fees and then pay it only if a physician keeps referral rates low. So when a situation crops up that the doctor can't handle, she may resist passing you on to a specialist.

PCP's are becoming specialists, but are they up to the task? "It's unclear whether they're adequately trained in disciplines such as dermatology and gynecology," says Carolyn Clancy, M.D., director of the Center for Primary Care Research for the Agency for Health Care Policy and Research in Rockville, MD.

Some doctors are less equivocal. "I'm an internist, and I feel uncomfortable with a lot of dermatologic and orthopedic procedures," says Jane Orient, M.D., executive director of the Association of American Physicians and Surgeons in Tucson, AZ. PCP's may also be on shaky ground in other areas. A family physician or an internist who does a flexible sigmoidoscopy (inserting a tube for a colon cancer check) may have learned how to do the procedure at a weekend seminar.

People with chronic conditions or serious illnesses such as lupus or complicated sickle-cell disease are especially at risk if they're in a plan that lacks a doctor who has particular expertise in their condition. Relying on a PCP for mental health care may also be risky. Research has shown that although family physicians are the top prescribers of antidepressants, they are less likely than psychiatrists to diagnose depression and more apt to undertreat it when they do prescribe medication. And most family physicians lack both the training and the desire to diagnose addiction problems, according to another recent report. The bottom line: Be prepared to pester your PCP for referrals to specialists and to do background reading about your specific condition if you think it will help you plead your case.

"ONE FREE OB/GYN VISIT PER YEAR" Whether it's free or requires a minimal co-payment, the no-hassle, no-referral-needed gynecologist visit is held out as a big bonus by Cigna, U.S. Healthcare and certain Humana Group health plans. The flip side of this sweet deal is not mentioned, however: If gynecologic symptoms develop after your free visit, you're expected to see your PCP, who may not give you a referral to an ob/gyn and won't necessarily have the expertise to handle your problem. "I know plenty of internists who haven't done a pelvic exam in years," says Dr. Orient.

If the basics aren't assured, what about an unusual symptom? "I haven't felt many ovarian tumors," Dr. Orient admits. "Nor am I comfortable taking a tissue sample from the uterus of a postmenopausal woman with unusual bleeding. I'd much rather refer that woman to a gynecologist." If you're able to choose your insurer and you have a chronic condition, such as fibroid tumors or endometriosis, consider a plan such as Oxford's that lets women see an ob/gyn anytime, or one of the Kaiser Permanente plans that allow women to choose ob/gyns as PCP's.

"MEDICALLY NECESSARY" This term pops up in reference to treatments and procedures that will be reimbursed. You're better off considering what *won't* be covered. "The term 'medically necessary' is undefined and undefinable," says Dr. Orient. "There are many treatments that aren't necessary to save a life but can dramatically improve quality of life. There are also lots of diagnostic procedures that doctors don't know are necessary until they do them." When you sign up, you take your plan's word that you'll be covered for what's medically necessary for you. "You find out later that it's a lie," says Dr. Orient.

Insurers typically refuse to pay for newly developed devices and state-of-the-art treatments. The insurer may argue that only the older version of a device or treatment is "necessary," even if it isn't as effective or comfortable as a newer one. A woman who undergoes a mastectomy for breast cancer may find that her insurer won't pay for reconstruction of the breast. Bone marrow transplants for the treatment of advanced breast cancer also tend to be deemed unnecessary. Because the FDA hasn't yet approved these transplants for breast cancer, insurers consider them experimental, despite the fact that they have shown good results in studies. Dr. Clancy points out, "We have hard evidence for only about 20% to 30% of current medical practice." By refusing to pay for treatments that show early promise, plans are effectively stunting the progress of medicine. Your mission? If you're denied something you and your doctor feel is necessary, appeal the decision. It could take months of haggling, but your efforts may pay off.

"UP TO 30 MENTAL HEALTH VISITS PER CALENDAR YEAR" Sounds generous, huh? Not so fast. "Consumers are lucky if this translates into six or eight visits," says Paul K. Ling, Ph.D., a clinical psychologist in Quincy, MA, and spokesman for the Mental Health Consumer Initiative. "Insurers will stop paying for sessions by invoking the concept of medical necessity," Dr. Ling explains. A class-action lawsuit is already under way in Massachusetts to challenge this practice. It charges that Blue Cross and Blue Shield advertised 20 sessions per year, but that patients actually got only one or two.

Managed-care plans are especially unlikely to acknowledge illnesses that typically require long-term therapy; they're more likely to cover treatment for depression and substance abuse, because they respond to relatively short-term therapy and medication. Even in these cases, however, the restricted number of visits favors medication over psychotherapy. Yet mental health professionals agree that most mental illness is best treated with a combination of medication and psychotherapy.

All of this means that it pays to shop around for a therapist who will battle the insurance company on your behalf. In fact, that advice goes for your choice of health care providers in general. Says Dr. Ling, "Patients ought to get what they pay for without having to jump through hoops."

Contemporary Health Hazards

FRY NOW. PAY LATER.

There is a proven connection between sun exposure and skin cancer, as well as premature wrinkling. If you must be in the sun, use sunscreen and common sense.

AMERICAN CANCER SOCIETY

Living is hazardous to your health." This may seem like an unusual way to begin this unit, but it represents a fundamental truth about the nature of the world in which we live. This unit will examine a variety of health hazards that Americans must face on a daily basis and will include such topics as environmental health issues, infectious disease, and acts of violence.

Over the past 25 years, Americans have been inundated with health warnings about toxic substances in our air, water, and food. "How Much Are Pesticides Hurting Your Health?" dispels much of the hype suggesting that such chemicals in our food supply cause millions of Americans each year to develop cancer.

Of all the environmental health issues, atmospheric pollution by chlorofluorocarbon compounds (CFCs) and carbon dioxide seems to have generated the most concern worldwide. CFCs are synthetic products that have achieved worldwide acceptance as components of refrigerants, propellants, and solvents. These compounds, when released into the atmosphere, destroy the ozone layer that shields Earth from ultraviolet (UV) radiation. This protective layer appears to be undergoing a rapid depletion; consequently, there has been a steady rise in the amount of UV radiation to which we are exposed. Most experts agree that we will witness significant increases in the incidence of skin cancer because of this depletion. To protect ourselves against the damaging effects of this form of radiation, medical authorities have encouraged us to apply liberal amounts of sunscreen to our skin. But do sunscreens really work? While most sunscreens have demonstrated their effectiveness against UVB radiation, the same cannot be said with regard to UVA radiation. At the

UNIT 10

present time, the only sunscreens that have proven to be effective in blocking UVA radiation are the broad spectrum sunscreens. Unfortunately, UVA radiation constitutes 95 percent of our exposure and is associated with malignant melanoma, the most deadly form of skin cancer. Opponents of sunscreens argue that they disable our sunburn response and increase our exposure. "Quiz: Are You Ready for the Sun?" addresses this controversial issue.

Over the past 20 years, many Americans have come to believe that we have all but won the war against infectious illnesses. However, several recent reports suggest that we are currently in the midst of a microbial resurgence of frightening proportions. This point has been dramatized by the deadly outbreak of the Ebola virus and the discovery of *Streptococcus pyogenes,* also known as the flesh-eating bacteria. According to the Centers for Disease Control and Prevention, the spectrum of infectious diseases is growing, and many infectious diseases once thought to be under control are increasing. Just as frightening as the emergence of new infections is the fact that the antibiotics used to combat these illnesses are losing their effectiveness. Ironically, many of the antibiotic-resistant bacteria found today probably had their origins in our hospitals, where massive amounts of antibiotics are used. "'Wonder Drugs' Losing Healing Aura" discusses how misuse has rendered many antibiotics practically worthless and has contributed to the resurgence of diseases such as ear infections, STDs, and tuberculosis. "The Bad News Bugs" examines the threat posed by deadly viruses such as Ebola and discusses where these viruses came from and why they appear to be on the rise.

The infectious illness that consistently gets media coverage is AIDS. But other sexually transmitted diseases (STDs), such as chlamydia, human papilloma virus (HPV), genital herpes, gonorrhea, and hepatitis B, are infecting Americans at the rate of 12 million new cases a year, with 66 percent of the new cases affecting people under the age of 25. Based on current statistics, the infection rate of these STDs is 10 times that of AIDS, and infected individuals are more susceptible to AIDS if they are exposed to the HIV virus. Nor is AIDS the only STD for which there is no cure. HPV, hepatitis B, and genital herpes are also currently incurable. Women appear to be much more likely to become infected than men, and the health consequences of such infections are greater for them. In fact, it is estimated that by age 30 over 50 percent of all Americans will have been infected at least once. "Prevent Sexually Transmitted Diseases" presents the reader with a discussion of the six most common STDs.

Another health hazard that warrants inclusion in this unit is violence. Violent acts may take many forms, but the most common are violent acts against women by men, including sexual assault or rape. Date rape or acquaintance rape has recently emerged as a major security issue at colleges and universities nationwide. It is difficult to determine whether this form of sexual violence is relatively new or has been quietly going on for years, like wife beating or sexual harassment. We do know that the number of reported cases is growing rapidly. "What Every Woman Needs to Know about Personal Safety" discusses the safety measures women can take to reduce their risk of becoming victims of rape or some other violent crime. "Why Is Date Rape So Hard to Prove?" discusses why it is difficult to make a rape charge stick.

While this unit focuses on exogenous factors that influence our state of health, it is important to remember that health is the dynamic state representing the degree of harmony between internal and external factors. Given the intimate relationship between people and their environment, it is impossible to promote the concept of wellness without also safeguarding the quality of our environment, both physical and social.

Looking Ahead: Challenge Questions

What do you consider to be our greatest environmental health hazard today?

Are you concerned about the damaging effects of UV radiation on your skin? What steps are you taking to prevent such damage?

How has our use of antibiotics contributed to the resurgence of infectious illnesses?

What could the government do to help combat the spread of STDs? What are you personally doing to reduce your risk of contracting them?

What safety measures can you take to reduce your chances of being a victim of date rape or some other form of violent crime?

Are government regulations concerning the use of pesticides and the safety testing of consumer products strict enough? Explain your answer.

Do our laws governing violent acts need to be changed? If so, in what ways?

Are Your Shades Good Enough?

Don't get burned: Choosing the right sunglasses now can mean better eyesight later.

Patricia Long

WHEN L.A. EYEWORKS opened in 1979 on trendy Melrose Avenue, a hotshot movie director was one of the first customers to stroll through the door. "He came in wearing $10,000 worth of clothing—Armani, a Gaultier leather jacket—but he had on the ugliest glasses I'd ever seen," says Barbara McReynolds, cofounder of the Los Angeles optical shop. "He had a sense of his looks only from the neck down." But McReynolds and partner Gai Gherardi helped him see the light, and soon he had himself some snazzy new shades that begged for a whole new set of clothes to match.

"We could write a psychology book about what happens when someone puts on a really good pair," says McReynolds. "First thing you know they're getting a new haircut, then new clothes, and before long they're opening up to other people." Sunglasses, in other words, are nothing less than a tool for self-invention, a personal statement of who you are or want to be.

Of course, they're also there for protection—or had better be if you value your vision. The sexiest sunglasses in the world are worthless if they won't block out enough light—not just the kind that makes you squint, but ultraviolet light, which can cause cataracts. Within the next year, regulations from the Food and Drug Administration will require all nonprescription sunglasses to block at least 99 percent of UVB rays and 95 percent of the less-damaging UVA. In the meantime, these guidelines can help you shop for a smart pair of shades:

Check the label for UV protection. UV rays are invisible, but long-term exposure to them can speed the formation of cataracts, a clouding of the eye's lens often compared to a fogged-up window. A study of Chesapeake Bay fishermen found that those who wore brimmed hats or otherwise avoided direct sun were three times less susceptible to cataracts than those who didn't. (None wore sunglasses because the lenses would have become fogged and salt encrusted from sea spray.) And recent figures show that nearly one in five Americans have poor vision due to cataracts by age 75; by age 84, it's one in two.

Even a few hours of intense UVB contact can burn the cornea, the transparent covering of the eyeball, although this painful condition, called photokeratitis, usually goes away within 24 hours.

For maximum protection, look for labels that read "100 percent UV absorption" or "UV absorption up to 400 nm." Look askance, though, at sky-high claims of over 100 percent or promises of protection against UVC rays, which don't even get through the ozone. And don't go by the darkness of the lens: Most UV-blocking chemicals and coatings are colorless. Generally, you can count on expensive sunglasses to be good UV blockers, but cheapies can do just as well. In one Canadian study, a 65-cent pair was just as protective as the pricier shades.

Make sure they snare the glare. Your natural reaction to visible light is to squint, which can cause headaches, eyestrain, and crow's-feet. That's why even sunglasses for casual use, like strolling city sidewalks at lunchtime, should have medium-tinted lenses. Before buying, try them on outside and see if the muscles around your eyes relax. If you'll be near water, sand, or snow, your glasses should be dark enough that someone can't see your eyes—blocking about 85 percent of visible light. For exceedingly bright conditions—say, climbing a glacier or lounging on a beach near the equator—look for 90 to 97 percent.

Don't worry about blue light and infrared. Amber-tinted glasses that promise protection against blue light, the band of visible light bordering UV on the light spectrum, are selling you something you don't need. For starters, it's controversial whether exposure to blue light is especially harmful (though some experts believe expo-

50. Are Your Shades Good Enough?

sure to those rays can eventually lead to macular degeneration, an irreversible condition that causes legal blindness). But even if those rays do prove hazardous, any lens that absorbs at least 80 percent of visible light automatically blocks most of the blue, so special blue-blocking glasses aren't necessary.

Similarly, you don't really need extra protection against the sun's infrared rays, which can't be seen but are felt as heat. In theory, infrared energy can speed up the damaging effects of UV rays. But that isn't a problem if the glasses are screening out enough UV to begin with.

Stick with gray, brown, or green. Red, orange, blue, or yellow lenses—especially if deeply tinted—can make it hard to distinguish traffic signals and ambulance lights. Gray or smoky tones give the truest colors. Brown makes colors more contrasty ("an advantage in the Sahara," says Gherardi). Green lenses make everything brighter ("great for places like Seattle and New York").

Go for large, Jackie O–sized frames. Small granny frames may look hip, but they let in UV light at the sides, not only upping your risk for cataracts, but exposing the delicate skin nearby. The same goes for tinted clip-ons over small-framed prescription glasses. Large, round lenses give better protection. If you're out in bright sun for hours, wear wraparounds or add a brimmed hat.

By year's end, the Skin Cancer Institute hopes to identify the most protective sunglasses with a "seal of recommendation." To qualify, sunglasses must be big enough

> Small frames may look hip, but they let in UV from the sides, upping your risk for cataracts.

to shield the eyes, eyelids, and nearby skin; absorb at least 99 percent UV; be shatterproof; and be dark enough to block most blue light as well.

Get shades that suit your life. Some shades are specially designed for particular uses. Gradient lenses, for example, are tinted darker at the top to block light from overhead—especially helpful for freeway driving because they let you clearly see the speedometer. Double-gradient lenses, darker on top and bottom, are good for tennis players and others who contend with light reflected off the ground. Polarized lenses come in handy for fishing or aquatic sports since they eliminate the glare reflected off water. And photochromic lenses, the kind that darken when you go outside, are handy for anyone who's in and out of the sun. (Note: These require some UV in order to darken, so they don't offer total protection.)

What about those mirrored shades so popular with skiers? Experts differ on whether these lenses, which reflect visible light, cut glare any better than regular sunglasses, which absorb it. There is one definite drawback: They're easily scratched.

Choose glass or plastic. Plastic lenses are more durable for athletic use. Of these, the polycarbonate are the most fracture-proof. But they're prone to scratches, so buy ones with scratch-resistant coatings. Lenses made of glass do resist scratching and give a truer picture of the world, but they're typically heavier and more likely to shatter when hit.

Beware of a warped picture. To avoid optical flaws, look for lenses that are "ground and polished." Or try this test: Hold the pair at arm's length and look through a lens with one eye, focusing on a rectangular pattern, like a tiled floor. If the lines get wavy as you move the glasses up and down or from side to side, buy a different pair.

Get a good fit. For maximum protection, it's important that the glasses sit well on your face. Besides, you won't wear 'em if they don't feel right. So even if you bought your pair at a drug or department store, you may want to go to an optician to get them adjusted. Or go ahead and spend some bucks at an optical shop for sunglasses you'll really love.

Is it worth that kind of trouble? Absolutely, McReynolds says. "When you put on your sunglasses and someone says, 'Wow, those are really cool,' you can't help but feel good about yourself."

Quiz: Are You Ready for the Sun?

May is National Skin Cancer Detection and Prevention Month, so it's a good time to test your knowledge about the subject. Answer true or false to the following questions.

___ **1.** About 70,000 Americans develop skin cancer each year.

___ **2.** Basal cell carcinoma is the most dangerous type of skin cancer.

___ **3.** You should do a self-exam for skin cancer every six to eight weeks.

___ **4.** A mole that is wider than the diameter of a pinhead may be a sign of malignant melanoma.

___ **5.** Skin cancer is most often caused by exposure to ultraviolet (UV) rays.

___ **6.** Fair-skinned people are at greater risk of developing all types of skin cancer than are darker-skinned people.

___ **7.** One or more blistering sunburns during childhood or adolescence can double one's risk of developing malignant melanoma.

___ **8.** People who spend time in the sun only on weekends are at greater risk of developing malignant melanoma than those who are in the sun every day.

___ **9.** Since the sun's rays are strongest between 10 a.m. and 3 p.m., there's no need to take precautions at other times.

___ **10.** Unlike ultraviolet B (UVB) rays, ultraviolet A (UVA) rays are harmless.

___ **11.** If you burn without protection after 10 minutes in the sun, wearing a sunscreen with an SPF of eight would allow you to stay in the sun eight times longer (80 minutes) before you'd burn.

___ **12.** You should wear a sunscreen even on overcast days, since 80% of the sun's rays pass through clouds.

___ **13.** A sunscreen with an SPF of 50 is 67% more effective than one with an SPF of 30.

___ **14.** You should apply sunscreen 15 to 30 minutes before going outside.

___ **15.** A UV index reading of 15 is very high.

___ **16.** The sun can penetrate some types of clothing.

___ **17.** You can get a sunburn even sitting under an umbrella at the beach.

___ **18.** The UV rays in tanning booths are safe.

___ **19.** It's okay to use a sunscreen that's been sitting in your medicine chest for a few years.

___ **20.** In addition to sunscreen, a baseball cap provides good protection for your face.

ANSWERS

1. *False.* Every year, more than 800,000 Americans develop skin cancer, and some 9,300 die from it.

2. *False.* Basal cell carcinoma is the most *common* form of skin cancer, affecting some 560,000 Americans each year. BCC's usually take the form of translucent nodules and are frequently found on the face (especially the nose), neck, hands and torso. Rarely deadly, BCC's grow slowly and usually don't spread to other organs; if treated early, they can be cured in at least 95% of cases.

Squamous cell carcinoma is the second most prevalent skin cancer, affecting about 150,000 people every year. SCC's are red or pink scaly nodules or wart-like growths that ulcerate in the center; they're typically found on the face (especially the lips), the ears, the hands and other sun-exposed parts of the body. SCC's can be deadly, grow-

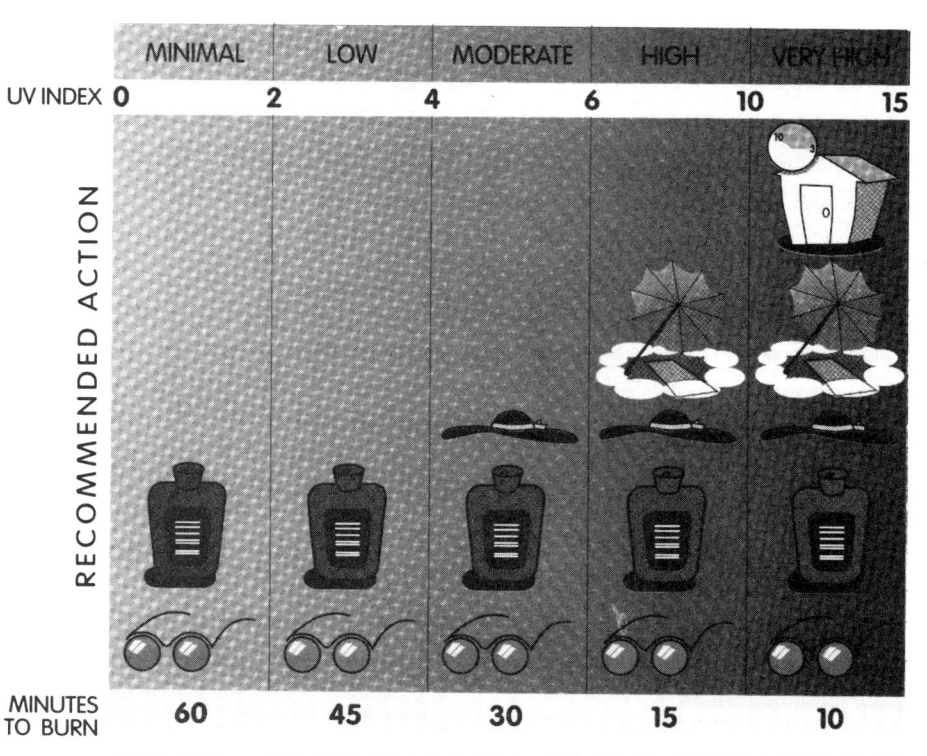

	MINIMAL	LOW	MODERATE	HIGH	VERY HIGH
UV INDEX	0	2	4	6	10 ... 15
MINUTES TO BURN	60	45	30	15	10

THIS CHART SHOWS THE LEVELS OF THE UV INDEX, HOW LONG IT TAKES TO BURN IN THE SUN *WITHOUT* SUNSCREEN AND WHAT YOU CAN DO TO PROTECT YOURSELF.

ing quickly and spreading to other organs. But if treated early, SCC's also have a 95% cure rate.

Malignant melanoma is the least common skin cancer—about 32,000 cases each year—but it is the most dangerous form, accounting for 75% of skin cancer deaths. Melanomas are cancerous moles that most frequently appear on the upper back, torso, lower legs, head and neck. Melanoma is likelier than other skin cancers to spread to other parts of the body, making it more difficult to cure.

3. *True.* Use a full-length and a hand mirror to look for any new skin discolorations or growths and any changes in the shape, size or color of moles, birthmarks and freckles. Don't forget to check your palms, soles and scalp and the spaces between your fingers and toes. If you notice anything unusual, see your primary-care doctor or a dermatologist right away. And fair-haired people especially should have an all-body exam by a doctor every year.

4. *False.* A mole that is wider than the diameter of a pencil eraser (a quarter-inch) may be a sign of melanoma. To distinguish normal moles from pigmentations that could be melanoma, use the "ABCD" guideline:

Asymmetry. Does one half look different from the other?

Border irregularity. Are the edges of the mole ragged, notched or blurred?

Color. Does the color vary within the mole, including shades of tan, brown or black and sometimes patches of white, red or blue?

Diameter. Is the mole wider than the diameter of a pencil eraser?

5. *True.* In one recent study, melanoma incidence was 68% to 97% lower in people or body sites (such as the buttocks) with little or no sun exposure.

6. *True.* Fair-skinned people, especially those with blond or red hair, have less melanin, a pigment in skin cells that helps prevent burning and longterm skin damage.

7. *True.*

8. *True.*

9. *False.* The sun is still strong enough to cause damage at other times of day.

10. *False.* Two types of UV light reach the Earth: UVA rays, which primarily cause premature wrinkling, and UVB rays, which primarily cause burning. Researchers now believe that both UVA and UVB light cause cancer. For this reason, a "broad-spectrum" sunscreen, which protects against both UVA and UVB rays, is the best choice. (Note: A sunscreen's SPF refers only to UVB, not UVA, rays.)

11. *True.* To figure out how long a sunscreen will allow you to stay in the sun, multiply the amount of time it takes you to burn without protection by the sunscreen's SPF.

12. *True.*

13. *False.* A sunscreen with an SPF of 50 is actually only 1% to 2% more effective than one with an SPF of 30. "After SPF 30, you tend to reach a point of diminishing returns," explains microbiologist Jeanne Rippere of the office of over-the-counter drugs at the FDA. For this reason, the agency plans to limit sunscreen ratings to SPF 30.

14. *True.*

15. *True.* Many newspapers and local TV stations now report the day's UV index, a measurement of the sun's intensity for a particular region. Developed by the Environmental Protection Agency, the National Weather Service and the Centers for Disease Control and Prevention, the index rates UV levels from 0, or "minimal," to 15, or "very high." For each number, consumers are advised on the best actions to take to protect themselves from harmful rays (see chart).

16. *True.* Fabrics that are loosely woven, such as crepe or knit, allow UV rays to penetrate. (A rule of thumb: If you can see through the fabric, it won't protect you.) Opt for silk or denim, fabrics with dark colors or special sun-protective clothing, such as the Sun Precautions Solumbra line (800-882-7860). And keep in mind that clothes of any kind are less protective when wet.

17. *True.* Sand, like pavement and snow, reflects UV rays.

18. *False.* The UV rays emitted by tanning booths and sun lamps can cause burning, skin aging and cancer.

19. *False.* A sunscreen's active ingredients are effective for only about two years. And any sunscreen you buy may have been sitting on the store shelf for a long time. So it's a good idea to replace your sunscreen every year.

20. *False.* A broad-brimmed hat is better, since it protects the cheeks as well as the nose.

—CYNTHIA MOEKLE PIGOTT

The Bad News Bugs

Peter Radetsky

Peter Radetsky teaches science writing at the University of California at Santa Cruz and is the author of The Invisible Invaders: Viruses and the Scientists Who Pursue Them.

Ebola is notorious, little understood and lethal. It first surfaced in 1976, killing some 400 of the 550 people infected in Zaire and neighboring Sudan, an appalling death rate of over 70%. And it wasn't just the fact of the killing that was so frightening: It was the way the virus killed, striking within days of infection, literally disintegrating the flesh, causing blood to ooze from every orifice in the body. There was no vaccine. There was no cure. When people died from Ebola, they decomposed, in madness and agony, before your eyes.

In 1979 Ebola struck again, killing 22 people in Sudan. And in 1989 the virus made its way to our shores. Research monkeys in Reston, Va., just a few miles down the highway from Washington, were discovered to be infected with Ebola. Four of the five regular workers in the facility swiftly became infected. But while Ebola methodically killed off the monkeys, this time it spared the people. They barely became sick. Why? No one knows. And there's much more no one knows about the virus. Where does it come from? When and where will it show up next time? When it does reappear—for surely these outbreaks are just the beginning—how great will the devastation be?

Similar questions surround more than just Ebola. It's only one of a number of new or reemerging viruses that are causing alarm around the world. For example, dengue, a relative of yellow fever, commonly causes severe joint pain—it's also known as breakbone fever—and other flu-like symptoms, and in later stages, bleeding, shock and finally death. Dengue is knocking on our door. In South and Central America there have been major dengue epidemics every year since the late 1970s. U.S. travelers routinely bring dengue back to this country, and mosquitoes carrying the virus inhabit much of the southeastern U.S. So it may be just a matter of time before dengue breaks out here.

Hantavirus already has. This group of viruses first came to the attention of Western scientists during the Korean War, when a mysterious disease, Korean hemorrhagic fever, afflicted thousands of United Nations troops. It began with flu-like symptoms that escalated to internal hemorrhaging, shock and kidney failure. In roughly 10% of those cases, the illness was fatal. Soon, however, it became clear that this "new" disease wasn't new at all: In China, for example, over 100,000 cases occur every year.

All that seemed exotic and remote until the spring of 1993. It was then that people in the Four Corners area (where New Mexico, Colorado, Arizona and Utah meet) began dying quickly and mysteriously of what at first seemed to be nothing more dangerous than a mild flu. Frantic work by local health officials and the Centers for Disease Control and Prevention (CDC) revealed that the deaths were caused by a previously unknown and far more deadly variety of hantavirus, one that attacked the lungs, boring holes in capillaries to cause internal bleeding. As of this writing, the Sin Nombre ("no name") hantavirus has surfaced in 23 states and attacked 111 people, 55 of whom have died.

Other emerging viral diseases—Lassa fever, Rift Valley fever, Orungo, Ebola's cousin Marburg—have gained a foothold throughout the world. Yellow fever itself is gaining strength. And, of course, the most notorious of all new viruses, HIV, the cause of AIDS, is projected to infect 40 million people worldwide by the end of the decade. It has already claimed more than 250,000 American lives.

Not too long ago such a siege was unimaginable. In the late 1960s Surgeon General William Stewart was so confident of the future that he declared it was time to close the book on infectious disease. But the future has not cooperated, and it's partly our own fault. We've created a world ideal for the fostering and spread of infectious disease, an enormous "microbial superhighway," in the words of virologist Stephen S. Morse of Rockefeller University in New York City. "Almost all of the viruses we think of as new are 'new' only because they haven't been in a human population before," says Dr. Morse. "Ebola, hantavirus, HIV—they came from other species where they or a close relative had existed for a very long time. Something happens to put them in contact with people."

That something involves our own behavior. By invading parts of the world never before inhabited on a large scale—the Jungles and rain forests of equatorial Africa and South America are prime examples—we unleash these hitherto unknown viruses. Because of modern transportation, the viruses can hitch a ride inside an infected person, animal or insect to appear thousands of miles away in a matter of days or even hours. Their destination may be one of the world's overcrowded and undermaintained megacities. With the influx of people exceeding supplies of clean water and adequate housing, these cities provide an unparalleled environment for disease to flourish. A burgeoning number of people, from those infected with HIV to chemotherapy patients to transplant recipients, have immune systems impaired to the point where they become walking incubators for viruses. And many of these people inhabit our enormous hospitals, which can become fertile breeding grounds for disease.

52. Bad News Bugs

Provided such openings, viruses are making dramatic inroads. Lest we forget, these outbreaks are a graphic reminder that we're in deadly competition with the microbial world. "The problem is our competitive evolution," declares Rockefeller University microbiologist and Nobel laureate Joshua Lederberg. "Our microbial competitors have occupied themselves with every imaginable trick of rapid genetic adaptation, mutation and evolution. I label the scenario 'wits (ours) vs. genes (theirs).'"

Genes, indeed. A virus is little more than an inert, and incredibly tiny, bag of genes—aptly referred to by British Nobel laureate Lord Peter Medawar as "a piece of bad news wrapped in protein." We and this piece of genetic bad news have identical goals: to survive and propagate. "They want to survive. They want to reproduce. They have the same imperatives we do. They're just taking advantage of opportunities," says Morse. "That's what life does: You see grass growing up through cracks in the cement." But viruses have one distinct disadvantage. Whereas we are able to maintain ourselves and give birth to offspring, viruses are virtually helpless, the ultimate parasites. In order to survive and propagate, they must commandeer the machinery of living cells to produce new viruses.

The process works like this: When, purely by chance, a virus encounters a suitable cell, an astonishing transformation takes place. By various subterfuges the virus deposits its genes inside. The viral genes then usurp the cell's genes, providing new blueprints that transform the cell into a virus factory. After being assembled within the cell, young viruses burst free, sometimes tearing away a piece of the cell's membrane for an overcoat, ready to infect more cells and make more viruses. And the violated, decimated cell? More often than not it dies. An infection, therefore, is the result of a virus trying to make a living.

How well any particular virus makes a living—that is, how profligately it reproduces—determines whether or not we become sick or die. The more cells that become infected, the worse off we are.

"If we die, it's irrelevant to the virus," says Morse. "Unless, that is, we die before the virus has a chance to spread to other people. If you're highly virulent but not highly transmissible, you're an ex-virus." The best viral strategy therefore is a long-term relationship, a more or less peaceful coexistence between the infected and the infector.

Frightening as it is, Ebola, as well as some of the other emerging viruses, would appear to be an unsuccessful virus. Ebola is simply too dangerous, and not contagious enough for its own good. Because it kills with unmatched efficiency and speed, it must spread quickly so as not to be buried with its dead host. But it's not very good at spreading. Ebola infests blood and bodily fluids; people become infected by handling Ebola victims. It's not enough simply to be in the same room with an infected person; you must have close, direct contact. The virus isn't particularly durable either, so it probably can't survive for long outside the body—on contaminated clothing, say, or on the ground. It has been possible to contain Ebola by providing caregivers with gowns, gloves, goggles and masks. With nowhere to go and no way to infect, the virus dies along with its victims. Thus, like the 1976 outbreak, the latest Ebola eruption came under control quickly, with 282 people infected and 222 deaths.

While they appreciate the terror and suffering caused by the virus, many scientists therefore discount it as a widespread threat. "I would say that Ebola virus is going to be a fizzler," says Amherst (Mass.) College evolutionary biologist Paul Ewald, a leading authority on emerging viruses. "It will create problems for a matter of weeks, but it will quickly fizzle out on its own, because it doesn't have the right combination of characteristics."

Likewise, Dr. Ewald doubts that hantavirus will be a widespread problem. Like Ebola, it's extremely virulent, but not very durable. Because it's spread

HIV: A Moving Target

Of all emerging viruses, the greatest menace remains HIV, the virus that causes AIDS. One reason is HIV's ability to mutate quickly. The virus evolves so fast that the HIV that infected you yesterday bears little resemblance to the HIV that continues to infect you today. With each cycle of replication, HIV's genes mutate. That changeability keeps the immune system—and, presumably, ongoing attempts at a vaccine—at bay. It's hard to fight off a virus you can't recognize. Add to its mutational skills a combination of different degrees of virulence and transmissibility that perfectly exploits today's social environment, and it's no wonder that AIDS threatens to rival the bubonic plague that killed off a third of Europe in the 14th century.

At first glance, though, HIV doesn't look that formidable. It's highly virulent, yes, killing perhaps every person infected (this plague is so new that we simply don't know yet if death is inevitable). But it takes its sweet time about it, on average some 10 years after infection. Also, because the virus is not very durable and depends on the exchange of bodily fluids, HIV doesn't transmit very readily. Abstinence, safe sex, clean needles, purified transfusions—all these can stop the virus in its tracks.

Nevertheless, HIV prevails. Why? Because social conditions turn its weaknesses into strengths. "Today's social changes have allowed a very wimpy microbe like HIV, with very poor transmissibility, to ride on the back of intravenous drug use and changes in sexual habits," says virologist Stephen S. Morse of Rockefeller University in New York City. "It's a good example of something that's able to take advantage of certain circumstances that have allowed it to spread."

—P.R.

10. CONTEMPORARY HEALTH HAZARDS

through the droppings and urine of mice, its transmissibility is limited; one must be in proximity to mouse excretions to become infected. "Hantavirus will pop up now and again, but the attention we're giving it is greatly out of proportion with the threat," Ewald says. 'I'd put it in the category of Ebola: Some people will get infected, and it's very bad for those people, but it's not going to cause a massive outbreak."

Dengue, on the other hand, may be the real thing. "It's a long-term problem," says Ewald. "It will cause several orders of magnitude more death than we'll get with Ebola and hantavirus." The reason has to do with the way it's transmitted: by mosquito. An infected person can be isolated and bedridden, completely immobile, and if there are mosquitoes droning around, the threat of widespread infection still exists. And it doesn't even matter that dengue is not particularly durable in the outside environment; sequestered inside a mosquito, it doesn't need to be. "Even though the death rate is much, much lower than Ebola's—one in 1,000—because it's vector-borne, dengue is probably a disease organism that's here to stay," Ewald says.

For a virus, one characteristic may come at the expense of another. It's a constant balancing act, a trade-off. For example, the smallpox virus, perhaps the most devastating ever, presented a formidable combination of survival qualities. It was extremely deadly, killing hundreds of millions of people throughout history, but not so virulent that it prevented transmission. Like the common cold or influenza, the virus spread through the air, in droplets from the nose and mouth. So although people readily died from the virus, it also spread readily. And it was very durable: You could pick up the virus even when an infected person was no longer around.

But smallpox has been eradicated, the only viral disease ever to suffer that fate. Despite its strengths, the virus had too many chinks in its armor. Perhaps the most glaring was its inability to mutate (change) in order to elude detection and destruction. "It's a stupid virus," says Ewald. "It doesn't change its surface proteins. So you can use its coat as a target." By inducing the immune system to aim antibodies at the virus's coat, that is precisely what the smallpox vaccine does. The last case of smallpox occurred in 1977.

Mutation is the wild card in the viral game. Like us, viruses ply their trade in a hostile world. One way to survive is to change. But while we might change our behavior deliberately, viral mutation is random, a consequence of minuscule mistakes in genetic replication. Mistakes that help the virus tend to persist, allowing it to replicate more successfully. Mistakes that hinder it disappear, along with the unfortunate virus itself.

Humans and other animals evolve too, in that our genes mutate over time. But because we're so large and complex, our evolution is measured in millions of years. Viruses, on the other hand, are such tiny, simple, fast-replicating organisms, and there are so many of them (the population of any one type of virus within any one person may number in the trillions), they can mutate and evolve like lightning. And lightning mutation is something these emerging viruses have in common, with HIV being the champion.

Few other viruses rival HIV's ability to mutate. One such example, however, is influenza. Although it's been around for a while, causing history's most ferocious pandemic in 1918 by infecting 1 billion people and killing at least 20 million, flu is still considered an emerging virus. The reason has to do with its mutability. In contrast to HIV's single strand of genes, flu genes come in a packet of eight separate links. Like pickup sticks, those genes tend to get swapped around pretty easily—especially as flu makes its yearly pilgrimage from ducks to pigs to people. The result is a different flu virus every year, and the need for a new flu vaccine every year. Scientists are concerned that one of these years the virus might mutate to cause another devastating pandemic like the one in 1918. "If there's one certainty in this business," says Morse, "it's that we should worry about influenza."

Scientists also worry that these mutable viruses might change so dramatically that they become something fearsomely new. For example, what if HIV should mutate into a virus spread by mosquitoes? There are precedents for viruses changing their hosts. Hantavirus belongs to a family that's normally insect-borne, so its lodging in a mouse may be an example of recent evolution. And what if HIV should suddenly become airborne?

Ewald considers either scenario difficult but possible. In fact, the transmission of virus on a mosquito's snout, just as on a dirty needle, a "reasonable expectation" in his view, might function as a stepping-stone to HIV's setting up shop in the insect. If HIV should become airborne, however, the eventual consequences of such a mutation might not be as horrific as one might suppose. Again, the trade-off among viral characteristics would come into play. An airborne virus, like the common cold or flu, requires an active host, such as an infected human, to spread it around. Because too much virulence would kill the carrier, to be successful a dangerous fluid-borne virus mutating to an airborne form would have to calm down. "If HIV or Ebola became airborne, in pretty short order you'd probably get a mild virus," Ewald says. "But it's hard to be sure. You can't anticipate all the possible features viruses could develop through mutation. It's beyond our comprehension."

What is real and pressing is the need for a strategy to deal with the emerging viruses already assailing us and those down the road. To that end, groups such as the CDC, the Institute of Medicine at the National Academy of Sciences in Washington, the National Institutes of Health and the World Health Organization have created proposals to increase our capacity to recognize, treat and prevent emerging diseases. Implementing the proposals will be a daunting task. While it's certainly possible to increase surveillance, and while mosquito and rodent control efforts are feasible, it's not at all clear that new diseases will lend themselves to vaccines or antiviral protection (such as gloves or condoms), that people will be willing to modify their behavior, or that the social conditions contributing to such an onslaught can be changed. And, however well intentioned, these proposals have no guarantee of adequate funding, which means they may have no teeth.

What seems certain, in any event, is that new diseases are on the way. We can only wonder how potent they will be. "Is AIDS a last-gasp pandemic?" asks Rockefeller University's Dr. Lederberg. "Or is it the forerunner of new tidal waves of the magnitude of the bubonic plague of the 14th century?"

In the meantime, like the two Zairean boys in the graveyard, we peer uneasily into the future.

THE ABUSE OF ANTIBIOTICS
BACTERIAL RESISTANCE EVOLVES

'Wonder Drugs' Losing Healing Aura

With Much Treatment Unnecessary, Officials Fear Health Toll Will Be Great

David Brown

Washington Post Staff Writer

In 1933, an antibiotic called sulfanilamide cured a 10-month-old German infant dying of a bloodstream staphylococcal infection. It was an event that began a revolution in medicine and a transformation of consciousness.

In less than a lifetime, whole classes of infections ebbed from the industrialized world.

Women no longer died of childbed fever. A ruptured appendix wasn't a death sentence. Pneumonia rarely killed the young and the healthy.

Vaccines, improved hygiene and a rising tide of wealth were the main reasons for the epochal change. But antibiotics provided the drama. More than anything, those drugs are responsible for the aura of protection that modern medicine has today.

Now, many scientists and physicians are wondering if this is all an illusion.

Antibiotic resistance is on the rise. Every year, more and more bacteria are able to survive assault by what used to be called "wonder drugs." Everyone pays for it in money and inconvenience. A few pay in illness and death. The bill is going up every year.

The source of antibiotic resistance is no mystery: It is the use of antibiotics themselves. The forces of nature guarantee that some bacteria will overcome some antibiotics, sooner or later. The proliferation of resistant microbes, however, is fueled not only by use but by overuse and misuse of the drugs. Behind the second two problems lie the unreasonable expectations of patients, the unquestioning habits of doctors and the relentless advertising of pharmaceutical companies.

Once emerged, resistant bacteria spread quickly, sometimes via a single infected person traveling between countries. Similarly rapid diffusion occurs in the microbial world itself. Genes that confer resistance to antibiotics can pass from bacterium to bacterium, evolving in one enterprise, such as agriculture, and soon showing up in an unrelated one, such as medicine—even if the bacteria themselves don't move.

In the United States, resistance is everywhere—in childhood ear infections, in venereal diseases, in tuberculosis, in surgical wounds and among the 60,000 deaths each year from hospital-acquired infections. But the problem is not confined to places that are rich and medically sophisticated.

In the developing world, antibiotics are the most common pharmaceuticals, and they often can be bought without a prescription. Many people take them when they're not needed or don't take them long enough to cure an infection completely. Such practices, combined with high rates of infectious disease, make developing countries especially fertile breeding grounds for drug resistance.

In one high-profile example, the outbreak of dysentery that killed up to 15,000 Rwandan refugees last summer might have been less deadly if the strain of *Shigella dysenteriae* hadn't been resistant to five common antibiotics. Relief workers ordered 4 million doses of nalidixic acid—the cheap, first-choice drug—only to discover it wouldn't work.

Epidemics, however, are not what experts fear from drug resistance. Instead, they fear the slow erosion of history's most useful medicines and the myriad small changes that will bring to everyday medical practice. They fear that treating simple illnesses will become onerous and expensive, and that the number of mild illnesses taking complicated turns will rise.

"The old people in the nursing homes are going to die, and the young kids with ear infections are going to progress to mastoiditis, sinusitis, meningitis," said Calvin M. Kunin, a professor at Ohio State University School of Medicine and past president of the Infectious Diseases Society of America. "I think there ought to be a new organization called MAMA, Mothers Against the Misuse of Antibiotics. Because it's the mothers' children who are going to die."

"There is a very large group of potential victims," said Stuart Levy, director of the Center for Adaptation Genetics and Drug Resistance at Tufts University School of Medicine.

"This is a problem that is not getting less serious. It is getting more serious," said Alexander Tomasz, a biologist at Rockefeller University who has studied microbial resistance for years.

Part of the reason it is getting more serious is that illnesses for which doctors often prescribe antibiotics are becoming more common.

About 150 million courses of oral antibiotics are prescribed each year in the United States. Childhood ear infections are the single leading reason. Doctor's office visits for that complaint rose 175 percent between 1975 and 1990, according to the National Center for Health Statistics. Sinus infections—an ailment more often found in adults, and the fifth-leading reason for antibiotic prescriptions—more than doubled from 1985 to 1992.

Ironically, the three other leading reasons for antibiotic use—colds, bronchitis and sore throat—are not good candidates for the drugs. Those ailments are usually caused by viruses, not bacteria. Viruses are not killed by antibiotics. Use of the drugs in those infections nevertheless fuels the engines of drug resistance by exposing bystander bacteria to high doses of antibiotics.

Some experts estimate as many as half the prescriptions written for antibiotics in the United States are not needed or warranted on diagnostic grounds. Forces other than the drugs' usefulness are driving doctors to write prescriptions. A study done in 1986 suggested, for example, how strong a force patients expectations may be.

Investigators wanted to know whether antibiotics were useful in acute bronchitis; previous research suggested the benefit was minimal or nonexistent. Patients were assigned at random to take either an antibiotic or a placebo. However, it proved very difficult to recruit people for the experiment. Sixty percent of eligible patients declined because they didn't want to take the chance of getting a placebo.

At the doctor's end, writing a prescription often provides the illusion that "definitive" treatment is at hand. It is also quicker than talking to patients. A study published last year in Canada hinted at this. It found that doctors in New Brunswick who saw many patients per day wrote more prescriptions per patient than did colleagues who saw fewer patients.

Commenting about the problem, two editorialists wrote recently in the journal The Lancet: "The combination of fixed patient expectations and pressures on physicians to limit appointment times has encouraged antibiotic prescribing as the path of least resistance."

Whatever their source, drug-resistant germs are now such an unavoidable part of the environment that children get them as a birthright.

In a study published five years ago, researchers analyzed the intestinal bacteria of infants and toddlers in three widely separated places. They found that 42 percent of samples from children in Qin Pu, China, were resistant to three or more antibiotics. Multiple-drug resistance was found in 30 percent of children sampled in Caracas, Venezuela, and in 6 percent of children in Boston. None had been recently exposed to antibiotics.

How Resistance Evolves

Curiously, genes that permit microbes to survive antibiotics predate the use of antibiotics as medicine.

The reason is that many antibiotics are products of nature. They are synthesized by bacteria and fungi (and harvested by pharmaceutical companies on an industrial scale). They evolved for self-defense, and probably also to regulate critical cellular events. (The latter function may actually be the more important one.) Not surprisingly, antibiotic resistance evolved right along with antibiotics.

Modern medicine, however, has exposed many more species of bacteria to far higher concentrations of these compounds that ever occurred in the primordial world. This has done two things: It has helped disseminate ancient resistance genes widely, and it has encouraged the evolution of new resistance genes.

The emergence of antibiotic resistance is a textbook example of Darwinian "survival of the fittest" compressed into weeks and months, rather than eons.

Like all inherited traits, antibiotic resistance evolves by chance. It arises through the mutation of genes, the strings of DNA that encode a cell's inherited instructions. Mutations of any sort are

53. 'Wonder Drugs'

rare. Given enough time, however, it's inevitable some mutations will occur that enable microbes to bind up, break up, lock out or pump out specific chemical molecules. And some of those chemicals will be antibiotics.

Under normal circumstances, those organisms might survive as a tiny fraction of the microbial world or, like most mutants, die a natural death. Antibiotics, however, change the picture utterly. They kill off "susceptible" microbes and create a world free of competition, which resistant strains—should any exist—can repopulate at their leisure. Sooner or later, some will exist.

Resistance doesn't evolve with equal speed for all antibiotics. It depends on the chemistry of the drug and the genetic endowment of the organism facing it. Sometimes a single mutation renders a germ resistant; in other cases an accumulation of them is necessary. For reasons that are quite mysterious, some microbes develop resistance to many antibiotics simultaneously.

Though mutation is a random event, the emergence of resistance as clinical problem is intimately bound to where and how a specific antibiotic is used—a fact that helps explain some curious observations.

One of the more important disease-causing bacteria in human beings is called *Streptococcus pneumoniae*. Its resistance to penicillin is a huge problem in Europe and a growing one in the United States. Penicillin-resistant *S. pneumoniae*, however, was originally found in Papua New Guinea.

In the 1960s, the Australian army gave New Guinean villagers monthly penicillin shots in order to prevent yaws, an infection resembling syphilis that is spread by casual, not sexual, contact. Over time, the campaign created a large human population in which penicillin-resistant *S. pneumoniae* could flourish should such a bacterium emerge by chance. One did, in 1967.

Once they have evolved, human behavior combines with chance to move resistant microbes around. The best-documented example involves the spread of penicillin-resistant *S. pneumoniae* in Iceland.

The bug surfaced in Iceland in December 1988, at a hospital in Reykjavik. DNA fingerprinting revealed it was similar to a strain found in Spain, a popular winter vacation spot. Within three years, 20 percent of the *S. pneumoniae* in Iceland was resistant to penicillin, apparently all descended from the single Spanish import. Dissemination almost certainly occurred through day-care centers, where more than half of Iceland's children spend their preschool years.

Common Bug Fights Back

As a threat to the public health, *S. pneumoniae* is currently the greatest object of concern. The bacterium is the leading cause of illness and death from infection in the United States. It is responsible for roughly 7 million cases of ear infection; 500,000 cases of pneumonia; 50,000 cases of bloodstream infection; and 3,000 cases of meningitis each year. Penicillin has always been the drug of choice against it.

In a study that chilled the blood of public health officials, the Centers for Disease Control and Prevention (CDC) last year reported high rates of penicillin-resistant *S. pneumoniae* in two southern communities.

In Memphis, about 10 percent of children in clinics and doctors' offices carried the bug. In a town in central Kentucky, epidemiologists found that 25 percent of the children at the largest day-care center carried it. (Many samples also were resistant to the alternative drugs, erythromycin and trimethoprim/sulfamethoxazole.) A survey of southern Ontario published this year found 8 percent of samples resistant to penicillin. Few experts doubt they could find the problem in many other places if they looked.

In general, drug-resistant bacteria are not more dangerous or likely to cause disease than drug-sensitive bacteria. In the case of *S. pneumoniae*, the immediate effect of penicillin resistance will be greater use of broader-acting and more expensive drugs, some of which must be given by injection, not pill. Inevitably, though, a greater number of cases will become "complicated"—an ear infection, for example, can occasionally spread to the skull or the brain—as physicians fail to control simple infections with the usual drugs. And because *S. pneumoniae*-caused illness is so common, a sizable number of people will be affected by such once-rare disasters.

Only slightly less troubling is growing antibiotic resistance in bacterial species that rarely cause illness among healthy people but can be deadly to the ill or debilitated.

Each year in this country, about 2 million cases of infection are contracted by people while they are in the hospital. The problem is far more common that in the past, as critically ill patients are kept alive, many connected to tubes and ventilators that give microbes easy portals of entry.

A common cause of these infections is a family of bacteria known as "the enterococci," which infect surgical wounds, the urinary tract, the heart and the bloodstream. Over recent decades, these germs have developed resistance to a half-dozen antibiotics.

10. CONTEMPORARY HEALTH HAZARDS

RESISTING ANTIBIOTICS

MECHANISMS OF RESISTANCE

Most antibiotic resistance genes are actually mutant versions of genes that originally served another purpose in a cell's life. In some cases, however, genes evolved specifically to protect an organism from an antibiotic. This appears to be the case with some bacteria in the Streptomyces genus, which make compounds called aminoglycosides. The producing bacterium shields itself from an aminoglycoside molecule's toxic effects by attaching a chemical structure called a "protecting group," which is clipped off just as the molecule exits the cell. Instructions for making the enzyme that attaches the protecting group are contained in a gene. This gene has been passed to entirely different kinds of bacteria, which use it to disarm incoming aminoglycoside molecules—in other words, to become antibiotic resistant.

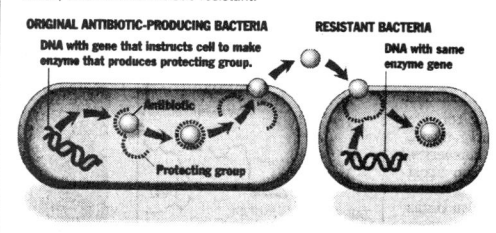

1 Streptomyces kanamyceticus naturally produces the antibiotic kanamycin. It also possesses the gene for an enzyme that puts a protective group on the antibiotic.

2 Staphylococcus aureus, another bacterium, becomes resistant to kanamycin after acquiring the gene for the enzyme that puts on the protecting group.

TRANSFER OF GENES

Bacteria acquire antibiotic resistance genes three ways. They can exchange small loops of DNA, called plasmids, with other organisms. They can be infected by viruses carrying genes. They can also vacuum up free-floating DNA from the environment and incorporate the information into their own genetic record.

HOW BACTERIA ACQUIRE RESISTANCE GENES

1 Direct exchange of genes between bacteria in a process known as conjugation.

2 Viruses can carry genes between bacteria.

3 DNA from the environment can be taken into a bacterium's own DNA.

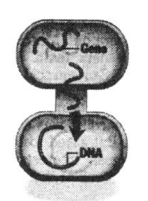

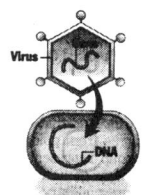

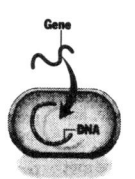

Medical practice theoretically could have played a role in spreading resistance genes via this third method. Julian Davies and Vera Webb, of the University of British Columbia, found that in many samples of antibiotics made from bacteria there were detectable amounts of DNA contaminating the drugs. Surprisingly, some of this DNA encoded antibiotic-resistance genes. An official at the Food and Drug Administration said there is no evidence such contaminating genes are functional. He added that most new antibiotics are either completely or partially man-made, making DNA contamination unlikely.

PACKAGES OF MULTIPLE-DRUG RESISTANCE

Some bacteria possess DNA structures called "integrons," which assist in the accumulation and dissemination of antibiotic resistance genes. An integron functions a bit like a bracketed phrase in an enormous DNA sentence. The brackets can be separated to accommodate more words—genes—and the entire integron can pick up and move to a different part of the sentence. Integrons can accumulate up to half a dozen different resistance genes. A bacterium receiving such a structure instantly becomes multi-drug resistant.

HOW INTEGRONS WORK

1 Integron containing two antibiotic resistance genes.

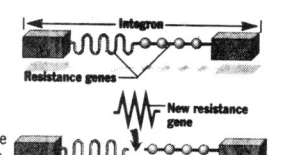

2 A third antibiotic resistance gene can be inserted like a cassette into the integron.

3 The entire integron can be incorporated into loops of DNA, called plasmids, which are passed between bacteria.

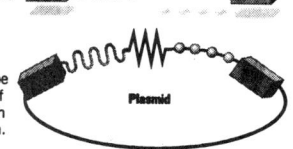

THE WASHINGTON POST

However, they remained susceptible to vancomycin, an expensive and occasionally toxic intravenous antibiotic.

Between 1989 and 1993, the fraction of hospital-acquired enterococcal infections that cannot be killed by vancomycin rose from 0.3 percent to 8 percent, according to a surveillance program run by the CDC. Mortality among people with the resistant organism in their bloodstreams was 37 percent, more than double that of enterococcal infections susceptible to vancomycin.

The biggest cause of hospital-acquired infections—the family of *Staphylococcus* bacteria—currently is resistant to everything but vancomycin in 40 percent of cases in large teaching hospitals. Experts fear the day that drug becomes useless in staph infections—though few doubt it will arrive.

Overuse

Antibiotics' reputation for reliability has led some patients to demand them and some physicians to dispense them even when they are not needed. The drugs serve many purposes, not the least of which is reassuring both patient and doctor.

Physicians often prescribe antibiotics for illnesses, such as bronchitis, that are rarely caused by bacteria so they can be certain to catch the small percentage that are. Ironically, the equivocal performance of antibiotics in such circumstances (combined with fear that the odd bacterial case will be drug-resistant) often drives practitioners to use the most powerful "broad-spectrum" antibiotics from the outset. Those drugs are almost always the newest and the most expensive and often the most convenient for the patient. Their popularity—even cachet—in doctors' offices helps lay the groundwork for their obsolescence as soon as they arrive on the market.

"If we are too quick on the trigger to use the newest drugs, we may be fostering resistance, and they may be less effective in the few instances where we truly need a new, big gun," said Jerry Avorn, a physician at Harvard Medical School who does research on drug-prescribing behavior. "But often the siren song the doctor gets from the [drug company] sales rep is, 'Give them this, and you and they will be protected.'"

The problem, though, is not just overuse, but misuse.

Patients who stop a course of treatment early (or take short courses of leftover drugs on their own) create the right conditions for "selection" of drug-resistant mutants. The seriousness of this problem is nowhere more obvious than in tuberculosis, where at least six months of treatment is necessary for success. Nearly all multidrug-resistant TB organisms evolved in patients who stopped taking their medicines early or took them sporadically.

Changing both patients' and doctors' habits would slow the emergence of resistant strains and might even turn back the hands of the clock somewhat. There is some evidence that susceptible strains of bacteria slowly return to the throat, skin, intestines and other body sites when antibiotics are less frequently encountered. In Hungary, for example, 50 percent of S. pneumoniae were resistant to penicillin in the early 1980s. By 1992, after a campaign against indiscriminate antibiotic use, the number had fallen to 34 percent.

A Social Problem

More than most problems in medicine, antibiotic resistance is a social problem.

"Antibiotics are unique among pharmaceuticals in that they treat populations as well as individuals," Stuart Levy wrote five years ago in the New England Journal of Medicine. "One's bacteria are not solely one's own. Rather, they are shed, excreted and otherwise spread into the environment, where they become part of a common pool."

Solving the problem, however, will not be easy, for antibiotic resistance is a "tragedy of the commons."

In 1968, a biologist named Garrett Hardin wrote a now-famous essay of that name. His subject was overpopulation and pollution, but it could just as easily have been the intemperate use of antibiotics.

He asked the reader to imagine a pasture—a "commons"—available to the public for the grazing of animals. For a period of time, it will be able to accommodate every herdsman's needs. For every additional sheep or cow there will be sufficient grass. But eventually, as the population grows and more people herd animals onto the commons, the land will reach its carrying capacity. Even then, however, every herdsman has more to gain by adding another animal (because the gain is all his) than he has to lose by the overgrazing that results (which is shared by everyone).

"Therein is the tragedy," Hardin wrote. "Each man is locked into a system that compels him to increase his herd without limit—in a world that is limited." Eventually, the commons is barren.

The microbial world is also a commons.

When a person has a bacterial infection, there's no question he has more to gain than lose by using antibiotics. But what if the infection is unlikely to be bacterial, or if the illness—whatever its cause—is minor and self-limiting? Many people would still say: "Yes, take the antibiotic, because there's nothing to lose." Nothing to lose, that is, until the commons is so full of resistant organisms that suddenly there's nothing to gain from antibiotics, either.

Preventing this will take a new way of calculating risks and benefits. It will take a community-mindedness not common in medicine. It also will take new antibiotics.

In the world of infectious disease, humankind is armed with the twin arrows of wit and will, and bacteria with the battering ram of evolution. We may learn in our lifetime whose weapon works best.

Prevent SEXUALLY TRANSMITTED DISEASES

Lauren Picker

Shortly after graduating from college in 1988, Sara Lewis* noticed a constellation of small red bumps on her vagina. She assumed they'd go away by themselves, but instead they became larger and more plentiful. She finally went to her gynecologist, who diagnosed a sexually transmitted disease (STD)—in her case, genital warts.

"I just lay there crying in the stirrups," recalls Lewis. At 21, she'd had few sexual partners and she had never seriously considered the risks of sex beyond an unwanted pregnancy. "This shouldn't happen to me—I'm a 'good girl,' " she remembers thinking. It's an attitude that's all too common.

"Most people think of STD's as something that happens to the other guy, but they're really everybody's problem," says Dr. H. Hunter Handsfield, director of the STD control program at the Seattle–King County (Wash.) Department of Public Health. "It's a fair bet that half of us acquire an STD at least once by age 30."

AIDS is the STD that receives the most attention. This lethal and incurable disease is caused by a virus, HIV, that currently has infected more than 1.2 million Americans, killing more than 220,000 of them. But the AIDS plague has overshadowed other important STD's that are spreading at a rate of 12 million new infections per year in the U.S., with two-thirds of new cases affecting people under 25.

*Name has been changed.

The most worrisome of these are, like AIDS, caused by viruses and are incurable. These viral STD's can have devastating health impacts and can even prove fatal. Genital warts, for example, are caused by the human papilloma virus, the most common STD. HPV is now believed responsible as well for most cases of cervical cancer, a disease that kills more than 4,000 American women each year. Add in cases of herpes and hepatitis B, and the proportion of Americans infected with an incurable viral STD other than HIV may approach 50%. For just one STD, genital herpes, "we know that about a quarter of all Americans become infected by age 35," says Handsfield.

Unfortunately, someone with almost any STD runs a much greater risk of contracting AIDS through sex with an HIV-infected partner. Herpes and syphilis cause sores or ulcers that facilitate HIV's entry into the body, but even nonulcerative STD's such as chlamydia and gonorrhea promote HIV infection, presumably because they allow the virus to enter the body through the microscopic lesions they cause. In fact, these much more common diseases, says Handsfield, "may contribute more to HIV transmission than do the ulcerative STD's." Preventing and controlling them, he adds, "is emerging as one of the most important but least appreciated ways of preventing the transmission and spread of AIDS."

STD's are blatantly discriminatory. Not only are women likelier than men to become infected (through sex with an

HALF OF ALL AMERICANS WILL ACQUIRE AN STD AT LEAST ONCE BY AGE 30

54. Prevent Sexually Transmitted Diseases

- A new detection test is available for chlamydia, and another one should be widely available soon. The new tests require just a urine specimen and will encourage many more people to be screened.
- Several vaccines for preventing genital herpes are being tested in clinical trials. Experts predict that a herpes vaccine will receive federal approval within a few years.
- A very effective vaccine for hepatitis B has been available since 1982, though it is vastly underused.

Here's a guide to some of the most important STD's.

CHLAMYDIA

During her senior year of college in 1984, Nancy Hartman* was stricken with such severe abdominal pain she could barely walk. She didn't connect her agony to a brief fling several weeks earlier. Then the campus doctor told Hartman that her pain was due to pelvic inflammatory disease caused by a chlamydial infection.

Chlamydia, a bacterial infection, strikes more often each year—about 4 million cases in the U.S.—than any other bacterial STD. The infections respond readily to antibiotics, but if they persist, they can cause devastating complications, especially for women.

"I was lucky the pain got severe," says Hartman, who was promptly treated and cured with antibiotics. Actually, she was lucky to have felt any discomfort at all. As many as 75% of women and 25% of men with chlamydia have no idea they're infected, a situation that can lead to unwitting spread of the microbe as well as to serious complications.

For many women, the first sign of a chlamydial infection is an inability to get pregnant. An examination may then reveal chronic tubal inflammation, a sign the infection has festered in the genital tract and scarred the fallopian tubes. Chlamydial infections account for up to 40% of all cases of female

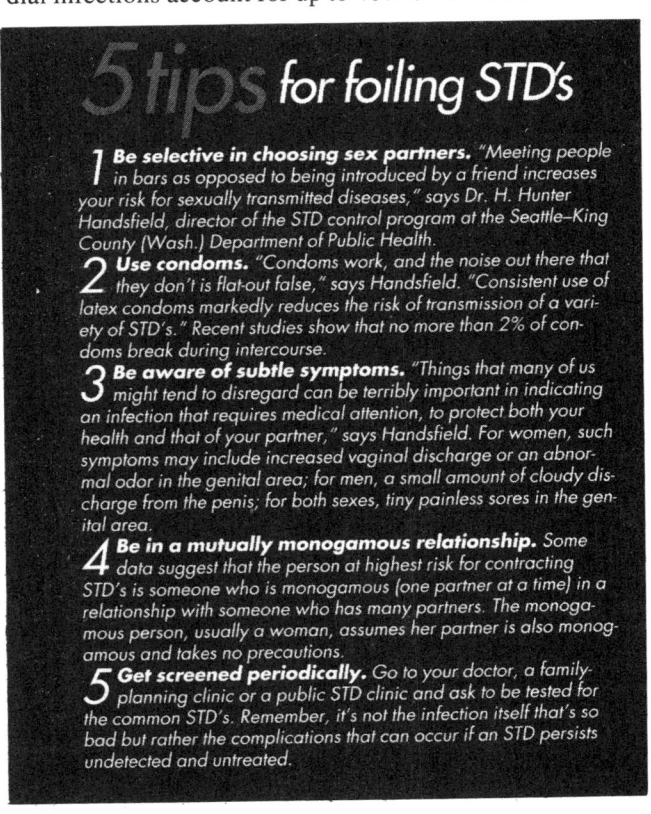

---

infected partner), but the consequences of those infections for women are also much more severe.

A woman has a greater susceptibility than a man to almost all STD's, including AIDS, for two reasons: She has a larger genital surface area that can be breached by microbes; and during sex, the man's secretions are deposited directly into the woman's body. In a single act of unprotected heterosexual intercourse with an infected partner, for example, a woman has a 50% or greater chance of contracting chlamydia, while a man runs only a 20% to 40% chance of being infected by a woman with the disease.

Once infection occurs, effective treatment for women is often delayed, partly because early symptoms of STD's are usually more subtle in women, so they don't seek treatment as promptly as men do. And when a woman does seek medical attention, the diagnostic tests don't work as well as they do for men, so an infection can persist for months or even years and cause extensive damage, particularly to reproductive organs, before being detected and treated.

"Women *far* more than men have serious long-term consequences from STD's," says Handsfield, who lists as examples infertility, life-threatening tubal pregnancies, sick infants and cervical cancer. "Unfortunately, women can't assume that their sexual partners will assume responsibility for the woman's sexual health."

Not all the news about STD's is bleak. Some bright spots:
- STD's are preventable by using latex or polyurethane condoms. The first male polyurethane condom, Avanti, is now available west of the Rockies and will be nationally distributed this fall. The FDA approved these "plastic" condoms so that people allergic to latex could have a way to prevent STD's, as well as pregnancy. Because testing has been limited, however, product labels state that "the risks of pregnancy and STD's ... are not known for this condom." Polyurethane condoms are thinner than latex and therefore provide greater sensitivity and heat transfer between partners. The new male condoms cost $1 to $1.50 each, or about twice the cost of a latex condom. Reality, the female condom, also made of polyurethane, has been available since 1994.
- While rates of viral STD's (genital herpes, hepatitis B, genital warts) are rising or showing no signs of decline, rates of some key *bacterial* STD's (syphilis, gonorrhea and possibly chlamydia) have fallen significantly in recent years, due to behavioral changes as well as public health efforts to educate people about prevention and screen them for infection. Another reason for the falling rates is that bacterial STD's can be cured with antibiotics once they're detected.

---

5 tips for foiling STD's

1. **Be selective in choosing sex partners.** "Meeting people in bars as opposed to being introduced by a friend increases your risk for sexually transmitted diseases," says Dr. H. Hunter Handsfield, director of the STD control program at the Seattle–King County (Wash.) Department of Public Health.

2. **Use condoms.** "Condoms work, and the noise out there that they don't is flat-out false," says Handsfield. "Consistent use of latex condoms markedly reduces the risk of transmission of a variety of STD's." Recent studies show that no more than 2% of condoms break during intercourse.

3. **Be aware of subtle symptoms.** "Things that many of us might tend to disregard can be terribly important in indicating an infection that requires medical attention, to protect both your health and that of your partner," says Handsfield. For women, such symptoms may include increased vaginal discharge or an abnormal odor in the genital area; for men, a small amount of cloudy discharge from the penis; for both sexes, tiny painless sores in the genital area.

4. **Be in a mutually monogamous relationship.** Some data suggest that the person at highest risk for contracting STD's is someone who is monogamous (one partner at a time) in a relationship with someone who has many partners. The monogamous person, usually a woman, assumes her partner is also monogamous and takes no precautions.

5. **Get screened periodically.** Go to your doctor, a family-planning clinic or a public STD clinic and ask to be tested for the common STD's. Remember, it's not the infection itself that's so bad but rather the complications that can occur if an STD persists undetected and untreated.

10. CONTEMPORARY HEALTH HAZARDS

infertility and also increase the risk for ectopic pregnancy (when the embryo develops in one of the fallopian tubes rather than in the uterus).

For the one in four infected women who experience them, symptoms generally appear one to three weeks after exposure and may include an abnormal vaginal discharge, a burning sensation while urinating, abdominal pain or pain during intercourse. Men may notice a discharge from the penis or burning when urinating.

Since symptoms so often are absent, all sexually active women should have a chlamydia test as part of a yearly pelvic exam and whenever suspicious symptoms appear. Experts also recommend frequent testing for men and women under 25 who have more than one partner.

Until recently, doctors tested for chlamydia by culturing genital secretions, an accurate but time-consuming (up to one week) procedure that is uncomfortable for men. The two tests recently developed for chlamydia can detect the microbes in a couple of days. Treatment of chlamydia has also improved, with just a single dose of the antibiotic azithromycin able to cure most infections.

GENITAL WARTS/HPV

HPV, the infection that caused Lewis's genital warts, is the most prevalent viral STD. As many as 40 million Americans have it, and up to a million more contract it each year. A 1991 study found that 46% of the women who used a health clinic at the University of California at Berkeley were infected with this highly contagious virus: If someone is infected with HPV, there is at least a 70% chance that his or her partner is also infected.

Genital warts generally appear as fleshy, cauliflower-like growths on the genitals or around the anus. Warts tend to surface within three months of exposure, but they sometimes don't appear until several years later. Although the warts HPV causes sometimes clear up on their own, more typically, people have them removed, because they often itch and are unattractive.

Treatments to remove warts include liquid nitrogen (freezing), electrocautery (burning), podophyllin (a caustic liquid) and, when warts are widespread, surgical or laser excision. The immune compound alpha interferon, which is injected into warts, has also received FDA approval, but it can cause flu-like symptoms. Unfortunately, getting rid of visible warts may not get rid of the virus particles, which are much more extensive, and so many patients who have warts removed need repeat treatments for new ones.

The main danger from HPV infection is not warts but cervical cancer. In a recent international study, more than 85% of women with cervical cancer were found to be infected with HPV. Ironically, an HPV infection expressed as warts is relatively good news. "As a rule, warts don't turn into cancer," notes Dr. Mark Schiffman, a medical epidemiologist at the National Cancer Institute and an expert on HPV.

Of some 70 types of HPV that have been identified, the two mainly responsible for genital warts, types six and 11, are only rarely implicated in cervical cancer. At least 10 other types of HPV cause cervical lesions that may ultimately develop into cancer.

These precancerous lesions usually don't cause symptoms, and the first sign of infection is often an abnormal Pap test. "I thought if I contracted something there would be some form of warning," says Alisa Spitler, a 32-year-old woman from Oakman, Ga., who was stunned to learn she had HPV after a Pap test detected abnormal cells.

Fortunately, regular Pap tests can detect cervical cell abnormalities, or dysplasia, well before the condition progresses to cancer. Mild dysplasias often go away on their own, without treatment. But if lesions persist or worsen, physicians can remove them, greatly reducing the risk of cancer without impairing a woman's ability to bear children.

HEPATITIS B

In 1982 Joe Brown* went to his university health center complaining of dizziness and fatigue and assuming he had mononucleosis. But a blood test revealed that his problem was hepatitis B, a viral infection that damages the liver.

Few people think of hepatitis B as an STD, but more than half of the 200,000 new infections each year are contracted through sex. This highly contagious virus, which is much hardier than HIV, can also spread through casual contacts such as sharing a toothbrush or razor blade. Like Brown, half of people newly infected with hepatitis B become acutely ill (about 5,000 of them die from it each year). The rest of those infected show no symptoms (or trivial ones perhaps mistaken for a cold) and don't realize they're infected.

Where to Get Help

The American Social Health Association, a nonprofit organization, operates several hot lines about sexually transmitted diseases. For information and referrals, call:

The National AIDS Hotline (800-342-AIDS)
The National STD Hotline (800-227-8922)
The National Herpes Hotline (Research Triangle Park, N.C., 919-361-8488)

Whether they get sick or not, the great majority of infected people manage to lick the disease completely. But 5% to 10% of infected adults can't shake the virus and become hepatitis B carriers; they not only can transmit the infection to others but also may develop chronic hepatitis, a progressive disease that kills an additional 5,000 people each year, mostly from cirrhosis (scarring of the liver), but also from liver cancer.

Brown, who went on to become a carrier, was upset to learn there is a vaccine that could have prevented his infection. In fact, the safe and highly effective hepatitis B vaccine has been available from family doctors and many public health clinics since 1981, but it hasn't been widely used.

Those who could benefit most from the vaccine are sexually active young adults, both straight and gay, since three-fourths of all cases affect people between 18 and 39. Yet only 1% of Americans in this age group have been vaccinated against hepatitis B. In an effort to protect young adults, the American Academy of Pediatrics recommends that all adolescents be routinely immunized against hepatitis B. The Centers for Disease Control and Prevention takes things a step further by recommending that all infants be vaccinated.

54. Prevent Sexually Transmitted Diseases

The Major STD's

CHLAMYDIA
Estimated New Cases Yearly: 4 million.
Who's at Risk: People with multiple sexual partners; most prevalent among young people; cuts across all socioeconomic groups.
Symptoms: None in most infected women and up to half of infected men, but abnormal genital discharge or burning during urination (in both sexes); abdominal pain or pain during intercourse (women); testicular pain or swelling (men).
Consequences: For untreated women, pelvic inflammatory disease, which can lead to chronic pelvic pain, ectopic pregnancy or infertility; for untreated men, may lead in rare cases to sterility. Increased risk of HIV infection if a person with chlamydia is exposed to the virus.
Treatment: Antibiotics (azithromycin, doxycycline, ofloxacin).
Prevention: Condoms; probably some protection from spermicides.

GENITAL WARTS/HUMAN PAPILLOMA VIRUS
Estimated New Cases Yearly: 500,000 to 1 million.
Who's at Risk: People with multiple sexual partners; most prevalent among young people.
Symptoms: Fleshy, cauliflower-like growths or warts on and inside the genitals and anus; may appear on the throat when acquired through oral sex; abnormal Pap test.
Consequences: Some strains of HPV believed to cause cervical cancer; HPV also linked to vulvar, vaginal, penile and anal cancers.
Treatment: Warts removed by freezing with liquid nitrogen, burning with electrocautery, applying caustic liquids or by surgical or laser excision for cases where warts are widespread. The precancerous lesions caused by HPV can also be removed.
Prevention: Condoms, though they offer no protection against uncovered lesions.

GONORRHEA
Estimated New Cases Yearly: 500,000.
Who's at Risk: People with multiple sexual partners; most common among teens and young adults in poor inner city areas and in rural southeastern U.S.
Symptoms: None in many cases, but discharge from the vagina, penis or rectum; burning or itching during urination; low abdominal pain (women).
Consequences: Same as with chlamydia.
Treatment: Antibiotics; some strains are resistant to penicillin, but alternatives (such as cefixime and ceftriaxone) are available.
Prevention: Condoms; probably some protection from spermicides. Vaccine in development.

HEPATITIS B
Estimated New Cases Yearly: 200,000, with slightly more than half of them sexually transmitted.
Who's at Risk: (sexually transmitted cases only): gay men; people with multiple sexual partners.
Symptoms: None in about one-third of those infected, but fever, muscle aches and fatigue and, as the disease progresses, dark urine and jaundice in the skin and eyes.
Consequences: For the chronically infected, possibly cirrhosis of the liver or liver cancer.
Treatment: No effective one.
Prevention: Condoms; hepatitis vaccine.

GENITAL HERPES
Estimated New Cases Yearly: 200,000 to 500,000.
Who's at Risk: People with multiple sexual partners.
Symptoms: Recurring blisters or sores usually in the genital area; fever, nausea and genital pain often occur during the first episode; in two-thirds of those infected, herpes symptoms are so mild they don't realize they have the virus.
Consequences: Increased risk of HIV infection if a person with herpes is exposed to the virus.
Treatment: Acyclovir to reduce symptoms and outbreaks.
Prevention: Condoms, though they offer no protection against uncovered sores. A vaccine could be available by 1998.

SYPHILIS
Estimated New Cases Yearly: 120,000.
Who's at Risk: People with multiple sexual partners; most commonly occurs in poor urban communities.
Symptoms: Syphilis sores, or chancres, in the primary stage of the disease; can appear anywhere on the body but are often hidden from view.
Consequences: If untreated, can lead to mental illness, blindness, heart disease and death. Increased risk of HIV infection if exposed to the virus.
Treatment: Penicillin.
Prevention: Condoms, though they offer no protection against uncovered sores.

Sources: Centers for Disease Control and Prevention and the Alan Guttmacher Institute

GENITAL HERPES

In a 1982 cover story, *Time* magazine proclaimed herpes "today's scarlet letter." Though AIDS soon pushed herpes out of the headlines, the ranks of herpes sufferers continue to swell. Today about 60 million Americans, or one in four, are believed to be infected with herpes simplex type 2, the virus that causes genital herpes. In 1992 Megan Smith* contracted the disease from her boyfriend.

"We always used a condom, but somehow I got it," says Smith, 29. Her symptoms: swollen glands and a lesion so tiny that "I practically had to use a magnifying glass to see it," she says.

Herpes symptoms usually show up two to 21 days after exposure and can vary enormously in severity from one person to the next. Many people associate genital herpes with recurring bouts of blisters or sores in the genital area, accompanied by pain, fever and nausea. But it's now clear that most people with herpes are not seriously affected.

Some two-thirds of herpes cases are so mild that people don't even know they're infected. Although herpes is most contagious during an outbreak, when sores are visible, it can also be passed by asymptomatic shedding of viruses from someone who feels perfectly fine, a fact that helps explain why up to half a million new infections occur each year.

The oral drug acyclovir, available since 1985, can reduce the frequency, duration and severity of outbreaks. A vaccine against genital herpes is now in clinical trials and could be available by 1998.

10. CONTEMPORARY HEALTH HAZARDS

GONORRHEA

Although gonorrhea is waning, it still causes more than half a million new infections each year, primarily in impoverished urban areas and in rural southeastern communities, where nearly one in ten 15- to 19-year-olds may have it. Women have a 50% chance of contracting gonorrhea in a single act of unprotected intercourse with an infected partner.

Symptoms of gonorrhea, which is caused by gonococcus bacteria, mirror those caused by chlamydia and usually surface two to five days after infection. In fact, the two infections are virtually indistinguishable without a microscopic exam of genital discharge (for men) or a culture of cervical secretions (for women).

Untreated, gonorrhea can lead to fever, pain and, in women, pelvic inflammatory disease, which can cause infertility. Infectious disease experts are concerned about the growing number of gonorrhea cases that are resistant to one or more antibiotics. The antibiotics penicillin and tetracycline have historically been used to cure the infection, but cases resistant to these drugs have risen rapidly, from fewer than 1% of infections in the U.S. in 1980 to 10% at present. Work on a gonorrhea vaccine is under way.

SYPHILIS

The introduction of penicillin in the 1940s sharply curtailed syphilis as a public health problem. But from 1970 to 1985, syphilis surged among gay men, and in the late 1980s cases soared once again, to their highest level in 40 years, due to the practice among crack addicts of trading sex for drugs. Syphilis cases are now declining rapidly again in most of the country. But they remain prevalent among blacks in lower socioeconomic groups, who have an infection rate more than 60 times higher than whites. The good news about syphilis: A course of penicillin can still cure the disease.

How much are pesticides hurting your health?

Pesticides. Just the word conjures up images of ruined cropland and diseased wildlife. For many consumers, even scarier than those images are the things they can't see: potentially cancer-causing chemical residues tainting otherwise healthful-looking fruits and vegetables.

It's a catch-22. At the same time that health experts keep pushing for more consumption of fruits and vegetables to lessen cancer risk, alarming headlines and news stories warning of the risks of dietary pesticide residues constantly leach into the public stream of consciousness.

Are pesticides the cancer threat many are afraid of? Should you spend the extra money on organically grown produce? What about children? Should they be given anything but pesticide-free food? Following is a look at some of the common beliefs about pesticides in the food supply—and the realities behind them.

> To find out everything from how to dispose of an insect repellent used in your garden to whether the chemicals your exterminator is using are safe, call the National Pesticide Telecommunications Network's toll-free hotline at 1-800-858-7378. Operators are available from 9:30 a.m. to 7:30 p.m. Eastern time, Monday through Friday.

Myth: Pesticides and other chemicals rank as the most significant diet-related cancer threat.

Reality: In the United States, diets too rich in calories, fat, and alcohol pose a far greater cancer threat than pesticides and other chemical residues, according to a 400-plus page report just released by the National Research Council, which scrutinized the data on more than 200 known carcinogens in food. What's more, a wealth of research indicates that a diet rich in fruits and vegetables protects against cancer. Thus, the risks incurred by avoiding fruits and vegetables for fear of ingesting pesticide residues far outweigh any risks that come from eating a produce-rich diet.

Myth: The only cancer-causing compounds found in produce and grains are synthetic chemicals added during farming and processing.

Reality: The number of naturally occurring chemicals found in the food supply probably exceeds a million, and some of these are known to be potent carcinogens. For example, a class of substances called mycotoxins, which are produced by fungal growth on food crops either in the field or during harvesting, are highly toxic and play a role in liver cancer. Many countries, including the United States, impose strict limits on the levels of mycotoxins allowed in foods.

Myth: To determine the amount of pesticide residues allowed in foods, the Environmental Protection Agency finds out what dose of the chemical is toxic and then sets the legal limit slightly below that level.

10. CONTEMPORARY HEALTH HAZARDS

Reality: To come up with limits, the EPA looks at animal studies that help project the maximum amount of a pesticide residue that a person could consume daily during a 70-year life span without suffering any harm. Once they determine this level, they set the legal limit at just a small fraction of that amount—generally 100 times lower—just to be on the safe side.

Myth: Pesticides are more toxic to children than to adults.

Reality: While most people assume that children's small size leaves them much more vulnerable than adults to the effects of pesticides and other chemicals, that's not necessarily the case. The ability of a child's rapidly developing body to metabolize, detoxify, and excrete chemicals is profoundly different from that of adults and plays a major role in their vulnerability to pesticides. Children's metabolic rates are much higher than adults', which may allow youngsters to excrete certain pesticides and other chemicals much more quickly.

That's not to say pesticides do not pose a problem for youngsters. Infants and children eat a far less varied diet than adults and so consume much more of certain foods for their body weight, which could boost their exposure to certain pesticide residues. This difference and others are not considered thoroughly when the government determines what levels of pesticides will be allowed in the food supply, according to a major report from the National Research Council issued in 1993.

Still, the report concluded that when it comes to pesticide exposure and physiologic responses, differences between children and adults are usually less than 10-fold. Given that the EPA typically factors in a 100-fold margin of safety, the problem certainly doesn't warrant keeping fruits and vegetables out of a child's diet.

Myth: All fruits and vegetables should be washed in detergent and peeled carefully to eliminate all traces of pesticide residues.

Reality: All fresh fruits and vegetables should be rinsed thoroughly with water to remove any dirt, bacteria, and surface chemicals that may have come into contact with the food. Fruits and vegetables with edible peels should also be scrubbed thoroughly with a brush, and the outer leaves of lettuce, cabbage, and other greens should be removed. Most experts advise against cleaning produce with detergents, however, because soapy products may leave behind traces of other chemicals not intended for consumption.

As for peeling, it does help rid produce of pesticides, since some chemicals tend to remain on or just under the skin of fruits and vegetables. That's particularly true of waxed products, like cucumbers; the wax that gives the fruit or vegetable its shiny appearance sometimes contains fungicides. On the other hand, you might not want to make a habit of peeling every vegetable and fruit you eat; much of the fiber and cancer-fighting nutrients in produce concentrate in or just beneath the skin.

Myth: Media reports that caution consumers about pesticide residues in certain foods should be taken as warnings to avoid those foods.

Reality: Headlines and news bites alarming consumers about pesticide residues should be viewed with a skeptic's eye. Scientists have developed sophisticated techniques that enable them to detect residues of pesticides so minute as to be virtually meaningless in many cases. In other words, the mere presence of a pesticide doesn't mean it's concentrated in a large enough dose to do any harm. The real question to ask is whether the pesticide level exceeds federal limits.

Keep in mind that residues are expressed in parts per million (ppm), parts per billion (ppb), and parts per trillion (ppt). Just what does that mean in practical terms?

- 1 ppm = 1 cent in $10,000, *or*
  1 pancake in a stack four miles high

- 1 ppb = 1 second in 32 years, *or*
  1 inch in 16,000 miles

- 1 ppt = 1 second in 32,000 years, *or*
  1 square foot of tile in a floor the size of Indiana

Myth: Once the government determines that a pesticide is unsafe for the public in any amount, its production in the United States is prohibited.

Reality: Unfortunately, between 1991 and 1994 alone, U.S. companies exported some 58 million pounds of pesticides banned for use in this country to other nations with more lax pesticide laws. This practice creates what has been dubbed "the circle of poison." Pesticides prohibited in the United States can travel the globe, boomeranging back to us through wind, rain, waterways, even imported food products. The scenario raises numerous ethical questions and highlights the necessity of considering the global, rather than just the national, impact of pesticides and other environmental contaminants.

Myth: Foods labeled organic must meet strict federal standards.

Reality: The federal government has yet to set a legal definition of "organic." Granted, 11 states currently have their own organic certification programs in place, as do 33 private organizations. Nevertheless, these programs vary in their definition of "organic" as well as in the degree to which the standards are enforced. As a result, consumers have no assurance what an organic label means.

The major roadblock to an all-encompassing federal definition has been financial. While the 1990 Farm Bill called for establishment of a national "organic" standard, funding for a staff to work out the details

55. Are Pesticides Hurting Your Health?

was not allocated until 1994. Officials at the National Organic Standards Board, the group of experts assigned to the issue, are still working away at a set of proposals to present to the governmental powers-that-be. Once a proposal has been made, it will likely be critiqued and revised before finally being set in stone—a process that could easily take another year or two.

Not in my backyard

Most people think farmers are the only people who need to take responsibility for pesticide use, but many suburbanites regularly dabble with lawn and garden chemicals that affect the environment as well. In fact, 64 million pounds of pesticides were spread on lawns and golf courses last year—amounting to 10 percent of all pesticides used in the United States. Keeping lawns green also wreaks havoc with the environment in other ways. Running a power lawn mower for one hour spews as much smog as driving a car 50 miles. And watering lawns regularly can contribute to water shortages.

Homeowners who want to care for their lawns in an eco-friendly manner can apply some of the same integrated pest management techniques currently used by farmers. The Environmental Protection Agency offers an excellent, free 18-page primer on the subject: *Healthy Lawn, Healthy Environment*. Write or call the National Center for Environmental Publications and Information, P.O. Box 42419, Cincinnati, OH 45242-2419; phone: (513) 489-8190.

While you're at it, you also might want to request another free publication, the *Citizen's Guide to Pest Control and Pesticide Safety*. This comprehensive 49-page resource covers everything from steps to control pests in and around your home; alternatives to chemical pesticides available to homeowners; ways to use, store, and dispose of pesticides safely; how to choose a pest control company; and what to do if someone is accidentally poisoned by pesticide exposure. Since pesticides are in everything from kitchen and bath disinfectants to pet collars to swimming pool chemicals, it's a booklet worth having.

WHY IS DATE RAPE SO HARD TO PROVE?

SHEILA WELLER

Sheila Weller is the author of Marrying the Hangman, *recently published by Random House.*

WITH ACQUAINTANCE RAPE cases now a TV spectator sport, lots of women I know are having some variation of this black-humored fantasy: You're on the witness stand, watching an expensively suited defense attorney pace around as he spits out accusations: What about those one-night stands six years ago? Your taste for double margaritas? Is it true that you met this man at a nightclub? And weren't you wearing a lace camisole under your blouse? That's the last straw. You stand up, rip the fuzzy blue dot off your face and say, "I give up! Let the bastard walk. It's not worth this trying to convict him."

After the past year's parade of well-publicized rape cases, such fantasy seems all too black and none too humorous. First there was the William Kennedy Smith case, during which the *New York Times* implied that rape complainant Patricia Bowman's speeding tickets bolstered a schoolmate's claim of her "little wild streak." More recently, when a young Manhattan architect accused three New York Mets of rape, her ex-boyfriend, Mets pitcher David Cone, reportedly told her that no one would believe her and her reputation would be ruined. He turned out to be right on both scores. The *New York Post* trumpeted the headline: "Mets accuser was 'No Vestal Virgin.'" And in early April, the Florida state attorney, pointing to a lack of physical evidence, decided to drop the case. The message to women has been clear: Many of us would not make believable accusers.

Not that a woman who says she's been raped shouldn't be scrutinized. After all, what about the reputation of the accused?

There's no getting around the fact that acquaintance rape is a crime in which the victim and the sole eyewitness are often one and the same. Both sides admit they had intercourse. The only issue is consent. When it's her word against his, it's only fair that her credibility and ulterior motives be questioned.

But that doesn't mean the woman is the one who should go on trial. All too often the legitimate question "Did this woman consent to intercourse?" leaps dangerously to "Was she leading him on?" In another recent case, a group of young men from prominent Tampa families admitted to drugging a woman and then raping her. The defense argued that by willingly accompanying the men after a night of drinking, she invited the ensuing events. The men were acquitted.

No wonder so few women actually report being raped. A new study by the National Victim Center estimates that one in eight women in the United States has been raped, in most cases by someone she knew, but that only about 16 percent of the rapes were reported. Of those cases that are reported, the majority are dropped by the prosecutor, according to Gary LaFree, a sociologist at the University of New Mexico and author of *Rape and Criminal Justice*. Only the rare resilient case, roughly one to 5 percent of all rapes, actually reaches the courtroom.

The road into and out of that courtroom can be so treacherous that even some rape counselors question whether it's worth it. "When I first started working here," says Colleen Leyrer of the Washington, D.C., Rape Crisis Center, "I was uncomfortable not encouraging a woman to prosecute. Now, after seeing victims go through a second trauma as a result of prosecuting, I urge the woman to decide for herself."

It's a tough decision—one that a woman should make with both eyes open. "If it's likely the case will end in acquittal, and if the woman's wavering, then I probably wouldn't recommend prosecution," says Andrea Parrot, a rape expert and psychologist at Cornell University.

But how does a woman know whether her case is likely to end in acquittal? How can she know if it will even make it to the courtroom? The people who deal with acquaintance rape cases daily—prosecutors, judges, defense attorneys—know firsthand why so few of them end in conviction. Here's what they say makes acquaintance rape so hard to prove.

UNLESS THE WOMAN IS A GIRL SCOUT OR VIRGIN, THE JURY WILL GIVE MORE WEIGHT TO HER CHARACTER THAN TO THE EVIDENCE.

EVEN THE MIKE TYSON conviction seemed to confirm this theory: Wasn't Desiree Washington a naive, churchgoing teenager? "A woman who has a good reputation, does not dress suggestively, has a nine-to-five job, and goes home after work will be looked on more favorably by a jury," says Brooks Leach, sex crimes prosecutor in Columbiana, Alabama.

In a study of 880 rape cases, sociologist Gary LaFree found that a complainant's "questionable" character was the best predictor of a defendant's acquittal. "We found that juries were most swayed by things like whether she had been drinking or even if she had birth control pills in her pocket," says LaFree. Juries find it more important that a woman frequents bars than that the man had a gun; more important that she had sex outside of marriage than that she was physically injured in the rape; more important that she was a "party girl" than that her clothes were torn that evening.

But you don't have to be a wanton woman for your morality to be suspect. Anyone who's had multiple sexual partners or an abortion is vulnerable. Even though 40 states now have "rape shield" laws making details of an accuser's past sexual life inadmissable in trials, such legislation is hardly foolproof. "There's an insidious way to get around the law," says sociologist Susan Caringella-McDonald. "Defense attorneys question the woman about her past sexual activity; the prosecutor objects; the judge sustains the objection—but the jury's already heard it so the damage is done."

Many well-off defendants hire private investigators to scout for information on accusers that can either be "leaked" at the trial or used to derail a case before it reaches the courtroom. "We'll do a surveillance of a rape complainant to find out: Does she go to parties and bars? Leave with somebody? Come home drunk?" says attorney Marshall Stern of Bangor, Maine. "You can't use these findings on the stand, but it's a bargaining tool with the prosecutor. If you say, 'See, she smoked dope here . . . ,' he may not think he has the winning case he once had."

Even a woman who's been sexually abused in the past might be considered less credible if that comes out in court, says Nancy Hollander, president of the National Association of Criminal Defense Attorneys: "If she has a history of abuse, we can use it to suggest that it's left her misunderstanding signals and thinking she was raped when she wasn't."

JURIES DON'T HAVE MUCH SYMPATHY FOR A WOMAN WHO WAS A WILLING PARTICIPANT UP TO THE TIME OF THE ALLEGED RAPE.

THE MORE ROMANTIC contact the woman had with the man, the tougher her case is to win. "You can almost diagram it," says Nancy Diehl, assistant prosecuting attorney for Detroit's Wayne County. "Fair to good is: The woman was in her or his house with him voluntarily, but she didn't have a previous relationship with him, it wasn't late at night, and she didn't kiss him. The more of those conditions that change from negative to positive, the harder it gets to win the case."

Patricia Bowman's case, for instance, was crippled by the lateness and the kissing. "When a woman has been acting in a way that juries see as encouraging a sexual encounter, they tend to say, 'Lady, you can't act like that and then change your mind,'" says Rock Harmon, deputy district attorney in Oakland, California. One of the most outrageous examples of this kind of bias occurred in the Tampa case. A defendant (later acquitted) explained at the trial that the complainant used profanity, smoked cigarettes, and dressed in green stretch pants: "She was not commanding as much respect from the guys as we would normally give other, more ladylike females."

Women jurors can often be hardest on women, perhaps because they want to deny that they too could be victims. Larry Donoghue, head of one of the sex crimes units of the Los Angeles district attorney's office, finds that female jurors are especially biased against assertive, ambitious women. Men are often surprisingly empathetic. "Fathers and grandfathers seem to take a protective attitude toward the victim," says Des Moines–based trial consultant Hale Starr. "But religious homemakers are the worst jurors for the victim. Their attitude is, 'I would never have gone to that room with that man . . .' They're unforgiving."

Still, there are some surprising exceptions. In a recent Detroit case, jurors convicted a man for the rape of a topless go-go dancer who had accepted a ride from him, changed into her street clothes in the back of his van, and driven with him in search of cocaine. Nancy Diehl says an eyewitness's testimony and strong physical evidence pushed the jurors past the tendency to believe that the woman "got what she deserved."

UNLESS THERE'S PHYSICAL EVIDENCE, IT'S HER WORD AGAINST HIS.

RARELY ARE THERE broken bones with acquaintance rape, but that doesn't mean there's no physical evidence. Even if a woman is uncertain whether she wants to pursue a complaint, she should go immediately to a doctor's office or the hospital for an examination. Forcible as opposed to consensual sex *is* often medically verifiable, even in long-sexually-active women. "When a woman is having consensual sex with a man, she needs to do what is referred to as a 'pelvic tilt' to accommodate his penis," says D.A. Donoghue. "In forcible sex, the last thing that she wants is to accommodate him. His force can lead to anything from reddening to bruises to lacerations. If it's just reddening, you've got to identify it fast, or it fades. It's not perfect evidence, but it can make the difference between winning and losing."

Immediate report of the assault also makes a rape victim appear more genuine. "Juries look for an immediate outcry. They want to see that she wasted no time telling the authorities," says Barry Levin, a defense attorney in the St. John's College case in which seven men were charged with gang-raping a black woman student. Levin, who plea-bargained his client down from a felony to a misdemeanor, says he got his biggest boost from the complainant, who waited a month before reporting the rape. The same holds true for the woman who accused the three Mets players a year after the rape. The prosecutor said her long delay and the resulting lack of physical evidence meant she didn't have a case.

"If you delay, the defense is going to say, 'See? She made it up to get back at the guy,' and the jury will believe it," says D.A. Nancy Diehl. "My advice always is: Report first, *then* decide. If you choose not to pursue the complaint, you can always back out of it."

EMOTIONAL OR CONFLICTING TESTIMONY CAN DESTROY A WOMAN'S CREDIBILITY.

THE ACCUSER should be calm but not robotic, testifying with feeling but not appearing overly emotional. Despite the harrowing experience she's endured, a victim who cries may be viewed as unstable. A calm but concerned woman, able to summon up the trauma without relapsing into it—like Desiree Washington—appeals more to juries.

Believability is crippled when the accuser tells a story that contains even a few loose threads, which defense attorneys use to unravel her entire story. Many prosecutors say that this is what most damaged Patricia Bowman's case: Her story was inconsistent and prosecutor Moira Lasch did her no favor by letting those inconsistencies reach the courtroom. "I did not find Bowman's story credible, and Lasch did not confront this before trial," says Karyn Sinunu, head of the sexual assault division of the Santa Clara County, California, district attorney's office. "I listened to Bowman say that she kissed him 'but it wasn't sexual' and I thought, 'You can kiss a husband of twenty years good-bye in the morning and it isn't sexual, but you don't kiss someone you've just met and it isn't sexual.' When you try to make your story sound better, the jury ends up seeing through it."

Even when a prosecutor catches all evasions well before the trial, they can come back to haunt the complainant and end up destroying her case. D.A. Donoghue tried a case in which a very credible woman had initially told police she was forced into the rapist's car: "She was too embarrassed to admit she had misjudged the man's motives when he offered her a ride home and had gotten into the car voluntarily." Though she corrected her story by trial time, the original falsification was bandied about by the defense attorney: If she had lied about that, then she could have lied about the whole thing. The defendant walked.

A skilled prosecutor plays devil's advocate early on, gently pushing the woman past her urge to apply face-saving spin control to her memory of the ordeal. "The woman needs to convince me that she was raped," says D.A. Nancy Diehl. "I say, 'Look, I need the whole truth. No matter how bad you think it looks, if you tell me, I'll be able to explain it to the jury.'"

These days, with Desiree Washington's success as inspiration, prosecutors say more women are deciding to press charges on a crime that has mostly been endured in silence and shame. But individual women can't be expected to live their day-in-and-day-out lives as political symbols, or as statistics in a war against apathy. In the end, the decision to pursue prosecution is deeply personal. "Victims and psychiatrists tell me it's therapeutic to prosecute," says Donoghue. Wanda Jones, who became a victims' service officer in Birmingham, Alabama, after she was raped by seven men, says the experience of seeing her rapists brought to justice was empowering. Says sociologist Andrea Parrot: "Some women, even understanding the likelihood of the man's acquittal, need to go through with prosecution to feel whole and vindicated. In those cases, I'd say go ahead."

what every woman needs to know about personal Safety

Are you scared silly? It's time to get scared *smart*. Trade fear for caution by understanding when and where you're most at risk and how to protect yourself against crime.

Lauren David Peden

Are you afraid to walk down the street alone at night? Let a repairman into your house when your husband isn't home? Accept help from a stranger if your car breaks down on the road? More women than ever answer yes. They're scared, and for good reason. One violent crime is committed every 17 seconds in the United States, with the number of murders and rapes each increasing 9 percent from 1989 to 1990.

And everywhere a woman turns, it seems, she is reminded of the danger. Switch on the television or go to your local movie theater and you're confronted with a slew of "jep" movies—the name that the entertainment industry gives to films in which a woman is in jeopardy of being raped, mugged, beaten, duped or worse. Movies such as *Cape Fear, Sleeping With the Enemy* and *The Hand that Rocks the Cradle* send shivers through female viewers by implying that they could be next. Even everyday life seems more dangerous. Newscasts, top-heavy with stories of crime and tragedy, compound the scare factor with "special reports" on the perils of everything from eating fresh fruit to shaving your legs.

The result of such menacing messages? Mean World Syndrome, a perception that danger lurks around every corner and that one is perpetually on the verge of being victimized. "Basically we're terrorized by the media," says George Gerbner, professor emeritus of communications at the Annenberg School for Communication in Philadelphia, who coined the term and has studied the phenomenon extensively. "Television shows are full of violence, and news programs dole out risk information without comparison, context, perspective or other relative values. It makes people panicky, particularly women." According to Gerbner, women are afflicted with the syndrome more than men and children primarily because of Hollywood's unnerving depiction of females. "On a typical TV drama, male characters outnumber females by three or four to one, but when there's violence, women are more often portrayed as victims," he explains. "In turn, women perceive the world as fraught with more danger than really exists." And Gerbner's studies have shown that the more hours women log watching TV, the more they suffer from Mean World Syndrome.

But experts are quick to point out that while these fears are exaggerated, they are still very real. It's how women put them in perspective that makes the difference between being reasonably cautious and hyper-afraid. The fact is, a woman *does* have a one in three chance of being raped in her lifetime and a one in 348 chance of being murdered. But when these statistics are stacked up against other odds, they're easier to live with. Overemphasized risks may be inconsequential, and underemphasized ones may deserve more attention. For instance, while you have only an 82 in 100,000 chance of being struck by lightning (an oft-depicted tragedy on reality-based TV shows like *Rescue 911*), your chances of drowning are significantly higher at 4,199 in 100,000.

The key, then, is knowing where your real risks lie and keeping your guard up in those situations but relaxing in others. Statistics show that terrible things happen to good people, but they're not inevitable. In fact, sometimes they're *very* unlikely. We'll discuss the most common dangers you should be concerned about and what you can do to minimize them. So you can learn to look over your shoulder prudently, not constantly, and concentrate on the good things in life.

10. CONTEMPORARY HEALTH HAZARDS

How to Feel Safe in Your Home

Crime hits hard on the home front, and Americans know it. We spent $3.4 billion on home burglar-alarm systems in 1991. Are such security systems worth the money? Maybe, but before you get out the checkbook, consider this: When criminals were asked what *they* would use to protect their homes, they said dogs, not alarms. Here are the biggest risk factors and some smart measures to keep you safe and sound at home.

• **Fifty-five percent of all burglars enter homes through an unlocked door or window,** says the National Crime Prevention Council. Keep all points of entry locked at all times. And be vigilant about it. Instill the habit in your kids too.

• **In almost all other cases, burglars enter homes through forced entry**—bashing in a window, prying a door away from its frame. Make sure the locks on doors are heavy-duty dead bolts and that the doors themselves are made of metal or solid-core wood that is at least 1 3/4 inches thick. Bolster window safety by installing specially designed pins through the casings to prevent windows from being opened from the outside (contact your local fire department for instructions). In suburban areas, thieves often enter houses by kicking in a basement window. Install bars over cellar windows that thwart break-ins.

• **A criminal may disguise himself to get into your home.** Criminals have been known to masquerade as salespeople, police officers and even victims of car accidents. *Never open your door to strangers.* First look through a peephole or window to see who it is. If you don't know the person, either ignore him until he goes away or ask what he wants through the locked door.

A New Kind of Street Smarts

Even if you don't live in a big city where street smarts are the way of the land, chances are you don't feel completely comfortable walking down the street alone at night (or even during the day in some areas). In fact, according to the National Victim Center, women are so concerned for their safety that 75 percent of them say they limit the places they go by themselves. Over half of all robberies and muggings occur on a street or highway, and driving doesn't afford any additional protection. Carjacking (stealing cars from drivers at gunpoint) is a growing phenomenon, so new that statistics on it aren't yet available. Here are three common crimes that women need to be on guard against.

• **Purse snatching.** The safest way to carry your purse is tucked snugly under your arm like a football with the strap wrapped around it. If the bag has a clasp closure, carry it clutched in your dominant hand, clasp side down. Should someone try to grab it, release the clasp and let the contents spill on the ground. A thief usually won't stop to sift through the mess.

• **Robbery by force or weapon.** Criminals scope out *easy* targets. Appear confident by walking with a strong gait, your hands out of your pockets. If you suspect you're being followed, don't go home. Even if the criminal passes you up, he'll learn where you live. Instead, cross the street, abruptly change direction or head toward an open store, restaurant or well-lit residence and call the police.

• **Carjacking.** According to the FBI, more than 1.6 million cars were stolen in 1990, a jump of over 50 percent since 1981. Increasingly, thieves are stealing cars from their owners right on the road. When you're driving, always keep doors locked and pay attention to other cars and pedestrians around you, particularly at traffic lights and stop signs. If a suspicious person approaches your car, lean on the horn and drive away, even through a red light if necessary. If the person threatens you, relinquish your car to minimize your chances of being hurt.

How to Feel Safe at Work

According to the U.S. Department of Justice, a surprising 13 percent of all violent crimes and 20 percent of all thefts occur on the job. Why the office? It's a contained environment where people spend at least eight hours a day—and it's easy for a criminal to blend in with the crowd or hide in isolated areas, such as rest rooms and stairwells. Here are two concerns to be especially aware of in the workplace.

• **Theft.** The simplest deterrent: Hide all valuables. Keep your purse and other important items in a locked desk or file-cabinet drawer, *not* on the floor under your desk.

• **Physical assault.** In this case, you're most at risk before and after regular hours. Stay alert when coming in early or staying late. Lock your office door while you're working if you're alone or in the company of other employees you don't know well. Keep the phone number for building security taped to your telephone. If your building doesn't have guards at the main entrance, make sure that door is locked too, if possible. And wait to use the bathroom until co-workers arrive or, if you'll be working late, use it before everyone has left for the day.

Index

absolute risk, 14
acetaminophen, 98–100, 101, 103
acquaintance rape, 236–238
Actron, 98–100
adolescents, depression and, 44, 45, 46
adult-onset diabetes, 80; heart disease and, 142. *See also* diabetes
Advil, 98–100
aerobic exercise, 11, 74, 75, 76–77, 140, 202; cancer and, 144–145; heart disease and, 144, 145–147
aflatoxin, 22
Agape love, 119–121
age, health care rationing and, 170
AIDS, 29–30, 129–130, 151, 158–159, 160–165, 220, 221, 222, 228
air pollution, cancer and, 152
Alar, 20, 22
alcohol, 109–110, 111–113, 149–150
Aleve, 98–100, 101, 102, 103
allergies, elimination of, 195
ALS, 210, 211
alternative therapies, 191–197
ambulance authorization, managed-care plans and, 212
American Council on Science and Health (ACSH), 18
anaerobic exercise, 144
angina, 138
animal studies, 22, 205
antacids, 101, 208
antibiotic resistance, 223–227
antidepressants, 44, 45, 46, 105, 107
antihistamines, 101, 103
anxiety, 16, 118
anxious-ambivalent relationships, 121
apoproteins, 138
appearance, body image and, 92–96
Arizona, medical savings accounts in, 175
Aron, Arthur, 116, 117
Art of Loving, The (Fromm), 124
arthritis, pain relievers and, 98, 99
aspirin, 98–100, 102, 103, 143
atherosclerosis, 137–138, 140
attachment theory, 121
avoidant relationships, 121
Axid AR, 207, 208
AZT, 163, 164

baldness, heart disease and, 142
barrier methods, 127, 128
basal cell carcinoma (BCC), 218
beef, 51
behaviorism, 116
Berk, Lee, 34
Bersheid, Ellen, 116, 117
beta carotene, 156
bipolar disease, 46
birth control: STDs and, 129–131; types of, 126–128
birth control pill, 127, 151
blocking agents, 154
blood tests, 186; PSA, 185
Blumstein, Philip, 125
body image, 92–96
body work, 192
brain, mental exercise and, 11–12
Brandon, Thomas, 105–106

breast cancer, 111, 113, 144, 155, 157, 185
bubonic plague, 138
buttermilk, 52

calcium, 156
calories, weight loss and, 84–85
cancer, 109; aerobic exercise and, 144–145; foods that fight, 154–157, 202; minimizing risks of, 148–153. *See also* specific type
carbohydrates: mood and, 37–38, 39; weight and, 50–51
cardiovascular disease. *See* heart disease
carjacking, 240
carotenoids, 156
Carter, Stephen, 125
cats, love and, 125
CD4, 162
Center for Science in the Public Interest, 55, 56
cervical cancer, 148–149, 185
cervical caps, 127–128
change, stages of, 15–17
"character disorders," 169
chelation therapy, 196
chest X-rays, 186
childbirth, 26, 28–29
children, 158; abuse of, 28; pesticides and, 234
chlamydia, 229–230, 231
cholesterol, 8, 52, 137–140, 141
Cimetidine, 207, 208
CKR5, 158–159
clinical trials, 14, 205–206
cognitive science, 29, 116
colon cancer, 144, 148–149, 157, 185
colonic irrigation, 196
Colorado, medical savings accounts in, 175
combination therapy, 160, 164
commitment, 118, 124
condoms, 126, 127–128, 129–130; female, 126, 127–128
Consumed: Why Americans Love, Hate, and Fear Food (Stacey), 59
coronary heart disease. *See* heart disease
cortisol, 26
Cowan, Connell, 125

date rape, 236–238
Delaney clause, 22
dengue, 220
Depo-Provera, 126, 127, 130
depression, 44–47, 105, 107; walking and, 41–43
Derks, Peter, 34
diabetes, 79; aerobic exercise and, 144; alcohol and, 111; atherosclerosis and, 140; heart disease and, 142
diaphragm, 127–128
diet, 7; cancer and, 150–151; mood and, 37–40; myths about, 50–52
dietary supplements, 53–60
doctors, Internet and, 210–211
dogs, love and, 125
dominant genes, 134
double-gradient lenses, 217
drug interactions, OTC drugs and, 207–208
dysthymia, 46

earlobes, heart disease and, 142
Ebola, 220, 221–222
electrocardiogram, 185–186
electronic fetal monitors, 170
emergency rooms, managed-care plans and, 212
emerging viruses, 220–222
endometrial cancer, 145
endorphins, 41
environment, cancer and, 152
epidemiological studies, 13–14, 205
epinephrine, 26, 28
equality, love and, 125
Eros love, 119–120
estrogen replacement therapy: heart disease and, 142; osteoporosis and, 202
eustress theory, 34
exercise, 6–7, 11, 76–77, 140; cancer and, 144–145; cholesterol level and, 140, 202; mental, 11–12; myths about, 74–75; weight control and, 78–79
experimental studies, 205–206

familial hypercholesterolemia, 134
family trees, 135, 136
famotidine, 207, 208
fast food, fat in, 64–66
fat, 39–40, 64–66, 140
Fehr, Beverly, 118–119
female condom, 126, 127, 129
fiber, 61, 62
Fiore, Michael, 104–105, 107–108
fish, 202
Fisher, Helen, 124
flavonoids, 155
flexibility, strength training and, 75
flu shots, 7–8
folic acid, 156
Food and Drug Administration (FDA): condom labeling requirements of, 130; female condom and, 129
food and mood movement, 37–40
Food Guide Pyramid, 61–63
food therapy, 192
Foreyt, John, 84, 85
Freud, Sigmund, 116, 169
friendships, love and, 118–119
Fromm, Erich, 124
fructose, 51
fruits, 233–235

Gallo, Robert C., 158
gastroplasty, 91
gatekeepers, 212
gene mutation, 222, 224–225
genital warts, 228, 230, 231
Glassman, Alexander, 105, 107
glycogen, 90
Golden Rule Insurance Co., 174–175
gonorrhea, 129, 231, 232
Gordon, Lori, 123, 124
Gottman, John, 124
gradient lenses, 217
grains, 61, 62, 63

hantavirus, 220
HDL (high-density lipoprotein) cholesterol, 111

health care: expansion of, 168–171; inversion of priorities in, 18–23
Health Employer Data and Information Set (HEDIS), 181, 182
health insurance: HMOs and, 177–184; loopholes in managed-care plans and, 212–213; medical savings accounts and, 172–176
health maintenance organizations. See HMOs
heart attacks, 138
heart disease, 111, 113; aerobic exercise and, 144, 145–147; alcohol and, 142–143; cholesterol and, 137, 141; prevention of, 141–143; snoring and, 204; stress and, 27–28
heartburn, 207, 208
Heidelberg Appeal, 22–23
height, heart disease and, 142
hemorrhagic fever, 220
Hendrick, Susan, 119–121
Henningfield, Jack, 105, 106, 107
Henry the Eighth syndrome, 82
hepatitis B, 151, 228, 230, 231
herbal remedies, 192
heredity, 14, 82, 84, 87–88, 106, 141, 134–136
high blood pressure. See hypertension
Hirsch, Martin, 162
HIV. See AIDS
HMOs (health maintenance organizations), 177–184, 212–213
Ho, David, 160–165
homeopathy, 193
hormone replacement therapy: heart disease and, 142; osteoporosis and, 202
hospitals, surviving stay at, 187–190
H2 blockers, 208
human clinical trials, 205–206
human papilloma virus (HPV), 228, 230, 231
humor, health and, 33–36
hunger, exercise and, 75, 85
hypertension, 9, 51, 79, 140, 141, 203

ibuprofen, 98–100, 103
Idaho, medical savings accounts in, 175
Illinois, medical savings accounts in, 175
illness, stress and, 26–32
immune system: aerobic exercise and, 144; laughter and, 34
impotence, 203
influenza, 7–8, 222
insulin, alcohol and, 111
insurance. See health insurance
intelligence, mental exercise and, 11–12
Internet, doctors and, 210–211
intimacy, 123–124
intrauterine devices (IUDs), 127, 128, 130
iron, 52, 142
isoflavones, 187

Jarvis, William, 194, 196
Johnsgard, Keith, 41, 42, 43

Kataria, Madan, 33–34, 35, 36
ketoprofen, 98–100
Klagsbrun, Francine, 124, 125
Korean hemorrhagic fever, 220
Kostas, Georgia, 84–85
Krokoff, Lowell, 124

labeling, 102, 130
"lactose intolerance," 51
Laughing Clubs International, 33–34, 36
laughter, health and, 33–36

leptin, 86, 89, 90
Leuchtenberg, William, 170
life events, critical, illness and, 26–32
lignans, 155
Limits of Medicine, The (Golub), 54
linoleic acid, 157
lipoproteins, 138
listening, couples and, 123
liver, alcohol and, 113
longevity, humor and, 35
Lou Gehrig's disease, 210, 211
love, 116–121, 122–125
Ludus love, 119–121

magnesium, 52
magnitude, risk and, 14
major depression, 44–47
mammography, 152, 185
Mangiardi, John R., 210–211
mania love, 119–121
manic depression, 46
Markowitz, Martin, 164
Marohn, Richard, 46
massages, 192
McAdams, Dan, 123
mean world syndrome, 239
meat, 62
medical procedures, 185–186
medical savings accounts (MSAs), 172–176
Medicare HMOs, 179–180
Medigap insurance, 179–180
meditation, 193
melanoma, 219
mental exercise, 11–12
mental health, managed-care plans and, 213
metabolism, weight loss and, 84
Michigan, medical savings accounts in, 175
milk, 51–52
Mississippi, medical savings accounts in, 175
Missouri, medical savings accounts in, 175–176
Monistat 7, 101
monoterpenes, 156
mood, diet and, 37–40
Motrin IB, 98–100
mutuality, couples and, 122
mycotoxins, 233

naproxen, 98–100, 101, 102, 103
National Committee for Quality Assurance (NCQA), 181, 182
"natural allergy elimination technique," 195
naturopathy, 191–197
Nauru, 86
nervous system, 110
Neuropeptide Y inhibitors, 89, 90
neuroses, 169
neurotransmitters, 45
nicotine patch, 106–107
nizatidine, 207, 208
Noller, Patricia, 121
norepinephrine, 26, 28
Norplant, 126–127, 128, 129, 130
nuclear power accidents, illness and, 29
nuts, 52, 203

obesity, 86–91
Olestra, 90
Olson, David, 122
omega-3 fatty acids, 202
oral contraceptives, 127
Oregon, rationing of health care in, 171
organosulfur compounds, 156
Orudis KT, 98–100

osteoporosis, 202
ovarian cancer, 145
over-the-counter (OTC) medications, 101–102, 207–209

pain relievers, 98–100
Pap smears, 185
passion, couples and, 124–125
passionate love, 117
Pearsall, Paul, 124
pelvic inflammatory disease (PID), 131
Pepcid AC, 207, 208
Perelson, Alan, 164
pesticides, health and, 233–235
pets, love and, 125
phlebitis, 188
photochromic lenses, 217
photokeratitis, 216
physical therapy, 192
phytochemicals, 54–55, 155
pill. See birth control pill
Pima Indians, 87
Pittman, Frank, 122, 123, 125
plague, 138
Plan 3 Insurance, 175
PMS Escape, 37
pneumonia, 188
polarized lenses, 217
politically correct science, 21–23
pollution, cancer and, 152
popcorn, 52
pork, 51
Pragma love, 119–121
preauthorization, managed-care plans and, 212
pregnancy, 26, 28–29, 170
premenstrual syndrome, diet and, 37, 38
preoperative tests, 187
primary-care physicians (PCPs), 213
Prochaska, James, 15–17
Propagest, 101
prostate cancer, 185
protease inhibitors, 160, 163, 164
protein, 50, 52
prototype approach, to love, 118
Proxmire, William, 116
PSA (prostate-specific antigen) blood tests, 185
psychiatry, expansion of, 169; managed-care plans and, 213
psychoneuroimmunology, 26, 30
psychosomatic disorders, 169

race, weight, and, 82
ranitidine, 207, 208
rationing, of health care, 170–171
recessive genes, 134
reciprocity, love and, 118
Reich, Wilhelm, 169
relative risk, 14
relaxation therapy, 193
repetition, in studies, 14
resilient children, 28
Rio Summit, 22–23
risk: basis of, 13; studies, 13–14; types of, 14
routine medical examinations, 185–186
RU-486, 128
"runner's high," 41

saccharin, 20, 22
Sachs, David Peter, 107
salt, hypertension and, 51
saponins, 156
saturated fat, 140

Schacter, Stanley, 117
Seasonal Affective Disorder (SAD), 46, 104
selenium, 156–157
Selye, Hans, 26
serotonin, 38
sexually transmitted disease (STDs), 129–131
Shaver, Philip, 121
Shaw, George, 163–164
shortness, heart disease and, 142
sigmoidoscopy, 185
Sime, Wes, 42, 43
sit-ups, 204
smoking, 7, 15, 16, 19, 20, 21, 149–150
social support, illness and, 27–28
Sokol, Julia, 125
soluble CD4, 162
spermicides, 127–128
sports drinks, 74–75
"spot reduction," 74
Sprecher, Susan, 117, 118
squamous cell carcinoma (SCC), 218–219
starches, 50–51
Stare, Frederick J., 18
Sternberg, Robert, 124, 125
stomach upset: heartburn and, 207, 208; pain relievers and, 98, 99
Storge love, 119–121
strength training, 75, 77, 85
stress, 7, 52, 201; diet and, 37, 38; illness and, 26–32; laughter and, 33–34
strokes, 137, 138

sugar, 39–40, 51, 52, 202
sunglasses, 204, 216–217
sunscreens, 219
Superfund, 19
supplements, dietary, 53–60
suppressing agents, 154
surgery: for obesity, 91; surviving hospital stays and, 187–190
"survival days," 169
sweating, 74, 84
Swensen, Clifford, 119
syphilis, 129, 228, 231, 232

Tagamet HB, 207–208
tamoxifen, 152
teeth, 202, 203
Tennov, Dorothy, 117
Thompson and Associates, 175
3TC, 164
treadmill test, 186
triglycerides, 138–139, 140
trust, love and, 125
tryptophan, 38
tubal ligations, 127
Tucker, Raymond, 119
Tylenol, 98–100, 101
Type A personality, 142
tyrosine, 38–39

ulcers, 52
urinary tract infections, 188

UV light, 216, 219

vaccinations, 7–8
vasectomy, 127
vegetables, 62, 63
vegetarianism, myths about, 52
verapamil, 102
Virchow, Rudolph, 26–27
viruses, 220–222; cancer and, 151
vitamin A, 157
vitamin C, 201
vitamin D, 157
vitamin E, 202
vitamins, 52, 193

walking, 41–43, 76, 77, 79
Walster, Elaine, 125
water therapy, 193
Watson, John B., 116
weight control, 6, 16, 78–79, 80–83, 84–85
willpower, 15–16
women's magazines, health issues in, 19
World Wide Web, doctors and, 210–211
Wurtman, Judith, 37–39

X-linked disorders, 134
X-rays, chest, 186

yogurt, 52

Zantac 75, 207, 208

Credits/Acknowledgments

Cover design by Charles Vitelli

1. Health Behavior and Decision Making
Facing overview—Dushkin Publishing Group illustration by Mike Eagle.

2. Stress and Mental Health
Facing overview—Photo by Cheryl Greenleaf.

3. Nutritional Health
Facing overview—WHO photo.

4. Exercise and Weight Control
Facing overview—New York State Department of Commerce (Albany) photo.

5. Drugs and Health
Facing overview—American Cancer Society photo.

6. Human Sexuality
Facing overview—WHO photo.

7. Current Killers
Facing overview—Photo by Pamela Carley Peterson.

8. America's Health and the Health Care System
Facing overview—Middlesex Hospital photo.

9. Consumer Health
Facing overview—Dushkin Publishing Group photo by Frank Tarsitano.

10. Contemporary Health Hazards
Facing overview—American Cancer Society photo.

PHOTOCOPY THIS PAGE!!!*

ANNUAL EDITIONS ARTICLE REVIEW FORM

■ NAME: _____ DATE: _____

■ TITLE AND NUMBER OF ARTICLE: _____

■ BRIEFLY STATE THE MAIN IDEA OF THIS ARTICLE: _____
_____

■ LIST THREE IMPORTANT FACTS THAT THE AUTHOR USES TO SUPPORT THE MAIN IDEA:
_____
_____
_____
_____

■ WHAT INFORMATION OR IDEAS DISCUSSED IN THIS ARTICLE ARE ALSO DISCUSSED IN YOUR TEXTBOOK OR OTHER READINGS THAT YOU HAVE DONE? LIST THE TEXTBOOK CHAPTERS AND PAGE NUMBERS:
_____
_____
_____
_____

■ LIST ANY EXAMPLES OF BIAS OR FAULTY REASONING THAT YOU FOUND IN THE ARTICLE:
_____
_____
_____
_____

■ LIST ANY NEW TERMS/CONCEPTS THAT WERE DISCUSSED IN THE ARTICLE, AND WRITE A SHORT DEFINITION:
_____
_____
_____
_____

*Your instructor may require you to use this ANNUAL EDITIONS Article Review Form in any number of ways: for articles that are assigned, for extra credit, as a tool to assist in developing assigned papers, or simply for your own reference. Even if it is not required, we encourage you to photocopy and use this page; you will find that reflecting on the articles will greatly enhance the information from your text.

We Want Your Advice

ANNUAL EDITIONS revisions depend on two major opinion sources: one is our Advisory Board, listed in the front of this volume, which works with us in scanning the thousands of articles published in the public press each year; the other is you—the person actually using the book. Please help us and the users of the next edition by completing the prepaid article rating form on this page and returning it to us. Thank you for your help!

ANNUAL EDITIONS: HEALTH 97/98
Article Rating Form

Here is an opportunity for you to have direct input into the next revision of this volume. We would like you to rate each of the 57 articles listed below, using the following scale:

1. Excellent: should definitely be retained
2. Above average: should probably be retained
3. Below average: should probably be deleted
4. Poor: should definitely be deleted

Your ratings will play a vital part in the next revision. So please mail this prepaid form to us just as soon as you complete it.
Thanks for your help!

Rating	Article	Rating	Article
	1. A Picture of Health		32. Cholesterol
	2. Healthy Habits: Why Bother?		33. Rating Your Risks for Heart Disease
	3. Risk: What It Means to You		34. The Heart of the Matter
	4. "Just Do It" Isn't Enough: Change Comes in Stages		35. Strategies for Minimizing Cancer Risk
	5. Challenging America's Inverted Health Priorities		36. Cancer-Fighting Foods: Green Revolution
	6. Critical Life Events and the Onset of Illness		37. Mutant Gene Can Slow AIDS Virus: Cancer Institute Study Indicates Some People May Be Impervious
	7. Can You Laugh Your Stress Away?		38. The Disease Detective
	8. Good Mood Foods		39. Health Unlimited
	9. Out of the Blues		40. Medical Savings Accounts: A Solution to Financing Health Care?
	10. Depression: Way beyond the Blues		41. Can HMOs Help Solve the Health-Care Crisis?
	11. Dietary Gospel—or Phony Baloney?		42. Examining the Routine Examination
	12. Food for Thought about Dietary Supplements		43. Your Hospital Stay: A Guide to Survival
	13. The Food Pyramid: How to Make It Work for You		44. The New Doctors of Natural Medicine
	14. Fast Food: Fatter than Ever		45. How Health Savvy Are You?
	15. Snack Attack		46. Nutrition in the News: What the Headlines Don't Tell You
	16. Fitness Fiction: Working Out the Facts		47. The Switch to OTC: No Prescription, No Protection?
	17. Which Exercise Is Best for You?		48. The Doctor Is On
	18. Fat Times		49. Health Insurance Hazards: How to Spot Hidden Pitfalls in Your Plan
	19. Test Your Weight-Loss IQ		50. Are Your Shades Good Enough?
	20. Gaining on Fat		51. Quiz: Are You Ready for the Sun?
	21. Body Mania		52. The Bad News Bugs
	22. How to Pick a Pain Reliever		53. 'Wonder Drugs' Losing Healing Aura
	23. OTC Drugs: Prescription for Danger?		54. Prevent Sexually Transmitted Diseases
	24. Kicking Butts		55. How Much Are Pesticides Hurting Your Health?
	25. Alcohol and Tobacco: A Deadly Duo		56. Why Is Date Rape So Hard to Prove?
	26. Alcohol: Spirit of Health?		57. What Every Woman Needs to Know about Personal Safety
	27. The Lessons of Love		
	28. The Indispensables: 10 Key Reasons Why Love Endures		
	29. Choosing a Contraceptive		
	30. Preventing STDs		
	31. Family History: What You Don't Know Can Kill You		

(Continued on next page)

ABOUT YOU

Name _____ Date _____
Are you a teacher? ❏ Or a student? ❏
Your school name _____
Department _____
Address _____
City _____ State _____ Zip _____
School telephone # _____

YOUR COMMENTS ARE IMPORTANT TO US!

Please fill in the following information:
For which course did you use this book? _____
Did you use a text with this *ANNUAL EDITION*? ❏ yes ❏ no
What was the title of the text? _____
What are your general reactions to the *Annual Editions* concept?

Have you read any particular articles recently that you think should be included in the next edition?

Are there any articles you feel should be replaced in the next edition? Why?

Are there any World Wide Web sites you feel should be included in the next edition? Please annotate.

May we contact you for editorial input?

May we quote your comments?

ANNUAL EDITIONS: HEALTH 97/98

| BUSINESS REPLY MAIL |
| First Class   Permit No. 84   Guilford, CT |

Postage will be paid by addressee

Dushkin/McGraw·Hill
Sluice Dock
Guilford, Connecticut 06437

No Postage
Necessary
if Mailed
in the
United States